American Women Playwrights, 1900–1950

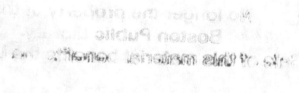

PETER LANG
New York • Washington, D.C./Baltimore • San Francisco
Bern • Frankfurt am Main • Berlin • Vienna • Paris

Yvonne Shafer

American Women Playwrights, 1900–1950

PETER LANG
New York • Washington, D.C./Baltimore • San Francisco
Bern • Frankfurt am Main • Berlin • Vienna • Paris

Library of Congress Cataloging-in-Publication Data

Shafer, Yvonne.
American women playwrights, 1900–1950/
Yvonne Shafer.
p.   cm.
Includes bibliographical references (p.   ) and index.
1. American drama—Women authors—History and criticism.
2. Women and literature—United States—History—20th century.
3. American drama—20th century—History and criticism. 4. Women in
literature. I. Title.
PS338.W6S48   812'.5099287—dc20   94-45719
ISBN 0-8204-2142-1

Die Deutsche Bibliothek-CIP-Einheitsaufnahme

Shafer, Yvonne:
American women playwrights, 1900–1950/ Yvonne Shafer. - New York;
Washington, D.C./Baltimore; San Francisco; Bern; Frankfurt am Main; Berlin;
Vienna; Paris : Lang.
ISBN 0-8204-2142-1

Cover photograph of Martha Morton, c. 1901, Museum of the City of New
York, The Byron Collection. Permission granted by the Museum of the City of
New York.

Cover design by James F. Brisson.

The paper in this book meets the guidelines for permanence and durability
of the Committee on Production Guidelines for Book Longevity
of the Council of Library Resources.

© 1995 Peter Lang Publishing, Inc., New York

Printed in the United States of America.

To Oscar G. Brockett and Theodore W. Hatlen
who first encouraged me to pursue
graduate work in theatre

Acknowledgments

I would like to thank Wendy Wasserstein and Ted Shine for their contributions to this book. I am particularly grateful to Susan Kelley, Thomas Shafer, Marvin Carlson, Nahma Sandrow, Oscar G. Brockett, Tommie Stewart, Don Marlette, Ron Willis, Theodore W. Hatlen, Rose Bank, Natalie C. Schmitt, Claude File, Gordon Wickstrom, and Barbara Van Holt for their continuing assistance, encouragement, and feedback through the several years of work. Kathy A. Perkins and Addell Patricia Austin graciously offered me information and advice about African-American drama. Students and former students who generously assisted me in various ways include Terry Burnsed, Doug Gordy, Joyce Aldridge, Daniel Raymond Nadon, Beth Osnes, David Reifschneider, and David Schuler. Assistance from Louis Rachow at the International Theatre Institute, Barbara Feeley and Kathryn Talalay at the American Academy of Arts and Letters, Marty Jacobson at the Museum for the City of New York, the staff of the Lincoln Center Library for the Performing Arts, and the staff of the Inter-Library Loan office in the library at the University of Colorado at Boulder is highly appreciated. I am grateful for several grants which assisted me in my research: a summer research grant from the University of Southern Maine in 1988 allowed me to begin the work. While at the University of Colorado at Boulder I was able to continue with two grants from IMPART and additional grants from the Committee for Research and Creative Work and the Graduate Commitee For Arts and Humanities. I was pleased to have support for these grants, and in other ways, from my chairpersons Walter Stump (University of Southern Maine) and James M. Symons (University of Colorado at Boulder).

Contents

Foreword by Wendy Wasserstein xi

Introduction 1

Part One 13

Rachel Crothers (1870?-1958) 15

Susan Glaspell (1876-1948) 36

Zoë Akins (1886-1958) 58

Edna Ferber (1885-1968) 79

Rose Franken (1895-1988) 102

Lillian Hellman (1905?-1984) 121

Summary 148

Part Two 155

Ted Shine: "Opportunities for African-American
              Women Playwrights" 157

Clare Kummer (1873-1958) 162

Josephine Preston Peabody (1874-1922) 176

Gertrude Stein (1874-1946) 190

Rida Johnson Young (1875?-1926) 203

Zona Gale (1874-1938) 216

Georgia Douglas Johnson (1880-1966) 229

Alice Gerstenberg (1885-1972) 241

Sophie Treadwell (1885?-1970) 255

Eulalie Spence (1894-1981) 271

Ruth Gordon (1895-1985) 284

Lula Vollmer (1898-1955) 296

May Miller (1899-) 309

Bella Spewack (1899-1990) 322

Clare Boothe Luce (1903-1987) 334

Mary Coyle Chase (1907-1981) 346

Fay Kanin (1916-) 356

Summary 370

Part Three 375

Martha Morton (1865?-1925) 377

Alice Moore Dunbar-Nelson (1875-1935) 383

Anita Loos (1893?-1981) 388

Dorothy Heyward (1890-1961) 395
Zora Neale Hurston (1891-1960) 403
Anne Nichols (1891-1966) 409
Mae West (1892-1980) 414
Dorothy Parker (1893-1967) 421
Marita Bonner (1899-1971) 428
Maurine Watkins (1900-1968) 433
Cornelia Otis Skinner (1901-1979) 440
Elsa Shelley (1905-?) 446
Carson McCullers (1917-1967) 451
Summary 456

Conclusion 459
Appendix: Prizes and Awards 465
Works Cited 469
Index 529

Foreword by Wendy Wasserstein

December 3, 1993 was the high point of my playwriting career to date. While I was off having dinner with a friend, a policeman from Albany won Double Jeopardy by answering the following question: Name one of three women who won the Pulitzer Prize for drama in the 1980's.

The three possible answers were Marsha Norman, Beth Henley, and me. Of course as I was told of the events (you wouldn't believe how many of one's best friends and relatives watch *Jeopardy* on a Friday night), the two losing contestants answered "Heidi Abramawitz", the name of a comic character created by Joan Rivers and Lillian Hellman". But the grand prize winner answered me.

I am not telling this story because I am hoping to make it on *The Price is Right* or *The Wheel of Fortune*. I suspect my last name is far too long for *The Wheel* anyway—Vanna can only turn so many letters. Nor do I think the ultimate theatrical accolade is becoming a *Jeopardy* clue. Rather, after reading these extraordinary accounts of the lives of American women dramatists of the early twentieth century, my hope was someday we wouldn't only be the obscure category Double Jeopardy super prize, but finally recognized as a mainstream of modern American drama.

I remember when I was a student at the Yale School of Drama in the 1970's, the only woman dramatist ever mentioned was Hrosvitha of Gandersheim, a tenth-century canoness whose plays were never produced. In other words, she was a "closet dramatist," not a role model. How I wish that at the time this book, with the theatrical lives of diverse writers such as Claire Booth Luce, Rose Franken, and Gertrude Stein existed. I would have turned to it for comfort and guidance nightly. I didn't want to be a tenth-century canoness, I wanted to be a working woman playwright.

I am touched and astonished by these stories. They are so different from mine and yet so similar. In drama school, I studied plays by men. I encountered Jacobean tragedies in which men would drop dead instantaneously after kissing the poisonous skulls of women. Of course I had trouble identifying with that. I wrote my first play, *Uncommon Women and Others*, in the hopes of seeing an all-female curtain call in the basement of the Yale School of Drama. A man in the audience stood up during a post-show discussion and announced, "I can't get into this. It's about girls." I thought to myself, "Well, I've been getting into *Hamlet* and *Lawrence of Arabia* my whole life so you better start trying."

This is not to say that the lives and works of the playwrights in this book are valid because they are women writing women; that would be an inept simplification. In fact, they are valid because they wrote in many cases ground-breaking work—the wit of Dorothy Parker, the storytelling of Edna Ferber and Lillian Hellman, the deconstruction of Gertrude Stein—that set standards in American drama.

The women discussed in this book haven't just written plays intriguing for a given moment in history; they've written intriguing plays, period. Plays which remain aesthetically compelling today. Most compelling, however, are the lives these writers led. They were a remarkable breed, self-reliant but often self-deprecating. They came from all backgrounds. They deserve to be the answers on *Jeopardy* nightly.

Introduction

Determination, hope, and compassion characterize the women in this book who represent the many American women playwrights between 1900 and 1950. For each of them it was an act of determination to attempt to become a professional playwright in a theatre dominated by white male producers, directors, theatre critics, and playwrights. Specific examples of assertiveness will be given throughout the book, but two may be given here. In 1930 May Miller wrote *Stragglers in the Dust* which posits the idea that the Unknown Soldier in the tomb in Washington might possibly be an African-American. In 1943 Rose Franken proceeded with determination to produce her own play dealing with homosexuality after it was rejected by the critics in Boston and her producer withdrew.

The plays discussed are informed by hope—even those which depict in tragic form the consequences for women who step outside the accepted norms of society. In Susan Glaspell's *Inheritors* the heroine goes to prison for her beliefs, but the playwright writes with the hope that such a play will cause Americans to search for the real democratic ideals and the true American way. Similarly, in *The Little Foxes* Lillian Hellman showed a family which in Alan Downer's words, "exemplified the inhumanity and vices of capitalism" (60). Yet, through writing such a play Hellman expressed her hope that Americans would realize the danger of these vices.

Finally, the playwrights viewed their characters with compassion. One of the most obvious examples is Sophie Treadwell's *Machinal* in which, as Judith E. Barlow commented, the heroine faces "a phalanx of male characters with the power to determine her life. Helen's only alternative, as she herself recognizes, is constantly to 'submit'" (xxvii). In the midst of World War II, with attention focused on the horrors of the war, Elsa Shelley called upon Americans to have compassion for young female juvenile delinquents led into hopeless affairs, pregnancies, and venereal disease because of the turbulence of wartime. Compassion for the victims of racism caused Georgia Douglas Johnson and others to join in the anti-lynching campaign and to write anti-lynching plays such as *A Sunday Morning in the South* in the 1920s.

Most of these women and their plays from the first half of the century have been forgotten. Such names as Edna Ferber, Zoë Akins, Fay

Kanin, and Anne Nichols were once as familiar to Americans as Neil Simon, Lorraine Hansberry, Arthur Miller, and Marsha Norman. Fortunately, in recent years attention has been drawn to the absence of plays by women playwrights of the past in anthologies, on stage, and in theatre histories. A number of books have appeared, such as *Notable Women on the American Stage* and *Women in American Theatre* which have created interest in many of the American women playwrights. This book will present an analysis of the work of women playwrights from the period in which they first produced important plays up through the time in which several hundred plays were written by women and the presence of women playwrights in the theatre was an accepted, and important, factor.

In the first half of the twentieth century a large number of women earned a living in the commercial theatre, received critical acclaim, and achieved a popular following. The range of their plays included drama, comedy, musicals, poetic tragedy, and folk drama. Most people think that there were few or no women playwrights at the turn of the century. In fact, there were many, but they attracted little notice because women such as Martha Morton wrote formula plays, generally tailored for an outstanding actress or actor. It was surprising and controversial when women such as Susan Glaspell, Josephine Preston Peabody, and Alice Gerstenberg began to write plays which broke with formulae and challenged the accepted conventions of a largely realistic, male-dominated theatre. Their plays introduced feminism, presented women who were determined to fight social injustice, and replaced the negative stereotype of "the old maid" with the positive depiction of a career woman, single by choice. Their plays were innovative in themes and techniques (the use of Expressionism, for example). They often focused on the position of women in American society in an unconventional and startling way.

Many of the women playwrights of this time were feminists, or at least shared with feminists goals for the liberation of women. June Sochen detailed these goals in *The New Feminism in Twentieth Century America*:

> The feminists envisioned an open society where each human being, in this land of infinite opportunity, could develop his or her potential to its fullest.... Women who wanted a career, with or without marriage, could do so. The society would rearrange its institutions to provide for this. Collective nurseries,

flexible residence requirements for graduate studies, and husbands that accepted equal responsibility in the home would enable the feminist dream to become a reality. (*The New Feminism* ix-x)

Playwrights espousing these ideals had an uphill battle against entrenched beliefs. In *A Man's World*, Rachel Crothers created a woman writer who chooses to be the single parent of an illegitimate child, to reject marriage for a career, and to denounce the double standard of sexuality. America's foremost playwright, Augustus Thomas, was so appalled by the viewpoints expressed in Crothers' play that he wrote a play attacking them. He received great praise for his hit play, *As a Man Thinks* (1911), in which he defended the double standard of sexuality and the disempowerment of women.

One obvious element of great importance in the plays by women was that many of the women in the plays had careers. Women were depicted as writers, artists, scientists, and business-women. Edna Ferber introduced a traveling saleswoman and Ruth Gordon created a successful screen-writer loosely based on Dorothy Parker. Fay Kanin depicted a journalist-turned-congresswoman modeled on Clare Boothe Luce. In addition to the characters in the plays, the playwrights themselves, obviously, had careers. Many of them devoted their lives to their writing, in contrast to the majority of the women in their audiences who were, foremost, wives and mothers. Thus, on and off stage, the women playwrights established role models for the rising generation of women. As Doris Abramson wrote in an article about Crothers, her plays "reflect the conflict arising at that moment in our history when women were beginning to assert their individuality in careers, and when some were trying either to have an equal partnership with men or to find a way to sustain an old-fashioned marriage while being a New Woman" ("Rachel Crothers: Broadway Feminist" 61). The whole question of role playing, role models, and standards established in childhood was treated by women playwrights in many plays. In Crothers' *He and She* and in Glaspell's *The Verge* the heroines are career women who want to create and work as equals with men. Their convention-bound families condemn them for their behavior and ask them why they can't be like other women. To quote Sochen once more, the attitudes expressed by such playwrights as Susan Glaspell and Neith Boyce (both with the Provincetown Playhouse) moved beyond the simple urge to get the vote:

> The expansion of woman's roles was tied to another element in the feminist ideology: the re-education of roles in childhood. The new attitude toward women would begin by retraining all children according to the emancipated values of feminism. Crystal Eastman said that, "it must be manly as well as womanly to know how to cook and sew and clean and take care of yourself in the ordinary exigencies of life." No role ought to be regarded as solely a feminine role. It should not be womanly to cry when deeply moved, and manly to repress one's tears. It should not be womanly to change a baby's diaper and manly to refuse to do it. (*The New Woman* 31-32)

Not surprisingly, many of the women playwrights who challenged traditional thinking about the role of women were living in Greenwich Village and working in what were later known as off-Broadway theatres in the Village. Sochen describes this milieu, saying,

> Greenwich Village was the setting for much feminist thinking, talking, and writing in the 1910s. Male and female Bohemians naturally accepted the latest ideas of Freud, Edward Carpenter, and Havelock Ellis. They believed in sexual freedom, individual determination regardless of sex, equal educational opportunities for women, and treating women as human beings and not sex objects. (*The New Feminist* viii)

In addition to having careers, women in plays by women were often sophisticated, well-read, and assertive. Women in the plays frequently initiated the action and were the dynamic characters in the plot. Even in such a charming, light comedy as *Good Gracious, Annabelle*, Clare Kummer contributes to the changing view of women. She presented an attractive, intelligent woman who conceives of a plan for herself and her impoverished artist friends to accept temporary jobs in a rich man's home. The witty Annabelle proceeds to manipulate the household, the rich man, and to achieve what she wants for herself and her friends. Different in type, but equally dominating, is Lillian Hellman's murderous Regina in *The Little Foxes*. Circumstances seem to set her up as the victim of her brothers' greed, a woman who can only get what she wants by pleasing a man. Through her own intense drive for power, Regina succeeds in outwitting her scheming brothers and ending up with the power in her hands. The range of women in plays who chose their own way, and got it, increased as the number of women playwrights increased. As early as 1910, as Sharon Friedman has noted, in *A Man's World*, "Crothers portrays a woman who challenges sexual politics—the power relationship based on sex—and sacrifices her union with a man who resists her challenge, thereby affirming her sense that it is a man's world" ("Feminism as Theme" 78). That fact, of course was changing. As Florence Kiper wrote in 1914, "It is hoped that they [women playwrights] will feel impelled . . . to set forth sincerely and honestly, yet with vital passion, those problems in the development and freedom of women that our modern age has termed the problems of feminism" ("Some American Plays from the Feminist Viewpoint" 931).

Naturally, the plays by women also focus on women who are disempowered. The Young Woman in *Machinal* is so overwhelmed by an indifferent, male-dominated world that she sees the murder of her husband as her only escape—in fact, her only true escape comes with her death in the electric chair. At the end of *The Member of the Wedding*, Berenice, a black woman marginalized in a racist society, bereft of comfort, says, "I just don't know what I have done to deserve it" (114). Zona Gale's *Miss Lulu Bett*, although she eventually revolts, represents the poor, tired women Gale saw around her, who were virtually slaves in the home of a husband or relative. The highly liberated playwright Susan Glaspell often chose to write about women who were unable to enjoy the freedom and independence she had gained. Likewise, Eulalie Spence, who received an M.A. from Columbia, wrote *Undertow* which depicts an African-American woman unable to achieve happiness because she cannot escape from her past as a prostitute.

Many male playwrights addressed these problems, but there are a number of reasons why it was important for female playwrights to do it. Most importantly, women are likely to view themselves and their roles in society in a markedly different fashion from men in terms of their capabilities, their intelligence, and their needs. This dramatic disparity is the central theme in one of the most popular plays by women, Glaspell's *Trifles*. In 1941 Moss Hart wrote *Lady in the Dark* which shows a woman suffering from a psychosis because she is the boss at a magazine instead of a married woman. About the same time in Ruth Gordon's *Over Twenty-One*, when a man doubts whether a successful woman writer can edit a major newspaper, the woman advises him to wake up and quit sounding old-fashioned. He doubts that she can do it, but she *knows* she can. As Friedman points out, "Feminist criticism underscores the need to listen to women recreate their own experiences through art, and to discern areas of commonality which grow out of their designation as a group" ("Feminism as Theme" 70). Along the same line, Patricia Meyer Spacks writes that, "Women dominate

their own experience by imagining it, giving it form, writing about it"
(*The Female Imagination* 413). The significance is not only in the innovative subject matter, but in that it is perceived and presented by a
woman. In the following chapters the characterization of women as
perceived through the eyes of women playwrights will be presented. It
is particularly important to draw attention to the work of African-
American women playwrights and the vision of the world seen through
the eyes of a black female. As Brown-Guillory states, "Early black
women playwrights offer much to American theater in the way of content, form, characterization, dialogue, and heart. These women mav-
ericks who have come from a long and efflorescent tradition were
instrumental in paving a way for black playwrights between the 1950s
and the 1980s" (*Their Place on the Stage* 3).

In the analysis of the plays the response of the critics is an important
element. The hundreds of reviews cannot all be quoted or noted, but
dozens of reviewers such as Heywood Broun, Alexander Woolcott,
Richard Watts, Jr., and Howard Barnes are quoted to give an indication of the response of these important figures who influenced their
readers. Unfortunately, of course, most of the critics were men, but a
number of women, such as Wilella Waldorf and Euphemia van Rensselaer Wyatt critized plays over a long period. The influence of the
critics is not only important in the original production, but in the rare
revivals of the plays under discussion. Critics such as Brooks Atkinson
and John Coleman saw plays in their original productions which were
revived many years later and were able to contrast the productions
and the effect of the plays in different periods of history. A major
source of information and criticism is the writer Burns Mantle, partly
because his career lasted so long. A more important reason for
referring to him is that his volumes of the best plays of 1899-1909,
1909-1919, and the subsequent annual volumes contain significant
information regarding length of runs, general critical and popular
response, complete casts and other useful facts. His collections and his
book *American Playwrights of Today* focused attention on *American*
playwrights (in contrast, for example to the Theatre Guild which in
the 1920s emphasized foreign plays). Through Mantle's publication of
condensed versions of current plays and the survey of the theatre in
New York and elsewhere in the country, many Americans outside of
New York were able to acquaint themselves with the many playwrights
emerging in the first half of the century. As a reviewer and editor he

gave attention and encouragement to many women playwrights who did not receive it elsewhere. His enthusiasm for such playwrights as Sophie Treadwell, Rose Franken, and Clare Boothe Luce was an important element in their careers.

The book is divided into three sections of analysis and production history of the plays by women playwrights in the period under discussion. These categories were decided on the basis of many factors including critical and popular response to the plays, impact of the plays at the time of production and later, the influence of the playwright as a perceived role model in terms of innovative subject matter and techniques, number of plays produced, and present-day attitudes about the playwright's work. Naturally, there will be differences of opinion about the appropriateness of these categories and the playwrights which appear in them. The first section is composed of in-depth coverage of notable playwrights including Rachel Crothers, Susan Glaspell, Zoë Akins, Edna Ferber, Rose Franken, and Lillian Hellman. All of these women wrote a number of plays which were successful with critics and audiences and which permeated the public consciousness. Such plays as Rose Franken's *Claudia* achieved almost undescribable success—at one point she was casting three companies for tours and later the play was transformed into a successful film. Lillian Hellman's *The Little Foxes* provided a fine acting opportunity for many actresses including Tallulah Bankhead and Elizabeth Taylor. Although most of these playwrights are nearly forgotten, their work had a major impact on the American theatre and some of their plays are being presented today.

The following sections will analyze the work of playwrights who wrote successful plays but for one reason or another did not have fully developed careers as playwrights or never fulfilled the full potential of their playwriting abilities. Zona Gale was the first woman to win a Pulitzer Prize for playwriting, but she achieved her major successes as a short story writer and novelist. Mae West wrote a number of plays which were usually successful and controversial, but she never really developed any depth or variety as a playwright. Many of the women in this section could have written many more successful plays, but found themselves drawn in different directions: Ruth Gordon preferred to devote herself to acting, Dorothy Parker wrote in several other areas, and Clare Boothe Luce ran for congress and won.

In this group are a number of minority playwrights who often found great difficulty in getting their plays produced. Alice Moore Dunbar-

Nelson, May Miller, Zora Neale Hurston, Marita Bonner, and Georgia Douglas Johnson created visions of the world of African-Americans which were unfamiliar to society as a whole. Some minority playwrights were able to find an audience during the short-lived Federal Theatre Project and some through the one-act play festivals which introduced many women playwrights to American theatre. However, most of the plays never were produced professionally and were only available to a wide reading public in the last few years. Denied opportunity in their own time, they must be recognized today both in terms of historical importance and theatrical effectiveness. In the early part of the century many African-American writers took what Brown-Guillory calls the "best-foot-forward" approach, avoiding dialect and questions of race "in order to demonstrate that blacks were not different than whites, and thus when whites read about these characters, who are only painted black, they would be receptive to such writing. . . . Many black writers who wanted to reach a broad market compromised, perhaps sacrificing the flavor of their works" (*Their Place on the Stage* 11). In contrast to these writers of the genteel school, were the women who depicted with graphic detail the history of slavery, blatant racism, lynching and other social problems. They played an important role, especially in awakening northerners to the actuality of mob rage against blacks. (Brown-Guillory quotes a figure of 4,736 blacks, men and women, who were lynched, burned, or otherwise murdered from 1882 to 1962). Many of the women who wrote these plays were denied production, by the Federal Theatre Project for example, because the play readers believed the social problem was exaggerated. Today the pioneer work of these women is finally being acknowledged and many of the plays are being published.

Most of the playwrights in this book had several strings to their bows. Many balanced playwriting with short story and novel writing, scripting for the radio and films, and/or acting and directing. Rachel Crothers and Rose Franken, for example, wrote, directed, and sometimes produced their plays. Many playwrights married, managed a home, and raised children. Often their careers were nurtured through the interaction of actresses, playwrights, directors, and producers. For example, Alice Gerstenberg devoted her life to theatre, choosing never to marry, and worked with other women to establish several companies in Chicago where women were encouraged to write plays. The actress Maxine Elliott encouraged the young playwright Rachel Crothers, who in her turn encouraged women playwrights and actresses when she achieved success. Eva Le Gallienne selected Susan Glaspell's *Alison's House* for production, directing it and playing the lead. Their work together led to the Pulitzer Prize. An area which has received little attention is the successful interaction of women playwrights in transforming stage plays into films. A good example is the highly successful adaptation of Hellman's *The Little Foxes* by Dorothy Parker.

The playwrights discussed in the book include some of the dozens of women who simply wrote plays for the commercial theatre, as David Belasco and Avery Hopwood did, and had no pretensions to literary merit. Rida Johnson Young's modest self-appraisal would stand for many other women playwrights: "I have never undertaken anything really big; I have contented myself with writing plays that are popular and within my ability" ("A Woman Dramatist" n.p.). Beyond this limited commercial view were many playwrights who wanted to create literary masterpieces, reintroduce poetry into a largely realistic theatre, and/or instigate social and political change. Even Young's self-deprecation must be questioned since she created a number of lively heroines who engaged in female self-actualization and she herself served as a role model for other young women desiring a career and independence. At a time when many professions were closed to women, female playwrights showed that a woman could successfully compete with men, earn considerable money, and have the pleasure of a career in the theatre. They were often awarded literary prizes for their work, presented a positive image of career women, enjoyed prestige, and had the satisfaction of participating in social change through their plays. For all of them, the possibility of independence and equality with men was important.

The role of producing groups and particular producers is an important element in the history of women playwrights. As Barlow points out,

> Around the time of World War I, so-called "little theaters" began to spring up, providing new outlets for women's talents. Little theaters—such as the Toy Theatre in Boston, the Little Theatre in Chicago, the Washington Square Playhouse, the Provincetown Playhouse, and the Neighborhood Playhouse in New York—rejected the pallid Broadway offerings. They favored either controversial European playwrights or unknown American authors. Since women often helped found these groups, artistic decisions were not solely in the hands of powerful men whose main interest was box-office receipts. Further, because participants and playwrights were unsalaried or minimally paid, these little the-

aters could scarcely afford to exclude women. The most important of these the-
aters was the Provincetown Playhouse. During the heyday of the Provincetown,
1916-1922, roughly one-third of the plays produced were by women. Women
were also actively involved in play selection and direction, as well as in the
business end of the theatre. (xix)

Special note should be given to a little-known group which produced many plays by women as part of an effort to assist the blind. For
many years the Lighthouse Players annually produced plays performed
by blind actresses for blind audiences. In 1931, for example, Winthrop
Ames donated the Booth Theatre to the group which raised $2,600
with the production of three one-act plays, including *La Divina Pastora*
by Eulalie Spence ("Three Plays Offered by Blind Actresses" 2).

In addition to the little theatres, professionals active in the commercial theatre encouraged women playwrights. Actresses such as Maxine
Elliott sought women directors to direct them in plays written by
women. Several men were very active in producing women's plays
including Arthur Hopkins, Brock Pemberton, and John Golden. In
1941 Burns Mantle wrote,

> John Golden is for women. Women playwrights in particular. In play produc-
> tion, especially with domestic comedies, he believes in the feminine touch. And
> because he has been wise enough to admit it, he has made a good deal of money
> and added considerably to his Broadway prestige. ("Watching a Stage Wife
> Grow Up" unidentified clipping, Lincoln Center)

The book concludes with a summary and analysis of the contributions of American women playwrights to the theatre in the first half of
the century. In the Appendix are listed the honors women playwrights
have received including Pulitzer Prizes, selection as one of the ten best
plays of the year, awards from *Crisis* magazine, the New York Drama
Critics Circle Award, and other awards. Many of the playwrights discussed received honorary degrees and were invited to lecture on playwriting in prestigious universities. Despite these honors, their names
are little-known today. Perhaps the publication of this book about the
women who contributed plays to the American theatre in the first fifty
years of this century will lead to publication of more of the plays, particularly in anthologies used in classrooms. Many teachers say they
want to discuss the works of women playwrights, but the scripts are not
readily available and too few of them are included in the textbooks
they use. Certainly the plays deserve our attention and deserve pro-

duction. There is no longer any excuse for the American women play-wrights of the past to be forgotten—the scripts are waiting to be read and performed.

PART ONE

Rachel Crothers (1876?-1958)

Rachel Crothers (1876?-1958) achieved popular and critical success with her earliest plays. She produced a large body of successful plays and became one of the most notable figures in the commercial theatre. From the early part of the twentieth century throughout the forties, she was an active participant in the theatre scene, writing and directing plays, organizing activities, lecturing on playwriting, and occasionally acting. Of her more than thirty plays, most were successful and were performed by outstanding actors and actresses. She was important in the theatre both as a woman writer and as a woman writing about women.

Crothers' background was one likely to have produced an independent, unconventional woman. Her childhood in Bloomington, Illinois may have been somewhat lonely, but she had the advantage of growing up in a home in which education and culture were valued. Her father, Eli Kirk Crothers, was a doctor. After Crothers' birth, her mother, Marie de Pew Crothers, returned to school, earning her medical degree in Pennsylvania in 1883. She then returned to her family in Bloomington. She had a successful practice as her daughter grew up, in contrast to the majority of women who had no career. Crothers was precocious and started writing plays at the age of 12. Her first play was *Every Cloud Has a Silver Lining*, or *The Ruined Merchant* in which she and a friend played all five roles (Crothers "The Construction of a Play" 131).

Crothers was an astonishing teen-ager. After graduating from high school at about 13, she went to Boston to earn an M. A. at the New England School of Drama. (There is uncertainty about her age and the accuracy of dates in her youth.) She remained to act as an instructor at the school for one term after her graduation in 1892. In 1896 she was quite experienced in the theatre for such a young woman, and decided to go to New York to try her luck. With no contacts, she wrote to Belasco and Frohman who answered her letters, but had no work for her. She studied in the Stanhope-Wheatcroft acting school for a year and taught there for several more. This was an important period as she had the opportunity to write one-act plays and direct students in them (Forman 56). Crothers used some of her experiences as a single woman living in a boarding house and trying to make a career in the New York theatre in her play *Thirty-nine East* which she wrote in 1904.

By the turn of the century Crothers had experience as an actress, a director, and a playwright. At this point she determined to make a career in the largely male-dominated American commercial theatre. She wrote a number of one-act and full-length plays from 1899 on. Most of these early plays fall below the quality of her mature works, but the subject matter and characterization are interesting. An example of the unconventional approach she often took in her early playwriting is *The Three of Us* (1906). Her heroine, Rhy (note that the name does not indicate gender), is an independent, strong woman, somewhat masculine, but very attractive to men. Living in a small Nevada silver town she finds herself in a compromising position. She defies two men when they urge her to marry to save her honor, pointing out that her honor is in her own hands. The play was palatable because at the end she turns to her brother for support and assistance and she marries one of the men she earlier defied. Nevertheless, the role of Rhy is unconventional, and at least explores the characterization of the New Woman. The play was successful in New York and on tour and featured Ethel Barrymore in the role of Rhy in London. With her first professionally produced full-length play Crothers attracted positive attention from audiences and critics and indicated her interest in exploring the changing world for women in America.

Myself, Bettina (1908) was a social drama examining sexuality in relation to American women. The central figure is an unmarried woman who has traveled in Europe, seen life, and had an affair. Crothers is ultimately ambiguous about the question of the double standard and the play is weak in construction. Despite the short run of thirty-two performances, the production was important because the star Maxine Elliott bought the play as a starring vehicle for herself and gave Crothers her first chance to direct a professional production. It was a major breakthrough in that period. Crothers wrote that Elliott, "had such an admiration for and faith in the work of women, that she was delighted to find a woman who could shoulder the entire reponsibility" ("Troubles of a Playwright" 14).

The support and encouragement she received from Elliott were important and Crothers subsequently helped and encouraged other women in their work. During Crothers' career she directed and staged (chose the costumes and settings, etc.) all but two of her plays. She also directed plays by other playwrights including Zoë Akins. Speaking to Djuna Barnes, Crothers noted the importance of women working together, saying, "For a woman, it is best to look to women for help; women are more daring, they are glad to take the most extraordinary chances. . . . I think I should have been longer about my destiny if I had to battle with men alone" ("The Tireless Rachel Crothers" 18).

Crothers' next play was quite literally a battle with men. Following the relative lack of success of her last play, she might well have chosen a popular subject and written a play which was compatible with accepted outlooks. Instead, in *A Man's World* (1910) she wrote a play with controversial subject matter and an ending which did not pander to popular taste. The subjects treated are the double standard, the question of illegitimacy and shame for the woman and child, and the problems of women of the streets.

In *A Man's World*, as in many of her plays, the leading figure is an attractive, successful woman who feels a conflict between her career and romance. Frank Ware writes novels, and has been perceived by the critics as a male writer until the day the play begins. Her identity has been discovered by a critic who writes:

> "The Beaten Path" is the strongest thing that Frank Ware has ever done. Her first work attracted wide attention when we tho't Frank Ware was a man, but now that we know she is a woman we are more than ever impressed by the strength and scope of her work. She has laid her scenes this time on the East side in the wretched poverty of the tenement houses, and the marvel is that any woman could see and know so much and depict crime and degradation so boldly. Her great cry is for women—to make them better by making them freer. It is decidedly the most striking book of the year. (12-13)

The play reflects Crothers' sympathy for women who encounter difficulties in the world, particularly women who have had affairs, and possibly illegitimate children, and are considered "fallen women" by society. Her heroine is raising a child whose mother suffered in this way. She has a deep hatred for the unknown man who seduced the woman and fathered her child. The man did not suffer, but the woman died in disgrace. The long arm of coincidence figures heavily in the plot, somewhat weakening its impact: Gaskell, the man Frank Ware has come to love, turns out to be the villain in the case. Crothers wrote a strong scene between the two in which their moral outlooks are contrasted. Frank is appalled that he has no sense of guilt and perceives nothing wrong in judging a woman harshly for having an affair, while excusing the man. In an exchange which is echoed in later Crothers' plays, the antithetical points of view are made clear:

> Gaskell— No woman with that in her life could be the same to any man—no matter how he loved her—or what he said or swore. It's different. It's different. A man wants the mother of his children to be the purest woman in the world.
>
> Frank— Yes, and a man expects the purest woman in the world to forgive him anything—everything. It's wrong. It's hideously wrong. (99)

The basic reason for incompatibility between the two lies in Frank's belief that women are capable of succeeding in the world because they are equal to men; Gaskell believes that women are not equal and need the protection of men. He tells Frank, "Why this is a man's world. Women'll never change anything. . . . Women are only meant to be loved—and men have got to take care of them. That's the whole business. You'll acknowledge it someday—when you do love somebody" (40-43).

At the conclusion of the play Gaskell is proved wrong; Frank does love him, but she cannot accept his conservative, narrow-minded opinions and she rejects him. Crothers' ending surprised and disturbed many critics and audience members. Some of them agreed with the attitude Gaskell expressed early in the play: that Frank didn't really believe all she was saying and that her ideals weren' t deeply rooted. Some critics even suggested that the character would really change her mind and accept Gaskell when she cooled off. Although the play seems a challenge to accepted opinions, many conservative writers approved of it because it proposed one standard of decency for men and women. One critic wrote, "Miss Rachel Crothers in her wholesome play, 'A Man's World,' proves her case that there should be a single standard of morals as between men and women" ("A Man's World," *Theatre Magazine* 68). Some critics simply felt the play was unrealistic—"the dish of life is likely to be served otherwise for some time to come" (qtd. in Abrahamson 316). Most of the critics agreed, however, that the play was well-written and theatrically effective. The critic for *The Nation* wrote,

> Whatever may be thought of its philosophy, the fact remains that in "A Man's World" . . . Miss Rachel Crothers has written one of the strongest, most interesting, logical, and dramatic pieces on the now dominant topic of the relations of the sexes than has been seen in this city for years. For once sense has not

been sacrificed to sentiment, or the desire for a happy ending. ("A Man's World" 146)

The critics generally commented positively on her craftsmanship. However, it is clear that the play has artifice and that she is still relying on already old-fashioned techniques. For example, her colorful bohemians living in the apartment house with Frank are utterly stereotypical in accents, occupations, and dialogue. In her later plays she developed original and amusing characters in scenes with witty dialogue. She also mastered construction and, particularly, treated exposition more smoothly. In this play she still moves characters in and out of scenes in an artificial way and the exposition is heavyhanded. Despite the play's faults, however, the characterization of the heroine, her conflict with the prevailing mores, her social consciousness, and her decision to stand by her ideals and go it alone at the conclusion of the play reveal Crothers' skill and determination.

The controversy over the actions of Crothers' central character did not end when the play closed. In fact, the playwright Augustus Thomas was moved to write a play taking an opposing point of view which was presented a little more than a year after the opening of Crothers' play. His play, *As a Man Thinks* (1911), reflected the generally held views regarding the role of women in the household and the acceptability of the double standard (Shafer, "Whose Realism? Rachel Crothers' Power Struggle in the American Theatre" 201). It's success fully established Thomas as the most important playwright in the American theatre in this period. However, *A Man's World* established Crothers as the chief spokesperson for *women* in the theatre. She maintained this role throughout the 20's and the 30's, often focusing on women's liberation and generally exploring the complexities of women's lives in a period of social change. A major polemic element which found great support among the women in the audience, was the abolition of the double standard. Not, as many women would feel today, to allow sexual freedom for men *and* women, but to insure monogamy on the part of both husband and wife. Crothers aimed at the women in the audience because she felt that they really controlled the American stage, saying, "They are the prevailing part of the audience and therefore really largely decide what plays shall be seen (Abrahamson 170). The determining element in her work, however, was entertainment, rather than demand for social change. As Clark and Freedley wrote, "She was not a woman with a grievance who expected the public to condone poor play writing because her cause was just, but a skilled dramatist who knew that the best cause in the world could not be effectively pleaded unless the means of presenting it were acceptable to playgoers. Throughout her career. . . she has consistently borne in mind that though the theatre can be used to persuade, its function is not primarily hortatory" (*A History* 675).

In her next play, *He and She,* Crothers analyzed the conflict in a household in which the husband and wife compete in their careers. The play opened on the road in 1911. Crothers revised it as *The Herfords* for production in Boston in 1912, but it still wasn't ready for a New York run. In the following years Crothers continued revising the play hoping for a New York production. The play will be discussed below in relationship to the time in which it was presented on stage.

In *Ourselves* (1913) Crothers again utilized some seamy material which she researched at the Bedford Reformatory for women. In the terminology of the day, the play dealt with "white slavery." In this play a girl of the streets is brought into a high class home in an effort to reform her. Unlike the usual Crothers characters, Molly is vulgar and low. Despite her elevated environment, both she and her high society mentor are surprised to find that she is not safe from the attentions of a married man. The social experiment is to some extent a failure, but the society woman has learned a few things about the world and her own responsibilities in it and Molly leaves with the intention of improving her own life. The play was popular with audiences and critics. The *New York Tribune* critic said the play was "written by a woman of sophisticated intellect and fine feeling, who brings to it the passionate revolt felt by most American women of her class against a double standard of morality for husbands and wives (qtd. in Abrahamson 322). The critic for the *New York Times* called it "a gripping, living drama, full of interest and produced with much attention to detail" ("Ourselves"11). The most appreciative audience for the play was composed of the three hundred young women doing time in Bedford Reformatory. Crothers arranged a special performance for the unfortunate inmates who "laughed and wept at a clear-cut picture of their own lives" which included a scene set in a reformatory (qtd. in Abrahamson 70).

In 1917 Crothers was about thirty-nine years old, financially independent, unmarried, and successful in her career in the theatre. At this time she utilized her abilities in charitable work which continued throughout her life. She organized the Women's War Relief which involved the efforts of about two thousand women in the theatrical profession. They raised more than six million dollars to help families whose wage earners were in the army and also entertained at camps and hospitals. These activities continued for three years during which Crothers was highly praised for her organizational abilities and social concerns. Her success enabled her to stand as a role model for women who wished to move into administrative areas of the work force in the theatre and elsewhere.

In 1919, possibly because she was busy with the Women's War Relief, she produced not a new play, but *Thirty-nine East* which was fifteen years old. It is ironic that the although the play related to Crothers' earlier experiences as a single, independent woman seeking a career in the theatre, the denouement and the characterization of the heroine are in sharp contrast to Crothers' own life. Penelope Penn (even her name seems silly) tries for a career, but concludes by marrying a man who will protect her. The play is definitely of the period in which it was written, and the characterization and the conclusion reveal that it was written before *A Man's World* and *He and She*.

The play ran for 150 performances. John Corbin noted that the opening night audience "was frankly and very heartily responsive" to the play and the excellent acting. He said that in the play "Miss Crothers' touch was everywhere deft and lifelike. From beginning to end the play is without a really false touch, and it has many and many a delightfully true one" ("Wisteria Romance"1). In contrast Heywood Broun found the play old-fashioned and unrealistic. He considered it ludicrous that a successful playwright and "efficient organizer and executive in the Stage Women's War Relief" had written such a play: "It is a vehemently sentimental play and the heroine is held up as an adorable person because she is naive, coy, and refined." He continued that he would bet ten cents against ten years profit from the theatre that Crothers, herself, did not believe that "The most admirable and adorable quality in womanhood is helplessness" ("Thirty-nine East" n.p.). Broun was not the only critic to see a disparity in this and other plays between Crothers' own approach to life and what she put in her plays. The clear implication in Broun's criticism is that Crothers should take a more realistic approach, and not pander to the conservative, sentimental elements in the audience.

Broun's dissatisfaction continued in the next year with Crothers' production of *He and She* (1920) in which a woman gives up her career to devote herself to her child. Doubting that "soup tastes better when opened by loving hands rather than hired help or that girls become entangled in love affairs because their mothers are painting or giving lectures" he concluded, "Indeed, we feel so strongly on this subject that as soon as we have a couple of weeks to spare we are going to write a pro-feminist play in which the young girl of the house marries a street cleaner because her mother is too busy baking apple pies to take proper care of her daughter" (qtd. in Abrahamson 356).

He and She presents the difficulties of sculptors Ann and Tom Herford which occur when they compete for a commission and she wins. Ann's father, husband, and friends—virtually everyone except another career woman—seem to think she has done something deplorable in competing and winning. Ann identifies a major factor in the failure of women to create successful careers. "You've always fought me, Father. You've never thought I had any right to work—never believed in my ability. Now that I've proved that I have some—Why can't you acknowledge it?" In response, her father says that Tom has had a blow that no man on earth could stand, and that she should offer to give up the commission (919).

Whether her father is correct in saying no man could put up with it, he is right about Tom. He first asks what is to become of Millicent when she is home from boarding school for the summer, and then says he will never touch a penny of the money Ann earns from the commission. As they discuss the problem, Tom says, "You're a woman and I'm a man. You're not free in the same way. If you won't stop because I ask it—I say you *must* (921). The discussion is interrupted by the sudden arrival of Millicent who has run away from boarding school. In the next act it comes out that she wants to marry the chauffeur at her school. In the end, Ann's decision is made on the basis of concern for her child. She decides to give up the commission, and apparently her career, as long as the child needs her. Crothers seemingly agreed with the men in the play who say that if a woman marries, then she must accept the responsibility of raising children rather than having a career. This is a conclusion which many of the women, and at least some of the men in the audience found unacceptable. It is not a "happy ending." Ann says her husband will have to make her sculpture while she takes care of her sixteen-year-old daughter. Even Tom realizes at this point that she is making a sacrifice which she will regret and which is not necessary. Ann responds that she will at times hate Tom and the daughter, but she feels she must make this choice.

The response of both critics and audiences to the ending was mixed. Louis R. Reid, called the play "a drama on women's rights which is solved in favor of the home rather than the career" ("He and She" *New York Dramatic Mirror* 310). He noted that the men laughed and applauded the male views and the women responded favorably to the defense of career women. Although the ending seems weak because the problem of the child is somewhat contrived, Crothers' exploration of the problem of a career mother was complex and significant in its time. It is an interesting point that Crothers, herself, played Ann. While Alexander Woolcott admired her honest performance, he felt that her inexperience as a professional actress marred the production. Calling the play a "tragedy of the New Woman," he applauded the ideas but felt that the play often lapsed into debate ("He and She" 16). The play ran only 28 performances, but in 1925 Arthur Hobson Quinn selected it for inclusion in his *Representative American Plays*, describing it as "one of the most striking plays which deal with the general question of woman's rights and responsibilities, of which its author has stood for some time as a representative in drama" (893).

He and She has occasionally been revived with success. In 1980 it was presented by the BAM Theater Company in Brooklyn. Reviewer David Sterritt found it necessary to tell readers who the author was: "Rachel Crothers is no longer a name to conjure with, especially among younger playgoers. Yet she was a major force in the American theater between 1905 and 1940, writing nearly 40 plays, and producing and directing many of them herself." He said the play, starring Laurie Kennedy, was a triumph.

> "He and She" came out in 1910. Aside from some archaic slang and a few obscure references, however, it seems astonishingly contemporary. The subject is women's liberation, and equality between the sexes. The perspective is personal and familial, rather than social and political. The approach is thoughtful, emotionally sensitive, and exquisitely balanced. Indeed, comparing it with its current movie equivalent, "Kramer vs. Kramer," I submit that "He and She" is every bit as funny, sad, provocative, and enlightened. It's also a sight more sophisticated in its complex web of family ties, rivalries, and loyalties. ("A Strikingly Modern Look at Feminism" 19)

The several plays discussed above have divided critics regarding the extent of Crothers' feminism. After studying her plays and criticism of them, Doris Abramson concluded by asking, "Was Rachel Crothers, then, an ardent feminist?" Her answer was,

> Speeches in *A Man's World* and *He and She* make her seem so, and yet one hesitates at the word ardent. A woman who had her eye on Broadway success—and who achieved it over a long period of time—had to disguise her ardor for a feminist message. She put critics off guard at times by giving them the polished comedies that Broadway audiences wanted, and inserting into them some questions about women's position in American society. She took time-worn themes and breathed new life into them by approaching questions a bit differently, always from a woman's point of view. Her popularity in her own time should not keep us from acknowledging her contribution to American theater. (64)

A major event in this period was the passage of the nineteenth amendment to the constitution in 1919. Achievement of the right to vote was symbolic of other freedoms as well. Howard Taubman noted a change in Crothers' plays at this point: "She used the stage to articulate the case for women's freedom. When the battle was won she did not shrink from poking fun at the liberated woman's pretensions. Her work had sanity and humor, often sophistication and maturity. Although she did not dig deeply into the question of marriage, the new place of women, the rebellion of the young, she was always timely and bright" (*The Making of the American Theatre* 157).

The new freedom in the twenties, particularly for women, led to a series of satirical plays. In 1921 *Nice People* opened with an outstanding cast. Francine Larrimore, Tallulah Bankhead and Katharine Cornell played young flappers—excellent roles which revealed their talent. The men's roles are less interesting and more conventional, as is the story.

The best scene is the first in which the three young ladies and two of their beaux are waiting for the most sought after of the young men in their crowd to arrive. Here as they drink, dance, smoke, and play the piano Crothers reveals their shallow, self-indulgent characters. The gossipy, barbed dialogue is in the line of *The School for Scandal*. The scene concludes with a spirited argument between the outspoken, smart young heroine, Teddy, and her father and aunt because she wants to go dance, stay out till morning and breakfast with her fast friends at Childs.

The rest of the play really is not memorable. Teddy and a shallow young man, Scotty, drive to Connecticut. Their behavior appears to be licentious and her "friends" spread the scandal. Teddy meets a man with real qualities, but nearly marries Scotty to save her name. By the last act Teddy has changed through spending time in the wholesome countryside raising chickens, she and her family are reconciled, and she marries the appropriate man.

Again Crothers pleased the audience, but a number of critics were displeased by the message conveyed by the highly conventional ending. Alexander Woolcott thought the beginning a "pointed and genuinely interesting play" but found the conclusion "painfully threadbare and shopworn in the theatre. . . . The only trouble with the country air is that it is heavy with the memories of a million last acts ("The Severe Miss Crothers" 11)." Louis V. De Foe wrote in the *New York World* that Crothers' ending was "cheaply and hopelessly melodramatic" and that she should have looked at the newspapers to see what was really going on in American society: girls like Teddy "plunge straight into the unhappiness which is the logical end of the course she pursues." He further suggested that Crothers didn't give the play an honest ending because it might alienate the class of people depicted in the play and concluded, "We recall no play of the current season more inept and irritating—inept because it is so flagrantly false in logic" ("Wild Youth" n.p.). Crothers' play appealed to audiences because it was ultimately "naughty, but nice." She made the play slightly controversial and titillating by the discussion of kissing, the questioning of the double standard and other such elements of contemporary interest, but she reinforced the norms of American society. These flappers, she seemed to say, appear to be wild and cynical, but they really have good values and will conform.

Nice People was the first Crothers play to be selected by Burns Mantle as one of the ten best plays of the year. In *Best Plays of 1920-21* he wrote that he had selected it although "the critics were inclined to patronize it" (224) because "it is of vital importance today, we feel, because of its sincere treatment of a present-day theme, though it does slip into the grooves of the theatrically conventional American comedy before it is concluded" (v).

The critical response was even more positive for Crothers' next play. *Mary the Third* (1923) has an amusing structure, delightful visual effects, and some telling satire on women, along with sympathy for their problems. The first two scenes show a young woman deciding to marry after being courted on a sofa which is in a sharp spot of light center stage. The first scene is in 1870 and the girl, Mary, is the mother of the second young woman seen in 1897. Act I focuses on the third Mary and her conflicts with her mother and grandmother over morals and marriage. She wants to go camping for a couple of weeks with two young men she likes in order to see which one would make the best husband. She actually sets out on the trip in a speeding automobile (which was shown on stage), but secretly returns and discovers how unhappy her mother's marriage has been. The play is significant in that it contains a serious discussion of the possibility of divorce. Vowing that her life will be different from the first two Marys, Mary the third idealistically declaims:

> I shall have my own money. I'll *make* it. I shall live with a man because I love him and only as I love him. I shall be able to take care of myself and my children if necessary. Anything else gives the man a horrible advantage, of course. It makes the woman a kept woman. . . . The biggest, fairest, most chivalrous man on earth can't feel the same toward a woman who lives with him only because she has to be taken care of—as he does to one who lives with him because she loves him. (92)

However, in a surprising denouement, Crothers satirizes the New Woman, by making her act just as women before her have done. Despite her determination to be different, Mary the third does just as her mother and grandmother did—she surrenders to the passion of the moment, and agrees to marry an attractive man in the usual "old blind accidental lottery" (96).

Critics praised the acting and the delightful production. John Corbin expressed the general opinion that the play was "abundantly amusing" and that the satire would draw an audience ("The Sphinx, Three Marys" 1). Several critics felt the play was Crothers' best work so far. Burns Mantle selected it as one of the ten best plays of the 1922-23 season. It should be noted that the choice meant much more in this period when many plays were being produced. Crothers was in competition with 189 other playwrights.

Crothers turned her satire in another direction in her next major play. *Expressing Willie* (1924) satirizes the tendency to leap at new religions and fads. The particular vogue she mocks is the cult of self-expression and the belief that every human being has a "Divine Power". In the play, Willie Smith (the name clearly signifying an ordinary man) has made an immense amount of money because he got in on the "toothpaste game" through the continual urging and direction of his strong-willed mother. Crothers' play is similar in its comical situation to Molière's *The Would-be Gentleman*. The strongest of Willie's new arty friends is Frances Sylvester, a determined, glamorous woman of the world willing to condescend to him because of his wealth. His equally determined mother perceives this and invites Minnie, his former sweetheart from the middle west, to save him from the calculating fortune hunter.

Crothers' depiction of the hangers-on is very funny. Their sneering reaction to poor, plain Minnie when she slips on the highly waxed floor on her way to the piano is amusingly portrayed. They alternate between back-biting and obvious flattery of one another and Willie. He *seems* to swallow all their new ideas of finding greatness and God within yourself, but Minnie actually *does*. At first scorned by them and embarrassing to Willie, she rises to spiritual heights and a sense of personal freedom. She plays the piano in a way which thrills most of the hangers-on, annoys Frances, and impresses Willie. At the end of the play the insincerity of his money-hungry friends has been revealed to Willie. He wants to dump them and the new religion, marry Minnie, and further her career. She is not at all disenchanted with the new religion, however, and says she doesn't want him: she wants freedom and self-expression. Willie kisses her, Frances appears, everyone talks at once and Willie has the last line, "I'm expressing myself all right— and I'm going to keep right on" (79). A few critics again objected to the conventional happy ending, but it is much more logical and realistic than some of Crothers' earlier denouements. True, Minnie has come out of her shell, but is she really a great pianist? Minnie and Willie end up together as they should, but she will never revert to the same plain Minnie because she has moved to a plane of self-confidence, beauty, and assertiveness. This is a very funny play, with playable characters and a satirical theme which is applicable to any age. It is a period play, but the satire is still valid.

John Corbin's review indicates the success of the play. He stated that he couldn't have anticipated, "the perfect conjunction of playwriting, acting, and stage management that unfolded itself like a miracle." Noting the audience's response to Crothers' satire, he wrote, "the sallies of wit took the audience by storm; it fairly shouted with laughter" ("Rachel Crothers Triumphs" 22). Critics all praised Crystal Herne for her performance as Minnie. Arthur Hornblow indicated some surprise at the high quality of Crothers' play, noting the "clever and hilarious situation, her unusually witty dialogue, the excellence of the acting and the admirable stage direction took everyone by surprise, and enabled the new piece to register as one of the biggest hits of the season" ("Expressing Willie" 15-16). Alexander Woolcott called it "a gay and engaging play acted to perfection by a cast happily chosen and expertly directed [by Crothers], it is a comedy which made these old ribs ache as they have not in many a week" ("Rachel Crothers Outdoes Herself" n.p.). Heywood Broun called it "one of the best plays of the year and among the most skillful of all American comedies" ("Expressing Willie" n.p.). The play ran for 281 performances and Crothers stated in later years that it was her favorite of all her plays (qtd. in Cordell, ed., *Representative Modern Plays* 499.) It was revived in 1978 by the Off-Off Broadway Encompass Theatre.

Crothers' next important play followed the moderately successful *A Lady's Virtue* (1925) and the complete failure *Venus* (1927). Neither play was printed. *Let Us Be Gay* was produced in 1929 and provided another fine role for Francine Larrimore. This play is rather the opposite of *Nice People* in that the first scene is the most conventional and the least memorable, and the rest works quite well. The role of Kitty Brown is witty, attractive, and complex. The first scene is a standard scene of a betrayed wife weeping and telling her husband it's all over. The rest of the play takes place several years later during a weekend in a ritzy country house where couples are flirting, drinking, swimming, and playing bridge. The play almost seems a problem play treatment of *Private Lives*, complete with a balcony where the former husband and wife meet under a full moon.

Crothers mirrors the tensions regarding divorce, adultery, and virginity in a changing society. For example, a young woman and her fiancé discussing the double standard have the following exchange:

Bruce: When a man wants to marry—pick out a mother for his children, he
          wants the straightest, finest cleanest thing in the world.
Deirdre: And if a girl wants the darling boy she marries to be the same
          thing—where the hell is she going to find him?
Bruce: It's not the same thing at all for you and me. (145)

The play combines qualities of a serious problem play with the witty, often ironic dialogue Crothers wrote so well. The ending is one which might provoke argument today, but which probably reflects the reality of the time in which it was written and our time: after carrying on affairs to see what Bob and other men found so attractive in idle romances, Kitty knows after three years that she has had freedom, gaiety, and independence, but a great deal of loneliness, disappointment, and restlessness as well. Bob never did want to leave her and in the conclusion proposes that they reunite. Their commitment at the end is to a remarriage based on a more honest appraisal of the nature of marriage and a vow of faithfulness—whether that is realistic is a question which can always be asked. It is indicative of the change in outlooks that the husband is glad to have her back despite her affairs; twenty years earlier in Pinero's *Mid-Channel* the wife was rejected and committed suicide.

Once again Crothers was in the *Best Plays* and had quite a hit. The critics were favorable, Benjamin de Casseres expressing the general opinion that Crothers never bored and was witty, "She is one of the few really clever . . . American women writers of the day" ("Let Us Be Gay" 64). Tribute was paid to her ability as a director by Robert Little in *Theatre Arts Magazine* who said that the success of the play was at least fifty percent due to the direction. "We do not have enough good directors. Miss Crothers is one of them. I wish that between plays of her own she could more often be induced to slap and pull vigorous life into the plays of others" ("Let Us Be Gay" 333). Similarly, Brooks Atkinson wrote, "Playwright Crothers keeps the ball of comedy gaily in the air and director Crothers stirred up the actors so skillfully that they bubble with entertainment" ("Two Bites" 19). Again, this is important in that Crothers demonstrated her ability in an administrative capacity. After the success in New York, the play went on to a successful run in London with Tallulah Bankhead in the lead.

In an interview regarding her play When Ladies Meet (1932), Crothers expressed the opinion that the world was still a man's world: "He's made all the rules. When women juggle them and do so for this so-called freedom they still must lie and cheat and deceive. They can't yet be frank and open and impersonally free as a man" ("Rachel Crothers" n.p.). Much of the play involves discussions between women, and between women and men, about the position of a single woman in a world in which the old rules no longer seem to apply.

Again Crothers has a novelist as the heroine, but Mary is not depicting the tough social problems that Frank Ware was. She is writing a novel about a woman in love with a married man who lives with him for a year to see if it is really love. At the end of the year she proposes (if it is) to go to the wife and explain it all. She assumes the wife will give the man a divorce so the love can be made public. Several characters point out that neither the single woman nor the wife would behave in that way. Mary believes they would, for the novel is about her life and her love for her publisher. The action of the play builds to a fine scene between Mary and the publisher's wife, neither of whom realizes the true identity of the other. The discussion of marriage, promiscuity, and other subjects is frank, interesting, and amusing. One idea which certainly must have been ahead of its time was that women would not necessarily be rejected by potential husbands if they weren't virgins. The publisher's wife says, "Don' t you think if a man *knows* in the first place a woman has had other men—if he loves her he doesn't give a damn—he just does? And if it's the real thing he wants to marry her. Why not?" (107).

When the ladies each perceive each others' identity (as the publisher enters Mary's room), the play moves to a darker mood and ends with a condemnation of the double standard. As usual in Crothers' plays this is not a plea for more sexual freedom for women, but for an end to adultery and seduction on the part of men. The play presents no solutions to the problem raised, but the two ladies have become more realistic about the world. Each has the opportunity to make an honest appraisal of the other without the husband's male glance as a distorting factor. The wife realizes the other women were not tramps as she had always thought, but sympathetic, intelligent women like Mary, who also suffered from her husband's selfishness. Although she has condoned her husband's affairs for years, she now rejects him. Mary, realizing her romance wasn't a unique, idealistic experience, does the same, and we assume she also alters her novel. The relationship of the women, their mutual respect, and their determination to alter their male-centered approach to life are important elements in this play.

Brooks Atkinson remarked on the "gusto of Miss Crothers' thinking" and said the play had "relieved the gloom of Autumn playgoing." After praising all aspects of the production, he discussed at length the high quality of Crothers' directing and her ability to train actors in their craft ("Three People and Miss Crothers"1). Critics pointed out the appropriateness of serious discussions of social problems in the theatre as well as the comedy and the play was performed for 173 perfor-

mances to sold-out houses (*The Best Plays of 1932-1933* 105). The play
won the Megrue Prize for Comedy and was revived in 1933. A review
of the 1933 production in London headed " 'When Ladies Meet' With
Strong Cast, Rapturously Greeted," called it a "notable addition" to
the season which received a "rapturous welcome" ("Crothers Play in
London" 15).

Within the play a novelist is relating events which have occurred in
her life and her own reaction to being a single career woman. Crothers
was now over fifty years old and had never married, nor had she had
any known lovers. Speculation would naturally arise that Mary was a
representative of Crothers and that her own life was a choice between
marriage and a career. Her statements about marriage in "The Stage
and the Modern Woman" seem to indicate that was the case. She
stated that strong, independent women had a narrow group of men
from which to choose a husband, because superior men found it hard
to accept superior women. She said that such men continued to
believe they should provide for women, and that "the superior man
will not have the superior woman—not on the superior woman's
terms" (qtd. in Gottlieb 120).

There was no doubt that Crothers was a superior woman. During
the run of *As Husbands Go* in the 1930-1931 season newpapers had
carried a story saying that she had achieved the distinction of being
America's foremost woman playwright. She was the only woman
invited to take part in a seminar on playwriting at the University of
Pennsylvania. In addition to her work in the theatre she utilized her
organization and administrative skills by engaging in many charitable
activities. In 1931 she worked with Brock Pemberton, Sam Harris,
Antoinette Perry and others to establish the Stage Relief Fund and
acted as its president. In 1933 she was elected to the National Institute
of Arts and Letters. Her success in the theatre and some work in films
had brought her a very large income, she was quite at home in society,
and she had a beautiful home in Redding, Connecticut. Still ahead was
one of her greatest successes, *Susan and God*.

Crothers worked for six years in Hollywood, but wrote few things
which she thought were worthwhile, so she returned to the stage with a
comedy called *Susan and God* (364). With this play she returned to the
social satire which had been so successful in the past. As *Expressing
Willie* debunked the cult of self-expression, her newest play debunked

the many cults of pseudo-religion which particularly attracted wealthy, bored women.

The Susan in the case has just returned from Europe and in the first act it is apparent why she had gone: she is bored by her adolescent daughter and her alcoholic husband. One of her friends quips, "I've never been sure whether Barrie drinks because Susan's tired of him— or Susan's tired of him because he drinks" (6). When Susan arrives, she is giddy, charming, chic, and utterly delightful. She babbles with enthusiasm about her wonderful spiritual experience with Lady Wiggam's new movement, interlarding her comments with inquiries about somebody's dogs, the latest gossip, and information that she has brought someone exquisite silk panties. Her friends are enormously amused by her description of her conversion, and her description of a chat with a gardener ("in one of the most marvelous tulip beds") who had also been converted after he had tried to kill his wife, "and now he actually *likes* his wife—very much indeed" (8). Barrie and his gawky daughter arrive seeking Susan, but he is told she isn't there. Later, Susan has irritated everyone with her talk of the movement, Lady Wiggam, and God and they decide to pretend to go along with it and then reveal their joke. As one of them starts to confess, Susan encourages him with assurances that he can conquer his problems, and with God's help be made over. Barrie enters in time to hear this, and seems to be the only convert to the movement.

In the ensuing scenes Barrie convinces Susan to give him another chance, and to spend the entire summer with him and their daughter. By the end of the play Susan realizes that her commitment to the movement was shallow and that she really does love her husband. Faced with losing him to another woman, she asks him to let her try to become a real wife, and concludes that the help they need lies not in God, but in themselves. The play is a clever satire with many amusing types. The role of Susan was one of the most memorable played by the exquisite Gertrude Lawrence. The handsome settings described in the script were designed by Jo Mielziner. All in all this was a very elegant, successful production.

The play was very popular and ran for 288 performances. Critics found it delightful. Brooks Atkinson wrote, "Given a current fad for a subject it is reasonable to suppose that Miss Crothers will make a refreshing play out of it. For Miss Crothers is one of our most sagacious women, not only about fundamentals in people but about fundamentals in theatre. By planning a play deliberately, she knows how to draw her theme out of her characters, not forgetting to keep her story entertaining" ("Susan and God" 26). Edith Isaacs said it might not be the "best of Crothers' many good plays, but with Gertrude Lawrence's acting it seems to be. . . . Rachel Crothers has theatrical skill and a sense of universality in the particulars" ("Susan and God" 918). It was inevitable that some of the reviews sounded like the summing up of a long career. Grenville Vernon wrote in *The Commonweal*, "Her successes have been many and well earned. 'Susan and God' is among them and the most delightful play the season has yet given" ("Susan and God" 606). Not surprisingly, the play was picked as one of the ten best of the year.

Susan and God was subsequently revived in 1943 and was later chosen for the opening production of the City Center Theatre. It was made into a film directed by George Cukor in 1940 starring Joan Crawford. It has been performed in recent years, notably at the Rapport Theatre in Los Angeles. Robert Koehler found the acting in this production disappointing, but commented that the play still speaks to audiences today, "Think of New Age devotees or born-again Christians, and the play becomes a commentary on how Americans are particularly vulnerable to spiritual trends" ("Stage Beat" 10).

Crothers had written her first play as a twelve year old girl in 1890. By the time of her last production, *Susan and God*, the world had changed almost unbelievably. She was disturbed by the coming war and could not write, so she turned her attention in 1940 to the organization of the American theatre Wing of the British Relief Society. She worked with Gertrude Lawrence, Antoinette Perry, and other women to set up an organization with more than a thousand women who worked in the New York theatre and more than 2000 in the rest of the country. This organization was very important in helping England in the fight against Hitler. After 1945 she wrote two more plays but they never appeared on the stage. Crothers spent her last years encouraging other women in the theatre, particularly young playwrights, and occasionally producing or directing. In 1958 she died in her home in Connecticut at the age of eighty. Her long career was filled with many dazzling successes.

When Crothers lectured at the University of Pennsylvania in the playwriting seminar organized by Arthur Hobson Quinn, she spoke about "The Construction of a Play." While she did not say anything very profound, the lecture reveals her attitudes about playwriting and her method. She was a great admirer of Shaw and had an early interest in Ibsen, rewriting *A Doll House* slightly for performance by her high school drama club. Her early grounding, then, was in realism and plays with social concerns. She stated in her lecture, "Personally I believe that great realism—realism at its best is the highest form of dramatic writing" (126). Many of her comments were conservative. Most of the new movements in theatre she condemned as destructive of drama. She mocked the small art theatre, saying it was usually made up of neither the best amateurs or professionals, "but people with dreams and ideals who raise money and produce the play they think too good for the commercial theatre.... The scenery is arty, the acting is immature, the direction weak, but each little group has a cult and a following" (133). She did say that she believed in a true art theatre which would be endowed, and free from commercial pressures.

As to her own method of composition, she emphasized careful construction in which the actions grow from the seeds planted in the first act. She began with an idea, developed a story and characters, but kept the construction open and fluid, "Because in the writing itself unexpected developments come as the sparks catch fire from each other; and too fixed a framework stops that growing thing which may have better stuff in it than one knew". Finally, she created the dialogue "where the characters take the whole thing into their own hands and say to me what they think" (129-130).

Crothers was certainly no groundbreaker in her technique and did not deviate from her realistic construction and realistic staging. Her innovations lie in the subject matter which she introduced: concerns of women as the century changed and opportunities for careers, freedom, and sexual license appeared. She was successful in pleasing audiences as she seemed to be able to walk a fine line between introducing unpleasant subject matter and alienating audiences. She was occasionally criticized for ending her plays with a conventional solution which would appeal to the audience. In the decades following her death her plays seemed less daring and unusual; the plays dealing with women's concerns hold up less well than her comedies which satirize cults, pretensions, affectations, and shallow approaches to life. Given the circumstances of the commercial theatre, it was amazing that a woman could have the success she had. One of the most important elements of her career was opening the doors for women playwrights and directors. Compared to the playwrights who inspired her, Shaw and Ibsen, she was not a great playwright. Nevertheless, she stands out as a highly successful playwright who believed in tackling difficult subjects, and examining the problems of current society on stage. Her career was effectively summed up in 1943 by Arthur Hobson Quinn: "She is, above all, a practical playright with a keen sense of what is theatrically effective. She directs her own plays and, with a feminine interest for detail, presents a stage setting in which there is rarely a jarring note. Yet she has steadily declined to be merely entertaining, and in consequence her plays form a body of drama whose significance grows under inspection and whose unity of purpose becomes steadily more apparent ("Rachel Crothers and the Feminine Criticism of Life" 50) .

Susan Glaspell (1876-1948)

Susan Glaspell (1876-1948) was one of the most talented and original women playwrights writing in the first half of the century. Her name is closely associated with the famous Provincetown Players which she and her husband George Cram Cook founded. Most of her plays were forgotten from the thirties to the eighties in the United States although her one-act *Trifles* was frequently anthologized and performed. In recent years Glaspell has attracted the attention of scholars and some of her plays have been revived. During her lifetime she wrote thirteen plays, fourteen novels, and over fifty short stories, essays, and articles. In 1931 she became the second woman playwright to receive the Pulitzer Prize. After receiving this award for *Alison's House* she wrote no plays which were produced, and this mysterious withdrawal from a successful theatrical career has perplexed historians and critics. An examination of Glaspell's life and career provides a tenable explanation for her withdrawal from playwriting, and also reveals the extent to which she was influenced by German Expressionism but remained the quintessential American in her philosophical and social outlooks.

Glaspell was born in Iowa in "the heartland of America" on July 1 during the centennial of the founding of the United States. American history and democratic ideals are an important part of her writing. She was one of the few women attending Drake University in the late nineteenth century. There she published stories, acted as literary editor of the college newspaper, and won prizes in oratorical competitions which frequently had set topics dealing with the nature of Americanism. After finishing her education, Glaspell worked for two years as a reporter for the *Daily News* in Des Moines. By 1889, only two years out of college, she was earning her living by writing short stories.

Living in her hometown, Davenport, she was involved in radical groups which believed in the New Thought and opposed conservative, small-town politics and social outlooks. Far from being oppressed by a melancholy *fin de siècle* feeling, Americans were imbued with a feeling of growth, the sense that progress was inevitable, and that a new century with great possibilities was around the corner. Although, as one writer puts it, Glaspell was "raised in the 19th century tradition that idealized patriotism, piety, and competition, progress, and respectability" (Noe 66), she was, in fact, quite a rebel who shocked her friends and family by carrying on a romance with George Cram Cook, a married man with a divorce in his past. With Cook she shared the many interests which were reflected in her novel *The Visioning* (1911). These included biological and social Darwinism, divorce laws, trade unions, prison reform, socialism, pacifism, and feminism. These interests inform her plays and give a depth and richness to the characters.

Glaspell's upbringing in the Midwest gave her a great admiration for the strong pioneers who created the cities by the rivers where she was raised, and she emulated them in breaking new ground in her playwriting and fighting for what she believed was *truly* American. According to Lawrence Langner, she was a "delicate woman with sad eyes and a sweet smile who seemed fragile as old lace, until you talked to her and glimpsed the steel underneath" (*The Magic Curtain* 70). A final element in what might be described as progressive Americanism was the strong belief in democracy she shared with Cook, whom she married in 1913. So strong was this belief that she and Cook ultimately went to Greece to find the source of democracy and there Cook died.

Shortly after Cook and she were married they went to Provincetown, Massachusetts. There they associated with bohemians, writers, artists, and radicals such as John Reed. They established the Provincetown Players in 1915 and worked with Robert Edmond Jones and others who were excited by experimental theatre and by German Expressionist plays in particular. Jones was an important influence on Glaspell, for he spent the time before World War I in Germany and brought back sketches of scenery and descriptions of plays. He contributed greatly to the enthusiasm for the New Stagecraft in America. Glaspell had traveled in Europe while Cook was getting his second divorce and had seen European productions. One of the central artistic impulses which permeated the productions of the Provincetown Players was that of Expressionism, most clearly seen in the plays of Susan Glaspell and Eugene O'Neill, the two outstanding playwrights produced by the group. In her use of Expressionism Glaspell was far ahead of most American playwrights, and it is only through a realization of the significance of Expressionism in her plays that they can be fully understood.

Expressionism developed as a formal movement in Germany after World War I, but the techniques utilized in Expressionism appeared earlier in such plays as Strindberg's *Ghost Sonata* and *A Dream Play*. Seeking a new, deeper realism, the Expressionists wrote plays (often called monodramas) in which everything was viewed through the perspective of the protagonist. Since the protagonist was usually suffering from the indifference or brutality of society, the settings mirrored her/his angst, and were sharply angled and distorted. Shafts of light and an intense use of chiaroscuro were typical. Characters were purposefully presented as types, not individuals, and were given names such as The Boss, The Wife, or The Poet. The language involved sharp staccato exchanges and telegraphic monologues. Glaspell often used Expressionistic techniques and was one of the first playwrights in America to do so. She began before the general awareness of Expressionism was developed through the showing of the film *The Cabinet of Dr. Caligari* in 1921, the Theatre Guild presentation of Kaiser's *From Morn to Midnight* in 1922, and the performance of O'Neill's Expressionist plays, such as *The Hairy Ape* (1922).

In 1914 Glaspell wrote a one-act play called *Suppressed Desires* with Cook, but had no intention of becoming a playwright. She was enjoying a lucrative career writing short stories and novels. However, Cook wanted a play to complete a bill with O'Neill's *Bound East for Cardiff*. When she responded that she had never written a play alone, he answered, "There is a theatre there waiting—go look at it!" (*The Road to the Temple* 130). The result was her highly acclaimed play, *Trifles*. Not enough attention has been paid to this imperative expressed by Cook: there was always "a theatre there waiting" for both Glaspell and O'Neill. Plays were both welcomed and needed, and experimental approaches were encouraged by the Provincetown Players in marked contrast to the American commercial theatres. The idealism, the yearning for excellence, and the belief in the possibility of great American art was expressed in many statements put forth by Cook and others.

As Cook left Provincetown to go to New York to find a theatre for the group, he shouted to Glaspell from the train, "WRITE . . . ANOTHER . . . PLAY!" (*The Road to the Temple* 250). Between 1915 and 1922 she wrote eleven plays, worked on the productions, and acted in most of them. One can fairly say that because of the Provincetown Players she gave herself entirely to the creation of American plays influenced by German methods of writing and staging. When the Provincetown Players seemed to move in a more commercial direction and there was dissension among the members, Cook and Glaspell left for Greece and she turned away from the theatre.

Suppressed Desires, the first of the Provincetown plays can seem merely a frivolous satire on Freudianism in America, but is, in fact, a carefully crafted comedy which has held the stage for over seventy-five years. As Sievers has noted, it "is an ingenious and delightful satire on the effects of amateur psychoanalysis in the hands of a giddy faddist" (*Freud on Broadway* 53). It still delights an audience and does not seem dated although it was very much a response to the intense interest in Freud when it was written. Glaspell once exclaimed, "You could not buy a bun without hearing of someone's complex" (qtd. in Sievers 53). The source of the comedy is Henrietta's obsession with psychoanalysis and her adulation of Dr. Russell. When her sister Mabel comes to visit, she describes a dream of being a wet hen who is commanded to "Step hen! Step hen!" Henrietta interprets Mabel's dream as an aversion to her husband and a suppressed desire for a writer. Throughout the action she urges both Mabel and her own husband Stephen to go to Dr. Russell with their dreams, pointing out the dangers of suppressing desires.

However, the tables are turned when to Henrietta's dismay Dr. Russell informs Mabel that she indeed has a suppressed desire, but it is for Stephen (Step hen). The final blow comes when Stephen goes to the psychoanalyst and returns with the information that he has a suppressed desire to leave Henrietta. She is shocked into a repudiation of the doctor and psychoanalysis and it seems that her marriage will take a more reasonable course. As for Mabel's suppressed desire, Stephen tells her, "You just keep right on suppressing it" (341). The amusing characterizations, the witty satire, and the clever dialogue combine to make this play a most effective comedy which maintains its appeal despite the passage of time. In contrast to many of her later plays, it is essentially realistic.

Trifles was first performed in Provincetown in 1916. Since that time it has become famous as is the short story based on it called *A Jury of Her Peers*. The situation in the play was suggested to Glaspell by a murder case she covered when writing for the newspaper in Des Moines. The basic situation is that a man has been found strangled in his bed and his wife, Mrs. Wright, claims not to know who killed him. The play begins as the County Attorney and the Sheriff have come to investigate the murder and find the motive. With them are the Sheriff's wife, Mrs. Peters, and the wife of the neighbor who discovered the murder, Mrs. Hale. Although the men mock them for their attention to small domestic details ("just like women!"), the two wives piece together a picture of the painful, lonely life Mrs. Wright has led, and what probably caused her to murder her husband. A major fact is the discovery of a murdered song bird—the only element of pleasure in the household. They also feel very guilty because they did not try to help Mrs. Wright with their friendship. Mrs. Hale cries, "Oh, I *wish* I'd come over here once in a while! That was a crime! That was a crime! Who's going to punish that?" (701). In the end the men, in their attention to "important" matters, have missed the explanation of the crime, and the women, bonded by their sympathy and understanding, do not reveal it. As Ozieblo observed, "Although Glaspell never again used female bonding as the main theme of a play, it surfaces in *Bernice* and is significant in the later Alison's House" (74).

The play is of note for its effective mood, realistic dialogue, and dramatic impact. Despite the absence of overt dramatic conflict, the play does not seem static and there is suspense in the action. It is notable in Glaspell's career as it is the first of several plays in which the central figure in the story does not appear in the play. By the end of the play Mrs. Wright's character is as vivid and detailed as if she had been in the play, but all of the material is presented through skillful exposition. Her husband's character is also developed in this manner. This technique was later used by Glaspell in *Bernice* and *Alison's House*. As Sharon Mazer has recently commented, the unusual construction of the play may not be noticed today:

> Its radicalism may be as easy to miss for the modern audience as the details of Minnie Foster's story are for its male "audience." But by leaving the primary female character off-stage and then reconstructing her through the eyes of the women on the stage, Glaspell effectively and theatrically exposes the construction of "woman" and the way women are perceived, and provides a vivid opportunity to begin to see the way these women do. (Mazer 88)

The influence of Strindberg is seen in this play and in other works produced by the Provincetown Players—O'Neill was particularly impressed by his plays. Like *Miss Julie*, the action of this one-act play is set in a kitchen and domestic details are important in the setting and the action. Also the servant Jean kills Miss Julie's finch which causes her to reveal her intense hatred for him. Glaspell makes the murdered song bird an element which leads to Mrs. Wright's murder of her husband.

Trifles has received praise from critics throughout the years, especially for the structure. Writing in 1916, Heywood Broun said, "The play is a striking illustration of the effect which may be produced by a most uncommon method. It shows that indirection need not be denied to the playwright if only he is clever enough to handle this most difficult manner of telling a story for the stage ("Best Bill Seen at the Comedy" 7).

Writing in 1962, Donald Fitzjohn also praised the playwright's technique:

> [*Trifles*] is not simply a play of detection, in which the two women discover the missing motive for a murder and decide to suppress the evidence. That is the plot on the surface level only. Fundamentally it is a play about compassion; although this is never mentioned specifically. In fact, one of the most interesting things about *Trifles* is the use made of implicit rather than explicit dialogue. By this means a vivid picture is created for the audience of the lives of two people who never appear. (*English One-Act Plays of Today*, viii-ix.)

After its initial performance in Provincetown the play was produced in New York. Its success led to productions throughout the United States and in other countries. In 1928 a Scottish group won the first prize in the Little Theatre Tournament with the play.

The People was written in 1917 and produced by the Players at Macdougal Street with Glaspell in the major role of The Woman From Idaho. (She was considered one of the best actresses in the group.) The setting and the subject matter are typical of Expressionism. The play takes place in a newspaper office of a liberal newspaper, *The People*. At a time of financial crisis the progressive editor (appropriately played by Cook) is about to give in to various pressures and close the paper. As if called up by his mind, abstract characters arrive from the entire United States—one country, despite its regionalism—and prevail upon him to continue to inspire Americans everywhere. Reluctant to listen to their pleas (i.e. the pleas of his own enlightened consciousness), he is nonetheless moved to continue his work by The Woman. She is a character who has come in response to an idealistic editorial written by the Editor. Her speech, written long before *Our Town*, presents a message similar to that in Wilder's play, emphasizing the importance of seizing and experiencing life and the beauty of nature:

> We are living now. We shall not be living long. No one can tell us we shall live again. This is our little while. This is our chance. And we take it like a child

who comes from a dark room to which he must return—comes for one sunny afternoon to a lovely hillside, and finding a hole, crawls in there till after the sun is set. I want that child to know the sun is shining upon flowers in the grass. I want him to know it before he has to go back to the room that is dark. I wish I had pipes to call him to the hilltop of beautiful distances. I myself could see further if he were seeing at all. Perhaps I can call you; you who have dreamed and dreaming know, and knowing care. Move! Move from the things that hold you. If you move, others will move. Come! Now. Before the sun goes down. (10)

This and her other long speeches are typical of the nonrealistic mono-logues found in Expressionistic plays by Walter Hasenclever, Georg Kaiser, and other German playwrights. When properly read, they do not sound like realistic dialogue, but have a stylized, staccato rhythm.

Unfortunately this play has been viewed as an unsuccessful attempt at social realism. Even Rachel France, while generally appreciative of the experimental approaches used by Glaspell, wrote, "*The People* is one of Glaspell's more obviously flawed efforts. Aside from its static quality, the play never settles on any one form, be it burlesque or straight satire. And the cast, made up mostly of cartoon characters, are all too often given to lofty, serious pronouncements" ("Susan Glaspell" 218).

Although *The People* is a minor work, it represents an effective the-atrical challenge to realistic playwriting and is still moving when pro-duced. In the early part of the play there is an amusing use of satire with such characters as Earnest Approach, Light Touch, and The Anarchist. So little attention was paid to the non-realistic approach in this and other Glaspell plays that a few years later when Thornton Wilder began writing such plays as *The Long Christmas Dinner* and *Pullman Car Hiawatha* many critics treated them as entirely new and original—and many theatre historians still do.

Close the Book (1917) is a mildly amusing satire which is chiefly of interest now because of its setting in an Iowa University town and the characterization of the central character, Jhansi. In both of these ele-ments it prefigures the later and more important Glaspell play *Inheri-tors*. The play presents the results of a conflict between a rebellious young woman student, an important family in the community, and the administration of the university. Jhansi revels in her position as an out-sider, an adopted gypsy child with outlaws for ancestors, as much as she scorns the proper family ancestors whose pictures adorn the walls of her fiancé's home. When documents are produced to prove she is really quite respectable, she is furious: "So this is what I was brought here for, is it? To have my character torn down—to ruin my reputation and threaten my integrity by seeking to muzzle me with a leg at Bull Run and set me down in the Baptist Sunday School in a milk wagon! I see the purpose of it all. I understand the hostile motive behind all this—but I tell you it's a *lie*. Something here (hand on heart) tells me I am not respectable!" (58)

When she is forced to admit to her heritage, she and her fiancé start digging through the records to find out disreputable things about their ancestors. Finally the grandmother suggests that they all "close the book." The point of view seems to be that we should be proud of our ancestors, but not deny their humanity by elevating them to saint-hood. As Ozieblo observed, "As a result of her first-hand experience, Glaspell was never tempted to sentimentalize pioneer life" (68). Glaspell, of course, was proud of the pioneers who established the towns and universities in the midwest. Some of the material for the play may have been suggested by her experiences at Drake University and the University of Iowa where Cook was a professor. As Bartholow V. Crawford commented, "The work of Susan Glaspell reveals considerable variety in form, setting, and style; but there is also a degree of continuity and coherence in ideals and point of view. . . . The Middle Western scene was for her not something to be lived down or forgotten, but one of her richest resources" (518).

Arthur Hornblow fairly described the effect of the play in his review for *Theatre* Magazine, noting that it was "far fetched and futile, a sad falling-off from either *Trifles* or *Suppressed Desires*." He concluded, "The skit started off well and the character of Jhansi . . . was a well-drawn character, but long before its close the story faded into nothing but talk" (356).

The Outside (1917) is a far more impressive play whose power has not been diminished by the passage of time. In addition to its own merits, it is interesting as a study for the later play *The Verge*. The setting provides immediate interest in the play. Glaspell's description is typical of her interest in the visual aspects of a play which contribute to its theatricality and symbolic qualities. Her detailed description takes up nearly a page of the script. The setting is an old life-saving station, now bleak and cheerless, with a barn type door at the back which opens to reveal the sand dunes: "At another point a sand-hill is menacing the woods . . . through the open door the sea is also seen" and outside the door the stiff beach grasses "struggle; dogged growing against odds" (69).

As the play begins two men are seen attempting to resuscitate a drowned man. The highly symbolic play is developed with a number of paradoxes. For example, this place devoted to saving lives is now housing a dead man and is the home for two women dead in life. Outside, the sand dunes continually kill the trees and plants, yet they are covered with new plants. This play is a good example of Glaspell's belief in social and biological Darwinism.

The apparent conflict in the play is between the captain who wants to keep trying to bring the dead man to life and Mrs. Patrick who insists she must have her home to herself. Beyond that, however, is the deeper conflict between Mrs. Patrick and nature: she wants to deny life and growth because she has been deserted by her husband. She has spent the winter in the station with only a servant, Allie Mayo, a Provincetowner hired particularly because she rarely speaks.

However, the attempt to restore life to the sailor has moved Allie. She starts to come back to life herself—come in from the outside—and to convince Mrs. Patrick to do so. Although the play is not Expressionistic in style, this character who has been silent for so long finds difficulty in speaking and utilizes a telegraphic style of speaking typical of Expressionism. As she tries to convince Mrs. Patrick she says, "I know where you're going! ... What you'll try to do. Over there. (Pointing to the line of woods.) Bury it. The life in you. Bury it—watching the sand bury the woods. But I'll tell you something! They fight too. The woods! They fight for life the way that Captain fought for life in there! (Pointing to the closed door.)" (76)

Ultimately, her stilted eloquence and nature, itself, convince Mrs. Patrick against her will to come in from the outside. Death leaves the house as the drowned sailor is carried away. Mrs. Patrick tries to mock the others, but as Allie has said, life grows over buried life and the "Spring will return when she is ready to know it is Spring. Life and the outside must meet" (79). Mrs. Patrick's final line indicates the struggle she is undergoing and what the result will be: "(bitter, exultant) Savers of life! (To Allie Mayo) You savers of life! "Meeting the Outside"! Meeting—(But she cannot say it mockingly again; in saying it, something of what it means has broken through, rises. Herself lost, feeling her way into the wonder of life.) Meeting the Outside! (It grows in her slowly.)" (80).

Not surprisingly this mood piece with little action received a mixed critical response. Glaspell's usual supporter, Ludwig Lewisohn commented, "Her attempt to lend a stunted utterance to her silenced creatures makes for a hopeless obscurity" ("The Drama and the Stage: 'The Outside' "103). Maurice Maeterlinck received much the same criticism for his Symbolist plays such as *Pélleas and Mélisande* and *The Intruder*. In recent years Pinter's plays baffled the public and critics when first performed. Glaspell, like these two playwrights created a mood of mystery and explored human relationships utilizing silence, pauses, mystery, and indirection. Glaspell's use of setting, language and characterization contribute to a moving and theatrically effective play which might be even more poignant on the stage now than when it was written. It should be noted that the idea for the setting was suggested by the life-saving station (remodeled by Mabel Dodge) where O'Neill and his wife entertained their friends, and where, one stormy day, Susan Glaspell and Jig Cook listened to O'Neill reading *The Emperor Jones*.

Another one-act play in the Expressionistic mode is the comedy *Woman's Honor* (1918). Whereas in many of her plays prison reform and feminism are treated as central, serious concerns, here Glaspell touches lightly on the subjects. The play is a comical treatment of a standard subject: an innocent man is awaiting trial for murder because if he revealed his alibi he would destroy a woman's honor. When his lawyer makes this public, abstract personifications of Woman come forth offering their help: The Motherly One (who enters knitting), The Scornful One, The Silly One, and others all offer to give up their honor and say he spent the night of the murder with them. The characters are essentially products of the vision of women held by The Prisoner and, by extension, men in general. Each woman exists only as a type, perceived, and to a degree created by men.

Glaspell used a great deal of humor in this play. German Expressionism was generally very serious, but in Glaspell's plays and later American Expressionist plays such as Elmer Rice's *The Adding Machine* (1923) and Kaufman and Connelly's *Beggar on Horseback* (1924) there is a strong emphasis on comedy. An example of a comic scene in *Woman's Honor* is the arrival of The Mercenary One. She appears to be a prostitute which causes the women to reveal their scorn for her. The scene concludes:

Scornful One—	Woman's honor doesn't play much part in your young life, does it? Or woman's self-respect, either.
Mercenary One—	(Rising) Say, you think you can sit there and insult me? I don't know what you are, but I'll have you know I'm an honest working girl! I heard they were going to take on another stenographer down here, but I don't like the *atmosphere* of this place. (She leaves.)
Silly One—	(Settling herself with relief.) It was a misunderstanding. Ah, life is paved with misunderstanding. (141-143)

The women have committed the same "crime" as The Prisoner in prejudging the woman and interpreting her responses in a precon-ceived fashion. The Prisoner is forced to listen to the stereotyped speeches from the women because he has perceived women as types, rather than respecting them as individuals. As the play rises to a cli-max, the women voice their objections to the roles in which The Pris-oner, The Lawyer, and other men have cast them. In desperation, The Prisoner rejects all their offers of aid and cries in frustration, "Oh, hell, I'll plead guilty (156). (This line, of course, relates to more than the false accusation of murder.)

In this play the abstract characters of Expressionist drama help to make the point that men's perceptions of women marginalize them and prevent them from perceiving reality through their own eyes. The play is at once a comic presentation of the feminist viewpoint and a light parody of the many realistic plays in which a woman sacrifices her honor to save a man.

As in *Trifles* and *The People*, in *Woman's Honor* Glaspell played an important role, The Cheated One. Since she directed *The People* and acted in both plays, the necessary Expressionistic style was created by her, so there was no possibility the audience would perceive the plays as realism. Again, from the point of view of realism, the play is not suc-cessful. France dismisses it by saying that it was less experimental than *The Outside*, and that Glaspell "turned to a device already overworked at the Provincetown Players—characters with abstract names" ("Susan Glaspell" 219).

Glaspell again collaborated with Cook on *Tickless Time* (1916). It is typical of a number of early Provincetown plays which related to the types of people in the group and their interests, and which are set in homes in Provincetown or apartments in Greenwich Village. As in *Suppressed Desires*, the play satirizes an obsession of one character which threatens to ruin the household of an otherwise happily married couple. Ian Joyce has worked for weeks to create an accurate sun-dial. Carried away by the idea that a sun-dial relates to truth and nature, Ian convinces his wife Eloise that they should bury all their clocks and live by the sun-dial.

Having set up a funny situation, the playwrights then initiated a series of misadventures resulting from it. Funny pieces of business, such as the cook dashing in and out of the garden trying to time the browning of onions and the cooking of beef, and the sounds of the alarm clock and the cuckoo from their graves at the foot of the sun-dial enliven the action. A funny visual effect is created, too, with her return after Ian has buried the sundial: "Annie and Ian appear and march across from gate to house, Annie triumphantly bearing her alarm clock, Ian—a captive at her chariot wheels—following with suit-case, shawl-strap and long strings of bags around his wrist. A moment later Ian comes out of the house, looks at each dug-up thing and stands by the grave of the sun-dial. His idealistic concept of time has been undercut by the pragmatism of the cook, who has the last word, calling in a flat voice from the house, "It's dinner time!" (150-151).

The play was another effective comic collaboration between Glaspell and Cook. It may have been self-satire in part, with Ian repre-senting Cook going off on a half-cocked idea and Glaspell supporting him. While it does not have the depth of her works written alone, it was a pleasing satire which would still be effective on-stage today. First performed in 1918, it was revived in 1921. When O'Neill's *The Emperor Jones* was moved to Broadway and then taken on tour, it replaced Lawrence Langner's *Matinata*. (Either of the plays must have seemed a rather odd curtain raiser for O'Neill's powerful play.) Fol-lowing the American tour the play was part of the bill in London and a subsequent revival in New York.

Glaspell's first full-length play was produced in 1919. *Bernice* is a realistic three-act play unusual in that the figure of Bernice never appears. The play is really a type of mystery play in which the several characters search for the explanation of Bernice's death. Visitors to the house, Margaret and sister-in-law, converse at length about the baf-fling circumstances of Bernice's death. The servant, Abbie, falsely tells Bernice's husband Craig that she committed suicide because she loved him too much to bear his infidelities.

Glaspell's examination of the character of Bernice gives an interest to the play and also provides a comment on the expectations regarding the conduct of a wife in this period. The sister-in-law (as in the later play *Alison's House*) speaks for the standard conservative viewpoint of society. She condones her brother's affairs because she thinks Bernice was too independent to be a good wife. Craig shares this view, saying, "Margaret, I wish I could tell you about me and Bernice. I loved her. She loved me. But there was something in her that had almost nothing to do with our love. . . . Well, that isn't right, Margaret. You want to feel that you have the woman you love. Yes—completely. Yes, every bit of her!" (58). In the concluding scenes Margaret decides to let Craig believe that he really did have all of Bernice. She sees that Bernice, in her great compassion and understanding, gave him in death what she was incapable of giving him in life. Glaspell created the image of a woman too intelligent and independent to act only as the pillar of support for a weak husband.

The play was not a major success and was not revived, but it reveals Glaspell's growing ability to move beyond the one-act form. Some critics described it as simple and cleverly constructed. The reviewer for the *Nation*, while praising the play as a whole, noted some of its problems: "*Bernice* is not for the commercial stage. It is too subtle, too slow, too real. The characters actually talk, they do not speak for the benefit of the audience. They grope for the solution of their problems with a reality that is actually painful. And their problems are not the problems of the stage but of souls today, the souls of young people seeking reality, and the souls of old people escaping it" ("Bernice" 702-703).

Two years later, Glaspell produced a full-length play which had considerable success and demonstrated her capabilities as a playwright much more clearly than in *Bernice*. Although *Inheritors* was produced in 1921, and is very much rooted in the society of that time, the themes in it seem very contemporary. In the play Glaspell presented her concerns about the nature of American society, academic freedom, the effects of war on society, the treatment of Indians by the pioneers, and twentieth century antipathy toward foreigners in America. The style of the play is realistic, but the three-act structure has an interesting element. The first act takes place on the Fourth of July in 1879 and concludes with the decision to found a college, and the second and third acts are set in the college in 1920. The effect of the structure is to emphasize that American society faces the same problems and concerns despite the passage of time. Again, Glaspell's Darwinism is in evidence: Silas, a rich farmer, wants to found a college in order to help all the children, not just his own, and to improve America. He says with asperity to the people who oppose him, "Why the buffalo here before us was more than we if we do nothing but prosper. God damn us if we sit here rich and fat and forget man's in the makin'" (42).

In the first act there is an emphasis on war, with concern expressed by Silas's mother that men never tire of talking about war, "Seems like nothing draws men together like killing other men" (p. 8).Various points of view about America are expressed through the arguments about what Silas should do with his land. At the end of the act, he gives the deed of land to Fejevary, a revolutionary nobleman who fled from Hungary to make a new start in America. Fejevary will organize the college to pay his debt to his new homeland.

In the second act the conflict concerns the question of free speech and the right to protest. Glaspell was reacting to the recent oppression related to the World War I. She was appalled by the 1917 and 1918 Espionage and Sedition Acts. Hundreds of IWW members and 95 leaders of the radical organization were found guilty on charges of draft evasion and conspiracy to cripple the war effort by fomenting strikes. They were given long jail sentences and heavy fines.

Glaspell's central figure, Madeline is the granddaughter of Fejevary, and shares his idealism. Another idealistic character is Professor Holden, who has been criticized by a state senator for defending conscientious objectors. The senator has come to celebrate the fortieth anniversary of the founding of the college, but the day is marred by student protests led by a Hindu. In the course of these, Madeline assaults a police officer and she and the Hindu are put in jail. The complexity of society is mirrored by the complexity of the characters. Madeline seems at once admirable and painfully naive. One character talks about how as a foreigner his father was welcomed to America and in the next breath says the Hindus should be deported. The question of freedom of speech is emphasized because the college wants money from the state to expand, but the money will not be forthcoming if professors speak their minds. The senator expresses his view very clearly, "Oh—a scholar. We can get scholars enough. What we want is Americans" (48).

The third act is one of decisions. Professor Holden decides he must keep his mouth shut because of his sick wife. Madeline has become less naive and realizes the future that awaits her if she stands up for her beliefs. She has been warned, "Do you know that in America today there are women in our prisons for saying no more than you've said here to me!" (113). In a dramatic scene, she chalks out on the floor the small space of a prison cell. Nevertheless, she refuses to compromise, and at the end of the act puts on her hat and coat and walks out facing a future in prison.

The role of Madeline was a major opportunity for Ann Harding and was a turning point in her career. Glaspell understudied her and was praised highly by William Archer who saw her perform the role. The critics praised the acting, particularly that of Harding, but generally did not praise the play as a whole. Terms such as preachy, dull, turgid, and wordy were used by many critics. O. W. Firkins was one of the enthusiastic critics, and praised the themes and technique: ""Dramatic movement may not assimilate the propaganda, but is continually active around and beneath it; the dialogue is hardly describable by any tamer adjective than brilliant, the play of intelligence is keen and varied, and the work while anything but impartial, is at least entitled to the solid praise of generous and thoughtful partiality" (344-345).

Eva Le Gallienne admired the play and decided to revive it at the Civic Repertory Theatre in 1927. Brooks Atkinson wrote that the play was verbose, but "Miss Glaspell's pure understanding of the American pioneer tradition remains as a quality rare in the theatre" ("Pioneer Traditions" 1). Writing in *Vogue*, David Carb expressed the view that the play had not dated:

> The assertion that it concerns mainly the injustices and fetishes in the wake of the World War I requires explanation—they cause the explosion, but the explosives are conditions which are as true today as they were seven years ago and seven decades ago and seven decades before that. The arrogance of wealth, intolerance, the smudging of a fine idea by the soiled hands of politics and finance, education having to lower its banner before economic necessity, the bold dream of one generation made ugly and perverse by the compromise of the next—all of those conditions remain. (138)

Although *Inheritors* is overwritten, it is a dramatic and courageous piece of work which remains of interest today. It is less exciting than some of her other plays in part because of its three-act, realistic structure. There was talk of a New York revival in 1967 when it would have been very topical, but it failed to materialize. Unfortunately, it was given a weak revival in 1984 with Geraldine Page, surrounded by lesser actors, playing a very small role. The play suffered because of the production (Lipsius 10). Given the contemporary quality of the themes and the characterization it is likely that a carefully pruned script might succeed today in a university theatre.

In 1921 Glaspell wrote (*The Verge,*) one of the most daring and demanding American plays written in this decade. Here her Darwinian beliefs and her idealism come together in a serious, innovative play which puzzled many critics who could only perceive in it a realistic depiction of a neurotic feminist. The settings for the play by Cleon Throckmorton emphasized the non-realistic, Expressionistic style: the first is a strange greenhouse in which the architecture and the exotic, strangely hybridized plants express Claire's visions and aspirations:

> The Curtain lifts on a place that is dark, save for a shaft of light from below which comes up through an open trap door in the floor. This slants up and strikes the long leaves and huge brilliant blossom of a strange plant whose twisted stem projects from right front. Nothing is seen except this plant and its shadow. A violent wind is heard. A moment later a buzzer. It buzzes once long and three short. Silence. Again the buzzer. Then from below—his shadow blocking the light, comes Anthony, a rugged man past middle life;—he emerges from the stairway into the darkness of the room. Is dimly seen taking up a phone. (58)

The second setting is a tower in which Claire works. This is her private place and can only be reached by a difficult climb up a spiral staircase. She seeks relief in this bizarre room from the world which is stifling her. It is, "A tower which is thought to be round but does not complete the circle. The back is curved, then jagged lines break from that, and the front is a queer bulging window—in a curve that leans. The whole structure is as if given a twist by some mysterious force—like something wrung" (78).

Claire, who breeds new species of plants (including the Edge Vine), wants to become something more than people have been, to think things never thought before, to dare things women have never dared. She is caught in the social situation of the America Glaspell rejected: rigid, static, intolerant, uncreative, and provincial. Claire represents the American woman who has the potential for something great. But the constraints of a patriarchal society have warped and perverted her so she can no longer interact with people. She has rejected her family (including her daughter whom she regards as an unsatisfactory experiment), she rejects her first and second husbands, and a lover. In the final scene (which, like most of the action, would be quite ridiculous if played as realism) she strangles the man she loves because she realizes that to accept his love would be to stop, to find a wall instead of a gate. She says, "I'm fighting for my chance. I don' t know—which chance" (98). As the play ends, she has stepped into the madness which she rightly perceives as the only way she can move beyond the life—and the men—she scorns. Had it not been for the Provincetown Players it is highly unlikely that Glaspell would have written this play or that it would have been produced: the theatre was there waiting.

The Verge proved puzzling and irritating to many critics in 1921. However, there were a few critics who wrote appreciative notices. Ludwig Lewisohn wrote, "Susan Glaspell has a touch of that vision without which we perish" ("The Verge" 709). Kenneth Macgowan tried to find things to praise, but had to conclude that, "The play is clogged, not only with a figure that affrights so many, but with abstruse phrases and very lengthy talk" ("Seen on the Stage" 49). A typical review was written by Robert A. Parker, who characterized Claire as "the type of erotic, neurotic, ill-tempered, and platitudinous hussy who dramatizes herself into a "superwoman" and even 'puts it over' on her gentlemen friends. . . . If she [Glaspell], like the feminine majority of her audiences, accepts this fraudulent female as an authentic "superwoman", we can only express our opinion that Claire is not convincing" (296).

Many years after the play opened, O'Neill biographer Louis Schaeffer dismissed it as one of Glaspell's lesser efforts (325) . It is not hard to see why critics found the play difficult (although apparently there was a sympathetic audience). The opening dialogue sets the expectation of a witty comedy which is not fulfilled, the dialogue shifts from prose to poetry in several scenes, and the setting is peculiar to those accustomed to realism. Finally, Claire's character is hard to accept. (Several critics noted that Margaret Wycherly gave a beautiful performance in a difficult role.) She tries to strike her daughter with the thorny Edge Vine, she makes incredible demands on people, and she tells her sister she is "a liar and thief and whore with words!" (82). In 1921 the general public was not prepared for Glaspell's searing, passionate, non-realistic exploration of the position of women in society. Stephen Rathbun predicted the play would find acceptance in the future, saying, "Mayhap a century or two from today . . . *The Verge* will be as much of a stage classic as *Hamlet* is today. Perhaps in those future years thought will count more than plot and the exploration of the soul will be more important to theatregoers than action on a mundane plane"

(4). There have been some revivals in recent years and contemporary appreciation of the play may lead to others. Sievers said the play "is one of the truly remarkable pieces of psychological literature of our times. The author draws a terrifyingly real portrait of manic-depressive psychosis. . . . *The Verge* is possibly the most original and probing play that had been written in America by 1921" (70-71). In an extended analysis of the play Ozieblo wrote that at the end, "Claire, a female Faust, now is her own God and cannot be reached by societal structures and compunctions; she has broken out and is free existentially, alone in the transcendental beyond. Like the protagonist of *Inheritors*, Claire rejects the laws of the patriarchal world, but unlike her she refuses to deal with them on their own terms" (71).

With the play *The Comic Artist* (1928) Glaspell again collaborated with a man, this time Norman Matson, whom she had met after Jig Cook's death in Greece. The play has something of the style of S.N. Behrman's high comedy critiques of American society without his wit, unfortunately. It was performed in London in 1928, then at the West-port Playhouse in 1931, and finally on Broadway in 1933. The play ran for only 21 performances despite the presence of the talented Blanche Yurka in the leading role of Eleanor. The conclusion of the play differs from the published version (1927), which may indicate a compromise in an attempt to please the public with a happy ending.

The plot of the play is fairly simple: into the seaside home of a hap-pily married painter comes a cynical woman of the world, her daughter who is beautiful but materialistic and selfish, and the idealistic car-toonist who is married to her and is the brother of the painter. Through the action and exposition it is revealed that the mother was attracted to the painter in Paris, but that he fell in love with her beau-tiful daughter Nina instead. He subsequently left Nina, so she married his brother Karl, as second-best. The key figure in the play, however, is Eleanor, a compassionate, nurturing woman, slightly older than her painter husband, Stephen. Throughout the play she supports her hus-band and Karl, even when the passion between Stephen and Nina again ignites. In the published ending, Karl is frightened into believing Nina has thrown herself in the ocean, and in trying to save her is killed. However, in the Broadway version nobody dies and Karl takes Luella and Nina back to New York, leaving Eleanor and Steven alone trying to rebuild their lives (Papke 81).

The play may be read as an allegory about a Paradise based on old, earthy, honest American values which is invaded by a serpent in the form of Luella, the worldly-wise American who has raised her daughter, the temptress Eve figure, to emulate her Parisian life of luxury and decadence. Although the play is not successfully or convincingly constructed, it has interest because there are some elements in it which relate to Glaspell's life and her outlook. The character of Stephen seems to have been modeled on her exuberant, Dionysian, would-be artist, Jig Cook. Cook mixed the powerful wine punches for the Provincetown Players' parties and Stephen pours the wine he makes from beach plums; Cook wanted to be a playwright, but he was a weak writer next to Glaspell and O'Neill, Stephen wants to be a modern Da Vinci, but concludes he is a mediocre painter; Cook and Stephen share a tendency to philosophize about the meaning of life. Perhaps most importantly from Glaspell's point of view, Cook was strongly attracted to women as is her character Stephen. The setting for the play is an old home redolent of American values, like many of the homes in Provincetown.

It is not surprising that the play was a failure. It was a weak collaboration to begin with, the altered ending seemed contrived, and the play was presented in New York when Glaspell's reputation was at a low ebb. As Papke commented, "This last major production on the American stage of a Glaspell work, then her collaboration with Matson, that fact elided by most critics who treated the play as if Glaspell must bear all responsibility for it alone, did not serve to shore up her reputation as a dramatist or stand as a strong finale to her experimentation with that art form" (84).

The reason for the decline in Glaspell's reputation was her play *Alison's House*, which was written after *The Comic Artist*, but produced before it in 1931. This play was the most controversial that Glaspell wrote because it won the Pulitzer Prize for 1930-31. It is ironic that this honor brought the critics down on Glaspell and on the Pulitzer Prize Committee.

The play was inspired in part by Glaspell's interest in the life of Emily Dickinson. The play is about a character similar to Dickinson. As in some of Glaspell's earlier plays, the "central" character is not in the play. The play opens eighteen years after the poetess Alison Stanhope has died. Her house is being cleared and sold by her relatives. The crass new owners plan to modernize and set up an inn for tourists.

As in *Inheritors*, the play involves a struggle between the values of two different generations. But in this case, the sympathy is with the younger people who are more honest and more devoted to Alison's memory. The play has a realistic three-act structure, and shows the influence of Chekhov's *The Cherry Orchard*. There is very little story line and the characters discuss their differing viewpoints at length. In the first act it is established that Alison loved a married man, but renounced her love and shut herself up in the house to write poetry. In contrast, her niece, Elsa, did not renounce her love for a married man, but ran off with him. The family is surprised when she appears late in the first act. Stanhope's unpleasant daughter-in-law, Louise, represents the conservative, narrow-minded American values Glaspell rejected throughout her writing career. She refuses to stay in the house if Elsa does.

In the course of the three acts, Elsa's Aunt Agatha attempts to burn down the house in order to destroy Alison's unpublished poems, then changes her mind and gives them to Elsa just before she dies. The last act is taken up with the discovery that the poems reveal Alison's love for the married man, her loneliness, and the depth of the love affair. Arguments are presented for and against destroying the poems, and the play concludes with the decision to publish the poems.

One of the obvious differences between this play and *The Cherry Orchard* is that Chekhov peopled his play with many fascinating characters but Glaspell's seem rather familiar types. Elsa is the most interesting character and she is only in the first and second acts briefly. She dominates the last act and then the interest rises because the spirit of Dickinson/Alison is present. Richard Lockridge wrote, "In the struggle between centuries, between ideals, Miss Glaspell has found the material for at least one act of clear and moving drama. For that act alone *Alison's House* is infinitely worthwhile" (32). In fact, Glaspell might have been able to create a very successful one-act play on this subject. Another problem with the play is the scandal of divorce and the disgrace of unmarried people living together. This element was very quick to date in a period of changing social values. Of course these subjects were close to Glaspell's heart: she had fallen in love with a married man who divorced his wife to marry her and at the time she wrote the play she was living with Norman Matson and was not married to him.

The unusual element in the play for many critics was the absent heroine. Most critics felt Glaspell was unsuccessful in creating the presence and vitality of the Dickinson figure. Mark Van Doren reflected the majority opinion, writing, "Miss Glaspell has written before, and written better, about the influence of a dead woman upon her family and friends. It is an interesting theme, if a somewhat artificial one, and much might be done with it. But very little has been done in the present instance, and the little that has been done is offensively false" (590-591).Those critics who did not see the play at the Civic Repertory Theatre and went to see it uptown (after the award) were generally baffled about why it had won over such plays as *Once in a Lifetime* and *Elizabeth the Queen*. Their negative reviews, which panned Glaspell, her play, and the prize committee, killed ticket sales and the play closed after two weeks.

Contemporary critics could not understand how the play won the Pulitzer Prize, and this has continued to puzzle some people. There were several factors which contributed to the committee decision. The first is in the nature of the award (which has since been changed). The award was for the play which would best represent the high values of American life. Despite its faults, *Alison's House* fulfilled that quality admirably. As a Los Angeles reviewer wrote when Le Gallienne presented it on tour, "[It isl a drama of an intense realism, a realism which somehow exudes the spirit of a real American, an America which still bears herself with dignity and reverence" (Blon, n.p.) Another factor was the outstanding performance given by Eva Le Gallienne as Elsa. Yet another factor was the wish to encourage intellectual drama of the type presented by Le Gallienne at the Civic Repertory at low prices. Defending the decision in 1944, committee member Walter Prichard Eaton wrote of the choice between a Theatre Guild production and "Miss Le Gallienne's struggling Civic Repertory Company." He concluded that he had no apologies as *Alison's House* was a good play, and that seeing it again in 1941, "it was still a moving and provocative play which deserved a recognition Broadway refused" (qtd. in Toohey, 93). The play was selected by Burns Mantle as one of the ten best of the year. Ultimately the quality of the play was summed up by the title of John Mason Brown's review: "*Alison's House*. Some Fine Moments, But a Disappointing Play by Miss Glaspell" (12).

Glaspell was naturally disappointed in the critical and popular response. She returned to her career as a novelist. She wrote only one more play, *The Big Bozo*, and it was never produced. Her last involvement in theatre was as head of the Mid-west Federal Theatre Project in the late thirties. Her play *Inheritors* was produced by the Federal Theatre Project in Jacksonville, Florida.

When Susan Glaspell died in 1948 her theatrical activities were largely forgotten. She was a talented actress, an outstanding playwright, and an idealistic intellectual who made many contributions to the American theatre. She wrote theatrically effective roles which provided opportunities for many fine actresses including Ann Harding, Blanche Yurka, Eva Le Gallienne, and herself. She was inspired to work in the theatre through connection with three idealistic theatrical organizations: the Provincetown Players, the Civic Repertory Theatre, and the Federal Theatre Project. Unlike most playwrights, she had no wish for Broadway success and did not seek financial success in Hollywood. Many of her plays have held the stage and others should be produced. Glaspell was technically proficient and highly imaginative. Some of her longer plays were criticized for verbosity, but a good director could easily cut them for production. When her plays appeared in a new edition in 1988, critic Michael Goldman called her "the only playwright of her generation worthy of comparison with O'Neill" (n. p.). He called his review "The Dangerous Edge of Things" and that was where Susan Glaspell worked. Because of the experimental approach taken by the theatres with which she worked she was free from commercial pressures and able to apply various techniques to subjects which reflected her idealism and her belief in the potential greatness of America. Edythe M. McGovern recently summed up Glaspell's career by saying,

> Because her work in the theater was of necessity much more experimental than her work in other genres, Glaspell's main significance stems from her Provincetown connection, not only as a playwright, but, more importantly, as an innovator instrumental in changing the course of American drama forever. The most striking hallmark of her best writing is her consistent emphasis on the need for human beings to fulfill their highest potential by utilizing what is desirable from the past and applying it with faith and courage to the future. (146)

Zoë Akins (1886-1958)

Zoë Akins (1886-1958) is a perplexing figure in the history of American theatre. For most theatre scholars, she exists only as the playwright who won the Pulitzer Prize in 1934 when Lillian Hellman should have won it and who made a reputation writing hack drama filled with purple prose. She is omitted from most histories of American theatre. As with Susan Glaspell, winning the Pulitzer Prize over a play preferred by most critics was a serious piece of bad luck. Writing in 1941, Freedley and Reeves expressed the general opinion of Akins and her play, The Old Maid: "The fact that so poor a play as this received the Pulitzer Award stimulated so much criticism that the New York Critics Circle instituted its own award for the best play of the season, feeling that the Pulitzer judges had either lost their critical standards or were too likely to be overruled in their judgements by the Advisory Board" (587). In fact, Akins was a playwright with imagination and skill who held a place in the theatre from 1919 to 1944. Her plays include romances, satire, and experimental drama. An examination of her life and career reveals an interesting playwright who has been mistakenly dismissed.

Akins was born in Humansville, Missouri. Her parents were Thomas Jaspard and Elizabeth Green Akins. The family moved to St. Louis when Akins was eleven because her father had received an appointment as postmaster (Londré, "Zoë Akins" 11). The family was prosperous and she was taken to the theatre and encouraged to enjoy the arts. Akins was drawn to the theatre as a child. She wrote plays and poetry and one of her plays was performed in her school, Hosmer Hall, when she was twelve. At seventeen she wrote a play called The End of the Strike and at nineteen a verse drama called Iseult, the Fair. She hoped to enter Radcliffe or the University of Chicago, but a serious illness prevented her. Although her father, by this time a well-known politician who moved in good society, had encouraged her interest in the arts, he was dismayed when she joined the Odeon Stock Company. She played many roles, including Juliet, and learned the basic elements of stagecraft. She also wrote for the St. Louis Mirror, interviewing visiting celebrities. One of these was the actress Julia Marlowe. She was an important influence on the young writer, giving her friendship and advice on her career. She also encouraged Akins to study the great

European dramatists ("Brief Sketches of Winners of Pulitzer Prizes" n.p.).

Akins' father finally allowed his debutante daughter to go to New York in 1909 to try to make a career as an actress, hoping she would get tired of it ("Miss Zoë Akins," St. Louis *Mirror*, n.p.). She didn't have much of a chance to get tired of it because she was told she had no acting talent (Yongue 13). She submitted poetry to journals and became acquainted with Willa Cather who was managing editor of *McClure's*. Cather told her she should write for the stage. She wrote a number of plays but none were produced and only one, *Papa* (1913), was published. She also published volumes of verse and several novels. She was grouped with such writers as Sara Teasdale, Edgar Lee Masters, and Carl Sandburg who contributed to the Renaissance of American poetry before World War I. She longed to move into the theatre and write plays using the exalted language of poetry.

Her first theatrical success came with *Déclassée* in 1919. She continued writing plays and spent time in Hollywood writing such successful screenplays as *Morning Glory*, which provided Katherine Hepburn with her first Academy Award winning role. Scheuer wrote "Astringency is the main ingredient of the film's charm" (708). Another major film success was *Camille* (for Greta Garbo) which has become a film classic. In 1936 she wrote the screenplay for *Showboat,* based on playwright Edna Ferber's novel, which Scheuer describes as "the definitive version of the landmark musical" (952).

In 1932 Akins married Captain Hugo Rumbold, a noted painter and scene designer, but he died within a year. She didn't have much success in the theatre after winning the Pulitzer Prize, but she continued to write plays until 1944. Criticism throughout her career was mixed. At heart she was a poet, praised for her poetry in America and England. Theatre Arts published a brief biography in 1927 saying, "Perhaps Zoë Akins real gift as a poet, which no one can doubt who has read her verse, is not at home on Broadway" ("Some Playwright Biographies" 532). Like Josephine Preston Peabody and William Vaughan Moody, she tried to write plays that were theatrical and poetic in dialogue. Unfortunately she was writing at a time when realism was the most admired form of writing. Nevertheless, when she died in 1958 she could look back on a long and active career. She achieved popular and critical success for many of her plays and was a real woman of the theatre.

"In 1916 the Washington Square Players put on a one-act play in verse called *The Magical City* by an unknown playwright named Zoë Akins. Everybody wanted to know who she was and where she came from" ("Some Playwright Biographies" 532). The play was a one-act tragedy in free verse. It was praised as the best of the four plays on the bill (Londré 11). Arthur Hopkins subsequently produced the play in vaudeville and it was published in *Forum* in 1916.

On the basis of her one-act Akins was perceived as a playwright of promise. Aline Barnsdall and Norman bel Geddes produced her play *Papa* in Los Angeles. *Theatre Arts* described the play as a "brilliantly satirical play" ("Some Playwright Biographies" 531). The play had been published a part of the modern drama series edited by Edwin Björkman. In his introduction, he described the play as "a little masterpiece that places its creator with such representatives of the genre as Arthur Schnitzler [and] the Dane Gustav Wied." He concluded by saying that on the surface it seems to be only for amusement "while to the penetrating mind it yields a social satire which, in spite of its good temper and its exquisite playfulness, buries its biting lash beneath the callous cuticle of our modern 'dronedom'" (ix).

The satire is aimed at the household of Papa, his two daughters Chloe and Doris and their society friends. The two daughters adore their charming and handsome Papa. They are all urbane and sophisticated. Chloe had an illegitimate child by an opera singer, but everyone behaves charmingly about it and the child is being raised by a French governess. Because Papa needs money, the girls decide to marry rich men. Doris misinforms her fiancée and says that the affair with the opera singer and the child are a part of her past. He receives the news with kindness and immediately suggests that they get the child and raise it. Chloe is distressed to be robbed of her child and her romantic past, but as they all live together in a villa in France, it doesn't matter much. The opera singer shows up, fails to recognize which of the girls he seduced, but is very happy to learn about the child. By the end of the play everyone is very well pleased that Papa is going to marry a beautiful and wealthy lady, and the opera singer says he wants to take the little girl for the summer. The only one who doesn't know the circumstances fully is Dick, Chloe's husband. One of the last lines is his question, "Why is everyone so keen on the kiddie?" (93).

Akins shows a society in which good manners and charm (and, of course lots of money) make everything all right. All the characters are hopelessly shallow and have no morals (Akins called the play "An Amorality in Three Acts"), but they praise each other and glow in the use of such terms as "noble," "gallant," and "magnanimous." The amusing picture of these people is really similar to plays about high society by Somerset Maugham and Noël Coward, though the influence of Schnitzler is clear. Writing in 1921, Ludwig Lewisohn remembered the play as "a slight but witty and glittering comedy" ("Homespun and Brocade" 325). The subject matter of the illegitimate child raised in ignorance of its true mother foreshadows the subject matter in Akins' adaptation of The Old Maid.

Following the successful production in Los Angeles, Oliver Morosco produced Papa at the Little Theatre, which he was leasing from Winthrop Ames. It ran for only 12 performances and Akins blamed the production. It probably would have fared better under Ames' sensitive direction and with more care in the production aspects. It was rushed into production to take advantage of the stunning success Akins had with Déclassée earlier in 1919. Papa was well received in published form and was performed in other countries (Chapman "Zoë Akins—Experimenter in the Drama Laboratory" n.p.) Several months after the unsuccessful production in New York, George Jean Nathan reflected on its merits, saying,

> [Akins'] play, "Papa," . . . is perhaps the best thing of its eccentric kind in the theatrical writing of our day. I know of nothing in Europe to equal it: not even Schnitzler has a suaver piece of work to his credit. . . . It is, in essence, a play as Viennese as the Prater and yet it is neither imitative nor hybrid. Unmercifully ridiculed by reviewers for the New York gazettes upon its local presentation, "Papa" surpasses in imagination, fancy, style and grotesque humour ninetenths of the plays written by Americans since Americans began writing for the theatre. (The Theatre, The Drama 87)

The success of Déclassée was important for Akins and Ethel Barrymore. The playwright provided a fine dramatic character for the actress and achieved her own first major success. As Barrymore's biographer Peters wrote, "Ethel needed a hit; the failure of The Lady of the Camellias still rankled. And this first [sic] play by a young woman from Missouri would be one of Ethel Barrymore's greatest successes" (The House of Barrymore 190).

The play is very much in the style of Arthur Wing Pinero and is even reminiscent of Mid-Channel, his story of a wife who leaves her husband, suffers scandal and dies in the last act. The play is plot-heavy and coincidence figures enormously. The most memorable quality in the play is the characterization of Lady Helen Haden. In the first act there is a bridge party which has been interrupted by Sir Haden's accusation that the Lady Helen's latest young man, Ned Thayer, has been cheating at cards. In a series of entertaining speeches she talks about herself as the last of the "mad Varicks"—the aristocratic family who lived madly and did not mind dying. "There were quite a lot of us once, and now I'm the only one that's left. We were at our best about five hundred years ago. But even then we were a little mad, too, I suppose. And we kept on being gay and mad" (14). By the end of the act she knows that Ned is a cheat and that if she reveals it he will give her letters to her husband. Through her "mad" behavior she has turned her life into a shambles.

The second act takes place in New York where the same people all turn up in a fashionable restaurant. There is an air of fate and star-crossed relationships which Akins intends to explain the coincidence of all the major characters meeting again in New York. In the final act the setting is the luxurious mansion Rudolph Solomon has furnished by buying furniture and art from impoverished aristocrats, including Helen. Solomon proposes to Helen and makes her promise to change her ways and be a respectable wife. He also gives her back the string of pearls she has been selling one at a time to live. Ned (now a respectable owner of diamond mines in Africa) arrives, and Solomon decides to give Helen up so she and Ned can marry. Unfortunately, she believes he has realized that to marry a woman like herself would be a mistake. In a very theatrical conclusion, she puts the pearls back in the box and exits. There is noise and confusion, all of her friends rush back on stage and she is brought in bleeding and near death, having been run over. It is a theatrical death scene in the tradition of *Camille*. Ned is there, but too late, she has dramatic lines to speak and dies loving life to the end like the "mad Varick" she was. A famous line from the last scene was "One more cigarette—and just one more glass of champagne" (101). She dies looking at the portrait of her grandmother (a duchess who died young) with the line "It's like the theatre—when they turn out the lights before the curtain rises—on the next act" (102).

The play is undeniably sentimental and artificial, but it moves swiftly from one scene to another and there are interesting characters and theatrical dialogue. For example, when Solomon asks Helen what happened to her in the past, she answers, "I ran very hard, and played very recklessly, and fell down and soiled my frock, that's all" (63). The roles provided the actors with excellent opportunities for comedy and drama. Barrymore's success was such that audiences shouted and applauded for so many curtain calls that she made her famous statement, "That's all there is, there isn't any more."

The play was Akins' greatest success. Lawrence Reamer noted in his review that she was the youngest writer with such a success to her credit. While admitting to the "theatrics" present in the play, he admired the structure and said Akins had presented the public with the "most absorbing bit of stage fiction that the present year has brought to the theatre. Then her language possesses a fiery distinction which no other writer for the theatre has shown this year" ("Déclassée" n.p.). Alexander Woolcott, who became a staunch supporter of Akins, praised the play much more than it was worth (in fact, a number of critics did), saying it gave Ethel Barrymore, "the richest and most interesting play that has fallen to her in all her years upon the stage." He wrote that it was "difficult to remember when a play came this way with a text so continuously interesting to hear. Many of the passages have a genuine beauty. All of them are clean-cut, sound and true" ("'Déclassée a Brilliant Play" 22). *Vogue* noted that a major part of the success of the play was Barrymore's performance and that the construction was weak. Despite the cheers of the audience, "it is not a great play—it is not even a good play as there is too much narration of off-stage events." However, the critic concluded, "The mere fact that an American author endowed with indubitable literary talents has made a sincere effort to write a worthy play, and that this earnest effort is attracting large audiences to the Empire theatre affords an opportunity for jubilation" ("Zoé Akins of St. Louis" n.p.).

Akins had a major triumph. Burns Mantle selected the play for his best plays volume. The play was revived in 1935 at the Berkshire Playhouse in Stockbridge. Ethel Barrymore again enjoyed a triumph as Helen. With *Déclassée* Akins earned the first of the huge sums she would eventually earn from theatre and movies. She netted $300,000 on the Broadway production (Inge n.p.).

Akins was not so fortunate with her next production. In 1921 a reviewer commented on her play *Foot-Loose,*

> Zoë Akins, who did so well by Ethel Barrymore (and, incidently, by herself) in
> writing "Déclassée" was engaged by George Tyler last winter to make a modern
> version of that old drama called "Forget-Me-Not." In its original form, we
> gather from the reviewers of the time, this was the sort of play those ladies of
> the stage gifted with an emotional temperament and a generous torso took
> great delight in playing, being the story of a scarlet sister who forces her way
> into a respectable home and insists on being introduced as an old and dear
> friend of the family. (Unidentified clipping Lincoln Center)

Tyler was a successful producer who tried from time to time to make
a windfall with a new version of some immensely successful piece of
clap-trap from the nineteenth century. He hoped to get Eugene
O'Neill to refurbish his father's money-maker, *The Count of Monte
Cristo*. In his efforts with Akins, he hoped to cash in on her recent success and provide a vehicle for the young actress Emily Stevens. *Foot-
Loose* offered the actress scenes in which she could act (as one reviewer
wrote) like "a heartless, vindictive, defiant super-cat" and make a dramatic exit when she is ordered out of the house because a man from
her past tracks her down. The reviewer continued, "She is ever so glad
to sneak out of the house, clutching at the furniture and the drapes for
support as she passes" (unidentified clipping Lincoln Center). The
quote gives the tone of the play, which *Theatre Magazine* described as
"a very talky old-fashioned drawing-room melodrama" ("Foot-Loose"
526). Reviewers favorably noted the acting of a young ingenue named
Tallulah Bankhead who had recently done well in Crothers' *Thirty-
Nine East*.

    Foot-Loose, following on the heels of *Déclassée*, led critics to sneer at
the aristocratic aura Akins seemed to enjoy. There were comments
about the usual champagne and caviar and scented cigarettes in the
play. She defended herself by saying, "I have been accused of chroni-
cling the life of only aristocrats. Well, the aristocrat to me is the best
dramatic material. . . . Some of the best drama has been written around
the upper strata, as, for example, the works of Shakespeare" ("Zoë
Akins—Experimenter" 2). The play was not the success Tyler had
hoped for: it closed after thirty-two performances. Like *Déclassée*, it
looked to the theatre of the past. In her next play, Akins was to move
away from the counts and princesses of the conventional nineteenth
century theatre and take a look at modern life.

    While she was an aspiring actress, Akins told a reporter she wanted
to play Ibsen's dramas "as these contain the intellectual element which
she believes should enter into the theatrical profession" ("Miss Zoë

Akins" St. Louis *Mirror*, n.p.). Akins' 1921 play *Daddy's Gone A-Hunting* was much more in the tradition of Ibsen than Pinero, echoing some of the elements of both *A Doll House* and *The Wild Duck*. The story deals with a marriage which the wife, Edith, thought was wonderful, but which the husband, returning from a year in Paris studying art, realizes was stifling for both of them. Bored by domesticity, his child and wife, he proposes an "open marriage."

By the second act this arrangement—pleasing to him—has blown up because his wealthy lover's husband threatens to sue for divorce. In a very good scene, the wealthy woman comes to see Edith, saying she hopes Edith will not divorce Julian because then her husband will have to go through with it. She is a very interesting character, extremely worldly, and not very upset about the events. She exits, saying that, as a woman of the world, she advises Edith to stay married. "Once is enough. . . . Getting divorced and remarried all the time is so *dégagé*. Don't you agree? . . . Good-bye, I'm not sorry I came—although you seem so—so *hostile*" (153).

Edith has been patient because she felt Julian was hunting for something elusive in life and that when he found it they could recapture their love. But when she pretends to have accepted jewelry from a rich man, he is unconcerned and she realizes that his love for her is dead. Like Nora, she leaves him, but her exit is one of bewilderment.

In the last act it is clear that she is a changed woman. She is attractive and sophisticated because of the life she has been leading. The rich man, Walter Greenborough, saved her from suicide, took her to live with him in luxurious surroundings, and is in love with her. He would like her to divorce so that they can marry. At this point, however, Edith's daughter, like Ibsen's Hedvig, dies and Edith believes that her death will bring Julian back to her. The conclusion is realistic and intense in contrast to that of *Déclassée*. Greenborough leaves and Edith is alone with his friend. Like Greenborough, the friend supposes that she is going back to Julian. She answers that she was wrong, that Julian doesn't want her. When asked what she can do, she responds simply, "God knows" (198).

The production was very impressive and reviewers noted the change in Akins' work. Arthur Hopkins was the director and Robert Edmond Jones provided three excellent settings. *Theatre Magazine* said, "Again, Zoë Akins has scored a triumph. She has invested a Mother Goose title with an almost allegorical meaning, and has retold an old story with an art, a simple beauty of language, and many deft twists of a vivid imagination that give it an absorbingly fresh interest" ("Daddy's Gone A-Hunting" 315).

Writing about the play in 1979, Yongue commented on Akins' "extremely sharp and sympathetic understanding of human foibles in general and of female folly and frustration in particular" (14).

> Although the play is recognized for its unorthodox focus on the troubled quest for personal freedom, it is more powerful for its quiet repudiation of woman's considerable dependence on man and for its unhappy admission that women like Edith—most women for that matter—find life "unsafe" when their traditional sources of security are taken from them. Neither Edith's initial decision to remain true to her adulterous husband, nor her later decision to live with Greenborough in the face of society's censure is completely admirable according to Akins. Her keen irony underscores Edith's appalling lack of personal identity and purposiveness, and the reader experiences her horror when she realizes that she cannot expect men or children to provide meaning and identity for her. (14-15)

Ludwig Lewisohn wrote a long, thoughtful review in which he praised the play highly, but also criticized its construction. Noting the excellence of the second act conclusion when Edith makes the final test of Julian, he said, "The American drama has yet to show a truer and profounder moment than that. The physical spheres of sex are here defined and delimited with extraordinary insight and precision. The protagonists who are both in the right, both admirable, and, acting from the innermost necessities of their nature, confront each other across a bridgeless chasm." He also praised the conclusion of the play, saying, "Here again, Miss Akins shows a peculiar grace. A shoddy, happy ending was within her grasp." However, he pointed to the weakness in the play, the third act as a whole. He felt the action should have moved to a climax within an hour of Edith's departure—in other words there should have been a continuity of time and action between the second and third acts ("Homespun and Brocade" 325). A more serious problem, which he did not note, is the death of the child which seems a mere contrivance of the playwright. In Ibsen's *The Wild Duck*, Hedwig's death arises from the action of the drama, whereas Akins' little Janet seems "to die of the third act." Despite this weakness, the play is good and reveals Akins at her best.

The Varying Shore opened in 1921, just a few months after Akins' successful Ibsenian drama, and ran for 66 performances. Akins said, "I conceived the idea of writing a play about the varying shore of a woman's life. I wanted to write about what sends people down hill" (Chapman, "Zoë Akins" 2). Lawrence Reamer described the action as a love story seen through the eyes of an old man who has been a faithful lover: "the spectators witness the life of the woman he has loved so many years. In the epilogue he is found dead at the table" ("Miss Ferguson the Lovely Heroine" n.p.). Akins engaged in the unusual experiment of placing the action in reverse, with the third act first. The challenge of moving from forty to thirty to sixteen provided a superb opportunity for Elsie Ferguson. However, New York audiences didn't care for the unconventional structure of the play. Akins was irritated by the negative response which caused her to rewrite the play in chronological order after the play had opened in New York. She said people didn't like to see a woman "middle-aged in the first act, mature in the second, and young in the third, because it is too hard to follow the action. That seems to me a silly reason. . . . The people in Newark had no difficulty in that respect" (Chapman, "Zoë Akins—Experimenter" 2).

Most of the critics praised the play and said Akins was more capable at writing such a romance than most of her colleagues. John Rankin Towse wrote that there was a crowded house which applauded the play strongly. "It is not a masterpiece by any means, but it is an uncommonly good specimen of modern emotional romance, ingeniously devised, and better written than most of its class. It is on the whole well-acted and in many respects a superior show. In the ingenuity and insight in one or two poignant and pathetic passages, it occasionally assumes the aspect of genuine and sincere drama" ("The Varying Shore" n.p.). Alexander Woolcott wrote that the evening was interesting "thanks chiefly to the play itself, which is told by a dramatic story-teller who has been many things in the theatre, but never a bore" ("The Varying Shore" n.p.).

After the opening of *The Varying Shore*, Akins had one play in New York, one in Chicago, and one on the road. John A. Chapman called her the "most popular of our women playwrights" and noted that she was not content to rest on her laurels, but had many plans for other plays: "She believes she has much to find out about the theatre, and she has gone at finding out very industriously." He quoted her as saying, "Most of the plays I have done have been experimental. I want to find out everything I can as to what makes for artistic success in the theatre" ("Zoë Akins—Experimenter" 2).

Londré wrote of Akins' next play, "Most critics agreed that Akins' finest work was *Greatness*, first produced in New York in 1922 under the title *The Texas Nightingale*. She wrote this comedy about a temperamental, often-married opera singer especially for her friend, the actress Jobyna Howland ("Zoë Akins" 12).

The Texas Nightingale is a very amusing play with a marvelous central role. Madame Canava, formerly Hollyhock Jones, the Texas Nightingale, is a great success professionally, but her personal life is a mess. She comes to visit her second husband, Stevie, who left her because she was accepting diamonds from a count, causing him to feel like an unnecessary appendage. It seems from the beginning of the play that they should get back together, but she is engaged to a violinist about the age of her son. The son, Raymond, is the reason she has come to Stevie: she reveals that he is the father and that the child was born six months after he left. Raymond wants to marry a dumb, slightly older, unsuccessful actress. Madame Canava wants Stevie, as Raymond's father, to stop the marriage. Through a series of comic scenes she weeps, shouts, talks baby-talk, appreciates food, sings, and generally displays artistic temperament.

Stevie loves her voice and what he perceives as her "greatness." He also likes the new-found son, Raymond and thinks if he loves the girl he should be allowed to marry her. By the end he and Raymond have convinced Ducky, as they call her, to allow the marriage. Left alone, Stevie and Ducky consider the future. She says that Raymond can get a divorce when he wakes up to the girl's dumbness or that she may be able to knock some sense into her head and teach her at least to answer the phone.

> Stevie: Yes, she may develop unsuspected virtues as the daughter-in-law of a
>   prima donna. She may even learn to autograph the photographs.
> Canava: [With her usual sarcasm] She'd have to know how to write to do that.
>   No other woman in this world could go through what I've gone
>   through today and sing Brünnhilde the same night. (289)

But she regains her cheerful humor, and, taking things in hand in her usual fashion, proposes to Stevie. He responds that he is too poor at the moment, but otherwise willing. She exits happily, wondering if she shouldn't take over Sieglinde as it might be a better role.

The reviewers liked the play. An unidentified critic wrote that Akins was making fun of the artistic temperament which had been done before, "but never in quite so erratic and whirlwind a style as this rowdy and romantic nightingale." He also noted that the central role was very difficult (unidentified clipping, Akins file, Lincoln Center). Heywood Broun called the play "The most important and interesting work which Zoë Akins has ever done" and said that "it touches emotional complications easily recognizable yet not often brought into theatre" ("The Texas Nightingale" n.p.) John Corbin wrote a review which praised nearly all aspects of the play and the production, calling it Akins' best play since *Déclassée*, "a flashing and scintillating comedy—a worthy play by one of the foremost American writers for the stage." He was most impressed with the characterization:

> In drawing her tempestuous prima donna, in probing into her illogical mind and revealing her many and sudden changes of mood, Miss Akins has been particularly skillful. It is for this character and that of a 19-year-old boy, her son, that the play has been written. It is, of course, purely an artificial comedy—a thing of character and dialogue, with nomore real heart than could be pressed between the leaves of a book. But those things which Miss Akins knows how to do she does supremely well. ("The Texas Nightingale" 15).

Other critics liked the play but felt that Jobyna Howland was inadequate in the role—some of them comparing her unfavorably to Ethel Barrymore in Akins' first success. The play remains very funny, and it is surprising that it has never been turned into a musical. It was an unfortunate production for Akins in that it was a critical success, but only ran for 32 performances. It was published under the title, *Greatness*.

Akins had even less success with her 1923 play *A Royal Fandango*. This was a slight comedy, with elements of fantasy, in which a princess falls in love with a matador. It played off the current craze for Valentino. Akins sent it to Ethel Barrymore who wired back, "IT IS DIVINE. I AM CRAZY ABOUT IT" (Peters *The House of Barrymore* 271). When it closed after 24 performances, she had changed her mind about it. Percy Hammond said the play was too slight, serving only as a vehicle for Barrymore's charms ("It is Well for 'A Royal Fandango' that Miss Barrymore is Present" n.p.). Alexander Woolcott called it a "shaky and uncertain little play" ("A Royal Wild Oat" n.p.). Heywood Broun called the first act a triumph for both the actors and the playwright, but said that after that it went steadily downhill with a weak plot. He concluded, "Grace and wit of line are all that remain" ("Ethel Barrymore" n.p.) Alan Dale gave the play mild praise, saying, "for the most part its gentle humor and its fevered attempt at the unconventional titillated agreeably. It was the work of Zoë Akins, who is industrious, clever, and often frolicsome" ("Royal Fandango" n.p.). John Corbin felt the plot was weak, but said, "In all, there is a certain charm and humor, an originality of humoresque fancy which is Miss Akins' own" ("Princess and a Matador" 25).

Akins was in for a run of bad luck. Her next play, *The Moon-Flower* (1924) ran only 48 performances, *First Love* (1926) only 50, *The Crown Prince* (1927) only 45, and *The Furies* (a modern retelling of *Hamlet* produced in 1928) only 45. Many critics thought the last play was overwrought, but it was a very interesting experiment on Akins' part. As Sievers has written,

> *The Furies* is notable as one of the few attempts in serious drama to depict subjective forces in external staging. Miss Akins used the technique introduced by O'Neill in *Strange Interlude* (which had opened one month before) of having the characters freeze while each in turn speaks his inner thoughts. Scenically also the author attempted to visualize the warped mind of the killer by having the walls of his room sloped, the table legs fantastic, and the candles and staircase surrealistically contorted. (78)

Akins was in bad odor with the critics after so many failures and her play utilized Expressionistic techniques which were felt to be passé. Nevertheless, the play reveals her imaginative approach to theatre and provided a fine role for Laurette Taylor.

Finally she had a success with *The Greeks Had a Word for It* in 1930. The comedy focused on three women who had been Ziegfeld Follies performers, but were now dependent upon generous gentlemen friends. When one of the three decides to marry, it seems like spoiling the fun to the other two. But, as Brooks Atkinson described it, "just before the wedding ceremony in a private suite in the Ambassador Hotel, she looks with envy upon her two sisters in sin who are just starting off on a harum-scarum adventure to Paris. She pulls off her wedding dress and joins them" ("Vine Leaves in a Heap" 16). The play lifted the gloom of the Depression for many theatre-goers, the critics found the play funny, it was performed in New York with Dorothy Hall and on tour by the enchanting Ina Claire. The play ran for 253 performances in New York.

Akins was part of a literary circle which included novelists and poets. She enjoyed giving dinners for such people as Elinor Wylie, Carl Van Vechten, Willa Cather, and Edith Wharton. When she dramatized *The Old Maid* (1935), Wharton trusted her so much that she never asked to read the script. Akins made a faithful adaptation of the poignant story, and provided Judith Anderson with one of her finest roles, that of Delia, the wealthy woman who rejects a poor suitor, Clem, but later finds her greatest happiness in her love for his illegitimate child, Tina. She sees the child in Charlotte's school for poor children and is immediately drawn to her. When Charlotte must choose between marrying Delia's brother-in-law and giving up her school, she confesses to Delia that she comforted Clem and bore his child in secret. Jealous of Charlotte and eager to have Clem's child, she breaks off the engagement by saying that Charlotte is too ill to marry. She then takes mother and daughter into her house and adopts Tina so she can make a good marriage.

The development of Charlotte's character from a good, generous, kind woman into a nit-picking, critical old maid is a very interesting aspect and gave Helen Menken a fine role. Tina grows to hate her, unaware that she is her true mother. On the evening before Tina's marriage, Charlotte flies out at Delia, saying that she knows Delia hates her and that she never wanted to help her, but that it was all for Clem Spender and his child:

> I'm not wicked. I wouldn't have done to you what you've done to me. From the beginning, you've deliberately divided me from my daughter! Do you suppose its been easy all these years to hear her call you *mother*? Oh, I know that it was agreed between us that she must never guess! But you needn't have perpetually come between us! If you hadn't, she'd have had to love *me*! But for all your patience and generosity, you've ended by robbing me of my child. That's why I can talk of hatred here before this altar tonight! And that's why—before she's his tomorrow: tonight, just tonight, she belongs to me! That's why I won't let her call anyone else *mother* tonight! (179-180)

Charlotte goes to Tina's room to tell her the truth, but realizes it would be useless: Tina's father loved Delia and the child loved Delia and Charlotte has turned into an embittered old maid for nothing.

There was an unfortunate circumstance regarding the first reviews. The opening conflicted with the opening of Robert Sherwood's *The Petrified Forest*. So the reviewers were taken by bus to Baltimore and reviewed a matinee while it was still in out-of-town try-outs. Most critics felt the performances were not particularly good—they obviously improved by the time the play was performing in New York because they were later remembered as outstanding. A typical reaction was expressed by William Boehnel who called it a good play which was neither great nor significant ("Akins Play at Empire" n.p.). Almost all the critics praised the denouement, which, according to Arthur Ruhl, left the men moved and the women weeping. He called it "an affecting work, beautifully played" and said "it never creaks and the atmosphere is excellent" ("The Old Maid" n.p.). The critic for the *New York Sun* summed up his response in the title "Valentine of Yesteryear." He called the play "a pretty water-color of yesteryear with an aura of wistfulness and sentiment which is affecting, but the play is more tableau than drama." He noted, which most critics did not, that it was unfair to judge the acting at the matinee in Baltimore (n.p.).

One problem with the play is that the original material is not inherently exciting—Wharton's novel is a low-key, intense picture of the relationship between two women in a society which has no forgiveness for a woman who has an illegitimate child. The critic for the *New York American* called the adaptation neat, straight-forward, restrained, and well-tempered, "which will probably imply to you that it is not a notably exciting one, however. It isn't. Perhaps it couldn't be" ("The Old Maid" n.p.). Arthur Pollock said Akins was too faithful to the novel which he called "stiff and old-fashioned" ("The Old Maid" n.p.). Some critics praised the work of director Guthrie McClintic and everyone praised the beautiful settings of Stewart Cheney. One of the few really negative reviews (which may have been written by George S. Kaufman) appeared in *Variety*. The reviewer described it as "a bad play which should make money . . . a woman's play from every standpoint. It had charm, lavender and old lace, and the scenery and the costumes were the high point of the show" ("The Old Maid" n.p.).

There were almost no rave reviews, but most had some good things to say about the production and *The Old Maid* pleased audiences. The Pulitzer prize committee awarded it the prize for the year's best play and there was an intense and unpleasant reaction. Clayton Hamilton said on the radio "The Pulitzer prize committee has labored and brought forth a mouse. Miss Zoë Akins herself very likely would be the last to claim that this is an original American play." He concluded that the major elements were all Edith Wharton's. Percy Hammond called it a "first-class second rater" and said the award should have gone to Hellman's *The Children's Hour*. Hellman's director, Herman Shumlin, intemperately said, "I think it's quite the worst selection the committee could possibly have made from all the plays now current on

Broadway" (qtd. in Toohey 127). The committee was attacked on all sides and Akins was criticized as well. The newspapers had a field day printing comments from critics and writers. Only George S. Kaufman, who had won a Pulitzer Prize three years earlier, refused to comment, saying, "I'm in a swell place to keep my mouth shut" (qtd. in Toohey 128).

For Akins the award brought a mixture of pain and pleasure, as it had Glaspell. However, Akins did not withdraw from the theatre, but went to Hollywood, her worth increased by the prize, and planned more plays for the future. She was able to salve her wounds with the knowledge that the play ran 305 performances. She also received the annual award from the Theatre Club Incorporated which described the play as the "most outstanding and dramatic production of the season" ("Brief Sketches of Winners of Pulitzer Prizes" n.p.).

Akins returned to the theatre in 1936 with O *Evening Star*, regretting in an interview the loss of about $26,000 which she could have earned in Hollywood during the rehearsal period. She happily stated that she didn't need to worry about the money, however, as *The Old Maid* was a big success on its national tour and she was receiving about $500 a week from it. Her new play was another vehicle for Jobyna Howland, whose performance failed to please in *The Texas Nightingale*. The play was variously said to be loosely based on the careers of Mrs. Leslie Carter, Marie Dressler, and Lillian Russell.

Commenting on working in Hollywood, Akins said she found it "a grindstone, but it's fascinating" ("The Author of Twenty Plays" 4). Part of the fascination seems to have been in observing the various types who worked there. In a review called "Hollywood Misery," the critic for the *Literary Digest* wrote that Akins dismissed the point of view that "the place and its people are funny." He summarized her depiction in O *Evening Star* by saying, "To her, it and they are shallow, miserable, and sordid, a vulgar concourse of overpaid humanity" (19). Akins' play contrasted the hilarity of Kaufman and Hart's *Once in a Lifetime* and pre-dated the dark view of Hollywood in the 1937 film *A Star is Born*. The play was successful in performances in Philadelphia, one critic saying she had written "simply and directly" [i.e. she had no purple prose], and another saying "she put her story across the footlights and that's what counts" (qtd. in "Hollywood Misery" 19). Most of the Philadelphia critics were impressed by the acting of Jobyna Howard and others, as well as the direction.

New York critics praised the handsome production with sets again by Stewart Cheney. Percy Hammond found the play over-dramatic and concluded, "If you like your drama to hit you full in the face, with broad and onerous exertions of atmosphere and conversation, you will be fonder of 'O Evening Star' than I am" ("O Evening Star" n.p.). Brooks Atkinson found many faults with the play, but admitted that he and the audience were moved by it. "Maundering and cluttered and completely undistinguished, nevertheless, it has its moments of emotional triumph all through the evening. Even though your mind rebels, your emotions betray you into acknowledging that Miss Akins knows how the character feels and can write it for the theatre" ("Jobyna Howard" 24). Many of the critics felt the production was not as good as it could have been. The audience response was weak and the play closed after 5 performances.

Akins was no more successful with her next play, produced in 1941. This was an adaptation of Claude-André Puget's comedy *Les Jours Heureux*. The work had been successfully performed for three years in Paris and seemed a likely play for adaptation. In the midst of the unhappy news of the war, shortages of consumer goods, and fears for the future, a light-hearted comedy about the trials of young people falling in love seemed just the right thing. Five cousins are spending their usual summer holiday on an island in the St Lawrence river. One of the girls invents a handsome aviator to make her male cousin jealous. At that point, an aviator who fits the bill arrives, having crashed in the vicinity. The young people fall in and out of love, one of the girls tries to commit suicide, and the pilot flies away, leaving all of them slightly changed.

Critics generally remarked on the artifice of the plot and the slight quality of the original script. There were a number of extremely negative reviews. Richard Watts, Jr. felt that the characters were so tedious that the play brought the season to a close "amid a great lack of excitement." He noted that the only benefit was that "it has persuaded me that youth perhaps isn't as admirable a quality as I had thought it was" ("Youth" n.p.). Similarly, John Mason Brown noted that aging critics might get some comfort from seeing these "empty little egoists, with their incessant chit-chat about nothing" and feel that the passing of youth was not all that bad. He stated "Miss Akins has never worked on a more trivial script" ("Diana Barrymore Seen" n.p.). John Anderson said that in Paris a dozen or so years ago, the play might have impressed the audience as having "tender wisdom" but that now it seemed like "a voice from another world": "the small upheaval on the island in the St. Lawrence occurs in a peaceful vacuum, too remote in time, place, meaning and emotion to be very pertinent. . . . Aviators these days are destroying more than illusions" ("The Happy Days" n.p.). Ralph Carey fell in between the pro and con critics, saying that it was pleasing to have Akins back in the theatre after a long absence in Hollywood. He said the return was disappointing compared to Rose Franken's return with *Claudia*, but that the play was a "pleasant, but undistinguished end to the season" ("Among New York Theatres" n.p.).

There were a number of critics sympathetic to the venture who noted the problems of presenting it in 1941 after the German occupation of much of France. Brooks Atkinson remarked that the play's success occurred in France before the Blitzkrieg and surrender, and that "to avoid rueful considerations" Akins had changed the setting from Europe to Canada. He was part of a group of critics who found the young people charming. He believed that Akins' "kindly adaptation may have given the play a tender sincerity out of her own regard for people. When these girls open their hearts, they occasionally speak pure poetry. They are very sweet children ("'The Happy Days'" 24). Richard Lockridge found the play one "to inspire affection and to be regarded tenderly," that it had "tinkling charm, prettily handled dialogue. . . . and a gentle appreciation of youth" ("The Happy Days" n.p.).

The critics, then, were clearly divided as to whether the young persons were "downright intolerable" or "sweetly charming." The play as a whole was disappointing for many people. First, for Akins, of whom Burns Mantle wrote, "The author of 'Déclassée,' 'The Greeks Had a Word for It,' and 'The Old Maid' has done and can do a lot better than this" ("The Happy Days" n.p.). It was also a great disappointment in that Akins hoped to provide a fine role for Diana Barrymore, even as she had for her aunt in 1919. While the critics were sympathetic to the young actress, she could not claim a success and Sidney B. Whipple wrote, "I do not believe her distinguished auntie, even in her own youth, could have done anything with such a play" ("Diana Barrymore in Play" n.p.). Finally, the play was a great disappointment to the producers, Raphael and Robert Hakim, who had been driven by the Germans from Paris and were hoping for success in America. This was clearly a weakly charming play presented at the wrong time. Just before the play opened Akins told an interviewer that all of her plays had covered operating expenses at least. This, her twenty-first play, ran only twenty-three performances and was a real financial failure.

Akins' theatrical career ended with moderate success, in contrast to many playwrights. At the age of 58 she wrote *Mrs. January and Mr. Ex* which was produced in 1944. George Freedley, among others, said that Akins had a very clever idea for her comedy ("Billie Burke, Frank Craven Provide Entertainment" n.p.). The play is a satire on a wealthy, often-married lady (so often married that she got a court order so she could use her maiden name and quit changing it) who is attracted to the little she knows about Communism, and decides to move into a small country cottage and get used to doing without. Although she anticipates the coming revolution with pleasure, her three children do not. She has raised them to be deliberately rude and selfish so they can succeed in the new society, and so they let her do all the work when the servants quit. Watching all this nonsense with a benign eye is a former Republican president of the United States, a character based somewhat on Coolidge. As he comes under her influence and she under his, they decide they would like to marry, but circumstances seem to make that hard. Her brother manages all her money (perhaps not quite honestly), and hates Mr. Ex who once had him investigated for fraud. Mr. Ex is drafted to run for president, but nobody thinks the public will vote for him because there would be a "red first-lady." But the American public surprises them all. They like Mr. Ex and his newly liberal, idealistic ideas and they like Mrs. January for her courageous experiment. Delighted to be engaged again and to be in the White House, she still can't quite believe it. The future president explains, "Countries change, you know. Like the people who live in them. Even like myself" (125).

The play had considerable charm which was expressed to the fullest by Billie Burke and Frank Craven. Young Barbara bel Geddes (whose father had produced *Papa* twenty-eight years before) was delightful as the daughter. The play was both a social comment and a merry comedy. When Mrs. January's children start acting nicely towards her, she remarks to Mr. Ex, "Something has changed them! But whatever it is, they are sweet when they're insincere, aren't they?" (114). When she exits at one point to get an aged bottle of champagne, she remarks that it is symbolical: "That champagne's at its very best—when the bubbles are almost ready to stop bubbling! Like us, Martin" (67).

Robert Garland in a largely positive review warned that there was social criticism in the play, saying that it is so deftly handled that "you can eat your Communism on 44th street, and have it too." He said that in Akins' play, "it's three cheers for the red, white and blue—red for the Russians, white for us, a blue for the way dissenters are going to feel about it." Like most critics, he praised the handsome production directed by Elliott Nugent and the costumes by Adrian. And, like all the critics, he praised the acting: "The co-starring of Billie Burke and Frank Craven . . . was a wonderful stroke of genius. [The play] is wise. It's witty. And it's wonderfully well-acted in the title roles" ("Mrs. January" n.p.). Wolcott Gibbs called his review "A Very Nice Piece of Work" and described it as "a funny and pleasant play" which was literate and entertaining (44). Several of the critics complained, quite rightly, that the play was too long. Some felt that the play was too fantastic or whimsical, Howard Barnes concluding that the actors kept the "whimsy palatable" ("Flimsy Whimsy" n.p.). The reviews on the whole gave the impression that the play was a lightly amusing satire on post-war greed and the conflicting views between liberals and conservatives, which was largely attractive because of the acting. The play ran only forty-three performances, so it could not be considered a commercial success. But it showed Akins still capable of devising a comic situation and developing it with funny characters and witty lines. It just wasn't funny enough. Ward Morehouse wrote, "I wish Miss Akins could have done more with a delightful notion" ("Mrs. January and Mr. Ex" n.p.). As she did throughout her career, Akins provided actors with roles in which they could show their abilities and delight the audience.

Although many of her plays were experimental, Akins had the reputation of writing largely commercial pieces. In fact, she did not choose the safe commercial path which beckoned to her, nor did she choose to stay with the big money in Hollywood as many other of the playwrights did. Her first love was the stage and she wrote many different types of plays which reflected the changes in society. Unlike Lillian Hellman, she was not involved in sharp criticism of American society, but her plays do often satirize or put the spotlight on such subjects as the plight of the "fallen woman," economic impossibilities for a woman without a husband or a career, hypocrisy, the intolerant attitude toward illegitimacy, the viciousness often encountered in the theatre, and, at the

very end, of the conflict between the views of liberals and conservatives in America. Her great love was poetry, and she often attempted
to write poetic dramas which were (as for Sophie Treadwell, Eugene
O'Neill and others) unsuccessful. The comparison with O'Neill is useful, for he was often criticized for daring, overblown dramatic experiments as was Akins. But in his case these are looked upon as aberra-
tions of a great playwright, whereas she has been described as "the
chief romancer of our stage. . . . Voluptuous in taste" (Saylor "Some
Playwright Biographies" 532), and many of her fine plays have been
forgotten.

In her best work Akins displayed wit, intensity, and an understanding of human nature. Even her lesser works often attracted audiences
because Akins was capable of blending sentiment and melodrama to
create a play with popular appeal. Actors were drawn to her plays by
the highly theatrical characters she created and the dynamic speeches
she wrote for them. The enormous financial success of such Akins
plays as *Déclassée* and *The Old Maid* led producers to take a chance on
her later plays. Directors such as Arthur Hopkins, Guthrie McClintic,
and George S. Kaufman admired the excitement present even in her
weaker plays. As Benson Inge wrote near the end of her career,
"Hasn't Akins discovered the direct route between the purse and the
heart? Emotion is the name of the highway. Emotion in frills and old
lace, but keep it beautiful. People want to be stirred . . . to forget.
There's gold in that emollient" (n. p.). Akins wrote easily, sometimes
completing an entire act in one twelve hour stretch and she often
worked on several plays at once. This very facility in writing may have
been a problem, leading her to toss off plays lightly without the necessary discipline of editing and polishing.

Starting as an ingenue from St. Louis, Zoë Akins made her way to a
highly successful career in theatre. She never collaborated, claiming
that no collaborator would put up with her temper (Inge n.p.), but it is
more likely that she simply preferred going her own way. She was an
independent woman whose friendships were largely with other women
in the theatre and the literary world. Her late, surprising marriage did
little to change her life; she continued as Miss Akins. High-spirited and
witty, she overcame negative criticism, was wholly involved in theatre
and film, and enjoyed life thoroughly.

Edna Ferber (1885-1968)

Edna Ferber (1885-1968) was whole-heartedly involved with theatre throughout her long career, writing her first play in 1915 and her last in 1948. Writing in 1940, one critic said, "Miss Ferber is probably more solidly steeped in the American theatre than any other contemporary writer" (Duval 7). She was born in 1885 in Kalamazoo. Her childhood may be divided into two parts. Her early years were in Ottumwa, Iowa where she suffered because of anti-Semitism and was taunted by such epithets as "Sheeny." She wrote that she resolved to become a success and "show them" (A *Peculiar Treasure* 41). When she was seven the family moved to Appleton, Wisconsin. There the mayor was Jewish, the school was very progressive, and the town as a whole provided a wonderful, liberal environment for a young girl. One of her good friends was a young black girl. Ferber said there was less racism in Appleton than in any other town she knew (A *Peculiar Treasure* 103).

As a child she was fascinated by a toy theater her grandfather operated on the dining table after dinner. She wrote plays which were "mostly blood and thunder. Edna acted, directed, improvised the sets and costumes and sold tickets for so many pins" (unidentified clipping, Lincoln Center). Much of her time at school was spent reciting and acting in plays. She took elocution lessons and as a high school student won first prize in the annual state-wide declamatory contest. Her family were avid theatre-goers and despite a general lack of money, Ferber and her relatives went to the theatre constantly, seeing Lily Langtry, Henry Irving, and all the major stars of the time. She wrote, "God bless the theatre for what it gave a frightened, fun loving family" (A *Peculiar Treasure* 56). Given her strong interest in the theatre, it was inevitable that she would be attracted to acting. However, her family could not afford to send her to Northwestern University to prepare for a career on the stage. She never got over the disappointment, saying, "The stage was my one love. To this moment I feel sure . . . that I would have been The Actress of my day. . . . I write plays for the theatre because I love it." Regarding herself as a "blighted Bernhardt," she became the first woman reporter for her hometown newspaper (A *Peculiar Treasure* 101). A 1968 obituary noted the importance of her newspaper work as preparation for her playwriting: "she developed a supercamera eye, a sense of the dramatic, and a vast storehouse of practical and psychological knowledge" ("Edna Ferber, Novelist, 82, Dies" 1). She began writing short stories and novels and achieved success fairly swiftly. When her family moved to Chicago she attempted to continue her career as a newspaper reporter, but could not get a job with the *Chicago Tribune* because they didn't want women reporters. Ironically, the man who refused her a job was Burns Mantle, who later selected several of Ferber's plays for his yearly volumes of best plays.

Ferber's most popular early stories were about an American businesswoman, Emma McChesney. She was regarded as a new and original type in fiction. Ferber based the character on her own mother, a strong-willed woman who took over her husband's business when he went blind. Inspired by her mother's example, Ferber was a strong, independent woman who did not accept entrapment in a male-oriented society. A typical Ferber statement was, "I believe woman's place, as well as man's place, is in the world" (Michaelson n.p).

She chose not to marry, but found satisfaction through her career as well as financial and critical success. She negotiated a payment of $1,500,000 for her novel *Giant,* the greatest single pay-off for a literary property in the history of moviemaking up to that time ("Edna Ferber's %" n.p.). Her role in the family was one normally taken by a male—she managed her finances, negotiated contracts, supervised the building of her home, and provided thousands of dollars for her relatives throughout her life. Through her writing she presented the reality of American society, both good and bad. She wanted particularly to express her pride as a Jew and to work against racism. She received the Pulitzer Prize for her novel *So Big* in 1924, and critics called her the greatest American woman novelist of her day (" Edna Ferber, Novelist, 82, Dies" l). Reviewing her career as a novelist and playwright, W.G. Rogers wrote that she would be a model for future writers, "She is the 24-hour a day professional, forthright and uncompromising. As a working woman writer she has no superior" (n.p.).

Ferber used her position to fight for various causes both through her playwriting and speaking. She was outspoken, determined, and often hot-tempered. At one point she was barred from Mexico because of her criticism of the country. She campaigned for liberal candidates such as F. D. Roosevelt and opposed conservative politicians. She was opposed to the policies of playwright/actress/politician Clare Boothe Luce, and wrote a letter in 1943 to the *New York Times* attacking her isolationist position and her attitude toward Hitler. Luce was the congresswoman for Ferber's district, but Ferber said that Luce did not represent her in the congresswoman's "most appalling statement to date." The letter concluded that if Luce and others like her were only moved to action by the attack on Pearl Harbor, "then she is a self-confessed condoner of Hitler and the Hitler regime and the Hitler plan from 1933 to 1941, and for all I know to this day" ("Mrs. Luce is Contradicted" n.p.). Ferber expressed her social concerns and her attitudes about fascism in most of her plays. She often spoke out for higher salaries for teachers, and her second play focused on that issue. In 1947 she gave a speech at an author's luncheon in which she stated, "I'd like to see bank presidents try to live on teacher's salaries" ("Speakers at Book" n.p.). Returning from Europe in 1953 she was greeted as usual by many reporters and took the opportunity to say that New York was the most disgustingly dirty city she had ever seen. This created a furor which resulted in a major clean-up campaign ("A Broom for Miss Ferber" n.p.).

Ferber's professional career in the theatre began with a play called *Our Mrs. McChesney.* Ethel Barrymore wanted to play Mrs. McChesney in a dramatization of the stories which depicted a strong, clever business woman who traveled alone to many cities. In 1915 this type was distinctly unusual. Although the stories were essentially light, Ferber was concerned with the role of women in society and the opportunities for careers—she had not forgotten her rejection by Burns Mantle. She collaborated on the play with an established playwright, George V. Hobart. Her comments on the collaboration are interesting because they reveal Ferber's approach to playwriting and her desire for realism in characterization and dialogue. She had contempt for much of the commercial playwriting of the period by such writers as David Belasco and Avery Hopwood and admired the plays done by the Washington Square Players and the Provincetown Playhouse. She had formed the habit of speaking the dialogue in her fiction out loud, then writing it down. This was very useful when she wrote plays, because it tested the actability of the lines. When she worked with Hobart she felt the dialogue he wanted to put in the play was artificial: "His idea of stage dialogue offended my ear. I said over and over, not very politely, 'But people don't talk like that'" (*A Peculiar Treasure* 216).

Ferber was not satisfied with the play (which was not published), but it was a success and Ferber earned the first of the many thousands of dollars she was to receive from the theatre. The simple story of a brisk, charming, girlish widow in her late 30's who is so successful selling women's petticoats that she becomes a partner in the firm appealed to audiences and critics. The critic for *The Nation* wrote, "The play may be recommended for its wholesome lightheartedness and entertaining situations ("Our Mrs. McChesney" 527). For Ferber the experience was important because she had the chance to watch rehearsals and work on rewriting. She had learned about theatre previously by reading plays and studying them in performance from the audience. As she later wrote, "I wanted to learn about the theatre. I wanted to watch these people in rehearsal" (*A Peculiar Treasure* 217). With her reporter's eye she was also observing and storing up ideas about theatre and acting which would later be used in plays such as The Royal Family and Bravo.

Ferber continued writing fiction, but took an avid interest in the work of the Washington Square Players. She was also very involved with the war effort, and during World War I traveled through the U.S.A. giving speeches, particularly urging women to play a greater role in society and in the war effort. She continued in this effort throughout her life, remarking with satisfaction in 1943, "The war has awakened women to the need the world has for what they can give" ("Edna Ferber Sees Better" n.p.).

Not until after the World War I did Ferber return to the theatre. A playwright named Norman Levy suggested that they collaborate on a play which focused on the deplorably low salaries for teachers. They began the play, but in the final stages she had to work on it alone because his father was dying. $1200 a Year is a story of a young professor who quits his job at a university in a factory town to work at the factory for higher wages. He becomes notorious as a labor organizer and travels to other cities making firebrand speeches. Meanwhile, his wife has a higher standard of living, but is unhappy because she misses her intellectual friends and does not enjoy the company of immigrant factory workers. The factory owner is modeled somewhat on Andrew Carnegie and is the most interesting character in the play. He is shown to be a shrewd business man, but far from the stereotyped cigar smoking, top hatted tyrant usually depicted in popular literature. He is the benefactor for the university, but believes in low salaries for factory workers and university professors. The ending of the play is rather fantastic. Just as the teacher seems to be beaten by the factory owner, a movie producer bursts in offering him a fabulous salary to come and play himself in a series of movies depicting poor working conditions and the plight of the workers. Rather than suffer more bad publicity, the boss offers to increase salaries at the university so the professor will go back to work there. Two typical Ferber characteristics inform the play: an interest in depicting ethnicity in a realistic manner and a belief that America is the land of opportunity and superior to Europe.

The play ran just a week in Baltimore in 1920. Ferber said that it wasn't bad, but just not good enough. She also felt that the play was wrong for the time: "A world fatigued by war and its horrors didn't want to hear about the class struggle between a group of college professors and their neighbors, the mill workers" (A *Peculiar Treasure* 250).

In fact, there are several weaknesses in the play. The chief problem is that it is a play which seeks to treat a serious problem in a comic manner but the comedy is not very effective and the play seems like many other second-rate imitations of Bernard Shaw's plays. Another difficulty in the play is the lack of reality in details. At one point a worker says eggs cost a dollar a dozen which is certainly not accurate for 1920. Lack of reality in the milieu is even more glaring. Ferber's reporter's eye could not help her for she had never been in either the university milieu nor the factory milieu. In her later plays she would draw on her observation of actual people and situations during her extensive travels in America and Europe. Although $1200 *Year* was a failure in its commercial production, Ferber was surprised by its success in amateur and little-theatre groups.

In 1918 Ferber wrote a short story called *The Eldest*. She discovered two years later that the Provincetown Players, whose work she admired, had announced a production of a play by the same name. She made inquiries and discovered to her fury that some other woman had dramatized her story. She then dramatized the story herself and it was presented by the group. The play is a simple treatment of a woman who was the eldest daughter in a family of selfish, greedy people. When her mother became ill (or too lazy to get out of bed), she assumed the responsibilities of the household and gave up her chance for romance. Throughout the play she tends to mother, whose whining is heard from off-stage, and reveals her sorrow over her lost love. When her fiancé reappears, it is to take out Rose's pretty sister (who now resembles the young Rose). Avoiding a false happy ending, the final scene shows Rose alone, carrying on the tasks of cleaning by habit. Only once does she reveal her anger, saying to her flashy brother, "Don't you think I ever get sick of slaving for a thankless bunch like you! Well, I do. Sick and tired of it, that's what. Coming around and asking me for money as if I was a bank" (73) The grim story is relieved by some humor, and the characters are depicted with interesting touches, and lively dialogue.

After *The Eldest* was produced she received what may have been the most important letter of her whole life. George S. Kaufman (later known as "The Great Collaborator") invited her to collaborate with him on a play based on her story *Old Man Minick*. Ferber was thrilled to be working with Kaufman, but was afraid the story was not dramatic enough to make a play.

In the event Ferber was wrong: the play was successfully performed and was selected by Burns Mantle as one of the ten best plays of the 1924-1925 season. Perhaps the low-key quality of the play appealed to audiences weary of sensational melodrama and attracted to realism. The story is very simple. As the play begins a pair of young, attractive, socially active women are talking about some committee work they are doing, problems with maids, and the imminent arrival of Old Mr. Minick, Nettie's father-in-law. After some comic confusion, Fred and his father arrive. He is a very amusing character, given to long, detailed descriptions of the train trip, his wife's last illness, and the disadvantages of eating on the train.

In the second act, it is apparent that the arrangement is not working well. Minick is lonely and bored and his two friends from the old folks home are rudely sent away when Nettie finds them mussing up the living room before an important committee meeting. The committee meeting is treated hilariously, with everything a shambles: women are late, there isn't a quorum, the minutes can't be read because the secretary isn't there, points of order are endlessly argued, and finally, as one of the women begins to make her presentation, Old Man Minick interrupts her and gives her his opinion of the situation. The women are furious and leave Nettie and Minick alone with a plate of sandwiches and a huge pitcher of orangeade. In this scene Ferber and Kaufman presented an effective satire of dilettante women who engage in social work in a very shallow way.

In the conclusion, Minick, who overheard Nettie saying that as long as he was there they wouldn't be able to have children, plans to move join his friends in the old folks home. In the last scene, Old Man

Minick packs up and moves out despite the protests of the new maid who says Nettie won't let him go. He answers, "Let me? I'm not a child. I know what I want to do, and I'm going to do it. Think I was a plumb fool." As he exits the maid asks him what to say to Nettie and he answers, "You tell her I said, 'Nettie—call me Grandpa'" (122-123).

The play was handsomely produced by the prestigious Winthrop Ames. Kaufman and Ames directed, but the former was often away, working on another play. Therefore, Ferber was the playwright who handled rewriting and problems which occurred in rehearsal. A noteworthy element in the production was the casting. Ferber wrote, "We thought ourselves rather daring to use a Harlem actress rather than a white girl in blackface. White and colored actors did not then ordinarily mingle. The stage has grown in that direction at least" (A *Peculiar Treasure* 287).

After out-of-town try-outs (which included an infrequently used theatre where bats flew at the actors and the audience during the performance), the play opened in New York in September of 1924. This was the first of many openings of plays by Ferber and Kaufman. After the New York run *Minick* was performed in Chicago and other American cities and in London.

Stark Young praised the play, but noted that it lacked plot complications and might not please everyone. He also noted that O.P. Heggie was not really good enough for the finely written role of Minick. Describing the play, itself, he said,

> The atmosphere, the tone and the writing of "Minick" are admirable. The whole tone of the play is constantly funny, loving and tragic altogether. The long gap between the generations of these people, the lack of any ideas that might bring them closer to each other; the barren mediocrity of their lives, their good intentions, their good hearts, their stupid interests, and most of all the dumbness of human beings toward each other no matter what they feel, these are the themes that are woven into the texture of the piece. The household ills, the meeting of the ladies' club, the visits of the neighbors, all are done to the life. The types are caught with a kind of gay precision. ("Two Generations" 20).

When Burns Mantle selected the play as one of the year's ten best, it was a very significant tribute to the play. Also included in the volume were *What Price Glory, They Knew What They Wanted,* and *Desire Under the Elms* and there were more than two hundred new plays produced in the season. Mantle felt that the 141 performances in New

York indicated only a moderate success, and personally felt the play deserved better as it contained "so much artfully elaborated detail and so much recognizable human nature." He selected it as representative of the "lighter American home dramas which are purposeful in intent and entertaining in performance ... and honestly concerned with everyday human problems" (*Best Plays of 1924-1925* x). Although she never felt the leading actor or the play itself were as good as they should have been, Ferber had made a big advance in the theatre and earned substantial royalties.

The remaining plays which Ferber wrote were with Kaufman, and it is important to look at the nature of the collaboration. Since his was the bigger name, the tendency has been to consider him the dominant writer in his collaborations, especially when working with a woman. Both Kaufman and Ferber stated many times that theirs was a true collaboration from the plot through the writing, casting, and production. However, the initial idea for four plays came from Ferber and Kaufman had the initial ideas for *Stage Door* and *The Land is Bright.* In an article headed "It Appears Two Persons Wrote Latest Kaufman-Ferber Play" the writer noted, "It is always assumed ... that whatever sentiment is found in any of their plays is contributed by Miss Ferber, and that the comedy is contributed by Kaufman. Miss Ferber insisted vehemently the other day that the blame for every line spoken on the stage must be jointly shared. (Unidentified clipping, Lincoln Center). The gender biased view that a woman must be responsible for sentiment and the man for comedy was irritating to both authors. Their shared work on the plays was analyzed in detail in this and other articles. Ferber noted that all of the lines were discussed and often acted out as the play was written. Some collaborators write separate scenes and then put the play together from them. Ferber and Kaufman worked on each speech together ("Edna Ferber's Notion of Fun is Playwriting" n.p.). She also stated often that she found the idea of a writer waiting for inspiration ludicrous: "Professional writers go to work daily as a bricklayer does" (Unidentified clipping, Lincoln Center).

Kaufman also wrote about their collaboration in a sarcastic letter to the *New York Times*:

> There is a tendency on the part of reviewers to assume that Miss Ferber is some sort of cook's assistant in the preparation of these little dishes, and that I dash them off single-handed, while Miss Ferber sharpens the pencils. Also, they seem

to have the idea that Miss Ferber is then sent to the Orient or some place while I attend to casting.

Certainly Miss Ferber needs no championing from me or anybody else at this stage of her career. It seems incredible that it should be necessary to remind reviewers that these plays have been written with Edna Ferber, not with Lottie Mifflepoor. But obviously it is necessary. My collaborations with Miss Ferber have been collaborations in the fullest sense of the word, from beginning to end. ("From Mr. Kaufman" n.p.)

In an article about Kaufman, Carl Carmer wrote that *Minick* "emphasized the complementary talents which, united, became a powerful alloy. The play served as a trial flight for the two dramatists who were soon to produce that modern classic, *The Royal Family*" (809). This play dazzled audiences in 1927 and has continued to do so. The play is a witty, often hilarious, depiction of a family of actors who have a long tradition and a great name in the theatre. It is dominated by Fanny Cavendish whose barbed wit and elegance have amused thousands of audiences and provided a brilliant role for many actresses, including Ferber herself!

The play is set in the luxurious Cavendish apartment in New York with a large portrait of the late Aubrey Cavendish. His widow, Fanny, is recovering from an illness, but planning to go on the road in a revival. Her daughter Julie is starring on Broadway and keeping in shape by taking boxing lessons. Her daughter Gwen is expected to carry on the family traditions, but is inclined to marry a well-to-do young man from a conventional family and give up the theatre. Fanny's brother Herbert Dean is also on the scene with plans for a new play which are hampered by the desire of his aging, never very good, actress wife to play the ingenue. About to appear is Gil Marshall, whose love Julie rejected in favor of a career and marriage to an actor. He has been sending roses every day, and Fanny dryly remarks, "If there's one way to take the romance out of roses it's knowing that you are going to get them every day" (35). Julie's brother, Tony, is also expected. It was widely supposed that the play was based on the Barrymore family. The writers denied that, but admitted that the character of Tony was based in part on John Barrymore whose amours, marriages, lawsuits, and eccentricities had made him notorious.

Tony does arrive, desperately seeking to escape the country and another breach of promise suit. He makes a stupendous entrance with enormous amounts of luggage, golf clubs, dueling swords, and a violin case carried by an entourage of bellboys. Reporters trying to find him surround the apartment house. At the end of the second act Tony makes a hilarious exit disguised as a bellboy.

By the end of the play the family traditions are clearly going to continue. Gwen, married and a mother, is going to return to the stage, Julie has a new role and will not marry Gil, Tony returns from Europe claiming he has bought "the God-damndest play I ever saw in my life"—a modern passion play in which he will play Christ (115). Even Gwen's baby is going to be cast in a play—as Julie says, "Gwen, he'll have to start sometime" (116) Cocktails are served and Fanny makes a toast to the newest actor in the family, commenting that the Cavendishes always carry on and always will—when one drops out another takes his place. As the family goes into the library, Fanny remains in her chair and soon the cocktail glass falls to the floor from her lifeless hand.

Ferber and Kaufman and producer Jed Harris were determined to get an excellent cast. (They naively thought that Ethel Barrymore might play in it, but she was furious about the supposed satire on her family and didn't speak to them for five years.) They performed the play out of town until they had what they wanted, then opened in December 1927 in New York. Otto Kruger played the role of Tony and Haidee Wright was Fanny. Critics and audiences were delighted by the production which ran 245 performances and then toured the country. The critics praised all aspects of it when it was initially performed, and have continued to do so in it many revivals. Alexander Woollcott said it was the most enjoyable play he had experienced in weeks and that the audience "is often weak with laughter at the unbelievable preposterousness of the great tribe that frets and struts through the turmoil of the House of Cavendish" ("These Be The Players at Home" 25).

Assessing the play in 1932 Carl Carmer noted Ferber's positive influence. He wrote that the characters were more individualized than in Kaufman's previous works.

> Probably due to Miss Ferber's skill as a narrator, this is the most workmanlike of the dramas to which her collaborator has devoted his abilities. It moves forward briskly and efficiently, never stopping for the effective speech—a weakness sometimes noticeable elsewhere in Kaufman's work. The wise-crack is supplanted by the shrewdly thought-out dialogue in character, the bludgeonings of satiric burlesque by the keen wit of comedy. The over-sentimental emotionalism into which the story might easily have led, however, is avoided with a sureness of treatment and a business-like theatricality which is attributable with a

fair degree of certainty to the more experienced dramatist. *The Royal Family* remains, a few years after its original production, a thoroughly enjoyable, not dated play, more than can be said of much of the other work for which Kaufman has been at least partially responsible. (810)

At the time the play opened, critics praised the collaboration, most calling it Kaufman's best play to date. Richard Watts, like many other critics noted the resemblance to the Drew/Barrymore family, but concluded, "it is so charmingly done that you feel all the Barrymores should be delighted that their names are coupled with this delightful play" (qtd. in "These Be the Players at Home" 26). Brooks Atkinson said, "Writing wit as well as humor the playwrights fill a long evening with the rigamorole of their dizzy off-stage existence. 'The Royal Family' makes for steady entertainment" ("The Royal Family" 26). Burns Mantle selected the play as one of the best of the year.

In 1930 the play was made into a film directed by George Cukor with Fredric March and Ina Claire. It has been revived many times since. Two of these revivals were particularly notable. In 1940 Cheryl Crawford cast Edna Ferber as Fanny Cavendish in a production in Maplewood, New Jersey. This attracted enormous attention from the press. The reviewers gave her positive reviews, but not raves. There was unanimity in the enthusiastic response to the play, Brooks Atkinson saying, "It is a remarkably absorbing play today and has been given an uncommonly good cast in Maplewood" ("Edna Ferber Begins" n.p.) Cheryl Crawford was impressed enough that she tried to get Ferber to play the lead in Kaufman and Hart's comedy *The Man Who Came to Dinner* under the title *The Woman Who Came to Dinner*. This would have been an interesting production, with Ferber quite right for the role, but she found acting disappointing. After wanting to act for so long, she found it boring to do the same thing every night, and also felt as if she were showing off (Duval 7). She donated all of her salary to the British Relief Fund. Another major revival took place in the 1975-76 New York season directed by Ellis Rabb. Rosemary Harris played Julie and the great Eva Le Gallienne (at age 76) played Fanny—a role which might have been written for her. The highly praised production drew crowds in New York and on tour (Shafer "Eva Le Gallienne" 542). Walter Kerr noted that the production created the aura of 1927, but that the play itself did not seem old—far from it, it was still able to create a sensation ("A Truly 'Royal' Revival" 1). Clive Barnes wrote that the play was still successful "because it is written so well. It is the kind of play that makes a craft into an art, and crafty itself becomes artistic" ("The Royal Family" 1).

Many regional theatres have produced the play with success since the Rabb production. In 1985 it was produced at Williamstown and by the Pegasus Players in Chicago. It was produced again in Chicago in 1988 by the Body Politic Theatre. Critic Steven R. Strahler noted that an important theme in the play was "women's special problem of choosing between a career and family" ("Theater" 37). In 1991 the play opened the Caldwell Theatre Company's festival season in Orlando, Florida and in 1992 it was produced in Waukegan by the Bowen Park Theatre Company. Reviewers for these revivals frequently commented on the pleasure of seeing a cast of twenty-two actors in contrast to most modern plays with few characters. They also noted the expense of such a play, and suggested that the excellent play would be revived more often if theatres could afford it.

Ferber loved working with Kaufman and loved writing plays. She told a reporter, "Playwriting is a gay adventure. Novel writing is a task, a hard, grinding task" ("It Appears" n.p.). Ferber's own feelings were expressed in *The Royal Family* in several speeches. When Julie hears that Gwen wants to quit acting in order to marry, she says, "Gwen, if I could only make you realize that the thrill you get out of doing your work is bigger than any other single thing in the world! . . . . It's everything. It's work and play and meat and drink. They'll tell you it isn't—your fancy friends—but it's a lie! And they know it's a lie! They'd give their ears to be in your place. Don't make any mistake about that" (82-83). Ferber never regretted being unmarried, and once remarked, "I don't know what people do who don't work" (" Edna Ferber Dies at 82" n.p.).

Miss Ferber was definitely "Miss Theatre" in 1927. In addition to *The Royal Family, Show Boat* was a smash success as a musical. It was based on her 1926 best-selling novel of the same name. Ferber's creation of the novel once again reflected her passion for theatre and her instinct for detail. She went to North Carolina and spent time on the James Adams Floating Palace Theater. She found it enchanting, "In those days I lived, played, worked rehearsed, ate with the company. I sold tickets at the little box-office window, I watched the Carolina countryside straggle in, white and colored" (*A Peculiar Treasure* 298). The former reporter captured all the realistic details of life on a showboat which later appeared in the stage and film versions. The novel seemed such a natural for adaptation on the stage that Ferber had many offers. Unaware that Jerome Kern was already writing the music, George Gershwin told Ferber he wanted to turn the novel into a musical. The libretto followed Ferber's novel very closely, even using extended portions of her dialogue. Brooks Atkinson noted in his glowing review, that the musical was "faithfully adapted from Edna Ferber's picturesque novel" ("Show Boat" 1).

The novel and the musical relate the sorrows and happiness of yet another theatrical family, and also the tragedy of the mulatto, Julie, who violates the laws of miscegenation. Ferber's liberal outlooks are reflected in the creation of Julie, doomed to sorrow because of her mixed blood, and in her sympathetic depiction of the black characters in the novel and the musical. Ferber's characters and story inspired some of Jerome Kern's most wonderful songs. The musical itself, because of the serious story line and realistic characterization, was a major element in the development of the musical in America.

An example of Ferber's business acumen was her own handling of the film rights: she sold the rights, but shrewdly negotiated their reversion to her after the film was completed. In that way she sold the film rights three times, as there were two more versions. Ferber loved the musical and went to see it in several countries as it was frequently revived. In 1982 Michael Kahn directed a beautiful production which was sold out at the Kennedy Center and on Broadway. Although Ferber had no direct connection with the dramatization, the musical so closely followed her book that she received billing and shared in the praise.

The third play written by Ferber and Kaufman was the enormously successful *Dinner at Eight* produced in 1932. There are comic lines and situations, but the whole of the play is quite dark and an aura of death is present. When the play was revived in 1966, Ferber told a reporter, "When George and I wrote that play, we wrote it not just as a high, swift comedy, but as a comment on our world in that critical and really dreadful period just before we went over the cliff" (Dudar 25). Discussing the collaboration, Ferber said that the play was conversationally planned and outlined, and written in nine weeks. "We'd wander all over the room deciding on positions and we'd experiment with the spoken lines. I might add that we didn't spare our voices in the dramatic scenes. One of my maids and the man who cared for my lawn are still, I think, a little suspicious of our sanity" ("Dinner at Eight Thirty" n.p.).

Ferber had the idea for the play, but she and Kaufmann put off writing it because the need for eleven settings seemed problematic. Ultimately the problem was solved by using a revolving stage. In his introduction to the play Burns Mantle noted that the use of the turntable stage was still unusual, and that the structure of the play appealed more to younger audiences used to film than to older audiences accustomed to conventional three-act plays (*Best Plays of 1932-1933 ix*). The play is cinematic in its structure, and it was made into a superb movie directed by George Cukor.

The basic situation in the play is very simple: a wealthy, shallow woman, Mrs. Jordan, decides to give a dinner party because she has snagged Lord and Lady Ferncliffe as honored guests. In the first scene she is indifferent to her husband and concerned only with gossip columns and setting up her dinner party. The second scene takes place in Oliver Jordan's old-fashioned office. He is in financial difficulties and if the stockholders in his shipping company sell off, he may be ruined. Two of the guests invited to the dinner arrive. First Carlotta Vance, a former stage beauty, now heavy and wrinkled. She needs money and wants to sell her stock. A ruthless businessman, Dan Packard, promises to try to help Jordan, but really intends to ruin him and take over the business. In each of the succeeding scenes the characters, who supposedly lead lives of glamour and luxury, are shown to have sordid or tragic secrets which would surprise the newspaper readers who envy them their luxurious homes and fancy Park Avenue dinner parties.

The play is notable for the array of interesting characters—including the servants in the Jordan home—which provided roles for notable actors in the original and subsequent productions. By the final scene each has been seen in her/his own environment interacting with the other characters, and their sorrows have been revealed: Jordan has heart trouble and Dr. Talbot reveals to him that he may die soon, Dr. Talbot's wife reveals to him that she knows about his latest affair with Dan Packard's beautiful, but vulgar wife, but that she also knows he is tired of her and planning to end it. Packard's wife spitefully tells him she is having an affair but won't name the man, leaving herself open to blackmail by her maid. Paula Jordan is hopelessly in love with an alcoholic, over-the-hill actor, Larry Renault. In one of the most effective scenes, Renault loses his role in a play, realizes he has no future, and is told he must leave the hotel where he never pays his bills. He carefully stages his death scene, turns on the gas and sits so that he will be seen in profile when his body is discovered. (Of course the parallel to John Barrymore, "The Great Profile" and his career is obvious.)

The play (and the turntable setting) has come full circle at the end. The Jordan home is the scene of merriment as red-jacketed musicians play gypsy melodies. But the dinner at eight is a total disaster. The Ferncliffes have gone to Florida, and Mrs. Jordan's poorly-dressed sister and brother-in-law have to substitute, Jordan is at death's door, Carlotta has sold the stock in his company to Packard, and the audience knows that Larry Renault is dead in his hotel room.

This behind the scenes satire on the lives of the rich and famous was one of the most effective collaborations of Ferber and Kaufman and one of his best plays with any collaborator. They decided on the cast together, and critical opinion was that it was "doubtful if any play on Broadway in recent years was so carefully cast" ("Dinner at Eight Thirty" n.p.) Constance Collier was particularly praised as the aging actress. Ferber was closely involved in rehearsals, and personally selected the properties for the play. She said that everything had to be first class and she bought the best from Fifth Avenue stores. It became the vogue for wealthy women to buy china patterns, etc. which she had selected for the play ("Edna Ferber's Shopping Splurge" n.p.).

When the play opened it was apparent that the authors had another big hit. Nevertheless, a few critics, including Stark Young and Joseph Wood Krutch, felt that although the play was very theatrical, beautifully performed and would certainly be popular with theatre parties, it was not a play with any true depth ("Booth, Adelphi, Music Box" 51 and "Dinner at Eight" 464). Richard Dana Skinner wrote a review which represented the majority of the critics in which he pointed out the fact that the play was much better than *Grand Hotel* (with which it would be compared), that it was rich with irony and that the cast portrayed perfectly the various characters in the play. "There are many weaklings in this play, but the authors never lose sight of honest values—a comment that could not possibly fit 'Grand Hotel'" ("Dinner at Eight" 49). As noted above the play perplexed some people who expected a well-made play with all the threads neatly tied up at the end. Skinner and others appreciated the Kaufman-Ferber ending as an innovative, lifelike treatment which was theatrically effective:

There has been some criticism of this last scene, to the effect that it leaves everything at loose ends, and that its irony fails to score. I do not agree with this objection. The scene is a forceful comment on the complete futility of most worldly standards and ambitions. The false face of the world hides realities and tries to rob them of their meaning. It is thoroughly appropriate to the purpose of the play—a devastating portrait of city life—to have loose ends scattered all over the stage and tragedy impending in the midst of vacuous gaiety and of hurt souls concealed by frigid smiles. ("Dinner at Eight" 49).

The play was a success in New York and then on tours. It was performed throughout California with Hollywood stars including Hedda Hopper and Louis Calhern. The movie version directed by Cukor with Marie Dressler, John Barrymore, Wallace Beery, Jean Harlow, and other stars is a classic which rates high with film critics today. The continuing appeal of the play is demonstrated by another film version made for television in 1989 with Lauren Bacall, Marsha Mason, and Charles Durning. Among many stage revivals, two were of particular interest. In 1988 director Arvin Brown assembled an excellent cast at the Long Wharf Theatre in New Haven. Mel Gussow praised the production and the fact that Brown "recognizes that the authors were intent on commenting on the emotional and moral impoverishment of the Depression aristocracy. Behind the pithy dialogue are serious questions of bankruptcy, financial chicanery, bigamy and death" ("Dinner at Eight" 9). The 1993 ACT production with the fine Peter Donat in the "Barrymore" role was a success despite the three-hour length of the play. Steven Winn praised the play, saying, "The play's gradually accruing energy comes from its ironic juxtapositions—one man's fatal heart disease and the 'tragedy' of a botched lobster aspic, a washed-up silent film actor's despair and his teenage lover's willful snit—snapshots of America's 1920s joyride coming to a crashing end" ("'Dinner At Eight' Is a Stylish Affair" 3).

After two big successes Ferber said that she was definitely turning to theatre. When she returned from a European trip, a reporter wrote, "She is not writing any more books because she prefers writing plays: 'I do not know why I ever wrote novels when there are so many plays to be written.'" ("Edna Ferber: Novelist Returns" n.p.). She did not care to write plays alone and felt very happy working with Kaufman (naturally, there was always speculation that she was in love with him). However, during his career Kaufman worked with two dozen collaborators and Ferber often had to wait.

By 1935 Kaufman had a good idea for a play to write with Ferber. He wanted to set it in a club where actresses live. In preparation for writing it Ferber went to the Rehearsal Club in New York and pretended to want a room for her niece. She interviewed the manager for two hours, asking about every phase of life and inspecting the club from the lobby to the attic. The reporter describing the incident correctly observed, "Miss Ferber has a passion for correct detail, both factual and atmospheric" (Stinnett n.p.).

Stage Door opened in October 1936 with the lovely Margaret Sullavan in the leading role. The play is a bouquet to the live theatre. It is essentially about the joy and anguish of the acting profession. The plot interweaves the stories of several young women who are trying to become actresses. Over a couple of years they face rejection and poverty. Some succeed, but most of them fail. The play has a dark mood despite the comedy throughout. One of the women hopes to succeed as an actress so she can escape her physically abusive husband—an unusual topic in that time. After losing one role after another she commits suicide rather than return to him. Another actress gives up and becomes the mistress of a wealthy married man. Yet another goes to Hollywood because she is more interested in money than in acting. One writer noted that Ferber certainly was responsible for "the scene in which a disappointed young actress who has failed to make the grade . . . is going back home to Appleton, the home of Miss Ferber's own girlhood" ("Miss Ferber's Fox River Valley" n.p.).

The leading figure, Terry, is not beautiful but has the inner fire and kind of looks which could make her a star. She speaks of her mother, who left the stage to marry, saying, "I know now that she missed it every minute of her life" (20). Terry becomes involved with a playwright who wants to give a message to the world. But by the end of the play she says goodbye to him because he has sold out to Hollywood. He is described by another character as "one of those guys who started out on a soapbox and ended up in a swimming pool" (85). But Terry, who has been selling blouses at Macy's, does not accept when a Hollywood producer offers her a chance. Seeing her determination and talent, he urges her to stay in the theatre and buys a play for her. The Cinderella-like ending is off-set by the surrounding failures and sorrows of the hopeful young women.

There was a metatheatrical quality in the play in that the part of Terry related so closely to the life of the actress who played the role, Margaret Sullavan. The critic for *Newsweek* commented that *Stage Door* was a "comedy-drama that is almost the story of her life" ("New York's Rehearsal Club Inspires Adroit Comedy" 24). Although the critics in general felt that the play did not reach the level of earlier plays by the collaborators, they gave it high praise. One critic wrote, "we know what Mr. Kaufman and Miss Ferber accomplished in *The Royal Family* and *Dinner at Eight* but there is no doubt that as a good show *Stage Door* rings the bell. It will appeal to most of the theatre-going public because it is an amusing, well-acted and skilfully staged little comedy" ("Stage Door" *Commonweal* 51). Although Joseph Wood Krutch felt the play was "Too Good Not to be Better" he wrote "yet Mr. Kaufman and Miss Ferber have hit off [the characters] with such crisp, amusing strokes that they seem quite fresh, and the whole thing moves with such perfect ease in such a perfectly calculated tempo, that one is carried irresistibly forward on a ripple of laughter." He concluded that the jokes and business are "as smart as a night club which won' t open till tomorrow and as quotable as what the *New Yorker* will say next week" (558). Few of the critics noted the pessimistic tone regarding the possibility of a career in the theatre. When the play was turned into a movie, much of the darker quality was removed and it became mostly a delightful vehicle for Katharine Hepburn and Ginger Rogers. Kaufman said it should have been called "Screen Door." The play still holds appeal, particularly for younger actresses in universities, and is frequently revived. (The cast of 32 has obviated most professional productions because of expense.) A successful production at the Columbia College reviewed in the *Chicago Tribune* was praised by Richard Christiansen who enjoyed the three-hour production with its snappy wit. While he praised the acting and directing, he concluded, "The greatest heroes of the evening, however, are Ferber and Kaufman, whose script is a model of good story-telling and rich incident. This makes it an old-fashioned play, perhaps, but if so, so much the worse for new fashions" ("'Stage Door' Opens on an Old-Fashioned Treat" 6).

The Land is Bright was written in 1941 before the entry of America into World War Two. Both Kaufman and Ferber were anguished about the war and about Hitler's treatment of Jews. In 1938 Ferber wrote her first volume of autobiography, *A Peculiar Treasure*, in which she placed great stress on her Jewish heritage and the anti-Semitism she had encountered as a child and as an adult. As she and Kaufman wrote the play, they interrupted their work to listen to speeches by Roosevelt and Winston Churchill on the radio. They wanted to say "Wake up!" to the American public with their play (A *Kind of Magic* 137).

The play provides an interesting challenge for the actors. The first act is set in the late nineties, the second in the early twenties, and the third in 1941. Some of the actors moved from extreme youth to old age, and Arnold Moss played a middle-aged man in the first act and his son in the third act. The play had an unusually large cast of thirty-one, a grandiose setting by Jo Mielziner which changed in style with the passage of time, and luxurious costumes which were designed by Irene Sharaff. The play traces the lives of a family from the period in which fortunes were being made by American robber barons (5). The family is headed by Lacey Kinkaid who has unscrupulously acquired mines and is now cheating his oldest friend out of a railroad. His daughter, Tana, is being married off to an impoverished Count, but his son, Grant, has disgraced him by marrying a tart. In the final scene Kincaid is shot by the man whose railroad he just acquired. The act presents an amusing picture of *nouveaux riches* Americans.

By the second act Mrs. Kincaid is an old woman in a wheel-chair, the tart Flora a fairly acceptable young matron, and her husband Grant the head of the family. Their children Linda and Wayne are typical twenties hell-raisers, and their son Theodore is an effete young man who is thrown out of college. Tana is embarking on her fourth marriage to a European aristocrat and hates America. In contrast her daughter loves the country and wants to marry an American writer. The act comes to a climax when the family discovers that Linda has been involved in a murder and has brought her gangster lover home to hide him from the police. This act ends with the murder of Theodore by Linda's lover.

The third act reflects the many changes in the world and in the family. Countess Tana and her friends are all back from Europe raving about the availability of butter, cream, shoes, and frocks which had disappeared from war-torn Europe. She is eagerly awaiting the arrival of her son Waldemar who has been held a prisoner in a concentration camp. The occasion is Grant Kincaid's seventieth birthday. He is angered by the fact that his son is going to work for the government instead of taking over the business and that the family wants to sell the "mausoleum" in which they live. He is further incensed when Linda returns for the first time since her gangster lover shot her brother. She is now a first-rate citizen, working hard with her husband on a ranch in the west. There is a sense that the family—symbolic of American society as a whole—has matured, and that the younger generation will work to win the war and improve America, rather than plundering it. There is shock and horror when Waldemar appears—a young man broken by the Fascists. However, the play ends with the family finally unified, and determined to stop the enemies of freedom.

Life described the play as first rate theatre in which the family at first holds the view that there's nothing that money can't fix, then "under the impact of a national crisis, rededicate their lives to the country that gave them their wealth" ("The Land is Bright", n.p.). There was praise for the actors, particularly Diana Barrymore as Linda (at last Ferber and Kaufman got a Barrymore in a play!). Richard Watts described the play as a valuable panorama of American life and called it "an arresting melodrama, a first-rate show and a shrewd picture of the attitude of the time toward our past and present" ("The Land is Bright" n.p.). Surprisingly, none of the critics viewed the subject matter as seriously as the authors. John Mason Brown wrote a rather flippant review saying audiences would undoubtedly want to see it, "Although hokum it is, it is hokum slickly presented and an engrossing show" ("The Land is Bright" n.p.) He was wrong about the audiences—it lasted only 79 performances. Ferber later wrote that the play was written too soon, that until Pearl Harbor the American public was uncommitted. But she said it was, "powerfully written, in parts, by two people who wanted terribly to say something that they deeply felt should be said" (*A Kind of Magic* 137).

Ferber had hoped that Kaufman would write a play for the Lunts set in Saratoga, but he couldn't get excited by the idea, so she reluctantly turned the material into the novel *Saratoga Trunk* in 1941. During the war she gave speeches promoting war bonds and suffered listening to news of the war. Following the war she visited Buchenwald and the shock and horror kept her from writing for several years.

In 1948 she and Kaufman wrote *Bravo.* Like their other plays it has a large cast of interesting characters, many of them involved in show business. Its dark theme related to the actual situation in America after Hitler's take-over in Germany. Great numbers of actors, playwrights, composers, dancers, and aristocrats, were forced to flee to America. Audiences seeing the play were familiar with such names as Kurt Weill, Elizabeth Bergner, Lotte Lenya, and Peter Lorre. Some of the immigrants, such as Thomas Mann and Max Reinhardt achieved success in America, some, like Brecht, managed to hang on, and some, like Stefan Zweig (in South America) despaired and committed suicide.

In the play a famous playwright, Zoltan Lazko and his leading lady, Rosa Rucker, live in a run-down apartment, along with several other immigrants trying desperately to make a living in the land of opportunity. There is a good deal of comedy, especially in the satire on some American show business types and in the depiction of a handsome prince reduced to selling ski equipment in a department store. Lazko is a bravura character, shouting for his coffee, wistfully playing Viennese songs, and trying to make a success by writing an American play. Unfortunately his ignorance of America and his poor English cause him to write lines such as, "I love you, little podner. Your hair is as silky as cactus" (95).

The play seemed headed for an ending as pessimistic as *Dinner at Eight*, with Lazko foreshadowing his suicide with a series of speeches in which he refers to Stefan Zweig. But the authors, perhaps because of an urge to offer hope to the world through their play and to affirm the dream of America.as a land of opportunity, provided happy endings for all the characters except a bitchy Russian ballerina who tried to get the immigration officers to send a young actress back to Germany.

In addition to the referential quality of the play to known artists forced to escape from Germany, there was a metatheatrical quality in the casting of Christine Grautoff as the actress nearly forced back to the country she had fled. Grautoff had escaped Germany in 1934 and had begun a new career in America.

The critics found the play very disappointing. As Harold Clurman noted, Ferber and Kaufman had a valid idea, but their grasp was shallow. They never came to grips with the subject matter ("Alien Corn" 29). Likewise Wolcott Gibbs noted that there was pathos, but it was not believable. Although there were "some funny bits, the total effect was mechanical, reminiscent, and dull" ("The President's Husband" 61). The critic for *Newsweek* summed up the general critical response by saying that altlough Oscar Homolka, Lili Darvas, and Christine Grautoff were excellent, "unfortunately all these characters are in search of a play" ("Everything But a Play" 80). A number of critics registered disappointment that two authors of proven ability, who had complemented each other so well in the past should write a play which was so weak. Public response was similar—possibly influenced by a kind of war weariness which rejected plays with this type of subject matter. The play ran for only 44 performances.

Few playwrights who live a long life manage to keep up with the changing taste in the theatre and with the changes in the society it reflects. When Edna Ferber wrote her last play she was sixty-three years old and had experienced two world wars, women moving into the business world, women gaining the vote, the Depression, and the post-war changes in American society. In an interview in 1952, she expressed her difficulties in accepting the work of younger playwrights: "They have no uplift. They are powerful plays, like prussic acid is powerful. I have the greatest admiration for the young playwrights who write with such power, but I wish they could feel that life has more than one dimension" (Nichols "Talk with Edna Ferber" n.p.). After *Bravo* Ferber wrote no more plays. Ferber would have written more plays throughout her career if Kaufman had been more available. According to Teichman, Kaufman enjoyed writing with some of his other collaborators more than he did with Ferber as he was often afraid of a fight with her. Toward the end of his life, and after their last play was a failure, they did quarrel and he told her he would write no more plays with her (90).

Throughout her career, Ferber used her writing as a means of propaganda for many causes, especially improving circumstances for ethnics, blacks, women, and teachers. She often said that if America was ever wrecked, it would be because of intolerance. In 1963 she told Judy Michaelson, "I was protesting the greed, the false standards, the callousness, the carelessness—I mean the not caring . . . the NOT living, which is the crime of all crimes" (n.p.). In this interview and elsewhere, Ferber expressed her liberal outlooks, her remembrance of anti-Semitism in her childhood, and her sympathy for oppressed people. In her long career as a writer she expressed her views in nine plays. Of these only one was a complete failure, eight were performed with varying degrees of success, and three (*The Royal Family, Dinner at Eight,* and *Stage Door*) became classics on stage and as films, and are still performed. In her work with Kaufman she brought out the darker questions of life in contrast to the largely farcical or comedic quality of his plays with other collaborators. In his biography of Kaufman, Howard Teichman wrote, "With Miss Ferber, Kaufman plays always had a larger variety of plot and a broader spectrum of color and characterization. Their plays darted back and forth between drama and comedy. Although he wrote an occasional drama with Connelly or Hart, Ferber made him dig deeper into what he called "the rich red meat of playwriting" (89-90).

The plays Ferber wrote contributed to the American theatre and co1.tinue to do so. She was honored by degrees from Columbia University and Adelphi College. She was one of only two women to serve on the advisory board of the Dramatists Play Service which was established to encourage publication of high quality plays. Although she won a Pulitzer Prize for her novel *So Big*, she never won any awards for her plays. Ironically, her novels are now mainly regarded as of interest only to younger readers, but her plays are still highly regarded. Her love for the theatre permeated all aspects of her life and her writing. She never wrote for Hollywood (although she had many offers) and only went there as a consultant for movies made from her novels. Her feelings about the live theatre as opposed to the "piecework" done in Hollywood were expressed in <u>*Stage Door*</u>. As she told a reporter, "Plays have always been my life and always shall be. They may call me and my books what they like, but when they say I'm a stage-struck girl—that's true!" ("Novelist Back From Europe" n.p.).

Rose Franken (1895-1988)

Rose Franken (1895-1988) was born Rose Lewin in Gainseville, Texas, to Hannah Younker Lewin and Michael Lewin. When she was quite young, her mother left Franken's father, taking the child to New York City. Franken had a very close relationship with her mother which was later reflected in her writing. She lived with her mother's family and received a fine education at the School of Ethical Culture. Unlike many young women at the time, she had the opportunity to attend college. However, despite her family's wish that she continue her education, on the day she was supposed to enter Barnard College in 1915, she married Dr. Sigmund Franken. She had three sons and involved herself in domestic duties for many years, living in the New York area where her plays are set.

Following her overnight success with her first Broadway play, Another Language (1932), Franken liked to give interviews in which she presented herself as a featherbrained, impractical housewife who only started writing because her husband bought her a typewriter and she thought she ought to do something with it. Based on her information, Burns Mantle wrote, "Miss Franken is . . . the mother of three children and a homebody at heart. Really likes to cook and keep house" (Best Plays of 1943-1344 397). In reality she had a very practical, hardheaded approach to life and her career. She successfully balanced the activities of playwriting and writing novels, and she was an immensely popular and prolific short story writer. Like Rachel Crothers, she not only wrote plays, she also directed and produced them. Her plays reveal intelligence, education, and a strong interest in serious social questions.

Before writing for the theatre Franken established herself as a novelist and author of short stories. In 1925, when she was thirty years old, she wrote a novel called Pattern which was successful enough to encourage her to follow a career as a writer in spite of her busy domestic life. Partly autobiographical (as are most of her novels), Pattern is the story of a young girl who grows to womanhood and marries but finds her great love for her mother an obstacle to complete maturity and to fulfillment in her marriage. This problem appears again in the characterization of Franken's most popular heroine, Claudia. Franken became one of the highest-paid short story writers in America, but critics characterized her short stories and her novels as "sentimental," "light" and "candidly feminine." Franken, who wrote very quickly and did little rewriting, explained her point of view by saying, "In a love story it is always the woman's relationship to the man that is the more interesting, that makes the story" (qtd. in Shafer, "Rose Franken," 281).

The year after *Pattern* was published, Franken became interested in writing for the theatre, and wrote a play, *Fortnight* which was never published or produced. Next, she and her aunt, Jane Lenin, wrote a children's play, *Mr. Dooley Jr.*, which was not produced, but was published in 1932. Franken claimed that her next play, The Hallam Wives was rejected by almost every producer in New York. However, it was successfully produced at a summer theatre in Greenwich, Connecticut in 1929. Following the run in Greenwich, Franken made revisions and changed the title to *Another Language.* When this was produced in New York in 1932, reviewers gave the work lavish praise. With almost no theatrical experience, Franken seemed to have conquered Broadway.

The play was usually described as a comedy which angered Franken because she had written with a serious purpose. She said she had intended to write a play which "would upset people and make them think" (personal interview 1976). Her point of view is certainly very clear to the present-day reader. Following in the footsteps of Sidney Howard's *The Silver Cord* (1926), Franken launched a broad attack on tyrannical mothers and proceeded to question the value system of the typical American family in relationship to the historical entrapment of women.

The play begins with preparations for the Hallams' regular Tuesday night family dinner at the grandparents' home in Manhattan. The usual crowd of the three older sons and their submissive wives (treated as comic characters) appear, and there is speculation that two seldom-seen family figures may also attend: Stella, the wife of the youngest son, Victor, and Jerry, a grandson who troubles the family by his artistic interests and his wish to be an architect. Despite a slight difference in age, when Stella and Jerry meet, it is obvious that they speak "another language" from the rest of the family. In her excitement, Stella puts aside her aversion to the family and invites everyone to dinner for the next Tuesday. This is a faux pas as the Tuesday night dinner is Grandmother Hallam's personal property. Franken indicated the problems and tensions in the first act, but also used considerable humor in the characterization and dialogue.

In the second act there is a darker mood as the family dinner predictably turns into a disaster. Victor is highly enmeshed in the traditional Hallam view of life. At this point he is incapable of responding to his artistic wife's attempts to draw him into a broader outlook on life and a more liberal attitude toward the relations between a man and a wife. The Hallams believe that wives should have children, cook, and take care of their husbands—and, incidentally, bow before Grandmother Hallam's every wish. When the family arrives, the conflict intensifies, Grandmother Hallam feigns illness out of pique, and the family leaves. Victor refuses to stand up for his wife and goes with them.

In the final act, when Victor discovers that Jerry has spent the night with Stella, he behaves with unexpected dignity. The shock jars him into an awareness of his need for Stella and his past insensitivity. Franken did not present an easy or sentimental solution to the problems in the play: whether or not Victor can save his marriage and whether the family can accept Jerry's artistic tendencies are questions which are left open. The play made a strong statement about the insularity, provincialism, and intolerance of the middle-class family and challenged the accepted view of the role of women in American society. It is reminiscent in its impact of Crothers' *A Man's World*. The play was important both in terms of its popular and critical success and because of the themes expressed in it which continued to inform Franken's plays.

Critics were unanimous in praising *Another Language*. Robert Coleman in the *New York Mirror* described Franken as "the most amazing figure to flash across the theatrical horizon this season—or any other season for that matter" ("Woman Author of Hit," 20). Brooks Atkinson wrote in *The New York Times*, that the play was "one of the finest plays of the season. A psychoanalytical drama, a remarkably evocative play, subtle, beautiful, tender, and as real as truth" ("'Another Language'" 25). Atkinson was so impressed by the play that he followed up his review with an analysis of the play a month later which emphasized the three-dimensional quality of the characters. He said in part, "Although it is the first play by her to go to Broadway, it is a singularly complete revelation of character and a remarkably workmanlike achievement. Here is a play that belongs to the theatre. It is written for actors. . . . Although Mrs. Franken is new to the theatre, she has an instinct for theatre expression. . . . Mrs. Franken has completed a play in three dimensions. It is a microcosm, it is the whole story of the Hallams and their kind" ("In Three Dimensions" 1). The play was selected to be in *The Best Plays of 1931-32*. It ran for 344 performances in New York and enjoyed a long run in London as well. The role of Stella was played by Dorothy Stickney in New York and Edna Best in London. This was the first of several Franken plays which would serve as vehicles to enhance the careers of notable actresses. The play was bought by MGM and turned into a film (with the same title) starring Helen Hayes. Writing in 1992, Leonard Maltin praised the film, describing it as, "Vivid, devastating picture of American family life (based on Rose Franken's play), with Hayes as an outsider who marries Montgomery and faces hostility from matriach Hale and her gossipy offspring" (44).

Although generally pleased by the enthusiastic critical response to the play, Franken revealed her somewhat vituperative nature when she discussed the use of the term "comedy" which was often loosely applied to any play not clearly a tragedy. Speaking to Lucius Beebe, she said, "The only people who infuriate me utterly are those who have said to me 'What a delightful comedy you have written!' I could tear them limb from limb. Anyone who is stupid enough to think I meant the comedy interludes to dominate the play really ought to be. The people who have really appreciated what I have tried to get at are those who have been most upset and distressed by the drama. They are the people I want to have see it" ("Translating Another Language" n.p.).

At this point in Franken's career her ambivalence about her role as a professional playwright was apparent. In an interview with William Engle called "Rose Franken wrote New Play in 6 days, & so she says 'out of plain cussedness,'" she said that she did not take her writing seriously, "The children laugh at me, and really I don't care much about it myself. But my friends and Dr. Franken are lovely about it" (n.p.) Lucius Beebe noted that that sort of comment did not reflect her true attitude:

> She asserts that she only became a writer because her husband once bought her a typewriter and she felt she ought to do something about it. But when Rose Franken begins to talk about *Another Language* it becomes at once apparent that, for all her casual airiness about the play, it was something more than a tour de force in creation and represents to her a whole system of ideas which

must have been carefully evolved and considered, no matter how easily dialogue, motivation, and plot construction may have come to her. ("Translating Another Language," n.p.)

Throughout her career she felt uncertain about the proper role of women in society, and this became a problem in at least one of her plays.

Despite her amazing first success, Franken did not have another play on Broadway for nine years. Her husband died shortly after the play opened in London and she accepted offers to go to Hollywood. She wrote some screenplays and enjoyed continuing popular success with her short stories and novels. She received screen credit with John Balderston and William Brown Meloney for the script *Beloved Enemy* in 1936. A year later she married Meloney who was a lawyer as well as a writer. While in Hollywood Franken earned thousands of dollars. Particularly remunerative were her ten stories about a young woman named Claudia written for *Redbook*. These were a staggering success when published as a novel, *Claudia*, in 1939. Franken stated that the novel reflected "the loveliness of my own young marriage" and she also stated that if she had known she would write seven more novels about Claudia, she would not have killed off Claudia's mother in the first one (*When All Is Said and Done*, 74).

In 1941 Franken capitalized on the success of her first Claudia novel by writing, casting, and directing a play based on it. After auditioning more than two hundred actresses, she cast the then-unknown Dorothy McGuire in the leading role. Franken, who had a sharp tongue, later referred to her as "that little dough-faced nobody" (personal interview 1976). McGuire achieved stardom as the rather naughty child-wife who does not want to behave like or assume the responsibilities of an adult, but has a strong curiosity about sex. Despite the serious undertones of the play, it is essentially comic, and audiences responded enthusiastically.

Claudia and David Naughton lead a pleasant life, but their relationship is unfulfilled because of her immaturity and her dependence on her mother. As the play progresses, Claudia's behavior is explained by the fact that both her husband and her mother have made life so easy for her that she has never had to face any difficulties and does not want to. In the first act she reveals that she has created havoc with the checkbook, has bought a pair of pajamas the wrong size and in attempting to alter them has cut off one leg twice, and that she constantly listens in on the telephone party line.

Claudia is clearly intrigued about sex, but hardly seems to be a married woman. In one scene she tries to find out more about sex in a conversation with her husband saying, "David, let's talk about sex for a minute.... Take Majesty. She doesn't have to have any personal magnetism. Nature does it for her. But nature doesn't do one thing for a woman but make it harder. You let a woman go without a girdle like a cow and see what happens. . . . Have I got sex appeal?" (38-39) But when her husband kisses her passionately, she says, "You make me feel like a bad woman!" (77). The implication, of course, is that she thinks that only "bad women" enjoy sex.

In the course of the action, Claudia dresses up in a sexy manner and is alone with an attractive bachelor neighbor, Jerry. When he kisses her, she asks him to do it again, and David enters as Jerry does so. But, Claudia has a perfectly simple explanation: "Kissing Jerry made me more in love with you. I even asked him to kiss me again, to make sure I was crazy about you. . . . Can't you understand the way it worked?" (144-145)

Claudia's guileless behavior pervades the play which is largely a framework for the presentation of her character. In the end an awakening sense of sexuality, the revelation of her mother's imminent death, and her own pregnancy lead her toward a more mature approach to life.

The critics rejoiced that Rose Franken had returned to Broadway. Many critics, including the exacting George Jean Nathan, called *Claudia* the best play of the season, and several felt it should receive the Pulitzer Prize. Richard Watts, in the *New York Herald Tribune* expressed the attitude of the majority of the critics:

The best new American play of the season is, by all odds, Miss Rose Franken's *Claudia*. Written with rare sensitivity and delicacy, this latest work by the author of *Another Language*, has a quality of graceful, skimming humor and a deftness of touch that might have made it seem light and insubstantial, but there is about it such a fine sanity, compassion, subtlety of characterization and honesty of emotion that it becomes a drama of distinction and depth.... In addition, Miss Franken's direction is as good as her playwriting which is high praise. . . . In a few words words *Claudia* is the first new American play of genuine quality to arrive this season and it deserves both success and commendation. ("The Theatre," 23)

Arthur Pollock, writing in the *Brooklyn Eagle* said,

> This is it! The play everyone has been crying for all season. The first really fine American-made play so far: *Claudia* by Rose Franken. . . . When the end came it was greeted by the season's most enthusiastic audiences. . . . New at the business of directing and author of only one successful play before this, *Another Language*, Rose Franken nevertheless directs her comedy herself, achieving a performance very nearly flawless. . . . There is no sense in going to the theatre at all this season if you don' t see Claudia. ("*Claudia*" n.p.)

Rowland Field welcomed Franken's return to Broadway, saying,

> It was nine years ago that this same Mrs. Franken's name appeared on a playbill as an author of a memorable comedy called "Another Language" on this very stage and she returns now with a second play that is a truly superb example of craftmanship. In a necessarily brief report of the many virtues in Miss Franken's play it is difficult to do justice to the honesty and eloquence of the writing and performance. Everything about *Claudia* is on a high plane and the author's direction of the work seems inspired, as is the acting of the superb cast. ("Broadway" n.p.)

A review which must have been particularly pleasing was written by Eleanor Roosevelt in her column "My Day": "I liked the Claudia of the book and I like her in the play. The acting in the play is good. The cast is well chosen and does a fine piece of work" (n.p.).

It is difficult to describe the dimensions of the hit Franken had written. It was so popular that she had to cast three road companies at once, and it successfully toured the United States, Australia, and England. An unidentified clipping in the Franken file at Lincoln Center states, "That engaging little lady Claudia has done quite comfortably for the little lady who created her—namely Rose Franken. In fact, Claudia should be worth a modest half-million dollars or more to her creator during the next few months. . . . Royalties of $1000 week go to Miss Franken. . . . A movie bid was $125,000 . . . plus radio and serial rights." The play was financially successful and was honored by being in *The Best Plays of 1940-41*. The impact of her play was described by one of many articles written about Franken at this time: "Not content to write a play, and a good one that has kept sophisticated New Yorkers in the best of spirits and critics honey-toned in their reviews, Mrs. Franken undertook the difficult job of directing the cast. She had no actual dramatic directing background, but simply knew how she wanted the play to be done. So right was she in her judgment that her performance was voted the best by Mr. George Jean Nathan. The play was almost a Pulitzer Prize winner this year and did manage to get its share of medals and glory. ("Claudia Royalties Pay for Farm" n.p.)

Despite the positive response to *Claudia*, there was an element which ultimately decreased Franken's reputation as a writer. People tended to remember only the rather cute quality of the young wife who has trouble adjusting to marriage, forgetting the deeper exploration of the nature of a woman's role in life. In 1941 the play was shocking because of the frankness of the language and the focus on a sexual relationship hindered by the wife's inability to forsake her position as her mother's child. As time went by, this element no longer seemed shocking, and only the superficial humor remained significant. There have been no significant revivals of the play, no doubt because changing attitudes about sex make Claudia's naive character seem inexplicable today.

The success of *Claudia* heightened Franken's interest in theatre, and she and William Brown Meloney acted as co-producers for the remaining plays she wrote. When Meloney read her next play, *Outrageous Fortune*, he exclaimed, "Good God, Rosie, this is damned censorable stuff!" (*When All is Said and Done* 277). The play was presented in 1943 despite many difficulties but did not receive the unanimous acclaim accorded Franken's first two plays.

When the play was produced in 1943, several critics considered it the most controversial and the most intelligently written of the early season plays. It resembles Franken's other plays in its plea for tolerance and its treatment of a dramatic and controversial problem which disturbed society, but which was not widely discussed. In this instance, the problem was homosexuality. The play is not about homosexuality, but about intolerance of any kind of love which existed outside the narrow middle-class view of propriety held by the central character in the play and by most of the audience. Franken was breaking new ground in this play. The limp-wristed, lisping caricature of a homosexual was occasionally presented on Broadway (in *Lady in the Dark*, for example), but *Outrageous Fortune* was one of the first plays to present a serious treatment of homosexuality. Only two major examples in American plays pre-date *Outrageous Fortune*: *The Captive* (1926) and *The Children's Hour* (1934).

The treatment of the subject of homosexuality is very frank in the play, both in discussion and overt acts, and in that sense, the play is distinctly unusual for literature of the period. When *Outrageous Fortune* opened, many reviewers mentioned the subject indirectly, and used phrases such as, "an ugly pathological problem." By choosing the subject, and then treating it sympathetically and in a direct manner, Franken set herself a very difficult task and one which was unlikely to bring commercial success. Writing in 1974, she wryly commented, "It was indeed quite a little ahead of its time" (Ltr. to the author qtd. in Shafer "Rose Franken's Outrageous Fortune" 10).

The play which seemed so offensive to many critics in 1943 seems inoffensive today, but not ineffectual. The action is placed in a middle-class Jewish home in which Bert Harris, the head of the family, symbolizes the conservatism of the average person in the society for whom Franken was writing. He is good and kind, but essentially distrustful of people who are not Jewish, and who do not live by his narrow standards. His wife respects him, but feels that sexually there is a wall between them because of his rigid propriety. (Franken's exploration of sexual problems in marriage in almost all of her plays was ahead of her time.) She is attracted to her protege, Barry, a younger man who teaches music. She has invited him for the weekend and he brings along a beautiful, older woman with a well-known past. Against his will, Bert is attracted to the shady woman, so tolerant of human frailties. Crystal Grainger sees that humans do not always choose to be what they are, but must accept, in Hamlet's phrase, "the slings and arrows of outrageous fortune." Her presence brings out the underlying conflicts in the house which involve Bert's marital difficulties, his homosexual brother, and the sexual uncertainty of the music teacher. Crystal seems to represent the author's point of view and her character was offensive to some critics. *The Catholic World* reviewer, Euphemia van Rensselaer Wyatt, stated,

> Her tolerance also has pity for an ugly pathological problem which is dragged into the picture. That, however, is treated with full repugnance [sic], but this is the first time to our knowledge that a woman, who is frankly a harlot, is held up as a torchbearer. Charity covers a multitude of sins, but this is stretching it to a very dangerous scuffing of standards. Mrs. Grainger, so beautifully played by Miss Elsie Ferguson, is certainly not pictured as anything but the heroine. Facing death with courage, kind and unselfish, the only completely poised person on the stage, why should her career not be emulated? Miss Rose Franken, the author, and her husband, Mr. William Brown Meloney, the producer, offer really a very poisonous mixture of "tolerance" and sentimentality. ("The Drama, 'Outrageous Fortune'" 298)

Two characters considered offensive were the two homosexual or potentionally homosexual figures. In creating the character of Julian, Bert's brother, Franken avoided the stereotyped "faggy" characteristics, and presented a person who was serious, attractive to women, and who had decided to make a convenient marriage for the sake of appearances. The description of the character at the beginning of the plays is: "He is handsome and well set-up, full of a smouldering animal magnetism which passes for an impressive masculinity. He has the sophistication and assurance of the successful man-about-town. He has advanced beyond his family and knows it" (2). In a scene with his fiancée, his outlooks are frankly revealed. He states that neither he nor Kitty are romantic, but both are getting what they want; she, security and glamour, and he, money and brains.

> Kitty: By the conspicuous absence of the word "love," I gather I'd better make
>   up a nice single bed and be prepared to lie on it most of the time.
> Julian: That's a little crude. I'm extremely fond of you, Kitty.
> Kitty: Don't worry darling. I'm smart enough not to ever get in your hair.
>   You'll have the name and not the nuisance. . . . At least I won't be dull.
>   You could never stand a dull woman.
> Julian: The point is, can I stand any woman? (80-83)

Later Kitty drinks too much and reveals her jealousy of the young musician, Barry. A scene between Barry and Julian is very interestingly written. It is explicit, but it was not written with the intention of shocking or disgusting the audience. Nonetheless, because of the attitudes of the time, and the novelty of the characterizations, the scene did have that effect.

> Barry: (Embarrassed) Look here—I know it's none of my business, but why
>   don't you go over and see Kitty for a minute? I Just left her. She's upset.
> Julian: I'm not interested in Kitty. She knows it. And you know it.
> Barry: That's a damn funny thing to say when you're engaged to a girl!
> Julian: Kitty called that off tonight. I was outside. I heard ler.
> Barry: She didn't mean it. She thinks you're coming over. She's in love with
>   you.
> Julian: (With implication) That's why she'd be a fool to go through with it. So
>   would I.
> Barry: (Stiffening) What are you trying to say?
> Julian: (Gently) I'll explain it to you in the garden—(He puts his hand on
>   Barry's arm. Barry finally gets the full significance of the overture, and
>   steps back quickly, knocking over a bronze ashtray. It falls to the floor
>   with a heavy thud. Crystal enters from Bert's study, and comes to the

> threshold of the living room. Julian hears the click of the door before he
> sees her. After a moment's conflict, he turns back to Barry.)
> Julian: (Grinding it out) In the future keep your hands off me—(He strides off
> to the terrace leaving Barry stunned by the accusation. Slowly, he bends
> to pick up the ashtry and in so doing, he sees Crystal. He starts upstairs
> without explanation." (143-144)

The scene which followed was also quite shocking. It is particularly interesting in that it pre-dates the famous scene between a sympathetic woman and an uncertain young man in *Tea and Sympathy* (1953). In this scene Barry reveals what happened between him and Julian and Crystal questions him about his past. He reveals that he has always feared and resented women, partly because of an incident in his youth when he felt a strong attachment to another young boy. He says, "A boy who lived on our block. In one of those big private houses. He went to France the second summer I knew him. My mother found a letter I was writing him. She thought it was to a girl—I never finished that letter. I never wanted to see him again. (With suppressed intensity.) And I hated my mother for what she did to me. She made me ashamed for no reason. She frightened me about myself" (149).

At the end of the scene, Crystal leaves to go to her bedroom and Barry follows. At the conclusion of the play, there is a sense that Barry has overcome his doubts about himelf and will find satisfaction in a heterosexual relationship. For Julian no change is indicated. This realistic ending was surprising to audiences at the time. He says goodbye to Bert and makes his plans so clear that Bert can no longer pretend that he doesn't understand what Julian is and does. Bert, the character symbolic of his society, will have to accept his brother as he is. The play as a whole is a thesis play demanding a broader acceptance of diversity in society, sexually as well as ethnically.

Franken knew she would be criticized for the subject matter and probably lose money on the play. Nevertheless, she chose to produce it without compromise. The production history of this play indicates Franken's many abilities, as well as her belief in the serious purpose of theatre. As usual, she cast and directed the play herself. She was able to attract outstanding performers including Madame Maria Ouspenskaya (who had been acting in film for several years), Margalo Gillmore, Margaret Hamilton, Eduard Franz, and Frederic Tozere. For the role of the homosexual she avoided stereotypical casting and used a former prize fighter. She took a real chance with the leading role by casting an actress who had been in retirement for fourteen years. Elsie Ferguson had been one of the great beauties of the stage and the silent screen with a reputation as a fine actress who was difficult to work with. At sixty she was still superb on stage and the critics unanimously praised her performance and her great presence.

When the play received negative reviews in Boston, the original producer, Gilbert Miller, chose to close the production. Franken and her husband decided to produce it themselves and bring it into New York. In *Outrageous Fortune* there is a plea for tolerance in life. The playwright was also putting forth a plea for tolerance in the theatre and the right to treat unpleasant subjects in an honest way. The audience was not ready, and most of the critics wrote what George Jean Nathan described as "idiotically bad notices" (qtd. in *When All is Said and Done*, 307), Franken could take satisfaction in the fact that although he was warned against it, Burns Mantle selected her play as one of the best plays of the year. One of the critics who liked the play wrote, "Her play will be violently denounced, violently upheld, loathed, liked and discussed with heat—which will attest to its vitality and to its interest as sheer entertainment. It is a play people will be talking about, and therefore one which everyone will want to see (Rascoe, "Outrageous Fortune An Exciting Drama" 237). E.C. Sherburne, writing for the *Christian Science Monitor*, was also positive: "In writing this play, Miss Franken has manifested the sort of daring that derives only from deep feeling. Seeing human beings as individuals, she evidently could not bear to cast them into stock stage patterns. She has written a drama of such insight that spectators to whom it appeals will have that best of all experiences in the theatre, a sense of sharing in the performance" ("Outrageous Fortune" n.p.). Another critic who praised the play was Wilella Waldorf. She said the acting alone was worth the price of admission and concluded, "'Outrageous Fortune' may be more of a clinical study than a play, but it has an enlightened and tolerant viewpoint on some old problems, and it dares to talk out loud in a sensible manner on subjects that are usually mentioned only in a whisper, or never mentioned at all. More than that, much of it is as entertaining as any of Miss Franken's earlier comedies. See it" ("Elsie Ferguson Returns to the Stage" (239). These critics were in a marked minority. Most claimed to find the play confusing (especially the nature of the wife's discontent) and unpleasant. Louis Kronenberger wrote, "I don't know who could do full justice, either psycho-

logically or philosophically , to this broad neurotic vista in which racial
and sexual frustration have some appearance of cause and effect; but
Miss Franken completely messes it up. She makes nothing seem significant or convincing" ("Very Fancy But Very Foolish" 237). Norman
Clark expressed a very common attitude toward the play: "Among
other things, perversion sticks its ugly head through the Harris' front
door. Just why this topic is introduced into the drama is another of its
baffling phases" ("Outrageous" n.p.).

George Jean Nathan was disgusted by the critical reception and
wrote at length about the play and its virtues. "All save three of the
daily reviewers denounced the play out of hand as both dull and
worthless. . . . At this point in the year her play proved to be the only
new one with the glimmer of a mind in it, the only one of even relative
size, the only one of any critical merit. What she has accomplished is
sometimes an ill-joined mosaic, but nevertheless a play whose delicate
imagination and inner wisdom bulk above its defects and constitute it
on the whole a credit to the American drama" (*The Theatre Book of the
Year 1943-44* 117). Burns Mantle, too, sided with the three positive
daily reviewers and selected the play (thus, inviting much criticism) for
the best plays volume. In his introduction, he summed up the history of
the run. An outstanding cast and Franken's well-established reputation were not enough to draw audiences to see a play of this type: "For
ten weeks arguments for and against the drama's statements were
freely spoken. When by that time a paying response one the part of the
public had not developed, *Outrageous Fortune* was withdrawn" (*Best
Plays of 1943-1944* 8). Franken could take consolation in the fact that
a few perceptive reviewers and audience members respected what she
had done, but she lost a great deal of money. Interviewed by Helen
Ormsbee after the play opened, she indicated her strong feelings about
it: "[It] has more of my own thinking and feeling in it than anything
I've done for years. It goes the deepest. So I haven't got over being
astonished when some of the critics said the play was confusing. If I've
chosen to let the public do its own chewing on the theme instead of
my handing out a predigested pachage neatly labeled, does it matter,
as long as our audiences are entertained and absorbed?" She said she
was very pleased by what one audience member said after the play,
"Whatever you are in life, you've got to accept it—and then do the
best you can" ("Rose Franken" n.p.). Ahead of its time in 1943, the
play has now been by-passed by playwrights treating the question of

homosexuality in a much more open manner and it is unlikely to be revived despite its high quality.

In 1943 Franken also directed her play *Doctors Disagree*. The first of her plays which was not selected for Mantle's annual collection, it ran only twenty-three performances. Franken chose not to publish it. This play received terrible notices, with some justification. The plot and characterization struck most critics and theatre-goers as clichéd and lightweight, and even Franken's staunch supporter Nathan wrote, "It was originally written as a serial for a popular women's magazine and it betrays its geniture" (*The Theatre Book of the Year 1943-44* 185). The play involved the difficulties a woman surgeon experienced in working in a hospital largely dominated by men. Wolcott Gibbs dismissed it very airily, writing, "The play is a variation of the old career-versus marriage dilemma; specifically she wants to know whether a promising female surgeon has any business cluttering up her life with a husband, who in this case happens to be a distinguished sawbones himself. My answer to this would be an emphatic no; Miss Franken's is a qualified yes. A hen medic, she says, and the phrase is her own, can reasonably provide love and companionship for her mate but she needn't be expected to darn his socks after a hard day in the abdominal cavity" ("Doctors Disagree" 23). Noting the sentiment and trite nature of the material, Kronenberger concluded, "The worst of it is that *Doctors Disagree* isn't even interesting trash" ("The Audience Takes Medicine" 188). Burton Rascoe chided Franken for what he perceived as an old-fashioned view of the world, noting that women surgeons had long been accepted in the medical profession and that women had been given the vote in 1920, "so the intellectual content of Miss Franken's play is about as exciting as the news that Queen Anne is dead" ("Old Conconctions Only" 189).

The critic for *The Commonweal* was much more harsh in the review: Indicating that it is often difficult to know where to fix blame for a theatrical disaster, he noted that in this case, since Franken wrote and directed and her husband produced, ". . . it is obvious that she must be prepared to face the consequences of staging a play which might possibly, just possibly, have been of some interest in 1902." The rest of the review gives an indication of the story line:

> Written, I believe, some ten years ago and originally designed as a story for one
> or other of the formula-magazines, the script presents a lady-surgeon torn

between the exaggerated alternatives of marriage and her job; surrounds her with a couple of medicos, one of whom is bright and young, plus a senior whose reliance on "ethics" merely covers a lack of skill; and finally provides her with the opportunity to prove both genius and womanhood over a hastily contrived operating table. All this accomplished through lines whose unrelated mysticism is indescribable, although perhaps such examples as "I love you too much to love you! and ". . . Science cannot fill loins molded for the bearing of children" will give you a fair idea. ("The Stage and the Screen," 328)

This unsuccessful play was based on a novel written by Franken and her husband under the pseudonym, "Franken Meloney." It is significant that all of her other plays, most of them successes, were purely her writing. The failure of the play and the tone of the reviews were very distressing to Franken. In particular, she was offended by the insinuations that she had merely hauled something old out of the trunk and put it on out of vanity. Nevertheless, she pursued her theatrical career and in 1944 presented *Soldier's Wife*.

In this play Franken continued her exploration of the change in the position of women in American society. Less controversial than *Outrageous Fortune*, the play appealed to audiences and most critics, and was selected for *The Best Plays of 1944-1945*. As usual, Franken was able to select an outstanding cast including Martha Scott, Glenn Anders, and Myron McCormick. In contrast to many plays written in the atmosphere of war, *Soldier's Wife* was humorous and light, in the vein of *Claudia*. Despite the tone, Franken was exploring a real social problem: the readjustments necessary between a man and wife after the man has been away at war and the wife has developed independence through a career. Retreating from her earlier position of championing the right of women to develop careers and financial independence, Franken presents another child-wife (quite similar to Claudia) who starts to develop independence to the extent of publishing a successful book of the letters she wrote to her overseas husband and being able to do household repairs. John voices the fears of many returning husbands, saying, "It scares the bejesus out of a man. We're coming home to women who've gone through their own kind of hell and who can take it the same as we have. Suppose I don't go back to fight. What do you need me for? The war's made a man of you" (45).

After John's return, Kate receives offers from film companies, and is asked to write a newspaper column. Her husband's reaction is similar to that of the husband in Crothers' *He and She* written in 1911. Talking to his sister-in-law, he says that his wife earns more than he does:

John:	I've gone over the whole thing with myself. What right have I? I can't put my foot down and say "You'll live on what I earn, young lady, and like it."
Florence:	She should!
John:	Whose in-law are you, anyway? (Gravely) No, but why should she Florence?
Florence:	Because your marriage is more important than all the success in the world. (126)

The conclusion of the play seems to leave Florence as the mouthpiece for Franken, the playwright. Although Franken, herself, wrote successful novels and plays and received encouragement from her husband, her play shows a woman who perceives that she must give up anything which might be a challenge to her husband's superiority. Even his manner of address to her as "young lady" is condescending and intended to deny her maturity and equality. Although John says he has no right to ask her to give up her career, he is clearly relieved when the electric plug she has mended fails to work, she declines the offer of a job, and informs him that she wants to have another baby.

In the aura of war-time society the play was welcome and few criticized Franken for a conventional or shallow point of view. The production played to full houses for 253 performances. Willela Waldorf spoke for most critics when she praised it as "simple, unpretentious, intelligent, and full of a warm understanding of human and decent values, plus a consistently diverting sense of humor. . . . in short, thoroughly civilized comedy" ("Two on the Aisle" n.p.). Franken was back in the running as a successful playwright. However, George Jean Nathan, one of Franken's staunch supporters revealed his increasing disenchantment with her playwriting: "Miss Franken has talent and even when she deliberately sacrifices it to the box office, as in this case, it can not entirely resist her. But it is to be regretted, since she doesn't need the money, that she does not continue to apply her gifts to the more reputable drama as represented by her last season's *Outrageous Fortune*" (*The Theatre Yearbook of 1944-1945* 87). *Soldier's Wife* is a particularly disappointing play since it looks at a serious social problem but makes no serious exploration of it.

Although she was deeply involved in the theatre, Franken had never ceased to write fiction. During the war she turned her attention to running a large farm as part of the war effort. She did not return to the stage again until 1948. That she was still highly regarded as a playwright was indicated by Ward Morehouse in his book *Matinee Tomor-*

row in which he listed the playwrights of importance in the contemporary theatre: "The dramatists who had emerged so vigorously in the
theatre of the twenties continued in their labors, and the newcomers
to their ranks now included Lillian Hellman, Clifford Odets, Rose
Franken, Lynn Riggs, Sidney Kingsley, Robert Ardrey, and Irwin
Shaw" (248-249). Franken was in very good company at that point,
but her next play was her biggest failure in the theatre and brought an
end to her career as a playwright.

With her last play, The Hallams (1948), Franken returned to the
family she created in her first success, *Another Language*. In this sequel,
Victor becomes the hero. The audience learns that following Stella's
suicide, Victor moved away from the family and never remarried. He
has turned against the narrow view that success (including profit from
the war), Protestantism, and family loyalty are the guiding forces in
life. As in the earlier play, the family gathers for the weekly dinner.
They gossip and complain about each other, and speculate about the
health of Jerry, the would-be architect who is now in a tuberculosis
sanitarium. As the play develops it is revealed that he has left the sanitarium to marry Kendrick, a young career woman completely
unknown to the family. By the end of the play the interference of the
family has caused Jerry's death. Juxtaposed with his death is the awakening of life in Victor as he perceives Kendrick as a recreation of
Stella. At the play's end Grandfather Hallam challenges his wife's
domination and intolerance and tells her that if Victor brings Jerry's
widow to the family as his wife, she must be accepted. One of the
problems of the play is that the grandfather is given to making wise
pronouncements. George Jean Nathan put his finger on the chief
problem in the play, saying, "The author deals honestly with most of
her people. They are, alas, essentially dull people." He also noted,
along with other critics, that the play had the tone and subject matter
of a soap opera. (*The Theatre Yearbook of 1947-1948* 316). The play
ran only twelve performances despite an excellent cast and good
direction by Franken.

Franken lived for forty years after this failure but never again
directed plays and not until 1971 did she write another. This was
Wings which was not produced. Instead, she continued her immensely
successful career as a short story writer and novelist. Reviewing her
popular autobiography, *When All is Said and Done* (1962), Brooks
Atkinson remarked, "She is not committed to any medium that does

not pay her well. . . . Broadway does not qualify" (*New York Times* 32). Lack of financial remuneration from *Outrageous Fortune*, *Doctors Disagree*, and *The Hallams* may well have been a factor in her exit from the theatre, but she had made large sums of money on the other plays, particularly *Claudia*. She was an astute businesswoman and highly concerned with her profits, but disappointment over the critical response to her plays was probably the chief factor in her decision to stop writing plays. As noted above, she had a sharp tongue and an unforgiving nature. In a conversation in 1978 she referred to John Golden, her former producer as "that son-of-a-bitch" and bragged about getting even with him financially for having done her out of some money. She referred to one critic as "that little bitch, down in the village" and complained that because she wouldn't court the critics and have lunches with them, she couldn't get good reviews (personal interview 1976).

Ironically, she spent most of her writing career on novels and short stories which were treated as lightweight, sentimental works essentially serving as escapism for the conventional woman reader. In contrast to her plays, she followed formulae, avoided controversial subjects, and provided a warm glow for the reader. Her plays generally aimed at an adult, thinking audience and introduced significant subject matter. What George Freedley said of *Outrageous Fortune* (which he went to see a second time) could stand for most of her plays, "Despite its faults, which still exist, a visit to *Outrageous Fortune* is imperative for anyone who cares for an adult theatre and a dignified portrayal of serious contemporary problems" ("Outrageous Fortune" n.p.). Most critics perceived Franken as an outstanding and challenging playwright when she was at her best, and entertaining and humorous when at her second-best. It should be remembered that her first play treated a serious subject and was able to fill a theatre for ten months in the depths of the Depression.

There is a paradox about Franken's work, however, which may have kept her from fulfilling her potential as a serious playwright. In her life and in her plays she never seemed to resolve her attitude toward the role of woman in society. As indicated above, she presented herself as a sort of Claudia, essentially a homebody, a giddy little woman involved in her family. In fact, she was a tough businesswoman, an excellent director, and a strong competitor. She scorned fashionable feminine dresses and usually dressed in slacks. In the period in which she wrote many changes took place in American society especially in terms of career opportunities. Franken shifted ground in her several plays and ultimately presented no clear view point about women and marriage versus women and careers. Nevertheless, her plays were carefully written and usually dynamic in terms of characterization and dialogue. She has not been revived often, but in 1975 *Another Language* was presented by the Equity Library Theater. The play held up despite the passage of forty-three years. Thomas Lask, writing in the *New York Times*, began his review with a tribute to the play: "'Another Language,' Rose Franken's warm and tender 1932 play, is remembered by everyone who saw it then for its nuanced and delicate account of the fate of an esthetic sensibility in the land of the philistines." Despite weakness in the cast, he concluded, "The heart of the play is not destroyed in this revival; the warring factions are set clearly against each other, the bittersweet yearning of the young is touchingly conveyed; the resolution leaves the viewer content" ("Another Language" 42). As Franken's plays are generally unfamiliar (indeed even her name is generally unknown) it is not surprising that there have been few revivals. Almost all of her plays are available in print and perhaps some adventurous directors will turn to them in the future.

Franken was an important figure not only because she was successful as a playwright, but because of her outstanding work as a director. She had no training as an actress or as a director, but she had a good eye for talent and she had an instinct for staging plays which always worked. She felt strongly that a playwright should direct her own plays, saying, "For an author to write a play and not cast and direct it is a little like having a baby and turning it over to a nurse as soon as it's born" (Franken "An Author's Slings and Arrows," n.p.). Franken's career in the theatre spanned sixteen years and in that time she was a major playwright, regarded as one of the bright hopes of the American theatre. She did not entirely fulfill those hopes, but she challenged the usual shallow Broadway fare in many of her plays and introduced important, often controversial subject matter to the theatre.

Lillian Hellman (1905?-1984)

Lillian Hellman (1905?-1984) was one of the most controversial and complex American writers. The theatricality of her life was not limited to a successful career as a playwright. She was the model for Dashiell Hammett's Nora Charles in the *Thin Man* stories which became a successful series of movies and a Broadway musical. She was also a character in Eric Bentley's *Are You Now, or Have You Ever Been?* and was recently portrayed onstage by Elaine Stritch. In 1985 Zoe Caldwell acted the character of Hellman in a one-woman play called *Lillian*. After a great deal of research and analysis she told a reporter, "There are two schools of thought about Lillian. One is that she was a liar. The other is that she was a saint who stood for decency and morality and was the greatest American ever investigated by the House Un-American Activities Committee. I think the truth lies somewhere in between" ("Bringing Lillian to Life is a Rough Acting Role" 11A).

Hellman's plays are generally clear and unambiguous (some would say overly didactic), but as a person Hellman was complicated, difficult, and ambiguous. Caldwell found the experience of acting her very wearing and even unpleasant (personal interview). There was a continual conflict between her need for independence and privacy and her yearning to be supported, loved and surrounded by friends. Although some critics have dismissed her plays as conventional and well-made, many people consider her the outstanding woman playwright of the first half of the century.

Hellman was born in New Orleans. Her German-Jewish father was named Max Hellman and her mother was Julia Newhouse Hellman. Her unconventional childhood was one likely to produce an adult with unreconciled attitudes about family and male/female relationships. For much of her youth her family spent half the year with the upper middle class Newhouse family in New York. Hellman was repulsed by their materialistic values, but was attracted by the comfort and style. This conflict was revealed in her adult life and in her plays. For the other six months she was in New Orleans with her father's adoring sisters who ran a boarding house. Hellman viewed her mother as a weak figure, but idolized her dynamic father until she found out he was unfaithful to her mother. When she discovered this, she purposefully fell out of a fig tree, breaking her nose. On other occasions she faked a heart attack, ran away to a boarding house for blacks, and generally engaged in rebellious behavior. Her youthful affection went to her black nurse Sophronia, and her plays are filled with sympathetic portraits of black people. She said that her life and feelings were to a large extent molded by her relationship with and love for her nurse: "Sophronia was the first and most certain love of my life" (*An Unfinished Woman* 14).

Because of her family's frequent moves, Hellman's schooling was interrupted and formal education had less impact on her than on most writers. Unlike many other playwrights, she wrote no plays in her youth and acted only once, in a high-school play. As a young woman she lived in New York, attending New York University and Columbia University. She didn't take her studies seriously and dropped out. However, she had an excellent mind and moved swiftly into the literary and theatrical world. In 1924, she was a reader and editor at Horace Liveright, Inc. She became pregnant as a result of a casual affair and had an illegal abortion. A year later she married writer Arthur Kober. During the two years they lived in Europe Hellman contemplated studying in Bonn, but was repelled by the anti-Semitism she saw in Germany.

In 1930 Hellman met and fell in love with the writer Dashiell Hammett while she was working as a script reader for MGM. Their attachment lasted until he died and he was a great influence on her work. Thirteen years older, confident and attractive, he read and criticized many of her plays and even wrote a major speech for *The Autumn Garden*. In 1934 he suggested that she read a short story based on a true case in Scotland in which a child claims her teachers are lesbians and their school is closed. Hellman took the basic story line and created her first play, *The Children's Hour*.

During the thirties she continued writing plays and screenplays. She was one of the most political of the women playwrights and her plays contain material referential to the Spanish Civil War, the rise of Nazism, and other events which filled the newspapers. She often covered political conventions and wrote articles for magazines and newspapers. She was a strong liberal and condemned economic inequities and injustice in the world. In 1941 she raised funds for the Joint Anti-Fascist Refugee Committee with a special publication of her play *Watch on the Rhine*. The edition featured an introduction by her close friend Dorothy Parker. In 1942 she was a speaker at a dinner arranged by Parker to honor Paul Robeson as one of the country's leading anti-Fascists. In 1943 she wrote the screenplay for *North Star* which has been described as "propaganda on the rocks thanks to our WWII alliance with the U.S.S.R" (Scheuer 760). In 1948 she supported Henry Wallace in his third-party run for the presidency.

By the 1950's she and Hammett were called to testify before the HUAC committee. He went to prison for contempt of congress. Refusing to cooperate with the committee, Hellman delivered a now famous speech which included the statement, "I cannot and will not cut my conscience to fit this year's fashions" (qtd. in Robinson 412). She was blacklisted and no longer able to earn money from screen-writing. For some time she was in economic difficulties.

However, for most of her career she had a great deal of money. Although divorced, she remained close friends with Arthur Kober and was very generous to him and his family. She lived well and loved cooking, entertaining, and buying glamourous clothing. After her success with *Watch on the Rhine The New York Times* reported, "She bought a farm with the returns from *The Little Foxes*. Now she wants a fur coat" (Prize Plays, Critics & Such n.p.). Late in her life she was criticized for posing for an advertisement wearing a Blackglama mink coat and accepting the coat as remuneration. She was outspoken and intemperate and her relationships with Hammett and other men were often tempestuous. She was often involved in controversy and at the time she died she was suing Mary McCarthy for $2,225,000 for slander. McCarthy had called her a liar while being interviewed on the Dick Cavett Show.

In her late years Hellman taught, lectured, and was honored with degrees and awards from many organizations and universities including the American Academy of Arts and Sciences, Brandeis University, Yale University, the American Theatre Association, and the National Institute of Arts and Letters. She continued writing on political events, often criticizing others and receiving much criticism. She presented her interpretation of her life and the people she had known in three best-selling books of memoirs, *An Unfinished Woman*, *Pentimento*, and *Scoundrel Time*. In 1977 the film *Julia* was based on a chapter in *Pentimento*, with Jane Fonda acting the role of Hellman. Many people praised the memoirs, while others (such as Mary McCarthy) found them biased and self-serving. The playwright died in 1984 after a life filled with success, romance, controversy, and hard work.

The Children's Hour was an auspicious debut for a young playwright. It was performed in November 1934 and many people felt it should have received the Pulitzer Prize. In his history of the Pulitzer Prizes John Toohey wrote that the decision to give the award to *The Old Maid* was, "the silliest and most disgraceful decision in the 50-year history of the Prize, not because *The Old Maid* itself was an atrociously bad play (it was not), but because of the unmentioned censorship that eliminated consideration of a genuine American classic, *The Children's Hour*. Miss Hellman's play should have won in a walk" (128). Just before the Pulitzer Prize was awarded the odds were 9 to 5 that it would win. But the theme of lesbianism was still shocking and one drama critic was reported to have walked out of the theatre in disgust at the subject matter Hellman utilized (Toohey 128). Hellman, herself, often remarked that the play was not about lesbianism, but about a lie. Many critics objected to the indirect censorship which kept Hellman's play from winning the award. The incident contributed to the decision of the critics to create the Drama Critics Circle Award.

The lie is told by the spoiled brat Mary, who is a pupil in the boarding school run by Karen and Martha. The school has been limping along for eight years, with the encouragement of Mary's grandmother, Mrs. Tilford. At the time the play begins, Martha and Karen have been doing so well that they can anticipate some changes. Martha's aunt, Lily Mortar, a garrulous former actress of the old school, will be pensioned off and sent away, and Karen's long engagement to Dr. Joseph Cardin will finally end in marriage. But there are problems in the school. Mary is an unpleasant, if not neurotic, child who blackmails the other girls and lies to her instructors. Lily Mortar is critical of everything and foolishly babbles loudly that Martha has an unnatural attachment to Karen and is jealous of Joe. Two of Mary's friends hear this and report it to her. When she is reprimanded she runs away to her indulgent grandmother, explaining that she was afraid to stay in the school because of the unnatural behavior between her two teachers. Hellman's language was not obscene or graphic, but it was shocking enough to some audience members that Mary claimed to have seen the two women kissing and to have heard them in Karen's bedroom making "funny noises."

The lie is believed and the children removed from the school. Karen and Martha sue for libel, but lose because their chief witness, Lily Mortar, disappears until the trial is over. In the last act Martha reveals that she has discovered that she really is sexually attracted to Karen. Joe arrives and Karen, knowing that he has doubts about her relationship with Martha, breaks their engagement. The sound of an off-stage gunshot tells Karen that Martha has killed herself in despair. Mrs. Tilford arrives too late, revealing that the lie has been discovered. A bleak future stretches out for Karen, Mrs. Tilford and Mary, the cause of the tragedy. Hellman's play foreshadowed the lies and false accusations of the McCarthy era, and the hysteria which can be induced by insinuations of behavior outside the norm.

The critics praised the new playwright and the play ran for 691 performances in New York, then toured America and Europe. One criticism was that the play should have ended with Martha's suicide. Hellman agreed with her critics, admitting that "the last scene is tense and overburdened. I knew this at the time, but could not help myself. I am a moral writer, often too moral a writer, and I cannot avoid, it seems, that last summing-up" ("Preface" *Four Plays* ix). The play as a whole, however, was considered excellent. Robert Garland called it a "stirring tragedy in which the love of one woman for another and the love of that other woman for a man are dramatically portrayed" ("Shumlin's Production Completes" n.p.). Writing in 1944 Edith Isaacs noted that Hellman "burst into attention" with the play which "left no doubt of the talent that lay behind it. It had the essential elements of good drama—plot, character, conflict, movement, and words that were vibrant and active, good theatre words" ("Lillian Hellman" 19). The positive critical response was echoed by Burns Mantle, who selected the play for *The Best Plays of 1934-35*.

Hellman's success was such that Samuel Goldwyn hired her as a screenwriter. In 1936 she wrote the screenplay for her first stage success under the title *These Three*. Ironically, she had to change the lesbian theme to a love triangle. In 1960 she planned to write a new screenplay to be directed by William Wyler, but Hammett's death in 1961 caused her to withdraw from the project. As Bernard Dick notes, that was a great loss because the later film is a disappointment, "Hellman was her own best adapter, as she showed in *These Three*" (*Hellman in Hollywood* 49). The 1962 film was called *The Children's Hour* and starred Shirley MacLaine and Audrey Hepburn. Leonard Maltin commented "[this] updated version of Lillian Hellman's play is more explicit in its various themes, including lesbianism than the original *These Three*, but not half as good (207).

Hellman also directed a revival of the play in 1952. At that time it was an appropriate comment on the political situation in America and the many people who suffered during the McCarthy era. Brooks Atkinson congratulated Hellman on her directing and praised Patricia Neal and Kim Hunter, as well as Iris Mann as the "little sadist" Mary. He analyzed the play, which he said was still "taut and pertinent," in relationship to the changes in American society:

> Since Lillian Hellman's "The Children's Hour was a sound play originally, it is still powerful and lacerating in the production put on at the Coronet last evening. It may, in fact, have grown a bit in stature. In 1934 it was a self-contained story about two school teachers whose lives were destroyed by a false accusation of abnormal sexual relations; and that was sufficiently shocking at the time. But now we know that lives can be destroyed by other types of slander. Having been intelligently written for the values of 1934, "The Children's Hour" fits the world of today just as accurately. Literally, it is still the story of the two hounded school teachers, but the implications are much broader now and have new political overtones" ("The Children's Hour" 35).

The dramatic intensity in the situation and dialogue so apparent in *The Children's Hour* was not present in her next play *Days to Come* (1936). Focusing on a model factory town in which the workers have not unionized, Hellman explores the effects of a strike, the arrival of a labor organizer and a strike breaker, and the passion the factory owner's wife feels for the labor organizer. The critics were justifiably disappointed in the play. Despite a good subject, some strong dialogue, and a few interesting characters, it was not a success and ran only seven performances. Hellman wrote, "I spoiled a good play. I returned to the amateur's mistake: everything you think and feel must be written this time, because you may never have another chance to write it" ("Preface" *Four Plays* x).

Hellman's personality is revealed by her behavior on the opening night. She drank a great deal, vomited during the first act, went home to change her dress, then returned and paid an usher to buy her some brandy to drink during the last act. At the party following the play she shouted at Hammett, "You son of a bitch! Didn't you tell me just last week that *Days to Come* was the best play you'd ever read?" He answered "I did, but I saw it tonight and I've changed my mind." He then left the party (Wright, *Lillian Hellman* 124).

For two years Hellman's intense disappointment and feelings of inadequacy kept her from writing for the theatre. Then she made a triumphant return. Her next play was *The Little Foxes*. In this work she was influenced by the contempt she felt for the greed and materialism of her Newhouse relatives and for American society. These feelings may have been brought to the fore by the years she spent in Hollywood among the newly rich movie makers. She found the play difficult to write because she was delving into the roots of her past. She wrote eight drafts before Hammett "gave a nod of approval" (*Pentimento* 172).

The play opened in 1939 with an excellent cast headed by Tallulah Bankhead. Set in the deep South in 1900, it presents the picture of the Hubbard family, Ben and Oscar who inherited their father's wealth, and Regina who resents them because, being a woman, she inherited nothing. She hoped her marriage would bring her wealth and happiness, but she grew to loathe her husband because he did not have the strength and greed which could bring her all she wanted in material terms. As the play opens, the Hubbards are filled with hope because Mr. Marshall from Chicago has agreed to join with them in building a cotton mill in their town. Regina sends her daughter Alexandra to Maryland to bring back her hospitalized husband, Horace, to force him to invest his money in the mill.

However, when he arrives, he tells Regina he will not invest because he knows the profits will come from underpaid workers and corruption. Ben and Oscar arrange to "borrow" Horace's bonds from his safe deposit box and make the deal with Marshall, leaving Regina in the cold. When Horace tells her that the funds are missing, but he intends to do nothing about it, she deliberately excites him to suffer a heart attack, then refuses him his medicine. In one of the most dramatic scenes in the play she watches him struggle from his wheelchair and collapse on the stairs. When the brothers arrive, she has turned the tables. Horace dies and Regina says she will prosecute Ben and Oscar unless they give her 75% of the profits. Forced to knuckle under, they take their leave, but Ben philosophically says that "one loses today and wins tomorrow" and that he wonders why a man in a wheelchair was on a stairway (*Collected Plays* 204). Regina's triumph is soured by his suspicions about Horace's death and by the loss of Alexandra who says, "I am going away from you. Because I want to. Because I know Papa would want me to" (206).

The play is composed of interesting characters, strong dialogue, and memorable scenes. In the first act Oscar's wife, Birdie, is happy because of the party for Mr. Marshall, but the act ends with her husband slapping her face for opposing a marriage between their son and Alexandra. A softer mood occurs in the second act when there is a brief absence of the Hubbards from the house, and Addie, the sympathetic, intelligent black maid, Horace, Birdie, and Alexandra chat, play the piano, and drink elderberry wine. In this scene Addie gives one of the most frequently quoted speeches from the play. Speaking about the Hubbards, she says, "Yeah, they got mighty well-off cheating niggers. Well, there are people who eat the earth and eat all the people on it like in the Bible with the locusts. And other people who stand around and watch them eat it. (Softly) Sometimes I think it ain't right to stand and watch them do it" (183). Hellman's belief that decent people need to fight for social and political change is represented in that speech and elsewhere in the play. Her view of American society is represented in a frighteningly accurate speech by Ben to Regina: "The century's turning, the world is open. Open for people like you and me. Ready for us, waiting for us. After all this is just the beginning. There are hundreds of Hubbards sitting in rooms like this throughout the country. All their names aren't Hubbard, but they are all Hubbards and they will own this country some day" (204). This grim prediction is only slightly undercut by the conclusion of the play in which Alexandra—a Hubbard by name—determines to reject the Hubbard values and actions.

The high quality of the play and the production drew audiences and pleased critics. The play ran for 410 performances. Bernard Hewitt wrote that "When *The Little Foxes* was produced [Hellman] took her place among this country's leading playwrights" He printed Richard Watts, Jr.'s rave review as typical. "Miss Hellman's new play is a grim, bitter and merciless play; a drama more honest, more pointed and more brilliant than even her triumphant previous work, "The Children's Hour". . . . Every portrait in "The Little Foxes" is mordant and masterly. . . . At last Miss Bankhead has a role and a play worthy of her" (*Theatre U.S.A.* 415).The acting opportunities for black actors were noted by several critics. The critic for the *Daily Worker* wrote, "Abbie Mitchell and John Marriott interpreted the two Negro servants, as they are written, with sympathy, dignity, and humor" (qtd. in Tanner 125). John Anderson's review placed Hellman in a high position in American playwriting, saying that Hellman was nearer to O'Neill than Maxwell Anderson or Clifford Odets. "She strikes to kill and in her third play 'The Little Foxes,' she proves her mettle, demonstrates that 'The Children's Hour' was no flash in the box office but the opening of a career, and establishes herself as an author of tragedy. It is a small field, occupied chiefly by O'Neill, Maxwell Anderson, and, occasionally, Mr. Odets, and Miss Hellman brings to it special gifts of her own" ("Lillian Hellman Establishes Self" n.p.).

Many critics noted the power and excitement of Hellman's dialogue. Barrett Clark wrote, "The dialogue is exactly right. It possesses a rhythmical quality which is never intrusive and a surface realistic quality that makes us forget it is the work of a conscious and determined and scrupulous writer" ("Lillian Hellman" 130).

The play was selected as one of the best plays of the year by Burns Mantle and has been successful in many revivals. Hellman wrote the excellent screenplay for the film directed by William Wyler which has been described as "a superb film" by Scheuer and others (Scheuer 617). The role of Regina provided an exceptional opportunity for several actresses including Tallulah Bankhead, Bette Davis, Anne Bancroft and, most recently, Elizabeth Taylor. It was turned into an opera called *Regina* by Marc Blitzstein (1949).

Its revival in 1967 at Lincoln Center with George C. Scott and Anne Bancroft was so successful that it was moved to a Broadway theatre for a long run. The newspaper reviewers were very enthusiastic, but Elizabeth Hardwick and John Simon attacked the play. The latter wrote, "That Hellman should be considered one of America's foremost playwrights speaks only of the dearth of American playwrights" (qtd. in Wright, *Lillian Hellman* 302). This production was notable in that it signalled the beginning of attacks on Hellman and her writing.

It was also significant because Austin Pendleton played the role of Leo. Writing in 1981, Frank Rich said, "Austin Pendleton, who played Leo in Mike Nichols's 1967 Lincoln Center revival of this play, was clearly born to direct it" ("The Misses Taylor and Stapleton in 'Foxes'" 228). The production which Pendleton directed was a major success in America and London, but was again controversial. According to Wright, "Many people, including some old friends of Hellman's, saw in her agreeing to Taylor in the part proof of her willingness to betray her artistic principles where big money was concerned" (*Lillian Hellman* 383). Austin Pendleton admired Hellman and the play, but found her argumentative and trying to work with, especially since she kept telling him to look at the movie when he had questions (Personal interview). Not surprisingly, the critics were divided about the play's merits. Rich said, "Miss Hellman knows how to tell a story at a breathtaking clip and how to stack her theatrical deck with well-placed narrative bomb-shells. . . . Most of all, she knows how to throw her actors the prime red meat of bristling language. If 'The Little Foxes' is Broadway melodrama, it's as good as the genre gets" ("The Misses Taylor and Stapleton in 'Foxes' 228). Clive Barnes said, "Miss Hellman's boulevard melodrama is not very good and never has been" ("Liz' Glamour brings glitter to 'Little Foxes' " 232) and Howard Kissel spoke of "the dead weight of the work itself, which veers between melodrama and soap opera" ("The Little Foxes" 229).

Despite critical controversy over its merits, the play remains popular and is considered by many to be one of the classics of the American theatre. Another criticism of Hellman, herself, grew as time went by: the unpleasant characters in the play gave rise to the belief that Hellman really didn't like human beings. John Gassner wrote that her characterizations in this and later plays were so alive "that the indictments she incorporates in her plays seem indictments of human nature itself, giving rise to the complaint that she does not like people" (*Best American Plays*, Third Series 206).

In her next play Hellman rather reversed the situation by creating a group of characters, most of whom were decent, some of whom were heroic, and one who is the embodiment of the evil which was so apparent in the world in 1941. *Watch on the Rhine* reflected Hellman's anti-Nazi attitudes, as well as her hatred of hypocrisy, lies, and blackmail. The play is set in the home of the wealthy Farrelly house outside Washington, D.C. The head of the household is the sharp-spoken grande-dame, Fanny, whose husband was a diplomat. An accomplished woman who speaks many languages and has international connections with high level people, she opposed her daughter Sara's marriage to a German engineer and has not seen her or her husband, Kurt Müller, for many years. As the play begins, Fanny, her son David, and their European house-guests Count Teck de Brancovis and his wife Marthe, are anticipating arrival of the Müllers and their three children. They typify the European refugees who were part of the American scene in the forties: poorly dressed, uncertain, unable to believe that such things as eggs and meat are readily available.

As the play progresses it becomes clear that Kurt Müller has been working as an anti-Fascist in Europe and that he is on a Nazi wanted list. He receives news that his colleagues have been captured and he must take $23,000 he has collected to Europe to try to help them escape the Nazis. However, Teck, who has strong connections with the German Embassy, tells the Farrelly family and the Müllers that he knows all about Kurt and wants $10,000 to keep quiet. He is not characterized as a black and white villain. He, too, has suffered from the war, and wants a visa and some help so he can return to his native Rumania. He also wants to keep his wife who is tired of a life of poverty and unhappiness. Barrett Clark used the character to illustrate the fact that Hellman's characterization was becoming more complex and subtle: "[He] stands forth a completely rounded characterization and Kurt, instead of being opposed by a conventionally wicked man who can be summarily killed and therefore eliminated from the picture, is seen by the audience as pursued by an idea and a philosophy which cannot be so conveniently disposed of" ("Lillian Hellman" 128).

Certain that Teck will not keep his word, Kurt knocks him unconscious and his son Joshua assists him in opening the door and getting him out on the terrace where he shoots him. The final scene is very moving. It is probable that Kurt will be captured by the Nazis on his return to Germany and that he is saying a last goodbye. He speaks to his children, referring to his reluctant murder obliquely: "The world is out of shape . . . and until it gets in shape, men will steal and lie and—(Slowly) and—kill. But for whatever reason it is done, and whoever does it—you understand me—it is all bad. . . . But perhaps you will live to see the day when it will not have to be. All over the world there are men who are fighting for that day. . . . In every town and every village and every mud hut in the world, there is a man who might fight to make a good world. And now good-bye. Wait for me. I shall try to come back to you" (275).

As the play ends, the Farrellys (who symbolize American people generally) have become accessories to a murder and realize that the future will not be easy. The reality of the world war and the personal experience of evil has changed their lives. Fanny says, "Well, here we are. We are shaken out of the magnolias, eh?" (276).

The play was a great popular and critical success, running for 378 performances. An article in the *New York Times* predicted it would win the Pulitzer Prize and that it was overdue: "Miss Hellman, in Broadway's opinion, deserved the Pulitzer Prize with "The Children's Hour" in the year the award went to the Zoë Akin's play "The Old Maid" ("Prize Plays, Critics & Such" n.p.). The critic for *Cue* wrote, "Lillian

Hellman has written a profoundly moving play of today, of Nazism, and done it in honest theatrical terms. Her play is made of the stuff of the theatre—plot and character and grand writing" ("Watch on the Rhine" n.p.). Burns Mantle noted that the Pulitzer Prize Committee would have a difficult decision and that Hellman was a major contender who had written the best of the many anti-Nazi plays. He also noted that whereas the characters in *The Little Foxes* were hateful people she ruthlessly exposed, in this play "her people are suffering humans for whom she has great sympathy and whose cause she declares with the burning enthusiasm of a crusader. The result is a drama that frequently glows with these virtues" ("Lillian Hellman's 'Watch on the Rhine' n.p). Richard Lockridge praised the play, noting in particular that it was "far and away the best drama on the anti-Nazi theme because it elevates that theme to the human level and keeps it there" ("Miss Hellman" n.p.). Although the play did not win the Pulitzer Prize, it won the prestigious Drama Critics Circle Award and was in the best plays volume for 1940-41. In his history of the Pulitzer Prize, Toohey wrote that *There Shall Be No Night* won, but "A much finer play, Lillian Hellman's *Watch on the Rhine*, opened on April 1, 1941, and may thus have technically missed the 1940-41 Pulitzer deadline by one day" (184).

Hellman's method of writing was to do a great deal of research about the society, politics, etc. which formed the background of her plays. When she wrote *The Little Foxes* she studied economic conditions in the South at the turn of the century including such elements as the exploitation of cheap labor by greedy factory owners. All of her plays show that she was well-informed and certain of her facts. In an interview before her next play, *The Searching Wind* was produced, she said that she had personal experience of the political and social events because of living in Germany and Italy in the1920s. Additionally she researched political events of the period: "Before I started writing this story I did a good deal of research into conditions in Germany that let Nazism grow." (Ormsbee "Miss Hellman All But Dares" 1).

In this play Hellman turned away from the three-act, Ibsenian structure which had served her so well. *The Searching Wind* alternates between scenes set in 1944, when the play was produced, and scenes set in 1922 as Mussolini is taking over Rome, in 1923 as Hitler is rising to power and the Jews are being attacked, and in 1938 as France and England are about to appease Hitler in Munich. Against the background of events which gradually and inexorably lead to World War II, the relationships between the Taney family, diplomat Alex Hazen, and Cassie Bowman are played out. In the first scene the old liberal, Moses Taney, formerly a powerful newspaper editor and his grandson, Sam, are discussing newspaper articles about the events in war-torn Italy written by Sam's father, Alex Hazen, a former ambassador. Sam has been wounded in the war and finds the articles, the war, indeed, the whole world difficult to understand. As the evening progresses, the events of the past are presented to him and he must judge the actions of the generation which preceded him. His mother Emily has invited her college friend Cassie to dinner after many years of estrangement. It soon becomes clear that Alex and Cassie have had a long-standing affair, and that Emily has tired of pretending not to know.

Through the flashbacks, we see that Moses foresees the dangers of inactivity and accomodation and that Cassie believes Alex, as a representative of the American Government should be an anti-Fascist. The irony in the play arises from the structure which begins in the present with a war in progress, and the inability of people in earlier years to recognize danger and make intelligent decisions. As Mussolini is taking over Italy, Cassie and Emily are involved in a rivalry for Alex which Emily wins. Cassie states a major motif in the play in this scene, "We're an ignorant generation. We see so much and know so little. Maybe because we think about ourselves so much" (300).

By the end of the play we have seen them play out their personal lives against a backdrop of horrendous political events. Hellman characterizes the calamity of the world by such elements as the anguish of Sam (beautifully played by Montgomery Clift) whose leg will be amputated and who watched his friends die in battles, a refugee couple, formerly well-to-do Europeans, now reduced to working as servants in the household, and the sense of waste and failure on the part of Cassie, Alex, and Emily. At the end of the evening, many things have been clarified for them, and for Sam. His feeling of shame for his parents extends to their entire generation and is an expression of Hellman's condemnation of American society.

Hellman clearly put her concerns in the play. Speaking at a luncheon (along with Edna Ferber) in 1940, Hellman warned of the danger of totalitarian governments and the failure of America to respond: "I am a writer and I am also a Jew. I want to be quite sure that I can continue to be a writer and that if I want to say that greed is bad or persecution is worse, I can do so without being branded by the malice of people who make a living by that malice. I also want to be able to go on saying that I am a Jew without being afraid of being called names or end in a camp or be forbidden to walk down the street at night" (qtd. in Wright, *Lillian Hellman* 168).

Once again Hellman had a major success. Elliott Norton expressed a view held by several critics, that the structure had some flaws, but he concluded the play was one "of serious purpose and strong feeling" ("Searching Wind" n.p.). Because it opened late in the season, it only had a run of 318 performances, but that was considered very good for a serious play. In his introduction to the best plays volume, Burns Mantle wrote, "Interest in the late season was considerably stimulated by the production of Lillian Hellman's 'The Searching Wind.' One of the few thoughtful dramas of the season, this exposure of the appeasers and the politicians who may have had something to do with bringing on the Second World War came as close to being the prize-winning play of the year as any, receiving six of the Drama Critics Circle thirteen votes" (*Best Plays af 1943-44* 14).

After *The Searching Wind* a major change took place in Hellman's career in theatre. She began to direct her own plays in place of Herman Shumlin who had directed the first four. In an article called "Herman Shumlin's Favorite Playwright," Shumlin described his work with Hellman. He said the work was not peaceful or calm, as both were intense people. She watched every rehearsal and they would sometimes fight about the direction. He also said that she often made suggestions about staging which would improve the production, but that he never contributed anything to the writing of the play "although some people assume so" (n.p.). (Even with a woman as strong and independent as Hellman, there was still an assumption that a woman playwright would need help from some man.) Hellman was also interviewed about the production process and said that she worked on the casting of all her plays and several of her movies ("Lillian Hellman Discusses Casting" n.p.). Having worked closely on the plays and films, Hellman felt capable of directing her own plays. Because of strong disagreements, she and Shumlin had broken off their professional and personal relationship, so she chose to direct herself, rather than find another director.

Hellman's 1946 play was a return in two ways. First, she returned to the Ibsenian structure and, second, she returned to the characters she had successfully created in *The Little Foxes*. She, herself, was in analysis for many years in the forties, and that may have stimulated her interest in looking into the Hubbards' family background. *Another Part of the Forest* presents the Hubbards of the first play in their youth, as they are making the decisions which determine their characters and their later lives. Regina is twenty and in love with a southern aristocrat, John Bagtry, who is thirty-six and eager to go to Brazil as a hired soldier. Ben is thirty-five, greedy, and entirely under the thumb of his sarcastic, egocentric father, Marcus. He and his brother Oscar work in Marcus' store at low salaries. Marcus bullies them and mocks them as he does his wife, Lavinia. His love is saved for his daughter, Regina, and it is clear that he does not intend her to marry, but care for him and travel with him to Europe. Hellman based the characters of two women in the play on that of her own mother: Lavinia who is weak and frightened of her husband and the young "ninny" Birdie Bagtry. (Lavinia's fate foreshadows Birdie's future.) Again Hellman creates a strong, admirable black character, Coralee, the servant who supports and protects Lavinia.

The tension in the town of Bowden between the aristocrats, who were impoverished by the civil war, and the Hubbards, who were enriched by it, underlies the action as does the hatred of the entire community for the Hubbards and their sharp business practices. Throughout the first part of the play there are hints that Marcus has a guilty secret, that he was nearly lynched during the war. The action of the play moves through a musical evening in which the contempt of John Bagtry for the Hubbards is clear, Regina's wish to meet him in Chicago and marry him, Oscar's desire to marry a whore who also has contempt for the family, Lavinia's pathetic desire to return to her small town and set up a school for the black people, and Ben's desire to negotiate a secret loan for Birdie Bagtry (part of which he will keep for himself), are all revealed to the audience and to Marcus. Sure of himself, Marcus sneers at the Bagtrys, orders Ben and Oscar out of the house by the next morning, and concludes the act by calling his wife crazy and saying he will never allow her to carry out her plans.

The last act, however, builds to a great reversal in which Ben moves into the position of power. In a tense, highly dramatic scene, he finds that Lavinia and Coralee know Marcus' secret. With patience, he finally manages to get the information that because of Marcus' trading in the north to buy goods to sell at inflated prices in south, the northern soldiers were able to trail him to a camp and slaughter twenty-seven soldiers from Bowden. In the end, Ben wins. In the final scene it is he who has the coffee served on the terrace and when his father reaches for the newspaper, Ben shakes his head no—all the privileges and power now belong to Ben. He has given the money to Birdie, thus providing funds for John Bagtry to travel to Brazil, he informs Oscar that he will marry Birdie to obtain the Bagtry plantation for the family, tells Regina she will marry the "quiet rich" Horace Giddons, and talks about his plans to make the family rich. Lavinia and Coralee leave, taking with them the Bible with the proof of Marcus' guilt, and Regina snubs her father to sit by Ben. The slight suggestion of an incestuous urge on the part of the father is also present in the relationship of Ben and Regina. Ben creates the Oedipal act of replacing the father: he has an urge to control Regina and marry her to a weak husband, and he, himself, never marries.

Critical response was generally enthusiastic and the play ran for 182 performances. Ward Morehouse headed his review, "Hellman's 'Another Part of the Forest' is a Fascinating and Powerful Drama" and concluded by saying, "Another Part of the Forest is full-bodied, vibrant theater, theater that Lillian Hellman can write. She has now done the trick five times out of six" (250). Richard Watts, Jr. praised her earlier plays, but said that the new one, "surpasses them all in sheer, overwhelming intensity of interest. It is also a brilliant and distinguished work, of enormous power and impact." He ended by saying it was one of the "most fascinating plays of the contemporary American theatre" ("Lillian Hellman's New Play" 250). Brooks Atkinson praised Hellman's directing and all the acting, particularly Mildred Dunnock as Lavinia, Patricia Neal as Regina, and Beatrice Thompson as "a merciful negro maid" ("The Play 'Another Part of the Forest'" 248). Robert Garland called it her most distinguished play, and suggested it should be performed alternately with *The Little Foxes* ("At the Fulton" 248). Burns Mantle selected it out of the sixty-six new plays presented as one of the ten best, telling his readers, "You will find a gifted dramatist's skill impressively employed" (*Best Plays of 1946-47* vi).

Some critics felt the play was too morbid and nasty and that there were too many crises in a short period or time. An anonymous critic summarized *Another Part of the Forest* as "the story of four scoundrels, two half wits, one insane woman, and a whore" (qtd. in unidentified clipping Lincoln Center). Several critics angered Hellman with charges of blatant melodrama so that she ignored the tradition of never responding to critics by writing a response which was a defense of her work and an attack on Brooks Atkinson ("An Author Jabs Her Critics" n.p.). Yet, as Carol MacNicholas has commented, "even the unfavorable reviews compliment Hellman for her consistent ability to create vivid characters . . . and to pit them against one another in individual scenes of great dramatic intensity" ("Lillian Hellman" 285). The play was successsfully performed on PBS in the early 1970's with Robert Foxworth as Ben and Barry Sullivan as Marcus. It has also been revived in regional theatres such as the Immediate Theatre Company in Chicago in 1986. An anonymous critic praised the opportunities Hellman had provided for actors, saying, "The venom in these characters is so rich that mere competency in the play's performance will keep it potent enough" ("Feral Foxes in Hellman's 'Forest'" 3).

Montserrat (1949) was the first of four adaptations by Hellman. Emmanual Roblès wrote the play in French. It has a very simple plot line and is in only two acts in contrast to Hellman's original plays. It is an effective dramatic situation rather similar to that of Georg Kaiser's *The Burghers of Calais* (1913), Sidney Howard's *Paths of Glory* (1935), and Arthur Miller's *Incident at Vichy* (1964). The play is set in 1812 in Venezuela, at the time Simón Bolivar was leading a revolution against Spain. Six citizens, selected at random, are brought into the General's palace to be executed unless Captain Montserrat reveals the hiding place where he took Bolivar the night before. The cruel officer Izquierdo tells them they have one hour to convince Montserrat to save their lives by revealing Bolivar's location.

As they speak to him, some begging, each of the characters reveals her or his character. One is a single mother who has left her two babies alone in a locked room, one is an artist who is to carve statues for a cathedral, one is a wealthy business-man with a young, beautiful wife, one is an actor from Spain, one is a young Venezuelan who had planned to join Bolivar in a year, and one is a young woman who sympathizes with Bolivar. In the first act they reveal their various backgrounds and outlooks. The actor from Spain is a staunch Royalist. Hellman puts in his mouth a theme heard many times as Hitler pursued the war (and even now): "I am sorry. These atrocity stories do not convince me. Down through history one reads of these matters and one never believes them" (447). But like the others, he is doomed to suffer an atrocity. Izquierdo is unmoved by their pleas, saying, "As much as you want your life, I want Bolivar" (463). Montserrat suffers as he hears the pleas, but stands firm, saying that God has told him, "It is nothing to give one's life if millions can be saved by so doing" (455).

In the second act the six are taken out one by one and shot. The drama is heightened by the off-stage sounds of drumming, many shots, then the single shot (*coup de grâce*). Throughout Montserrat never wavers, although he pleads with Izquierdo to shoot him instead. Then as the young man who wanted to fight for Bolivar is to be shot, he nearly gives Izquierdo the information, but the young woman tells him to be faithful to Bolivar and goes with dignity to her own death.

Izquierdo is still intent upon getting the information and in a dramatic speech reveals his particular hatred for Bolivar and all those like him. He had been captured by Bolivar and tells of what was done to him:

> They buried me up to here (touches his chin) and packed the earth tight. Then they counted out ten men and ten men and ten and so on. And each ten came to me and pissed in my face. That was twenty-five months ago: there hasn't been a night since that I haven' t heard their laughter and felt my face to see if—that laughter fills the world for me. The rest I've almost forgotten: the four days and four nights, my head like a stone placed in an empty land. That is the story as you heard it . . . about a miracle survival—but nobody knows what they did to me. Only you. (Violently) I can't live unless they don't live. (477)

In the PBS production of the play in 1971, Rip Torn played the role. Throughout the early part of the play he squeezed lemon juice over his head and face and this speech revealed his reason. The play provides excellent roles for the actors. Torn played opposite Keir Dullea on television. In the original production Emlyn Williams played Izquierdo and Julie Harris made her mark in the role of the heroic young woman.

In a review headed "Grim", Robert Garland, said that there was a certain fascination about the play, but that it should have been better: "Both as the adapter and the director of her adaptation, Lillian Hellman would seem to have let Emmanuel Roblès down" (246). Robert Coleman called it obvious melodrama and said, as many critics did, that Hellman didn't provide enough information to find the murders understandable ("'Montserrat' Well Acted But Script is Bumpy" 246). Ward Morehouse praised the acting (most critics singled our Julie Harris and Emlyn Williams), but said the play was "a sharply disappointing venture" ("'Montserrat' Disappoints" 245). MacNicholas summed up the failure of the adaptation, saying, "The dialogue is often abstract and philosophical; most of the characters are underdeveloped; and the summary executions of each become mechanical." She quoted one critic who said the play was so static one could hardly wait to have all the victims shot ("Lillian Hellman" 286). The play closed after sixty-five performances.

Two years later Hellman returned to the American scene for one of her best plays, *The Autumn Garden* (1951). The play has often been described as Chekhovian and plotless; the play is less complicated in structure than her previous plays and there is no grand secret to be revealed at the climax as there is in the usual well-made play. The mood of the play, the absence of violence, and the final scenes are less Ibsenian than Chekhovian: there is no major confrontation which arises from a surging action leading to an inevitable, highly dramatic conclusion. All in all, the play is simply a lower key play than those dealing with war or the Hubbard family. It is certainly Hellman's wittiest play, revealing qualities in the playwright which appealed to Dashiell Hammett, among others, and which he utilized in his characterization of Nora Charles.

The setting is the Tuckerman house, on the Gulf of Mexico, about one hundred miles from New Orleans. Constance Tuckerman's father died broke and so she maintains the house by renting rooms. A familiar element in the play is the presence of a poor person from Europe who acts as a servant. Constance has brought her niece from Germany to educate her and help her live in America. What she doesn't realize is that Sophie would rather be in Europe with her family and only poverty keeps her where she is. She has contracted a marriage with Frederick, the son of the very wealthy Ellis family. His mother and grandmother approve because he has had an attachment for a male writer. Also present in the home is a General Griggs and his wife, Rose, a giddy, foolish woman addicted to babbling, over-dressing, and flirting. Ned Crossman is an old friend of Constance, thought to have been in love with her, who comes every summer. Into this group suddenly arrives Con's old beau, Nick. He is a portrait painter who left her to marry a very wealthy woman, Nina.

Nick is like Gregers Werle in Ibsen's *The Wild Duck* in that he likes meddling with other people's lives, giving them advice, and feeling that he is a wise counselor. He differs from Gregers in that he is charming—purposefully charming, and that he can't stand being unable to charm people. On Sunday Nina goes for a picnic, leaving Nick alone to drink champagne and be bored. By the end of the evening he finally does something which is worse than his prying and meddling. After everyone has gone to bed, and Sophie has made up her bed on the sofa, he returns, makes advances, and then passes out on her bed.

The play seems about to end on a doleful note for everyone. Rose comes back to tell Griggs that she has found out she really is seriously ill, and he will have to nurse her, so his plans for a new life are over. Nina is leaving Nick. The marriage between Sophie and Frederick is off because people believe Nick slept with her, and Con finds out that Ned never did want to marry her. But Hellman has a surprise for the audience. Nick and Nina reconcile, plan a luxurious trip to Europe, and he slips out of the house leaving her to pay up and take care of the luggage and the farewells. Sophie, who has been so deferential throughout the play, tells Nina she wants $5000, or she will lie and say Nick seduced her. She is very clear and unemotional about the matter, but says she will not take it as a gift, only as blackmail. Everyone departs leaving Con and Ned alone. She is sad that Sophie will go back to Europe and that Ned will not return the next summer. He describes the dreary, empty, alcoholic life he leads and says he lied to himself saying that if she had married him, things would have been different: "I not only wasted myself, but I wanted it that way." The play concludes with her line, "Never mind. Most of us lie to ourselves. Never mind" (572).

It is unavoidable to see elements of Hellman's relationship with Hammett throughout the play. Particularly since he wrote a long speech for Griggs in which he concludes that he has frittered away his life and that he has largely been useless. Hammett was frustrated in his writing in his later years, and his off-again-on-again relationship with Hellman, the alcoholism which affected both of them is reflected in the two marriages seen in the play and the relationship between Ned and Con. In 1951 Hellman was forty-six and Hammett thirteen years older. It was certainly the autumn of their lives, and their relationship had continued for seventeen years. Many of the lines in the play must have been spoken between them more than once. Nick says to Nina, for example, "Come back to me, Nina, without shame in wanting to. Put up with me a little longer, kid. I'm getting older and I'll soon wear down" (557). As he leaves, he says, "Think what you want and I'll be what I am. I love you and you love me and that's that and always will be." (559).

As with most of Hellman's plays, the production was excellent. Florence Eldridge and Frederic March (soon to create the roles in *Long Day's Journey Into Night*) played the major roles. Surprisingly, on the whole the critics were not enthusiastic. Many seemed surprised at the lack of Hellman's usual fireworks. Richard Watts, Jr. wrote, "In a somber, Chekhovian mood, Lillian Hellman has written a brooding, philosophical play. . . . Despite its adult virtues, however, it lacks the biting and overwhelming theatrical power that we have come to expect of Miss Hellman" ("Lillian Hellman's Latest Drama" 326). Several critics callecd the script scattered and diffuse. John Chapman and William Hawkins both liked the play. Chapman's title gave the purport of his review: "Hellman's 'Autumn Garden' Meaty Comedy Played by Flawless Cast." He called the play "kindly, humorous, and profound" and noted the "fine, funny lines" (327). Hawkins called it "utterly absorbing" and said it was a rare play which made him want to see it again ("'Autumn Garden' is Rich and Mellow" 325). The play closed after 101 performances. As time has passed the play has been successfully revived at Arena Stage and elsewhere, and it is generally regarded as one of the author's best plays—Hellman regarded it as the best (MacNicholas 288).

Hellman returned to adaptation for her play in 1955. *The Lark* was adapted from *L'Alouette* by Jean Anouilh. His play is about Joan of Arc and the collaboration of the French with the English. He was making a comment on the collaboration of French with Germans during the occupation of France during the Second World War, and through the character of Joan, voicing the antipathy of people in an occupied land toward the occupiers. Like most of Anouilh's plays, the influence of Pirandello is clear. Joan is on trial, but seems to have been tried already—she sometimes loses the sense of where she is as she re-enacts a story the judges already know. The line betwen illusion and reality is not clear: after the trial she says, "They think I dreamed it all. Maybe I did" (626). Like Shaw's *St. Joan*, the play ends on a comic note with a scene following Joan's burning at the stake. Joan says the play should end with her happiest day. So, Joan chooses the coronation day, because that was the day France was returned to its people. She says, "Let's end with it, please, if nobody would mind" (630)

For Hellman the play must have been intended as a comment on the collaboration of so many people with the McCarthy committee. She had a success, with the play running 229 performances. The role of Joan was a triumph for Julie Harris. Many critics credited Hellman with altering the play to fit the American taste. (Those who love Anouilh feel her adaptation is thin and lacks wit.) John McClain said he felt Hellman's contribution was considerable, "for the lofty speech and towering phrases which are usually injected into any such ecclesiastic exercise are happily missing ("July Depicts a Vital Joan" 208). John Chapman's review was similar to the other critics, headed "Julie Harris Simply Magnificant In a Beautiful Drama" (208). Richard Watts, Jr. wrote "How wonderful the theatre can be when everything goes right!" and concluded that the play was "a moving dramatic experience" ("A Stirring Play" 207). Walter Kerr paid tribute to the characterization of Joan, saying, "It has remained for a woman dramatist to give us the first really tough-minded Joan of Arc" ("The Lark" 206). Despite her success with the play, Hellman had little chance for a major award. Julie Harris received a Tony, but *Anne Frank* swept away all competition for playwriting.

Hellman's next play was another adaptation. In 1956 there was great anticipation regarding the operetta *Candide*. Many great talents were involved in the project: Leonard Bernstein wrote the music and the lyrics were written by poet Richard Wilbur, John Latouche, and Dorothy Parker. Tyrone Guthrie directed, Oliver Smith designed the settings, and Irene Sharaff the costumes. With such a prestigious group of theatre artists collaborating on Voltaire's witty satire success seemed very likely.

The script Hellman wrote followed Voltaire's work in terms of its story line and satire on society. Candide, his love Cunegunde, and his tutor, the optimistic man who believes this is the best of all possible worlds, move through war, the Inquisition, shipwreck, and other disasters, only to return to their native Westphalia. They find it in ruins and look back on a life of foolishness and senseless idealism. Wilbur's last lyric sums up the view of life expressed in the operetta: "We're neither pure nor wise nor good; We'll do the best we know; we'll build our house, and chop our wood, and make our garden grow" (712).

There is a widely held belief that the failure of *Candide* lay with Hellman and that the reviewers all praised everything about it except the book. In fact, a number of reviewers liked everything about the production. Brooks Atkinson wrote, "Pooling their talents, Lillian Hellman, the literary lady, and Leonard Bernstein, the music man, have composed an admirable version of Voltaire's philosophical tale"

("The Theatre: 'Candide'" 40). John Chapman called the operetta a "work of genius" and said that Hellman "has fashioned a strong, clear, and humourous libretto" ("'Candide' an Artistic Triumph" 176). Tom Donnelly said the operetta was wonderful in most aspects, but felt there were problems with the book. However, he said, "Only Burton's 'The Anatomy of Melancholy' could conceivably offer more problems" ("Best Musical News of the Year"). In contrast, Walter Kerr and a number of other critics felt the production was severely flawed. Kerr criticized the book saying Hellman "found nothing to laugh at" and called the event "a really spectacular disaster" ("Candide" 179). The operetta was one of the most expensive failures in the American the-atre and ran only 73 performances. It was a long evening in the the-atre, although Hellman was bitter that her script had been severely cut (MacNicholas 289). Probably Robert Coleman's review touched on the major reason for the failure: "If you're on the town, in search of fun and frolic, 'Candide' is not your dish. Rather it's for those who don't demand lacy icing on their entertainment cake, who can stand a lot of bitter with a little sweet" ("Musical 'Candide' Is Distinguished Work" 179).

The very popular recording of the operetta (and the immensely popular overture by Leonard Bernstein) continued to draw attention to the work and many people bemoaned its failure. In 1974 a new book was written by Hugh Wheeler and the operetta was successfully performed. It has subsequently been a part of the repertoire of the New York City Opera and has been performed elsewhere with success. This would seem to give weight to the critical opinion which based the blame for the failure of the expensive project on Hellman's book. The failure was very humiliating to her and was a contributing factor in her move out of the theatre. She wrote, "I think now that I began to leave the theatre with *Candide*" (*Pentimento* 205).

With the encouragement of her friends and her own inner strength, Hellman returned to the theatre. It is an interesting insight into her character and her writing that she took an idea initially suggested by Hammett, but altered it. He suggested a play about a man who wants to do good, but in trying to please people fails. Hellman began the play, but then told Hammett, "I can write about men, but I can't write a play that centers on a man. I've got to tear it up, [and] make it about the women around him, his sisters, his bride, his mothers (*Pentimento* 206).

Toys in the Attic opened in 1960 and ran for 556 performances. Hellman develops the theme of incestuous desire only suggested in *Another Part of The Forest* and introduces another daring theme, that of love between whites and blacks. The play is more of a psychological study of several characters than some of her clearly didactic plays. It has been suggested that her two aunts and her father were the models for the three central characters, Carrie, Anna and Julian Berniers. To the extent that her aunts adored her father, this is true. In the play Carrie and Anna are aging spinsters who have given their love, attention, and savings to their luckless brother Julian. Not having heard from for a while, they are staggered when the wealthy Albertine Prine, accompanied by her supposed servant, Henry, appears to say that her daughter, Lily, and Lily's husband Julian are in town.

Julian and Lily made a dramatic entrance with a taxi driver carrying many boxes of expensive presents. He says he is rich, but that what he has done to get the money is a secret. In fact, he has bought a piece of land on a tip from a Mrs. Warkin, who is married to a vicious landowner who abuses her. Julian was formerly her lover and knows her to be part black.

In a strong confrontation between the sisters, the truth about Carrie is revealed. She is raging that Julian is married to a "crazy little whore" and is "the daughter of a woman who keeps a nigger fancy man. I'll bet she paid Julian to take that crazy girl away from her." She challenges Anna to ask him, saying that when you really love "you take your chances on being hated by speaking out the truth." The act concludes with the following lines:

> Anna. All right. I'll take that chance now and tell you that you want to sleep with him and always have. Years ago I used to be frightened that you would try and would watch you and suffer for you.
> Carrie. You never said those words. Tell me I never heard those words. Tell me, Anna. (When there is no answer.) You were all I ever had. I don't love you anymore.
> Anna. That was the chance I took. (766)

The play ends as Julian, beaten and humiliated, returns to the house. Thugs set on him and Mrs. Warkin, took the money, slashed her face, and beat him. Albertine Prine foresees that Carrie will tell Julian that Lily secretly informed Warkin and that Julian will send her back to her mother. Carrie is perfectly satisfied with the situation as she plans to make soup for Julian and help him recover.

Once again Hellman had a hit—in fact, one of her biggest. Robert Coleman's review was typical. Noting that the subject matter could have been depressing, he said that Hellman had leavened it with 'flashes of humour" and concluded by saying, "the play is exciting, electrifying theatre. From the rise of the curtain to its final fall, it is a stirring experience in play-going. It's the stimulating tonic that the Fabulous Invalid has been needing this season. A word of warning: rush to the Hudson box-office immediately if you expect to see it this year. It's a hit, hit, hit!" (" 'Toys in the Attic' Sure-Fire Hit" 346).

Most of the reviews were in this vein. Walter Kerr said that going to the theatre often made critics forget what good writing was like, but that Lillian Hellman reminded them. He described her work as "the splendor of straight-forward, uncompromised writing" ("Toys in the Attic" 348). Jason Robards, Irene Worth, Maureen Stapleton, and all the other actors were highly praised, and Anne Revere won a Tony. Arthur Penn's directing was also praised as was the setting by Howard Bay. The play won the Drama Critics Circle Award. It was made into a film in 1963 with a fine performance by Geraldine Page. The play is Hellman at her best and in recent years it has been performed in a number of theatres. A 1985 performance at Ashland, Oregon was praised as the best play of the season by Gerald Nachman. He noted the strong theatrical qualities of the play, the positive treatment of the black characters, and the fine opportunities Hellman provided for the actors ("Strong Staging of Hellman Play at Ashland" 3).

It seems unfortunate that Hellman's career didn't continue past her next play or stop with the success of *Toys in the Attic*. Her last play was an adaptation of Burt Blechman's novel *How Much*. In 1963 *My Mother, My Father and Me* opened. Hellman's biographer, Doris Falk, describes it as a fiasco, "an off-beat, zany, satirical comedy about middle-class Jews . . . alien to Hellman's talent" (84). The play focuses on the Halpern family. Their son is a failure, the grandmother lives with them, but has to be put into a home, and their apartment is open to all sorts of peculiar characters who wander in and out. The play is not really interesting enough to be puzzling, but what is puzzling is what made Hellman choose the material. The play lasted seventeen performances. One review will suffice to give the tone of the critical reaction. Robert Coleman's was headed "Lillian Hellman Play is Depressing Farce." He began by saying the play started "as though it were going to be fun, but rapidly deteriorated into tasteless, far-fetched and often depressing farce" and concluded by saying the large cast of twenty-eight "and the script have been too much for director Gower Champion to cope with" (303-304). The play seems to have been an attempt to write something in the vein of the Theatre of the Absurd which failed utterly.

In *Pentimento* Hellman discusses it very briefly. She said she still thought it was funny, and that although audiences would not accept the shift from farce to drama, she believed it was viable. This was the last time she was to sit in a hotel room making changes in a script. Bidding farewell to the theatre, she wrote, "The playwright is almost always held accountable for failure and that is almost always a just verdict. But this time I told myself that justice doesn't have much to do with writing and that I didn't want to feel that way again. For most people in the theatre whatever happens is worth it for the fun, the excitement, the possible rewards. It was once that way for me and maybe it will be again. But I don't think so" (209).

Four years after the failure of her last play Hellman told an old friend, "I don't like the theatre anymore and yet it is what I do best. I have cut myself away from it, don't go much, don't learn, don't even want to. And I am getting old and I can't understand how that happened to me" (*An Unfinished Woman* 207). Her writing career continued, but she never worked in the theatre again. Nevertheless, hers was a long career, from her first success in 1934 to the failure in 1963. Of her twelve plays, most were successful and she had more long runs than most other American playwrights. Her plays often utilized daring subject matter and she sought to bring integrity and social relevance to the theatre. Her treatment of black characters was ahead of its time and she provided a number of black actors with excellent roles. Not only did she earn awards, respect, critical acclaim, popular success and a great deal of money as a playwright, she was a successful director, and the only woman playwright to write successful screenplays of her own plays alone. She is generally considered the most important woman playwright of the first half of the century. She interacted with other women in the theatre of her own age, and was helpful to younger playwrights as she grew older. Although there are still many critics who consider her plays melodramatic and old-fashioned, Hellman is a sort of heroine to others. But proof of the theatrical effectiveness lies in the successful revivals of *The Little Foxes, The Autumn Garden, Toys in the Attic* and others. It should also be noted that several of the filmscripts she wrote, such as *Dead End* have been highly praised.

After her first ten years of playwriting, Barrett H. Clark wrote an overview of her work and summed up her purpose in writing:

> Though she never wrote a play merely to entertain an audience, to win fame, or to make money, she never wrote a line without trying to say something that would help man escape or offset the effects of ignorance and wrong thinking. In a word, she is an idealist and a philosopher. But, if that were all, she would hardly be worth talking about: she is also an artist, a playwright whose "message" is invariably, though not always, skilfully integrated into works which hold us by those qualities of truth without which all the good ideas in the mind of man are of no avail. ("Lillian Hellman" 127-8)

In *Critical Essays on Lillian Hellman*, Mark W. Estrin states,

> Arguably the most important American playwright next to O'Neill in the first half of this century, Hellman has been the subject of an astonishingly small number of book-length studies devoted exclusively to her work. That major symptom of critical condescension and neglect began to change significantly following the publication of her memoirs, by which time, however, primary attention was being addressed to the life-writing, not to the life in the theater. Hellman's plays deserve the sustained scholarly analysis that will extend the revisionist view initiated in this volume and restore her to her proper place in the American dramatic canon. A number of longer studies, most of which were published within the past decade, do suggest that the balance is finally being redressed. (8)

Summary

The women discussed in this section wrote plays from the turn of the century to the late fifties. Naturally, their work both reflected and influenced the volatile American society during this period. All of these writers were a major part of American theatre, not only in New York, but throughout the country. Plays toured through the United States to California and back. Plays such as Franken's *Claudia* were so successful that several touring companies were performing the play at the same time. Later, through the radio program "Theatre Guild on the Air," the publication of Burns Mantle's annual editions of best plays, and other media channels, Americans listened to and read plays by these American women. It is easy to imagine the anticipation in cities as diverse as New York, Columbus, Ohio, and Los Angeles when announcements appeared for new plays by Akins, Hellman, and the others. Their popularity indicated pride in American playwrights who were in competition with established British playwrights such as Arthur Wing Pinero, Somerset Maugham, and J. M. Barrie who had previously provided the leading roles for Ethel Barrymore, Maude Adams, and other stars. The women playwrights were part of the rapid development of American playwriting nurtured by such critics Stark Young, Joseph Wood Krutch, George Jean Nathan, Alexander Woolcott, and Kenneth Macgowan. In this development women playwrights played a major role. Their plays both documented and criticized the dynamic changes in American society.

Writing in 1910, Shirley Burns, herself a minor playwright, wrote, "This is the day of Woman in the theatre. More plays have been presented on the American stage in the past two years than ever before in a like period" (632). This explosion of playwriting by women took place at a time when women were constantly stereotyped both on and off the stage. An unidentified male writer assessed the successful careers of Rachel Crothers and other women writing in the period before 1920. He began by noting that women were acquiring distinction not only as playwrights, but as lawyers, physicians, and politicians: "The trend of the times is toward giving the reputed "fair" sex an opportunity to do things that have long been monopolized by men" (n.p.). The writer even conceded that, in contrast to the general "calumny that women have no sense of humor," they could write com-

edy very well. He then went on to note that, "Women like sentiment
. . . women, bless their hearts, have never wept so much that they cannot, on brief notification and any array of mournful fact, weep some
more. This persistent, perennially ready 'weepfulness' hails an undying
sentimentality that the feminine writer of plays can utilize and appeal
to" (n.p.). Given this perception of women, it was no wonder that surprise greeted the characterization and plotting in such plays as
Crothers' *A Man's World*, Glaspell's *The Verge*, Akins' *O, Evening Star*,
Ferber and Kaufman's *Dinner at Eight*, Franken's *Another Language*,
and Hellman's *The Children's Hour*.

Another stereotypical perception under which these playwrights
labored is indicated by the same critic who predicted that women
would always be second-class playwrights treating the lighter elements
of life:

> Women will achieve more and more success as writers of comedies and dramas.
> But they will never exclude men. In fact, I do not believe that the best, the
> most worthwhile plays will ever come from a woman's pen. The horrors of war
> have produced the inevitable reaction on the stage. We have had so many
> gruesome incidents paraded in print before our eyes, so much, indeed, of blood-
> shed and "hate" and bitterness, that women authors of frothy comedies and
> sentimental dramas are in the ascendent. We want to laugh as a relief from the
> miseries of world war. We want lovemaking to offset the slaughter of the bat-
> tlefields." (n.p.).

How surprised this writer would have been if he had lived long enough
to know that women discussed above won awards from the Pulitzer
Prize Committee and the Drama Critics Circle as the best plays of the
year and that their subject matter ranged far beyond froth and sentiment.

During this period women playwrights were facing stereotypical perception not only from male writers, but from women as well. As professional career women, they constantly faced the fact that they would be
judged not on the quality of their work alone, but on their relationship
to the accepted norm of feminine behavior and appearance. For
example, in 1919, Shirley Burns praised playwright Anne Crawford
Flexner for her "feminine qualities": "She is a most charming young
woman, with baby blue eyes, and has a soft little voice and a gentle
way with her that wins you immediately. And there is nothing about
her that suggests the professional woman. Your impulse would be to
place her in the center of a domestic picture and not to imagine her

anywhere else. She would be entirely at home, there, too, for she is the
mother of two lovely little girls" (635). Contrasting this description
were the women playwrights described above who created independent female characters, and who also presented images of independence, administrative abilities, and assertiveness in their lives and
careers.

These playwrights were mirroring the society of their time in the
plays and also taking part in the development of realism in the American theatre. In the nineteenth century the influence of Ibsen was clear
in the work of James A. Herne and other male writers. The influence
on Crothers and other twentieth century women playwrights is equally
clear and set them apart from the many women writing artificially contrived, conventional plays. As Abramson observed,

> It is not easy to imagine what it was like for Crothers when she began her career
> as a Broadway playwright. There were many women writing plays for Broadway
> at the turn of the century, so many that one Washington critic was quoted as
> saying: "Women don't write plays; they put them in a squirt gun and push the
> plunger." They were turning out plays written to formula for the stars of the
> day. To get an idea of how they were viewed by the newspapers, one need only
> notice that interviews with and articles about "lady playwrights" were often
> placed on the society page. . . . Rachel Crothers, Zoë Akins, Susan Glaspell,
> and a few others had to get off the society pages to be taken seriously as play-
> wrights. . . . As late as 1941, Charlotte Hughes wrote that "Rachel Crothers,
> Zoë Akins and Rose Franken are inordinately proud of being good housekeep-
> ers." (58-59)

In contrast to the authors producing facile entertainments, the
women playwrights discussed so far wrote plays which presented a truer
picture of life—particularly the life of American women. Friedman has
commented, "In the early part of the century, the insistence upon the
truth, the goal of verisimilitude, the 'desire to get closer to the fact' was
the dominant chord in American drama,and women playwrights did
not hesitate to draw upon the 'facts' of their lives as women" (74). In
the plays by Glaspell, Akins, Ferber, Crothers, Franken, and Hellman
the reality of change was presented.

As Stanley Cohen has written, between 1870 to 1920 the types of
jobs held by women changed radically. The numbers of ill-paid women
working in manufacturing (usually only until they married) dropped,
and the numbers of women "working as secretaries, stenographers,
typists, and clerks multiplied by ten." He also noted that women
"virtually took over the occupations of librarian, nurse, elementary

school teacher and telephone operator. . . . By 1920 more women were employed in white-collar jobs than in manufacturing" (100-101). Thus, plays in which women had a choice of a career or marriage, or a combination of both, were more realistic than conventional plays in which a woman's only choice, and her highest duty, was to be a good wife and mother. Many people were shocked or disgusted by Crothers' frank treatment of an independent woman in *A Man's World*, but the characterization appealed to those men and women who espoused social change and believed the theatre was an appropriate arena for the realistic depiction of the problems of American society.

Many other examples of theatrical realism mirroring the changes in society could be given, but let one more suffice. The traditional attitude toward divorce in American society was being undermined by the resolution of women to escape unacceptable marriages. In 1870 there were 29.6 divorces per thousand marriages. By 1900 the number had risen to 81 and by 1922 there were 131 divorces per thousand marriages and the number was rising. By 1929 71.3% of divorces were sought by women (Kolb 152). This change was reflected in such plays as Akins' Ibsenian drama, *Daddy's Gone a-Hunting*, Crothers' *Mary the Third* and *Let Us Be Gay*, Glaspell's *The Outside, The Verge*, and *Alison's House*, Ferber and Kaufman's *Dinner at Eight*, and many other plays by women.

Changes in career opportunities, relaxation of strict divorce laws, increased education, and other societal changes inform the realism which came to dominate the American stage, and to which women playwrights contributed through their personal visions of life. Thus, Glaspell presented her view of a woman who had murdered her husband in *Trifles*, a play deeply grounded in realistic details, Akins' turned Wharton's realistic novel of a woman judged as an "old maid" into a realistic period drama, moving in its central theme and its details, Edna Ferber showed in grim realism the plight of a woman who fulfills her perceived duty to her family by turning her back on any hopes of personal fulfillment in *The Eldest*, Rose Franken used both comedy and drama to reveal the position of the wives in *Another Language*, and Lillian Hellman dared to present her view of a society which drives a lesbian to her death in *The Children's Hour*.

Although women playwrights contributed to the development of realism and social drama, women discussed in this book were often involved in experimentation and avant-garde drama. Of the women discussed above, Glaspell and Akins must be praised for their daring, not always successful, plays which utilized Expressionism and other non-realistic forms. Free from commercial pressures, Glaspell was able to experiment with Expressionism and to direct successfully her own plays at the Provincetown Playhouse. In contrast, when Akins wrote plays for the Broadway stage, such as *The Varying Shore* and *The Furies*, she received a full blast of criticism. She altered the former play to a more realistic style, but the latter was a complete failure. Whatever the immediate result of the experimentation by these women, however, they created plays which broke the bounds of realism and led the way for women playwrights discussed below to write plays on innovative themes with non-realistic methods. Critics and directors need to be more aware of the purposeful use of non-realistic elements in plays by these women and appreciate them as experimental plays rather than condemning them as poor efforts at realistic drama.

Two final elements related to the careers of the six playwrights under discussion may be considered. As Kiper observed in 1914, in Crothers' play *A Man's World*, the significance lay not only in the innovative subject matter, but in the fact that the subject matter was presented as perceived by a woman: "*A Man's World* is honest, well-built drama, interesting to feminists not only because of its exposition of a modern sex-problem, but also because it is written by a woman—one who does not attempt to imitate the masculine view-point, but who sees the feminine experience through feminine temperament" (928). Friedman speaks of a "sense of sexual differentiation, a recognition of experience that may cause women to view themselves and the world differently from the way that men do" (75). While a man such as Augustus Thomas could present his vision of a woman's role in society through his observation of life, the women playwrights were writing of the changes they had both observed and *experienced*. This aspect, and the importance of their experience was noted as early as 1913 by critic Richard Burton, who wrote about the social, political, educational, and economic changes affecting the American woman: "Within our generation she has been and is undergoing a triple revolution in these particular aspects of life. . . . and although at present her political enfranchisement would seem the burning question, when it is settled, the political phases of her new life will be seen as one fact of that general evolution of the sex into social freedom in the broadest sense" (qtd. in Friedman 87).

One of the final elements which allowed the women playwrights to pursue questions of "social freedom," was the economic independence which they achieved through their playwriting. Crothers earned vast sums of money from 1910 to 1927, so that she was able to produce Akins' unusual play *Thou Desperate Pilot*. Unfortunately, the play lasted only a week, and "absorbed all Miss Crothers' ready money, put a mortgage upon her house and sent her some fifty-five thousand dollars into debt" (Forman 56). Dismayed, but undeterred, Crothers proceeded with her career and soon built up another fortune. Glaspell not only earned money with her plays and other writing, she was the major wage earner during her marriage to Cook. When her lover, Norman Matson, left her for another woman she was able to continue to support herself as she had always done. Akins, Ferber, Franken, and Hellman were similarly financially successful. The significance is not that these women became wealthy, but that despite changes in circumstances and various misfortunes in their lives, they were able control their lives through economic success usually enjoyed only by men. This enabled them to exist as models for other women, particularly aspiring women playwrights, and to infuse reality into their depictions of career women.

Another quality which is evident in all of these women is their deep concern for moral questions and their examination of appropriate responses on the part of both men and women to changes in society. These concerns led them to write plays which moved beyond concerns of feminism and a close examination of women's problems and opportunities. Their writing ranged over a wide area of subjects including race prejudice, difficulties of union organizers, homosexuality, problems created by war, and political questions. What Friedman wrote of Lillian Hellman applies to the others as well:

> Though Hellman has referred to herself as a "moral writer," these morals are often played out in a political arena. Her book *Scoundrel Time* is a subjective response, nevertheless, moral, to the McCarthy era, when she herself had been blacklisted. Although Hellman did not write a play that treated the issues raised by McCarthyism, her earlier plays have been considered controversial, politically charged drama. As Alan Lewis notes, "her plays of the 30s and 40s were, in some ways, a response to the Depression and World War II." Certainly the greed of the Hubbard family in *The Little Foxes* and *Another Part of the Forest*, and their exploitation of the poor, though portrayed at the turn of the century, reflect her concern with poverty and the rising industrial classes. (73)

Many of the plays analyzed here are still performed: *Trifles* has held the stage for 78 years and has recently been turned into a musical by Jean Marie Ackermann and Michael Cook ("Theatre and Social Change" 3): Hellman's *The Little Foxes* (also turned into an opera by Marc Blitzstein) has been revived frequently, is presently in the repertoire of a theatre in Riga, Latvia, and was presented with *Another Part of the Forest* by the Cleveland Playhouse in 1994; *Showboat*, closely based on Ferber's novel has just been revived by Harold Prince and her plays have become American classics. The Hunger Artists' 1993 production of *Stage Door* in Denver received particular praise for the characterization of women and its overall theatrical quality. Crothers' plays have not been revived often, but there is increasing interest in them and *He and She* attracted positive attention in a recent revival. Akins and Franken, both successful over a long period of years, deserve to be reevaluated both in analyses and through productions of their plays. Along with Hellman, Crothers, Glaspell, and Ferber, they showed that women were capable of creating major careers as playwrights, that they could successfully compete with male playwrights for awards and audiences, and that they could treat a wide range of subjects in a variety of styles.

PART TWO

Opportunities for African-American Women Playwrights by Ted Shine

This book focuses on women playwrights between 1900 and 1950, and includes several African-American women who sought through their works to present an honest portrayal of African-American life and characters. Prior to 1917 black characters created by white playwrights were basically self-effacing stereotypes, ridiculed for the sake of laughter. It was believed that this depiction might change following the successful presentaton of Ridgely Torrence's one-act plays, *The Rider of Dreams, Granny Maumee,* and *Simon the Cyrenian,* which presented African-American characters who emerged as real and believable. By the 1920s African-American artists were in a creative renaissance that produced an abundance of work that should have had a greater influence on the general perception of African-American art and artists, but that was certainly not the case as far as the playwright was concerned: ". . . there was the hope that if true black characters could be presented on stage, the old Negro stereotypes could be driven off the boards. However for another twenty years a kind of Gresham's law of the theatre was to prevail: bad characterization will drive out good" (Hatch and Shine 210).

As late as 1947, two years before the works in this book conclude, African-American stereotypes were still being used for the same purpose—laughter, as this excerpt from John Kirkpatrick's one-act farce, *She Married Well,* attests:

EDITH.   (Coming down from landing, carrying two glasses. There is a twinkle in her eye as she shuffles across the stage like a darkie and speaks with a Southern negro drawl) Iz y'all talkin' 'bout me? 'Cause ef you iz, somepun's wrong. (To Peterson, handing him one of the glasses) Heah you iz big boy. Give it to yer pappy!
SALLIE.   Louise!
EDITH.   (Blinking at her) Ma'am?
SALLIE.   *Louise!*
EDITH.   'Scuse me, lady, but you done made a mistake. "Louise" wuz de one you had las' week. 'Member? Me—Ah'm name Lillybelle Brown—one o' de *dark* Browns fum Mimphis, Tinnysee. (Kirkpatrick 37)

In this scene, Edith, a pretty twenty-two year-old white girl, has disguised herself, pretending to be a maid in order to impress her mother's guests.

Prior to the 1960s only a limited number of African-Americans were able to earn livings exclusively in theatre. The frustration of trying to find work led many to abandon theatre completely, others with degrees in theatre sometimes found work in public schools or colleges. This was fortunate, particularly for the Southern segregated schools since there usually was no qualified person to teach drama or to direct plays. Drama clubs were organized in these schools providing a creative and cultural outlet for the students. The major problem faced by these directors were the lack of facilities, technical support, and budgets. Lack of budget in most instances meant no budget at all. These same problems prevailed at many of the African-American colleges. Play selection became a problem. Administrators sometimes encouraged directors to select works that would not offend or enrage the audience, the superintendent or the Board, the latter two being exclusively white in most Southern and some Northern communities. If the director had freedom of choice in play selection, a popular Broadway play might be staged, or a classic, or perhaps an original work. If royalty was not available, groups sometimes created their own productions. These were generally special occasion events centered around a holiday such as Thanksgiving or Independence Day, and used the talents of a large number of students including the band and the choir. They could be structured as pageants with a narrator and a series of scenes. Other original productions might be in the form of variety shows consisting of skits with a connecting theme, and focusing on the talent of the participants. These original productions often received greater response from the audience than did legitimate plays since the audience could relate directly to what was being said and done, and because the subject matter and characters were drawn from their own experiences.

Directors wanting to do plays by and about African-Americans found that very few scripts were available prior to the sixties. The NAACP and the National Urban League attempted to remedy this by sponsoring playwriting contests, and publishing winning plays. Both organizations aimed to "define directions and to encourage artistic productions," (Fabré 214) the NAACP in *Crisis*, the Urban League in *Opportunity*. These magazines were major sources for the publication and distribution of plays by African-American playwrights during the 1920s and 30s.

The 1920s also saw a number of African-American community the-atres developing with the purpose of presenting the works of black playwrights to counter the stereotypical portrayals that had dominated the American stage since the eighteenth century. Since the original plays that they produced were seldom published, directors who might have presented them did not know that they existed, and if they did know, it was often difficult to obtain a copy of the script. The same held true for the playwright seeking a production. Unless the writer lived in the immediate area, there was no way of knowing that these companies solicited original scripts.

Montgomery Gregory, Alain Locke, Marie Moore-Forrest, and Cleon Throckmorton organized the Howard University Players in 1921 with the following aim: ". . . to establish on an enduring basis the foundations of Negro drama through the institution of a dramatic labo-ratory where Negro youth might receive sound training in the arts of the theatre. The composition of original race plays formed the pivotal element in the project" (Locke 158). Since its inception the Howard Players have always placed a great deal of emphasis on playwriting. The founders and other faculty members who followed them such as Sterling Brown, James Butcher, Anne Cooke-Reid, John Lovell, and Owen Dodson, heartily encouraged and nurtured the writing talents of students.

Owen Dodson's playwriting class attracted students from all disci-plines, as well as individuals from the city who came to Howard just to enroll in his course. Students were required to bring in vignettes each Thursday which were read and critiqued in class. These assignments provided students with opportunities to perfect dialogue, characteriza-tion, plot structure, or any specific aspect of playwriting that they were particularly concerned with at that time. In addition to these weekly assignments, students were working on their final assignment for the semester, the completion of a one-act play. Although most of these plays were originals, adapations were permissible. The instructor worked with each student individually on the development of her/his play. At the end of the semester each play was read and evaluated before the class. Three or four of the best works would be selected for production, or given staged readings. Students at an advanced level worked on full-length plays.

This type of playwriting activity was taking place at other African-American colleges under the guidance of playwrights and directors.

Prominent among these individuals are Randolph Edmonds, Thomas Pawley, Fannin Belcher, Carlton Molette, Joan Lewis, Alexander Marshall, Ethell Pitts, Allen Williams, Robert West and Glenda Dickerson.

Randolph Edmonds was the motivating force behind the development of the Negro Intercollegiate Dramatic Association and the Southern Association of Drama and Speech Arts, both professional organizations in theatre for African-American colleges. Original plays by students and faculty were presented at their annual conventions, which was another way of making new scripts available for production.

The impact that drama has had on the African-American community, particularly in the Southern states, can be directly attributed to the theatre programs established at African-American colleges. These colleges not only introduced theatre to communities where none existed, but they also provided training for aspiring playwrights and offered opportunities for their work to be seen. Graduates of these colleges returned to their communities establishing drama clubs in schools, recreation centers, and churches. For the first time African-American audiences were able to see themselves, their lives and experiences on stage in comedies, tragedies, musicals, and melodramas with a kind of honesty that radio and film had never offered—*real* African-American life as seen through the eyes of African-Americans.

The African-American women included in this work were a part of this movement to change the image of blacks on the American stage. The characters that they created were drawn from all facets of African-American life; from the illiterate poor to the middle class sophisticate, and from both Northern and Southern regions of the country. They are bound, no matter what their class or where they are from, by the humiliating effects that racism inflicted on their lives. None of these women's primary interest was playwriting, and although their works have merit, Sterling Brown felt that three of them, Georgia Douglas Johnson, Eulalie Spence, and May Miller, were "apprentices" who were disadvantaged because they had no laboratory theatre where they could see their plays performed (Brown 128). Marita Bonner's militant voice foreshadows the protest works of Martie Charles, James Baldwin, Sonia Sanchez, Amiri Baraka, and Aishah Rahman, that accompanied the civil rights struggle of the sixties. The controversy concerning the appropriate language for African-American characters, whether the dialect in the folk plays of Zora Neale Hurston, or the "raceless" dialogue used by Alice Dunbar-Nelson, appears to have given way to a new concern: has dialogue become *too* naturalistic, *too* offensive today. Apparently so, since many colleges and community theatres, including professional ones do not hesitate to change the language in plays if they believe that it would offend their audiences. All of these women paved the way for the African-American playwrights that followed them: Lorraine Hansberry, Alice Childress, Adrienne Kennedy, Judi Mason, Endesha Ida Mae Holland, Celeste Walker, proving that plays could as simple, complex, or diverse as the artist's imagination allowed so long as *truth* was the source from which the work sprang.

Clare Kummer (1873?-1958)

Clare Kummer (1873?-1958) was described early in her playwriting career as a writer of mad, nonsensical plays—Alexander Woolcott referred them as an exemplification of "this very madness" ("Good Gracious, Annabelle!" 9). Her first play was directed by the noted producer Arthur Hopkins who described Kummer as "An Alice in Wonderland sort of person." Kummer said that probably meant that she saw life from a "fanciful point of view" (Mullett, "Clare Kummer's Experience" n.p.). Her career as a playwright did not begin until she was about thirty-nine years old, but she had been preparing for it for many years.

Kummer was born Clare Rodman Beecher, the grand-daughter of a minister, and related to Henry Ward Beecher and Harriet Beecher Stowe. She grew up in a happy home filled with artistic endeavors such as amateur theatricals. Her mother was described as brilliant and fascinating, and Clare apparently inherited these same characteristics. An amateur theatre club was organized in the home, so Clare was in contact with actors and would-be actors and met William Gillette as a young girl (Kummer, "The Essence of Drama" n.p.) Clare married Frederick Kummer, but later divorced him. She turned to writing songs in order to earn a living and became famous for "Dearie" which sold 1,000,000 copies of sheet music in 1906 (Osnes 103). In addition to writing songs, she worked as a play reader and polished up many plays before she turned to writing them herself. Having written some bits of dialogue for musicals, she proceeded to adapt a musical based on a German operetta with two collaborators in 1912. This encouraged her to continue and she wrote an original libretto for a musical. Arthur Hopkins decided to produce it as a straight play and in October 1916 *Good Gracious, Annabelle!* scored a major success. She proceeded to write other comedies until 1944. Initially acclaimed as fresh and original, Kummer never mastered plot construction and failed to change her style, despite changes in the theatre and in society, so her later plays were perceived as dull and silly. Writing in 1938 in an article headed, "She Used to Write Delightful Comedies," Arthur Pollock wrote, "Miss Kummer's plays used to be delightful, irresponsible little things full of strange quirks and comical irrelevancies. They began an era of graceful nonsense in the American theatre. The theatre has now gone on to other things, but that is no reason Miss Kummer should not continue to write plays" ("Spring Thaw" n.p.). The reasons for the failures of her later plays will be considered below.

After her divorce, Kummer married Henry Arthur whose cousin was William Gillette. Kummer wrote one her her most successful plays, A Successful Calamity, for Gillette, whom she called "uncle" (Mullet n.p.). The British actor, Roland Young, appeared in Kummer's first play, and after that in many roles she tailored to develop his understated comic style. (This was later displayed to perfection in the Topper movies and the television series.) After Young acted with Kummer's daughter, Marjorie, in Rollo's Wild Oat, they married, so Kummer was writing roles for her son-in-law for many years. After her early successes, Kummer went to Hollywood to write a few films for Fox Studios, but she soon returned to the theatre.

Kummer's plays never won awards, but two of her plays were selected for the best plays volumes. For many years her plays were greeted with excitement and she was considered one of the brightest hopes for the American theatre in her first decade of playwriting. The central characters in her plays were often charming, unconventional young women who were similar to the playwright, herself. Writing about her Annabelle, Kummer asked, "Have I made Annabelle sweetly irresistible, loveable, and yet worldly wise? For that is what I tried to do. I have met many girls like Annabelle. She is an American type. She could exist nowhere except in this funny land of extremes" ("Clare Kummer Wins Success" n.p.).

Kummer's first straight play was typical of most of her work: she started with a funny situation, created whimsical characters, moved them through a fairly simple plot with funny scenes (usually based on misunderstandings), and created hilarious comedy with her dialogue. In Good Gracious, Annabelle, Annabelle Leigh finds herself without money and she and some other artistic, penniless friends try to find someone to pay for their lunch in a hotel restaurant. Hearing that a millionaire needs to hire servants for his country home, Annabelle passes herself and her friends off as cooks, gardeners, etc. and they all look forward to a splendid summer. The situation is complicated by the fact that the butler, anticipating the absence of the millionaire from his Long Island home, has rented it. The situation provided many opportunities for scenes of comic misunderstandings, and all comes right in the end when Annabelle falls in love with the rich renter, who turns

out to be a man she had previously married under peculiar circumstances.

When the maid Lottie questions Annabelle about her life and her
friends (disguised as servants), she wants to know why Mrs. Jennings
slept with Annabelle instead of her (supposed) husband. The
exchange between them is full of non sequitors and humorous elements.

> Annabelle.   Oh, yes—it was on my account. I was nervous—yes—when I'm in
> a new place I'm apt to think of Mr. Postlethwaite.
> Lottie.   Oh—your poor, dear husband, I suppose. . . . Didn't he treat you
> right, or is he dead?
> Annabelle.   (After a moment's hesitation) Both.
> Lottie.   Don't we poor women have it hard? But what can we do but just
> go on and do the best we can? (Takes a nip from a bottle she
> carries in her pocket, and explains as Annabelle sees her) It's just
> a little headache cologne.
> Annabelle.   And do you swallow it, Lottie?
> Lottie.   It acts quicker. (53)

When the owner of the house returns, he is surprised by his new staff,
in particular the pretty cook, Annabelle. Getting a little worried, she
has the following conversation with him:

> Annabelle.   Mr. Wimbledon, you must think me a very strange cook—
> Wimbledon.   They're all strange, if you ask me. I think you're a dashed
> good-looker!
> Annabelle.   Don't you get the idea that I may have seen better days?
> Wimbledon.   No. You never saw a better day in your life than this—and I
> never did. (77)

After the play opened, Kummer was the toast of the town, with
everyone asking who she was and where had she come from. The critics were generally dazzled by the great fun of the play, Arthur Hopkins'
direction, the beautiful setting by Robert Edmond Jones, and the acting. Critics considered it an "all-around success" in which Hopkins was
sharp enough to recognize "the nonsense note in the farce and emphasize it" ("Kummer's Success" n.p.). Woolcott wrote, "Its appeal lies not
only in flash after flash of distinctly feminine wit, but in this very madness. . . . Her airy and very feminine wit is quite her own, and it is just
because she uses none of the familiar formulas that her work is so hard
to measure and describe" ("Good Gracious, Annabelle!" 9). Charles
Collins, writing from a man's point of view, wrote, "The truly feminine

sense of humor, as a rule, is too subtle, indirect and delicate for successful expression in the theatre; this Miss Kummer, however, is the exceptional case. This piece alone would mark her as a decidedly unusual lady. . . . Here is winsome humor beside which the pranks of the average farce are merely vulgar clowning" ("Ideas on Stage Affairs" n.p.). Heywood Broun gave a warning note in his review. Noting that her work had been compared to Carroll and Wilde, he suggested that her story line was deficient in logic and that characters such as the Red Queen and Algernon are passionately logical—the fun "lies in the successful invention of plausible reasons for doing preposterous things." He concluded his review by saying, "Miss Kummer is often deficient in justifying the mad actions of her characters, and there is every bit as much need for motivation in farce as in more serious dramatic endeavor. Nevertheless and notwithstanding, we laughed a great deal at 'Good Gracious, Annabelle'" ("Good Gracious, Annabelle" n.p.) An anonymous critic was even more negative about the weakness of the plot, saying that the author "does not even know enough about the craft of making plays to motivate the entrances and exits of her characters . . . and [it] is about as bad a play as one could see." Despite its plot, however, the critic agreed with everyone that Kummer had provided a delightful evening in the theatre because of the dialogue. Betraying his male vantage point, he enthused, "Mrs. Kummer writes as some women talk,—the sort of women that one goes a second time to see" ("Good Gracious, Annabelle!" *Vogue*, n.p). The capstone to Kummer's surprising conquest of Broadway was the selection of the play as one of the ten best plays written between 1909 and 1919 for the first volume of Burns Mantle's best plays series. This selection was from literally hundreds of plays.

Kummer was quick to capitalize on her success. In six weeks she wrote a play with a starring role for "uncle" Gillette. *A Successful Calamity* is again a simple story populated with amusing characters. He played a brilliantly successful millionaire businessman whose smart young son and daughter spend money recklessly, and whose young second wife insists on fancy clothes, jewelry, and a night on the town every night. In order to get a quiet night at home with his family, he takes a tip from his butler's comment that the poor don't get many nights out, and tells his family he is ruined. They all feel sorry for him and want to help. Mrs. Wilton says, "Isn't it a good thing we bought the new car, for now we can sell it and get almost as much as we paid for it!" and he answers "I hadn't thought of that. What a pity I didn't buy half a dozen of them." (29) Kummer tailored the role of Wilton to Gillette's famous dry sense of humor. At one point his character tells a nosy maid, "Your habit of listening at doors is not a desirable one. I knew a man who tripped over a girl listening at a door and hurt himself very badly" (59). In the end several misunderstandings are straightened out. Mrs. Wilton clears away the suspicion that she is romantically interested in a bohemian artist doing her portrait and reveals her love for her husband by pawning her jewels. The basic family problem is also cleared up when she reveals that she wants to stay home, too, but a venomous friend had told her she was too dull and uninteresting to keep her husband unless she took him out to parties all the time. By the last scene everything is very merry in the Wilton household.

Everything was very merry for Clare Kummer, too. She had two hits running in the same season and was in the foreground of women dramatists. Audiences and critics who had loved her first comedy were even more pleased by this one. One critic praised the fact that she turned a potentially sentimental play into a comedy, because "she handles it in a vein of bantering and almost gossamer burlesque, with a unique and individual wit." He went on to praise the "beautiful simplified settings by Robert Edmond Jones and said, "The whole affair is a delight to the mind and the senses" (Unidentified clipping Lincoln Center). Hopkins was praised for his work, and, in turn, praised his playwright, saying, "Not in years has a fresher or more individual sense of humor found voice in the American theatre" (qtd. in "Gillette Returns in a Brilliant Play" 10). Another critic quoted chunks of dialogue to support his contention that, "Better than any other native author she can reproduce the repartee of the drawing room and can spin gossamers of humorous small-talk. Keen observation and a fine sense of nonsense are reflected in the conversation" ("Clare Kummer's Smart Dialog, n.p.). Many critics noted the special qualities required to play Kummer's characters, and the superb mating of the actors Hopkins had chosen with the roles. In particular Estelle Winwood, Roland Young, and William Gillette were praised. An unidentified critic made an analysis of the acting approach required to perform Kummer well:

> First the actor has to create a character quite seriously and realistically, or the play has no solid base. Then, without getting out of this character, he has to speak the lines, which often poke ironic fun at the very character he is creating, as if he didn't know they were funny. . . . Mr. Gillette knows how to play it, too,

quite solemnly and seriously creating his character and never disclosing in any way that he knows what he says and does is funny. He plays with that double edge so necessary to the art of the acting of ironic or fantastic drama. (Unidentified clipping Lincoln Center)

The play was such a success that it ran through the summer (without air-conditioning) into the fall, and then Gillette performed it on tour. When it left New York, Kummer was ready with a replacement called *The Rescuing Angel* (1917). This was not the success which had been expected by Kummer and audiences. Critics noted that it had much of the charm as her earlier plays, but not enough. There was also considerable disappointment in the leading role performed by Billie Burke: "Alas, Miss Burke is not William Gillette! She has not the faintest conception how to act it, or, at any rate, the technical ability to do so" (Unidentified clipping Lincoln Center). The play ran for only three weeks. For the modern reader, this is no surprise. The first act is very slow and the character played by Billie Burke is not fanciful and amusing, but peculiar and artificial.

Kummer was undeterred and came back with a better play in 1918 called Be Calm, Camilla! She was in the front ranks of American playwrights and critics wrote at length about her style. The "nonsense" in the play was generally recognized by the critics as something unusual and delightful. Many tried to analyze the nature of her comedies and what made them rise above her pedestrian construction. She was compared to Lewis Carroll, Edward Lear, J.M. Barrie, Wilde, and Shaw. In a lengthy analysis in 1918, an anonymous critic wrote, "To write such comedy successfully, you have to be something of a genius as were Barrie, W.S. Gilbert, Wilde, and Shaw" and continued by saying that all of those writers were individual and readily identifiable. "And the work of Miss Kummer impresses you in the same way. Her wit and her mimic world are her own. She is as individually flavored as Wilde or Barrie." In trying to analyze Kummer's comedy and place it in a genre, this critic concluded, "It is most assuredly not farce, but is is just as surely not comedy as we have traditionally known comedy in our theater. Perhaps 'fantastic comedy' describes it as well as any tag can do (Unidentified clipping Lincoln Center). John Corbin was another critic who tried to analyze Kummer's comic technique: "[She] has a style all her own. Of ideas she seems guiltless, and also of wit in any ordinary acceptance of the word. The laughter which her plays evoke (and it is incessant) is not a matter of epigram, or of phrase-making of any sort, but of the subtle yet inerrant revelation of human nature" ("Sentimental Comedy" n.p.). Other critics noted the difficulty of indicating the comedy by quoting lines, since the lines were generally only funny in context—because they were out of context, in effect. Much of the comedy arose from non sequiturs or lines which were unexpected in terms of the situation.

In *Be Calm, Camilla!*, Kummer again created a lively, charming heroine. The play was dubbed a Cinderella story by many critics because it told the tale of a down-and-out would-be piano player who comes to New York to make a success, but hasn't the talent. Dazed by hunger, she is run into by a wealthy man in an automobile, who puts her into a luxurious hospital to recover, then takes her to his camp in the woods. Here Kummer chose to introduce a switch in the Cinderella story: by now Camilla is in love with him, but he is married. Interestingly, Kummer defied tradition by having her heroine pursue her man until he got a divorce in order to marry her. Critics pointed to an incipient sentimentality, but most felt she avoided it by the continual comic dialogue. John Corbin and others praised not only the dialogue, but the characterization. He wrote,

> The amazing thing about it is that the people in the story are the freshest, the most authentic that have appeared on our stage since the previous plays of Clare Kummer. Every character in it is acutely felt and distinctly realized, down to the last word and accent. If the heroine's conduct seems bizarre and strange—well, it is congenital to her. Even in childhood her mother taught her, when beset by emotional storm and stress, to grasp her bosom and say: "Be calm, Camilla!" ("Sentimental Comedy" n.p.)

The critical response indicated that Kummer had maintained her good qualities, and that her plotting had improved. The critic for the *Christian Science Monitor* wrote that her new play "shimmers with all the charm of "Good Gracious, Annabelle." and "A Successful Calamity," and is marred by none of the faults of "The Rescuing Angel" ("Be Calm, Camilla" n.p.). The critic for *Vogue* praised the play as a whole and the fact that Kummer had created "more than half a dozen characters that seem astonishingly true to life." He went on to praise the acting, the winning combination of Kummer, Hopkins, and Jones, and, at great length, the dialogue: "A wise and witty woman has felt herself impelled to talk; and we are very glad to listen. '*C'est une originale*'" ("Be Calm, Camilla" n.p.). Heywood Broun noted improvement saying the play was either the best performance or the brightest play in town, or perhaps both. "Kummer has gone beyond 'Annabelle' or 'A Successful Calamity' in her new comedy." He felt the difference lay in an improved story line, and "glints in its gayety of things which are not so gay" ("'Be Calm, Camilla' Marks New Best for Clare Kummer" n.p.)

Astonishingly, Kummer followed up the success of *Camilla!* with yet another hit, Rollo's Wild Oat. This play with its amusing title provided Roland Young an opportunity to display his comic ability fully. (His role in *Calamity* was good, but small.) Rollo is perfectly willing to go into business as his wealthy grandfather wishes, but he wants to sow one wild oat first. He rents a Broadway theatre, hires a stage manager and a company and prepares to play Hamlet. His stage manager is definitely reluctant, suspiciously asking about his new ideas for the play. In response to Rollo's suggestion for "extreme simplicity" he responds, "It's been done to death. Unless you've got some new kind" (14). Rollo also wants steps leading to the audience so that any "gifted auditor" can join in—he doesn't want to be separated from his audience. But Stein says, "It's a good thing to be separated from them, Mr. Webster. It ain't the gifted ones usually that want to join in" (15).

The scene of the rehearsal is very funny and complicated by the fact that Rollo's sister, Lydia (pretending not to be his sister), is to play the Prologue, and that Rollo's attraction to the Ophelia is rebuffed because she thinks Lydia is Rollo's mistress. On the opening night, just as he launches into his big speech, Goldie as Ophelia, rushes onstage to tell him his grand-father is dying and they leave the cast flat. All turns out well, however, as the impresario went to the runway "and asked 'Is there a Hamlet in the house?' the response was almost unanimous, and a favorable comment on the classical education of our English speaking public" (104). When the role was actually taken by Rollo's valet, the house went into an uproar as the play was "the biggest laughing hit in the world" (105). In the end Rollo realizes that the world was saved from another bad actor and reconciles himself to life without Hamlet, but not without Goldie. She is so moved to learn that Lydia is his sister and that he wants to marry her that she bursts into tears. He starts to propose, but concludes, "I'll ask you to marry me again when we both feel more like it" (116).

Kummer's gentle satire on the urge of many non-actors to act, and the urge of most of them to play Hamlet had great appeal. Most of the reviews read like those of her earlier successes. The critics praised the overall effect, the dialogue, the acting, and the general sense of fun, but noted that the structure was not all it could have been. Kenneth Macgowan, a very intelligent critic usually inclined toward experimental drama, praised the play saying "of such absurd and highly intelligent stuff is the humor of Miss Kummer" and concluded, "It is charming and elusive art; twinkling rather than brilliant, all the more delightful because its casual, modest little jokes seem always trying to escape you" ("Clare Kummer and Roland Young at the Best" n.p.) Burns Mantle noted, "Few writers of comedy can fuse the real with the ridiculous as gracefully as Clare Kummer" and called her many fans "Kummerites" ("Rollo's Wild Oat" n.p.). Several critics suggested that Kummer had killed the mother-in-law joke because of the role she had written for Young: "No star ever had a better fitting vehicle for his talent" ("Clare Kummer's Comedy" n.p.). Writing a few weeks after the opening, Alexander Woolcott praised Kummer for her delicious and original sense of comedy, commenting particularly about the distinctive quality of the dialogue. He also said that in the midst of her feather-light touch, she successfully introduced intelligent criticism about the general acting of Shakespeare's plays ("Second Thoughts on First Nights"1).

Despite the praise, the critics were starting to expect more from Kummer and to comment on her failure to improve the structure of her plays. An anonymous critic noted that despite the great laughter, the play just didn't have enough plot ("'Rollo's Wild Oat' Has Suggestion" n.p.) The critic for the *Christian Science Monitor* tried to analyze the failure of Kummer to write really first-class comedy. He concluded that the problem was that the clever dialogue was "only a casing that covers a mechanical plot and persons" ("Rollo's Wild Oat" n.p.). Rebutting that type of comment was the critic writing under the pseudonym "The Highbrow" who said that although people could find fault with the structure, Kummer was a fool to listen to them because "every dialogue spoken in public that pleases an intelligent audience is a play. . . . The wiseacres will continue to declare that they are not plays. Who cares? Miss Kummer can afford to be at ease. She has an authentic and original talent. That is the best thing there is" ("'Rollo's Wild Oat' at the Punch and Judy Theatre" n.p.). That was the worst sort of criticism Kummer could get—she must have been aware of her lack of ability in structuring a play. After all, she had had no training and there had always been negative comments about her plotting. But the success of this play overshadowed any negative criticism and according to one critic, she had written "the most original play of her remarkable career" and was "safely enthroned in the heights of play-writing" ("Rollo's Wild Oat," unidentified clipping Lincoln Center n.p.).

Kummer spent some time in Hollywood, then assisted Florenz Ziegfeld with a musical version of *Good Gracious, Annabelle*. His wife, Billie Burke, scored a success in this Kummer play in the title role of Annie. In 1926 Ernest Truex helped Kummer's highly contrived play *Pomeroy's Past* to receive good reviews and a fair run. But it was not until 1933 that Kummer had another major success. Kummer had no plays on Broadway for several seasons, then in September 1933 her play *Amourette* opened to negative reviews. It was a "warmed-over vaudeville skit called 'The Choir Singer'" (Mantle, *Best Plays of 1933-1934* 256) which did not occupy much of Kummer's time as she was occupied with her next one. It ran for only twenty-two performances and was so memorably disappointing that critics attended Kummer's play which opened in October with some reluctance.

Fortunately, *Her Master's Voice* was a delightful play which made up for *Amourette*. The plot deals with Ned Farrar who has married a would-be opera singer, Queena. They are both unhappy as the play begins as they have little money, the mother-in-law is visiting (that must have been an amusing in-joke), and Ned Farrar has lost his job. "It wasn't a very good job anyway—I only made just enough for us not to get along on.... I can get something just as bad—maybe worse" (15) Queena's imperious, wealthy aunt swoops in and takes Queena away for a rest and a return to a singing career. She mistakes Ned for a servant, and unknown to Queena, hires him. Also unknown to his wife is the fact that Mr. Twilling, head of a radio station, wants Ned to have a career as a singer. After many scenes of misunderstanding and disguise, Ned succeeds as a singer, and the couple is reunited. The charm of the play is enhanced by some romantic songs. The play was carefully produced by Max Gordon and brought Roland Young and Laura Hope Crews back from Hollywood.

Richard Lockridge's review was typical: "A continuously diverting comedy, worthy to be the vehicle which brings back Laura Hope Crews and Roland Young to the stage." Noting that Kummer had filled the play with disguises and tricks, he concluded, "She has, unimpaired, the light and pretty wit of old. The evening is a feathery pleasure for those who will be content with feathers" ("Her Master's Voice" n.p.) During the dark times of the Depression, many were, indeed, content with feathers. Brooks Atkinson said, "The world in which Miss Kummer dwells is bright and pleasant, secure from the realities that vex most of us. Her people speak in a bubbly brand of nonsense. It is good to hear it again" ("Her Master's Voice" 24). John Mason Brown noted that it was hard to believe she wrote *Amourette* after seeing this "ingratiating trifle acted with unusual skill." He noted, as did most of the critics, that the play was "slight as her better comedies are apt to be, but as felicitious a bit of fooling as it is her special talent to produce when her dialogue is at its giddiest" ("Max Gordon Presents" n.p.). Gilbert W. Gilbert said there was hardly any plot but he didn't care because it was so pleasing and funny, "a really beautiful brand of humor midway between sympathy and absurdity." He contrasted it to *Amourette,* "a period play with old beaver hats and lace bodices" ("Her Master's Voice" n.p.). Burns Mantle joined heartily in the chorus of approval, praising her as mistress of "the sly and the subtle, the smart and the observing, the human and the hilarious lines and situations that have previously given quality and wholesomeness to her stage writing" ("Bright New Clare Kummer Farce" n.p.) He went on to include it as one of the year's ten best plays in his annual volume.

Clare Kummer enjoyed this triumph. She was now sixty years old and still capable of creating funny situations and dialogue which relieved the gloom of the Depression. However, it was the last time she was able to produce work at this level. In 1936 Max Gordon produced her new comedy *Spring Thaw.* Even the presence of Roland Young could not warm up the audience to this story of a woman who runs off with a composer, but later returns with the composer to her husband's bed. Many critics punned on the title and noted the wintery reception the play received. Richard Lockbridge observed that the author had had trouble with the plot out of town and had done a great deal of rewriting, but all to little avail ("Spring Thaw" n.p.). John Mason Brown summed up the reaction to to play by calling it "one of the season's silliest and most unsmiling scripts" (" 'Spring Thaw'" n.p.). Even Roland Young was criticized, and as the lover, Guido Nadzo was singled out for criticism, with most of the critics unable to resist George S. Kaufman's old pun "Guido Nadzo is nadzo guido." By now Kummer was unable to overcome "her old-time frailties" with enough comedy (Watts, "Unhappy Spring" n.p.). The play ran only eight performances.

Kummer was at the end of her successful career. Yet, she made one more effort. When *Many Happy Returns* opened in 1945, Kummer was seventy-one and had been writing for the stage for thirty-three years. Her play was intended as a vehicle to return Mary Astor to the stage. The story of a woman who flirts with a son because she is in love with the father was a complete disaster. It ran only three performances and was a dismal end to a bright career.

Kummer made important contributions to the theatre. She was notable in her original, difficult-to-categorize comedy—and notable that she was a woman writing successful comedies. Writing in 1990 for a conference on women and humor, Beth Osnes summed up Kummer's style by saying,

> Clare Kummer's humor created authentic nonsense that brought to the fore-front, in a most delightful way, a world view that acknowledged the seeming absurdity of the human situation, but maintained a dignified and sincere cast of characters. She seems to endorse faith in impulses as the best indicator of what to do when and where. Perhaps more comedy of this type could ease our ratio-nal minds from the need to understand the incomprehensible, and to give order to disorder and nonsense. Escapism? Or is it a conscientious, and perhaps giddy, form of enlightenment. ("Good Gracious, Miss Kummer!" 106-7)

At her best Kummer was an excellent comic writer, but not as good as she might have been. Her best full-length comedies and her one-acts which were successfully performed in vaudeville provide the mod-ern reader with great entertainment. Her abilities and her flaws were analyzed by Richard Watts, Jr. when he reviewed *Spring Thaw:*

> It is not that we expect much of a plot from Miss Kummer. In her past suc-cesses, such as "Good Gracious, Annabelle!," "A Successful Calamity," and "Rollo's Wild Oat," she revealed little interest in story but considerable talent for a friendly, easy-going sort of whimsicality that seldom quite slipped over into excessive archness. She could draw pleasantly scatter-brained characters and set them down in situations that were serviceable, if not striking. At her best she was capable of a brightly humorous sort of gay chatter that often seemed brilliant and epigramatic, particularly when spoken by Mr. Young. Yet in *Spring Thaw* she reveals all of her old-time frailties, without any of her erstwhile skill. ("Unhappy Spring" n.p.)

Along with the problem of weak plotting, there was the problem of increasing familiarity. Even as late as *Her Master's Voice* her characters were still perceived as fresh and delightful, but by her last two plays they had become conventional and familiar, particularly with Roland

Young playing basically the same type each time. John Anderson wrote that the audience had seen all these characters before, "They are old retainers in the play factory and deserve a pension." He went on to blame Kummer for her poor plot and concluded, "I'm having a relapse from merely writing about it" ("Spring Thaw" n.p.).

Beginning her career late in life, Kummer nevertheless delighted audiences and critics for many years. Writing in 1941, Freedley and Reeves stated that "Among the comic writers of a generation ago, none of the men . . . was able to reach the sheer delight of the dialogue of Clare Kummer" (586). Along the way she earned a great deal of money from her songs and plays. She began when many comedies were sleazy plays which invited a leer rather than a laugh, and she was often praised for the wholesomeness of her comedies. She was able to create many comic characters and to write amusing dialogue without resort-ing to cheap, salacious effects. Her plays did not relate to the changing situation for women except in presenting several dynamic young American women like Annabelle and Camilla. In fact, it was charac-teristic of her plays not to relate to the actuality of American society at all—in a way, the plays are less dated than those of her contemporaries on that account. Her creation of a world of comedy which did not relate to social problems was praised, rather than criticicized. The critic for *Vogue* wrote, "Her plays are all the more delightful because they are not weighted down with any purpose more serious than to amuse the public by the momentary flashing of flitting sidelights on humanity" ("Be Calm, Camilla" n.p.). Despite her success, after her last plays Kummer was virtually forgotten except for an unpublished dissertation (Finizio). There are no entries for her in either the *Cambridge Guide to the American Theatre* or *The Oxford Companion to the Theatre*. Not until the publication of *Notable Women in the American Theatre* was her career examined in recent times. Noting both her good and bad quali-ties, Duskey Loebel concluded, "In her day Kummer's work was both distinctive and popular enough for Alexander Woollcott to claim that she was 'the only American playwright with a style so recognizable that you could spot her authorship by listening to a single scene'" (516). It is really unfortunate that Kummer did not, or could not, heed the voices of warning and develop an ability to write a well-structured comedy which supported the characters and the dialogue. Plot is not only the soul of tragedy, it is the underpinning of the classic comedies. Kummer was a good playwright, but if she had mastered the technique of play construction, she would have been one of America's finest comic playwrights. Writing in an age in which there was actually an article entitled, "Do Women Have a Sense of Humor?", Kummer convinced critics and audiences that women could be as funny, or funnier than men. Her best works still move the reader to laughter and could be performed successfully today.

Josephine Preston Peabody (1874-1922)

Josephine Preston Peabody (1874-1922) was one of the earliest women to achieve notable success writing for the American theatre. She was primarily a poet and wrote only a few plays. However, she achieved fame throughout the world for her play *The Piper,* a retelling of the legend of the Pied Piper of Hamelin. Her other poetic dramas were important and highly visible elements in the struggle against the domination of realism in the theatre.

Peabody was raised in Brooklyn, New York. Both her father, Charles Peabody and her mother, Susan Morrill Peabody lavished time on Josephine and her sisters in a home in which beauty, courtesy, music, poetry, and theatre were all important. In later life Peabody spoke of the major role theatre played in the family discussions:

> Our father and mother saw all the great actors and all the best plays. It was interesting even to us children to hear them discuss the contrasts in the acting of Modjeska and Bernhardt or the psychological differences in the Hamlet of Booth and Fechter. They saw the same plays repeatedly, always from the standpoint of criticism and analysis, and my mother said they had seen "Richelieu" at least ten times and she could not remember how many times "Hamlet." I know my father had it almost by heart, as well as "Lear," and much more of both drama and verse. He showed his gay side to his children with whom he was almost never too preoccupied or too tired to play. And when we played, we played "Plays" and when he was merriest we "did Shakespeare." (Qtd. in *Diary and Letters* 4)

The children were encouraged to paint, to write, and to read poetry, good novels and plays. Their father died when Josephine was only eight and her mother never recovered from the blow. Sorrow over the father's death and the lack of money ended the happy homelife Peabody had known. The family moved to Peabody's grandmother's house in Dorcester, Massachusetts and the theatre became an unaffordable luxury.

The young girl kept up with her work, later describing her life as "the old tale of reading and solitary writing . . . and the effort to climb over environment" (*Diary and Letters* 6). Despite poor health, which caused her to drop out of high school, Peabody was able to enter Radcliffe College in 1894. There she took great pleasure in courses on Elizabethan drama and Miracle and Morality plays (*Diary and Letters* 3-5). In 1894 Horace Scudder, editor of *The Atlantic Monthly*, accepted a poem for publication. He was something of a father figure for her, providing friendship and encouragement in her writing (*Diaries and Letters* 6).

After leaving Radcliffe in 1896, Peabody received praise from all quarters for her poetry and her poetic dramas. She was soon considered in the forefront of American poets. From 1901 to 1903 she taught English literature at Wellesley, helping to support relatives with her small salary (*Letters and Diaries* 159). In 1906 she married Lionel S. Marks, an Englishman who had emigrated to America and who taught engineering at Harvard. She had a daughter in 1908 and a son in 1910. She was in an unusual position for a woman of that time in being able to continue her writing with the full support of her husband ("American Play Wins Prize" n.p.). It was typical of the period that she was not only praised for her writing, but for her feminine appearance and charm. An article in the *Toledo Times* concluded by saying, "Mrs. Marks shows rare personal charm, being an ideal mother and perfect in her home life" ("One of America's Foremost Writers" n.p.). Walter Pritchard Eaton, too, wrote that she was well-bred and well-dressed which proved that "Genius does not have to be 'queer,' nor the women of creative powers unsexed. Mrs. Marks has the imagination of a poet, the sympathetic insight of a dramatist—and the common-sense of a housewife" ("Josephine Preston Peabody" 192).

But beneath this conventional exterior was a very unconventional woman. Shortly after her second child was born, she traveled alone, without any assistance, to England to see the premiere of *The Piper*, taking the two babies with her. She was disgusted by the popular "conception of woman as at once the inspiring angel and the inevitable victim of man" and responded with a "burning intolerance of legal injustice to women. This impersonal indignation impelled her advocacy of Suffrage and later of the Woman's Party" (*Diary and Letters* 8). Peabody was strongly in favor of education and careers for women. When she began teaching she wrote in her diary, "This is a thrilling experience;—to be a wage-earner *and* to get your wages! (*Diary and Letters* 159). She was also unconventional in being a vegetarian. She responded fully to life, love, and nature and one diary entry in particular typifies her enthusiasm: "Nothing I have done gives me such delight as swimming without clothes. I just feel born again" (155). She wrote and worked for causes in which she believed, expressing "her conviction that peace and a more humane social order might be achieved if women could have equality of influence and participation in world affairs" (Eliasberg, "Josephine Preston Peabody" 358). In her last years she suffered great pain from a fatal illness, but still wrote beautiful, exuberant letters to friends. As Wendy Wasserstein would say, she was an "Uncommon Woman."

Peabody's play *Marlowe* was completed in 1901 and she was eager for a production. It was published and available, but she was discouraged about her chances of seeing it onstage. She wrote a letter indicating her lack of knowledge of the theatre and her straitened finances which kept her from seeing plays: "You read of dramatists writing a play with a certain actor in their eye, going to see him, night after night, and dogging dress-rehearsals. While I go to the theatre once in two weeks as a treat" (*Diary and Letters* 123). She sent the script to several actors, including E.H. Sothern, but had no success. A diary entry reads, "I have almost bled to death in the struggle to get 'Marlowe' done, against the hosts of the world, the flesh and the devil (154). Finally in 1905 the play was produced at Radcliffe College with George Pierce Baker playing the eponymous hero. She wrote him saying she had been so pleased to see it on the stage and to see how "deeply impressed" the audiences were (*Diary and Letters* 195). She continued to hope for a commercial production, but was disappointed.

The play follows the known facts of the life of Marlowe fairly closely and surrounds him with characters based on other playwrights of the time. Peabody posits his love for a lady of the court, who eventually betrays him, and his admiration and non-sexual love for Alison, a simple, angelic young woman he knew as a child. His denunciation as an atheist and his subsequent death are explained by the jealousy of a rival also in love with Alison. Like her later play, *The Piper, Marlowe* contains Peabody's sympathy for actors who are frequently scorned by respectable citizens. Marlowe's rival, Bame (a fictitious character), says vindictively,

> I told you he is lay'd for. . . . You shall see
> The law upon him and upon yourselves
> To fellow with him. He,—a lying player,
> A conjurer, an atheist, that drinks
> And wagers with a swarm of outcast knaves,
> Thieves, ruffians, and the women worse than all! (152)

The play has an authentic sense of atmosphere, particularly in the scenes with Robert Greene, Thomas Nashe, and the characters based on real people. The dialogue is playable and the verse retains its interest. Writing in 1911 after the success of *The Piper*, Walter Pritchard Eaton praised the play by noting the "man's language" in which it was written—it was typically assumed, of course, that women's language would be more delicate. Eaton said,

> "Marlowe," [was] published in 1901. This tragedy of the unhappy author is full of the surge and sordidness, the poetry and the charm of Christopher Marlowe's life. We venture to think it actable; at any rate it is readable only as good plays are, by a process of visualization into stage terms, almost by an oral process as well. The dialogue is most often dramatic, not lyric. "Marlowe" is a man's part, and it is written in man's language. ("Josephine Preston Peabody" 190)

The Piper was written in 1910 for actor Otis Skinner who wanted a stage adaptation of Browning's popular poem based on the legend of the pied piper of Hamelin. When the play was completed he was busy with other commitments and so Peabody sent the play to a competition in England. Out of 350 plays submitted, hers was selected to win production and the $1,500 Stratford-on-Avon Shakespeare Memorial Prize. Unfortunately only a day after the festival opened, King Edward died and all was postponed. She wrote in her diary, "The Play won't be produced till the Summer Festival. If Ever, if Ever, if Ever! Heigh-ho! So the clock, indeed, struck twelve; and Cinderella scattered!" (231). Her concern came to an end in July 1910 when the play was performed with great success and almost immediately translated into French, German, and Swedish. Naturally, there was tremendous publicity regarding the American poet who had won a prestigious prize with such a wonderful play and there was strong interest in an American production.

Peabody took a familiar, simple story and turned it into a highly visual, entertaining play with dramatic language. One of the most effective elements in the play is the characterization of the Piper as one of a group of strolling players going from town to town presenting *Noah's Flood*. The visual element is charming and imaginative. The actors are costumed as animals within the ark and there is a Hell-Mouth at the side into which a devil is thrusting sinners. Surrounding the actors are colorfully costumed townspeople and the delightful buildings which still exist in Hamelin. As the play begins, the crowd of children and adults are watching the presentation in the market at Hamelin. Everyone is very happy because of the play and because of the removal of the rats and mice three days earlier. Here we see the wisdom of Peabody's point of attack. Whereas the familiar story begins with the arrival of the Pied Piper, she picks it up with his return with the touring actors and quickly moves to his struggle with Jacobus, the mayor, to get the promised 1000 guilders. The audience was immediately drawn in by the conflict between the artistic figures and those representing philistine, hypocritical society in the small town. Peabody also foreshadows a plot complication by dramatizing the beginning of love between Michael-the-Sword-Eater and Barbara, the daughter of Jacobus. The politicians reveal their contempt both for the Piper (because he is an actor) and for the bargain they made with him. Kurt the Syndic says,

> What do ye, mewling of this fellow's rights?
> He hath none! —Wit ye well, he is a stroller,
> A wastrel, and the shadow of a man!
> Ye waste the day and dally with the law.
> Such have no rights; not in their life nor body!
> We are in no wise bound. Nothing is his.
> He may not carry arms; nor have redress
> For any harm that men should put on him,
> Saving to strike a shadow on the wall!
> He is a Nothing, by the statute-book;
> And by the book; so let him live or die,
> Like a masterless dog! (240-241)

The politicians are unaware that they have touched a tragic chord within the Piper. His mother was a player "a thing so trodden, lost and sad,/I cannot think she was ever young" (240). In asking for the large fee, he is asking for some justice from the "smug towns that drive us forth/After the show" (240), and intends to share the money with his companions. As everyone knows, the town refuses to pay, and the Piper lures the children away. In a highly dramatic scene, the children run from the houses, many in their nightgowns, delighted to follow the beloved Piper, the citizens pour forth seeking them, the alarm bell rings, and an old woman cries, "Ye'll never have them back.—I told ye so!" (242).

In the succeeding scenes, the audience sees the children happily playing and sleeping in a grotto-like cellarage of a ruined monastery with the Piper and some of the actors. Peabody introduces an interesting element into the play which relates to her love for children and her concerns about their proper education. Unlike the simple legend, in which the Piper acted out of revenge, here the Piper has abducted the children so that they can be brought up to believe in love and generosity. Earlier in the play many of the parents had expressed the view that children were an expensive nuisance.

What stops the Piper's plans to keep the children and raise them is the discovery that in anger at Jacobus, the town has demanded that he send his daughter Barbara to a nunnery, as penance for the town's guilt. In a marvelous scene, reminiscent of many fairy tales, the Piper pipes magically so that all the citizens escorting Barbara to Rudersheim must dance against their will "round and round like corks at first, with every sign of struggle and protest" and then onward to Rudersheim while Barbara is saved (249). The Piper bewitches Babara, too, but his plan temporarily miscarries because she falls in love with him. In the end, Barbara and Michael are united and the Piper, moved by the genuine love of the mother Veronika for her lame son, Jan, brings the children home to Hamelin. He makes his decision when he prays for guidance before a crucifix with "the Lonely Man." He returns to the market place carrying Jan, then pipes for the others to come. The scene becomes one of mad spectacle, with parents rushing from the houses, laughing and crying, the childen capering and dancing, and the Piper standing by the crucifix in the center of the market, identified now with "the Lonely Man" who tries to spread good throughout the world. The thousand guilders are offered, but the Piper asks that they be given to Michael, exits, and the sound of piping is heard in the distance.

The play was first produced at the Stratford Memorial Theatre Festival in July 1910. E.F. Benson directed and played the role of the Piper in a very handsome, skillfully acted production. When the first performance ended, the curtain closed, then opened again to reveal Peabody center stage, surrounded by the Governors, the Mayor, the Vicar of Stratford, the cast. The audience cheered wildly, threw bouquets, and she was presented with a silver casket with her prize of $1500 inside (*Diary and Letters* 233). The opening, of course, was covered in newspapers throughout the world. After the Festival, Benson produced the play in London for special matinees ("Well Known Daughters of Famous Men" n.p.).

The next great event for Peabody was the production in America. Winthrop Ames was the director of the New Theatre which had opened in 1909. An enormous theatre, nicknamed the "Millionaire's Theatre," it had so far been unsuccessful despite lavish staging and outstanding stars. *The Piper* struck Ames as an appropriate choice for the theatre and an opportunity to score a success because of the quality of the play and the immense amount of publicity it had received. Peabody traveled to New York, leaving her children at home, and worked through the rehearsals making cuts and writing dialogue for the crowd when the ad-libs proved jarringly modern. When the play opened on January 30, 1911, it proved not only a success for the theatre, but was hailed by many critics as a play which marked a new era in American playwriting. John Black observed that after several failures it was pleasing that "the New Theatre certainly scores in its latest effort." Calling the play a big hit, he praised the verse and concluded, "in no production at this house so far have there been so many exquisite stage pictures" (Metcalfe's New York Gossip" n.p.). The critic for the *New York Tribune* wrote, "*The Piper* is a play of strength and beauty, of dignity and tenderness, a play of movement aglow with living dramatic interest" (qtd. in "'The Piper' Charms" n.p.). Several critics noted that this was the third dramatization of Browning's poem and the first successful one. Walter Pritchard Eaton commented that many poor plays win prizes, so it was more important that the play was a success on stage than that it was a prize winner. He noted also that Peabody had studied dramatic technique and had succeeded in creating a popular play with humor and dramatic dialogue: "She has accomplished what no male poets in this country have succeeded in doing, lo, these many years. She has written a popular poetic drama" ("Josephine Preston Peabody" 192). Summing up the importance of the play, an anonymous critic wrote,

> Of all the plays which The New Theatre has produced during this passing season, "The Piper" most adequately fulfills the real object of that institution. It is a play by an American author in poetical form, full of grace and charm and yet with just the sort of frailty that would endanger both its acceptance and its performance on our commercial stage. Just now, when literature and drama are still so widely apart, all plays that lean towards literature need careful fostering. (Unidentified clipping Center)

Other critics praised the themes and ideas with which Peabody invested the simple story:

> It is a delightful bit of work, fresh in concept, and full of humor and true poetic fancy. But the inspiration is entirely modern, and its satire, direct and vigorous, is as timely today as ever it could have been in Hamelin. The Piper's denunciation of the selfishness and greed of commercialism, the wrongs of blighted childhood, the heartlessness of many mothers, the dead formalism of the churches, and man's inhumanity to man, has its present and immediate application. ("The Piper" *Evening Post* n.p.)

The only element of the production which was criticized was the casting. Most critics felt the play called for a masculine figure as the Piper, and, as Eaton put it, "hence the sin of casting Miss Edith Matthison in the title part" ("Josephine Preston Peabody" 192). Matthison was praised for her acting and many people liked her, but others felt the play was diminished by her lack of masculinity, particularly in the scene in which Barbara expresses her love for the Piper. But the critics' reaction was pale compared to that of Peabody. In her letters, she spoke of the outrage of casting a woman in the role, and said that she and her husband were "jaded beyond thinking" because of it. She saw the play and wrote, "how *wan* we both felt just over the pale semblance of the play to the thing we know to be *in* it for *vividness* and strength." Nevertheless, she was pleased by the critical response, the calls for the author at the end, the bouquets, the "wild pleasure of the actors," the attention of reporters, and, perhaps, most of all, that the play had been published in Braille ((*Diary and Letters* 235-237).

The poet was compared favorably with Edmond Rostand and Maurice Maeterlinck, and the play was subsequently produced in New York with A.E. Anson as the Piper in 1920 and enjoyed a popular run. This inspired a performance in Boston by the Community Players in a "modest little theatre, which, by coincidence, bears her name of Peabody." The article describing this production bemoaned the fact that it had taken ten years for the play to be produced in Peabody's home town, despite the fact that there had been twenty-one editions of the play in English and that it was popular reading in America, France, Sweden, Denmark, and Germany ("After Nearly Ten Years" n.p.). However, as Londré notes, the play would probably have been performed much more but the stringent child labor laws made it extremely difficult to produce because of the many roles for children

("Josephine Preston Peabody" 723). In fact, Peabody once travelled to Milwaukee to testify that the children in the cast of *The Piper* were taken care of "beautifully and got good education" (Unidentified Clipping, Peabody File Lincoln Center). Peabody, herself, told a reporter "'The Piper' presents unusual difficulties, having a very large cast. There are sixteen or eighteen speaking parts, thirty-one children, and crowds of supers" ("Tells of Her Prize Play" n.p.).

The success of the play at the New Theatre (which was the only major success in this ill-fated theatre until it was converted into a cathedral for *The Miracle* years later) fed Peabody's passion for playwriting and despite her continuing failure to get *Marlowe* produced, she wrote another historical verse drama called *The Wolf of Gubbio* in 1911. Peabody was deeply religious and her favorite saint was St. Francis. She described it as "a play for children (and their grown folks they take with them); it is in prose and poetry for the common folks talk in prose, but Saint Francis and the wood creatures and the Epic Wolf, of course, speak in rhymed verse; the wolf's is four-legged, of course. But I like it very much." At this time her work, her "glorious and shouting-healthy children," and her husband all gave her so much pleasure that she wrote a friend, "Life is full to bursting; —bursting into millions of clouds of little star-worlds again" (*Diary and Letters* 239-240). But by 1912 her writing was halted because of a nervous breakdown. In 1913 she completed the play and sent it to her publisher Houghton Mifflin for publication the next year.

The Wolf of Gubbio again reveals Peabody's delightful imagination, her enlightened outlooks, and her skill at dialogue and setting. The play begins in the forest outside Gubbio. The stage is framed by "two towering pine-boles like pillars" and shows in the valley in the distance (3). The Wolf's cave is seen as well as two Pine Dryads (nature divinities) whose appearance is fantastic: "Their auburn hair is long and straight; their hanging drapery is filmy green." They are joined by a Vine-Dryad who "appears over the edge of the cliff at back, reaching her way with long arms, from a tree-top just visible. She has dark hair in tendrils; and a garment of green and violet" (405). They are listening to The Wolf, whose words blend with the sound of the wind:

The World is cold; the World is cold.
The snows are round us, fold on fold
Only the flocks are stalled within;

The kine are gathered, kith and kin.
. . . I must be growing old. (4)

Throughout the action of the play it is revealed that The Wolf longs to be a man, that he suffers for the vicious killings he committed in Gubbio in his youth, but that he holds men responsible for his actions. His mate was slaughtered for her pelt and he was forced into his role by men's preconception of the nature of a wolf. In particular, he hates to hear men speak of "the wolf at the door." He tells Francis,

Yet have I not deserved to be
Their by-word for Misery.
Men cast their wolfishness on me!
Big wolves and little,—hutch and hall,
Raven upon each other, all;—
Each on the lesser, —day by day,
They snatch and cheat and rend their prey;
. . . Yes, warring all!—
The very bread they struggled for,
They spill and waste in war—war
. . . War! (136-37)

In the first scene The Wolf is waiting for Saint Francis to pass through the woods on his way to celebrate Christmas in Gubbio. Two criminals appear who have attacked a couple with their baby, and are hurrying with their meagre gains to Gubbio. The Wolf finds the baby and hides it in the cave while the Dryads lean from the trees and watch. When Francis appears he is loving and friendly and invites The Wolf to join him. Happy, but uncertain about the baby in the cave, The Wolf exits with Francis while the Dryads lean from the trees and point accusingly (52).

The rest of the play is set in the quaint market-place of Gubbio with its medieval buildings and "stone arcades shading the little house-fronts, with humble wares hanging out, and a few caged blackbirds and pigeons" (58). The atmosphere of thirteenth century Italy is created by the period costumes and the activities of The Baker, The Potter, The Furrier, and The Dyer. The action of the play involves trying to get the townspeople to contribute something so Francis and his companions can cook a Christmas meal for all in a giant kettle. Eventually, they do, but The Wolf, in anger, at their comments about him, eats it all up. Francis still believes in him, and continues with the preparations for a play about the birth of Jesus. The man and woman victimized by the thieves in the forest are dressed up as Mary and Joseph and the little children bring their presents. But the cradle is empty for their baby is still missing. In a true conversion to goodness, all of the people, even the criminals, join in worship and The Wolf brings the baby to the cradle. The people cry out that it is a miracle: the Christ child is found and The Wolf is transformed into Fra Lupone. Francis says,

> Oh, and the very stars shall sing
> For joy of this glad thing.
> Lo, Love is born!
> Though we crown Him yet with thorn,
> Though we laugh Him all to scorn,
> Love,—Love is born! (194)

In an Epilogue, Frances comes through the curtain, peers out at the audience, and says,

> And if there be out yonder any Wolf,
>   Or great or small, behold,—
> Come, little brother Wolves, come in, come
>   hither,
>   Out of the cold! (195)

Peabody became so involved with the character of Saint Francis and the animals that she became a vegetarian. She had high hopes for the play, especially after it was published. She tried to interest the commercial producer George Tyler in presenting it, but heard nothing from him. It is not surprising, as the major role in the play is that of The Wolf, and what leading actor would have been eager to dress in a wolf skin and walk on all fours? Again the production was complicated by the presence of many little children. The play was successful in print and became known throughout the country.

In 1912 the Toy Theatre produced Peabody's one-act play, *The Wings* along with a dramatization of a Robert Louis Stevenson story and a play by the Swedish playwright Hedberg. She had written the play in 1904 but was unable to interest anyone in production. The play deals with illusions in a mystical fashion. A hermit, Cerdic, lives in a hut by the northern sea, in a grim waste-land. He dreams of carving a statue of the virgin Mary. As he sits listening to the sound of the wings of seagulls, he comes to believe that she will appear to him. When there is a knock at the door, and a woman appears, he falls to his knees to pray to her. However, he is disillusioned when the woman turns out to be the beautiful mistress of the King. She had him banished from court for criticizing her, but unsatisfied with her revenge, has now brought the King to kill him. When he tells her of his illusion, she is moved and vows to reinstate him in court. At the end of the play he sits sadly, his illusion shattered, holding a sea-gull with a broken wing. There is beautiful poetry, but the play is essentially a mood piece notable chiefly for its characterization of Cerdic. It was rarely produced after this presentation. The play was praised as a "truly poetic, a truly dramatic piece" in the *Boston Transcript*, although the critic noted that it was "somewhat beyond the power of the players" ("Miss Peabody's Play" n.p.). Another reviewer that the play contained "the finer things of drama [and] true humanity" but regretted that "the illuminating and the exalting speech necessary to such poetry and emotions lay somewhat beyond its players" (H.T.P. "Toy Theatre" n.p.).

Peabody made a major contribution to the theatre with *The Piper*, but it was her last play to be produced in New York. The play was part of what Freedley and Reeves described as the "American Renaissance" of playwriting. She and William Vaughan Moody and Percy MacKaye were noted by these authors as the three most important figures in the movement (583). However, she and MacKaye, in writing poetic drama, were swimming upstream against the tide of realism in the American theatre.

Although no other plays were produced after *Wings*, Peabody continued to write plays. By today's standards the most important of these was *Portrait of Mrs. W.____* which was published in 1922, the year of Peabody's death. Her continuing interest in social causes and women's role in society are reflected in this, her last play. Through a dramatization of the lives of Mary Wollstonecroft and her daughter, the author presents a vital plea for equality for women. In this prose play Peabody attempted to "bring into close range a name and a face" which was little known in 1922, but which has come to be known in recent years because of Wollstonecroft's importance in the struggle for women's rights. In the foreword to the play Peabody wrote, "Dramatically, it is wilfully built against traditions of stage structure. But the plea of all that Mary Wollstonecroft had to leave unsaid and undone, the tragedy of death at the hour so looked to for deeds, or utterance, that clamor of unfulfilment, made it impossible for this chronicler to deal with the story according to more obvious stage possibilities" (*Collected Plays* 636).

In stating her feelings about the subject, Peabody put her finger on a problem with the play. It was an excellent subject for a play, but her structure places much of the interesting material about Wollstonecroft's life off-stage. Wollstonecroft's dramatic story, her romance with a libertine in Paris during the revolution, her illegitimate child, and her return to England following the publication of *The Vindication of the Rights of Women* in 1792 are all revealed in exposition during the first act by such notables as Mrs. Sarah Siddons, the playwright Mrs. Inchbald, John Phillips Kemble, and the poet Robert Southey. The central conflict—the decision of Mary and philosopher William Godwin to marry against all their published opinions about the negative impact of marriage on both men and women—is not developed dramatically onstage. In the final act the death of Mary (after the birth of a child) takes place offstage. The best moments in the play are those in which Mary presents her viewpoints about the lot of women in society and her hopes for improving it. Shortly after her marriage she says to a woman friend,

> Once, of course, people would say to me, 'When you have a home of your own, then you'll think no more of these wild projects for reforming the world.' —Reforming the world, Amelia!— Simply to desire *truth to be true; love to be love; thought to be thought;*—for the poor;—for women and for men. Simply to desire the human to be human!—and while that passion burned in me, my own blood-kindred,—my mother, my brothers and sisters,—yes, and our father, too, our wretched abject father,—God forgive him,—were crying out to the hearing of my body,—for . . . husks. (*Collected Plays* 708)

The play ends with an epilogue in which Peabody amplified her thesis. Godwin has remarried and has become conservative in his views and distant toward his and Mary's daughter. Mary appears to her daughter in a dream and speaks feelingly of love. At the end of the play the daughter happily and courageously leaves her father's home to run away with the poet Shelley. Like her mother, she will defy convention and seek her own way in the world. Her choice negates the sorrow with which her mother had greeted her birth. Because of the absence of equality for women, she despaired at having produced a "girl-child" and questioned her future: "My girl-child . . . what will you be? . . . Something solitary? Be Something for us . . . be something . . . steadfast" (*Collected Plays* 749).

This last effort at dramatization can be seen both as a tribute to Mary Wollstonecroft and the women's movement and as Peabody's own regretful farewell to life and her young daughter. Peabody knew that marriage had brought her happiness and great support for her career, but she knew that was not the case for most women. She left her daughter a message of hope for the future of women. It is unfortunate that the play itself did not have more dramatic value. The choice of subject related closely to her beliefs and the emerging concerns about women in American society, but she was nearing death, and did not have the opportunity to see it in performance and work toward improving it. It stands, nevertheless, as an early effort to infuse the American theatre with a belief equal rights for women and respect as human beings.

Josephine Preston Peabody was an important figure in the development of American theatre despite the fact that few of her plays were seen on the stage. When *The Piper* was revived in New York in 1920, Alexander Woolcott wrote, "This is the play which won the prize at Stratford and which, together with a finer achievement called 'Marlowe,' is responsible for her unrivalled eminence as an American writer of poetic drama." Woolcott also noted that her contribution was significant because in the increasingly realistic theatre, there were few contributors to that genre ("Mrs. Marks' Play Revived" 14). She was an excellent role model and an inspiration for other budding women playwrights. She was the only American woman playwright to write poetic drama successfully. The great popularity of *The Piper* placed her at the forefront of American playwrights in 1910. Although largely forgotten today, *The Piper* remains a theatrically effective play with much of the same appeal as the ever-popular *Peter Pan*. If she had not been virtually alone in her efforts to write non-realistic plays, or if she had been writing at a different time, she might have been a major American playwright. In a period in which dozens of women were content to write hack plays for commercial profit, Peabody aimed higher. Although her plays were not widely produced, they were widely read in many countries and both her plays and poetry received praise both from critics and other poets including Swinburne ("American Play Wins Prize" n.p.). Through her life and her plays she promoted equality, justice, and love.

Gertrude Stein (1874-1946)

Gertrude Stein (1874-1946) is one of the most controversial playwrights discussed in this book. For some critics her plays are brilliant examples of modern theatre, whereas others feel they are merely self-indulgent expressions of her giant ego. In recent years there have been increasing numbers of productions of her plays and many contemporary playwrights acknowledge the importance of her playwriting upon their works. In her lifetime she was very drawn to writing for the theatre, and in the three periods of playwriting between 1913 and the time of her death, she wrote more than seventy plays.

Stein was the youngest child of seven born to Amelia Keyser Stein and Daniel Stein. Although she was born in America, her father took the family to Europe when she was a baby, so she spent her early years there. In 1879 they returned to America and ultimately bought a large home in Oakland, California. Both Stein's parents died while she was an adolescent and she formed a close bond with her brother Leo. Stein's parents were of German-Jewish heritage and her mother had a strong interest in the arts. Later in her life Stein wrote that in her youth she had enjoyed touring companies of standard melodramas such as *Uncle Tom's Cabin, Secret Service, Alabama,* and *Shenandoah*. She remembered seeing such notable performers as Edwin Booth, Sarah Bernhardt, and William Gillette (*Last Operas and Plays* xv). The latter had a profound effect upon her view of theatre. She wrote,

> Gillette had conceived a new technique, silence stillness and quick movement. . . . Gillette had not only done it but he had conceived it and it made the whole stage the whole play this technique silence stillness and quick movement. One was no longer bothered by the theatre, you had to get acquainted of course but that was quickly over and after that nothing bothered. ("Lectures in America" 116-117)

At the time of her father's death, her brother arranged the inheritance so that all the children were given an income for life. Untroubled by financial concerns, and utterly independent, Stein felt "a sense of release from firm restraint" (Townsend "Gertrude Stein" 714). Although she had never completed high school, she was admitted to Radcliffe College (then the Harvard Annex) in 1893. Leo was a student at Harvard and they enjoyed the exhibits, concerts, and theatre, sometimes both in the afternoon and evening (Leach 11). While at

Radcliffe she studied with William James who encouraged her to pursue the study of psychology at Johns Hopkins University. According to one of Stein's admirers, Thornton Wilder, at Johns Hopkins she undertook a research project which involved automatic writing. She asked several hundred fellow students to engage in this activity. "Her interest, however, took an unexpected turn; she became more absorbed in the subjects' varying approach to the experiments than in the experiments themselves" and she became highly absorbed in the process of observing and describing all types of human characters ("Four in America" Bloom, ed. *Gertrude Stein* 27). According to her biographer, Townsend, B.F. Skinner, the noted behavioral psychologist, believed that her "innovative writing style is in essence automatic writing" and rooted in this experience ("Gertrude Stein" 153).

Stein did not complete her medical studies but traveled, lived in New York, and then joined Leo in Paris where he was pursuing his study of art. They lived together and collected art. In 1905 Alice B. Toklas arrived in Paris and she and Stein began a relationship which lasted throughout Stein's life. She did not publicly admit her lesbianism, but it informs much of her writing in a disguised form. Leo moved out, and the two women maintained the home which became a famous salon. Stein had started writing, but Leo disparaged her work. In contrast, Toklas encouraged her writing and typed her manuscripts for her (Townsend 153). In this period Stein and Toklas were in close contact with the major avant-garde painters including Picasso, Matisse, and Braque whose paintings Stein bought before they became fashionable. Her work was influenced by this contact as Brinnin notes in his introduction to her selected operas and plays:

> In spite of a certain shyness that seemed to overtake her whenever her own work was referred to as cubist, Gertrude Stein was technically and temperamentally committed to the aesthetics of that movement. Her famous exercise in abstraction entitled *Tender Buttons*, wholly a product of the cubist dispensation, met with ridicule and exasperated comment when it first appeared in 1914, but at least it was widely noticed and discussed. When, by way of cubism, she brought abstraction to the drama, only embarrassed silence and total neglect ensued. As the primary form of art where ideas are made flesh, drama was naturally the very last of the arts to accomodate the inventions of Picasso and Braque. (xii)

In addition to the art of this period, Stein was aware of the interesting surrealistic plays being performed and written. Such works as

Apollinaire's *The Breasts of Tiresias* (1917), Cocteau's ballet *Parade* (1927) with music by Satie, and Cocteau's *The Ox on the Roof* (1920) were typical of the experimental, multi-media productions which excited Paris after World War I. Stein's first period of playwriting pre-dated and overlapped this period. In 1913, following an interesting dinner party, she wrote *What Happened*. As Ryan has written, "It renders the images, rhythms, and qualities of an evening dinner party without suggesting a story line. Typical of her first period of playwriting, it is an attempt to capture the essence of relationships and subtle movements between things without telling what happened, but rather to make a play the essence of what happened" ("Gertrude Stein" 832). Since this type of play was innovative when written and hard to understand, as it remains today, it is useful to examine Stein's explanation of what she was doing. She felt it was useless to tell a story in a direct narrative fashion because that had been done so much. In contrast, she wanted "to tell what could be told if one did not tell anything" (qtd. in Brinnin xii). As Brinnin notes, these qualities made her work "as remote as a planet from the American theatre until late in her creative life" (xii). A typical passage reads, "A cut, a cut is not a slice, what is the occasion for representing a cut and a slice. What is the occasion for all that. A cut is a slice, a cut is the same slice. The reason that a cut is a slice is that if there is no hurry any time is just as useful. A cut and a slice is there any question when a cut and a slice are just the same" (7). To the playgoers who wanted plot and realistic spectacle, as in the plays of Belasco and Augustus Thomas, Stein "was as hermetic and freakish as the newly imported paintings of Pablo Picasso" (Brinnin xii).

Despite negative response to her work, Stein pursued her own ends, saying, "I write for myself and strangers" and she later withdrew the "strangers" (qtd. in Van Vechten, "Introduction" viii). She published her first collection of plays, *Geography and Plays* (1922), and began a second period of playwriting which extended until 1931. These plays were still spatially arranged relationships and dialogue, rather than linear, chronological stories. As Ryan notes, her third period of playwriting, which began in 1932, was a narrative period "within which she depended for the first time upon some sort of story. Nevertheless, these plays depend less on causal connections between story elements than on sustained views of each element, subverting overt movement to the quality of the scene at hand" (833).

In the thirties, too, she enjoyed the success of her opera (with music by Virgil Thomson) *Four Saints in Three Acts* and an extended lecture tour of America which convinced people that she was not merely an eccentric. The lectures, which give insight into her playwriting, were published and widely read.

Stein continued living in Europe, even during the Second World War. During the First World War she and Toklas had spent much of the time in Spain. When they returned to France, Stein drove a truck for the American Fund for French Wounded (Ryan 832). Following the end of the war in 1944, Stein's bravery and assistance to service-men was recognized and soldiers came to see her in Paris. Among them were theatre professionals such as Alan Campbell and Richard Whorf. There was increasing interest in the production of Stein's plays in America. In 1946 Stein died of cancer, leaving behind an amazing art collection, a great body of work, and a reputation as an outstanding twentieth century writer. She had chosen to write largely about Americans, but felt she could do so by observing them at a distance.

It is obviously impossible to consider a large number of Stein's plays in a short space. A single scene in one of her numerous plays could be subjected to close analysis and yield a variety of interpretations. A few plays which represent her playwriting from several periods will be discussed in terms of possible interpretations, technique, and production. *Ladies' Voices* is representative of the early period of her writing for theatre. It is a curtain raiser which is two pages long. In it there are four acts, the last divided into two scenes. There are no stage directions, nor are the speeches in the play assigned to characters. It is a forerunner of the sort of short play with which Beckett was later to experiment.

The play is particularly interesting in that it is apparently a disguised depiction of the lesbianism Stein did not publicly admit during her lifetime. Unlike Radclyff Hall, Virginia Woolf, and others, Stein maintained privacy regarding her sexuality and it is only in recent years, with the opening of the boundaries regarding sexuality in life and literature that Jane Rule, Elizabeth Fifer, and Neil Schmitz have explored the relationship between Stein's sexuality and her prose. As Joyce Aldridge comments, however, "limited analysis devoted to uncovering lesbian references has been applied to Stein's drama" ("Gertrude Stein: Rose by Any Other Name" 1). Aldridge's analysis of *Ladie's Voices* is a good example of the difficulty of comprehending Stein's early plays, and the necessity for a word by word analysis: "Stein selectively alters grammatical structure in order to obscure references. Choosing to use pronouns instead of nouns allows Stein to include sexual references in her writings without endangering personal exposure" (2). Aldridge points to the "invention of a private language used to mask lesbian content." For example, "cows" is frequently used without any clear meaning. Stein says, "Cows are very nice. They are between legs." The term cows, meaning orgasms relates to the word "caesar" which stands for the vagina, and finally, the title, "ladies' voices" seems to represent women loving each other (Aldridge 3). Given these clues, the reader may comprehend more of Stein's intention in a section which is Act 3:

> Yes Genevieve does not know it. What. That we are seeing Caesar.
> Caesar kisses.
> Kisses today.
> Caesar kisses every day.
> Genevieve does not know that it is only in this country that she could speak as she does.
> She does *speak* [italics mine] very well doesn't she. She told them that there was not the slightest intention on the part of her countrymen to eat the fish that was not caught in their country.
> In this she was mistaken. (4)

Aldridge sums up the content of this act by saying, "Generally, Act 3 may be interpreted as being a conversaton between two lesbian lovers who have masked their sexuality from the public. The topics of their conversation are their ghettoized affair and Genevieve, another les-bian" (6).

Given the obscurity of the language, it is not surprising that many critics have attacked Stein, or at least indicated that her approach to theatre was not accessible. In her book *Art by Subtraction: A Dissenting Opinion of Gertrude Stein*, B. L. Reid speaks for many others when she objects to Stein's wish to inaugurate an art in which words are stripped of their received meanings. Noting that for the reader this means a "vocabulary of impenetrable, esoteric abstractions," she calls Stein's use of such a vocabulary an artistic blind spot: "The matter is as simple as this: the words do not mean the same things to us that they mean to her; she is writing in one language, we are reading in another" ("An Evaluation" 95). Obviously what is difficult for the reader, who has time to ponder associations and word play, is much more difficult for the listener in the theatre. The difficulty is compounded by the fact that in addition to the private vocabulary, as Brinnin has observed, "In only a minimal sense do typical plays of Gertrude Stein refer to anything." He continues,

> Yet while they are not "about" anything, they insist on being something—and that "thing" is Gertrude Stein's own, an almost improbable mixture of primitive mindlessness and sophisticated intellect. Their primitivism shows in ritual gesture, the sing-song incantations of children, sequences of talk, and exchanges of dialogue so little ordered that they might have been picked up at random by a tape recorder placed in the center of a crowd. Their sophistication lies in the fact that, without being ideological, they are always conceptual, always based in a governing idea even though that idea may be all but dissolved in the presentation. (xiii)

Despite the difficulty of comprehending any meaning, there is often a great deal of theatricality and fun in Stein's plays. One more example of an early play, *Counting Her Dresses*, will give an indication of Stein's satirical approach and her sense of play. Michael Hoffman suggests that this is the most playful of the works in *Geography and Plays*. "It is divided into Parts, with each Part consisting of Acts. Only a few of the acts have more than one line, the longest being part 1, act 1, which has three. There are forty-one parts in "Counting Her Dresses" and perhaps one hundred and fifty acts. This is as far as Stein goes in demonstrating the absurdity of conventional theatrical labels" (77).

A play from Stein's second period of playwriting was the most successful of her works in her lifetime. *Four Saints in Three Acts* was set to music by Virgil Thomson who worked very diligently to get backing for a production of the unconventional work. The production opened in Hartford in 1934 and went on to become a "legendary success." The all-black cast, the glittering settings which utilized colored cellophane created a theatrical effect which overcame the difficulties of comprehension. Despite the title, there are forty saints and dozens of acts, the scene and act breaks are nonsensical, and the plot is, as Hoffman writes, "like most Stein works of this period difficult to summarize . . . but the "action" of this opera-play is quite simple. . . . The text consists of a series of meditations primarily made by the narrator-chorus (Gertrude Stein) and some by the chorus of saints" (*Gertrude Stein* 78-79).

A typical speech goes,

Four saints are never three.
Three saints are never four.

Four saints are never left altogether.
Three saints are never idle.
Four saints are leave it to me.
Three saints when this you see.
Begin three saints.
Begin four saints.
Two and two saints.
One and three saints.
In place.
One should it.
Easily saints.
Very well saints.
Have saints.
Said saints.
And not annoy.
Annoint. (43)

In another passage we see the continuing use of a private vocabulary
which could have meant nothing to the audiences in Hartford or New
York:

Dear Sir. A play.
A great many people ask me in misery.
Have they come. . . .
   Why can't you accomodate yourselves and leave me alone. I don't mean to
day or yesterday or by counting. Everybody cannot count. An avenue goes
through a city and a street crosses it crosses the city. There is no use in pointing
out associations. A great many people can read. Not women. Not in some
countries. Not in some countries. Oh yes not in some countries.
        Caesar.
   Caesar isn't a name that is used. I have known that a great many people
have it. (12)

What accounts for the popularity of this sort of material on the New
York stage in 1934? One must remember the effectiveness of the music
and the voices. In the late thirties Stein wrote rather wistfully, "As yet
they have not done any of my plays without music to help them" (qtd.
in Van Vechten, "Introduction" xvi). But in his lengthy analysis of the
opera, Norman Weinstein provides more reasons. He quotes Stein's
comments that for her as a child, the theatre was like a circus. "For
Stein the stage area is analogous to a circus ring. Things happen at a
circus: clowns go through their paces." Continuing the circus analogy,
Weinstein says, "Into this timeless arena saints speak. What the saints
say is also timeless. Games and riddles, verbal melodies and textures,
need no precise temporal or spatial context in which to exist" (119).

Four Saints in Three Acts is one of Stein's most popular works. It has frequently been performed in opera houses, universities, and in smaller theatres. Recent productions have taken a tip from Stein's comments about the opera in their productions. In her lectures she said,

> Anyway I did write Four Saints and Opera to be Sung and I think it did almost what I wanted, it made a landscape and the movement in it was like a movement in and out with which anybody looking on can keep time. I also wanted it to have the movement of nuns very busy and in continuous movement but placid as a landscape has to be because after all the life of a convent is the life of a landscape, and it may look excited as a landscape does sometimes look excited but its quality is that a landscape if it ever did go away would have to go away to stay. (131)

Reviewing a 1986 New York production, Stephen Holden noted visual elements which reflected Stein's description. He quoted the director, John J.D. Sheehan, as saying, "It's a pageant. Just as you grasp Gertrude Stein's meanings not from what she says but from what her words summon in your mind, you get the meaning from the resonance of depicting ordinary activities in pageantry and tableau" ("The Opera Ensemble Has Fun With 'Four Saints'" 33). Reviewing a 1989 production at UCLA, Daniel Cariaga praised the design elements which contributed to the viewers' understanding: "In a plotless operatic entertainment, lighting, stage groupings and visual accents keep the listeners within the author's grasp." He also praised the bold, eclectic costuming and the "Large, unmistakably symbolic props—a huge and mobile elephant sculpture, giant sea horses in soft lavender, an oversize jukebox, among others—also proclaim the optimistic character of the piece" ("UCLA Forces Present 'Four Saints' Opera" 4).

Dr. Faustus Lights the Lights (1938) is a fairly comical treatment of the Faust legend which is really a serious analysis of the actuality of identity. Dr. Faustus has sold his soul (if he has one) to Mephistopheles in exchange for the ability to create light by means of light bulbs. Typical of the flippant tone is Faustus' speech to the Mephistopheles which concludes,

> Oh you devil go to hell, that is all you know to tell, and who is interested in hell just a devil is interested in hell because that is all he can tell, whether I stamp or whether I cry whether live or whether I die, I can know that all a devil can say is just about going to hell the same way, get out of here devil, it does not interest me whether you can buy or I can sell, get out of here devil just you go to hell. (Faustus gives him an awful kick, and Mephisto moves away and the electric lights just then begin to get very gay.) (206)

The question of identity and actual existence is explored through
Faustus' character and that of Marguerite Ida/ Helena Annabel. She is
a combination of the naive innocence of Marguerite and the sexuality
of Helena. She carries with her a serpent (a phallic symbol), which
Faustus uses to kill his accompanying figures the little boy and the dog
(who says thank you repeatedly). He does this in order to commit a sin
and thereby be able to go to hell taking Marguerite/Helena with him.
But she rejects that idea saying, "No one can deceive me not a young
man not an old man not a devil not a viper I am Marguerite Ida and
Helena Annabel and never never will a young man be an old man and
an old man be a young man, you are not Doctor Faustus no not ever
never never" (235).

Because of increasing interest in Gertrude Stein this play has been
performed in recent years. Like most of her works, it really demands a
director who will create her/his work out of Stein's work. As Leach
perceptively wrote in 1954, "The scenario and the details of performance are left to the creativity of the director and actor, to their own
creative 'recognition.' She did not think of them as only recreators or
interpreters, but as the ultimate makers of the reality of the performance that could only exist in the present time of each moment of
that performance" (174). Of course, that now sounds like a description
of the current view of postmodern theatre in which Robert Wilson has
been a leading director. His highly praised production of *Dr. Faustus
Lights the Lights* at the Hebbel Theatre in Berlin was part of the Lincoln
Center Serious Fun festival in 1992. Alexis Greene described the
approach Wilson took:

> Under Wilson's direction, Stein's short, repetitive word-bursts ricochet against
> alluring images: a giant female figure in a voluminous white gown, wielding a
> scythe; a delicate florescence of dangling light bulbs. Hans Peter Kuhn's fanciful
> score includes whistles, metallic crashes, barnyard sounds and cabaret songs.
> The whole was a typical Wilson mixture, offering esthetic bravura more than
> political insight, yet sensitive to Stein's vision of the evil in people who want to
> rule the world. (256)

Stein's influence on Wilson has often been noted, and his suitability as
a director of Stein's works was commented on by most critics. Stephen
Holden noted the division of the roles of Faustus, Marguerite/Helena
and Mephisto between several actors—very appropriate considering
Stein's questioning of identity—and noted the whole approach Wilson
took to the play:

His essential technique has always been to create a semi-abstract landscape for a piece, letting the text speak mostly for itself, while evoking mystery and surprise from the friction between the words and his broad theatrical concepts. And with Stein, whose open-ended exploratory sensibility and use of repetition foreshadowed modern-day Minimalism, he is playing against a sensibility that is closer than usual to his own. ("Gertrude Stein Interprets Faust" 15)

Two of Stein's most popular (if such a word is appropriate) plays are from her last period of playwriting. Both were written just before she died, and were subsequently produced in a number of theatres. Ryan says that in the two, Stein allowed "more concessions to traditional playwriting" (833).

Yes Is For a Very Young Man (1944-45) has a fairly lucid story line which may make it more interesting for some readers, and less for others. It is more like a conventional play than Stein's others. Stein wrote that she was inspired to create this work because of memories of the splits within families at the time of the American civil war. She had seen such plays as *Secret Service* and felt that similar tensions existed in France during the occupation by the Germans. She said, "I hope it will make you feel the French as they really were during the long years of the occupation" (qtd. in Van Vechten xv). The young man in the title is Ferdinand. At the beginning of the play his interests are focused on Constance, an American who supports the resistance movement. Ferdinand is torn between collaborating with the Germans or working against them because of the conflicting attitudes within his family. He expresses his feelings to Constance saying, "Constance, Constance what can I say, what is there to say but yes, no does not mean anything, no not now, but yes, yes means something. Oh my God, yes means you, it means you, yes it does, you do not want it to mean you but it does, yes, yes, yes." But Constance is involved in larger issues than love and answers, "Yes, yes is for a very young man, and you Ferdinand, you are a very young boy, yes you are, yes is for a very young one, a very young man, but I am not so young, no I am not, and so I say no. I always say no. You know, Ferdinand, yes you know that I always say no" (265). By the end of the play family loyalties have been torn, Constance has broken with Ferdinand's sister-in-law, and Ferdinand is not so young. He has seen his brother after three years in a German prison, his father has been murdered by the Germans, and he has worked with the resistance. Paris has been liberated, and he tells Constance the war is over for some, but not for the young people:

"Yes, look facts in the face, Constance, for you it is all over, for Henry it is all over, but for me it is just beginning, yes is for a very young man" (320).

Although the play relies to a certain extent on knowledge of political events in the forties, it is still an understandable portrayal of life in any period of political upheaval and tension. The portrait of Constance is interesting in itself, but additionally because it is based on Clare Boothe Luce and also reveals characteristics of Gertrude Stein. First produced at the Pasadena Playhouse during Stein's lifetime, it has since been produced in many colleges and universities including Princeton and Smith College, and in professional theatres from San Francisco to Paris. Writing a review of a 1949 production of the play, Brooks Atkinson said it "conveys those admirable, shining qualities of personal character that always made Miss Stein seem so much more vital than her work. To get the good things in this thin, sketchy drama you have to accept her theory of style, which is asking a lot of anybody who is in a normal hurry. But the style is not a bogus affectation. A certain freshness of truth does come through it in some elusive fashion" ("Yes Is For a Very Young Man" 27).

Atkinson and, in 1963, Howard Taubman point to an important element about this play, and by extension, all of Stein's plays: the director and the actors have to create the piece afresh ("Drama of Wartime Fails to Come To Life" 7). This is crucial to understanding Stein's plays. What she did was to suggest a play which must then be fully created and which may be created in a variety of ways. Her viewpoint could easily shift or be shifted. As Marc Robinson wrote of *Four Saints in Three Acts*, "Stein makes her commentary simply by choosing to see things one way instead of another, to look at her landscape from a specific promontory—say, a place that keeps Saint Therese in the foreground, closest to her, and others receding, or only partially visible. If Stein was 'standing' in another place, looking from a different angle, the contents of her picture and their relationships would change—and so change the meaning" (628).

Despite the fact that speakers are not always designated and the language is far from realistic, a story line can be deciphered in *The Mother of Us All* (1945-46). According to Brinnin, this play is "a kind of 'memory book' of the United States in the lifetime of Susan B. Anthony, whose struggles to gain the vote for women, like Miss Stein's struggle for artistic recognition, occupied almost all her long life." Virgil Thomson intended the score to be "an evocation of nineteenth century America, with its gospel hymns and cocky marches, its senti-mental ballads, waltzes, darn-fool ditties and intoned sermons" (Brinnin xvi). Stein's feminism and many autobiographical elements are present within this opera. In several passages Susan B. notes the difficulties of working with men because of their faults:

> In a little while they found everything very mixed. It is not really mixed said Susan B. How can anything be really mixed when men are conservative, dull, monotonous, deceived, unchanging and bullies, how said Susan B. how when men are men, how can they be mixed. Yes said Anne, yes men are men how can they be mixed yes how can they. Well said Susan B. let us go on they always listen to me. Yes said Anne yes they always listen to you. Yes said Susan B. yes they always listen to me. (170)

Another revelatory passage is the exchange in which Stein criticizes African-American men (who received help in getting the vote from Susan B.) for not supporting women's suffrage:

> Susan B.   Negro man would you vote if you only can and not she.
> Negro Man. You bet.
> Susan B.   I fought for you that you could vote would you vote if they would not let me.
> Negro Man. Holy Gee. (177)

At the end of the opera the vote has been won. Critics have likened the last lines to Anthony's life and to Stein's as well. In her last speeches, Anthony says, "Life is strife, I was a martyr all my life/ not to what I won but to what was done./ Do you know because I tell you so, or/ do you know, do you know./ My long life, my long life (202).

In her long life Stein received little recognition for her contributions to theatre, but she was not completely ignored. For example, Stark Young was moved to write several pieces of criticism about the 1934 production of *Four Saints in Three Acts*. He wrote with some exaspera-tion, "I wish I knew some way to make sure of being taken seriously when I say that 'Four Saints in Three Acts' is as essential theatre the most important event of our season" ("Might It Be Mountains" 246). In recent years her plays have been reconsidered and frequently pro-duced. For several years Al Carmines focussed attention on Stein through his productions of her plays at the Judson Memorial Church in New York. Lawrence Kornfeld, who has directed many of her plays successfully, received two Obies for Stein plays at the church. Kornfeld's view of Stein's place in the theatre is an apt summation of her work:

> I take Stein very seriously. She's a very important playwright on the cutting edge of experimental theatre. She set out to discover a new existence for the stage, for the dynamics of theatre, to see how audiences perceive what's happening onstage. She was in another world, opening a new space and surprises for us. Today's avant-garde theatre forces—Richard Foreman and Robert Wilson—are indebted to her. In his letters, Thornton Wilder said he could not have written the third act of "Our Town" without her influence. (Qtd. in Klein 24)

Stein wrote many plays, but saw few performed. One memorable occasion occurred in 1937 when she and Toklas traveled to London to see Lord Berner's ballet, *A Wedding Bouquet* with Robert Helpmann and Margot Fonteyn. The ballet was based on Stein's *They Must. Be Wedded. To Their Wife.* After seeing the delightful performance, she wrote, "And so I do write a lot of plays and they are things for somebody to see and somebody does see them, sometimes there will be lots more of them given" (qtd. in Van Vechten xvii). Although Stein did not live to see them, her prediction proved correct. Writing in 1958 B.L. Reid voiced a fairly common criticism of both Stein and her supporters, saying of her writing, "To say that this becomes tiresome is the grossest understatement; it is deadly, it is not art, and it is not fit fare for a sane reader. . . . There is no point in vilifying Gertrude Stein. She is the victim of her pathology rather than her villainy" (96-98). As the theatre moved away from realism, feminism came to the fore, and as attitudes toward sexuality became more liberal, interest in Stein increased and this critical attitude decreased. Her plays were republished and many critics have identified her influence on such writers as Thornton Wilder, Ionesco, Beckett, and Pinter. Ryan summed up her impact on the theatre by saying, "Her groundbreaking experiments in non-referentiality and non-linearity in literature and theatre are directly evident in work by theatre artists like Richard Foreman and Robert Wilson . . . who acknowledge her influence" (834).

Rida Johnson Young (1875?-1926)

Rida Johnson Young (1875?-1926) was one of the most successful playwrights of the twentieth century. Her plays and musicals included Brown of Harvard, Naughty Marietta, and Maytime. More than a million people bought the sheet music for her sentimental song Mother Machree. Her career in the theatre lasted from just after the turn of the century until her early death in 1926. She stumbled with her first efforts at playwriting, but soon found a formula and wrote twenty-six plays and musicals almost all of which were big hits. She was a shrewd woman who dressed in the most elegant style and knew how to keep her name in the papers.

Born in Baltimore to Emma Stuart Johnson and William A. Johnson, the young girl grew up in comfort and culture, despite a shortage of money. One of the many stories which appeared about Young after she made a success was headed, "Bloody Distinguisht" and informed the readers that the playwright had distinquished blood flowing in her veins, being a great-grandaughter of a Hungarian nobleman and a Rothschild. (n.p.). She began to write poems and short stories at an early age which were published in local papers. She attended Wilson College in Pennsylvania and retained pleasant memories of college life which she put into her plays. There were so many stories about her that it is a little difficult to separate fact from fiction. It was widely reported that she had attended Radcliffe for many years when Brown of Harvard was a success. She claimed to have won support from her parents to take her play about Omar Kayyam to New York when she was eighteen. Young apparently made an effort to appear younger than she was, so her real age is uncertain. However, it is known, and was frequently reported, that she did go to New York at an early age, at first supporting herself by selling furniture polish. She was obviously quite confident and courageous to go to New York with no contacts and no financial support. Nobody but E.H. Sothern responded when she sent her play, but he took the time to tell her kindly that a cast of more than a hundred, clumsily moved through many settings would not be a success. He helped her to get a job as an actress with Daniel Frohman and for two years she performed as a "rotten actress." She later said that she wanted to be a great actress, but soon saw that was not to be. These details of her life and career were given to Helen Christine

Bennett in a long interview in 1920. She said that after working for two years as an actress, she turned to writing songs. She worked in a "music publishing house, where we worked as a factory works, turning out songs at a rate that was bewildering. . . . When a song was needed to fit a particular play or concert, or actor, someone wrote the music, and I fitted words to them" ("The Woman Who Wrote 'Mother Machree'" 185). Young wrote more than 500 songs, many for more than a dozen musicals for which she wrote the books.

After working in the music publishing house, Young returned to acting, using the name Louise Jansen. She told Bennett, "I did better and got better parts, but I was no actress. Then I wrote another play; not so long as the Omar one, nor with so many characters ; but still pretty ambitious. This one was about Lord Byron, and it was actually produced and played, though not with much success" (185). While acting in a stock company the budding playwright acted with the atheletic looking, promising actor James Young, Jr. (the son of a Maryland senator). The play was added to the company's repertoire and she and he played the leading roles. They were married in 1904 and she assumed his name, which she maintained after her divorce a few years later.

Young's first two plays were ambitious period plays with a literary bent. She decided that she wanted to write a really successful play, so she wrote one with a contemporary college theme and had a stunning success with *Brown of Harvard*. After that she stuck with her boy meets girl formula and earned fantastic sums of money. She bought a home in Bellhaven, New York and a large estate in Stamford, Connecticut. There she worked, dividing her time between playwriting and gardening. She larded her discussions of playwriting technique with gardening terms such as pruning, weeding out, and tending and watering the growing idea. She said that writing a play was difficult for her, but that she spent every day from nine to one at her typewriter, even if nothing much came of it. Then she spent the rest of the day playing golf, or tennis, or gardening. She spent four to six months on each play. Although she did not actually direct her plays, she spent much of her time in rehearsals: "while I don't conduct all the practicing, yet I like to see things done just as I want them" ("A Woman Dramatist" n.p.) In her interview with Bennett she discussed at length the rigors of out-of-town work as a librettist, working late at night writing new scenes and lyrics for the rehearsal the next day. Young often indicated that she wished she had time to be idle and play, but that she had to keep working. In 1910 an article "Holds Record as Woman Playwright" indicated that in the past four years, Young had written seven plays and that she was "busily engaged on several works for next season" (n.p.).

Young traveled widely. When she wanted to write *Brown of Harvard* (1906) she went to Cambridge to spend six weeks on the campus. Charles Frohman, hoping for another such success, sent her to Oxford to study the British university. On another occasion, when she wanted to write a baseball play, she went to a training camp for several weeks and collaborated with pitcher Christie Mathewson on *The Girl and the Pennant* (1913). Her writing was noted for its authenticity of detail, atmosphere, and dialogue. In one of her numerous interviews she discussed the difference between her plays and earlier formula plays. She said that playgoers were more demanding regarding details in staging and performance, as well as in the writing. She studied actual locales and the people inhabiting them before writing her plays. As a woman moving in good society she felt her society plays were superior to those written by many men whose work made it painfully obvious that they wrote without real knowledge: "It is suggestive of men who are never, probably, inside the house of a woman who makes any pretensions to be in society" ("A Woman Dramatist Tells About Plays" n.p). Though she knew about society, she felt she had to study to learn about athletics because of the "steady improvement in athletic plays." She wanted to "become thoroughly imbued with the technical points and go about the scenario or framework not as a novice, but as one who knows what she is writing about" ("A Woman Dramatist" n.p.).

Authenticity certainly contributed to Young's success. Another factor was her charm and her sense of publicity. She had a great reputation for modesty which was enhanced by statements such as, "I don't call mine plays. They aren't my idea of a play. They are just amusing little things—I don't know what you'd call them" (Burns 634). Despite this modesty, she managed to keep her name in the papers continually. Not only did she grant frequent interviews and charm the writers, she sent cables and letters to such figures as the anonymous woman who wrote the column "Mlle. Manhattan" for the *Telegraph*. When she took dancing lessons in preparation to going to Oxford and going to parties with the undergraduates that was in the paper. When she was in Oxford she sent a cable to Mlle. Manhattan just before Shakespeare's birthday. She often sent out press releases which were published throughout the country under photographs showing her glamourously dressed in furs and large hats. One of these in 1910 read in part, "Mrs. Rida Johnson Young, author of 'The Lottery Man," which, with its original company is filling an engagement at the Shuberts' Masonic Theater, is a tall, stately brunette, and has the reputation of being the handsomest of the women dramatists of the country" ("Brilliant Dramatist of the South" n.p). So Young consciously contributed to the portrait of herself as a talented, modest, glamourous, independent woman who was fêted by high society wherever she traveled.

Young admitted frankly that she did not seek anything new or original, but that she wanted to write clean, wholesome plays which would be successful and earn her a great deal of money. In an interview in 1910 she said that she hated to work, "But I am after the money, although I don't keep it when I get it. But I do like the things money can buy." The interviewer commented "In winter, Mrs. Young, with her maid, lives at a fashionable hotel in New York, and in summer, much of her time is spent at her beautiful country home. All of the luxuries *she has gained for herself* [italics mine]" (Burns, "Mrs. Rida Johnson Young" 634).

She gave the public the kind of play she thought it wanted: "It does not have to have a new plot. Managers insist that the public demands novelty . . . but I have an idea that what people want most is an old story in a new dress" ("The Woman Who Wrote" 178). She was certainly proved correct. Many of her plays ran for years and were frequently revived and made into films. She was able to indulge herself in Paris dresses and hats, furs, and a luxurious life. She preferred to describe herself as a "play manufacturer" rather than as a playwright. In 1917, Helen Ten Broeck wrote that Young wanted to see a woman "write the GREAT AMERICAN PLAY. It is a perfectly impersonal ambition, however, for she has no aspirations toward giving the stage that masterpiece herself" (202). As for her own work, Young said, "There is a better chance for the playwright than ever before. Only—one must make it a business. That is the real reason I have succeeded. I have never undertaken anything really big; I have contented myself with writing plays that are popular and within my ability" (Bennett 187). She stuck to that outlook even after seeing plays in Germany, France, and England for three months in 1909. When she arrived in New York on the Mauritania she was naturally interviewed by many reporters including Mlle. Manhattan. She was so in love with the breadth of the French and German theatre that she said, "I am afraid I shall never be satisfied to write mere money-making plays for America until I divest myself of every one of the new ideas I have gained in three months' skimming of the theatre in Paris and London" ("Mlle. Manhattan" n.p.).

Despite her wholly commercial orientation, however, Young did have something which raised her plays above much of the commercial writing of the time. As she herself had charm, she was able to write plays which were charming. She often had quite amusing basic ideas, even if she followed a standard plot. She felt that she was capable of creating real women on the stage, not types like vamps ("I have never seen a real vampire, have you?") and "the woman who wears herself out in a riot of devotion." She walked out on a movie because an old woman scrubbing, cooking, etc. was held up as an example of the ideal woman. She said, "The ideal heroine has long been a silly little thing, who does exactly as she is told. Flights of independence are put down as petulance. The woman of spirit has been caricatured as masculine and a freak. Men have written, produced and judged the plays, and the nearer the heroines approached their preconceived notion the more approval they bestowed upon her and her creator." In creating modern, attractive, individualized women, she felt that she was able to write better love scenes than men—"normal love scenes, for normal, sane women" (Weinstein, "Real Love for the Stage; The Man Made Variety is Bosh, Women Dramatists Say" n.p.).

Young also felt that comedy was very important but that women had not previously convinced men that they had humor. Young said, "Women have not paraded their humor. They couldn't afford to when men were their main source of income. But there's a lot of laughter hidden away up the feminine sleeve. . . . Women will contribute comedy to the stage. They have a remarkable sense of humor, which, coupled with their uncanny insight into nature, should bring a rich harvest of laughs" (Weinstein "Real Love for the Stage" n.p.).

An examination of a few of Young's plays and musicals will demonstrate the type of plays she wrote which pleased the public for so many years. *Brown of Harvard* was actually modeled on George Ade's *A College Widow* (1904). It was more conventional than her later plays, containing both a clear villain and a more than virtuous hero who is mis-

takenly charged with a number of moral peculations. He is anony-
mously supporting a poor student through Harvard and seems to be
keeping his sister as a mistress. The villain lures the poor student away
from the big Harvard/Yale boat race and Brown has to fill his place on
the team. Needless to say, the team wins, misunderstandings are
cleared away, and Brown and his sweetheart, Evelyn, are united.
Today it is difficult to remember that this setting and the excitement of
the boat race were fresh in 1906. According to reports, much of
Young's time at Harvard was "spent at the headquarters of the Harvard oarsmen. She accompanied the crew to New London for the
annual race with Yale, and received from the Harvard rowing authori-
ties much assistance in the way of technical information" ("Miss Rida
Johnson Young" unidentified clipping, Lincoln Center, n.p.). Young
captured the atmosphere of the men's college rooms and used the latest college slang. When the men see some young women in a boat,
they say, "Look at that boat-load of peaches!" and "That one in the
red dress for mine" (59). The excitement of the mythical boat race
between an English team and Harvard was the high point of the
action. All of the characters are in the room looking out at the river.
As the race is nearly over, the English are ahead by a length. The finish
is described by the excited characters:

Evelyn.	Look! Look at Tom! He's going faster—he—they're closing up the gap. They're creeping up!
Mrs. Ken.	Our boys are creeping up!
Edith.	The coxswain is yelling to them.
Tubby.	What does he say?
Evelyn.	Pull boys, pull, faster. Oh, I wish they would hear me. They've got to win.
Everybody on Balcony.	They've got to win.
Thurston.	Oh, Oh! They're about even.
Edith.	That makes them work. That makes the Englishmen work.
Evelyn.	But our boys are not tired, and they are.
Edith.	Our boys are growing better every minute.
Evelyn.	Oh, such a little way! Pull, boys!
Everybody.	(on and off stage) Pull, pull, pull! They're ahead! (cheer, then immediately) Harvard! Harvard! Harvard! Rah! Rah! Rah! Rah! Rah! Rah! Rah! Rah! Rah! Rah! Rah! Harvard! Harvard! (Pistol shot from off R.)
Thurston.	They've won!

(As Harvard wins, everyone on stage starts to sing and dance. Colton [the vil-
lain] tears across stage and Exits at L. The orchestra plays "Star Spangled
Banner." At the height of excitement the crew rushes on from float at R.,

bearing Tom on their shoulders. As he comes under balcony, Evelyn drops flowers on him.) (73)

Audiences responded with enthusiasm to this scene, as they did to the scene in which Tom, in unconventional language, turned on those who misjudged his conduct. Springing to center stage, he shouts,

> Stop! Stop! Now you listen to me! I'm tired of being bullied. I'm tired having you sit in judgment on me. Now you've got to listen to me, and you've got to believe what I say. I tell you, my record's clean. I've never done a low trick in all my life. You, Madden, my room-mate for four years, you ought to be ashamed of yourself! And you, Thurston, and you, and the rest of you. I tell you you've got to stop sitting in judgment on me. I can't explain about the check and I'm not going to say anything more about it either, but every man in this room has got to say he believes me, or Damnation and Hell! I'll fight the whole damned crowd of you. (80)

This speech was widely quoted, with dashes taking the place of whole swear words. Audiences rose to their feet after hearing it. When the play toured to Chicago, the *Record* reviewer wrote that the audience loved every bit of it: "The plot and counterplot, the romance and the larks, the bright pictures of the Harvard demesne and of the historic Charles River, the gurgling girls and the giddy undergraduates, all—all were loved and acclaimed with so much fervor by the Sunday night crowd that, weather permitting, 'Brown of Harvard' bids fair to put in many a blithe week at the Garrick" ("Music and the Drama: "Brown of Harvard" n.p.). One element which appealed to audiences in not only this, but all the Young plays, was the use of songs. Many songs were heard off and on-stage, contributing to the college atmosphere. Young's "When Love is Young in Springtime" became a popular hit.

The reviewer for *Theatre Magazine* summed up the effect of the play and its appeal, saying that the playwright had captured "The joyousness of exuberant youth" and that the play had "much to commend it for its fresh and accurate character drawing and the breezy naturalness of the dialogue." He paid tribute to the authenticity of the script, saying, "It is in the little truthful touches of student life that Mrs. Young, herself a college-bred woman, is happiest. The title role is conventional, the epitome of all the virtues and long-suffering and self-sacrificing as well, but there are other types projected that are vital, true and satisfying. The earnest youth working his way through college, the gilded youth who finds study a bore, and the 'Tubbys' and 'Happys,' without which no regulated class is complete, are capital figures from life" ("Brown of Harvard" 87).

Young wrote the role of Brown for her husband, but a more experienced actor was cast. Young justified his wife's intentions by taking over the role in the second year and playing with great success. She went on to write a vaudeville sketch in 1910 called "Wanted—a Sister" in which Young again played Brown. In the sketch one of the characters suggests that they solve their problem of no chaperone the way the characters do in *Charley's Aunt*, by dressing one fellow up as a woman. This slight farce was a popular spin-off from the enormous success of *Brown of Harvard*. The latter ran for several years, toured the country, and was made into a film. The role of Brown established Harry Woodruff and James Young as stars.

It was during the process of rehearsing *Brown of Harvard* that Young really matured as a playwright. She had never studied writing and her play was crudely put together. She said afterward, "When I think of *Brown of Harvard* I think mainly of my quarrels with Mr. [Henry] Miller. When I was forced to rewrite and rewrite, to cut and elaborate, I felt that Mr. Miller was murdering my child. One day, after a vehement quarrel, he ordered me off the stage. But I can never thank him enough for having had the patience to put up with me at all" (Bennett 185). She went on to construct plays more tightly to support her sprightly dialogue and atmospheric locations.

A good example of her craft is *Glorious Betsy* (1908) a vehicle for Mary Mannering who played it for five years. The play was set in the time of Napoleon and featured elegant settings and gorgeous costumes. As usual, Young did research in order to make the play authentic. So impressed was the French playwright M. De Courcelles (whom Young met in Paris), that he made an adaptation of the play for the French stage. American audiences loved the story and critics praised the wholesome qualities of the script. An important element in Young's plays was the wholesome, exuberant quality of fun which contrasted the sordid stories in many realistic dramas and the off-color qualities of many farces. The reviewer for the *Washington Star* commented, "It required some courage to set a simple, wholesome love story like 'Glorious Betsy' before the public" ("Glorious Betsy" n.p.).

Naughty Marietta (1910) with music by Victor Herbert (who conducted the orchestra at the premiere) and libretto by Young was an instant success and has been performed ever since. In 1917 Young said it was very easy to write with Victor Herbert and that they made very few changes from the orignal libretto and songs during rehearsals (Young, "Life of the Poor Librettist" n.p.). The story of a young woman who runs away from a French convent and disguises herself as the son of a puppet master was tailored for Mlle. Emma Trentini. She had scored a success as the mechanical doll in *The Tales of Hoffmann*. The role gave her a chance to perform comic scenes and generally sparkle. The atmosphere of French New Orleans in the early eighteenth century delighted the audiences. One critic wrote, "Real comic opera is this "Naughty Marietta," perfectly proper notwithstanding the title, and with such a succession of pretty melodies in its score that it would not be fair to the others to single out any one for special mention" ("The Propriety of Naughty Marietta" 707). The big hit song was "I'm Falling in Love With Someone" with charming lyrics by Young. The operetta ran for 136 performances and then toured. It was revived in New York in 1929 with Ilse Marvenga, who, according to the *New York Times* critic, "gave the runaway Countess of Rida Johnson Young's book all the sparkle and dash and impertinent charm the part calls for, both in voice and action" ("Naughty Marietta Back" 26). This was one of many roles which Young created for actresses which were unlike the innocuous heroines the author so disliked. The operetta was also a vehicle for Jeannette MacDonald and Nelson Eddy (teamed for the first time) in the film version in 1934. There were also revivals in New York in 1931 and 1936.

By 1917 Young had written nineteen works for the stage, of which five were musicals. In that year she "topped the playwrights of the season with three productions": "Captain Kidd, Jr.," "Her Soldier Boy," and "His Little Widows" (introduction to Young, "Life of" n.p.). Arthur Hornblow praised "Her Soldier Boy" for all its qualities including songs with lyrics by Young and music by Emmerich Kalman and Sigmund Romberg. But what he praised mostly was the libretto because he felt it was so unusual. "Incredible as it may sound, "Her Soldier Boy" has a real honest-to-goodness plot . . . here is a musical comedy—real music and real comedy—with a PLOT!" ("Her Soldier Boy" 64). The plot seems sentimental, but was handled with a light touch and comedy which undercut the potential saccharine quality. A soldier was killed in Belgium and his friend was persuaded to go visit his blind mother. He reluctantly does so, falls in love with the dead soldier's sister, then all ends happily as the supposedly dead son appears. The horrible reality of the war was not yet clear to the American audience, and only the superficial reality of settings and costumes was present in this musical. The popular show actually opened in December 1916, but ran for 198 performances into 1917, so that Young had three productions on at once.

His Little Widows was a good example of Young's hand for a comic treatment of a basically funny idea. The story has to do with a young man, Jack, who inherits his uncle's millions, but with a catch: the uncle was a Mormon and the heir has to marry his widows in Salt Lake City! Mixed up in the action is an opera company, a mine in Utah, and all the widows. The marriage takes place, but then, to the disappointment of the widows is annulled and Jack marries the opera star he loves. Young wrote the libretto with William Cary Duncan and music was by William Schroeder (Schrader, "His Little Widows" n.p.). Young said that she really preferred to write plays by herself because she didn't like to split the profits. With musicals, of course, she had additional income from the songs. *His Little Widows* was not one of Young's major successes, but it ran 72 performances at the Astor Theatre.

1917 was an important year for Young. In August, following the other shows, one of her biggest successes opened. *Maytime* had a score by Sigmund Romberg which was very popular and "Sweethearts" was sung everywhere. The play was ideal for Young's talents as it moved from 1840 through a variety of settings up to the nineteenth century. It followed the lives of a pair of lovers who were separated when the girl's father forced her to marry a wealthy man. As they age, they see each other again, but it is too late for their love. In the final scene the happiness which eluded them comes to his son and her daughter. The reviewer for the *New York Times*, wrote, "Romantic stories that combine delicate charm and the native aroma of youth with those larger visions in which the tragedy of the individual blends with the eternal comedy of living come very rarely to any generation. Ours had "Alt Heidelberg" and "Milestones" . . . and now "Maytime" ("'Maytime' Scores at the Shubert" 7).

Unfortunately for Young, there was a controversy regarding the book. A year before the big Berlin hit *Wie einst im Mai* performed successfully in New York. By 1917 anything German was unwelcome, but the Shuberts thought an Americanized treatment of the story by Young would be popular. However, the fact that no credit was given to the original authors was noted by several critics. Lee Shubert attacked the critic of *The Green Book*, citing the review as "only another instance of the hostility with which you have treated the Shubert enterprises" ("In Rebuttal" 595). Outside of this, however, there was only good news. The production was praised, particularly the musically enhanced atmosphere of each period with authentic dances, settings, dialogue, and costumes. It ran 492 performances at the Shubert Theatre and then was performed throughout the country. Young was at the peak of her career and enjoying all of her success.

Sometime was an effort to utilize the techniques of film onstage. The play began with a group of performers rehearsing in a stage setting. As one critic wrote, "Now follows what the motion picture people call a cut-back and the audience is taken back five years in the story. In this manner the story runs, with the episodes in retrospect" ("Sometime" At Atlantic City" n.p.). The story continued to run backwards with a final scene back at the rehearsal and happy lovers united. The plot was criticized by Arthur Hornblow because he felt the structure (which was fresh when Elmer Rice had used it in his 1914 play *On Trial*) had been used too much: "'Sometime' is one of those hybrid things, sired by the motion picture, which has frequent 'cut-ins,' showing the past events in the life of the hero and heroine, very much like 'Forever After,' which, in turn is like 'Chu Chin Chow,' which, in turn, is like—but, great heavens! hasn't 'On Trial' a lot to answer for?" ("Some Time" 346). John Corbin dismissed Young's work saying, "Not much can be said for the book and lyrics of 'Sometime'" ("'Sometime' Comes, With Ed Wynn" 11). The songs by Rudolph Friml and Young and the hilarious performance by Ed Wynn drew in audiences, so the show ran for 283 performances at the Shubert. The play was also memorable because it provided Mae West with one of her first stage roles.

In 1918 Young returned to the war for subject matter with *Little Simplicity*. This was the first musical with the cast in khaki, as several reviewers noted. The novelty of ending the piece "somewhere near the trenches" was also noted. This was not unusual in drama, but as John Corbin noted, "it is a bit of a novelty to begin a musical piece in Algeria in 1912 and run it into the war for its denouement." Although the play was successful, critics were beginning to find Young's writing old-fashioned and conventional. Having noted the novelty of the story, this critic continued, "Otherwise, however, the piece is strictly Orthodox. It is concerned with nothing newer than the love of a man for a maid, and its three acts content themselves with separating the pair and bringing them together again." He concluded the review by saying, "The book and lyrics of Rida Johnson Young are workmanlike, albeit far from inspired, and if the proceedings are a bit dull on occasion, the fault must be laid to the extreme tenuousness of the story" ("War Romance in Musical Frame" 2). Arthur Hornblow was not impressed with this plot, remarking in a short review, "Rida Johnson Young's acrobatic libretto for "Little Simplicity" leaps from a Tunisian cafe to the Latin Quarter of Paris and thence to a Y.M.C.A. hut somewhere in France. Mrs. Young cracks the whip and all of the popular musical-comedy situations jump through the hoop" ("Little Simplicity" 347). The timely musical appealed to audiences enough to run 112 perfor-mances—a respectable run but not a smash success.

Young was nearing the end of her career and her life. In 1924 she essayed a straight comedy called *Cock O' The Roost.* By this time New York audiences and critics had seen plays by Rice, Glaspell, O'Neill, Gale, and others whose work ranged from experimental drama to intense realism. The formula play continued, but was viewed as the part of the theatre which looked to the past, rather than to the future. Stark Young wrote a review which was condescending in tone. Noting that the play was "brewed from a simple and oft-used recipe." He described the dutiful daughter about to be "sacrificed on the altar of Mammon" and the usual happy ending. "A good deal of the play has been written against the grain of plausibility. There are, now and again, scenes of truth and shrewdness, but for the most part there is merely a succession of theatricalisms unconvincingly arrayed." ("'Cock O' The Roost' Shown" 23).

Rida Johnson Young died in 1926 after a long illness. Her meteoric career caused scores of women playwrights to send her scripts to read. She was of her time in her approach to playwriting, but for most of her career her own fresh sense of humor, her attitude toward the charac-terization of women, her songs, and her sense of atmosphere made something special out of the formula, commercial play and musical. With the advent of modern playwriting, she was perceived as a play-wright whose day had passed. In the years to follow her death only her musicals were revived. There was talk of producing several scripts she left behind, but nothing materialized. A bizarre touch was added to Young's career after her death when her former husband told a reporter, "I was co-author of all the early plays of Rida Johnson Young—'Brown of Harvard,' 'The Lottery Man,' 'Naughty Marietta,'

'Glorious Betsy,' etc., but at that time I was an ambitious actor and, not desiring any literary distinction, I claimed no credit for my work" (unidentified clipping, Young file, Lincoln Center). Such a claim, coming so late after the work was done, and after Young had made a fortune on the plays named which he did not attempt to claim, was surprising to say the least. Her mark was clearly on all the plays which she wrote. If Young was not in the group of developing women play-wrights who would make bold experiments or significant social state-ments through her plays, she was nevertheless an extremely successful playwright who knew what she wanted to do and did it well. Her plays brought millions of playgoers happiness in the early part of the century, particularly during the war. For twenty years she played an active role in the American theatre both in writing plays and participating in their production.

Zona Gale (1874-1938)

Zona Gale (1874-1938) gained fame chiefly for her novels and short stories, but she contributed a few memorable plays to the theatre. She is an important figure in theatre history as she was the first woman to win the Pulitzer Prize for Playwriting. She is also important because she moved away from the standard urban settings so typical of the theatre, particularly in New York, to present regional characters and settings.

Gale was born in Portage, Wisconsin. Her parents were loving, if over-protective, and like Edna Ferber, Gale's life was dominated by her close relationship with her mother. After her mother died, when Gale was 49, she signed letters to friends with both their initials, and made efforts to contact her mother through spiritualism. She was also very close to her father, a railroad engineer given to writing philosophical thoughts in little notebooks. As Gale's biographer Simonson noted, "Absence, romantic love, career—nothing but death could sever these three" (16). It was difficult for Gale to leave her parents to attend the University of Wisconsin, but at their insistence she stayed until she received her B.L in 1895. She returned and received her M.L. in 1899.

Although frail and very delicate, Gale had determination and ambition. She persisted in applying for work at the *Evening Wisconsin* and was finally accepted. She covered society news, plays, and interviewed such notables as Ellen Terry and Sir Henry Irving. By the time Edna Ferber came to the same newspaper to begin her career, Zona Gale was a famous writer, first writing for the *New York Evening World*, then achieving success with fiction. Her writing was concerned with the mundane, often pathetic, lives of ordinary people living in small towns like Portage.

While in New York, Gale became involved with an artistic group of people including Hamlin Garland, Isadora Duncan, Louis Untermeyer, Richard Le Gallienne (father of Eva Le Gallienne), and, most importantly, Ridgely Torrence who was one of the first white writers to write plays for black actors. She had a platonic romance with Torrence for several years which involved many idealistic love letters. At one point she wrote that his "spirit, not his manliness, drew her to him" (Simonson 28). Although secretly engaged for a period of time, the marriage did not take place because of parental opposition, Torrence's mistaken jealousy of Le Gallienne, and Gale's hesitation to commit herself. It was not until a year before her father died that Gale, at the age of 54, married. Her husband was a 64 year old widower whom she had vowed to marry in her youth.

Gale was committed to writing throughout her adult life and wrote hundreds of short stories and articles as well as twenty-two volumes of fiction. She was very active in a number of causes such as women's suffrage, Theosophy, spiritualism, and pacifism. She was sincerely interested in education, particularly for women, serving for many years as a member of the University of Wisonsin's Board of Regents. She was one of the writers of the 1923 Wisconsin Equal Rights Law and was Wisconsin's representative to the International Congress of Women in Chicago in 1933. Gale was a close friend of Jane Addams and was active in the Women's Peace Party (Breitsprecher 97). Her writing, particularly her immensely successful 1920 novel *Miss Lulu Bett*, reflects her concern for equality for women.

In 1910, at the request of Thomas Dickenson, who was encouraging regional playwriting, Gale wrote a one-act play called *Neighbors*. In his foreword to *Wisconsin Plays* (which contains *Neighbors* and plays by two other playwrights, Dickenson explained the aims of Gale and the others involved in the Wisconsin Dramatic Society:

> In a strict sense it has been the ideal of the Wisconsin Dramatic Society to be a free-stage society, free, that is, in the sense of freedom from commercial necessities, from professional trammels, even from a too insistent social purpose; in other words, free to experiment with a rapidly changing art and to trace out in practice its growing social implications. The plays which make up this series constitute one factor of an experimental programme, which has been directed to the cultivation of a better dramatic art, by means of training actors, and the encouragement of the study, criticism, and writing of plays. (n.p.)

Superficially, *Neighbors* is a pleasant little play which features a number of small-town people, just folks who toil and move through their daily, repetitious activities. They are surprised and excited by the news that one of their poorer neighbors, Carry Ellsworth, is going to raise the son of her sister who has just died. They gossip, make plans of various types, and finally all get together to collect food and clothing in order to have a real party when the little boy arrives. All, however, seems for nought because the little boy will be raised by another relative. However, it proves that all the excitement has had a good effect: a shy young man finally talks to the girl he loves, and at the end they embrace to the satisfaction of all the neighbors. It looks as if all the children's clothing will come in handy in the future.

Beneath this tale of people moving away from their petty concerns over wood left on the lawn, buffalo bugs in the carpets, and aches and pains, is a depiction of the life of ordinary women in small towns. Throughout the play there are reminders of the constant toil of these women. The setting is a living room in which Mis' Abel is ironing, using the old-fashioned irons which are heated on a stove, and Grandma sits in a rocker rolling rags for rag rugs. Carry Ellsworth is a poor widow who has to work as a clerk to supplement her income of eight dollars a month from her dead husband's pension. Mis' Moran has worked all her life keeping the house clean, cooking, sewing, etc. and she is wracked by various types of pains and feels, "I dunno but my time is come and my grave is diggin' around the next corner. I feel that way. I told Jake so" (24). Many of the women have essentially empty lives, particularly old women like Grandma who used to be "folks" but is now just useless. She says, "Dum 'em. They've gone off to do things. And I'm so old, so fool old" (43). Carry Ellsworth has led a dreary life and will now have a child to support. Mis' Abel sums up the life Carry led, "Carry didn't have much of any wedding presents. And she never had a baby. I dunno as I ever set foot in her house to any real occasion excep' a funeral" (32-33).

It is very clear, too, that the women are not only dominated by the men, they are ignored or ridiculed because they are women. Mis' Moran tells of her husband's indifference to her pains, saying, when she told she felt she might die, he asked her if she had made the pancakes yet. "I'd been goin' to tell him about my back, but I hadn't the heart. I just laid and cried" (25). Mis' Abel tells her daughter Inez about the difference between her husband before marriage and after. She says that before marriage he didn't talk much and seemed awed by her. "After we was married, whenever he begun actin' like he knew it all, an' like I wasn't nothin' but the fly-leaf o' things, I used to remember how perfectly simple he did use' to act when I first knew him—when he was first makin' up. An' many's the time I've just laughed to myself and gone and done like he told me to, sheer through rememberin' how simple and scairt and green he did use to act" (22). A very self-important male neighbor, hearing the news that Carry is to take care of her nephew, says, "Well, ain't that just like a woman!

Always gettin' herself come down onto by a lot o' distant relatives to support" (40).

All in all, the picture of the life of uneducated, overworked women is clearly depicted. Although there is a gentle joy in the coming together of the neighbors and in the projected union of the young couple, it is undercut by the emptiness of Carry's past life and the disappointment of her hopes. The most poignant speech in the play occurs when she tells of the plans she had made for the nephew. She says in part, "it's goin' to be awful hard for me not to have him to do for. Last night—when I begun to plan—it come over me like it never done before what I'd missed in *not* bein' left with one." She describes her plans for a bed and for cooking his meals, then pathetically pulls out a little hat, "I just see this little cap in the post-office store and I bought it for him. I thought the feather'd look kind o' cute, stickin' up in front. And now here comes this [letter]—and it's all for nothin'— it's all for nothin'" (59).

The play was performed by the Wisconsin Dramatic Society, at the Neighborhood Playhouse in New York, and was then taken up by the Washington Square Players for production. Reviewing *Miss Lulu Bett* ten years later, the reviewer for the *New York Telegram* noted that New Yorkers had already had more than one chance to see the *Neighbors* and noted its "delightful folk quality, its warm, human touches, its homely humor and its pathos" ("American Folk Play" n.p.). One of the most satisfying performances of the play was that given by a blind cast for an audience of 250 blind people and invited guests. This was a production at Lighthouse 1 which was connected to the Association for the Blind. A reviewer noted, "The members of the cast moved through their roles with seeming confidence, and the country witticisms of Miss Gale's play produced laughter from the sightless audience" ("Plays Given By Blind" 23).

Gale continued her support of the Wisconsin Dramatic Society (which was later known as the Wisconsin Players) by giving them a donation of $500 and allowing them to produce *Neighbors* royalty free at any time. She also allowed any group which planted a tree in a community to present the play without paying royalty. Because of the play's simple appeal, it was popular, and because of the royalty conditions, it was put on more often in Wisconsin than any other play (Derleth 117). When Gale had completed the dramatization of *Miss*

Lulu Bett, she obtained the rights to allow presentation of the play by the Wisconsin Dramatic Society before its Broadway production.

Gale spent most of her life in Portage with her parents, gathering details of the society around her to use in her work. However, she maintained connections in New York and generally spent two months each winter there. She often invited guests and had a large circle of friends who were also women writers. Naturally, she knew people in the theatre as well. As soon as her novel *Miss Lulu Bett* was published in 1920 it became a great success and the producer Brock Pemberton asked Gale to turn it into a play. Later she said, "I'm ashamed to say how quickly it was done. I finished it in a week, but as I wasn't satisfied with the last act I held it over from Saturday to Monday to revise it. So I can say that it took me ten days, and that doesn't sound quite so bad" (Simonson, *Zona Gale* 84).

Many critics noted that the play was very faithful to the novel, and that many lines were the same. The story is simple, the characters homely, and the dialogue is often comical in its banality. Dwight Deacon is the head of a family and is very well pleased with his position. As a successful dentist and local magistrate, he lives well with his wife Ina, his two daughters Diana and Monona, his mother-in-law, Mrs. Bett, and his sister-in-law Lulu Bett. The thirty-four year-old Lulu is conspicuously *Miss* Lulu Bett, and is never allowed to forget that Dwight allows her a place in his home. She is the full-time cook, cleaner, and maid-of-all-work. She is poorly dressed and suffers from low self-esteem: she believes that she is treated as well as she deserves and imagines no man would be interested in her except for her cooking. She can't even recognize the attention an eligible suitor, Neil Cornish, is paying her. However, there is some foreshadowing of a rebellion to come when, after Dwight criticizes her for the wicked expenditure of a few cents for a pot of tulips, she picks the one blooming tulip, pins it on her dress, and throws the pot out the window.

When Ninian, Dwight's brother arrives for a visit, he makes Lulu aware that she is detestably treated and that she is attractive for more than her cooking. He plans a party for her in the city with dinner in a restaurant and a trip to the theatre. Dwight is pompous and ridiculous, as usual, as they kill time waiting for the train, and insists on some entertainment. Ninian and Lulu playfully pronounce the marriage vows, and Dwight realizes that they are, in fact, married, because he is a magistrate. He suggests they can have it annulled, but Ninian and Lulu decide to be married and leave for a honeymoon the next day. The confusion and comedy in the scene is enhanced by the silly little brat daughter Monona and old Mrs. Bett who can't seem to figure out what's going on. The scene ends with the typical confused, conversation which goes on throughout the play:

Ina.	They've just been married—Lulu and Ninian.
Mrs. Bett.	Who's going to do your work?
Lulu.	Oh, mother dearest—I don't know who will. I ought not to have done this. Well, of course, I didn't do it—
Mrs. Bett.	I knew well enough you were all keeping something from me.
Ina.	But, mama! It was so sudden—
Lulu.	I never planned to do it, mother—not like this—
Mrs. Bett.	Well, Inie, I should think Lulu might have had a little more consideration than this.
Lulu.	Mother dearest, tell me it's all right.
Mrs. Bett.	This is what comes of going to the theater. (124)

As they all rush for the train, Miss Lulu Bett is happy and unhappy, and by habit, mostly concerned about two pies she has left baking, Monona is dancing and chanting, "I was to a wedding! I was to a wedding!" and Lulu calls back, "Mother, mother! don't forget the two pies!" (124)

In the second act the family is surprised by Lulu's return, and scandalized to learn that Ninian has revealed that he was married to another woman fifteen years earlier but believes her to be dead. Lulu has returned until he straightens things out. Dwight is ready to take Lulu back in her former servant role, on condition that she keep the first marriage a secret and let people think Ninian got tired of her. It is apparent that a week with Ninian in Savannah has changed Lulu. She argues forcefully that she has nothing to hide, and insists that Dwight write to Ninian to learn the truth. In the original ending, Lulu liberates herself from the family when she learns that the first wife is still alive, refuses the opportunity to marry Neil Cornish (although she leaves open the possibility for the future), and leaves to find a life of her own. In the novel, Gale had Lulu accept Neil and marry him. She felt that the ambiguous ending of the play made a clear statement of Lulu's own maturation, but more than that, she did not think another marriage would be acceptable to the audience. She said, "Lulu could not marry two men in the space of an evening, no matter how vehemently the program announced that time had elapsed. Two marriages in the interval of two and a half hours would have been, one critic observed, almost bigamous" (qtd. in Toohey 20).

Critics noted the difference in the ending of the play, with some praising it as artistic and truthful. Louis V. De Foe, noting that the play was more of interest as a character study than as a story, compared the ending positively with that of *A Doll House*, saying, "We venture that Miss Lulu Bett will know how to take care of herself" ("Miss Lulu Bett" n.p). An anonymous critic wrote, "She asserts the rights of her womanhood and, like Nora of the Doll's House, goes out to seek for herself" (unident. clipping, Gale file, Lincoln Center n.p.). Kenneth Macgowan called the novel a "small classic" and did not feel the play was as good. He observed that the play was more cruel than the novel, commenting on the "bitter realism that is surprising and disturbing" ("Miss Lulu Bett" n.p.).

Playgoers by the hundreds agreed with Macgowan and wrote to Gale to protest the unhappy ending. Amazingly, after two weeks of performance she wrote a new ending for the play. There was no proposal from Neil Cornish, Lulu declared, " I can't stay here in Dwight's kitchen a day longer" (141) and left for the train station. Ninian arrived with the news that his first wife was, indeed, dead, Lulu returned and they were joyfully reunited. Critics complained that the new ending was tacked on and Ludwig Lewisohn complained that the new ending, "destroyed Lulu's significant liberation" ("Native Plays" 189). Playgoers were pleased with the new ending, the controversy gave the play publicity, and the play was performed 600 times. The play then went on tour. Such was the popularity of the play and the novel that Paramount purchased the rights, and in December 1921 both the play and the movie were drawing audiences in Chicago (Derleth 151).

Aside from the ending, many critics had strong reservations about the play. Many of them felt Gale had created fresh, interesting characters, but that the plot was extremely weak. Alexander Woolcott called it "somewhat sleazily put together, with but a slight sense of dramatic values and no instinct at all for the idiom of the theatre" ("Zona Gale's Play" 9). Heywood Broun said Gale didn't seem to know how to write a play, that she had written one which "has action and suspense but never really seems to be a drama" ("'Miss Lulu Bett' Is of Fine Fabric Though Often Crude" n.p.). Certainly, the critics were right in noting

the absence of strong plotting. The sub-plot involving the older daughter is not fully engaging, the timing of the return of people, particularly
Ninian, is contrived, and there are passages which seem too thin for
dramatic effect. Nevertheless, the play is engrossing and the critics who
called it Dickensian were accurate. The roles would be delightful for
character actors and the role of Lulu is an attractive challenge which
was successfully met by actress Carroll McComas. The play seems to
have been dark and bitter in performance, which is surprising to a
present-day reader. There seem many opportunities for comedy, and
many funny lines. Gale commented quite amusingly on the boring,
Babbitt-like quality of life in the household by having two scenes of
after-dinner conversation between Dwight and his wife exactly the
same. The second ending of the play, although contrived, seems in key
with the rest of the play, given the attitudes expressed by Ninian and
Lulu and the development of her character. (Judith Barlow includes
both endings in her book *Plays by Women*.) The new ending also
improved the play in an important way. The first audiences were
notably patient during long scene changes. By eliminating the proposal
from Cornish and the setting in his piano shop, Gale reduced the scene
changes to one, from the dining room to the front porch. The settings
contributed to the success of the play in their folksy, home-town quality.

   The play is not great dramatic literature, but it is certainly an entertaining and engrossing play which draws forth strong sympathy for Lulu
and calls attention to the plight of such women. Gale replied to criticism of the grimness of the depiction, "I know them . . . overshadowed,
browbeaten women, wives or Lulus enslaved by duty, dead duty"
(quoted in Simonson, *Zona Gale* 85). In *Miss Lulu Bett* as in the earlier
play *Neighbors*, Gale combined the pathos of a small-town woman,
overworked and undervalued, with the comedy of "that curious distil-
lation of the pettiness ane exasperation of life," as Alexander Woolcott put it ("Zona Gale's Play" 9).

   With the success of the play to recommend it and with her old
friend and supporter, Hamlin Garland, on the selection committee,
Gale won the Pulitzer Prize for the 1920-21 season. The critics complained that few would agree with the choice. However, the only
strong competition that year was O'Neill's *The Emperor Jones*. It was
pretty much out of the running because O'Neill had won the prize the
year before and his play was not considered a full-length play. After all

the criticism and excitement, Gale was glad to return to the quiet of Portage. One final oddity about the production of Miss Lulu Bett may be noted: it previewed at Sing-Sing prison on December 26, the night before the opening in New York on a new stage provided by David Belasco. A wife-murderer and a bigamist were among the temporary stage-hands (Toohey 19).

With an increasing interest in the production of plays by American women, a number of productions of Miss Lulu Bett have been seen. In 1984 the Berkshire Theater Festival in Stockbridge, Massachusetts presented it with Carol Kane, Elizabeth Wilson, John Glover and Kathryn Grody. In 1985 Horizons Theater in Washington, D.C. presented the play with both endings, as Joe Brown said, "a decision that provides an insight into the playwright's creative process and leaves it to you to decide which is the real 'happy ending.'" Brown praised Lee Jacobson's "playful direction" which made for a "very funny evening, without scanting the play's proto-feminist underpinning." He concluded that "Carole Myers is a lulu of a Lulu, awakening visibly to assertiveness from mousy servility" ("The Enduring 'Miss Lulu Bett'" 11). In 1988 Richard Christiansen praised the play more than the production by the Center Theater in Chicago, which performed the original ending. He noted, "Beyond its contemporary feminist appeal, 'Miss Lulu Bett' still has the benefit of a keenly observed view of a small-town middle-class life in the early part of this century" ("'Miss Lulu Bett' Suffers at the Hand of Superficial Acting" 5).

Quite naturally, Brock Pemberton encouraged Gale to write another play in order to follow up on her success. She chose to dramatize her 1918 novel Birth which many critics consider her finest work of fiction. In a sense it was a rather peculiar choice for dramatization as its central character is a pickle salesman whose chief characteristic is his crude inarticulateness—so intense that one critic likened it to aphasia. Marshall Pitt meets a woman by chance, and, as John Corbin described it, "in walked Barbara Ellsworth, whose father has just died and left a number of debts. Barbara, a weakling, anxious to have some one help her shoulder these debts, lets the poor innocent Mister Pitt fall desperately in love with her, marry her—and suffer. She never loved him, but, oh, how he loved her" ("Mister Pitt" 1"). Corbin looks at it with a male glance, ignoring the complex situation Gale has set up. Certainly, Barbara marries Pitt for money and support—what else can she do? Gale establishes her as a woman with no abilities, no income, and nothing to sell except herself. She has a baby and she performs the duties of a wife, but after a year she can't stand her husband's totally boring character, lack of refinement and slavish adoration, so she runs away with a musician. Pitt is determined to prove he can be something, so he arranges for the child to be raised by a neighbor and leaves town determined to make a success. But when he returns two years later he hasn't changed. Sadly, he finds that his inherent insignificance is an embarrassment to his son as it was to his wife.

The critics generally found something positive to say about the play, but many pointed to weakness in the construction. Brock Pemberton suggested that Lula Vollmer might assist her in improving it. Gale later felt that the major benefit of the experience of *Mr. Pitt* was the friend-ship she formed with Vollmer.

The play opened in January 1924. John Corbin expressed the point of view which was shared by most critics: much of the play was true and moving, but Gale had not mastered dramatic technique ("Mr. Pitt" n.p.). John Ranken Towse, noting that in her curtain speech Gale indicated many hands had been at work on the play, said it was no surprise that it was a patchwork of "prolixity and feebleness" relieved by "several isolated scenes that are excellent and life-like" ("Zona Gale's Play Has Good Points" n.p.). Percy Hammond called the pro-duction, "more or less chaos" with many short scenes, long waits, and an unclear attitude toward the characters by the playwright. He sug-gested Augustus Thomas or another playwright might make it into a good play ("'Mister Pitt' by Miss Zona Gale is Good, Though it Needs to be Rewritten" n.p.). Another problem noted by the critics, and one which no doubt discouraged audiences, was that the central character was a bore who was boring. As E.W.Osborn complained, "Because nothing in Miss Gale's play relieves Pitt of his lowness of mind, we could not find the drama convincing" ("Mr. Pitt" n.p.).

One aspect of the play which was quite interesting was the presence of a chorus of gossiping women. Heywood Broun called the play more experimental and challenging than *Miss Lulu Bett*, saying, "between the episodes are interludes like a Greek chorus" ("Mister Pitt" n.p.). After a month Broun returned to see the play again, and made a very interesting observation. He wrote, "I don't feel that anybody can see 'Mister Pitt' by Zona Gale, without getting some glimmer of the nature of all that unrest which we know as feminism." He went on to say that the critics all wrote that the play was about an inarticulate man, but he felt it was about a woman. He compared Barbara to Nora (as critics had done with Lulu), and said that the play showed the psychology of incompatability and detailed why the woman could not endure her husband. Broun was alone in calling the play "the most subtle and the most thrilling piece of playwriting I have seen all season" ("It Seems to Me" n.p.).

The play ran for only six weeks, and even that brief run was in large part due to the attraction of young Walter Huston who had just come to the theatre from the vaudeville circuit and was virtually unknown. John Corbin remarked that he played the uninteresting character so well he made him interesting ("Mister Pitt" n.p.). But even Huston's performance couldn't hide the problems in the play. In the novel there were many other elements to surround the boring character and hold the reader's interest. With the compression required for a play, these were necessarily omitted. The chorus of women was an excellent idea, but it chopped the play into too many short segments and necessitated too much scene changing. All in all, the play revealed that Gale's understanding of human nature, her gift for dialogue, and her interest in feminism were better used in the writing of stories and novels. After the failure of Mr. Pitt, Gale never wrote a full-length play again.

However, Gale wrote a few short plays which were published and widely performed by amateurs. Among these, Uncle Jimmy was published in The Ladies' Home Journal, by Baker, and included in Hughes' Short Plays for Modern Readers and other anthologies. Like her other plays, it presents the quotidien lives of people living in a small town in the mid-west. A major motif is the conflict between the desire to travel (which is expressed in wonderment about how many miles it is to Idaho and how fast trains go) and the safety and pleasure of a small-town with familiar flowers and routine activities. Again the people are characterized as absorbed in problems of canning rhubarb, chopping wood, saving money for their funerals, etc. Uncle Jimmy is the sixty-nine year old jack-of-all-trades who has spent his whole life in Friend-ship Village. As the play begins he is discontent because Calliope Marsh is expecting her mother, called "Grandma", from Idaho. He complains to the neighbor Mis' Toplady, "Why, they's men that ain't been half that far. . . . I'm sick of this town, and I'm sick of running its urrants [errands]. They ain't anybody's cat dies that I ain't expected to ring the bell" (18) When he repeats his complaints to Grandma, she urges him to put on his "dyin' coat" and take the money he has saved for his funeral and go see someplace with palm trees. When an actual opportunity arises for him to go to Idaho all the women pitch in getting him a satchel, clothes, and lots of food for lunch on the train, but in the end he returns—the picture of ambiguity; he is spared the alarms of the trip, but sad to know he will never travel. As he sits with his chin on his chest, Grandma speaks sympathetically, "Couldn't you do it? Couldn't you go? You've waited too long!" He smiles faintly, takes off the funeral coat, and starts chopping wood (63).

The play is filled with charm and poignancy. The setting shows the two "back dooryards" with geraniums, morning glories, lilac, and wisteria. Uncle Jimmy is fond of picking a spray of flowers for his buttonhole, and wonders if they have "laylac" in Idaho. There are amusing discussions of minor activities which loom large for the characters. For example, Grandma carried her satchel across the city to the train, as usual, but "came within one of taking a hack." This provokes a lively discussion:

The Women. A hack!
Grandma.   I never took a hack across the city. So I says to one, "how much is it?" And he says, "Where do you want to go? And I says, "That depends on how much it is." And he says, "Well that depends on where you want to go to." And I says, "You needn't take me at all." Why if he'd known I was going out of town no telling how much he'd of charged me!
Calliope.   Of course not.
Mis' Sykes.   Why, of course.
Mis' Toplady. The rascal. (20)

The play is enlivened by the regionalisms and quaint expressions used by the characters. Uncle Jimmy refers to Friendship Village as "this little two-by-four, half-a-loaf, ten-cent, one-acre town" (24); Mis' Toplady is fond of exclaiming, "For the good land sakes alive!" and in a squabble Mis' Toplady accuses Mis' Sykes of being "dressy" and is herself criticized for "buyin' shelled nuts, when shelling 'em with your fingers costs twenty cents off" (61). The play maintains its charm and quiet humor and is worthy of production today.

Zona Gale cannot be considered a major American playwright either on the basis of the body of her playwriting or the quality. After reading her plays, one tends to retain the impression of cleverly written dialogue, low-key scenes with little action, and memorable characterizations. She was not temperamentally inclined to be involved with the theatre in New York, nor was she trained as a playwright. Writing short stories and novels brought her pleasure and success and allowed her to remain in Portage. Nevertheless, she made a break-through as the first woman to win the Pulitzer Prize and she established a precedent with her treatment of the character of Miss Lulu Bett. The theme and depiction are still appealing today. Writing when the play opened, critic Francis Hackett wrote, "Miss Gale has done authentically what perhaps only a feminist, and certainly what only an artist can do. She has shown in perfect American terms, the serious comedy of an emancipation" ("Miss Lulu Bett" n.p.). After Gale's death the people of Wisconsin expressed their gratitude for her encouragement of theatre in the state. The Zona Gale Memorial Dramatic Collection was founded in the University of Wisconsin Library. It's purpose was to collect "everything of interest having to do with Wisconsin drama in memory of Zona Gale, Wisconsin's most loved author and only Pulitzer Prize winner in drama" (Unidentified clipping Lincoln Center). Gale was also honored as a Doctor of Humanities from Rollins College and a Doctor of Literature from Wooster College. Throughout her life she was an example of intelligence, idealism, and productivity. She was always active and as a high profile feminist she drew positive attention to the inequalities suffered by women and the need for women to receive education and take an active role in social and political activities.

Georgia Douglas Johnson (1880-1966)

Georgia Douglas Johnson (1880-1966) was a poet, a playwright, and a social activist. Despite the fact that she wrote about thirty plays (Perkins 22), her theatrical work has been largely ignored throughout this century. Even in a book like *Negro Playwrights in the American Theatre* there is no mention of her. Yet her plays and her own personality contributed greatly to the development of African-American playwriting. As Winona L. Fletcher wrote in her article on the playwright in *Notable Women in the American Theatre*, "Georgia Douglas Johnson has earned a place of recognition in the early twentieth century literature and in the American theatre" (476).

Although there have been conflicting opinions regarding her birth date and place, recent accounts indicate that she was born on September 10, 1880 in Marietta, Georgia. Her mother was Laura Jackson Camp and her father was a wealthy, educated Englishman who was a little-known figure in the family. In her youth Georgia was often lonely because she had a working mother and had no brothers or sisters wholly related. Her education was excellent: in Atlanta she went to public schools and Atlanta University, and then studied music at Oberlin Conservatory. In 1903 she was married to Henry Johnson and they had two sons. Her husband was a successful lawyer who was appointed by President Taft to a government post in Washington, D.C. where the family moved in 1910. In Washington the Johnsons were very much involved in political and social activities. Johnson called their home "Half-Way House" and for forty years it was a major meeting point for writers and artists. In it she founded the "S Street Salon." Langston Hughes, May Miller, Zora Neale Hurston, Countee Cullen, W.E.B. Du Bois, Alain Locke and many others came to visit and exchange their views on literature. Johnson's Saturday Evening Soirees became famous in Washington because of the noted black and white political figures who were entertained by the Johnsons (Fletcher, "Johnson" 473-474).

Johnson found little time for her writing because she worked at the Department of Labor and took care of her family. Nevertheless, she started to write poetry, inspired by a poem by William Stanley Braithwaite. She was impressed by the poem and by the fact that the poet "had a drop or so of colored blood." The playwright May Miller's father was Dean Kelly Miller of Howard University and he was responsible for introducing Johnson to Braithwaite. They became close friends and he assisted her in getting her works published, which was certainly not easy for an African-American woman in that time (Perkins 22). She published several books of poetry including *The Heart of a Woman and Other Poems* (1918), *Bronze* (1922), *An Autumn Love Cycle* (1928), and *Share My World* (1962). She has been recognized as "one of the first black feminist poets and the most prolific black woman playwright of the Harlem Renaissance (Brown-Guillory, *Wines in the Wilderness* 12).

Another writer who encouraged Johnson to write was Zona Gale. This playwright encouraged Johnson to express her concerns as a black woman in plays. Johnson later wrote, "Then came drama. I was persuaded to try it and found it a living avenue and yet—the thing left most unfinished, less exploited, first relinquished, is still nearest my heart and most dear" ("The Contest Spotlight," *Opportunity* 204). Like other African-American playwrights, particularly women, Johnson found it very difficult to get her plays performed, let alone published. Of all her plays most have been lost and only five were published (Perkins 22). Writing plays in the early twenties, Johnson focused her attention on the problems of women in society, "As the Harlem Renaissance, with its emphasis on black pride, took on great importance, Johnson's concern for women focused on colored women and their families as was manifest in her one-act plays" (Brown-Guillory, *Wines* 12). Her depictions of African-American women, usually seen working and struggling in their homes, continue to move readers and audiences. Johnson's active participation in "most of the organizations in the Washington area committed to concerns of women and minorities" (Fletcher, "Johnson" 473) was reflected in the variety of subjects she treated in her plays: "Her plays encompassed a great variety of themes, including lynching, miscegenation, black history, passing, black folk life, and the empowerment or disempowerment of blacks" (Brown-Guillory, *Wines* 12).

Johnson received recognition for her play *Plumes* which was awarded the first prize in the 1927 *Opportunity* playwriting contest. The prize was $60.00 and publication by Samuel French. The play was then produced by the Harlem Experimental Theatre. This theatre had patterned itself after Krigwa and both groups wanted to "foster the development of the black folk play and to make these works available to the

Negro community in New York City" (France, *A Century* 75). The production drew attention to Johnson's plays and encouraged her to continue to attempt to find productions. During the period of the Federal Theatre Project she had high hopes because of the interest displayed in African-American playwrights in the Harlem Unit. Although a few plays by African-American men were produced, Johnson found no success. She submitted six plays but they were all rejected. These plays which dealt with rape and lynching of blacks and the attempts of slaves to escape were too shocking or forthright for the Project despite its proclaimed interest in "plays of social protest" (Fletcher, "Johnson" 475). In recent years the discoveries of Federal Theatre Project papers has enabled scholars to find out why Johnson's plays were rejected by the readers.

Johnson's next efforts at playwriting were concerned with historical figures. *Frederick Douglass* and *William and Ellen Craft* were published in 1935 in *Negro History in Thirteen Plays*. Willis Richardson and May Miller edited this book in an effort to bring theatre and African-American history to school children. Although these and other plays by Johnson received occasional professional productions and frequent productions by amateurs, she was "disheartened by the reception of her efforts to bring serious matters of black life to the American stage, gave up playwriting and returned to writing poetry in the 1940s" (Fletcher, "Johnson" 476).

In her later years Johnson became known as an eccentric. Although her husband had died in 1925, she maintained the house on S Street and continued to be hospitable and generous to unfortunate people, stray cats and dogs who came her way. In 1962, a few years before Johnson's death, Rosey Poole wrote a description of the writer and her life: "[She] lives in Washington amidst the most chaotic amassment of usable and broken-down typewriters, television sets, radios, furniture and piles of books and papers, among which she finds any single one with unerring instinct (qtd. in Hatch and Shine 211). S street was no longer the pleasant neighborhood she and her family had enjoyed—it had become one of the many slums in Washington. Only a few of the homes remained as they were and, during the 1950s, many of them were turned into expensive boarding houses for African-Americans moving up from the South. Johnson was always available to help those who needed it. She was "a beautiful, down-to-earth woman, who had no concern for appearances of material things" (Hatch and Shine

211). Ted Shine, who was teaching at Howard University, said that she became known as "the old woman with the headband and the tablet around her neck." Shine could not remember ever seeing her without a large yellow pencil and a blue notebook tied around her neck with a ribbon in case she had an idea for a poem" (qtd. in "Georgia Douglas Johnson" *Afro-American Writers* 163). She maintained her belief in work and her black pride and was ready to admonish those who did not exhibit the same qualities. Once she was outraged by the appearance of two young black men who walked by her house cursing. She shook her cane at them and shouted, "Such filth! Get those rags off your heads, and walk with your shoulders back! You're black men—you should be proud!" Startled, the two obeyed her and walked away looking the better for her advice. Satisfied, she called, "That's more like it!" (qtd. in Hatch and Shine 211).

Although Johnson is remembered more today for her poems than for her work in theatre, she made a major contribution to the theatre and was actively involved with other African-American women playwrights. In addition to her writing she accepted speaking engagements in which she talked about concerns of women and minorities. During World War II she worked to support the war effort and organized African-American women in several states to contribute. She died in a Washington hospital at the age of eighty-six.

Two events described by Brown-Guillory "marked a revolution in black theater in America and ushered in the Harlem Renaissance" (*Their Place* 2). These events led Johnson into an active participation in the literary and theatrical scene. The first was the establishment of the National Association for the Advancement of Colored People in 1910. The importance of this association can not be overstated, particularly in connection with the publication of *Crisis* magazine. W.E.B. Du Bois edited the journal which placed emphasis on the importance of theatre written by and for black people. There was an annual playwriting contest and playwrights were given an opportunity to publish their plays. "This maiden magazine served to create a networking of black authors across the country . . . many of whom were playwrights desperately in need of an audience. *Crisis* served as a laboratory for novice playwrights" (Brown-Guillory, *Their Place* 2). The NAACP also encouraged the production of plays. The second important occurrence was the production in 1917 of *Three Plays for a Negro Theatre* by the white playwright Ridgely Torrence. Johnson was one of many writers to take up the challenge of providing plays about her people for the public as seen from the perspective of the African-American, rather than through the eyes of white writers such as Torrence, Eugene O'Neill, Marc Connelly, and others. For Johnson and other women playwrights there was also the challenge of providing plays informed by a woman's point of view.

The date for A *Sunday Morning in the South* is estimated to be 1925 and the play is set in 1924. Johnson was a concerned and aggressive participant in the post World War I anti-lynching movement. The heartbreak experienced by African-Americans who read with dismay of the estimated 1,886 lynchings between 1901 and 1931 (Hatch and Shine 211) was expressed in editorials, books, novels, and plays. Johnson hoped to contribute to social change through the several plays she wrote in which lynching was theme. The action of the play begins quietly and cheerily: a seventy-year old grandmother, Sue Jones, is moving about her kitchen alternately singing and calling her grandchildren to breakfast. The situation is familiar, the children don't want to get up, the grandmother urges them to come and eat her "good hot rolls," saying, "It's as hard to git yawll out of the bed on Sunday morning as it is to pull hen's teeth" (213). As they breakfast a neighbor drops in on her way to church, and the pleasant atmosphere continues with a discussion of the plans of the grandchildren for the future. A dark note is sounded with a discussion of Sue's bad leg. Apparently, she is not receiving medical attention for it, and she says, "I won't never walk on it no good no mo. It eats and eats. Sho is lucky I'm right here next door to church. (To Tom) Open that winder Tom so I kin hear the singing. Folks don't like to set next to me in church no mo. Tinks it ketching—a cancer or somethin'" (214). Tom is also suffering because he sprained his back lifting heavy boxes for his white boss. There is joking about the fact that he was so tired that he fell asleep at eight o'clock and kept his brother awake with his snoring. The homey atmosphere established by the sympathetic, loving relationship between the characters and the sound of hymns from the church changes swiftly to concern and then despair as Sue and her grandchildren learn of an attack on a white woman and the conversation turns to lynching. Tom says, "They lynch you bout anything too, not just women. They say Zeb Brooks was strung up because he and his boss had er argiment" (214). They comfort him by saying that he has nothing to fear, as everyone knows him and nobody would bother him. Suddenly, the police appear with the young girl who was attacked. They brutally insist that Tom must be the man, as he fits the description and they bully the girl into identifying him. They tell Sue and Tom's brother to shut up as their testimony means nothing. Sue protests the obviously false charge, saying, "Mr. Officer, that white chile ain't never seed my granson before—All Niggers looks alike to her; she so upset she don't know whut she's saying" (215). Tom is hauled away, and within a few moments another neighbor comes in with the terrible news that "white mens wid guns a trying to take him away from the police—said he'd done been dentified and they want gointer be cheated outen they Nigger this time" (215). Sue asks what she can do, but the only for thing a woman with no empowerment in her society can do is to pray to Jesus. Now the sound of the hymns from next door has an ironic sound, especially the verse, "Jesus will help me, Jesus alone" (216). But no one will help these people: the play ends with Sue learning that Tom has been lynched. She falls in her chair dying as the church choir is heard singing "Lord have mercy over me" and the curtain falls (217).

This is a powerful play with richly developed characters and dialogue. In contrast to her early poetry which was "raceless," Johnson recreated the dialect of the Southern African-Americans to contribute to the reality of the scene. She effectively used music throughout. Despite its simple structure and brevity, it has a power for the reader and is still effective onstage. Hatch and Shine say that the play is not one of Johnson's best, but "the emotional impact of the piece cannot be ignored. . . . This is a protest play by a woman who wants to believe in law and order, but finds this belief more and more difficult to achieve when at every level the law has been unjust or unenforced" (212). This was one play Johnson submitted to the Federal Theatre Project which had a chance of performance. As Winona Fletcher notes, a reader praised it as "the first piece I have read about lynching that truthfully shows the futility of resisting the insane minds of a lynching mob with gentility. . . . Her characters appear as if from life. It has Tenseness [sic] and reality. It is not offensive to either group. It is a sermon against this national shame. I recommend for Little Theatre" (qtd. in "Georgia Douglas Johnson" *Afro-American Writers* 161). Despite the fact that the play was "not offensive to either group," it was never produced. It remained unpublished until 1990.

In 1926 Johnson achieved some welcome success with her play *Blue Blood* which won honorable mention in the contest held by *Opportunity*. It was produced by the Krigwa Players in New York and then published in 1927 in *Fifty More Contemporary One-Act Plays*, making it available for production in the many African-American theatres and in schools throughout the country.

The play has been described as Johnson's only tragi-comedy. Brown-Guillory describes the play as a commentary on "the sad state of black womanhood and how black men have taken on the responsibility of caring for their women who have been defiled by white men" *Wines in the Wilderness* 13). The setting is again a kitchen and there are merry preparations for the marriage between two light-skinned characters, May Bush and John Temple. When their mothers meet, an argument over the merits of each leads to the revelation that May and John both had the same white father. The noise and merriment of the offstage wedding guests is an ironic accompaniment for the anguish of the two mothers as they reveal the truth to May and her former suitor Randolph. There has been some foreshadowing that Randolph would be a more appropriate husband for May, and the play ends on a light note as Randolph leads May out the back door saying, "Mother Bush—just tell them the bride was stolen by Randolph Strong!" (25).

In the body of the play there are many lines which relate to the underlying anguish in this story. Mrs. Temple describes the scene in which the white man raped her after bribing her landlady, "I cried out. There wasn't anyone there that cared enough to help me, and you know yourself, Mrs. Bush, what little chance there is for women like us, in the South, to get justice or redress when these things happen! (22). Johnson also comments on the necessity for hiding such a crime against disempowered women, when the two mothers decide they cannot tell the truth to the guests or to the intended groom, "Keep it from him. It's the black women that have got to protect their men from the white men by not telling on 'em" (24). Brown-Guillory notes the significant aspect of the old problem of condescension of light-skinned blacks toward those with darker skins, "She cleverly makes Mrs. Bush and Mrs. Temple, who both brag of how close to white their children are, see that the very thing that they boast of divides the race" (*Wines in the Wilderness* 13). In this short play Johnson subtly comments on a number of social questions and problems in the African-American community.

Her next play was even more successful. As noted above, *Plumes* was a prize winner in 1927. Many critics note the folk quality of the play and relate it to the American tours made by the Abbey Theatre Company beginning in 1911. Their productions encouraged American playwrights to try to write folk plays set in various regions of the United States, and encouraged the formation of such groups as the Provincetown Players. As Rachel France wrote, "The notion of a Harlem Renaissance had inspired black scholars such as Alain Locke to champion (as William Butler Yeats had done in Ireland) 'folk' plays dealing with the poorest and the most economically and socially deprived natives in his own country" (*A Century* 75).

Plumes has an even simpler plot than the two plays described above. It centers on Charity Brown whose daughter is near death. She is torn between the views of Dr. Scott, who wants to perform an operation for fifty dollars and her wish to save the fifty dollars for a grand funeral if Emmerline dies. She expresses her concern to Tildy who arrives to ask about Emmerline, "It's me that's low-spirited. The doctor said last time he was here he might have to operate—said, she mought have a chance then. But I tell you de truth, I've got no faith a-tall in 'em. They takes all your money for nothing" (75). Her dilemma is symbolized by the dress for Emmerline which Tildy offers to finish while Charity continues with her back-breaking task of doing laundry for white people: if Emmerline lives she will want the dress short, if it is for her funeral it must be long. Tildy reads the coffee grounds and foresees a big funeral, then the doctor arrives to say he must operate at once. Charity is unable to make a decision because she doesn't believe the operation will help and she longs for the glory of a fine funeral with carriages and horses wearing plumes. The decision is taken out of her hands when she hears Emmerline groaning offstage, rushes off, and returns, saying to Tildy, "Rip the hem out, sister Tildy" (78). The dialogue through which the playwright effectively conveys the poverty and indignities of the lives of the characters is simple and moving. Again, offstage sounds add to the theatricality. The audience hears Emmerline in her suffering and also hears the sound of a church bell and the sound of horses. Charity looks out the window and cries, "My Lord! ain't it grand! Look at them horses—look at their heads—plumes—how they shake 'em! Land o' mighty! It's a fine sight, sister Tildy" (76). The play remains one of the best examples of an American folk play.

Safe is a much grimmer play which relates directly to lynching. It was apparently written in 1929 but was lost for many years. It is set in the front room of a cottage in which Liza and John Pettigrew are with Liza's mother, Mandy. The latter is ready to help when Liza gives birth to her first child, but she is exhausted from doing laundry all day. John reads in the paper that Sam Hosea has been put in jail because his boss slapped him and he hit him back. (Some readers may remember the shock which still occurred in *In the Heat of the Night* when Sidney Poitier slapped a white Southerner.) Mandy allows, "that's mighty unhealthy sounding business for this part of the country. Hittin' a white man, he better hadder made tracks far away from here I'm er thinking" (27). A neighbor comes to say that there is a mob downtown and there will be hell to pay. In her current state, Lize is more than usually horrified and says, "What's little nigger boys born for anyhow? I sho hopes mine will be a girl. I don't want no boy baby to hounded down and kicked 'round. No, I don't want to ever have no boy chile!" (28) John says he must go to see if Sam is safe. John's absence, the sounds of a mob dragging Sam to be hanged, and his pathetic cries operate to send Liza into a frenzy and immediate labor. The doctor arrives, and the sound of a baby crying is heard offstage. But the play concludes with the doctor telling Mandy that Liza has strangled her baby when she discovered it was a son. He is appalled and helpless as he says, "She kept muttering over and over again: 'Now he's safe—safe from the lynchers! Safe!'" (32). As usual, Johnson simply and effectively dramatizes a powerful situation closely related to the lives of African-Americans. Her use of offstage noises is typical of her work. Writing about the play recently, Patricia R. Schroeder observed the effect of interweaving the political with the personal:

> *Safe* illustrates the mutually influential relationship between social tensions (the lynching) and private lives (Liza's maternal fears). By bringing the chilling results of lynching into the Pettigrews' peaceful living room, Johnson protested the way racial violence hovered menacingly over even the joyful aspects of African-American family life—including the birth of a baby who is eagerly awaited. (10)

Johnson submitted the play to the Federal Theatre Project, but it was rejected by all three readers because they found the action unrealistic: "An extremely dramatic, tragic piece. But the glaring weakness of utter exaggeration is too bright—and it fails not because the idea is not dramatic, but because it follows from an absurdity—that they lynch Negro boys 'Down South' for defending themselves from thieves. In fact, the *crime that produces lynching is vastly fouler* [italics mine]." As Fletcher notes, the readers believed the myth that only rape produced lynching ("Georgia Douglas Johnson" *Afro-American Writers* 161). The play was first published in 1990, sixty-one years after Johnson's powerful plea for social change.

Blue-Eyed Black Boy (1930) takes a similar theme, but the focus is slightly different. In this, Pauline Waters is a fairly well-to-do black woman whose daughter Rebecca is preparing for her wedding to Dr. Grey. He arrives to see his fiancée and take care of Pauline's foot which she injured by stepping on a rusty nail. Again bad news disturbs the domestic scene. It appears that Pauline's son, Jack, a young man with surprisingly blue eyes, has accidentally brushed against a white woman on the street and is in danger of being lynched. Pauline frantically calls for a little box in her bedroom, finds a ring in it and tells Dr. Grey to run to the governor's house to give him a message. He must remember it word for word: "Pauline sent this. She says they goin' to lynch her son born 21 years ago. . . . Look in his eyes and you'll save him" (36). The play ends with the sound of the state troopers arriving to protect the jail and save Jack. Although Jack is saved, the play is nevertheless a statement about the powerlessness of black people. In this instance Pauline is able to save her son because his white father has become a powerful figure and has inherited his blue eyes. But for the ordinary black person no such aid was available and the accidental touch of a black man against a white woman could well lead to his death. Again, the Federal Theatre Project readers rejected the play as pointless melodrama, and said specifically, "Its rather unhealthful matter would interest and delight many loose-thinking, race-baiting persons both black and white" (Fletcher, "From Genteel Poet to Revolutionary Playwright" 53). Such were the handicaps under which Johnson labored. Still, she made a strong plea for justice and equality in all the plays above.

The other two published plays by Johnson have to do with slaves escaping their tyrannical masters. In *Frederick Douglass* (1935), the historical figure is planning to escape on the train with the money he has saved. His sweetheart Ann has baked him some "gingy bread" and they talk about their plans. The scene is filled with poignant realistic touches such as the fact that he only saw his mother once and that he had to put up with beatings and abuse from white people who wanted to stop him from learning how to read and write. "They caught me an' nearly killed me many a time. They took all my papers away, but pshaw! I whirled right around an' found some more an' learned harder than I ever had. Something inside of me just drove me to it! (152). Douglas is insistent that Ann learn to read and write and do arith-metic. He feels that education is more important than the activities normally thought of as appropriate for women, such as knitting socks: "Yo got to learn a lot cause you got to help me when we get way, honey" (151). When news comes that he is going to be sold down the river, he quickly concludes that he will dress up as a sailor and use Ann's brother's pass to escape. With the aid of old Jake, a colorful fig-ure who tricks Bud by pretending to read his tea leaves, Douglas is able to accomplish his plans, promising to send for Ann when he reaches the North.

William and Ellen Craft is similar in the tension surrounding an attempt at escape. Here, the eponymous figures intend to escape via the Underground Railway, but are frustrated by its discovery. William and Ellen represent figures who will no longer tolerate their fates. Old Aunt Mandy is at first willing to trust to Jesus and hope for the best, noting to Ellen, "life's moughty sweet if it is bitter!" (167). Sam repre-sents the figures who better themselves by betraying slaves who want to escape. In the end William kills Sam outside and he and Ellen escape by the above ground railway, she dressed up as William's master and William acting as her slave. The tension of trying to get the clothes for Ellen, cutting off her hair, and her fear that she cannot pass as a white person all contribute to an exciting short play. Both of these history plays accomplish what the editors of *Negro History in Thirteen Plays* intended. They bring to life incidents from history and create an aura of excitement and actuality through vivid characterization, dia-logue, and action. Additionally, Douglas indicates through the action in the play that women must take an active role in improving condi-tions, and cannot be held back by fear or lack of education.

Johnson's plays relate directly to the several periods in which they are set and are powerful statements of the actuality of the life of African-Americans in the South. Through the plays she expresses the desire for safety from lynching, better health care, protection for black women against rape by white men, the possibility of a safe future for the children, and a general need for equality for blacks. Unfortunately, she had little opportunity to see her plays in production except in amateur productions in the area of Washington. Had she received more encouragement and criticism, she might well have developed into one of the major women playwrights of the first half of the century. Certainly her plays are dramatic and the dialogue is lively and engaging. In the last few years of her life she was perceived only as an eccentric old lady living in a slum. As Fletcher has written,

> After a period of nearly sixty years, the judgment of knowledgeable critics has coalesced to grant Georgia Douglas Camp Johnson, poet, playwright, and composer, a place among the best writers of the early twentieth century. Omitted from the most popular anthologies and textbooks, even when her black contemporaries gained admission, she was labeled "minor" primarily because as a black woman of the genteel school she was over-shadowed by what J. Saunders Redding calls the "masculine literature of the 'New Negro.'" ("Georgia Douglas Johnson" *Afro-American Writers* (153)

Johnson's importance as a revolutionary writer who moved from the genteel school has now been noted by Fletcher and others. Recent publication of her plays has made her work available once more and she stands as a symbol of courage and a role model for women playwrights.

Alice Gerstenberg (1885-1972)

Alice Gerstenberg (1885-1972) is remembered chiefly for one play, *Overtones*, although she was active in the theatre from 1908 to 1943 and wrote more than forty plays. In 1915 she made the first successful adaptation of Lewis Carroll's Alice novels. The play was a success in New York and introduced new staging techniques to the commercial theatre. *Overtones* is frequently performed, but little attention is given to her other plays which remain interesting, playable, and imaginative in structure and style.

Gerstenberg was born in a well-to-do Chicago family. Like Josephine Preston Peabody, she enjoyed a childhood in a cultured home with loving parents who encouraged her to write and to perform. She started writing stories when she was eight. After high school she attended Bryn Mawr and took part in pageants and plays. Because there was no playwriting course, she learned playwriting by writing a series of plays for herself and her fellow students to perform. In 1908, while she was still a student, these were published under the title *A Little World* (which is sometimes mistakenly described as a novel).

After leaving Bryn Mawr, Gerstenberg returned to Chicago and pursued a career as a writer. She published two distinctly feminist novels which which were highly successful and catapulted her into the public eye. She also traveled extensively in America and Europe, seeing theatre wherever she went. She spent a winter in New York observing theatre, encouraged by David Belasco who allowed her to sit in on rehearsals of several plays. Ironically, the commercially oriented plays by Belasco, Augustus Thomas, and other male and female playwrights who catered to popular taste for formulae and sentiment were the very plays Gerstenberg would not only oppose with her experimental playwriting, but would, at least in one play, satirize. She created her own opportunities for writing the kinds of plays she wanted to write in Chicago and was very dedicated to making theatre of various types available to children and adults in that city.

Gerstenberg helped organize and develop the Players' Workshop of Chicago. At the time she began writing there were a number of outstanding writers, sometimes referred to as the Chicago School of Writers. Gerstenberg worked with Ben Hecht, Max Bodenheim, Kenneth Sawyer Goodman, and Elisha Cook in a tiny theatre where the

unusual was the norm. Here she was a leading spirit and had the freedom to write whatever she wanted. Besides her work with the Players'
Workshop, Gerstenberg joined with Annette Washburne to found the
Chicago Junior League Theatre for Children. She served as its director
and dramatized *The Land of Don't Want To* and *Water Babies*. These
productions and the theatre as a whole were so successful that the
Chicago organization became a model for Junior League children's
theatre in many cities.

In 1922 Gerstenberg founded the Playwrights Theatre of Chicago
and many of her plays were first produced there. The purpose of the
organization was to give local playwrights, especially women, a venue
for their plays. The organization served this purpose until 1945. In
1938 Gerstenberg won the Chicago Foundation for Literature Award
for her work in American Drama. Occasionally she wrote for the
commercial theatre in collaboration, but these plays were less successful than the plays she wrote alone. In fact, her last play, *Victory Belles*,
a play about women desperate to find husbands during the war,
surprised critics with its conventional quality. (Audiences found it
funny enough to extend the run to a respectable 87 performances.)
Gerstenberg died in 1972 in Chicago.

Alice in Wonderland was produced in Chicago at the Fine Arts Theatre and in New York at the Booth (one of Winthrop Ames' theatres)
in 1915. In his book *Freud on Broadway*, W. David Sievers describes
the impact of early plays which used Freudian symbols, dream plays,
suppressed desires, and other elements which were coming into the
public consciousness following Freud's lectures at Clark College in
Worcester in 1909 and the 1913 publication in English of Freud's *The
Interpretation of Dreams*. He also points out that playwrights such as
Strindberg, Wedekind, and Schnitzler had had little impact in America
so the plays written after 1910 which used some of the techniques of
the Expressionists were startling and theatrically innovative. Although
there were a few plays which used the concept of the dream, so important in Strindberg's work, Sievers writes that two years after the publication of Freud's major work on dreams Gerstenberg was the first
playwright "to give Broadway its first really authentic glimpse into
unconscious life" (49). Of course Freudian interpretations of Carroll's
Alice in Wonderland and *Through the Looking Glass* are familiar today,
but in Gerstenberg's time the translation to the stage of the sexual
symbolism and anxiety which run through the books was revelatory.

As Sievers says, "Alice finds constant threats in her dreams. Most of her anxieties center around oral repressions, changes in size of her body from eating things which make her larger or smaller, and sadistic (castration) threats—'off with her head'" (50).

Several other playwrights had attempted to turn Carroll's work into plays, but with little success. What is easy to describe in the novels— surrealistic distortions of space, swift transitions, characters who appear and disappear, long falls down holes, flying through the air, and the change of one character into another— was very difficult to put on the stage. The compression of the action of the two novels into a comprehensible play of reasonable length was also daunting. In 1915, Gerstenberg successfully met these challenges and excited audiences in New York and Chicago with the adaptation which was true to the novels and scenically stunning. Because the staging was so unusual it will be described in some detail.

Gerstenberg chose a framing device for the dream in which Lewis G. Carroll and Alice are in a large room with a fireplace and a mirror. The realistic elements which will take the form of phantasy in the dream are present or are discussed: Carroll is playing chess, and Alice wonders about the game and about a pack of cards, and talks about the mirror and asks Carroll if he doesn't ever wish he could go into the looking-glass house she can see over the fireplace. She becomes drowsy and he suggests a nap, leaving her alone in the room. Gerstenberg's stage directions throughout the play are very challenging for the designer. The first move away from reality occurs when Alice falls asleep: "A red glow from the fireplace illumines Alice. Dream music. A bluish light reveals the Red Chess Queen and the White Chess Queen in the mirror" (155). They call to Alice, who stirs in her sleep, and beckon her to join them, but she says, "I—don't—know—how—I—can—get—through. I've tried—before—but the glass was hard—and I was afraid of cutting—my fingers—(She feels the glass and is amazed to find it like gauze.) Why, it's soft like gauze; it's turning into a sort of mist; why, it's easy to get through! *Why—why*—I'm going *through!* (She disappears.) (156)

Gerstenberg's construction would be described as cinematic today, but this terminology was not familiar in 1915. Her characters are blown in or fly in, sets change swiftly from one location to another, and there is continual feeling of transition and alteration. A good example is the scene following Alice's amusing conversation with Humpty-Dumpty. He says good-by and immediately disappears.

> Alice. Oh!—I forgot to ask him how to——(She tries to open the doors. They all locked; she begins to weep. She walks weeping to a high glass table, and sits down on its lower ledge. She sits on a big golden key and picks it up in surprise. She tries it on all the doors but it does not fit. She weeps, weeps—and Wonderland grows dark to her in her despair. In the darkness she cries, "Oh! I'm slipping! Oh, oh! It's a lake. Oh! my tears! I'm floating! (A mysterious light shows a "Drink me" sign around a bottle on the top of the table. Alice floats up to it, panting, and holding on to the edge of the table, takes up the bottle.) It isn't marked poison. (She sips at it.) This is good! Tastes like cherry tart, custard, pineapple, roast turkey, toffy, and hot buttered toast—all together. Oh! Oh! I'm letting out like a telescope. (A mysterious light shows her lengthening out. Music) But the lake is rising, too. Oh! Oh! It's deep! I'm drowning. Help, help, I'm drowning, I'm drowning in my tears!
> Gryphon. Hjckrrh. Hjckrrh!
> (The Gryphon, a huge green creature, with big glittering wings, appears where Humpty Dumpty had been, and reaches glittering claws over to grab and save Alice.) (168)

The setting immediately changes to a place "symbolic of a wet and rocky shore in a weird green light. The Mock Turtle is weeping dismally" (169). Soon strange creatures come in to dance as the Mock Turtle sings his lugubrious song about mock turtle soup. Then the Mock Turtle and the Gryphon grab Alice and fly into the air, dropping her into the Mad Hatter's Tea Party. In the scenes which follow the Cheshire cat appears and partly reappears, the baby Alice is holding turns into a pig, the kings and queens appear, there is a croquet game with flamingoes for mallets and hedgehogs for balls, and the action comes to a climax in the trial scene where all the various characters appear. When Alice escapes from the Red Queen there is a particularly interesting stage direction:

> If there is a trap-door on the stage, Alice disappears down it, leaving the crowd circling around the hole, screaming and amazed. If the stage has no trap-door, a bridge is built across the footlights, with stairs leading down to the orchestra pit. When the crowd is chasing Alice, she jumps over the footlights on to the bridge, and, as the curtain is falling, dividing her from the crowd, she appeals to the audience, "Save me, save me, who will save me?" and runs down the stairs and disappears." (200)

This is one of the first examples of a character breaking through the proscenium and engaging in direct address to the audience in the American theatre.

The play not only has the structure of a dream, there are references to dreaming in the play. The Cheshire Cat tells Alice that she is only a sort of thing in the Frog Footman's dream, and that if he quit dreaming, she would cease to exist (188). As in a dream, the conclusion becomes a violent mixture of all that has gone before. Alice is protesting the treatment in the trial, characters are shouting and suddenly the scene shifts to Alice sitting in the chair asleep. Carroll returns to wake her up and at the same time, off stage, the characters repeat their most characteristic lines, a shower of playing cards come through the mirror and fall on Alice, and she wakes to say, "Why—it was a dream!" (218).

Reading the script, one is struck with the ease with which Gerstenberg compressed the many elements and characters into a swiftly moving three-act structure. The stage directions quoted above would be easily carried out today with modern technology, but in a theatre dominated by realistic scenery, with primitive lighting equipment, it was difficult to accomplish in 1915. Gerstenberg worked closely with the designer, William Penhallow Henderson, who used shifting platforms, lighting, trap-doors, and all the technical elements which were available at that time. Writers took note of Gerstenberg's own interest in new methods of staging, one saying that she "has been interestd in the new movement in the theatre since the first vibrations circling out from the Continental theatres reached this country" ("About Alice's Stage Mother" 5). The *New York Times* critic noted that she was influenced by "new styles in stage decoration"—referring to the New Stagecraft which had been developed in Europe, but not much used in America. He said, "It was a matter of supreme importance that the staging should be right and most of it is. This part of the work has been done with taste, understanding, and resourcefulness ("A Carroll Classic" 11). The importance of this innovative production using the New Stagecraft was indicated by the exacting critic Clayton Hamilton in his review. He noted that Gerstenberg wisely followed Tenniel in the costuming, but "called for a decorative treatment of the mise en scène, and Mr. Henderson applied the principles that have been exemplified recently in Germany and Russia. As a consequence, this non-commercial production of 'Alice in Wonderland' pointed along a path that must ultimately be pursued by our commercial managers" (qtd. in Austrian n.p.). In one of many articles about Gerstenberg published at the time of the productions, Delia Austrian noted that nearly thirty playwrights had tried unsuccessfully to dramatize Carroll's stories and "It remained for Alice Gerstenberg, a young woman still in the light of the '20s to dramatize this book successfully, to depict it as Carroll wanted it" (n.p.).

The play became the standard version of the stories and remained so until Eva Le Gallienne's version in 1932. It was so popular in New York and Chicago that daily matinees were added and thousands of children saw the play. It was performed in many theatres in America and widely anthologized. Naturally, Gerstenberg was flooded with hundred of letters from children and adults about the play. Le Gallienne's version was very popular for many years, but Gerstenberg's has recently been rediscovered. In 1992, for example, it was produced by the Lakeside Players in Ottawa, Canada. Critic Iris Winston enjoyed the production and found the visual elements particularly effective. In keeping with Gerstenberg's version, director Mike Harris added an apron to the stage and brought the performers into the audience from time to time ("Foray into Wonderland Worth the Visit" H7).

Overtones was first produced by the Washington Square Players in 1915. It featured scenery by Lee Simonson. Gerstenberg's play was on a bill which attracted wide attention as it also included plays by Schnitzler, de Musset, and Robert de Bracco. Despite the fact that these playwrights were quite well-known, Gerstenberg's unusual play drew much of the critical attention, not just in New York but throughout the country. Again, Gerstenberg was creating a play which was informed by Freudian psychology. Sievers observed that aside from Gerstenberg's and a few other playwrights' actual dream plays, "it marks the first departure from realism for the purpose of dramatizing the unconscious" (51). The play is very simple in structure, but within the superficial simplicity of the play are depths of characterization. Harriet, wealthy woman, is awaiting the arrival of Margaret, the woman who married an attractive but impoverished painter when she chose a rich man instead. Harriet is deep in thought, which Gerstenberg presents as a conflict between id and her ego. Her id, Hetty, is also present, wearing a dress of a slightly darker color and a veil over her face. Gerstenberg says in a stage direction that the costume and veil should be chiffon, "suggesting a possibility of primitive and cultured selves merging into one woman. The primitive and cultured selves never come into actual physical contact but try to sustain the impression of mental conflict" (483). The exposition is presented as an argument between the two selves. Hetty says "I am the rushing river; you are the ice over the current." Harriet answers, "I am your subtle overtones." Hetty sums their relationship up by saying, "But together we are one woman, the wife of Charles Goodrich" (485). Both hate the husband and envy Margaret for her marriage to John Caldwell. When Margaret appears with her other self, Maggie, the conflict between the women begins. Each woman wants the other to think she is very happy. Margaret brags about her travels and the great success of her husband in Paris, while Maggie urges her to take cream and eat a lot because she and John are starving. Margaret wants Harriet to commission a painting from John, who has no work at all, but she pretends disinterest. In contrast, Harriet wants John to paint her portrait, but claims to have another artist in mind. Throughout the play, the proper women mask their true urges and attitudes, even as Hetty and Maggie are masked. Hetty demands in anguish, "Do you love each other? Is it really true?" but Harriet smiles and asks, "Did you have all the romance of starving for his art?" (489). Maggie reaches her "claws" toward a cake when Margaret offers it, but Margaret delicately takes the cake, saying, "I really shouldn't—after my big luncheon. John took me to the Ritz," but Hetty exclaims, "Starving!" (490). At the end the painting is commissioned, and both of the unhappy women and their other selves are satisfied as the women kiss each other and say good-bye.

The play drew attention not only from the critics in New York, but from theatrical reporters across the country. Typical of the articles which appeared was one in the *Indianapolis News* called "The Significance of Overtones." The writer commented on the New York response to the play, quoting in particular the *New Republic* critic who called it "not the most interesting play produced in New York last week, but the most interesting event." The New York critic went on to discuss in detail "the orginality of choosing to incarnate the self which we are fully conscious of and as consciously wish to hide" (qtd. in "Significance of Overtones" n.p.). The critic for the *New York Times* called the play highly original, but thought the idea cleverer than the execution. Nevertheless, he called the evening more interesting theatrically than productions at the major theatres. He also commented on the fact that Gerstenberg was the only American playwright represented. ("Comedy Playlets at the Bandbox") Although many years have passed and Freudian theory reflected in plays is a commonplace,

Overtones is still regularly performed. The depiction of women suffering because of the pretenses they must assume still has appeal for today's audience. A recent production by National Taiwan Normal University students at the Taiwan Railway Station auditorium was very popular with the largely Chinese audience (Tai n.p.).

Gerstenberg's next New York success occurred in 1917 with her play, *The Potboiler*. Like most of her plays it was first performed in Chicago. It was described as a "delightful satire on hack methods of playwriting" which was one of "two notable achievements last night at the Theater Workshop." This article in the *Brooklyn Eagle* noted that the organization was striving to elevate the standards of the New York Stage and helping actors to improve by giving them good works to perform. It also noted that, "Although there was naturally great interest in the new Lord Dunsany play . . . it is a matter of local pride that Miss Gerstenberg's play received the lion's share of interest and applause" ("Theater Workshop Produces Dramas" n.p.). The play was subsequently produced in vaudeville and in theatres in many states.

The play was a satire on the type of formula plays written by the most important playwright of the time, Augustus Thomas. In fact, it may have been a direct satire on him and his methods of writing and directing. Remembering working with him in 1915, Edna Ferber wrote, "From the very outset his manner and conduct shocked me beyond belief. . . . He began by insulting everyone except Miss Barrymore" (*A Peculiar Treasure* 218). A close examination of this play reveals not only Gerstenberg's comic skill, but the type of commercial play she, Susan Glaspell, and many other women playwrights were revolting against.

The playwright in Gerstenberg's play is Thomas Pinikles Sud, who is condescendingly allowing a hopeful playwright to observe his technique. Mr. Wouldby says, "It must be wonderful to be the master playwright of our day. Everybody knows Mr. Thomas Pinikles Sud" and Sud replies, "Yes, it is a privilege to be a friend of mine" (146).

As the rehearsal begins, it is apparent that the plot is entirely predictable: Mrs. Pencil has had an affair with Inkwell, but Inkwell now loves Miss Ivory, whose father has lost his business and is in his power. Miss Ivory rejects the man she loves, Ruler, in order to marry Inkwell and save her father. The business Sud urges is also entirely conventional. He urges Mrs. Pencil to pound on Inkwell's chest, saying, "Seeing a woman pounding on a man's chest and hearing her scream is worth 3 dollars to anybody" (157). In this scene and throughout the play, the dialogue is entirely trite and conventional and the melodramatic style which Sud demands emphasizes it. He urges the actors to greater melodrama in one section which is comically rehearsed several times:

> Mrs. Pencil: Who is spying on you?
> Inkwell: You!
> Mrs. Pencil: I?
> Inkwell: You!
> Mrs. Pencil: I?
> Inkwell: You!
> Mrs. Pencil: I! (158)

Sud notes with pride that "there is nothing so effective as the repetition of the same words brought up to a climax" (157).

Sud is impossibly rude to the actors, swearing at them, and blaming them for the disorder of the rehearsal and the script. This confusion leads to a "Who's on first?" type of exchange between Sud and the actor playing Ruler:

> Ruler: Beg pardon, sir—I didn't hear my cue!
> Sud: It's your business to listen for it.
> Ruler: But they didn't give me the cue!
> Sud: Well, what is your cue?
> Ruler: What is it?
> Sud: I asked you what your cue was?
> Ruler: What is it?
> Sud: Is your hearing perfectly clear?
> Ruler: Perfectly.
> Sud: Then will you kindly tell me what your cue is?
> Ruler: What is it?
> Sud: I shall go mad! I'm dealing with lunatics! Lunatics—once again I ask you, Mr. Ruler—if you can *hear*! (Yells) Kindly read from your book and tell me what your cue is.
> Ruler: (Yells furiously) I've been trying to tell you my cue is "What is it?"—
> Sud: That line was cut long ago! The trouble with you actors is you can't forget.
> Wouldby: I always thought actors had to remember—
> Sud: Any fool can remember— (1670169)

The disorderly rehearsal reaches its comic climax in the final scene when all the characters have guns and threaten to shoot each other. In fact, Sud hasn't been able to decide who will be shot, and as Wouldby exits in disgust he says, "Oh, shoot the author!" and all the actors loudly agree, "Oh, shoot the author!" (186).

In this satire Gerstenberg anticipated the reaction of younger critics such as George Jean Nathan to the formula plays of the time, particularly those of Thomas. Writing in the tradition of *The Rehearsal* and *The Critic*, Gerstenberg challenged conventional playwriting with this play and with the experimental plays she wrote.

One of her most experimental plays was *Beyond* which must have been quite shocking in 1917. It shows the wraith of a woman who is wandering in a scene suggesting "limitless space and mist and is played behind a curtain of gauze" (*Ten One-Act Plays* 213). The woman presents an image more spiritual than physical. "She has died and is now passing upward to meet and to be judged by the All Powerful whom she cannot see but whom she supposes is high up off left" (213). As she speaks, she reveals a life which was filled with pain and she questions the reason for such things as her father's suicide and her mother's death in childbirth after having too many children. She, herself, married a wealthy man to care for her siblings and her life exemplifies the constraints imposed on women by a patriarchal society. Her only happiness was found in adultery and for that she was scorned by society. Nevertheless, she says that she found the beauty of God's world through her love. In the end she moves toward the throne appealing for justice. The idea that an adultress should not be punished, and that a woman had the right to question the order of the world and the intentions of God were innovative at the time. The simple structure and absence of plot, plus the setting, place the play outside the conventional theatre. The interest in the characterization of the women as a victim of male dominated society, as her mother before her was, reflects the changing views of women during this period. The play was one of several plays which are essentially one-woman pieces.

Another was *Attuned*, written in 1918. This play reflects the anguish and fear of Americans during the time so many men were fighting and dying in Europe in World War I. It is a simple play which shows a woman writing a letter to her husband who is in France. She writes of how attuned they are to one another and of her great love for him. As she is writing, the backdrop opens to reveal a pantomime (which she does not see) showing her husband going into battle, being shot, and dying. Then there is a strange aura onstage (created by lighting) and she cries out that he has been killed. She senses his spirit and draws understanding and courage from its presence. At the end of the play she receives a letter from him which concludes, "I am convinced that the soul survives the destruction of the body—and if it does I shall come straight to you" (*Ten One-Act Plays* 142). The play reflects concerns about the war as well as an interest in spiritualism and the afterlife which was current at the time.

Another unusual one-woman piece was *A Patroness*. This was written during World War I, but for unknown reasons, it was not professionally staged or published. Notations on the typed script indicate that it was performed. The play is of interest because much of the action is pantomime and there is no realistic setting. The play shows a day in the life of a society woman. The setting consists of a bare minimum of pieces which serve as furniture in many locations, and as the back seat of an automobile. The patroness wakes up in the morning with her head full of her countless charities. She has no time for her husband or children because of them. She mimes getting in the chauffeur driven car, going into an elevator, meeting people in a club room where she speaks of prison reform, having a dress fitting, going to the Red Cross to wrap bandages ("What poor wounded hero will need these! War is terrible!" n.p.), going to a lecture on feminism ("Feminists say such clever things! They sound so shockingly interesting!" n.p.), going to tea , changing for dinner, going to a play, to supper in a club, and then home with her husband. Gerstenberg has created a very comical character, utterly selfish and shallow, but convinced of her good works, and proud of being a delegate to Washington for the Suffragette League. No doubt the author observed many such flighty, society women in her family's social circle. The role provides the actress with many changes of mood and many amusing lines. At one point she observes, "We must uplift the Drama. I'm taking a playwriting course, it's the latest fashion. I'm writing a play already" (n.p.). The unusual staging methods pre-date many later plays which were considered highly original.

In contrast to this experimental play, *Fourteen* is a realistic comedy with a funny basic idea. Written in 1919, it quickly became very popular after its first production in San Francisco and its publication in *Drama Magazine*. The central figure, Mrs. Pringle, is a charming, giddy woman who is solely concerned with the success of her dinner party for the enormously wealthy and sought after Oliver Farnsworth. She plans to place her debutante daughter next to him and hopes for a marriage.

Unfortunately, she experiences considerable difficulty because there is a blizzard and guests call to say they can't come.

In her desperate efforts to keep the number of guests at fourteen (to avoid thirteen and the problem of putting women at the head of the table if there are only twelve), she madly telephones people inviting them and uninviting them, rages at the beasts who are cancelling, and calls out orders to the nearly hysterical maid to set more plates, take away plates, make new place cards, order more food, bring another board for the table, etc. The final blow falls when Farnsworth can't come. The room is a shambles, Mrs. Pringle is in despair and she cries that she'll never entertain again: "I'm going to live for myself! I'm going to be selfish and hard—and unsociable—and drink my liquor myself instead of offering it gratis to the whole town! (*Ten One-Act Plays* 239). At this desperate juncture she receives a note from Farnsworth announcing that he has sent the Prince of Wales in his place. She orders her daughter to set her sights on the Prince and beams with delight as she says, "I always manage somehow to the be most successful of hostesses! Thank God for the blizzard!" (241). This delightful comedy reflected the giddiness of America over the visit of the Prince of Wales, the difficulty of entertaining during Prohibition, and Gerstenberg's satirical view of empty-headed society women. It may also have given Kaufman and Ferber an idea for *Dinner at Eight*.

In his appreciative introduction to Gerstenberg's *Comedies All* in 1930, Alexander Dean wrote of her originality and importance in the American theatre and noted the range of her work from serious mate-rial to comedy. "The success of *Overtones, The Pot Boiler,* and *Fourteen* place Miss Gerstenberg in a distinguished class by herself. No other American playwright has written any three one-act plays which have been produced as frequently as these" (xi). That is an important statement considering the number of one-act plays written by Susan Glaspell, Lawrence Langner, Eugene O'Neill and other outstanding writers which were available at the time.

Dean also called attention to a very innovative idea Gerstenberg had in writing several of the plays in the volume:

> In her present volume she has included four plays created around a most origi-nal idea. *Facing Fact, The Puppeteer, Rhythm,* and *The Menu* were written to be played in homes, using the fire-place, the staircase, the davenport and the bay window for settings although there is no handicap for their production on a stage. She felt that such plays given without much expense in any home large

enough to seat an audience could be the means of raising money in many communities seeking funds to found a Little Theatre. (xi)

During her life-time Gerstenberg was an acknowledged success as a playwright from her earliest efforts on. When she had just turned twenty she was described in a New York paper as "a full blown teacher of simplified feminism whose writings are turning older heads" (Beckley "Girl Author" n.p.). This was based on her best-selling novel *The Conscience of Sarah Platt* (1915) which followed her success with *Alice in Wonderland*. Like many others, the writer was surprised by Gerstenberg's youth and appearance:

> Alice Gerstenberg has flashed out of Chicago and into New York so suddenly and so brilliantly that we are a little bit dazzled. In fact, she's dazzled herself. When you go to talk to her about her plays and her books, thinking to see a dashing authoress of confident mien, you find instead a small, quiet slip of a child who doesn't seem quite aware she has "arrived." (Beckley "Girl Author" n.p.)

This rather condescending description was written by a woman reporter and indicates the tone taken by male and female reporters toward Gerstenberg in this time. She was pleased that her work was so successful, but was never overwhelmed by her sudden fame. She continued to pursue her work with determination and imagination. She could have chosen to make a bigger name for herself by working and living in New York, but she wished to enrich her home town. Her many plays deserve re-examination on the basis of their interesting and unusual structure and the ideas which inform them. Such terms as "singular" and "audacious" were used to describe her plays. Her subject matter was in sharp contrast to the conventional, superficially realistic theatre of the time: she argued for divorce, for equal rights with men (especially in the area of sex), and rejected the idea of early marriage for women. She never married, but chose to devote her life entirely to the theatre and to improving the lives of women. When she was still described as a "Girl Author" she told a reporter, "There should be no condemning laws for women and condoning laws for men. There should be but one law for both, and that a clean, broad, uplifting, developing human law, a law of honest self-expression" (qtd. in Beckley n.p.) Gerstenberg devoted herself to improving society through the theatre and to improving American theatre. Writing in 1989, Debra Young noted, "Although her continuing literary reputation is based chiefly on *Overtones*, Gerstenberg's enthusiasm for the little theatre movement and for new playwrights was a significant influence on the developing American theatre" (326). As a young playwright she expressed her hope for a future in which "to smile, to work, to experiment along new lines, and to achieve" (Austrian n.p.) and she accomplished all of those things.

Sophie Treadwell (1885?-1970)

Sophie Treadwell (1885?-1970) is known to most theatre scholars as the author of a 1928 play, *Machinal*. Little else is generally known about a woman whose career spanned the years from 1922 to 1957. She wrote over thirty plays, only seven of which appeared in New York. They ranged in subject matter from the Mexican revolution to a 1954 character study of a homosexual car thief. Like so many of her plays, the latter was never produced. Her tendency to experiment with new approaches and unconventional subject matter placed her at the fringe of the commercial theatre. Although she rarely achieved commercial success, Treadwell made an impact on the American theatre through her adventurous approach to playwriting.

A study of her career reveals an extraordinarily interesting woman. Her ancestors were pioneers who crossed the plains to make a new life in California. Her mother was Nettie Fairchild Treadwell and her half-Spanish father was Alfred Benjamin Treadwell. The young girl learned to speak Spanish and several other languages. When she was six her father took her to the theatre to see Modjeska perform and she was thrilled by the actress and the theatre. Barbara L. Bywaters suggests that Treadwell's attitude toward marriage and her inclination to physical and mental breakdowns relate to her father's later ill-treatment. He and her mother separated when the child was eight and the successful judge failed to support them (110). Despite having to work as a teen-ager and suffering a breakdown while in high school, Treadwell managed to earn a B.A. at the University of California at Berkeley. She studied theatre, acted, and wrote several plays which were produced at the University in her senior year. She appeared in many plays including one which opened the newly constructed Greek Theatre on the campus. She then gained experience by acting in stock and vaudeville.

Through a coincidence Treadwell was introduced to her idol, Madame Modjeska. Treadwell lived for some time at Modjeska's ranch, studying acting and helping the actress write her memoirs. There she wrote her first play with Modjeska's encouragement. After the famous actress' death in 1909, Treadwell began work as a newspaperwoman. Writing for the *San Francisco Bulletin*, she covered crime news and reviewed plays. Between 1910 and 1920 she covered international news stories for national publication—a job for which she was particularly suited since she loved travel and spoke several languages. She covered boxing matches, murders, and wars. A strong feminist, and a member of the Lucy Stone League, she retained her maiden name after her marriage to sports writer W. O. McGeehan. She was the first accredited woman war correspondent for American newspapers for the First World War. She later traveled extensively in Mexico and sent scoop reports of the power struggles there. When it seemed nobody could locate Pancho Villa, she traveled alone by mule and a "Fordito" and spent several months interviewing him and getting to know him and his family. She was known as "La Amiga de Mexico." Her richly interesting life and background furnished her with materials for her plays ("The Theatre," *The New York Times,* 26 April 1925, n.p.).

Treadwell and her husband moved to New York in 1919 where she turned to writing plays, although she continued to do some work for the newspapers. In 1921 Treadwell copyrighted *Rights,* an unpublished play about Mary Wollstonecroft. Her first play to be produced was *Gringo* in which she drew on her experience in Mexico and her Spanish ancestry. Among her later plays was *Plumes in the Dust,* based on the life of Edgar Allen Poe. *Ladies Leave* was a lightly comic play about a woman seeking fulfillment through psychoanalysis. *Promised Land,* a naturalistic look at the negative aspects of the new Russia, flew in the face of the early 1930's pro-Russian stance taken by many liberal writers and such companies as the Group Theatre. *Million Dollar Gate* focused on corruption and exploitation in boxing, pre-dating Odets' *Golden Boy* and Irwin Shaw's *The Harder They Fall.* Her plays often featured unpopular attitudes, unfamiliar subject matter, or other elements which made commercial productions unlikely.

Nevertheless, it is important to remember that high quality producers and artists were interested in Treadwell's work throughout her career. In 1922 *Gringo* was produced by Guthrie McClintic. Having worked with Winthrop Ames at the Little Theatre, he was inclined toward unconventional, innovative plays. The element of particular interest in this play was the honest, detailed characterization of the Mexicans. Drawing on her close connection with Pancho Villa, Treadwell used him as a model for her central character, a Mexican revolutionary bandit. The critics were divided about the play as a whole, but all praised the refreshing actuality in the picture of Mexico.

A typical review read, "'Gringo' probably brings a more authentic picture of Mexico to the stage than any play which the American theatre has known" (The New Play at the Comedy Theatre 'Gringo'", n.p.).

The two central characters pleased the critics. The Mexican bandit was played with style and verve by Jose Ruben. Edna Hibbard created a memorable portrayal of a "half-breed" girl, the daughter of an American miner and a Mexican/Indian woman. Abducted by the bandit, she ultimately chose to reject her Gringo background and stay with him. Treadwell's depiction of these and the surrounding characters was admired by most critics.

A typical summary of the play stated, "Miss Treadwell evidently understands the peon and the bandit perfectly and seems to have an illuminating knowledge of the American, or the Gringo, as the peons call him. Out of an extended stay among our Southern neighbors she has written a play which compels attention and which tells a genuinely dramatic story" ("The New Play at the Comedy Theatre 'Gringo'" n.p.).

Few critics praised the play as a whole. Some described it as a melodrama, one as grim realism, and another as a ironic comedy. Some of the critics felt that the point of the play was unclear, but others felt it was about the difficulty of a person of mixed race in society.

For a first play, however, Treadwell did well. The production ran for five weeks, and many critics described Treadwell as a playwright to watch. Corbin expressed the view of many when he said with all its faults the play, "remains, however, an achievement of great distinction and of greater promise on the higher levels of the drama" ("Americans in Mexico," 26). The most positive review was by Alexander Woolcott who concluded that the play was much more than a mere melodrama: "It is truly and humanly written in all its minor colloquies and it reaches a final act that is more than merely theatrically effective—that is authentic and interesting drama" ("Miss Treadwell's Play" 14).

Treadwell's next play to be produced in New York had a rocky road. Originally produced under the title of *Loney Lee* by George C. Tyler as a vehicle for the young Helen Hayes, the play closed out of town. The playwright persevered, rewrote, and finally produced the play herself in 1925 under the title of *O, Nightingale*. Surprisingly, she found success. Treadwell fulfilled a life-long ambition by acting one of the roles and both her performance and the play were praised. Thus, against the odds and without much encouragement, Treadwell produced and acted in a play she had written and was rewarded with a long run in New York.

Although the production was greeted with praise, most of the credit for its success went to Martha-Bryan Allen who played with great charm and naiveté the role of a stage-struck girl who had played Juliet in Kansas and hoped for a career in New York. The familiar plot of a young actress seeking success, only to find she hasn't the talent, was developed by Treadwell with a number of interesting scenes in a realistic, three-act play set in a sculptor's studio. Here Loney Lee and a worldly-wise actress study dance with a Russian ballerina (played humorously by Treadwell). The teacher advises her she would be better off as a maid than an actress. Loney faints from hunger and is advised by her more experienced friend, "You gotta get a man first if you wanna succeed. It's men who can give you the boost because it's men that rule the roost" (qtd. in "O, Nightingale is Sprightly" n. p.).

Taking the advice of both women, Loney takes a job as a maid to the sculptor, but mistakenly believes him to be a wealthy French roué whom she elects to be "her man." A comical scene noted by the critics occurred in the last act when "her man" (who bought her clothes, etc. but got nothing but smiles in return) arranged a dinner with an important producer and his shallow actress wife. Treadwell created effective comic dialogue between the crass producer, the actress, and Loney who tries to spout Shakespeare to impress him. The last impression is that Loney will be able to marry the handsome, talented, wealthy sculptor and the stage will be spared another untalented Juliet.

The reviews of this "spring comedy" (it was produced late in the season after Easter) were generally very positive and predicted a long run. Many critics commented on the hearty laughter throughout the play. Noting that the action could easily have degenerated into farce, the reviewer in the *Christian Science Monitor* wrote, ". . . but the various characters are so well delineated, and the writing so fine, that Miss Treadwell is to be congratulated for her excellent addition to the theatre, as well as the fortunate casting of her play" ("'O, Nightingale,'" n.p.). The critic for the *New York Post* wrote that the playwright "deserves credit for a skillful, workmanlike, engaging piece of work that stands out above the usual Broadway comedy like a nightingale above a poll parrot" (Davis, "'O, Nightingale'" 12). That Treadwell had established herself as a playwright worth following was indicated by the major coverage of the play and references to her earlier play

Gringo. The critics were right in predicting a success for Treadwell. The papers were full of pictures of the youthful Martha Bryan-Allen and audiences filled the 49th Street Theatre. In order to keep extending the run the play was forced to move to the Astor and finally to the Ambassador where it completed its run.

Machinal was produced by Arthur Hopkins in 1928 with scenery by Robert Edmond Jones. It was Treadwell's only major critical success. The source of the play was a sordid story which Treadwell and others covered extensively for the papers. Edmund Wilson stated that more was written about the Judd Gray/Ruth Snyder murder trial than anything but the Harry K. Thaw murder and the Lindbergh baby kidnapping ("Judd Gray and Mrs. Snyder" 321). Americans were fascinated by the quiet, neighborly woman who helped murder her husband one night. They thrilled to the front page photo of her in the electric chair taken by a reporter with a camera secretly taped to his leg. The element which lifted this story above the ordinary love triangle murder was that the lovers who planned and executed the murder were such ordinary people. This provided Treadwell with the impetus to write the play—the first statement in the script is "the story of a woman who murders her husband—an ordinary young woman, any woman" (Gassner, *Twenty-Five Representative American Plays* 496). The brilliance of Treadwell's conception was to utilize Expressionistic universalized character types in place of the naturalistic approach which was the obvious approach for this material. Her "Young Woman" is a superb creation and provided the finest role Zita Johann performed in her career. The cold-blooded murderer from the front pages is transformed into a poignant figure who draws in the audience because it sees everything through her eyes—she is a victim of a machine-like, indifferent society. In 1955 Treadwell wrote a letter (in virtually the same sentence structure she used in the play) saying, "I would like to put down briefly for you the simple basic idea I had when I started to write the play. It is all in the title—"Machine-al"—machine-like. . . . A young woman—ready—eager—for life—for love— . . . I wanted to unfold her story in vital situations—teeming with life—but deadened—squeezed—crushed—. . . she is a woman innately unsuited to this mechanization of life" (quoted in Heck-Rabi 65).

The "vital situations" are nine episodes in which the Young Woman (Miss A in the "The Office") suffers from the oppression, dehumanization, and the mechanical noises of the modern world. Appropriately, she is ultimately killed by a machine: the electric chair. Treadwell uses the typical elements of German Expressionism well; throughout the play there is a continual use of offstage noise including typewriters, an adding machine, buzzers, telephone bells, telegraph instruments, airplanes, and radios.

In the first scene Miss A. arrives at the office late, craving air and freedom after a stifling subway trip. The Boss, a typical Expressionist character called Mr. J (for Jones) distresses her by his attentions and perplexes her by proposing marriage. Overwhelmed by the noise of the office and her loathing for Mr. J., she reveals her thoughts in a telegraphic monologue which concludes, "Oh don't!—please don't touch me—I want to rest—no rest—no rest—earn—got to earn—married—earn—no—yes earn—all girls—most girls—ma—pa—ma—all women—most women—I can't—must—maybe—must—somebody—something—ma—pa—ma—can I, ma? Tell me, ma—something—somebody" (Gassner 501).

The appeal to "somebody" is a motif which occurs throughout the play; but within her society there is nobody. Her co-workers are shallow, she finds no comfort from God, and her mother is a selfish nag whose chief interest is in being supported by the Young Woman. Her character symbolizes the crass materialism and false moral standards of society.

The third scene "Honeymoon" depicts the horror and despair of the Young Woman. Imprisoned in a stifling hotel room, she is tortured by Mr. J.'s pawing and continual dirty jokes. When she finally must remove her clothes and prepare for bed, she enters from the bathroom, "her eyes wide with a curious, helpless, animal terror (Gassner 506). Her last lines are, "Somebody—somebody—" (Gassner 507). Bywaters responded to the fact that the 1931 production in Britain was criticized because this scene was perceived as revolting. She comments, "Helen's plea for 'somebody' to help her suggests the possibility of a rescue, a revolution against a tradition that requires a woman to submit to a kind of 'legalized rape' that is truly 'revolting'" (103).

The fourth episode follows logically; it is "Maternal." In her poignant telegraphic monologue which ends the scene the Young Woman uses imagery of animal births, blood, guilt, and death. Episodes Five and Six are the only scenes in which the Young Woman experiences any happiness. She meets and makes love with The Man (appropriately the role which gave Clark Gable his big chance). In these episodes she feels free and delights in his stories of life South of the Border (background which Treadwell knew well). She is fascinated by his tale of escape from bandidos by filling a bottle with pebbles and killing his guard.

Episode Seven ("Domestic") shows the Young Woman back in her bourgeois prison contemplating killing her husband as he brags about his business deals. In Episode Eight ("The Law"), the Young Woman is tried for murdering her husband. There is the continual clicking of the telegraph instruments, and the words and movements of all except the Young Woman are mechanical.

The final episode is called "A Machine." Again the action is enhanced by off-stage noises including the singing of a condemned black convict who drowns out the words of the priest. The Young Woman is calm until barbers come to shave a patch of her hair where the electrode will be attached. As they cruelly force her to submit, she cries, "No! No! Don't touch me—touch me! I will not be submitted—this indignity! No! I will not be submitted! Leave me alone! Oh my God am I never to be let alone! Always to have to submit—to submit! No more—not now—I'm going to die—I won't submit! Not now!" (Gassner 527). As the play ends, the Young Woman is taken to the electric chair and against the monotone of prayers and the shallow chatter of the reporters her voice cries out for the last time, "Somebody! Somebod—" and her voice is cut off (Gassner 529). It was selected as one of the best plays of the year, was anthologized by John Gassner, and has been revived in New York and in regional theatres.

It might seem unsurprising that Treadwell chose an Expressionist mode for her play, but in fact, the style was already perceived as passé by the late twenties. As a Boston critic noted, "Some critics called Expressionism a dead dodo in the American theatrical pit, but she [Treadwell] has unexpectedly galvanized it" (unident. clipping, Lincoln Center Library). Critic James Craig rated *Machinal* above such plays as *The Adding Machine* and *The Hairy Ape* in its use of Expressionism, stating in *The World*, "Her method follows the pattern that the modernists set and called 'expressionistic'—that perilous form of distorted lights and brief vignettes and harsh staccato utterances. It burst on to our Broadway stage with Kaiser's 'From Morn to Midnight,' and not since that unforgettable production (1922) has its value been so completely realized" ("Machinal" n.p.).

Reviewers were so impressed with the work of this little-known playwright that some compared her writing favorably with that of O'Neill. In the *Herald Tribune* Arthur Ruhl wrote that while *Machinal* was not like *Strange Interlude*, "It deserves to be mentioned in the same breath with the O'Neill play as an example of modern technique in the theatre, and it does give the spectator somewhat the same sense of having seen all around its principal character and not so much spent an evening looking at something arranged for his entertainment as lived through another human being's whole life ("Machinal" n.p.).

Treadwell traveled to Paris, London, and Moscow to see *Machinal*. It the distinction of a production directed by Tairov at the Moscow Kamerny Theatre where it ran for a year. Following the success in Moscow it was produced in the Russian provinces as well. Treadwell spent several months in Russia in connection with these productions making notes and collecting material for *Promised Land*.

Proof of the continuing appeal of *Machinal* is shown by New York productions in 1960 and in 1990. Reviewing the 1960 production Brooks Atkinson (who had seen the first production) wrote, "It has lost nothing through the years. . . . Although Mr. Frankel's imaginative production gives 'Machinal' the astringent note that updates it, Miss Treadwell is still the source of its modernity. She was the person thirty-two years ago who saw the sordid murder of a commonplace husband by his panicky wife as the expression of a hostile environment. . . . After thirty-two years 'Machinal' remains an original theatre composition" ("Machinal 27).

The play had even more appeal in a very effective production at the Public Theatre directed by Frank Greif in 1990. Frank Rich wrote, "Like an archeological treasure preserved in a subterranean air pocket, 'Machinal' . . . is both an authentic artifact of a distant civilization and a piece of living art that seems timeless ("A Nightmarish Vision" 171). Douglas Watt began his review by saying, "Grab 'Machinal'" and concluded, "After following the sorry career of subjugation and crime bringing the Young Woman (tellingly portrayed by Jodie Markell) to the electric chair, you'll almost feel like rushing out to get the morning paper and readallaboutit. 'Machinal,' told in punchy episodes, is that immediate" ("'Machinal': Joltingly Executed Drama" 173). Concurring with most of the critics who praised the timelessness of the play, Clive Barnes wrote, "Here is a wonderful play so perfectly of its time that it transcends any such boundaries, and stands as a drama about a woman in a land of machines, a woman in a sea of men" ("Perfect Period Piece" 173).

After the successful New York revival, Machinal was performed in many regional theatres. Reviewing a 1991 production by A Fly's Eye in Chicago, Sid Smith wrote, "'Machinal' is an obscure 1928 drama enjoying rediscovery in recent years, thanks to its stylish experimentalism and playwright Sophie Treadwell's early feminist muscle and sexual frankness" ("Rediscovered 'Machinal' 5). Director C.David Frankel selected the play for a 1991 production at Saint Leo's College in St. Petersburg because of the Expressionistic style. He drew the audience into close proximity by putting the audience on the stage with the actors (Hayes, "After Words" 11). In an unusual gender-blind production by the Denver City Stage Ensemble, Jeff Bradley found the approach interesting and the play still gripping ("'Machinal' still jolting" 6). Peter Vaughan praised the 1993 Minneapolis production by the Frank Theatre. Describing the play, he wrote, "Helen becomes an Everywoman who leads a life of submission and powerlessness and is continually forced to make choices that only lead her from one form of subjugation to another. . . . Treadwell doesn't offer Helen's solution as either viable or logical, but she does make it understandable" ("Theater" 9E). After years of neglect, Treadwell's play has taken its place in the repertoire of theatres in America.

Less than a year after her success with the Arthur Hopkins' production of Machinal, Treadwell saw Ladies Leave produced by Charles Hopkins. The event was far from triumph of her last play: she had created a comedy which some critics thought notable only because of the elegant Robert Edmond Jones scenery. (Jones continued to be a great supporter of Treadwell through her successes and her failures.) Several critics noted that it seemed as if Treadwell had noted the potentially ridiculous aspects in the circumstance of a bored wife who takes a lover, and had created the obverse side of Machinal. In Ladies Leave, Zizi Powers is married to a wealthy publisher, but finds her life in her beautiful apartment boring. Intrigued by the ideas of a Viennese psychiatrist who advises that there may be morality in immorality, she decides to take a lover. Zizi drives both her husband and her lover to distraction while the affair is going on, but at the end concludes that she doesn't care for either of them, and leaves to catch up with the attractive psychiatrist in Vienna. Several critics noted a resemblance to the departure of Nora from her doll house, but the play had neither the intensity of Ibsen's play nor the wit necessary to carry it as a suc-cessful comedy. Stephen Rathbun put his finger on a major problem in the play: "Mrs. Zizi Powers is a feminist to the extent of insisting upon living her own life. She refuses to be submerged by her husband . . . and she refuses to be fettered by her lover. But it is hardly feministic of the frankly honest Zizi to be interested only in men. She lives in a man-centered world. Thus her newly acquired freedom is but an illusion. And that is why this drawing room comedy is an unimportant play and is just the fleeting diversion of an idle evening. ("'Ladies Leave' Opens," n.p.) The play closed after only fifteen performances, and did not enhance Treadwell's reputation in any way.

It was several years before Treadwell got another play, *Lone Valley*, on Broadway. She found it difficult to find a producer, and ultimately produced it herself in 1933. The critics were virtually unanimous in commenting on the familiarity of the material. The three-act, realistic play treated a "fallen woman" who left her house of ill-repute after inheriting a ranch from her aunt. She tried to create a new life, felt cleansed by the love of a respectable man, but was driven away by a sheriff who knew her past. Brooks Atkinson noted the familiarity of this legend, saying, "after serving the drama faithfully, man and boy for nigh on to fifty year, that legend must be true." He concluded his review by saying, "'Lone Valley' is out of the theatre's old clothes closet. In view of the mental agility that 'Machinal' disclosed, it is sur-prising that Miss Treadwell did not recognize the frailties of 'Lone Valley' before she placed it in production" ("Desire in 'Lone Valley'" 18). Wilella Waldorf reminded readers of *Machinal* ("an interesting, if unpleasant, drama"), and spent much of the review regretting the con-ventional story and characters: "'Lone Valley' is not brilliant enough either in the writing or playing to make up for the dreary familiarity of its plot. Much finer plays have been written on this theme and finer actors have played them" ("'Lone Valley' Arrives" n.p.)

Probably the most interesting thing about the production as a whole was Treadwell's approach to prices. Her unusual decision to sell tickets for $2.00 took nerve because it went against the wisdom of the male dominated theatre business and conventions. She concluded an article explaining her approach by saying, "This experience makes me wonder if there may not be a grain of useful truth in the idea that a good many of our activities, including those of business in general, might gain by a fresh consideration of them by persons—including women—who are

sublimely unconscious of the past and its rules and customs and conventions. Women like myself who are blessedly ignorant" ("Miss
Treadwell Explains" n.p.)

Despite the low ticket price, the Depression and the negative critical reception of *Lone Valley* caused it to close after only three performances. It was perceived as conventional and old-fashioned when it
was written and it has not been revived.

After the financial and critical failure in 1933, Treadwell turned
again to a more experimental approach with *For Saxaphone* in 1934. In
the preface Treadwell stated that the play is to have unbroken musical
accompaniment: contemporary Jazz, a Brahms symphony, Viennese
waltzes, and Hungarian gypsy music. Additionally, she uses off-stage
voices, and dialogue "written in a short repetitive rhythm, where I
tried to create the empty, blatant blah blah effect of most of our talk
today ("Preface," typed copy, Lincoln Center)." The play is composed
of a series of scenes in three acts. These scenes shift and blend with a
cinematic effect, relying on little scenery. As in *Machinal*, there is
extensive use of light and sound.

Treadwell again focuses on a female protagonist. Lily Laird, "a sort
of kaleidoscope of a beautiful girl in beautiful clothes" (1-1-1). Lily is
torn between the various pressures of her society and her own impulses
and urges. She marries a man whose dominating mother raised him to
find physical love repulsive.

The progression of scenes reveals the progressive misery of Lily, married to a sexually unresponsive man and surrounded by his dull friends.
There are 24 characters, plus extras and there are more than thirty
voices which are heard. Sexually frustrated, Lily is attracted by a
coarse, violent dancer. Ultimately, he kills her by throwing a knife at
her. Throughout the play the sexual symbolism of knives, and the relationship of sex and death is strong, Lily has said that "love is a compulsion like death—a little death" (2-5-3). Her relationship with the
dancer echoes Miss Julie's attraction for Jean. She says, "It's as though I
have to go down, deep down, down underneath, down" (3-3-30).

Treadwell tried to sell the work both for the stage and for film (for
which it would have been quite appropriate) but had no success. The
play prefigures the Elmer Rice hit play *Dream Girl* and the highly successful Kurt Weill/Moss Hart musical *Lady in the Dark*. The Expressionistic characters are effectively drawn and much of the dialogue is
engrossing and theatrical. Creatively staged, with filmed sequences to

add to the visual element, the play might fare well today. The theme of repressed sensuality and the fear of death as a result of sex is more likely to be appreciated today than when the play was written.

Treadwell intended to write a play about Edgar Allen Poe very early in her career. She wrote a play in the twenties and sent it to John Barrymore for his consideration—this would have been an exciting matching of actor and role. However, he later announced that his wife had written a play about Poe in which he would appear. Treadwell took him to court, and there was lengthy litigation. In the 1930's Treadwell, who had done laborious research on Poe and American society in his lifetime, revised her play and it was presented in 1936. Arthur Hopkins produced and staged it and Henry Hull, who had performed in *Ladies Leave* and in the staggeringly successful *Tobacco Road*, played the role of Poe.

The play is a straight-forward realistic treatment of Poe's life from 1826 when he was a student to the time of his death in 1849. The most interesting scene is the last in which Poe is in Washington Hospital at death's door. In a dilirium he quotes his poems and stories and speaks to people who are not there. The role as a whole and this scene in particular presented a fine opportunity for Hull. One speech ran, "No care—no hope—no effort. Just the chilliness of night—of the night without end—I shake as the quivering plumes upon a hearse. . . . Shrouded bodies in their sad and solemn slumber with the worm" (3-2-4/5).

Critics were generally negative about the play despite Hull's moving performance. Brooks Atkinson noted the outstanding cast and the seriousness of the effort, but concluded with most of the critics that the play did not succeed. He and others suggested that Poe's life was not amenable to theatricalization, despite its superficially theatrical quality. "If one is still ungraciously reluctant about 'Plumes in the Dust,' doubtless it is chiefly because the genius of Poe was secretive and shy" ("Plumes in the Dust," 14). One positive element of the production was the role it provided for African-American actress Laura Bowman who was praised in several reviews as the maid. The play closed after 21 performances and Treadwell left on a world cruise to overcome her disappointment over the failure of a work of many years.

The last major Treadwell play to be produced fared somewhat better than *Plumes in the Dust*. *Hope for a Harvest* was produced by the prestigious Theatre Guild and starred the notable acting team of Florence Eldridge and Frederic March. They performed it on a road tour and found success in Boston, Pittsburgh, Baltimore, and Washington. However, in New York most of the critics admired the subject matter, but did not give the play "money reviews" so it ran for only five weeks. Despite the short run it was selected for inclusion in the *Best Plays of 1941-42*.

It comes as something of a surprise to read *Hope for a Harvest* after considering earlier Treadwell non-realistic works. In its realistic format and its setting it is reminiscent of Sidney Howard's 1924 play *They Knew What They Wanted*. The simple story line has to do with a woman who is driven home by the war after many years of life in Europe. She yearns for the rural peace and the vibrant fertility of her family's old ranch.

Unaware of the economic problem of farmers and the effects of the Depression on the economy, she is disappointed in both her ranch and her relatives: both seem to be worn out failures. Her return and her hope for a harvest revitalize her cousin Elliott. Assuming a new courage and zest for life he proposes that they marry and work together to bring the ranch back to its old life. The interesting aspects of the play are not so much the story line or the structure, but the social comment Treadwell is making about a society which is oriented too much toward materialism and has slipped into desuetude. Three main themes are developed: the failure of the American people, prejudice against foreigners, and improper use of the environment.

The criticism of 1940's society is somewhat surprising since it sounds so much like what is often said today: it is a consumer society, conspicuous consumption abounds (along with destruction of the environment), money is the only criterion for value, and people buy everything on credit with little regard for the future. Pitted against this is the value of profit which comes from work, the pleasures of growing and eating one's own food, concern for the land, and the strength and pride appropriate to the American farmer.

The theme of prejudice against foreigners is expressed early in the play when Carlotta expresses her dismay about the condition of the land. The responses to her resemble comments heard today about the influx of Vietnamese and other ethnic groups and the effects of Japanese imports:

Lotta.   The trees cut down, the barns fallen in—the—What's happened?
Elliot.   Oh, nobody lives in 'em any more but Dagoes and Japs. They've driven
          us out, Lot!
Lotta.   How?
Elliott. Oh, undercut us, underlived us—overbred us—an inferior race will
          always breed out a superior one— . . . Wait till you see your mail
          box—there's a whole row of 'em there—where just our one Thatcher
          box used to be—Cadematori—Yamaguchi—Sanguinetti—Matsumoto
          —Cardozo—Ito—all living on what was just our one ranch—
          and all despising each other. (28-29)

The third concern expressed in the play was one to which Treadwell
was very qualified to speak. She had lived many years in California on
a ranch and was involved in its management. She was well aware of
the problem of farmers and the destruction of rich farm land through
real estate development and improper farming methods. In her play
the ambitious Italian immigrant Joe is contrasted with the persons who
view themselves as American, but who have failed to maintain the
farmland.

Treadwell used the metaphor of the decaying ranch as a symbol for
an America in decline: an immigrant country which wanted to shut its
doors to immigrants, a society abusing the resources inherited from
immigrant ancestors. She was expressing concerns not generally felt
when she wrote the play, and the recognition speech given by Elliott
might well have been written today: "There's something awful wrong,
Lot—about what people like us have let happen to our land. Two
hundred million of it just plain used up since we took it over from the
Indians. You see, the Indians respected the land—they knew there are
gods in it. We ain't got any gods anymore. Just a lot of machines"
(109).

Many of the critics expressed the point of view that the play was
worthwhile and they wanted to like it, but did not find it theatrically
effective. Richard Watts Jr. wrote, "Because 'Hope for a Harvest' has
something to say, and says it with unmistakable sincerity, one has from
the start a sympathetic concern with it and a far deeper respect for its
heart and mind than for more expert dramas af lesser integrity. It really
is striving to speak to the soul of America with gravity and idealistic
fervor. The unfortunate thing is that, in expressing its author's heart-
felt interest in the future of the nation in a time of desperate crisis, the
play goes in for some unpersuasive and undramatic theatrical matters
which destroy the great part of its effectiveness" ("California" 199).

Robert Coleman indicated his verdict in the title of his review, "'Hope for a Harvest' Pedestrian Play": "There's a fine play in such material, but Miss Treadwell hasn't been able to lift it above the commonplace. The result is pedestrian drama, often dull and seldom arresting" (n.p.). Wilella Waldorf disagreed, remarking that it was easy to see why the Theatre Guild had picked the "quiet, heart-warming play. Miss Treadwell has something to say that is worth saying and she says it simply but with a good deal of conviction" ("Hope for a Harvest" 198).

Another positive review was written by George Freedley, who called it first truly adult play of the season. Like many others he noted the effective acting, and praised Alan Reed who "won the hearts of the audience" as the Italian farmer. The characterization by Treadwell was also praised. Freedley concluded by saying, "All in all, 'Hope for a Harvest' is the kind of a play that the Guild should be doing. Congratulations, Miss Helburn and Mr. Langner" ("'Hope for a Harvest'" n.p.). Treadwell and the critics who believed in her play were vindicated when it was successfully produced on television by the United States Steel Hour in 1951.

Sophie Treadwell was a playwright with social concerns and an ability to write moving dialogue and create memorable characters. The problem in many of her plays was the structure. Seeking the appropriate plot and form she would often write twelve to fifteen versions with different approaches and different endings. Eager to try everything, she had no identifying style as Rachel Crothers, Lillian Hellman, George S. Kaufman, or George Kelly had. American critics and audiences like to pigeon-hole actors and writers. Treadwell would probably be known for more plays if she had developed an identifying structure and style early in her career. But if she had, she probably wouldn't have written her best play, *Machinal*. Despite her failure to repeat the success of that 1928 production, Treadwell was successful on other counts. She earned a living in the American theatre from 1922 to her death in 1970, she had plays successfully transformed into television productions in the early fifties, and the roles she created attracted actors such as Helen Hayes, Frederic March, Florence Eldridge, Laura Bowman, Clark Gable and Zita Johann. Through the production of her non-realistic plays she encouraged experimental techniques and made audiences aware of the theatrical effectiveness of such techniques. She drew attention to the serious problems of women in American society and created outstanding roles for actresses. She was ahead of her time in introducing sympathetically created minority figures based on actual people she had met throughout the world. Those who admired her work and encouraged her included such notable actors, directors, and designers as Paul Muni, Robert Edmond Jones, Theresa Helburn, Arthur Hopkins, and Lawrence Langner. Although in the end great success eluded her, she was true to her calling and was not afraid to follow her urge to write plays which were experimental in structure or subject matter.

Eulalie Spence (1894-1981)

Eulalie Spence (1894-1981) was a playwright whose works were informed by her feminism and whose career was actively oriented toward production of her plays. She was born on the island of Nevis in the British West Indies on a sugar plantation owned by her father. After the cane crop was destroyed by a hurricane at the turn of the century, the family moved to the United States in 1902 so her father could seek employment. Elements from Spence's childhood had a strong influence on her plays. She grew up in poverty in Brooklyn, but said later that she was unaware of being poor and unfortunate (Perkins 105). She was aware, however, that West Indians were not welcomed in this country. In her home her mother was the strong figure, the father yielding to her decisions. Spence herself grew up to be a strong person who often depicted powerful female characters. As Brown-Guillory stated, Spence was one of several "early black women playwrights [who] dealt successfully with the issue of the emergence of woman as an individual who has her own tastes, aspirations, and uniqueness" (*Their Place* 19). Spence's niece wrote of her, that she "was prim, proper and ultracorrect in her speech and dress, yes—but she was gentle, generous and loving and the backbone of a family of seven girls" (qtd. in Perkins 105). Despite the poverty in the home there was a loving, supportive atmosphere. Spence enjoyed hearing her mother read to her and became interested in writing as a young girl.

After attending the New York Training School for Teachers, she took courses in English and speech in the 1920s at the College of the City of New York and Columbia University. There she was fortunate to work with playwright Hatcher Hughes. She was a student briefly at the Ethiopian Art Theatre School in 1924. After she began teaching she continued her education, receiving a B.A. in speech in Teacher's College in 1937 and an M.A. in speech from Columbia University in 1939. She taught speech and directed the dramatic society at the Eastern District High School in Brooklyn. She could take pleasure in later life in remembering her students, including Joseph Papp (Peterson 178). The training she gave Papp must have been a contributing factor to his unconventional attitudes toward Shakespeare, particularly in the area of interracial casting.

As an adult Spence was actively involved in theatre, writing fourteen plays, several screenplays, and directing. Unlike many of the early
black women playwrights, she was not part of the Washington, D.C.
group and set her plays in Harlem. Because of her work and
continuing education, she did not join the writers in the Harlem
Renaissance. She corresponded with Alain Locke at Howard
University, and she may have met Zora Neale Hurston through her
work with the Krigwa Players. From 1926 until the demise of the
group, Spence wrote plays and participated in theatrical activities. She
worked with W.E.B. DuBois, but could not agree with him about her
playwriting. Spence emphasized that "her rationale for avoiding
propaganda issues was that she knew nothing about lynchings, rapes,
nor the blatant racial injustices in this country." DuBois tried to
"persuade her to use her excellent writing skills for propaganda" but
she felt that she could not write with no experience of the subject
matter he felt was important (Perkins 106). Although her father had
difficulty in finding employment, her family was never subjected to the
sort of actions present in the plays of Douglas and Miller which are set
in the south. Spence determined that she would write folk dramas
which essentially provided fun and entertainment (Perkins 106).

Another contrast to many of the early black women playwrights was
Spence's determination to see her plays produced. She wrote "A Criticism of the Negro Drama" for *Opportunity* in 1928 in which she
expressed her condemnation of plays written to be read:

> I have seen plays written by our Negro writers with this caption: To Be Read,
> Not Played!
> A play to be read! Why not the song to be read, not sung, and the canvas to be
> described, not painted! To every art its form, thank God! And to the play, the
> technique that belongs to it. (Qtd. in Perkins 105)

She was very active in community theatre, directing her plays and
those of other writers including Eugene O'Neill. As one of the
founders of the Dunbar Garden Players in the late 1920s, she directed
plays at the St. Mark's Church on lower Second Avenue. Brown-
Guillory sums up the importance of Spence's activities by saying that
her most significant contribution to the developing African-American
theatre "rests in her attempts at piecing together the cultural and spiritual fabric of black in general, and of Harlemites in particular. Her
involvement in the business of theatre—in writing, directing, and pro-

ducing—initiated a movement away from the 'plays to be read' written by the majority of black women of the period and a trend toward viable theatre with a viewing audience" (*Wines in the Wilderness* 40).

Spence never married, but maintained close ties with her sisters and their children. She directed her sisters Doralyne and Olga in her own plays, and coached Doralyne when she took over the leading role first played by Rose McClendon in *In Abraham's Bosom*. Through her teaching, playwriting, and directing Spence was deeply involved in the development of African-American theatre. Her work was chiefly in New York, but her plays were widely produced throughout the country.

Of the plays written by Spence, the first was *Being Forty* (1924) when the playwright was twenty-six. This one-act comedy was performed by the National Ethiopian Art Players at the Lafayette Theatre. It was not published, but *Foreign Mail* (1926), another one-act comedy, won the second prize in the *Crisis* contest, and was published by Samuel French in 1927 making it available to acting groups. As a prize winner, it was produced by the Krigwa Players in New York City at the 135th Street Library on *Crisis* "Prize Night" in 1926, and again by the same group in 1927 (Peterson 179).

In 1926 Spence wrote another one-act play called *The Starter*. This tied for third prize in the *Opportunity* contest in 1927. In this widely produced play, a young elevator starter wants to propose to his girlfriend on a park bench in Harlem. Initially enthusiastic and romantic he changes his views as the play progresses. His idealism is undermined by her realism regarding finances and responsibilities in marriage, and he decides not to propose. The play was published in *Plays of the Negro Legacy* in 1927.

Her (1927) is described as a mystery play in one act. It is, on the surface, a play of the supernatural in which an avaricious white man is punished for his cruelty to his Philippino wife by her reappearance as a ghost. However, there is a strongly developed picture of the realistic element of disempowerment of women who are foreign or black. The simple strory is revealed largely through the characterization of Martha. She has been victimized by both the white landlord, Kinney, and her husband, "crippled and an idler for fifteen years." Although she suffers from back trouble, she earns money for the rent and food by ironing for "very old families" (132). Kinney pays her a pittance to show empty apartments to prospective renters. But he suspects she has frightened away renters from the apartment above with her stories of ghosts, so he comes himself, for the first time in twenty years to show the rooms upstairs to a nice young couple. When he returns to the rooms alone, Martha describes his harsh treatment of his young foreign wife which caused her to hang herself upstairs. Martha and the young couple, Alice and Sam, go out into the hall to investigate a loud noise, and Martha rushes back in, saying, "Pete! Pete! yuh wanted a sign! Ah jes seen John Kinney walkin' down the stairs with *Her*! She had him by the hand an' she was laughin'! (The curtain starts to descend just as Alice's piercing scream rings through the room) (140).

Spence created interesting characters, and through her introduction of the element of the victimization of women gives added meaning to a familiar type of ghost story. The play was produced by the Krigwa Players in January and April in the 135th Street Library Theatre in Harlem. Once again, the simple elements required for staging, the strong characterization and dialogue make the play appealing to amateur groups.

Fool's Errand (1927) is a satire on gossiping zealots in the church who mistakenly suppose a young girl, Maza, is pregnant because they discover baby clothes hidden in the house. They tell her drunk father, who immediately expresses violent intentions toward his daughter and the two young men who have been courting her. In a sharply barbed scene Spence characterizes the parson and the members of the Council for the Suppression of Vice and Correction of Sinners. "A hard, fanatical, relentless look seems in some imperceptible fashion to stamp each face. Here, the gleam of an eye; there, the tight fold of a lip. The Sisters carry palm leaf fans for the night is hot. They are dressed in ill-fitting white frocks and ugly black hats" (124). Early in the play there is an amusing depiction of their critical attitudes toward the changing mores of society. Sister Cassie (Maza's aunt, who has found the clothes and brings the council to the home), says the Council has waited too long to crack down on the youth of the community: "It's mah 'pinion dey's bin outer han' a mightly long time. Whut wid dey cuts off de little hair Gawd gives 'em, an' den spends all dey's got tuh straighten it out—flyin' in de face uh Gawd, Ah calls it!" and the parson's wife answers, "Ef sech doin's keeps on, reckon our young people'll be jes' as brazen's white folks" (121).

The play is an effective combination of comedy and violence. When Doug hears about the baby clothes, he tears a dress into rags, and when he suspects a young man of being the father, he grabs him by the throat and flings him down. The play rises to a climax when the parson and the council, in shrill condemnation, exchange chants and shouts about the power of the devil and the desertion of the Lord when a sinner cries out for help too late. Maza's distress is genuinely moving. The sudden appearance of Maza's mother stops the persecution and the air is cleared when she announces that it is she who is pregnant, and the council leaves in shame. In the final moments she and Doug stand, listening to the council singing a song. Throughout the play Spence has made the point that women are attacking women instead of being supportive to each other. She emphasizes the point with the song at the end:

> Ah met mah sister de odder night
>   She call me by mah name.
> An; jus' as soon's mah back wuz turned
>   She scandalize mah name.
> Yuh call dat a sister?
>   No! No! (Chant the Council)
> Yuh call dat a sister?
>   No! No!
>
> Yuh call dat a sister?
>   No! No!
> Who'd scandalize mah name! (131)

The use of music, comedy, and the underlying threat of violence are effective throughout the play. It was first produced by the Krigwa Players in New York in 1927. It was later successfully produced at the National Little Theatre Tournament in New York City in 1927, winning the Samuel French prize of $200 as the best unpublished play in the tournament. The play was published by French and presented by many little theatre groups. There was a dispute about the prize which DuBois accepted to pay for production expenses, so it did not go to Spence (Peterson 179). This exacerbated the differences between them and may have led to the disintegration of the Krigwa Players shortly thereafter.

The Hunch (1927) is a comedy of Harlem life in which a young woman about to be married is informed that her fiancé is already married. Instead of expressing gratitude to the former lover who gives her the news, she attacks him for spoiling her happiness. Although it won second prize in the *Opportunity* competition in 1927, it has only been published in *Carolina* magazine. It was performed by the Washington, D.C. Krigwa Players at the time it won the prize.

In contrast to the comedy of many of Spence's plays, *Undertow* (1927) is a Strindbergian play of hate and thwarted love between a man and his wife and a woman who bore his illegitimate child. The play has a mood of darkness and anger from the beginning when the wife Hattie is frowning at the place setting for her husband Dan, who has not come home for dinner. She is described as a dark woman, wearing a dark dress, and frequently "frowning darkly." Her indulged, weak son, Charley, bursts in wearing fashionable clothes. She has obviously spoiled him and brought him up to have contempt for his father, whom she calls a fool. Remarking on the absence of his father for dinner, he says he will tell Hattie something if she will give him five dollars for gambling. Reluctantly, she gets out the bill, and sits with her fist on it while he tells that he saw his father apparently meet an old girl friend on the street a few days earlier. He describes the dazed look of his father, blithely takes the bill, and exits saying, "She warn't no chicken—but she was good tuh look at. Tain't no use mopin', Ma. Dad ain't de fus' husban' tuh take dinner wid his girl friend. Funny, though his never doin' it befo'. Well, s'long" (109).

Angry and suspicious, Hattie clears the table and when her tired, patient looking husband appears, she vents her anger on him and refuses to give him anything to eat: "Whar yuh been, dat yur ain't had nothin' tuh eat? Yuh kain't say, kin yuh? . . . Yuh keep outa thar! Keep outa mah kitchen! Ah kep yuh supper till eight o'clock. Yuh didn' come, and Ah's throwed it out!" (110). He leaves to get something to eat and one of the boarders enters. She is a nicely delineated character who typifies the other boarders who, as Brown-Guillory says, represent another element of the folk tradition, "with the constant stream of people flowing in and out of Hattie's boarding house" (*Their Place* 16). She has come to complain of the cold (although she says, "Co'se, Ah ain't complainin', Mis' Peters") and to say that a woman is waiting in the parlor (111). Soon Clem, the tall, lighter skinned third member of the triangle appears. She has suffered, but has raised her daughter to have an education and marry well. Now, she wants the happiness she and Dan have missed for twenty years. Audience sympathy is turned toward her and Dan. Clem says she knows Hattie hates Dan and has treated him cruelly, nagging him, forcing him to wear shabby clothes, and turning his son against him. Spence now turns sympathy toward Hattie, when she indicates the wrong which was done to her as a young pregnant wife:

> Funny—how—thoughtful yuh's got sence Ah's las' seen yuh. Yuh come inta mah house twenty years ago as a frien'—an' yuh took Dan when Ah hadn't bin married ter him a year. Yuh didn' give no 'nouncement den 'bout whut yuh was gwine ter do. Yuh jes' took him—an' me expectin' tuh be de mother uv his chile. Gawd! (a deep shudder runs through her body) But now—dat yuh's got mo' stylish—mo' lady-like in yuh ways yuh come tuy tell me ve'y politely, dat yuh's gwine tuh take him again. Is it mah blessin' yuh's waitin' fer? Yuh doan' need no permission. (113)

When Clem tells Hattie she is hard she answers, "Ah was soft 'nuff, when yuh fust stepped on me. Ef Ah's hard now, 'tis yo' fault" (114).

When Dan returns the play rises to it inevitable tragic conclusion. Laughing crazily, Hattie vows to spend her life if she has to to find the daughter and tell her her mother was a prostitute and her father a married man. In surprising frank language (both for the time and for the kind of woman Spence was), she refuses to say she will stay away from the daughter, "Never! An' yuh kain't make me! Ah'll tell her 'bout dis good woman! Dis thief! Dis dirty minded whore!" (116). The conclusion sees Hattie dead, after hitting her head when Dan knocked her down, and Dan and Clem once again separated. Dan says with anguish, "We's brung each other bad luck, Clem. Hattie was right" (117).

In this compressed, deeply felt play Spence has created an engrossing set of characters, and managed to direct sympathy at all three while yet showing all three to have negative or malevolent qualities. The title indicates the unavoidable power of past passions which still lie beneath the surface and will suck the three into renewed tragedy. The atmosphere of the clean room with snowy linen effectively contrasts the poisonous quality of the dialogue. An element which often occurs in African-American plays is the jealousy of darker people for lighter people. Not only does Hattie hate Clem for taking Dan away, she hates her for being lighter and more attractive to Dan.

The simple setting makes the play attractive to performers with limited funds and facilities. It is poignant without being sentimental. Brown-Guillory calls it a "jewel of a play" It has, however, been criticized because of its subject matter. Hatch and Shine note that few black playwrights attempted what Spence did: "to write a play whose characters were undeniably black, but whose problem within the play

was not ethnic" (192). Hatch and Shine do not criticize the playwright, but imply that others might say the characters are really white,
only "painted black." Their judgment is that Spence "may be one of
the first to write black characters into a non-racial plot" and that she
may be praised for enlarging the sphere of black experience on stage,
or "censored for avoiding it" (192).

At the time the play was written this point was debated, but the play
was praised and performed, nevertheless. In the 1927 *Crisis* competition, it won third prize with another play by Spence, *Hot Stuff*. *Undertow* was published in *Carolina* Magazine, and has recently been
anthologized by Perkins and by Hatch and Shine. It is the best-known
play by Spence because of its early availability, frequent productions,
and inclusion in recent anthologies.

Hot Stuff (1927) is less well-known and Peterson lists no known
productions of it. For the time in which it was written, it is a surprisingly sordid depiction of the squalid lives led by many African-Americans in Harlem. The story line is thin with the focus on the well-devel-
oped characters and their interaction. The play has to do with an
exceptionally beautiful young woman, Fanny, who lives an amoral,
careless life as a numbers runner, a salesperson for stolen clothing, and
a prostitute. She has a husband whom she finds boring but useful, as he
supplies the clothing from the firm for which he works, and she has a
lover she sees most evenings. Her taste runs to high-living and fancy
clothing. Into her apartment comes her girl-friend who also is a prostitute and buys clothes from Fanny to sell. The first scene is a lively one
between them in which they chat gaily about boyfriends, gambling,
making money, and clothes. Mary goes off to meet her out-of-town
date, then a young compulsive gambler comes in, having won for once.
But Fanny won't give him the two hundred and fifty dollars, claiming
she lost his slip and never played it. But in a swift reversal, his girlfriend
comes in pretending to want to buy a dress, then threatening to tell
Fanny's husband's employers about the theft of the clothes. She is a
tough, confident woman who disapproves of Fanny. She says, "I ain't
got no love fer Saltzberg and Olinsky, an' I ain't got none fer you. But
just the same, I ain't one fer doin' my own people like some folks I
know" (47).

Yet another interesting character appears, a rather stereotypical
Jewish peddlar of questionable reputation.He has brought what seems
to be a hot Ermine coat which he tries to sell Fanny. The scene

between these two hustlers is very cleverly written, with each trying to outdo the other. He tells her if he sells it to her for $250, he is giving it away:

Fanny: I know you're jokin'. (She takes off the wrap and hands it to Goldstein). Here. I ain't crazy if you is. Say, do I look like two hundred fifty spot cash?

Goldstein: You look like a million dollar kid to me. Say, would you pass up such a coat like this? It don't suit nobody but you.

After they haggle a little more, he moves a little closer and brings up a new idea:

Goldstein: Mebbe you got something what ain't money.
Fanny: What you mean?
Goldstein: You know what I mean. (He places his arms about Fanny's waist.)
Fanny: (without drawing away) Get out. I'm a respectable, married woman, an' don't you forget it.
Goldstein: Who said you ain't? If you wasn't respectable, I wouldn't make no bargain with you. (48-49)

Fanny kisses him and gets him to give her the coat for a hundred. She says she will pay C.O.D. and they exit into the bedroom. At this juncture, Walter King, her husband arrives. Spence effectively creates a real character, although she gives him no dialogue. He enters, sees the peddlar's suitcase, frowns, then "passes in his same quick manner into the bedroom." The violence which follows is indicated almost entirely by sound. King kicks the beaten peddlar out of the room, then returns for his revenge on his wife whose cries come quickly: "Lemme alone! I didn't do nuthin'. (She utters a loud scream. There is the sound of scuffling and other loud screams, sobs and moans. There is never a word from King.) Yuh's killin' me! Gawd! Oh! Murder! Murder!" Now King, still silent, reenters, ignoring the knocking on the hall door. "He walks up to the mirror and adjusts his tie and collar. He flicks a bit of thread from his coat and puts it on. He takes up his hat and puts that on. Then he walks to the hall door, opens it and goes out, banging the door behind him" (49). After a silence Fanny enters looking the epitome of a battered wife, but holding the coat. She pulls herself together and puts it on, saying "The dirty brute! Glad he didn't scratch my face none" and calls her boyfriend to say she can't meet him until the next night (50). Apparently, she is so hardened by the life she leads that she considers she got a good bargain for the coat. As Brown-Guillory wrote, the play makes a clear statement about life in the 1920s in Harlem in which everyone was hustling something, but at the same time it seems very much related to events today.

> Spence seems to be mirroring a society in which blacks do what they have to do in order to survive and to secure material things. Some of them, like John Cole, place all of their trust in the numbers game, hoping to win enough to make ends meet. Some make a living by stealing from corporate America. Some prostitute their bodies in order to live and to have the finer things in life. What permeates the play is a sense of urban poverty and the con games that are enacted in order to survive in a fast-paced, uncaring world. (*Wines* 40-41)

Peterson lists no production history of the play, but with its fast-paced dialogue, its realistically detailed picture of society, and its ironic viewpoint, it would be surprising if it had not been performed. The roles of Fanny and Goldstein are the most attractive for actors, but all the others, perhaps particularly the silent husband, present fine theatrical opportunities.

Episode (1928) is an ironic extended one-act with a situation which is mildly humorous. It shows a young couple, briefly married, in two scenes, six weeks apart. The play begins with what is apparently the nightly argument. Mamie wants Jim to stay home with her and keep her company, but he, as usual, is going to to join the boys—or girls? He leaves angrily, and she is immediately the recipient of advice from two older female neighbors on how to keep your man at home. She accepts the suggestion of one, to buy a radio. Jim unexpectedly returns with a friend and a cornet. He happily explains that *he* had decided to buy her a radio, but then kills her joy by saying his friend Walt talked into buying the cornet instead. So he will be home every night practicing. As Jim makes some pathetic efforts to get some sound out of the cornet, Mamie "begins to laugh, loudly, hysterically, painfully, the tears streaming down her face" (57).

In the second scene, Mamie is being consoled by Jim's friend Harry. In a reversal of the first scene, her life is now painful because Jim never goes out. Harry says she should come to dinner with him, or just tell Jim she is going to, and he will pay attention to her. But when Jim returns, his obsession with the cornet is the only thing on his mind. When she says the landlord called to say he must either stop playing or move, he answers, "Ah'd like ter see him or anybody else that kin make me stop playin'. Gawd! an' they calls this a free country!" (59). He laboriously and incorrectly plays a song, letting the audience see that he has no talent whatsoever. When Mamie intimates she wants to go out, he encourages her, saying Walt is coming over to give him a lesson. When she says she is going with Harry, he says that is fine. When she says she may not get back until morning, he reminds her to take her key. He seems impervious to her desperation and the failure of their marriage. When she slams out of the house, he looks relieved, "adjusts the cornet at a more convenient angle and blows once more a thundering blast from his beloved instrument" (60).

The play can be taken as a light spoof on the difficulties of marriage, but it is difficult to be certain. Brown-Guillory makes an analysis in which she sees the play as a serious statement about the evils of nagging and the failure of communication between the two people: "While Mamie has her two girlfriends as sounding boards, Jim chooses the cornet to articulate the depths of his pain as a black man in America. Spence intimates that the real music should be made between two people with as little outside interference as possible" (42). However, as the play begins, Jim seems to be leading a life of idle pleasure, not particularly troubled by money problems, unemployment, gambling, or any of the other problems which occur in Spence's other plays. There are clear comic effects in the play which mesh strangely with the anguish Mamie is suffering at the end. All in all, the story is not as effectively dramatized as Spence's others although it has many intriguing elements. It was originally published in *The Archive* and recently anthologized by Brown-Guillory.

Spence's other plays are not available for reading or production. *La Divina Pastora* (1929) is a play which was performed as part of a production by the Lighthouse Players of the New York Association for the Blind at the Booth Theatre ("Three Plays Offered By Blind Actresses"). It is a drama which centers on a blind woman who is to be married. Hoping to achieve a cure, she seeks miraculous help at the shrine of the Lady of a Thousand Miracles (Peterson 179). The play is interesting in that it is set in Trinidad rather than in Harlem.

The Whipping (1934) was a more ambitious effort by Spence than her earlier one-acts. It was a comedy which dramatized a novel by Roy Flannagan. It centered on a southern woman who becomes famous because the newspapers widely publicize her whipping by the Ku Klux Klan. The play was supposed to be presented by the Century Play Company in Bridgeport, Connecticut, but was cancelled (Peterson 179). Determined to make a success with her effort, Spence rewrote it as a screenplay. Surprisingly, considering the subject matter, Paramount Pictures purchased it in 1934 for $5,000. As was typical of Hollywood productions, the story was changed so that rather than focusing on the actions of the Ku Klux Klan and African-American characters in the south, the film was changed to New England. The title was changed from *The Whipping* to *Ready to Love* [!]. Instead of a whipping, the heroine, played by Ida Lupino was set in the stocks and ducked in a pond by Puritans. Despite the watering down, the film was at least produced and Spence did earn a large sum of money. Ironically, she claimed this was the only money she ever made from her writing for the theatre.

Given the opportunity, Spence could have developed into a major playwright. As it was she was extremely successful with her one-act plays. She also had the enjoyment of working as a director both in her high school and in the professional theatre. She won the respect of her peers through her own personal conduct and through the talent she displayed. Although her childhood was not filled with the advantages of wealth, she had the advantage of an emphasis on education and self-esteem. Her mother instilled in her daughters "a strong sense of pride, making them aware that they were important individuals regardless of how little they possessed materially" (Perkins106). Spence carried this pride with her and her plays are important because they were well-written and successful and also because they are vehicles for her feminism. Her characterizations of women suffering from the oppression of wealthy white men, as in *Her*, oppressed by a lack of compassion from other women, as in *Fool's Errand*, and sinking into prostitution, as in *Undertow* and *Hot Stuff*, represent her sensitivity to the problems faced by African-American women in American society. Although she claimed to be interested in writing folk plays for fun and entertainment, her works are shot through with the social issues surrounding her. Eulalie Spence has not received the attention her work deserves compared to May Miller or Zora Neale Hurston, but her plays have been anthologized recently and there is a growing appreciation of her many contributions to African-American theatre. Brown-Guillory commented on Spence in connection with her discussion of the importance of plays by black *women*. Noting that early black women such as Spence were "unwelcome in the commercial theatre of the period" she continues, by saying, "These authors are crucial to any discussion of the development of black playwriting in America because they provide the feminine perspective, and their voices give credence to the notion that there was a 'New Negro' in America" (*Their Place* 4). With the present availability of Spence's scripts more attention will be forthcoming, and years after her death she may receive the recognition she deserves. Perhaps Brown-Guillory is correct in her description of Spence as "a daring and vociferous woman playwright who might one day be credited with initiating feminism in plays by black women" (*Their Place* 4).

Ruth Gordon (1895-1985)

Ruth Gordon (1895-1985) is best-known as an actress whose range ran from classics, such as Wycherley's *The Country Wife* and Chekhov's *The Three Sisters,* to eccentric modern characters in the movies *Rosemary's Baby* and *Where's Poppa?*. In addition to her outstanding ability as an actress, Gordon was also a writer of great skill. She wrote several important screen plays, three fine comedies for the stage and books of autobiography. She went into the theatre as soon as she left high school and was active until her death.

Gordon was born in Wollaston, Massachusetts. Her father was a character fascinating enough for her to incorporate into a play when she was an adult. Clinton Jones, was a former sea captain given to strong language, and atheist beliefs, as well as a man interested enough in theatre to have worked as a stage hand in order to have seen Booth and other actors and actresses up close. He was a tyrant at home, and on one occasion threw cantouloupes all over the kitchen because his wife said she wished they were peaches. Gordon's mother, Annie Tapley Jones, was a typical housewife of the period, who worked to keep calm in a household with two such fiery personalities as Ruth Gordon and her father. In her autobiographical play, *Years Ago,* Gordon depicts the family as very poor. Either she exaggerated for dramatic effect, or the family somehow scraped money together to go to the theatre fairly often. At the age of two Gordon was taken to see the great actor William Gillette in his play *Secret Service.* She grew up seeing much of the conventional theatre of the time and when she saw the lovely actress Hazel Dawn, she wrote to her to express her wish to become an actress. Gordon's father insisted that she finish high school in Quincy, Massachussetts, but then gave her the money to go to New York to live at the Three Arts Club and study at the American Academy of Dramatic Arts. She was discouraged from returning for a second year because she had not impressed the instructors with her acting.

She was determined to pursue a career in the theatre and asked her father to support her in New York despite her failure. He did so, but she suffered poverty and rejection for a time. Finally she was cast as a lost boy in *Peter Pan,* was praised by Alexander Woolcott, and was on her way. Her subsequent career was rich in variety and monetary rewards. She was first married to an actor, Gregory Kelly, who died in

1927. She was unhappily involved with the producer/director Jed Harris, by whom she had a son, and in 1942 she married Garson Kanin, director/writer, who was sixteen years younger than herself. She starred in films, won an Academy Award at the age of 72, wrote screenplays, acted in America and England, and was once described as "a forest fire under control." From her rich experiences in life, determination, and love of the theatre, she fashioned three plays.

Gordon's first play was inspired by her experiences as an army wife. During World War II, Garson Kanin (along with Thornton Wilder) was trying to graduate from Officer Candidate School. She accompanied him and went through the various trials and tribulations involved when an older man is in competition with younger men more adapted to the rigors of the army. Since she had time on her hands, she wrote the play *Over Twenty-One*. In the process she wrote an excellent role for herself and a play which was directed on Broadway by George S. Kaufman. Talking about the experience she admitted that her husband had helped her block out some of the scenes. She said, "For the first time in years I found myself with nothing to do. I had been hoping to write a play some day and here at last the opportunity had come" ("Ruth Gordon Makes Bow" 1).

The action in the play moves from the arrival of celebrity novelist/screenwriter Paula Wharton to join her husband Max while he is in training until the day of graduation. Paula is a wise-cracking screen writer modeled on Dorothy Parker. Gordon is very clever at setting up scenes of comic confusion. Paula's arrival is complicated by the fact that the young couple who have supposedly left the crummy apartment where she is to stay are still in place. Their presence, while Paula meets her husband for the first time in a long while, provides opportunities for comedy which Gordon and director Kaufmann exploited to the fullest.

In the early scenes the young wife of the recent graduate, Jan, explains the vagaries of the cheap bungalow opposite the army base which was formerly rented by the hour. The light switches for each of the rooms are in other rooms, there is no sink in the kitchen, so the only water is in the bathroom, and to open the window one has to stamp hard on a particular spot in the floor. Paula's reaction is, "Well! And where is the place your skirts blow up?" (22) Jan also points out that her husband found the work difficult because he was so old—twenty-five! "A friend of Roy's in the Surgeon General's depart-

ment said that the Army has proved that over twenty-one you don't
absorb any more. He said they'd proved it scientifically" (17). The
action of the play has to do with the efforts of Paula to help her husband Max, who is nearly forty, to endure the difficulties he experiences
in "absorbing" enough to graduate. His efforts are first hindered by the
arrival of the owner of the newspaper who wants him to get out of the
army and come back to editing the paper, and second by a Hollywood
producer who wants Paula to come back to Hollywood to fix up
scripts. In the end, Max graduates, and Paula offers to edit the paper.
The owner remarks that she never did anything like it before, and she
responds, "Women never ran railroads or built airplanes or were
welders before. . . . This is a world of changes. The waltz is on the
wane, kiddo. You better oil up your joints, or you'll turn quaint" (138).

The play is a remarkable first effort. It could be viewed as mere light
entertainment, but it is also notable in reflecting the changing opportunities World War II brought for women. It reflected Gordon's views
on the place of women in society. She had taken a bold step in seeking
a career in the theatre and despite hardships won success in many
areas. She simply didn't see why a woman shouldn't edit a newspaper
as well as a man. She told a reporter, "I guess I am a determined
woman. I've had to fight for what I wanted all my life. Even as a child,
when anybody in the family was against my going on the stage, particularly my father, I battled vigorously till I wore them all down"
(Dorfman 1). A pleasing side note on Gordon's success was provided
by Ward Morehouse, who observed, "Our Miss Gordon, doubling as
playwright and actress, won approval from both sides of the proscenium last night, for upon the stage, quite recognizable in a photo-
graphic study was the face of an old and dear friend, Alexander Woolcott, watching the proceedings quizzically. And, I'd say, with vast
delight" ("Over Twenty-One" 297).

The critics viewed the play as an enjoyable experience and their
response to Gordon's performance as the Dorothy Parkerish character
was almost entirely positive. However, there was mixed response to
the play on its own merits. Ward Morehouse expressed a view which
speaks well for the play, "'Over Twenty-One,' as a play, will not cause
earth tremors. . . . But as entertainment the piece is immense, and it is
helped along mightily by the playing of Miss Gordon and her associates. The stage business is the funniest I've seen since "You Can't Take
It With You" (297). Everyone agreed that the story line was slight.

This is certainly the problem with the play; there simply isn't enough suspense and there is too little complexity in the plot. Nevertheless, as Morehouse said, "It's a hit, definitely. In 'Over Twenty-One' Miss Gordon has written a gay, glib, daffy, and enormously funny show, and the Music Box is back in old form and stride" (297). Howard Barnes noted that the play, as a first effort at playwriting, "betrays some ragged edges," but concluded that the play was not "all of a piece, but it adds up to considerable fun." Like other critics he praised the characterization which offered fine acting opportunities, first, for herself, and for the other actors including Loring Smith and Phillip Loeb, "Miss Gordon knows the people of whom she writes. She has conceived her characters wittily and at times maliciously" ("Miss Gordon's Night" 298). John Chapman compared the play to those of Dorothy Parker and Claire Booth Luce and concluded, "She has a critical eye and a sharp bite, as do these other two; and she has something one of the others hasn't in her joke department—an elliptical, off-center sense of what's funny that makes you relish all of your chuckles as well as your howls" ("Ruth Gordon Writes" 298). Robert Garland suggested that the dialogue was so funny, that it was like listening to George S. Kaufmann playing poker, "frequently as good as that, really" ("Over Twenty-One" 298). Finally, Wilella Waldorf, who was not alone in regarding Gordon as an extremely mannered actress, expressed the view that she was a better playwright than an actress, "As an actress she has her limitations, but as a playwright, she knows how to make her mannerisms pay dividends" ("Over Twenty-One" 230). The general feeling of the critics was that for a first play, Gordon had done very well, that she had written a role for herself which offered her showed her comic ability better than any she had played, and that the play provided hilarious entertainment. As was often the case with women playwrights, there were rumours that she need assistance from a man to accomplish all that. Of course, it was no secret that her husband, Garson Kanin, had established an outstanding reputation in the theatre. John Chapman addressed the point directly in his review:

> Before "Over Twenty-One" was produced certain wiseacres hinted that Miss Gordon didn't write the play, really, but that it was actually done by her husband, Lieut. Garson Kanin, one-time George Abbott aide who became a hotshot movie director. I'm willing to bet it isn't so. It's all Miss Gordon. Kanin probably talked problems with her, sure, but his wife has put her own stamp on the work. The stamp says "sterling." ("Ruth Gordon Writes" 298)

Not only was Kanin suggested as the actual playwright, George S. Kaufman was another candidate. It is almost inconceivable to read this type of comment now and realize how many male critics simply could not believe that a woman was as capable of writing a play as a man was. It is particularly ironic in this case, since no critic pointed out the underlying message in the play—that women can write, edit, weld, or whatever, given the opportunity. Kaufman (who was so very irritated by male chauvinist comments when he worked with Edna Ferber) was very annoyed by a comment casually tossed off by Louis Kronenberger. Commenting on how funny the play was and how juicy Gordon's role was, he added, "Finally, she has had George S. Kaufman's strong directorial right arm to lean on—as well (one may be allowed to suspect) as his agile right hand to scribble a good gag or two for her" ("Ruth Gordon is Twice Blessed" 299).

Thanks to good reviews and the outstanding performance of the comedy, the play ran for 221 performances and was enough of an encouragement to motivate Gordon to write another play, also based on her own life. She was also encouraged by the playwright Edward Sheldon. Many people are familiar with the tragic story of this early realistic playwright who, through illness, spent much of his life nearly paralyzed, a mask covering his eyes, lying in his elegant New York apartment. He encouraged many actors, most notably his friend, John Barrymore, but he also gave encouragement to playwrights, many of whom spent time reading their works to him. Gordon was introduced to Sheldon and, in order to provide him with some amusement, described her early life and read out some excerpts from her diary. He encouraged her to publish the material which she did in a series of articles for *Forum* and the *Atlantic Monthly* (Koon 161). She then took his suggestion to compress the material into a play and he lived long enough to know that she had successfully done so.

Years Ago opened in 1946. It was so closely related to Gordon's life that the characters are described as "Me," "My Father," "My Mother," etc. The father, domineering and short-tempered, dominates the action and is the most captivating figure in the play. Quite late in the play his bitterness and determination to control things is explained in a touching speech about the suicide of his mother and his subsequent harsh treatment by religious relatives who drove him to run off to sea at the age of eight. Contemporary concern about domineering males and the marginalization or subjugation of women in the household may create a problem for the actor playing this role.

As in her first play, the story line is very slim: we see Ruth and her friends reading *Theatre Magazine*, gossiping over actresses, and thrilled that Ruth secretly plans to be an actress and that if her father knew, he'd just kill her. We see the family at home, the father uncertain about his job, permanently angry because he has to grovel to the owner to be sure of getting his yearly bonus, and tantalized by memories of exotic places and fabulous meals when he was a sailor. At one point, furious over the high grocery bills (including cat food) and catching the cat on the heat register (which he claims brings back his old malaria), he threatens to "go lay down on the New York, New Haven, and Hartford railroad tracks! . . . And what's more I'm going to take that cat *with* me!" (27) At the end of the play, despite the fact that he has told his boss off, and seems to be without a job, he gives Ruth his treasured spyglass to pawn if she needs it, and she goes off to New York. He says, "If what it takes to be an actress is gumption, you at least got that! . . . Your mother says you take after me, and, better or worse, I guess you do. Of course I don't suppose you know what you're tacklin', but I'm willin' to give you the chance to find out" (169).

In her newest play, which was directed by her husband, Garson Kanin, Gordon did not provide a role for herself. She did provide outstanding roles for Fredric March and Florence Eldridge as the parents, and Patricia Kirkland as "Me." In 1953 Gordon received praise for her screen version of the play called *The Actress*, in which Spencer Tracy, Teresa Wright, Anthony Perkins, and Jean Simmons were delightful. Although the critics warmed to the charm of the play, there was mixed opinion as to how successful Gordon was as a playwright in her second appearance. They noted the moments of hilarity, as when the father first uses the telephone (which he had sworn he would never have in the house), and the the fact that it was a "generally enchanting period piece" (Barnes "Fascinating Yankees" 229). March was highly praised, and several critics noted, as Brooks Atkinson did, that it was an unusual approach to feature him, rather than the young would-be actress, "Probably the most original thing about this stage autobiography is the fact that the principal character is not the author but her father. Clinton Jones, one-time second mate in deep-water vessels, and now employee of a factory in Weymouth, somehow manages to epitomize the dreariness, plain ideas and feeling of frustration that seeped into most middle-class homes in the period Miss Gordon is recalling" ("The Play: Years Ago" 44).

The play was a success because of the charm of the dialogue and the evocation of the period, an excellent cast, and the positive response of the critics despite the slender story-line. As Ward Morehouse wrote, "'Years Ago' has warmth; it is folksy and charming. Ruth Gordon has paid her tribute to Wollaston and to her girlhood, with an entertaining, if somewhat aimless, comedy." Despite his reservations, Morehouse liked the play, saying, it "has atmosphere and characters, it has been written with an understandable affection, and Garson Kanin's keen direction brings forth all its values" ("Ruth Gordon's Autobiographical 'Years Ago' a Warming and Chuckling Comedy" 230). Richard Watts Jr. summed up the feeling of most of the critics by saying, "It is a warm and tender little comedy, gentle, sunny and gracious, and it is filled with a winning sort of simplicity and a rueful sense of the remembrance of the days of lost innocence. But is also slight, slender, and uneventful" ("Pleasant Memories" 232). Although the critics felt that March, in the role of Gordon's father pretty much stole the show, many noted the tender tribute Gordon paid her mother (and other women of the period) in the role exquisitely played by Florence Eldridge. Howard Barnes wrote,

> Aiding and abetting March at every turn in giving color and meaning to the show is Florence Eldridge. As the astonishingly patient Mrs. Jones, who puts up with a choleric husband and a completely self-centered daughter, puts her little hoard of silver under her bed at night, wangles a telephone, and cherishes a lazy tomcat, she adds immeasurably to this bit of domestic Americana. Her scene with March, when he confesses that he once lavished a fancy valentine on a French boarding-house keeper, is utterly beguiling. ("Fascinating Yankees" 229)

In a minority was John Chapman who gave a very positive review of the play and, by implication, urged Gordon on as a playwright. He called it, "a little treasure of a play" and said the actors "are giving performances that made me want to go right up on the stage last evening, give them a hug and say, 'Thanks.' Three seasons ago Miss Gordon . . . wrote for herself a comedy, 'Over Twenty-One,' which was theatrically slick enough to be a success. . . . [*Years Ago*] is much better than being theatrically slick, for it is a human comedy, and a human comedy is likely to be as close to tears as it is to laughter" ('Years Ago' 232). Louis Kronenberger praised the play, as well, noting, "one of its virtues lies in its never trying to swell up into anything larger than it is. It is an atmospheric play and it rightly relies on warmth and humor and homeliness to see it through. It is, indeed, more atmospheric than actual, with old songs and period furniture ... doing a good deal to help out" ("Ruth Gordon's Likeable Comedy About Her Youth" 231).

Critics were right in praising the aura and charming feeling of Gordon's play. Although the story line is simple, it is clearly developed with humor and suspense, and the dialogue is excellent. She recreated the period with great charm, but also demonstrated the prejudice, injustice, and lack of opportunities for women early in the century. Gordon pictured her down-trodden mother as a gently comic figure, not as pitiful. She does help Ruth become an actress, but she is not an assertive figure. In contrast, Gordon showed her own view of what women could do through her characterization of "Me." In recent years there have been a few revivals of this worthy play. The Germinal Stage in Denver had a popular production in 1983. Critic Abby Ellis noted the appeal of the play which related in part to the popularity of Gordon herself. She began the review by saying, "For 60 years actress Ruth Gordon has enjoyed an illustrious career on stage, screen and as a playwright." She praised the actress Janet Rayor who portrayed the heroine for modeling herself on Gordon. In conclusion, she stated, "'Years Ago' at Germinal Stage is, in all respects, a lively and handsome tribute to the beloved Gordon and to the richness and quality of the forever bygone era in which she grew up. It shouldn't be missed" ("Janet Rayor Winning, Effective in 'Years Ago'" 1).

Gordon went even further with her depiction of a woman who triumphs over circumstances to become a successful, fully developed human being in her next play, *The Leading Lady*, which was produced in 1948. As background to this play it is important to understand that Gordon worked with the talented, but notoriously egocentric and tyrannical Jed Harris, first in *Serena Blandish* in 1929, then later in a Thornton Wilder adaptation of Ibsen's *A Doll House* in 1937. She was in a paradoxical position in the Ibsen play—she was playing a woman who liberates herself from male domination, but Jed Harris was dominating her in the rehearsals and trying to make her believe that only with his help could she be a success. It is difficult to believe that her depiction of the actor/manager Gerald Marriot is not based on Jed Harris.

As in A *Doll House*, the *The Leading Lady* begins at Christmas time, typically a time of domestic happiness. But Gay Marriott, devoted actress and wife of Gerald, has anything but a happy time. She and her husband have just scored a great success with a trashy sort of popular play and are giving a party for friends. Set in 1899, the play features such recognizable figures as playwright Clyde Fitch. There is a drama critic who makes no secret of his platonic adoration of Gay. Helene Koon suggests that the role is "a nostalgic portrait of Alexander Wool-cott" (160). He offends Gerald by urging Gay to act in Shaw's *Candida* with Richard Mansfield. Gerald is furious, and openly insulting to Gay, the guests, and the servants. He is incensed by the fact that her name was mentioned first in a review, and (as his unhappy assistant Harry Train listens), he tells her, "Why, I picked you up from nowhere.... Made you into what the public takes for an actress. Takes for an actress because I say you are. ... Where would you be without me? You couldn't get by the stage doorman. You were a chambermaid at the Palmer House when I took you and you'd go back there again—a common slut!" (25). Because of her love for him, her concern for his heart condition, and the fear that what he says may be true, she begs him to be calm and tells Harry to pay no attention. Gerald continues in the same line, and at the end of the act has a heart attack and dies. Although the character is egocentric and cruel, he is a magnetic cre-ation and his death unfortunately leaves the play with an absence of dynamism.

In the second and third acts, we see Gay suffering failure, selling things to pay Gerald's debts, and completely unable to believe that she can be anything without him. He still controls her from the grave. However, the efforts of her friends finally wake her up. In particular, the maid played by Mildred Dunnock, has a series of speeches in which she lists Gerald's faults and his deliberate cruelty, concluding, "He did the worst thing one human being can do to another. He made you dependent on him. He died tellin' you so. He died tellin' you you'd be a failure, without him. So you went and lost your confidence and I lost my job. Throw him the hell *out*!" (75). In the end, with the help of actor friends and Richard Train, who is now a successful playwright with a leading role for her, Gay is able to find courage and indepen-dence, and, probably, happiness as Mrs. Train. Several recent biogra-phers credit Garson Kanin as co-author, but the play was published with Ruth Gordon as playwright, and the critics treated the play as hers when it opened.

Robert Garland's review was headed "A Brilliant Play Written, Acted by Ruth Gordon" and he praised all aspects of the play. " 'The Leading Lady' is the first wholly satisfying theatrical adventure the new season has supplied. Out of her great knowledge of, her even greater affection for, the world of pay-as-you enter-make-believe, Miss Gordon has fashioned a tragic-comedy for the theatre itself to cheer and cherish." He concluded by saying that the setting by Donald Oenslager, the costumes by Mainbocher, and Garson Kanin's direction made the play "a truly notable theatrical occasion, and of Ruth Gordon, player and playwright, the leading leading lady of the 1948-1949 season" (191).

Although he felt she had successfully recreated the atmosphere of theatre life at the turn of the century ("you can hear the hoofbeats on the quiet streets of the New York of 1900 and the hurdy-gurdy is at the window"), Ward Morehouse, like other critics, was less enthusiastic. Morehouse could not accept the ending. He wrote, "She finally gains her release from a domination that has come from the grave, but the transformation, as it is worked out in Miss Gordon's final act, is not convincing" ("Wonderful Atmosphere, Little Play" 190). John Chapman felt the play "comes off well only in parts" and he mentioned the pleasing secondary roles Gordon had written (" 'The Leading Lady'" 192). A number of critics felt the central role which Gordon played could not be a dynamic center for the play because most of the time she is unable to overcome her subjugation to her husband. In contrast, as William Hawkins observed, her husband Gerald invigorated the first act: "Gerald, who only lives till the first intermission, is, in the hands of Ian Keith, soaked with limelight. He is elegantly cruelly egotistical, and grandly unable ever to stop acting" ("'Leading Lady' Called Amiable but Aimless" 192). Most of the critics praised the colorful character roles which reflected Gordon's love for actors and the theatre. Brooks Atkinson summed up this element of the play, saying,

Miss Gordon loves the theatre, as patrons of "Years Ago" quickly understood, and the scenes with theatre people in "The Leading Lady" are warm, humorous and delightful. As Mrs. Gilson, a tart old character actress, Ethel Griffies is enormously enjoyable and crafty. . . . In the companion role of a fine old trouper, William J. Kelly is also richly amusing. These casual scenes are played with as much genuine affection as Miss Gordon has rubbed into the writing of them. ("Ruth Gordon Appears" 38)

The mildly positive reviews by some critics and the highly negative review by John Lardner, who spoke of corny jokes and bogus romance about the past ("Nostalgia of '23 Skidoo' Days" 193) did nothing to draw in audiences. Probably more important, however, was the fact that Gordon as playwright had slighted Gordon as actress. Audiences expected a role to allow her to "light up the sky" as she usually did and were disappointed. The play was clearly in trouble on the road, and some critics thought Gordon was a "good sport" to bring it into New York. In the end it ran only eight performances. The critics were certainly correct in noting that the second and third acts were not as strong as the first and that Gay was depicted in a low mood throughout most of them. However, one cannot help but wonder if the reception of the play might not have been more positive if the point of view of the playwright had been perceived and appreciated fully. Gordon deliberately set the play at the end of 1899, with a woman terribly dominated by a vicious husband. She clearly intended to say that in the twentieth century—the third act, specifically—women would not have to remain dependent and fearful. It is entirely possible that a good production of the play, rich in atmosphere and theatrical comedy, and offering excellent character roles, might very well find a more appreciative audience and a more positive response from the critics today than when it was written.

Gordon's only other Broadway effort at playwriting was an adaptation of a French play, *Les Joies de Famille* (by Philippe Hériat) as A Very Rich Woman. This was essentially another playwright's work which seemed to offer her a good role. The play opened to good notices in 1965, but despite praise for her acting, the play closed in two weeks. Only three years later, at the age of seventy-two, Gordon was at the peak of her popularity, winning an Academy Award for her role in *Rosemary's Baby*.

Ruth Gordon was a natural writer. In addition to her plays, she wrote three highly successful books of autobiography. She was particularly adept at writing screenplays. She and Garson Kanin wrote the engrossing script for the backstage story of an actor playing Othello called *A Double Life* (1948), *Adam's Rib* (1949), *Pat and Mike* (1952), and others. In an obituary in the *New York Times* in 1985, the writer commented "how much Ruth Gordon and Garson Kanin [contributed] to the symbiosis of the Tracy-Hepburn team is inestimable

("Grit and Wit" 10). Gordon had great wit, and strong ability to characterize with effective dialogue. Her weakness as a playwright was in
the sparseness of the story line and incidents in her second and third
acts. But as noted in the *New York Times* in 1985, "at least two plays,
"Over Twenty-One" and "Years Ago" bear reconsideration. . . . The
latter is an endearing romantic comedy of adolescent longing. . . . It is
time that the theatre looked again at early Ruth Gordon" ("Grit and
Wit" 10).

Time has passed, but this suggestion that Gordon's plays are undervalued has produced no result. No doubt part of the reason lies in the
fact that Gordon's acting overshadowed her other work in the theatre.
As her biographer Tolman wrote, "Those who worked with her were
impressed with her conscientiousness and her professionalism.
Although she wrote plays, screenplays, autobiographies, and a novel
and showed herself skilled as a speaker on the lecture circuit and on
televised talk shows, she will be remembered as a actress, an exuberant
comedienne, whose completely imagined characters thrilled many"
(349). Gordon's own life furnished the material for her plays which,
despite the humor, reveal the difficulties she faced, and, by extension,
faced by other women trying to achieve a career in the theatre. As
Koon wrote of Gordon's autobiography, "*My Side* is a vivid recounting
of Gordon's life, although not in chronological order. The emphasis is
almost entirely on her professional experience, and the personal elements are related only as they relate to the theater." Koon notes the
frank discussion of her unhappy affair with Harris, abortions, struggles,
and failures, and concludes, "It is an uneven, at times, confusing story,
but it is a unique view of a kaleidoscopic and genuinely theatrical personality. Gordon's work is neither profound nor timeless, but it is
amusing, distinctly theatrical, and representative of an important as
well as fascinating era of American drama" (160-161).

Lula Vollmer (1898-1955)

Lula Vollmer (1898-1955) was an important figure in the American folk play movement. Her career involved successes on the stage and on the radio. Few people know her name today, but in 1924 she was considered, "as much a pioneer in her field as Eugene O'Neill is in his" ("Lula Vollmer Dies" n.p.). In 1949 she was still so famous that an article appeared in the *New York Herald Tribune* describing her work as a volunteer water warden ("Water Warden's Day" 20). In addition to her writing for the theatre, Vollmer was a highly paid short story writer.

Vollmer was born in lumber camp in Keyser, North Carolina. Her father, William Sherman Vollmer, was a lumberman. Her mother was Virginia Smith Vollmer. Her family was well-to-do, but she had the opportunity to get to know the poor people in the mountains of North Carolina because the family spent each summer in the midst of them. After achieving financial success Vollmer did much to contribute to education in this part of America and to awaken Americans to the plight of the people there. As a young girl Vollmer was sent to Episcopal Church boarding schools and her religious training informs her informs her plays. They are also informed by the mysticism and superstitions she encountered among the uneducated North Carolina mountain women. She often talked with them when they brought their wares to the Normal and Collegiate Institute at Asheville where she was a student for three years (Quinn, *Representative American Plays* 983). There she began writing short plays for her fellow students, although drama was not a part of the curriculum and was frowned upon. She had been inspired to write plays when she saw *The Curse of Drink* on a family holiday in New Orleans (Smith, "Lulu [sic] Vollmer" 890). She also tried to learn about playwriting by reading Ibsen and Shakespeare (Mantle, *American Playwrights* 192).

For about nine years she worked as a secretary and then as an accountant in an Atlanta Hotel. All this time she was writing plays, short stories, and a column for the *Atlanta Pilot*. This was a theatrical newspaper for which she interviewed actors and actresses. She learned from them that if she wanted to succeed as a playwright, she must go to New York. One of her plays from this period, *Jule,* became a successful vehicle for Louise Coleman in vaudeville.

Vollmer went to New York and obtained a job as the treasurer in the box office of the Garrick Theatre, then worked for the Theatre Guild. She tried to interest producers in her play *Sun-Up*, but it took her five years to find a producer. Her early champion, Arthur Hobson Quinn, noted, "It is characteristic of the difficulties under which the American playwright labors that while Miss Vollmer was an officer of the Theatre Guild, which has devoted its powerful energies largely to the production of foreign plays, *Sun-up* should have been produced first by the Beechwood Players at Scarborough, New York." He noted that it was then produced by the Players Company in the Provincetown Playhouse in New York and was successful that its run was extended in two other theatres. Vollmer no longer needed to labor in box offices—she was a major success. Her first play opened in May 1923 and her second, *The Shame Woman* opened the next October, so she had two plays running simultaneously on Broadway (Quinn, *Representative American Plays* 984). Vollmer had many more plays produced, wrote for the films, and had a highly successful career in radio. Between 1930 and 1933 she wrote "Moonshine and Honeysuckle" and later "Grits and Gravy" and "The Widow's Son" ("Lula Vollmer Dies" n.p.). Her programs inspired others to write about folk life and common sense folk characters such as Lum and Abner. Ironically, her radio success and the many short stories probably contributed to the failure of her later plays: what had been fresh and engaging in 1923 had become familiar and conventional by 1938 when *The Hill Between* opened. The critic for *Time* noted tersely, "In the past 15 years hillbillies have lost much of their freshness on the stage" ("The Hill Between" 30).

Despite the failure of her later stage work, Vollmer continued to do well on royalties from *Sun-Up* and from other writing. When she died most obituaries wrote about her success with *Sun-Up* and the difficulty she had in getting it produced. Throughout her career Vollmer believed in the value of exploring the lives of the mountain people, particularly the women. She created a series of unforgettable portraits of women bereft of education, love, financial security, or self-knowledge. In her best work she truly expressed Quinn's definition of the folk-play movement, which "tried to interpret the life of those natives of America who have retained the primitive culture of their ancestors, and whose emotions have remained in that inarticulate and unsophis-

ticated state which allow them free expression and make them therefore well suited for the drama" (*Representative American Plays* 983).

Sun-Up is set in the two-room cabin of the Widow Cagle. She is
developed as a strong figure, staunch in her opposition to the law and
to rich folks. She has no education and knows nothing at all of the
world outside her small farm—she doesn't even know the name of the
nearby town and has never been there. Her time is spent working in
the cabin and smoking her corn-cob pipe while thinking of the past. In
her view, her husband was a brave man making a living selling moonshine who was unjustly murdered by the revenue agent. Cagle's only
son is different in that he has had enough education to learn to write.
In school he learned that he belongs to a whole country and that part
of that belonging involves obeying the law. He also differs in that he
doesn't want to shoot people and he is opposed to selling or drinking
liquor. His symbolic property in the play is a hoe, not a gun. The play
has to do with the Widow coming to a broader acceptance of his views
through his death in World War I.

When the play begins there is only some talk of the war as Pap
Todd (who spent twenty years in jail for selling moonshine) says he
heard something about it. His daughter Emmy and his son Bud appear,
and then Rufe Cagle. He has registered for the draft although he
knows nothing about the war. Most of the people think it is fighting
the Yankees again, but the Sheriff knows it is the Germans. Both he
and Rufe want to marry Emmy, but she chooses Rufe when she learns
he is brave enough to go and fight while the sheriff remains at home.
Cagle is opposed to Rufe's going, saying,

> Whut does Rufe or Bud owe the Guv'ment? The Guv'ment kept Bud's daddy in
> jail for twenty years 'cause he tried to make an honest livin' outen the corn he
> planted and raised. Whut did the Guv'ment do to Rufe's pap? Shot him in the
> back while he wuz a protectin' his own property. Fight? Well, I reckon if either
> one of them boys fights, hit will be their own fight, and agin' the Guv'ment.
> (990)

Immediately after marrying Emmy, Rufe leaves at sun-down for the
army camp. He does not know where France is, but has heard it may
be about forty miles on the other side of Ashville (997).

The arrival of a stranger creates a stir. There are two important plot
developments. Cagle learns that her son is dead, and then that the
man, who is a deserter from the army camp, is the son of the man who

shot her husband. Previously inclined to use her gun against the sheriff, she now intends to shoot him because that is the law of the feud. But she believes she hears Rufe's voice saying, "As long as thar air hate—thar will be—feuds. As long as thar air women—thar will be sons. I ain't no more—to you—than other mothers' sons are to them." Emmy and the stranger say they heard nothing, and the dead cannot come back, but Cagle simply answers, "No, I reckon my love went on—out yonder and reached him and he's told me what to do. I reckon ye better go, Stranger" (1008). At the end of the play the sheriff threatens to take her to jail for helping the deserter escape, but hasn't the heart to do it. Cagle sits holding her son's hoe and muses, "Hit wuz sundown when ye left me, son—but hit's sun-up now, and I'm knowin' God A'mighty is a takin' keer of ye—Rufe" (1009).

The most notable aspects of the play were the female characterization and the dialogue, which was new and engaging at that time. As Quinn wrote, "These characters are developed by conversation which is remarkably natural and in which every word tells. There is hardly a line in the play which is not definitely a step in the progression of the drama" (*Representative American Plays* 984). The three acts are tightly constructed, and the incidents are highly probable, excepting only the coincidence of the stranger being the son of the man who killed Mr. Cagle.

The modern reader, accustomed to plays and movies in the tradition of Vollmer's mountain people, will find it difficult to understand the excitement created by *Sun-Up* in 1923. It has been called the first American folk play, and as such raised great hopes for future plays in that line from Vollmer and others. A long article by an anonymous critic for *Current Opinion* summarized the critical response to the play:

> This "most beloved American folk-play," as so advertised by its producer, Lee Kugel, is admitted by the New York *Herald* to be comparable to the best offerings of the Russian players in their American invasion. The *World* critic calls it "a play rich in observation of American life"; the *Times* critic catalogues it as "the first demonstration of a play-writing talent that, undeniably crude and uncertain, nevertheless holds forth the promise of better things," and the *Evening Telegraph* parades it as "a masterly play, acted in a manner worthy of its content." This is the choral note. ("Such is Life in Carolina" 701)

The high praise which came from the critics was in spite of the production circumstances. Despite the fine acting, especially that of

Lucile LaVerne as the widow, many critics found it unpleasant to attend productions at the Provincetown Playhouse. The critic for *Theatre Magazine* concluded that it was impossible to make a fair judgment about the play because of the discomfort of the playhouse, which had once been a stable, and which was fitted out with benches in contrast to the plush seats in Broadway theatres. He spent half the review complaining about the theatre, and concluded after a brief summary of the story that the play, "Presented in a real theatre, *Sun-Up* might actually have shone" ("Sun-Up" 16). For many other theatre-goers, the Provincetown Playhouse was real theatre in contrast to Broadway, and one of the few places where outstanding, challenging plays by American playwrights, male and female, could be seen. The production was enormously successful, running for a year in New York before going on tour.

The success was not limited to America; the play was appealing in such diverse cities as Amsterdam, Paris, Budapest, and London. It must have been a particular thrill to the American playwright to read a story in the *New York Times* in 1925 headed "King and Queen See 'Sun-Up' in London." It appeared that they had been advised by friends that they must see the play, so they bought three boxes and attended with a group of friends (13). The attendance of the King and Queen probably increased attendance at a play which was already popular. It ran over two hundred and thirty performances in London. Vollmer made a fortune on the play, but she did not lavish it on herself. She donated what was then an immense sum, $40,000, for education among the mountain people ("Lula Vollmer Dies" n.p.). After the success of the national tour of the play it was revived in a cut version (about fifty minutes) by LaVerne for vaudeville. Today it is difficult to imagine this stark drama heading a vaudeville show which featured Louise Groody singing and dancing and the young African-American comedians, Buck and Bubbles ("Playlet at the Palace" 6). LaVerne next produced the play in Paris in 1929.

After waiting five years to see her first play produced, Vollmer was not slow with her second offering. *The Shame Woman* opened in October with much the same production history and critical response as *Sun-Up* had. Quinn described the play in his introduction to *Sun-Up*:

The Shame Woman is another tragedy laid in the North Carolina Mountains. Lize Burns, a woman who has suffered all her life the same of her early seduction by Craig Anson, who lives in the nearby town, finds that Lily, her adopted daughter, is meeting Anson, now a middle-aged roué and in order to warn Lily, she tells the story of her own career, which is represented in five scenes placed twenty years earlier. To her horror, she finds the warning is too late and Lily dies. To save her memory from the stain that has shadowed her own life, Lize kills Anson and goes to the scaffold without revealing the reason. (*Representative American Plays* 984)

The structure of the play is interesting, because the flashbacks provided excellent opportunities for the actors, playing themselves middle-aged, then as young people, then as middle-aged again. The theme of the play was both daring and unconventional. Vollmer was well aware of the helplessness of poor women in the society she was depicting. John Corbin felt that Anson was portrayed as a successful politician with a tactless insolence which would have made him unattractive to women. He suggested that the theme would only appeal to "a certain type of feminine playgoer" ("Betrayed and Scorned" 4). Certainly, he was correct in predicting the play would have appeal to women because of the depiction of two women mercilessly used by one man. However, he was perhaps ignorant of the actual lives of disempowered women who, not unnaturally, are often drawn to powerful, successful males, even if they are bullies.

Among the largely favorable reviews, Corbin was not the only one to find some faults in the play. Ludwig Lewisohn touched on a more significant flaw, noting "The death of Lily is simply incredible" ("Scramble" 587). Indeed, the death of Lily seems very contrived. However, Lewisohn felt there was much to praise in the play which was an advance over Vollmer's earlier play. "The dramatic texture of "The Shame Woman" is quite on a level with that of "Sun-Up." Again Miss Vollmer's presentation of folk life is rich and authentic; again she tells us what we are most eager to know—the inner truth of human lives. Again we see exemplified the recurrent experience that art most deeply rooted in a given soil has the best chance of attaining a universality of interest" (587-588). For audiences, the play provided insight into the lives of two women representative of their culture. For actresses, Vollmer continued to provide superb opportunities for acting in roles which were original, challenging, and disturbing. Lewisohn noted the importance of the roles which demanded animated, heightened acting which was still close to nature: "I know of no two examples of recent acting that illustrate this point quite as well as the per-

formances of Miss LaVerne and Miss Rittenhouse in these two folk-
plays of the North Carolina mountains" (588). Quinn concurred,
praising all the female characterizations, and noting that the midwife,
"drawn as a brooding figure of implacable fate, is as fine a creation as
anything that the Russian drama has brought to us" (*Representative
American Plays* 985).

Despite the success of her first play, Vollmer's second was perceived
as too narrow in appeal for a Broadway production, so it opened at the
Greenwich Village Theatre. Its success was such that it shortly moved
to the Princess Theatre and then the Comedy. Following the nine-
month run in New York, the play toured to Chicago, Philadelphia, and
other cities where it drew enthusiastic audiences. It was never published, which foreshadowed a diminishing interest in Vollmer's plays.

That was further indicated by the lack of success of her next play,
Dunce Boy (1925). Its theme was undoubtedly ahead of its time, but in
its construction it was perceived as a throw-back to melodrama. The
play deals with the problems of a mother with a "half-wit" son who
comes to sexual maturity. In subject matter, it is very like many present-day plays and movies which give attention to persons who are
mentally retarded or have physical problems which make the sexual
urge difficult to accomodate. Stark Young wrote that the play treated
the problem of the boy, who "had the mind of a poetic child, the innocence of a woman, and the body of a man. His mother tells him that if
he touches the girl he is attracted to she will die. This problem of the
touch and the disaster of it are uppermost in the boy's mind from then
on" ("Lulu [sic] Vollmer's New Play" 20).

The play has a rather complicated plot in which the young school
teacher to whom the dunce boy is attracted first fends off the
unwanted attentions of the boss at the sawmill, and then an assault
from her fiancé when she rejects him. The dunce boy rushes in to save
her, kills the man, and then runs out and throws himself on the wheel
of the sawmill.

Stark Young was one of many critics who felt the suicide was arbi-
trary. Nevertheless, he stated that of all the plays he had seen in the
year, *Dunce Boy* was "one of the most nobly and sincerely aimed. Its
themes were deeply taken; its movement was deeply felt." He stated
that the opening of the second act, with the mother's speeches about
her love for her son, was "one of the two or three finest moments that I
have found in the season's theatre" ("Lulu [sic] Vollmer's New Play"

20). The general view of the critics was three-fold: first, they praised the qualities of her first two plays; second, they praised Vollmer's sincerity and potential; third, they said *Dunce Boy* was a disappointment. Quinn, Vollmer's loyal supporter, only noted that the play was not a popular success, but that it had two-well drawn characters in the dunce boy and his mother (*Representative American Plays* 985).

Ironically, by 1925 Vollmer had achieved quite a reputation as a playwright and was often compared favorably with O'Neill. *Dunce Boy* play opened not in the Village, but at Daly's Theatre on Sixty-Third Street. However, it had a short run and was not published.

Vollmer was writing and publishing short stories, but she was determined to succeed as a playwright. Many of her short stories were quite sentimental which contributed to a diminution in respect for her work on the part of drama critics. Her play *Trigger* (1927) excited little critical enthusiasm and did not draw a large audience. Her play centered on a young woman who can read and write and is therefore different from her neighbors. The question of alcoholism which played a minor role in *Sun-Up* was in the fore here, because Trigger is the eighteen year old daughter of an alcoholic who was largely left to her own devices. An examination of the psychological and emotional problems of a child of an alcoholic was very unusual in the American theatre in 1927. In story, the play involves the superstition of the mountain people which would later form the basis of the very successful play by Howard Richardson, *Dark of the Moon*. In Vollmer's play the inhabitants of a tiny village believe that good witches have cast a spell which protects them from death and illness. In their ignorance and superstition they turn against Trigger, because of her wild behavior and because they are suspicious of her education. Two engineers from the world outside perceive something of value in the Trigger and protect her from the villagers' attempt to run her out of town. Vollmer's interest was in depicting a female different from the other women in town, who is filled with anger because of her environment and the rejection she suffers. Trigger is pursued by several men but prevents their advances by throwing bolts from the mine at them. She also shouts unpleasant things at the villagers such as "I am bad, but you ain't right in the head" (qtd. in "Presenting Claiborne Foster" 1). Underlying this hostile nature Vollmer wanted to suggest a spiritual, other-worldly quality.

Once again the playwright had an interesting idea for an examination of a complicated woman facing problems in her community, but she failed to develop it with a fresh story line. Critics generally tossed off the story as familiar and inconsequential. Perriton Maxwell wrote that the playwright wrote well of the mountain people, "so well, in fact, that her play becomes one of character rather than incident. . . . We haven't told you the story because there isn't much of a story to tell" ("Trigger" 39-40). The cast, in particular Claiborne Foster as Trigger and Minor Watson as one of the engineers, was praised. The *New York Times* critic was satirical about the plot, but felt that the performances justified a "slightly giddy evening amid witchcraft and the sentimentalities" occurring in the play ("Presenting Claiborne Foster" 32). Quinn was definitely dispirited by the failure of Vollmer to develop into a major playwright. In 1930 he said that Vollmer had drawn "the character of a wayward but spirited girl of the mountains who elicited sympathy in her struggle against the prejudices of her narrow community. The play, however, was hardly up to her standard" (*Representative American Plays* 985). In subsequent editions he continued to print *Sun-Up,* but did not discuss any of Vollmer's later plays. Susan Harris Smith wrote, "Vollmer's later plays could not match her earlier efforts either in subject matter of style. *Trigger* [was] a confused and sentimental play set in rural North Carolina" "Lulu [sic] Vollmer" 891). Aside from Vollmer's characterization of her heroine, the most interesting thing about the play is that it was made into a film starring Katharine Hepburn (1934). Vollmer collaborated on the filmscript with Jane Murfin. Despite the efforts of John Cromwell as director and an excellent cast, the film was not successful, and was one of the reasons Hepburn was perceived as "box-office poison" before *Philadelphia Story.* Film critic Leonard Maltin called it "boring melodrama with Hepburn sorely miscast in one of her oddest roles. . . . This one's only for the curious" (1165).

The film followed *Troyka* (1930) which was one of Vollmer's most unusual theatrical efforts. Possibly in an attempt to move beyond the mountain people with whom she felt so comfortable, but who were beginning to wear with critics and audiences, she wrote about Russians on the island of Sakhalin. No doubt she perceived some similarities between the prisoners working in the mines on this remote island and her primitive American types. The story dealt with the reaction of the prisoners when they were freed because of the death of the Czar. Imre

Fazekas, the Hungarian playwright who wrote the original, set a triangle of two men and the woman they both love within the violence which results from the sudden freedom. Vollmer adapted the story, putting it in dialogue which Brooks Atkinson described as "an argot clipped from the ten-cent American magazines" ("Troyka" 32).

The play excited attention before the opening because the role of the woman was to be played by Zita Johann—her first performance since her stunning success in Treadwell's *Machinal*. Her performance was praised, but the critics tore the adaptation to pieces, noting the effectiveness of the original idea and setting, and the hackneyed writing provided by Vollmer. By this time, it began to seem that her career in the theatre was never going to reach the heights critics had believed it would in 1923.

This feeling was confirmed by another short-lived attempt in 1931 called *Sentinals*. Once again Vollmer moved away from the primitive mountain people, setting her play among well-to-do southerners who have black servants very loyal to the family. So loyal, indeed, that when the scape-grace son kills a man, Mallie, the black servant who loves the boy as her own, talks her own son into confessing to the crime. He does so, but is saved at the last minute when the white boy confesses. The story seemed improbable in its own time, but seems ludicrous now. Despite the improbabilities of the characterizations, the roles of the black mother and her son provided good acting opportunities for Laura Bowman and Wayland Rudd who were both praised by critics. Brooks Atkinson said the play was filled with "spurious and short-lived heroics . . . and "Sentinals," both in the writing and playing, is only Broadway balderdash in a Southern setting" ("Sentinals" 15). Vollmer continued to be successful on the radio and in the magazines, but her plays *Sentinals*, *Shining Blackness* (1932), and *In A Nutshell* (1937) failed to receive acclaim or popularity in New York.

Still, Vollmer persevered. *Moonshine and Honeysuckle (1933)* closed in Boston despite the popularity of her radio show by the same name and with the same Romeo and Juliet type of characters. At least Vollmer had the satisfaction of seeing the play published by French, probably on the basis of the name value of the radio program. Several scripts of unproduced plays are in the Vollmer collection in the New York Public Library. Finally, she got another New York production in 1938. *The Hill Between* returns to the early settings which were so successful for Vollmer.

Brent is a doctor who grew up among uneducated people but who left for the city, managed to become a doctor, and to marry a sophisticated city woman, Anna. When they go to visit his home town, he feels an urge to stay and help his people. Bored and frustrated, Anna flirts with and kisses Brent's friend Larz. The barrier between the mores of the country people and the outlooks of the corrupt city people is made clear and nearly results in suicide for the innocent Larz. In the end, the doctor is urged to return to the city by Julie, the girl who loved him, but sent him away for an education. Her characterization represents the women Vollmer had met who only knew sacrifice and self-abnegation. Julie's speech to Anna and Brent in the final scene reveals the suffering she has endured,

> Love air greater only when it can sacrifice itself fer the thing hit loves. Brent's a-goin' back, Anna, because I'm a-sendin' him. Twelve years ago his life work was a-callin' him. I could a held him. I didn't then. 'Tain't likely I'd hold him now, when I know that the bindin' of him to me—the holdin' of his mind—air only destruction. Unashamed afore ye, I own I've loved ye, Brent, ever since we wuz little together. The night that ma died I left her and went a-walkin' miles through the woods to the mail box, a-hopin' fer a letter from ye. Hit didn't come. The waitin' dwarft me—unpowered my life. But my love has give me the strength to give ye up. That's why ye must go out there agin—yo' life work air still callin'. I'll stay this side and keep the love that can let ye go. Outen that has come peace. After a long journey, I'm near about home. (108)

Brent goes reluctantly, saying, "A man spends his youth dreaming out, and all the rest of his life dreaming back" (qtd. in "The Hill Between," *Time* 30). In the published version Brent's wife leaves and he stays with his people.

The play failed to please despite the characters who were generally praised. Brooks Atkinson began his review by a discussion of the characters:

> The folks are real. They adhere to customs, manners and character. They live a neighborhood life with affection and probity. They work in the fields, cook on the hearth, say grace at table and at parties they dance the Virginia reel, which is festive and lively. In the development of a theme Miss Vollmer is inarticulate; perhaps her mind is not as rich as her characters. But after a series of plays written out of the history books or taken off the stock shelves in the theatre's warehouses, it is refreshing to associate with characters who have come out of a playwright's personal observation. (12)

However, he went on to say that the story was inconclusive and the dialogue clouded with "mystical implications that sound like gibberish in her rigidly worded dialogue" (12). The critics agreed that the play was trite and oversimplified in its depiction of the city as evil and the folk ways wholesome. John Gassner wrote a very thoughtful analysis of the play in which he noted two elements which worked against its success. Noting Vollmer's play was a noble effort, "forthright and sincere and possessed of a humanitarianism that rarely intrudes itself into the cheap successes of the theatre" ("Two Folk Plays" 1120), he continued, "that it no longer comes with the force of novelty is partly due to the successful work of writers like Miss Vollmer in earlier years" (1121). The other element which negated success was the aura of the world in 1938: "We are not in a mood for the innocuous art of folkways while the whole world is burning with immediate problems of life and death" (1120). Gassner was right about the effect of the impending war—Vollmer's play seemed artificial and unrelated to the problems of the world at large. It only lasted eleven performances. One interesting aspect of the production was that it had been directed by Robert Porterfield of the Barter Theatre in Abingdon, Virginia. Gassner remarked that the director "who is closer to these provincials than most of us, directed the play without frills and with a good deal of sensitivity" (1121).

Despite the frustration of years of theatrical failures, Vollmer tried again. She wrote *Dearly Beloved* which was performed in Newark, New Jersey in 1946, but did not reach New York and was not published. In 1949, interviewed in connection with her volunteer work as a water warden, she said she was at work on a novel. She was also writing a radio program, *The American Story*. A few years later she died of heart trouble at her MacDougal Alley home.

It is ironic that Vollmer's subject matter was generally about the mountain people, but she spent her adult life in her home in Greenwich Village. Perhaps she was "dreaming back" like her character, Brent. She had never married and lived alone, but her close friendships with Zona Gale and other women in the theatre cheered her life. She seemed to live entirely for her writing. Her early success in the theatre led Burns Mantle to write in 1929 "she has been confidently looked to for bigger and better plays and will probably yet achieve them" (*American Playwrights* 192). It is ironic to read his prediction and realize how wrong he was. When Vollmer died few obituaries mentioned any of her plays except *Sun-Up*, written thirty-two years earlier. However, a number letters to the editors of various papers indicated that to many people throughout the country, Vollmer was a playwright who had touched them and affected their lives. A man named Robert Downing wrote to the *New York Times* saying that "amateur actors owed a special tribute to her because so many of them had acted in home town drama groups in her play *Sun-Up*" ("Drama Mailbag" n.p.) Robert Porterfield, who had directed *The Hill Between*, wrote a long letter saying that he had known and produced all of her plays with great success at the Barter Theatre. He summed up her accomplishments by saying "a woman who lived close to God has left us characters in her plays that will live as long as people are interested in the true American folk play. Few playwrights created characters who live as heroically as her Widow Cagle in her play 'Sun-Up'" ("Drama Mailbag, n.p.). Susan Harris Smith summed up Vollmer's merits by saying that she made important contributions to folk drama: "first, she took a sympathetic view of simple people, always refusing to use them as comic subjects and insisting that her sophisticated, cosmopolitan audiences accord them the dignity and attention they deserved; second, she dealt with difficult social topics such as sexuality in women and the handicapped, topics not often confronted directly in the drama of the twenties" (892). Vollmer contributed breadth to American theatre by writing in a mode quite different from the standard drawing room comedies set in London or New York which were so popular when she began to write. She cleared a path for such later playwrights as Lynn Riggs who wrote *Green Grow the Lilacs*, the basis for *Oklahoma!,* and Paul Green who wrote *Johnny Johnson.*

May Miller (1899-   )

May Miller (1899-) was one of the pioneers in African-American theatre. She was an actress, a playwright, an editor, and a teacher and in
all of those capacities she contributed to enlarging the sphere of possibilities for writers and for audiences. Miller began life with advantages
and she took care to fulfill her parents' expectations. Writing in 1982,
Isabel Wilkerson described May Miller as "a fragile-framed writer with
saucerlike eyes, [who] was a turn-of-the-century child born into the
protective palm of Washington's early black elite, reared among the
Negro intelligentsia in the old faculty quarters on the Howard University green" ("A D.C. Poet Reminisces" 1) Her father, Kelly Miller, was
an important sociologist who taught at Howard University and established the Moorland-Spingarn Research Center there. Her mother,
Annie May Butler Miller, was a teacher in the Baltimore area. She was
encouraged by her parents to learn and write poetry, to read widely, to
play music, and to value education. She and her four siblings spent
warm summer days acting out Shakespeare. Remarking on the difference between her childhood and that of present-day children, she said,
"You didn't have a TV in every room of the house back them." She
expressed some disdain for the TV dominated present, saying that she
and her siblings created their own entertainment by making up stories
to tell their parents and that her father would give a nickel for the best
one (Wilkerson 1). As Miller grew up she had the privilege of associ-
ating with the most important African-Americans of the time who
were guests of her parents. She was encouraged to have a career in
writing by W.E.B. Du Bois, Carter G. Woodson, Alain Locke, and
Booker T. Washington. Georgia Douglas Johnson had a very close
friendship with Miller's parents. Later, "Miller would become a member of the 'S Street' group' and a close friend. It was May Miller who
sat at Johnson's bedside during her last hours (Perkins, *Black Female
Playwrights* 15).

This background was enhanced by her training at the Paul Laurence
Dunbar High School where she had the advantage of studying with
playwrights Mary Burrill and Angelina Grimke. Miller's first publication was a poem in *School Progress* magazine for which she was paid the
munificent sum of 25 cents. She was fourteen at the time and was
encouraged to continue her writing with a play, *Pandora's Box*, which

was published in the same journal in 1914. The play was written under the supervision of Burrill.

Miller entered Howard University in 1916 and had training in theatre which was unusual for anyone, white or black, male or female in that time. She was involved in the Howard University Dramatic Club which was organized "to give students sound training in the arts of the theater" (Stoelting 242). She acted in many plays, including Clyde Fitch's *The Truth* in 1919. Her abilities were demonstrated not only by her writing and acting, but by her scholarship—she graduated at the head of her class in 1920 and determined to pursue a career as a playwright (Wilkerson 1). She was awarded a prize at her graduation for *Within the Shadow*. She also had an opportunity to see plays on stage, including the black folk play *Mortgaged* by Willis Richardson, one of the most successful black playwrights of the time.

In the 1920s Miller won awards for many plays and had the pleasure of seeing them performed. She knew she had to become someone on her own—not an appendage of her famous father, "There was a time when I couldn't be known as myself. I always had my father's name tagged onto mine. I'm proud of my background, but you have to make your own contribution in life. If you have any gift you're obligated to share it" (qtd. in Carter, "New Generation Discovers D.C. Poet" 12). Encouraged by Johnson, Burrill, and Grimke she went on to do exactly that. She was also encouraged in her writing by Paul Green and Frederick Koch. She was a member of the latter's drama workshops at Columbia University in the late 1920s (Stoelting 243). Belief in the importance of education and the significance of the work of many African-Americans in the history of America led Miller to work with Willis Richardson to publish an anthology of plays dramatizing the lives of black heroines and heroes. Anticipating the work of later playwrights such as August Wilson, Miller said, "We started to dramatize Negro history because it was a treasure trove and greatness has no boundaries" (qtd. in Hamalian and Hatch 307). In 1935 she and Richardson published *Negro History in Thirteen Plays* which included four plays by Miller. Speaking about the importance of black history plays, Miller noted that many students and many young leaders were not aware of the contributions of people such as Randolph Edmonds of Morgan College, who, "believed that productions on stage of those great Negro characters would help the students understand. For a number of years at Morgan College they gave one-act plays, and we wrote for those occasions." She also said, "We would have no Lorraine Hansberry if there had not been behind her those people who were slowly leading up to her great productions" (qtd. in Stoelter 243).

As it was impossible to earn a living as a playwright, Miller was a teacher of speech and drama at Frederick Douglass High School in Baltimore where she produced many plays she wrote (Hatch and Shine 353). "Keenly aware that her young students needed to see plays about black heroes and pioneers, Miller began writing one-acts—*Christophes's Daughters, Harriet Tubman, Sojourner Truth*. During the decades of the 1920s and 1930s, she authored nearly twenty one-act plays" (Hamalian and Hatch 307).

Miller's first important award as an adult was the third prize in the first literary contest held by *Opportunity* magazine in 1925. Her play *The Bog Guide* was one of 65 plays judged by Alexander Woolcott, Edith Isaacs, Montgomery Gregory, and Robert Benchley (Brown-Guillory, *Wines in the Wilderness* 62). In later years she loved to show momentoes of this honor and the ceremony in a Fifth Avenue hotel. She was very proud that in the same competition Langston Hughes won first prize for his poem "The Weary Blues," Countee Cullen won the second prize for poetry, and Zora Neale Hurston also won a prize for a play: Miller was in good company. "After that we all went down to the Greenwich Village and had a bang-up time. I can see Zora now, in that rapture-red shawl" (qtd. in Wilkerson DC1). Later, she saw the play produced by the Intercollegiate [Drama] Association at the Imperial Elks Auditorium in New York in 1926. In 1926 she won honorable mention for her play *The Cuss'd Thing* in a drama contest sponsored by *Opportunity*. Encouraged to write folk plays by Green and Koch, she wrote *Scratches* which was published in the *Carolina Magazine* at Chapel Hill in 1929.

She married John Lewis Sullivan, a high school principal. They were happily married for forty-one years, but she continued (with encouragement from her husband) to publish and act under her own name. In the summer of 1927 she had an opportunity to act with the Krigwa Players in Georgia Douglas Johnson's *Blue Blood*. Her last play was *Freedom's Children on the March* which she wrote in 1943. This dramatic folk ballad, with music by Llewellyn Wilson, was presented for the commencement at the Frederick Douglass High School. In addition to her plays, Miller was also writing short stories. She retired in

1944 from teaching and, unfortunately for the theatre, turned her
attention to writing poetry.

She was enormously successful with her poetry. Following the publication of many of her poems, she was invited to read at the inauguration of the first black mayor of Washington, D.C., Walter Washington,
and at the inauguration of President Jimmy Carter.

For over forty-five years Miller lived in "the same expansive apartment filled with antique furniture, art and memories. She writes at an
oak desk given to her when she was 10 years old by her father (Gaines-
Carter 12). She continued to refuse to give her age, but noted that
when she got to the point that when she wanted to go to Woodward
and Lathrop's to try on a hat and couldn't, her age really hit home
(Sutton B3).

Her last years were spent writing and giving poetry readings for children in schools and in public presentations with other notable poets.
She was recognized as a leader, not only in theatre, but in society as a
whole, and was praised for her quiet strength and dignity which were
often reflected in the female characters in her plays (Stoelting 241). In
1982, she was invited to read her poetry at the Folger Library and was
honored by the Women's National Democratic Club (Sutton B3). In
1983 she was invited to speak at Howard University on a panel called
"The Black Presence in Nineteenth-Century Washington" which was
held in conjunction with an exhibit at the National Museum of
American Art. She missed her husband and her friends who had
passed, but kept on working and "sharing her gifts" with school children and others. Her work was given great recognition after many
years of neglect, and in 1986 she laughingly remarked, "They must
think I'm going to die soon" (qtd. in Gaines-Carter B12). By 1993 she
was very frail, but summoned up the energy to give an interview to
Kathy Perkins for her forthcoming book.

Miller's plays run a gamut from folk plays, in dialect, to period plays,
in "genteel" or "raceless" language. One of her plays which has frequently been anthologized and performed is the comedy *Riding the
Goat* (1929). This play depicts the changes occurring in African-
American society, and the differences in generations. The title refers
to a part of an initiation ceremony into an African-American lodge.
Ant Hetty is a simple woman who speaks for the older generation. Her
granddaughter Ruth has been educated in a convent school, and
although she is employed to sew clothing for white people, she has

advanced beyond her grandmother's views about society. She wants to marry Dr. William Carter who is about to lead a parade as grand master of the United Order of Moabites. The conflict in the play is quite simple: Carter is tired of engaging in what seem to him foolish ceremonies for the lodge he joined in order to get patients. Ruth initially seems to support his point of view. In a discussion with Ant Hetty, she comes to see that in order to help the poor people of the community (and save them from a white doctor who prescribes pills which don't keep them from dying), Carter has to accomodate himself to his clients by participating in the ceremonies they value. When Carter throws his uniform on the floor and refuses to march Ruth secretly puts in on and marches in the parade. In the end, all parties are reconciled, and the young couple has Ant Hetty's blessing.

The position of women, and the changing attitudes of women about themselves is an important element in the play. Ant Hetty says to Ruth, "'Course I thinks Doctor's all right in some ways but the educated chaps always manages to think a little diff'rent. I guess that's where the trouble comes wid you—them sisters at that convent kinda educated you 'way from me" (70) and also remarks, "You young ones gits me. You'se too pert fo' your years" (69). Miller dramatizes the differences through the use of language. Ruth speaks without a dialect, as does Carter, but Hetty speaks the dialect of the poorer people. She remarks, "I 'clare wid all these hindrances nobody kin get a bite. Come now, Ruthie, 'cause I know you're most nigh starved to death" (72). The difference in generations is carefully presented visually as well as in their speeches Ant Hetty wears an old gingham dress and "a pair of well worn bedroom slippers . . . more off her feet than on (65), whereas Ruth's "smoothly brushed hair and the pretty checked gingham she wears bespeak personal care" (68).

Hetty is old-fashioned and uneducated compared to Ruth, but she is pragmatic about the capabilities of women, saying to Carter that it's too bad he doesn't appreciate his position as the grand master of the lodge: "A woman ought to have it; she'd know a good thing" (68). Throughout the play it is the women who take action, give good advice, and reveal common sense. The inability of women to participate as equals with the men is suggested by Ant Hetty's story of a woman denied denied admission to the lodge who hid in a closet and saw a secret initiation. To keep her from revealing the secrets, the lodge let her join.

The concerns of the different generations are clear: Ruth values education and improvement in living conditions for her people, but Hetty talks of the glory of a big funeral with the lodges represented by uniformed members with swords. She misses the reflected glory of her husband's position in the lodges and looks forward being able to hold her "haid higher 'n the res'" (158) through the connection the the grand master.

The effective use of costuming, the dialogue, and the theme contribute to the play's effectiveness. It has humor, vitality, and tight construction. As with many of Miller's play there is unity of place and action, and stage time is actual clock time.

Riding the Goat was produced many times. Of particular note was the production in 1931 when the St. Augustine College Players in Raleigh, North Carolina performed it as part of a festival in the Playmakers Theater of the University of North Carolina. Another production was that of the Krigwa Players in the Albert Auditorium, Baltimore in 1932. Writing in 1937, Benjamin Brawley noted in *The Negro Genius* the high quality of the play, and said that Miller's plays came closer to reality than others in the collection (qtd. in Stoelting, 243). Brown-Guillory noted the humor in the play, the practical viewpoint, and the introduction of class differences, saying, "*Riding the Goat* is one of the few early plays by black women that deals with the black middle class. Dr. Carter has to be taught . . . that it is unwise to ridicule those values and practices that are held in high regard in the uneducated black community in which he works" (63).

One of Miller's most provocative plays, *Stragglers in the Dust,* was written in 1930 but remained unpublished for many years. It is an original conception, and is treated with dramatic effectiveness. It is set at the tomb of the Unknown Soldier. An old cleaning woman, Nan, tells the watchman, Mac, that she loves to work there because her son is the unknown soldier: "Dey put him in dat marble box dere aftah dey fin' him on de field. Flanders, Ah think dey calls it" (146). She is a little concerned about a "creature wid de ghost like face and empty eyes what's been haunting dis place for two days" (147). Nan leaves reluctantly because she has nobody to go home to now that her son is dead.

A noted white politician appears seeking his son, apparently the straggler who has been haunting the place. He is a psycho-neurotic who was shell-shocked, and has now had another attack. His father says that his poor son would be better off dead. He is amazed to learn that Nan, whom he passed on the way, thinks her son is the unknown soldier. He says, "Why that isn't even possible. . . . But if it were—what a terrible joke on America" (148). In the most dramatic scene in the play the straggler describes what happened to him on the battle field. He was saved by a black man, and he now believes that he has spoken to the man who saved him and that he is Nan's son who is in the marble box:

> You see I met him in No man's land. It was just a few minutes after one of those infernal German shells had exploded near me. I was standing there a little dazed when he came to save me—did you hear me—to save me, I said. He was such a huge black one and it was so easy for him to carry me. We had gone some distance when he missed his gun and went back. A shell got him. (150).

At the climax of the action, the straggler has a mystical experience and describes the return of the soldier to the tomb, "Doesn't he stride like a king over the city and they don't even know he's there" (151). So compelling is his description (enhanced by sound effects and lighting) that the father comes to believe the vision is actual. His son explains that he was cheated of death and burial in the tomb, but that the black man who is there is going to help him: "I talked with him this morning when he left and he promised that I can go in with him tonight if I get there when the slab slides for him" (151). The straggler runs up the steps to meet the unknown soldier and meets his death—he collapses on the steps. His father seems to perceive some mystical union of his dead son and the soldier who saved him and tells Mac, "That was my son, but he went in the tomb you know. Thank you for your trouble. Good-night. I am sorry if I detained you" (152).

The play is unusual in its combination of realism and mysticism, its point of view and in the presentation of white characters. As Perkins has commented, "While most black women chose to utilize an all-black cast, Miller would incorporate white characters to stress a point" 144). The play has an intense, mystical quality which is quite effective throughout. The language effectively establishes the difference between Nan and the better-educated Mac and the other white characters. The irony of the mystery of the identity of the soldier, and the conceit that he could be black is quite original.

In 1930 Willis Richardson selected *Riding the Goat* and *Graven Images* (1929) for his important anthology, *Plays and Pageants From the Life of the Negro*. He described Miller as one of the most promising of the Negro playwrights, whose plays "have helped to make the Negro drama worthy of attention" (ix). Forty-four years later Hatch and Shine selected the latter play for their anthology, describing it as a play for eighth grade children inspired by an Old Testament verse, "And Miriam and Aaron spake against Moses because of the Ethiopian woman he had married" (353). The play is largely of historical interest today and Brown-Guillory associates it and *Samory* (1935), and *Christophe's Daughters* (1935) with the "genteel tradition" (*Black Women Playwrights in America* 12). She summarizes the action by saying, it "is a play in which the black son of Moses suffers abuse because he is different.As the play concludes, he puts his best foot forward and persuades his young enemies that he is very much like them, only tanned" (12). Much of the dialogue is stilted and artificial, but there are some lines which speak directly to the problem of discrimination. The children taunt Eliezer, but worse is the condemnation of his aunt Miriam, who says, "This child is no image of God, Jehovah. He is black like his mother" (357). For her actions she is cursed with leprosy, which Hatch and Shine describe as a "racial *coup de grâce*" (353). The most effective dialogue in the scene occurs when Miriam and Aaron argue as she tries to convince him to supplant Moses, saying, "He should lead Israel who is truly an Israelite, one uncontaminated by Ethiopian blood" (358).

Christophe's Daughters (1935) seems remote from reality, especially in the proper language spoken by Athenaire and Amethiste, the two princesses who are daughters of King Henry Cristophe. The setting and locale are inherently interesting: the island of Haiti, in the pretentious throne room. The question in the play is whether the two daughters will escape the anticipated attack of a rival or remain and support their father. In the end after he has shot himself offstage with a golden bullet, his body is brought onstage to be carried away by the daughters, their mother and a tutor. The play would probably have had more interest if the play had focused on Christophe, but Miller was interested in depicting black women of courage and dignity. The drum beats warning of the enemy and the bullet of precious metal are effective but had already been used by O'Neill in *The Emperor Jones*.

In contrast, *Nails and Thorns* (1933) is a realistic play which was part of the anti-lynching movement. However, unlike most of plays of this type, this focuses on a white family and the only African-American is the maid, Annabel. The setting is a living room of the sheriff's home.

An aura of tension is immediately established by the nervousness of his wife, Gladys, who stands anxiously at the screen door latching and unlatching the catch. The sheriff pretends to be reading the paper, but is really watching his wife. The cause for the anxiety is an attack on a white woman by an unknown assailant who may have been black or white. Simple Lem (who should have been in a mental institution, but was kept out because he was capable of field work), has been arrested and the sheriff refused to call the state militia to protect him. Annabel arrives with the news Gladys has feared: the men in the town intend to lynch and burn Lem. The sheriff exits to try to stop them, and is shortly followed by Gladys who is convinced that if she pleads with the men and shows them her baby, they will stop. In the end Lem is lynched and burned, and in the riot Gladys has been knocked down and the baby trampled to death.

The speech is strong and effective, and many of the sentiments usually heard from the African-American characters are heard from Gladys, the idealistic, concerned white mother. She voices the theme of the play: "Ugly things move in the dark" (311). She also voices the horror that a lynching produces, not only for the victim. She lived in a town where there was a lynching, and says, "It wasn't what they did to the unfortunate man alone. He was out of his misery. It was what they did to every soul in that town. They crucified everything that was worthwhile—justice and pride and self-respect. For generations to come the children will be gathering the nails and thorns from the scene of that crucifixion" (315). At the end of the play she expresses a sentiment similar to the black mother in Johnson's *Safe*, gladness that her child is dead. In Johnson's play the mother is glad that her son will not live to be lynched, but Gladys is grateful that her son will not live to see a lynching.

Annabel stands as a representative of the African-American community and movingly describes the fears of the ordinary people (in white terms "the good colored folks"), and the horror which has taken over the town. "Ma'm, it's happ'ned to all us cullud folks. Down there beyond the railroad tracks, there's nary a dark face about. They's gone in an' locked their doors an' pushed chairs an' tables up 'gainst 'em so as nobody kin git to 'em. Tomorrer mos' o' 'em what kin fine the money's gonna git way from heah" (313). The horror is intensified by the sounds of the riotous mob racing through the streets shouting, "They got him," "Lynch him!" Annabel knows the mob mentality better than the white woman, she says they won't hesitate in their vile action because of their children, "They's got chillun wid 'em. I seen some o' 'em pass down by the corner" (319).

The play was written to make a strong anti-lynching statement and does so. The unexpected focus on a white family and the death of the white child at the time of the death of the black man gives the play an unusual, memorable quality. In a period when lynchings were still common it was an important play, and it remains so as a reminder of that time. The play won third prize in a drama contest at Southern University, Baton Rouge in 1933.

Harriet Tubman (1935) is a vital depiction of the period in which slaves were escaping to Canada with Tubman's help. The plot is simple but dramatically effective. Tubman is known to be in Maryland about to take some slaves to Canada and safety. A "house slave," Sandy, is going to betray them for money and freedom. He promises freedom to the young slave Catherine, but she merely pretends to accept in order to get information from him. She reveals the plot to Tubman and escapes with her and the other slaves by boat. Once again the action is dominated by the women. Tubman and Catharine are both lively, outspoken, courageous characters. Tubman tells the frightened slaves, "Always they's trailin' you—clar to the line an' back. They was watchin' foh me today, but they ain't caught me. We's the fools an' they's the wise men; but Ah warn't fool 'nough to go down the high road in the broad daylight" (181).

The play successfully establishes the horrible power of life and death the white men have over the slaves and the shame a black person should have for siding with them against another slave. When the traitor Sandy discovers Catherine's duplicity, he says, "You two-faced devil! Ah'll tell Mas'r Charles, an' he'll break ev'ry bone in you' dirty, lyin' body!" Despising him for "tellin' on you own folks," Tubman tells him, "Shet up! Ah hates to lebe you livin' anyhow. If you yells out thar once mo', Ah'll choke the breath out o' you' worthless body wid mah bare han's" (184). The cruelty of the masters rebounds on the traitor in the final scene when two of the trackers appear and find Sandy tied up, and Tubman and the others on their way to safety. One says, "They got the key from this nigger" and the other says, "Mistah Charles's gonna sell you down the river" (185).

Throughout the play excitement is maintained through the creation of an atmosphere of danger and suspicion. Again Miller uses unity of time, place and action very effectively. Through the language and the subject matter Miller created a vivid, realistic portrayal of the period, the characters generally, and the historical heroine, Harriet Tubman. What could have been an overblown tribute to a real heroine, is a genuinely dramatic piece of theatre which informed black and white people about an important person in the history of the black race in America. One production of the play was at Dillard University, New Orleans in the 1935-36 season.

Sojourner Truth is Miller's depiction of another important figure in the history of America. The former slave, now turned to preaching and fighting evil is revealed sitting on her wagon singing a spiritual about Jesus. She is near a campground in Massachusetts and planning to address the crowd at the meeting. A white man, Clarkson, appears and asks her where she has come from. Her dialogue throughout the play is very vivacious or, as one of the white boys in play says, she is "real pert with her answers" (327). Clarkson's curiosity is aroused by Sojourner's answers and she explains her mission to him: "Years ago when I lived in New York City, my occupation was scourin' brass doo-knobs, but now I go 'bout scourin' sinners" (317). Clarkson lets her know she is not welcome to address the meeting, and tells her to leave the camp. However, in the ensuing scenes she preaches to a group of boys who plan to burn down some tents for fun. When Sojourner tells them they should not add evil to a world which already has enough they start to attack her and she runs away. But she courageously returns, mounts her wagon and converts them from their malicious plan. The high point of the play occurs when she describes her own experience of cruelty as a slave:

> I could tell you 'bout when I was a little girl an' how my master once whipped me 'til the blood streamed from my body an' dyed the floor beneath me. But whippings like that is common. Even now thousands o' my black sisters an' brothers are still barin' their backs to the bitin' lash. Still their children are snatched 'way an' sold where they never see nar hear o' 'em again; an' still they toil an' pray. Sometimes I say to myself, "Sojourner, is God dead that He cannot hear them? With pain like that in the world I couldn't hurt nothin'. I don't even want to see no fires 'cause they might be takin' food an' clothes way from poor people what has to struggle to git more. Whenever I see flames lickin' joyous-like at the heavens I say to myself, that's the devil's work. Who knows tomorrow heart-broken pappies and mammies may be rakin' them ashes for charred bones that was once happy, laughin' little children. No, lads, fires ain't fun; they's jes' a taste o' hell. (320-330)

When Clarkson returns the boys tell him they had planned to set
the fires, but that Sojourner had changed their minds. Now the white
man says the people at the meeting will be happy to hear the black
woman speak. She exits triumphantly singing the spiritual which began
the play and the boys stand spell-bound listening.

The play is not quite as effective as *Harriet Tubman* because the
boys and their plans are not as harrowing and immediate to the reader
as the picture of escaping slaves and their imminent danger. However,
it has a similar use of unity and a central figure which is depicted with
actuality and force. The setting and action relate to real events which
occurred in the nineteenth century and the depiction of the plight of
the slaves is very moving.

Miller's active role as a playwright occurred largely in the 1920s and
1930s, but her influence continued long after that time. Referring to
the Harlem Renaissance, she said, "You can call it what you will, but
there have always been Negroes writing, plenty of them. That time was
just a buildup that surfaced. We were products of the ages and there
had been contributions to it all along" (qtd. in Wilkerson DC1). Had
she not turned to poetry she might have written important plays in the
1950s and later when there were more opportunities for professional
productions. Winifred L. Stoelting wrote of her work as a playwright,

> May Miller early recognized the need to write and produce plays that would
> break away from the early crude renderings of blacks on stage and portray them
> with some measure of faithfulness to their daily lives. Encouraged by Carter G.
> Woodson, Alain Locke, and W.E.B. Du Bois, she is part of the movement of
> young writers whose literature reawakened racial pride and dignity and created
> an acceptance and a respect for blacks that had not before been afforded in
> drama. (241)

After she quit writing plays, her works were largely forgotten and
only in recent years have they been rediscovered and published. She
was perceived as old-fashioned when many black playwrights were
being performed in the 60s and later. She said , "The black movement
didn't recognize me because I wasn't black enough. . . . We did those
Negro plays before they even dreamed of rebellion" (qtd. in Wilkerson
DC1). In 1986 E. Ethelbert Miller, director of the Howard University
Afro-American Studies Resource Center said, "If she is not known it is
not the fault of the writer but the fault of those of us who are critics
and who teach literature" (qtd. in Gaines-Carter B12). In her last years
and at the time of her death, Miller was praised by many, including

Marita Golden of the African-American Writers Guild in Washington, D.C.: "She is someone who is a shining example of the endurance and resilience of the creative spirit" (qtd. in Gaines-Carter B12). Brown-Guillory summed up her impact on the theatre and on African-American culture by saying, "Her contribution to black drama is almost inestimable. . . . Many of Miller's play were presented in Baltimore schools and churches and at such places as Howard University, Morgan State College, Dillard University in New Orleans, and at St. Augustine College in Raleigh, North Carolina. . . . [They] gave Negroes a sense of pride in their black history" (*Wines in the Wilderness* 62).

Bella Spewack (1899-1990)

Bella Spewack (1899-1990) was an extraordinarily independent and capable woman whose major work, ironically, was written with her husband Samuel Spewack. Together they wrote twenty-six plays and twenty films. Their marriage and their work together lasted until his death in in 1971. Spewack is chiefly remembered for three major successes: *Boy Meets Girl, Kiss Me, Kate,* and *My Three Angels.* Writing for the commercial theatre, Bella Spewack was not experimental nor particularly innovative, but her work had wit, freshness, and a memorable zany quality.

Born Bella Cohen, the future writer was raised by a single mother, her father having deserted them while she was a baby. Her parents, Adolph Cohen and Fanny Lang Cohen were Jews who had emigrated to the United States from Europe shortly after their daughter was born (Hart 814). She grew up on the Lower East Side in New York and was a "born entertainer," acting in comedies and directing a play. While in high school she joined the Provincetown Players and performed a variety of jobs at their Macdougal Street theatre (Gould 136). After high school graduation she sought work on a newspaper at the age of seventeen. An attractive, petite, energetic young woman, she was disappointed when day after day she failed to find work. Despite her frustration, her cheap clothes, her fatigue and often wet shoes, she kept on and finally got a position at the *Yorkville Home News.* Later her "radical, pacifist views" took her to the socialist newspaper, *The New York Call.* Ambition drove young Bella and she published the amazing number of forty short stories by the time she was twenty-two, one of which was included in O'Brien's collections of the best short stories of the year. In 1922 Bella Cohen married another newspaper writer, Samuel Spewack who had, according to her, "fallen in love with her writing" (Hevesi 36). He was four or five years younger than she, but she later claimed they were both about nineteen (Alexander 31).

For four years they worked as reporters in Europe, gathering material in Moscow for a future play (Sam was born to Russian emigrants), then they returned to the United States and began trying to write for the theatre. While they established themselves as playwrights, Spewack worked as a press agent for Morris Gest, then a publicist for the Girl Scouts. In publicity, as in her playwriting, she was imaginative and original. For example, she was the person who conceived and actually developed the idea of selling Girl Scout Cookies as a publicity gimmick! She chose not to go back to writing for newspapers because "women reporters weren't well paid" (Alexander 31).

During the late twenties and thirties the couple scored their first successes in the theatre and subsequently went on to work in Hollywood despite their inherent dislike for the work and the place—the money was too good to refuse. The temptation to satirize Hollywood was also too good to refuse and their hilarious picture of life in a producer's office was called *Boy Meets Girl.* Spewack was closely involved in her writing career and the production of plays for most of her life, including revivals which occurred when she was no longer writing. Her work with her husband was very profitable so that her busy life was very comfortable. It was reported that when her husband died their estate was estimated to be worth as much as a million dollars. They were both very philanthropic and their early memories of poverty led them to share their good fortune with others. They were also very public spirited. Both took an active part in the war effort. Sam produced *This is Russia* and acted as head of the Rissian division for the OWI. Bella wrote programs for the American Broadcasting Company about the work of the United Nations Research and Relief Agency. She utilized her ability as a reporter to acquaint Americans with conditions in Berlin, Prague, London, Geneva, and Paris (Gould 139).

Growing up in stark poverty, Bella Spewack was determined to succeed. She devoted herself to her career. Her life and her outlook were unconventional and contributed to the eccentric comedy in the plays. After her death her close friend Lois Elias said, "She never thought like other people. She was witty, sharp, but with a quixotic approach to life, a great concern for others. [However,] she was a very good businesswoman; the one who made all the arrangements for the productions (Lois Elias, quoted in Hevesi 36). When her husband wrote *Golden State*, Bella produced it. Obituaries in 1990 noted the popularity and vigor of Spewack's "madcap" comedies ("Bella Spewack" *Variety* 319) and the awards she and her husband had won for their many contributions to theatre, film, and television.

The Spewacks' first play was written in Europe and called *Swing High Sweeney*. It was never produced as originally written. Their earliest efforts betray a difficulty in finding an appropriate style. *Poppa* was produced in 1928 and ran for 96 performances—a fair success. Critics praised many aspects of the play, but felt it was a peculiar mixture of comedy and drama. Howard Barnes called the play "the season's most engaging portrayal of New York's Lower East Side," but said the construction was frail. He and others praised Sam Jaffe in the lead as Pincus Schwitzky, an idealistic, impoverished Jewish man whose daughter wants to marry a rich man ("'Poppa' Amusing" n.p.) Brooks Atkinson wrote a description of the action which calls to mind the nineteenth century comedies of Harrigan and Hart, but with more realistic characterizations. He noted the authentic Jewish accents, the colorful neighbors, the involvement of local politics and the depiction of family pride. However, he implied that the authors hadn't made up their minds if the play should be hilarious or pathetic, noting that there was "cheap comedy" destroying the potentially effective "drama of Jewish-Americans" ("Alderman" 31). Other critics noted that the characters were true to life and interesting. One critic noted that the comedy was broad, but that it "convulsed a sympathetic audience which missed none of the characteristic Jewish humor" (L.W.F. "'Poppa' Opens" n.p.). In this play Spewack had drawn on the environment in which she grew up and contributed to the poignancy and comedy in the play. It was directed by George Abbott with whom she would work in the future.

The play which established the Spewacks as successful playwrights on Broadway was a rewrite of their first play. *Clear All Wires!* (1932) was an animated, detailed picture of the work of newspaper reporters in Moscow which was based on their own experiences. By this time the Spewacks had written several plays and had developed a style of fast-paced comedy with rapid-fire witty dialogue and outrageous characters. "The two worked so closely together that it was impossible, even for them, to tell which part of a play was contributed by one or the other. Bella, noted for her sharp wit, was always quick on the uptake in conversation, which may have resulted in the fast-paced dialogue" (Gould 138).

Herman Shumlin directed the play and wrote an introduction in which he praised the comic portrayal of the real Russians, "who are comical without making you cry" and who "visible under their own racial texture, are remarkably like you and me" (vii). The play is set in the only room with a private bath in the hotel where the foreign correspondents live in Moscow. The *Times* reporter, Pettingale, is celebrating in his room with several other reporters including Kate Nelson. She is a crisp, intelligent reporter who formerly worked for the legendary ace reporter, Buck Thomas. Pettingale has heard with delight that Thomas has been fired because his Chicago editor found out he was carrying on with Dolly Winslow, the editor's girlfriend from the Follies. Kate is pictured as a woman who expects to be treated as a colleague, not as a woman, and who is non-sentimental. When Pettingale proposes a toast to the downfall of Thomas, she answers, "I won't drink to his downfall! (She takes the glass from table.) But I'll drink!" (20). Within a few moments all is chaos as Lefty (a polite heavy who learned short hand in the state prison and works as Buck's secretary) moves in bag and baggage, informing Pettingale that Buck has taken over his suite and his Russian assistant, Kostya. Infuriated, Pettingale describes Buck as "a rank sensationalist . . . a faker . . . unscrupulous . . . a liar and a cheat" (30).

In the course of the play it is revealed that he is all that and more. He arrives with great plans and orders Kostya to get him a "a peasant, a worker, a soldier, a New Woman and the Foreign Minister" (26). Delighted to see Kate, he asks her help in keeping Dolly Winslow under wraps in another hotel, which she reluctantly agrees to do. In the frenzied action of the three acts Dolly appears, demanding attention, a piano, and fun, Buck puts into action an attempted assassination which he vividly covers before it happens, gets shot himself, is fired, lures people into taking a bath in order to lock them in the bathroom, and finally is rehired and sent to China, taking Kate along and marrying her at her insistence. All the while his fertile imagination is inventing new lies to cover his complex problems and to try to hold on to Dolly and his job.

A major part of the fun is the range of characters. Dolly Winslow finds it hard to to grasp that things are different in New York than in Moscow and ultimately decides to return to "Daddy" (Buck's rich editor). After Buck tries to keep her away from "Daddy" by putting her on a train to Siberia, she responds to Buck's pathetic description of his bullet wound by saying, "What about me? I haven't had my girdle off in three days!" (227). The various reporters have their vagaries and comic qualities and the Russians include a range of characters from the maids who speak no English to the suspicious bureaucrats, a ballet dancer, and a former Prince, now a streetcar conductor. Invited by Buck to have a bath and stay to dinner, he requests a few trifles including champagne, caviar, sturgeon, truffles, salmon, and roast goose (142).

Critics and audiences were delighted with the hilarious character of Buck, played to the hilt by Thomas Mitchell, and the other comic characters racing on and off stage. Several noted the effectiveness of having actual Russians, including Eugene Sigaloff as the last Romanov, playing all the Russian roles, and the outstanding Viennese actor Egon Brecher as the German reporter. These were elements of reality which gave a solid underpinning to the frantic farce. Critics also noted other details which were realistically treated (the routine of cable arrangements and official relations, for example) with which the Spewacks were familiar because of their work in Russia. Brooks Atkinson was delighted by Thomas Mitchell who was seldom absent from the stage—a very demanding role! Atkinson said he "careens through the part like a prizefighter in the ring" ("Clear All Wires" 1). Praising the play in two different reviews, he noted it was "brisk, noisy, extravagant and funny in 'The Front Page' and 'Broadway' tradition" ("Clear All Wires" 19). He concluded his first review by saying, "Sometimes you suspect that Mr. Mitchell and Mr. Shumlin are keeping the play in motion by application of sheer physical vitality. But they have something to work with. Mr. and Mrs. Spewack have given them a roaring yarn" ("Clear All Wires" 19).

The Spewacks went on to turn the play into a successful film in 1933 with Lee Tracy and Una Merkel. One critic described it as "a sharp and speedy vehicle for Tracy" Scheuer 105). When the play was turned into a musical *Leave it to Me!* by the Spewacks and Cole Porter it was one of the major successes of 1938. Critics praised the book and the songs, including "My Heart Belongs to Daddy" and "Get Out of Town." The Spewacks provided fine roles for Mary Martin as Dolly, William Gaxton as Buck, Sophie Tucker, and Gene Kelly (making his Broadway debut).

Despite the success of *Clear All Wires!*, it was not until 1935 that the Spewacks were categorized with the foremost American playwrights. In that year *Boy Meets Girl* was a riotous comic explosion. Based on their own experiences in Hollywood, the play was also thought to play off the screwball antics of their friends Ben Hecht and Charles MacArthur. The idea which is parodied is that all Hollywood producers want from their writers, whether Pirandello or the central figures Law and Benson, is a plot which can be summarized as "boy meets girl, boy loses girl, boy gets girl." The structure of the play is itself a joke, because framing the riotous activities of the two writers is a love story in which the boy meets girl formula is played out.

The incredibly fast, almost mercurial quality of the play is established by the two writers who are at once capable of churning out the hackneyed, clichéd plots and dialogue *and* expressing their contempt for the whole process, for ham actors, for vulgar producers, and for the atmosphere of Hollywood. Their characters are similar to that of Buck in *Clear All Wires!,* in that they are constantly inventing schemes to hold on to their jobs and their peculiar sense of comedy leads them into bizarre relationships and scrapes. Bored by their work, they enliven their days by pulling practical jokes such as leaving false messages for songwriters commissioning pieces of music, sending out a casting call for midgets, and getting a friend in London to send a fake cable offering to buy the studio. Throughout the activity they dance with the secretaries, mock the crass cowboy actor Larry Toms, and make up scenarios at a moment's notice. When they become interested in Susie, a single woman expecting a baby, they take over her life and turn her baby into a movie star in films with Larry:

Law.	He finds a baby—in the Rockies—
Benson.	(inspired; quickly) Girl with a no good gambler—out of Las Vegas—has a baby . . . gambler is killed. Girl leaves baby on the ranger's step. Larry is the ranger.
Law.	(dramatizing it all) My God, he says—a baby!
Benson.	(awed) A baby!
Law.	The most precious thing in life. The cutest, goddam little bastard you ever saw.
Benson.	Tugging at every mother's heart. And every potential mother.
Law.	And who isn't!
Benson.	A love story between Larry and the baby—
Law.	The two outcasts! Get it?
Benson.	And then he meets the mother!
Law.	She wants her baby back.
Benson.	She's been through the fires of hell.
Law.	The man she loved . . . let her down. . . .
Benson.	She hates men . . . all men. . . .
Law.	She won't look at Larry . . .
Benson.	Out on the rockies—
Law.	The hell with the Rockies—back to the Foreign Legion!
Benson.	Right! Larry's joined to forget. He's out on the march. We can use all that stock stuff—and he finds a baby! He's gone off to fight the Riffs.

Law.	We cut to the Riffs—
Benson.	Cut back
Law.	Right into the battle.
Benson.	(Really inspired now) His father's the colonel!
Law.	Talk about Kipling—
Benson.	Talk about scope—sweep—what a set-up! (32-33)

The Spewacks created a pair of characters who were unscrupulous, unethical, and unstable with whom the audience would identify. Henri Bergson's theory that in comedy the audience would rather identify with the trickster than the tricked is perfectly exemplified. Their antics were greeted with rejoicing by audiences and critics. As Spewack's biographer Hart wrote, "This lively satire on the Hollywood movie industry ran for 660 performances and won the Roi Cooper Megrue Prize (1936)" (815). George Abbott was a perfect choice as the director and critics praised his pace and sense of mad vertigo. The cast as a whole was excellent with Jerome Cowan and Allyn Joslyn in the demanding leading roles. Again Brooks Atkinson wrote two long appreciative reviews. In the first, he wrote, "By wooing the Hollywood muse with a slapstick, Bella and Samuel Spewack have succeeded in writing an extraordinarily hilarious comedy, 'Boy Meets Girl,' which was perfectly staged at the Cort last evening. . . . Their chief hilarity is the inspired sophomoric prank-dance of their brilliant leading characters whose passion for practical jokes exhausts the strength they should husband for their normal work" ("Boy Meets Girl" 38). In his second review, he placed the play high in the category of indigenous American humor: "Although 'Boy Meets Girl' is technically Hollywood satire, it is primarily the sort of impudent and breezy comedy most characteristic of America. We like it in this neighborhood" ("Holding Both His Sides" 3). In 1936 the play was a success in London and enjoyed a long run. An article indicted that it had an enthusiastic reception from the audience ("'Boy Meets Girl' Wins Applause in London; Critics Find it Full of Laughs" 18). The play was selected by Burns Mantle as one of the ten best plays of the season.

In succeeding years the play became a standard part of summer stock, university productions, and community theatres. It was revived in New York with the great comic Joey Faye as Benson. Wilella Waldorf commented that although the production was not up to the play, the evening was very funny because of the Spewack's dialogue: "Altogether, the current version should prove amusing enough to playgoers who never saw the play before, and positively hilarious to those who never saw any play before" ("Boy Meets Girl" 317).

Because the Spewacks were able to turn their own plays into films they were able to avoid the common experience of playwrights who see their works mutilated by the type of hack writers they were satirizing. Film critics described *Boy Meets Girl* (1938) as a delightful spoof which provided outstanding roles for James Cagney, Marie Wilson, and Pat O'Brien. Film critic Leonard Maltin wrote that the Spewack's own adaptation "has enough sharp dialogue, good satire in the tale of two sharpster screenwriters to make it worthwhile" (143).

Following their war work the Spewacks returned to the theatre with another collaboration with their friend Cole Porter. *Kiss Me, Kate* has one of the most literate, amusing books ever written for the musical stage and has become an American classic performed here and abroad. The authors were intrigued by the idea of turning Shakespeare's *Taming of the Shrew* into a backstage musical with the action offstage mirroring the action in the original. Katharina and Petruchio are played by a divorced couple, Fred and Lilli Vanessi who realize they are still in love as they bicker, rehearse, and sing "So in Love," "Wunderbar," and other memorable Cole Porter songs. Bianca and her lover are played by a free and easy chorine, Lois and her dancer boyfriend Bill, who would rather gamble than dance. The action is complicated by the arrival during opening night of some gangsters who want to collect on an IOU for "ten G's" lost by Bill who signed Fred's name to it. It is typical of the zany Spewack touch that the gangsters take part in the fun by singing "Brush Up Your Shakespeare." At the end all debts are settled, the lovers are reunited, and the play within a play is a success.

In this instance life paralleled art, and *Kiss Me, Kate* became the hit of the season. It opened just before Christmas in 1948 and critics and audiences regarded it as the best Christmas present Broadway could give them. Describing the opening, George Dale wrote, "As the *New York Times* later noted, it was raining too hard that night for dancing in the streets, but the critics adequately took care of the celebration in their columns. The public, too, gave every indication that this lavish and opulent musical comedy was exactly what it was looking for, and *Kiss Me, Kate* became the town's reigning hit and remained so for 1,077 performances" ("Notes" n.p.). It closed in New York in 1950, then moved on to London as the first Broadway musical to be performed at the Sadler's Wells Opera in London (Hart 815). Not only does the musical show the Spewacks in top form, their work with Porter led to what many critics consider his finest musical (Gill *Cole* xiv). Reviewing the original New York production, Brooks Atkinson praised Alfred Drake as Petruchio/Graham as "the heart of the show," and also praised Patricia Morison as Kate/Lilli and Lisa Kirk and Harold Lang as the younger couple. He said that using a few scenes from Shakespeare, "Bella and Samuel Spewack have contribed an authentic book which is funny without the interpolation of gags." As far as the songs went, he said that "Cole Porter has written his best score in years, together with witty lyrics" ("Kiss Me, Kate" 10). Porter and the Spewacks were given a Tony Award for outstanding contributions to the American theatre for their work on the musical.

The musical went on to become a best selling original cast recording and a film (in three-D and Cinamascope versions) which provided Ann Miller with her best screen role as Lois. The musical has since been revived in America and Europe with great success.

The next big hit for the Spewacks was an adaptation of Albert Husson's *La Cuisine des Anges* which they called My Three Angels. Many American playwrights had encountered difficulty in adapting French comedy for the American stage, but the Spewacks succeeded in creating a charming comedy with a fairy tale quality. The 1953 play is a very simple tale set in a convict colony run by the French. The Ducotel family, headed by a charming, but ineffectual and honest father, is trying to make a go of a general store owned by Felix' cousin, Henri Trochard, who lives in Paris. Marie Louise Ducotel is excited on Christmas Eve to learn that Henri and his nephew Paul, whom she loves, have arrived on the island. Her parents regard the arrival as disaster, since the hard-hearted Henri will undoubtedly fire Felix and it is apparent that Paul does not love Marie Louise. But all is well because this Christmas the Ducotel family is guarded over by three angels: convicts who are repairing the roof and overhear all the conversations. Joseph, a convicted forger and con artist, Jules, and Alfred, both doing life for murder, undertake to rearrange life. They effectively put both the Trochard's out of the picture by means of their pet, a poisonous snake. At the end Joseph says, "It's too much to ask destiny to send along the young man we're waiting for at this precise moment. Still it would have been neater somehow." Destiny (and the playwrights) send in "an attractive, even intelligent" young man to take the place of the duplicitous Paul in Marie Louise's heart (179).

This sweet tale could have been sentimental in other hands, but the Spewacks concentrated on comedy and the matter-of-fact way in which the criminals take over, discuss their crimes, and then go back to their ordinary lives. They also undercut the potentially saccharine story by the continual irony of the position of the "angels": intelligent and good-hearted, they have ended in prison because of chance. As Jules remarks, "Our world's just like your. All kinds. The only difference is we were caught" (42). Again, the play is full of various types of comic characters, and again, the authors presented a clever liar and trickster in the role of Joseph, which provided Walter Slezak and opportunity to display his wit and charm. Jerome Cowan, who was so successful in *Boy Meets Girl*, delighted critics and audiences in this as well.

A few critics felt that the play sagged a little after the first act, but all agreed that the basic situation, the dialogue, and the fine comic acting made the evening delightful. The strongest tribute to the playwrights came from John McClain, who wrote (apparently after seeing a number of dull plays)

> When you see it done well it all seems so ingenuous and simple. You take a conventional idea (borrowed, new or blue, it doesn't matter), you endow it with a bright and sometimes brilliant cast, a director of established merit, a tasteful and tolerant producer, and you come up with a sure-pop hit like "My 3 Angels," which opened at the Morosco Theatre last night. But when you begin wondering why it doesn't happen every evening on Broadway you appreciate the debt you owe Sam and Bella Spewack, who are responsible for the deft adaptation of an original French play by Albert Husson" ("A Brilliant Cast and a Sure-Pop Hit" 334).

Robert Coleman also praised their work, saying, "It takes great craftsmanship to make murder amusing or even palatable, but the Spewacks have achieved the tour de force with ingratiating success. . . . We advise you to rush immediately to the Morosco for your reservations. They'll be hard to come by if you wait too long. We predict that 'My 3 Angels' will be a top ticket by the time you read this" ("'My 3 Angels' a Wonderful New Hit" 335). John Chapman concluded his positive review by saying, "'My Three Angels' is a good Spring tonic; it's easy to take and will make you feel better" ("'My 3 Angels' a Smooth, Engaging Comedy" 334). William Hawkins began his review by saying, "'My Three Angels' turns out to be an entirely enchanting evening at the Morosco" ("'My 3 Angels' Stars Convicts with Halos"

336). The play ran 344 performances. The cap to the Spewacks' critical and popular success was the selection of the play as one of the year's ten best by Burns Mantle. Once again a successful film was made starring Humphrey Bogart and the play was frequently performed in schools, regional theatres, and summer stock.

The Spewacks had no more major successes, but continued working in theatre, film, and television. In nearly fifty years of writing Bella Spewack had succeeded in many areas of writing and was admired and respected by critics and colleagues. She was always a spunky and daring person and demonstrated that in 1955 when she surprised the cast of the Spewack's play *Festival* by appearing onstage after the second performance with an appeal to the audience. Irked by the negative response of the critics, Spewack asked each person in the audience to call up five friends and tell them to come to the show immediately. She then appeared on a dozen television and radio shows trying to draw attention to the play. She told an interviewer, "Having a failure isn't such a dreadful thing, but *Festival* is a good, clean show, and when I heard the audience laughing and applauding, I felt it must be something they wanted" (Hevesi 36). Her efforts led to an extension of the run, but only for six weeks.

Bella Spewack was a thorough theatre professional who was successful in all that she undertook. Her name is largely forgotten today, perhaps because the books of musicals are less often remembered than the songs, perhaps because the comedies related very closely to the periods in which they were written. However, her work stands up against the test of time—the plays still seem funny and are well-constructed. Although she wrote for films, she was never trapped into hack work work as so many playwrights were. When *Clear all Wires!* opened in 1932, she told a reporter in New York, "We had to come back, plays or no plays. Hollywood is just a lot of empty sunshine and pink houses. If you stay too long you're ruined. It's very easy to stay but if you do you compromise eighty-five different ways—intangible ways, but they result in the destruction of your soul, sentimental as that sounds" (Seeley n.p.). In addition to maintaining a connection with the live theatre and writing successfully for it for many years, Bella Spewack and her husband set a high standard for work in Hollywood and were nominated (with Leo McCarey) for an Oscar for the 1940 script for *My Favorite Wife*. Speaking of her philanthropic work with her husband and her career with him, she said in 1976, "We felt we had an obligation to aid those who needed help and to give the world a laugh" (Alexander 31).

Clare Boothe Luce (1903-1987)

Clare Boothe Luce (1903-1987) was active in the theatre for many years, but is chiefly remembered for one play which was a great success. This was her third play, *The Women*. In addition to writing plays, she was an actress, an editor, and congresswomen. She was also the model for several characters in plays. Her long, exciting life has inspired many articles and two biographies. Stephen Shadegg, the author of the latest biography wrote, "The abundance of material would support at least four lively books" (7). She was born in 1903 to Ann Clara Snyder, an aspiring actress, and William Franklin Boothe. Her father was an insolvent violinist who encouraged his daughter to read books beyond her years, introduced her to his bohemian friends, and raised her in an aura of atheism (Pederson 563). When Clare was nine, her father left his wife for another woman and Clare and her brother were informed that he had died. Like her mother, Clare was strikingly beautiful and her mother determined that she should be an actress. Belasco hired her as an understudy for Mary Pickford in *The Good Little Devil*. She did some other understudying as well as a walk-on in a movie. All this time Clare was reading the many books her mother bought her and acquiring culture in museums although she had little formal education. In 1913 she and her mother went to Paris to live. In Paris the young girl saw opera and theatre and went to museums. However, this pleasing life ended abruptly with the beginning of World War I.

At the age of twelve, Clare had become rather fat, but had a beautiful face and startling blue eyes, so she was nick-named "Angel Face Tubby." Her mother apparently received some financial assistance from an admirer, so she put Clare in the prestigious Castle School in Tarrytown. Here she took up swimming and other sports and lost weight. After she graduated she briefly studied acting in the Clare Tree Major School of Drama, but quit after her acting was greeted with roars of laughter. However, she did continue learning about theatre by reading Shaw, Wedekind, Wilde and other important playwrights. Her mother seems to have divorced Boothe and in 1919 she married Albert Elmer Austin who took his wife and step-daughter on a first-class trip to Europe.

By this time Clare Boothe had poise, education, great beauty, ambition, and self-confidence. The head of her school had repeatedly told her students, "You can do anything a man can do, and probably do it better" (Shadegg 27). Clare had written in her diary that her ambition was to speak four languages, marry a publisher, have three children, and write something that would be remembered (Shadegg 31). In Berlin she learned German, fell in love with a young man, and saw plays directed by Max Reinhardt. On her return to the U.S., Clare Boothe was on the ship with many other notables including actress Jane Cowl, the Barrymores, Otis Skinner, Max Reinhardt and the wealthy society woman, Mrs. O.H.P. Belmont. She knew how to make herself attractive and was taken up by the society figures on the ship. Reinhardt was getting ready to stage his great pageant *The Miracle* in New York and offered Luce the leading role, according to her report. She claims not to have taken it seriously because she was taken up as a protegé by Mrs. Belmont. She was an important figure in the Women's Party and believed that with her intelligence, charm, and looks, Clare Boothe could be a major assistance to the efforts of the party.

After returning to New York, Boothe did work with the Women's Party. Through her new connections Boothe met and married a very wealthy man named George Tuttle Brokaw, who was forty-two. The twenty-year old woman saw her marriage as a step toward the financial security which was lacking in her childhood and an opportunity to become a part of high society. She was angered by the fact that she was perceived by her husband's family and friends as "a fortune hunter who had somehow trapped George" (Shadegg 41). The unhappy marriage lasted six years. During this time Clare Brokaw, as she was known, had one child, Anne Clare, and established herself as a popular hostess and a major figure in the society columns. At the age of twenty-six, she went to Reno, spent the required time, and achieved the freedom she desired. She looked forward to a future in which she would achieve success as a career woman. She had a trust fund of $425,000 and many connections in the theatre and the publishing world.

In 1929 she became an editorial assistant at *Vogue* and moved on to become managing editor of *Vanity Fair*. In 1935 she began to turn some of the material she had experienced or seen in her colorful life into plays. Her biographer, Lucinda P. Gabbard, claims that, "As a writer, Luce's most significant body of work is her plays" (48). Her plays include *Abide With Me, The Women, Kiss the Boys Goodbye,* and *Margin for Error.*

In 1935 she married Henry Luce and assumed the name Clare Boothe Luce. She was again rejected by her husband's family. She was regarded as a flashy divorcée who had broken up Henry Luce's marriage. He had divorced his proper wife of many years in order to marry the glamourous writer. When she wrote her play *The Women* many people smiled knowingly at the line, "Don't ever marry a man who's divorced a good woman" (58). Luce acted and wrote plays off and on, but her husband didn't like to have her away in the evenings, so she turned increasingly to politics. She wrote articles and books and, thanks to her intelligence and beauty, plus her husband's support, she was twice elected congresswoman from Connecticut. She was later appointed ambassador to Italy. She was honored with many awards and degrees in her last years. Her final theatrical effort was a modern retelling of Ibsen's *A Doll House* called *Slam the Door Softly* produced in 1971 at the Mark Taper Forum.

Her first play produced on Broadway was *Abide With Me* (1935). The play concerned a heroine married to a sadistic drunkard (Boothe's vision of her own marriage) and had very little action. Gabbard describes it as "a somber melodrama about a sadistic husband who is finally shot by the old family servant" (48). Milton Mackaye called it a "dank melodrama about a young girl who married a sadistic and drunken older man and went to live in a gloomy New York mansion. It was pretentious and confused and a resounding failure" (13). The failure was clear on opening night, but Boothe compounded the disaster by coming onstage to take a bow when her friends called "Author!" The critics were disgusted by the play and many noted in their reviews that it was poor taste to take a bow for writing such a bad play. At the time she was waiting to marry Henry Luce, the multi-millionaire editor of *Time Magazine*. She received no preferential treatment on that account. The review in the magazine was as harsh as any other she received, concluding, "Where a neophyte might be pardoned for a good many slips in dramatic structure, it is not so easy to forgive sheer bad writing" (qtd. in Shadegg 91). Brooks Atkinson called it a "gratuitous horror play about an abnormal family" ("Abide With Me" 19). The play was, according to Richard Lockridge, "too horrible to be real" (qtd. in Shadegg 91). With such terrible reviews, it was surprising that the play even lasted 36 performances.

Because of the enormous amount of money she and her husband had, Luce didn't need to work, but her ambition drove her on. After her first failure, she returned to the theatre with another play in 1936, probably to prove she could make a success. Luce hit the jackpot with *The Women*. Probably because her first play was so bad, it was rumored that George S. Kaufman really had written her new one, but he just laughed at the idea. As he was a famous "play doctor," he undoubtedly gave her some good advice during rehearsals. Luce said she got the idea for the play when she went into a ladies' room and heard some rich, idle women engaging in malicious gossip. In writing it she also had the opportunity to satirize some of the women who snubbed her as she tried to break into society and some of her own experience in getting a divorce in Reno.

The Women was innovative in two ways. First, the cast was composed of 34 women and no men. Second, one of the women took a bubble bath on stage which was both new and titillating. The play sets a contrast between an amiable, loving, honest wife, Mary, and an avaricious fortune-hunter named Crystal Allen. Crystal manages to become the mistress of Mary's husband and Mary's bitchy friends make sure that she finds out. A typical exchange takes place in the first act when Mary's society friends are playing cards in her house. When Edith and Sylvia are left alone, Edith says she has been about to burst because she has some exciting news: "Stephen Haines is cheating on Mary!" She goes on to describe how she heard it while having her hair done: "Wait till you hear. You know I go to Michael's for my hair. You ought to go, pet. I despise whoever does yours. Well, there's the most wonderful manicurist there. (Shows her scarlet nails.) Isn't that divine? Jungle Red." Finally she works up to the point of disclosure that the manicurist knows the woman being kept by Mr. Haines. Edith is thrilled: "Someone *we* know?" but Sylvia answers, "No! That's what's so awful about it. She's a friend of this manicurist. Oh, it wouldn't be so bad if Stephen had picked someone in his own class. But a blond Floozy!" (14).

Of course they send Mary to the manicurist who gives her the news. At the beauty shop there is an encounter between Mary and the very unflappable Crystal:

Mary   He couldn't love a girl like you.
Crystal   What do you think we've been doing for the past six months?
           Crossword puzzles? What have you got to kick about? You've got
           everything that matters. The name, the position, the money—

Mary	(losing control of herself again)—Nothing matters to me but Stephen!
Crystal	Oh, can the sob-stuff, Mrs. Haines. You don't think this is the first time Stephen's ever cheated? Listen, I'd break up your smug little roost if I could. I have just as much right as you have to sit in a tub of butter. But I don't stand a chance!
Mary	I'm glad you know it.
Crystal	Well, don't think it's just because he's *fond* of you—
Mary	*Fond!*
Crystal	You're not what's stopping him—You're just an old *habit* with him. It's just those brats he's afraid of losing. If he weren't such a sentimental fool about those kids, he'd have walked out on *you* years ago. . . . Listen. Stephen's satisfied with this arrangement. So don't force any issues, unless you want plenty of trouble.
Mary	You've made it impossible for me to do anything else—!
Crystal	(rather pleased)—Have I?
Mary	You haven't played fair—!
Crystal	Where would any of us get if we played fair?
Mary	Where do you hope to get?
Crystal	Right where *you* are, Mrs. Haines!
Mary	You're very confident.
Crystal	The longer you stay in here, the more confident I get. Saint or no saint, Mrs. Haines, you are a hell of a *dull woman!* (26)

Ultimately, against all good sense, Mary goes to Reno to divorce Stephen. Once married, Crystal reveals her true nature and starts an affair with another man. Mary realizes that the glamourous, conniving woman seduced her husband and that he now regrets it and wants her back. Mary arranges it all with a clever plot, triumphs over Crystal, and regains her happy life with her husband.

The bare story is fairly ordinary, but the characterizatons and dialogue lift the play to another level. Burns Mantle said it exposed female bitchiness "with such surprising candor that it shocked and convulsed its first night audience" (quoted in Rebecca Morehouse n.p.). The play ran for two seasons, grossing more than $900,000. It earned more than any other play in that time period (Shadegg 101). The play was also a critical success (even though some critics disliked the subject matter) and Burns Mantle picked it as one of the ten best of the year. Luce was hired to go to Hollywood when Reliance Pictures paid $125,000 for the film rights. Earning $3,500 a week, she was a consultant on the film (written by Anita Loos and Jane Murfin) and did some screenwriting. The film was directed by George Cukor with an all-star cast and has become a classic. In 1956 it was made into another film called *The Opposite Sex* with screenplay by Fay and

Michael Kanin. Still later Rainer Maria Fassbinder made an unauthorized German version of the film called *Women in New York*.

It is important to note that some of the male reviewers took umbrage at the depiction of the women by Luce. Brooks Atkinson, for example, wrote that the playwright, "has compiled a workable play out of the withering malice of New York's unregenerate worldlings. This reviewer disliked it" ("The Women" 19). His attitude toward the play is shared by many women and men today, so it is interesting to examine Luce's intent. Was she titillating the audience, as Burns Mantle suggested, by revealing the secrets of the female sex (*The Best Plays of 1936-37* 219) or was she castigating a certain type of woman. She claimed that she was aiming her vicious satire against a category of women who deserved it.

> The women who inspired this play deserved to be smacked across the head with a meat axe, and that, I flatter myself, is exactly what I smacked them with. They are vulgar and dirty-minded and alien to grace, and I would not, if I could . . . cross their obscenities with a wit which is foreign to them and gild their futilities with the glamour which by birth and performance they do not possess. (Qtd. in Shadegg 100)

Although Luce was prone to take a revisionist view of her own intentions after her plays were produced, this is probably an accurate statement. She had worked with the Women's Party for Mrs. O.H.P. Belmont, and felt that as a woman she personally had to set an example for others. She said, "Because I am a woman, I must make unusual efforts to succeed. . . . If I fail, no one will say, 'She doesn't have what it takes.' They will say 'Women don't have what it takes' " ("Clare Boothe Luce Dies" n.p.).

Whatever her intentions, the play must be judged on the impression it creates. Unfortunately, her scathing, hilarious portraits of the high society women helped perpetuate stereotypes of women as selfish, scheming, idle creatures who spend their time in malicious gossip, and value their husbands only in monetary terms. In a long thoughtful analysis Susan E. Carlson explores the effect of the comedy, particularly the ending which she posits is "a conscious emphasizing of their hopelessness as redeemable human beings. The best Boothe can offer is Mary's unsatisfying final compromise because it is the best she *wants* to offer." Carlson explores both the play and Boothe's position in the world as role model and as playwright:

> In exposing the double standards under which her women function (as she could not avoid doing in comedy), Boothe allows us to witness their vulnerability. Yet Boothe, whose life patterned for others one way out of such a confining miasma of stereotyped roles, persists in denying a connection between a double standard and her empty women. Because of this blind spot, she also persists in misreading the effects of "comedy" in her play. Boothe's text is full of the social criticism comedy encourages, but its object—the women themselves—confuses that criticism. Boothe forgets that she is criticizing the double standard that has made these women mean-spirited *as well* as criticizing the women. The effect is that her lampooning of the women seems cruel because it is practiced upon characters who are already the victims of comic and social convention. Thus, when the play ends with Mary's ambiguous triumph, and Sylvia and Crystal's hand-to-hair combat, we respond with as much pity as scorn. (211)

This type of analysis reflects the response to the play, performed by an excellent cast, in 1973. Jack Kroll, writing in *Time* praised the production, but questioned the effect of the intense bitchiness. He noted the play's "ambiguous attitude toward women, whom it clearly despises as much as it loves" ("The Girls in the Band" 109). T.E. Kalem called it a "vigorous, thoroughly entertaining revival" and felt an element which attracted more attention than it did originally was the class distinction, "From the vantage point of 1973, one of the fascinations of *The Women* is that it is positively class-ridden" ("Witchy Laugh Potion" 88). In a long analysis of the play and its critics, Elenore Lester, writing in *MS.*, noted that "The male critics displayed their newly liberated consciousnesses and piously noted the sexist aspects" (44). She interviewed Luce and reported, "She told me that she had fought for women's rights before most of her critics were born. (Now 70, she marched in a 1922 parade for the national Equal Rights Amendment, and worked for Alice Paul who wrote that Amendment.) She contended that her play was never intended to be a 'profound sociological study—it is a comedy, a satire, and in satire you *do* use stereotypes—you work with a broad brush'" (44). It was obvious that the passage of time had altered the response to the play, funny though its lines might be, and the play did not have a long run despite the high quality of excellent actresses including Alexis Smith, Kim Hunter, and others.

Luce's next play was *Kiss the Boys Goodbye.* She got her idea for this satire from her work in Hollywood and David O. Selznick's nationwide search for the right actress to play Scarlett O'Hara in *Gone With the Wind.* She offered the play to Max Gordon (who had produced *The*

Women, but he turned it down. It really wasn't a completed play (it wasn't even laid out in acts), but producer Brock Pemberton said he thought he "could wrestle a play out of it" (Mackaye 13). So with a little help from her friends, including director Antoinette Perry, Luce had another success. The satire was very topical, since dozens of actresses, including Mae West, had been given screen tests for the role of Scarlett and the newspapers had a field day with the competition for the role.

The play centers around Hollywood producers, agents, actresses and actors, all of whom are willing to lie, cheat, steal, or sleep with somebody to get what they want. In this case, what is wanted is the role of Velvet O'Toole in the film version of a runaway best-seller called *Kiss the Boys Goodbye*. The director has ostensibly been seeking the perfect woman for the role throughout the South, and has brought back a Georgia peach named Cindy Lou. However, his scheme is to cast a slightly aged actress, Myra, because he is having an affair with her—as are several other men in the play. The characters all meet in a country home in Connecticut where they swap partners, discover each other's secrets, and make sarcastic remarks to and about each other. Outsiders in the household are Cindy Lou and a gallant young polo player named Top Rumson. After various shenanigans, Cindy and Top leave the world of corruption and lies, and Myra gets the role of Velvet.

The play opened on Broadway in 1938. Once again Brooks Atkinson indicated his displeasure with her characterization, saying, "Claire Boothe, *la belle dame sans merci*, is investigating the manners of a group of poisonous people assembled at a Westport house party, and she is impartially opposed to both sexes. She mows them down with a machine gun attack. When the characters of a play are rats and lice it is always a good plan to have a normal person on hand to provide a standard of comparison" ("Kiss the Boys Goodbye" 30). Vernon Grenville wrote, "Clare Boothe Luce in 'The Women' despised her fellow women; in 'Kiss the Boys Goodbye' she hates her fellow men. So at least the record is now even. . . . Miss Boothe has again soaked her typewriter ribbon in vitriol. There are many laughs but they are always cruel ones" ("Kiss the Boys Goodbye" 644). Writing about this play as well as *The Women* 1939, Milton Mackaye stated that her plays expressed her contempt and hatred not only for the group she was satirizing at the time, "but for the whole human race. No character who does not have a case of moral measles or a certification of spiritual bankruptcy need apply for work in the theatres where she holds forth. Her women are sluts, backbiters or dumb-bells. Her men are androgynes, lechers or sots" (50). Although critics continued to express dismay over the vitriolic depiction of human beings by Luce, the play received many positive reviews in terms of the comic effect and the high quality of the production. It ran for 286 performances and was again selected as one of the ten best plays of the year. In 1941 it was made into a reasonably successful musical film with Mary Martin, Don Ameche, Oscar Levant, and Connee Boswell.

As Ferguson notes in her study of American women dramatists, the play was treated by the critics as a funny satire on the search for Scarlett O'Hara, but "this play when published caused a mild sensation because of the playwright's declaration in the foreword that it is 'a political allegory about Fascism in America'" (255). Boothe wrote a long foreword describing Southernism as a form of Fascism which she exposed through her play. Critics and audiences certainly saw nothing of that in the play. As Ferguson observes,

> While Miss Boothe expounds some of these ideas [about the narrow thinking in the South] through the character Madison Breed, columnist, the farcical elements of the situation completely destroy any serious message the playwright may intend to convey. Indeed, if Miss Boothe is to be taken seriously in her statement of the intent of *Kiss the Boys Goodbye*, this play must be considered an outright failure, for no casual reader or viewer could possibly get the political implications that Miss Boothe believed she had written into her play. (255)

Luce's last major play came after she went to Europe with her husband who was engaged in studying world affairs. She talked with people who worked for *Time* and concluded on the basis of their opinions and what she had seen, that "until Nazism, Fascism, and Communism were all destroyed, the future of the world would be filled with dangerous uncertainties" (qtd. in Shadegg 111). Her concerns resulted in a play called *Margin for Error* which opened in 1939.

The play is set in the library of the German Consul in New York, complete with a bust of Hitler and a Nazi flag. The evil and merciless Consul, played by Otto Preminger, degrades his wife, takes money to help refugees out of Germany, searches out the fact that his aide had a Jewish grandmother, and engages in the sort of general behavior which might lead someone to murder him. He is under the protection of a series of Jewish policemen (allegedly Mayor La Guardia's idea of a joke!), but is murdered anyway. Suspicion falls on everyone, including the policeman, a comic character played by the young Sam Levene. The crime is re-enacted several times, and the good people are revealed to be innocent and the blame is fixed on a Nazi. The policeman tells his captain, "Well, Captain Mulrooney, it seems the Consul was shot, stabbed and poisoned." The captain responds, "Well, the son-of-a-bitch! Did it kill him?" The uneasy mixture of serious material about Hitler's Germany and the farcical techniques make this a very strange play.

In the time, however, it was chiefly perceived as wise-cracking comedy, welcome in the increasingly gloomy times. The *Time* reviewer commented that it was "a lively mystery melodrama peppered with wisecracks. 'Margin for Error' is much less propaganda than entertainment" ("Margin for Error" 58) Vernon Grenville, as usual, did not care for Luce's work, seeming to have decided that she could only successfully write bitchy plays about a limited range of society. Although he called *Margin for Error* very well acted, he thought it dull. He concluded, "Although she can write about the women of cafe society and their male counterparts with a pen of vitriol, she seems at sea when she attempts more masculine themes" ("Margin for Error" 118). His sexist comment must have been particularly annoying to Luce since she had claimed to be writing indirectly about Fascism in *Kiss the Boys Goodbye* and was writing directly about it in this play. George Jean Nathan was even harsher in his review, saying, "The Boothe dispensation is one of the most unblenching tournaments in box office hokum that has come to this notice in some time." He indicated his objections to the caricatures of Nazis, Jews, and newspapermen which he felt she had created, and the conclusion in which "not to miss a trick, the villain is murderously coveted not by one Hitler-phobe but by four." He felt the whole play was lacking in logic and reality: "So gluedly intent upon such profligate hoke has the fair Boothe been that she has neglected to provide her bijou with even the minimum of the basic sense and rationality demanded of melodramas" and concluded, "If this be treason, Clare, make the most of it, darling" ("Arrivals and Departures" 36). Of course, Nathan was notoriously sarcastic, but his response did reflect some critical concern that the treatment of Fascism in a comical way was a mistake. For most, however, the fine performances and the clever dialogue were welcome in the theatre and the play was a success and was selected as one of the ten best plays of the year. Otto Preminger directed the 1943 movie and again played the villainous Nazi, with Joan Bennett and Milton Berle also in the cast.

Child of the Morning (1951) reflected Luce's life-long interest in religion and her conversion to Catholicism. It was the story of a Brooklyn family intent upon their daughter entering a convent. Aside from the interest provided by Margaret O'Brien as the daughter, the play received little attention. Writing in *The Commonweal*, Richard Hayes noted the "high ardor of sanctity" of the play which related to canonization. The religious story, with its conflicting elements of chastity and desire, seemed to Hayes uneasily set in contemporary lower-class Brooklyn:

> A Brooklyn, moreover, complete with switchblades, marijuana, and various kinds of delinquency. It is an exotic impulse, and startling in a figure of Mrs. Luce's sophisticated sense of reality; indeed, the want of authenticity in "Child of the Morning" is a constant distress. The playwright has documented this dreary religious patois and haggling with energy but a very uncertain taste, and even in this theater season of familial recrimination and abuse, Mrs. Luce's raucous egotists are noisily distinguished. One is troubled, moreover, through the whole of "Child of the Morning," with that cool stress we would call elsewhere shrewd technical guile: it is deployed here with a dismaying ruthlessness sadly at odds with the lyrical and somber nature of Mrs. Luce's subject. ("Ceremony of Innocence" 153)

The play was not a success in its time and is usually not mentioned in a discussion of Luce's work as a playwright.

Luce occasionally acted in plays in the 1940s and 50s. While a congresswoman in 1945 she played in *Candida*, but not with great success. She also served as the model for several characters in plays by other women, including Constance in Gertrude Stein's *Yes, Is For a Very Young Man*.

Her last play, *Slam the Door Softly* (1970), was a one-act modern treatment of the subject matter in *A Doll House*. It was written at the height of the women's liberation movement, which was particularly active in New York City. Set in New York's suburbia, the play is an exchange between a coarse, macho husband, Thaw, and his wife, Nora, who is planning to leave him. As the play begins there is satire on Thaw and the feminists he is observing on television. He sneers at them as a bunch of battle-axes and "lesbos" and pays no attention to the comments of his wife. He becomes absorbed in a magazine which he reads as Nora says she is leaving him and going to get a job. The rest of the play is an attempt on his part to understand her, and on her part to explain that she is leaving him because she wants to exist as a person which she feels she can only do if she has a career. But as she leaves, she answers his statement that a man needs a woman of his own by saying, "I know. A sleep-in, sleep-with body servant of his very own." She leaves, but in contrast to the original Nora, says, "I'm not bursting with self-confidence, Thaw. I love you. And I also need . . . a man. So I'm not slamming the door. I'm closing it . . . very . . . softly" (20). The play is artificially constructed, in that neither even mentions hiring someone to clean the house—it's either be a house cleaner or have a career. Luce seems to be satirizing men who oppose feminism and women who comprehend it in a very shallow sense and can only quote books they have read. It exists chiefly as an oddity inspired by the events of the time in which it was written.

Luce merits attention because she wrote three hit plays and because of the world-wide success of *The Women*. However, as Gabbard has noted, "In the light of the women's liberation movement of the 1960s and 70s, however, the play comes across as false and unworthy" (48). Her dynamic personality made her a glittering part of the theatre world and she is one of the few women playwrights from the first half of the century who are widely-known. She established herself as an independent woman with several careers and the ability to challenge men in many areas. It is not surprising that several playwrights (including Gertrude Stein) chose her as a model for their characters, knowing that the audiences would relate the material to her personality. In the early 1950s a Gallup poll determined that she was fourth in line as the World's Most Admired Woman, following Eleanor Roosevelt, Queen Elizabeth II, and Mamie Eisenhower. This startling position was achieved through her work as a playwright, politician, war correspondent, and diplomat (France 186).

Mary Coyle Chase (1907-1981)

Although Mary Coyle Chase (1907-1981) wrote plays from the late thirties to the late seventies, she is chiefly remembered for three plays performed in New York in a space of eight years. She is still represented in the American theatre by occasional revivals of her Pulitzer Prize winning play, *Harvey*. She had a gift for comic characterization and dialogue which offered fine opportunities for actors such as James Stewart, Helen Hayes, and Fred Gwynne.

Chase was a native of Colorado. She was born in Denver and was highly influenced by her four Irish uncles and her Irish mother. Her Irish fancy pervades her writing. She attended both the University of Denver and the University of Colorado at Boulder, but failed to get a degree. She worked for several years for the *Rocky Mountain News* as a "sob sister" noted for getting photographs of people in the news even if she had to steal them. She ran with a hard-drinking, fun-loving group of reporters. After marrying Robert Chase (later editor of the paper), she had three sons and worked for a variety of causes including increased rights for Spanish-Americans. For a time she wrote a weekly radio program for the Teamsters' Union. She was a very devoted mother and housewife with no interest in sophisticated New York society. She remarked in 1952, "As soon as a play is launched, I immediately get on a plane and fly home to my family in Denver. I don't stay around Broadway long once that opening night curtain has gone up. I'm especially anxious to get back now that I have a granddaughter" (Barron, "Mrs. Chase" n.p.). Dorothy Parker met Chase in Denver and was so impressed by her that she described the fellow playwright as, "the greatest unacclaimed wit in America" (Melrose 1). However, at parties in New York, Chase couldn't think of anything to say and felt dull and uninteresting . In Denver she felt at home and was known as Colorado's first lady of theatre (Hutton 126).

Chase wrote her first play for the Federal Theatre Project in Denver. *Me Third* was produced in 1936 and directed by Antoinette Perry. The director interested producer Brock Pemberton in presenting it in New York in 1937 under the title *Now You've Done It*. After the failure of this play, Chase wrote a script for a movie *Sorority Girl* (1938). Undeterred by another failure, she wrote a new play incorporating Irish folklore, *The Banshee*. Pemberton felt it was too dark for presentation during the war, so Chase set herself to writing a play which would bring happiness to people in that sad time.

For two years she wrote at the dining room table, moving empty spools around a miniature stage as she envisioned the action of the play. Her idea was to treat the subject of a woman who takes up with a pooka—a large mischievous fairy spirit in animal form. Again, Chase drew on Irish folklore. At first she conceived the pooka as a large canary! After several drafts, she changed the central figure from a woman to the gallant Elwood P. Dowd, the pooka to a giant rabbit, and the title from *The White Rabbit* to *Harvey*. With these changes she created one of the biggest hits in the history of the American theatre.

Chase's central idea is simple, but unforgettable. Well-to-do Elwood P. Dowd has become an embarrassment to his socially conscious sister Veta and her daughter Myrtle Mae. He spends most of his time drinking and insists that he is accompanied by Harvey, a six foot tall rabbit. Elwood describes his pleasing existence to the psychiatrist Veta contacts. He usually passes his time sitting in bars with Harvey, drinking and playing the juke box, and meeting people: "Soon the faces of the other people turn toward mine and smile. They are saying: 'We don't know your name, Mister, but you're a lovely fellow.' Harvey and I warm ourselves in all these golden moments . . . soon we have friends. They come over to us. They drink with us. They tell about the big terrible things they have done. The big wonderful things they will do" (54). Ultimately, the pleasure of Elwood's life becomes so attractive to the psychiatrist examining him, that he determines to get Harvey for himself. Meanwhile, Veta attempts to commit Elwood to the sanitarium, but through a series of funny misunderstandings is herself, committed, stripped, and shoved into a hydro bath.

Chase develops the characters who represent proper society in sharp contrast to the easy-going, polite character of Elwood. As Albert Wertheim has noted, she exposes,

> the ridiculous stiltedness, meanness, and sterility of what one might call "normal" or "expected" social behavior. To foster her increasingly negative picture of normalcy, she makes her audience laugh at the comic posturing, insensitivity and stupidity of "good society" and of the arbiters of normalcy, the psychiatrist and his staff. (164)

After her experiences in the sanitarium Veta is doubtful about what to do, and has also come to feel more sympathy for Elwood. She asks her daughter, "Where else could I take him, I couldn't take him to jail, could I? Besides, this is not your uncle's fault. Why did Harvey have to speak to him in the first place? With the town full of people, why did he have to bother Elwood?" (60). As the psychiatrist is about to give Elwood a shot which will bring him back to reality and a responsible existence, a cab driver tells Veta about the change which will take place. He has noticed the difference between the patients he brings up and the ones he takes away: "Lady, after this he'll be a perfectly normal human being and you know what bastards they are!" (69). As the play ends, Veta decides she prefers Elwood as he is. As they leave the sanitarium Elwood sees Harvey, and says "Where've you been? I've been looking all over for you" and he and the invisible rabbit exit arm in arm (71).

The play was an immediate success and ran for four years. Frank Fay was the original Elwood P. Dowd, and although he enjoyed the success, he tired of telephone calls allegedly from Harvey, extra place settings in restaurants with lettuce and carrots, etc. Josephine Hull was hilarious in the role of Veta on-stage and in the movie (for which she won an Oscar). Later Elwoods included Jimmy Stewart and Joe E. Brown. Stewart was in the film version (1950) and the Hallmark Hall of Fame television production of the APA revival which also starred Helen Hayes. Chase did the scripts for both and was paid a record breaking million dollars for the film rights. Writing in 1951, Chase estimated that the play had earned her about eight million dollars.

Critics noted the wit in the play and the charm of the whole production. Howard Barnes' review was typical: "Fantasy has charm and infinite delight in Harvey. The new play is as wise as it is witty; as occult as it is obvious. It is full of laughter and delicate meaning. . . . It is stage sorcery at its whimsical best. A lively and utterly charming show. Frank Fay's performance of the bum is memorable; Josephine Hull's daffy dowager is not to be missed" ("Fay in Wonderland" 95). John Chapman wrote, "'Harvey' is the most delightful, droll, endearing, funny and touching piece of stage whimsey I ever saw ("'Harvey' is Just Wonderful" 95). Despite the general praise, and the critics' delight with the production, several critics suggested that much of its success was due to the performances and criticized the structure of the play. Louis Kronenberg said that the play gave him the "pleasantest theatrical lift I have had in a long time" despite is shortcomings. In particular he noted, "'Harvey' has a first act that keeps going way too long, and a last act that, in a sense, can't keep going at all" ("A Fine Night" 95). Ward Morehouse wrote, "It sags in spots, the first act is over-long and the third act is not up to the pace of the second" ("Mrs. Fay's Friend" 96) Wilella Waldorf was even more negative, stating, "Elwood is a delightful fellow and Harvey is an entrancing, though invisible rabbit. But the vehicle their creator has knocked together for them to wander around in is a slipshod farce in which all of the other characters are stock figures hacked rather crudely out of a very low grade of theatrical cardboard" (qtd. in Toohey 200).

The number of successful revivals and the high quality of the movie based on the play testify to its ability to please an audience. However, a present-day assessment must question the message the playwright was presenting. Even at the time, George Jean Nathan mocked the Pulitzer Prize Committee for giving the prize to *Harvey* instead of Tennessee William's *The Glass Menagerie*. He reminded readers that the award was supposed to go to a play "which shall represent in marked fashion the educational value and power of the stage, preferably dealing with American life." He went on to say that the educational value of Harvey consists "in the instruction that it is far more contributive to human happiness to be good and drunk, and to stay good and drunk, than it is to be dismally sober. The play is the greatest intemperance document that the American stage has ever offered" (qtd. in Toohey 200). Paradoxically, Chase was an alcoholic, but she may have realized this only later when she faced her own problems and gave up drinking for good. In 1971 she refuted the comments of critics to the effect that Elwood was a "happy drunk" or a "gentle tippler." She said most of the critics missed the message she intended, "It is not a play about an amiable drunk. It is a spiritual play written in farce terms. I never intended Elwood to be a drunk. Some people live in a different world than other people, and Elwood is such a man" (Syse 3).

A recent revival of Chase's biggest success demonstrated the many changes in American outlooks since she wrote the play. The production at the San Jose Repertory Theatre. As Steven Winn wrote, the production, "adds at least one wrinkle audiences wouldn't have encountered in the '40s: three of the 11 actors in the cast are black" ("'Harvey' Reappears" 1). Winn also commented that Chase's satire on psychiatrists seemed rather light-weight to "a contemporary audience that's been to the 'Cuckoo's Nest' and other black comic dens of insanity" (1). Assessing the play as a whole, Winn commented on the "magically timeless lines" which still drew laughs, but noted, "'Harvey' which beat out 'The Glass Menagerie' for the Pulitzer Prize in 1945, potters along for three acts" (1). The sense of the review was that the hilarious dialogue still held up, but that only when the best lines were given "the play sheds its years and feels newly minted" (1).

With the tremendous success of *Harvey*, Chase's circumstances altered considerably. One would have supposed that for a woman unaccustomed to wealth and praise, the change would have been for the better. But Chase told a reporter in 1971 that the success of the play had been "a painful experience, traumatic and actually frightening" (Syse 3). First, her problem with alcohol increased. (Later she was able to overcome her alcoholism and was proud of having founded a home for alcoholic women in Denver.) Second, the great success of the play created a writer's block. Finally, she felt that her former friends turned against her. She wrote that three witches always come to the feast: "Greed and the distorted faces of her sisters Envy and Malice" (Chase "My Life With Harvey" 58). The bitterness against supposed friends who let you down is a dark undercurrent in her later play *Mrs. McThing*.

The next play to appear in New York by Mary Chase was *The Next Half Hour*, a reworking of *The Banshee*. This opened in 1945, but ran for only 43 performances. In her play Chase told the story of a woman able to hear the wail of the banshee, and thus predict a death in the next half hour. When the victim is to be one her sons, she decides to try to avert the fate, but succeeds only in causing the death of another son. The critics thought little of the story line—Howard Barnes going so far as to say, "The general idea of the piece adds up to sheer nonsense" ("Mystical Confusion" 132). Burton Rascoe was one of the few critics to praise it as a "drama with even more substance than *Harvey*." However, he noted that the cast had done its best by "a melodrama that depends more on the way it is played than on the text" ("The Next Half Hour" 12). The play had been directed by George S. Kaufman, with a cast headed by Fay Bainter but their efforts could not disguise the weakness of the script. Ward Morehouse called it "gloomy, plodding, and quite exhausting . . . tedious and fumbling—and quite definitely her second best" ("Mary Chase's 'The Next Half Hour'" 130). In "Bad News for 'Harvey' Fans," Louis Kronenberger wrote, "The play is the limpest kind of theater, billowing and at length, just stagnating with talk. . . . Mr. Kaufman's direction is for the most part above reproach, but hasn't a chance of carrying the day" (130). It is unfortunate that Chase was unable to develop a workable structure to express her Irish mysticism and reveal the essentially interesting character she had created. She started out with a character and situation which, had the play been successful, might have led her to develop her abilities in depth.

Chase returned to fantastic comedy with her play *Mrs. McThing* (1952). The producer Robert Whitehead originally intended a run of a few weeks for the play described as a play for "children of all ages." That phrase, which has become such a cliché, is actually a rather meaningful description of not only this play, but all of Chase's work. *Mrs. McThing* is a type of fairy tale in which even crooks and gangsters are harmless. Chase based some of the play on her own relationship with her young sons.

One of the most interesting elements of the play is the double roles it provided for Helen Hayes, as Mrs. Larue, and the charming Brandon de Wilde, as her son Howay. Mrs. Larue is a wealthy woman, selfish in her desire to protect her son from any unpleasantness and discontent with his normal boyhood boistrousness. When Mimi, a poor waif, wants to play with Howay she is driven away. Her mother, Mrs. McThing, avenges Mimi by substituting a perfect "stick child" for Howay, and sending Howay to earn his living at a pool hall/lunchroom run by gangsters. She also substitutes a "stick woman" for Mrs. Larue who then must work as a cleaning woman at the pool hall. When Mrs. Larue calls her friends for help, they refuse to believe in her identity and leave her in despair. Later, with Mimi's help, she and Howay return to their home where the magical waif burns both the stick figures. Mrs. McThing appears, first as a hateful witch, then as a loving fairy, and bids goodbye to Mimi. The gangsters joyfully take away all the silver with Mrs. Larue's blessing (it's all insured anyway), and she promises to open her home and gardens not only to Mimi but to all children.

The play was successful in part because of the light touch with which the characters are created, and in part because it allowed Helen Hayes and Brandon de Wilde to play a wide range of emotions and switch costumes and characters as they alternately played the real people and the stick characters. The play was so well received that it ran throughout the spring, Hayes toured it through the summer and returned with it to New York in the fall.

The reviewers generally liked the play, but pointed out that it was very weak in its construction, several using the phrase "ramshackle construction." Brooks Atkinson noted its "innocent sense of comedy" and said, "It is delightful. Thank Ireland for Mrs Chase's rich make-believe sense of humor and her compassion for the needs of adults and children." ("Helen Hayes" 1). John McClain wrote one of the more negative reviews, saying that even the superlative performances of Hayes and de Wilde could not "sustain the meagre and frothy premise which the author endeavored to stretch into an entire play. . . . Mrs. Chase is a gifted writer, but this time I think she became entangled in a plot from which she never quite extricated herself ("Mary Chase Gets Snarled" 360). Robert Coleman praised the production, noted that the audience roared appreciatively throughout most of the evening, but described the play as something "J.M. Barrie and William Saroyan might have penned together in an off moment" ("'Mrs. McThing'" 361). Walter Kerr was "crazy about it" noting that the only flaw in the production or the play was the "comic strip mannerisms" of the gang-sters ("'Mrs. McThing'" 362). Despite its flaws, the critics chose it as the runner up to *I Am a Camera* for the Drama Critics Circle Award.

By November of 1952 Chase had quite a coup: she had two plays running successfully in New York City. *Bernardine* had opened with the attractive young actor John Kerr in a major role. Again, the play relates to Chase's life and background. In it she develops the relation-ship between a mother and her son when he has reached adolescence. The plot is really an exploration of the tricks and pranks which disturb a mother as she attempts to understand her teen-age sons and his friends. As Chase wrote in her introduction to the play, "I embarked on an impossible journey of penetration into a world where I did not belong—a study of the viewpoint of a crowd of teen-age boys. This was not easy" (viii). Critical response was mixed. Although critics found many faults, particularly with the first act, most found the play moving. Noting that the kids and grown-ups seemed caricatures, nevertheless, Robert Coleman said, "After a slow and disappointing start, 'Bernardine' becomes an amusing and moving theatrical experience. The best, the most rewarding comedy of the season" ("'Bernardine' is Moving" 231). Walter Kerr felt the play had a special appeal, but wrote, "As a dramatist, Mrs. Chase is loaded with faults. It is perfectly possible that she is the sloppiest scenarist now delighting the profes-sional theatre." In a staggering statement of male chauvinism, he concluded that the weakness in the structure was because she was a woman, "There never was a more feminine playwright, every bureau drawer is left open" ("'Bernardine'" 233). Richard Watts was one of the few critics who simply found the "antics in the back room of a beer hall" trying. But he noted, "I may be alone in being chill to "'Bernardine'" ("Trials" 234). He was nearly alone.

The play was made into a movie with Pat Boone, which was not particularly successful. It has seldom been revived. Perhaps this is largely to do with the change in times: both youth and youthful slang have changed since Chase depicted her teenagers. Critics in 1952 generally perceived the play as a touching and accurate depiction of the problems of adolescence. Brooks Atkinson was nearly alone in describing the teen-agers as "comic-book stereotypes" ("Mary Chase Studies Problem of Being Young" 233). Today, the young men seem not only stereotypes, but idealized and sentimentalized stereotypes. As Al Wertheim commented, "Where *Bernardine* falls short is in its ability truly to recapture this adolescent world" (170). Although it was amusing in its time, it added little to Chase's reputation. That was even more true of her next play.

Midgie Purvis, a vehicle for Tallulah Bankhead, was produced in 1961. In this play the eponymous heroine is a debonair lady with a fondness for furs and spectacular clothing. Her notion of fun is to build a giant snowman in the front yard and dress him in a bra. Her neighbors and family are embarrassed and irritated by her continual antics, so she runs away and disguises herself as an old, shabbily dressed woman and sets up as a baby-sitter for a working widow. Needless to say, the moral is clear and the ending is happy. Ms. Purvis' priggish son realizes how much he loves his mother and welcomes her home. The story is a little like *Mrs. McThing* in reverse.

Walter Kerr was definitely in the minority in his extravagent praise for the comedy and "advanced sociology" in the play. He professed amazement at the fact that although the nine scenes in the play "could have been played in almost any order at all" and that it rambled, nevertheless he enjoyed it immensely ("'Midgie Purvis'" 377). Howard Taubman began by remarking, "There is nothing more depressing than a fantasy that won't take wing" and concluding that the leading character, while initially comical "becomes thoroughly vulgar" ("Tallulah Bankhead in Mary Chase Play" 376). The feeling of the critics in general can be summed up by Frank Aston's conclusion, "For the understatement of the year, let it be said that the play is negligible" ("Tallulah Plays" 376). Despite the poor quality of the play, many critics raved about the performance of Tallulah Bankhead and her fans cheered each evening when she made her entrance. John McClain noted, "It's a pity the play's on the seamy side. It will be interesting to see if Miss Bankhead's personal draw will be sufficient to keep the play alive. I would guess not—but I hope I'm wrong" ("Tallulah's Fine— The Play? No!" 378). He was right, the play did not run.

Chase had no more plays produced in New York, although a few minor efforts were presented in some regional theatres. In 1979 the production of a play called *We Love You Denver!* was announced by the small Off-Center Theatre in New York. However, the theatre cancelled its season and expanded its bread baking operations instead! This was her last effort at a major production before her death in 1981.

Mary Chase spent the years following the success of *Harvey* coming to grips with her changed position in life. She was torn between her urge toward a career and the urge to be a full-time mother and wife. After writing her first play, she said she really didn't know if she could find time to write another one. She once told a reporter, "Rearing three sturdy youngsters is a job in itself" (Coleman, "Her Play" n.p.) Unlike many other women playwrights, she never acted or directed, and did not enjoy the rehearsals which kept her away from Denver. She also had a fairly casual attitude toward playwriting, remarking that any intelligent person should be able to write a play: "Just put things down on paper. Just write. If you have something to say, you will find a way to say it" (Coleman, "Her Play" n.p.). Perhaps this accounts for her failure to perfect the structure of her plays.

Chase spent her last years as a successful figure in Denver society, almost a "civic monument" in her beloved home town. She was awarded an honorary doctorate by Denver University in 1947. She served on many committees and was a member of the board of trustees of the Bonfils Theatre and the Denver Center for the Performing Arts. In 1944, when she failed to realize the immediate succcess of the opening night of *Harvey*, Frank Fay called her a "dumb Denver housewife" and this description stuck to her (Chase "My Life With Harvey" 54). She was a housewife, but she was far from dumb. Her plays are filled with witty lines and amusing situations. Her ability as a playwright was summed up by Lucina P. Gabbard, who wrote,

The best of Chase's work, despite uneven writing, reveals a world of whimsey, good humor, and kindness. Elwood in *Harvey* sets the tone with his dignified courtesy and his guileless friendliness in a crass, unacceptable world. *Mrs. McThing* adds a touch of magic as the witch turns into a beautiful fairy to bid farewell to her tearful daughter. *Bernardine* carries forth Chase's humor with the character of Wormy, who, by refusing to obey his mother's threatening commands, causes her to realize the value of boys as allies. Thus, Chase's vision is complete: love is victorious in a pleasant world of fancy. (Mary Coyle Chase 341-342)

It is unfortunate that Chase lacked the discipline or ability to develop a strong structure and avoid easy sentiment. Walter Kerr summed up her flawed playwriting in his review of "Midgie Purvis." He began his review by saying, "Mary Chase is unfair to drama critics" and explained that he felt he should be telling all the things wrong with the play: "the whole thing seems to have been composed on an out-of-order Ouija board, and all I can say is that 'Midgie Purvis' warmed the cockles of my heart" ("'Midgie Purvis'" 377) With the inherent charm which disarmed theatre critics and her ability to move an audience to laughter she could have been one of America's finest comic playwrights. As it is, her fame rests chiefly on *Harvey*.

Fay Kanin (1916-   )

Fay Kanin (1916-) is a woman who made significant contributions to the American theatre in several fields. Beginning at the age of nineteen, she learned all aspects of film, theatre, and television, performing in practically every capacity and achieving great success in many areas. She was a strong feminist who believed that women should seize opportunities and that young women should be encouraged to take an active role in society and government. In all her theatrical work she demonstrated the possibilities for women, as well as the need for them move beyond conventional roles. Looking back at her own career in an interview in 1980, she remarked, "No one ever told me I couldn't be anything I wanted to be" ("To the Top" 18).

Like Rachel Crothers, Kanin was an amazingly precocious young woman. Having grown up in Elmira, New York she attended Elmira College and completed her junior year at the age of 18! Her mother had given up a career in vaudeville to marry and have children. Her family was very supportive; when Kanin decided she wanted to spend her senior year at the University of Southern California, her father found a job in Los Angeles so she could do it. As a young student in Elmira, Kanin had written and produced a children's show for the radio. When she graduated from USC, she looked for a job writing for films and was hired at $65 a week. Almost immediately, however, in an economy wave, she was shifted to the position of play reader at $25 a week. At the age of nineteen, having studied theatre, she now began to absorb all the aspects of working in theatre. After her successful play *Goodbye, My Fancy* opened in 1948, a reporter wrote that Kanin,

> . . . watched them shoot movies, hobnobbed with the writers, technicians and script girl, and stayed on the sets and dreamed when the actors went to lunch. And she wrote—a screen play, short stories, a magazine novel, and did radio acting. With the war she sold NBC a network idea called "The Woman's Angle" which explained the war to women. She wrote it, did the commentary, and interviewed the guests she collected from the kid who sold war stamps to the big movie celebrities. (Fields, "The Playwright" n.p.)

The radio program was an early indication of Kanin's belief that women need to be informed and active. Although capable of working alone and earning her own living, she chose to marry Michael Kanin and write many screenplays and plays with him. They worked together and had two children and she assumed his name, but she always continued with her career. Of their films together, the most notable are *Teacher's Pet,* which was nominated for an Oscar in 1958, and *The Opposite Sex,* a version of Luce's *The Women* which won praise in 1956. Kanin was a woman with many abilities, and she exercised them fully. She mastered the techniques of screen-writing and radio work, then following World War II, she turned to the stage and television.

While many criticized television for its shallow content and the control of subject matter, Kanin plunged in to write several productions of real importance. In 1972 she wrote her first television film, *Heat of Anger,* which starred Susan Hayward. It is recognized as "a contributing factor in the emergence of strong women as protagonists in television dramas" (Korf 484). In terms of subject matter her 1974 *Tell Me Where It Hurts* was very important: she presented a mother (played by Maureen Stapleton) who feels superfluous because her children have grown up. She forms an informal group with other women in which they discuss their feelings of inadequacy and she subsequently helps her husband to understand her need to establish a role for herself in life. The script won an Emmy Award and the Christopher Award for television scripts. Kanin's next work, *Hustling,* involved prostitutes in New York. She told an interviewer, "When I was asked to write it, I said to ABC that if I was expected to write a pantywaist movie about prostitution, I just didn't want to do it. I asked them 'Are you willing to be as forthright about this subject as television will allow?'" The answer was yes, and after interviewing prostitutes picked up by the police, she wrote her highly successful script which was produced in 1975 and won the Writer's Guild Award for television. Another major contribution to television was *Friendly Fire* which exposed the accidental death of a soldier in Viet Nam who was shot by his own artillery. Kanin wrote and then co-produced the film which won the Emmy Award, the Peabody Award, and the San Francisco Film Festival Award in 1979.

Kanin pursued her interest in producing, which began in 1948 when her first play was rejected by a New York producer, by forming a female producing team with Lillian Gallo (Korf 484). One of their notable productions was the 1980 *Fun and Games,* an early study of sexual harassment of women at work. Before, during, and after this work for television Kanin was raising a family, writing for the stage, and taking a major step in heading organizations previously largely headed by men. In 1971 she became the president of the screen branch of the Writer's Guild of America—the first woman in that position for twenty years. In 1979 she became the first woman to serve at length as President of the Academy of Motion Picture Arts and Sciences. (Bette Davis had served for a month during World War II.) She contributed her expertise and served as a role model for young women playwrights in the American College Theatre Festival and was honored by the American Theatre Association in 1979. She traveled extensively in connection with American films and became "the principal woman ambassador of American films in the world" (Korf 485). Elmira College awarded her a Doctor of Humane Letters in 1981. She won many other awards and honors including the prestigious Internationalism Award from American Women for International Understanding in 1982. Her career brought her happiness, fame, fortune, and the knowledge that she was an active feminist putting her beliefs to effective use. As her biographer Jean Prinz Korf wrote, "Kanin's outstanding contribution has been to write about contemporary subjects pertaining to the problems of women or contemporary problems for both sexes as seen through the eyes of women" (485).

Kanin's first effort at playwriting came as a result of a personal experience. During a visit to her college in Elmira, she was forcefully impressed by a number of things. She asked herself, "What is this nostalgia that has so much power over us all? and what happens to the man or woman who goes back to look at the past and tries to recapture it?" Perhaps more importantly, "She found many young girls going into the world with a feeling of insecurity. She, a career woman herself, began to think seriously about the place of a girl in world affairs today" ("Milestone for a First Playwright" n.p.). Her musings led her to write the play which expressed her feminist point of view. She told an interviewer, "If it has a theme, it is that every adult in this world has to tell the truth to the young, if we are to have a world at all. By going back to the Elmira I knew so well I found that you can't go back to your past. You must live with the realities of the present" (Fields, "The Playwright" n.p.). In the same interview she expressed her pleasure in the response of women to her play: "I'm a feminist. I don't think women are better than men, but I think they are just as good. I've put into my play my feeling that women should never back away from life, and I think that the women who see it are challenged" ("Milestone" n.p.).

Goodbye, My Fancy presents a weekend in the life of a successful newspaper correspondent turned congresswoman in which the past is examined and the future decided. Agatha Reed has been invited to give the commencement address and receive an honorary degree at Good Hope College for women (in the terminology of the day "girls"). The college president, James Merrill appears, calling up memories of her romance with him before she was expelled from college after spending the night with him. She reveals that she has loved him all these years and only left so that his budding career would not be blighted. She is proud of her sacrifice and believes he has been a wonderful president.

However, reality comes upon her when her secretary looks into the past of the president and when her war-time lover, Matt Cole appears, covering the weekend for *Life*. (This was a joke which pleased theatregoers who related the characterization of Reed to Congresswoman Clare Boothe Luce, whose husband, Henry Luce, edited the magazine.) Although she has had a successful career, Reed realizes that she never committed herself to a full life because of her lost romance with her inspiring teacher. She imagines he has been an inspiration to generations of female students. In fact, he has subsided into a lackey of the trustees, never creating any problems, never doing anything controversial, successfully raising funds for new buildings, and wearing evening dress impeccably. And so she must say "Goodbye, my fancy," a line from a Whitman poem.

Reed fully realizes the emptiness of her dream when Merrill toadies to the highly conservative businessman who heads the Board of Trustees, by cancelling her controversial anti-war film. In the end he shows the film and offers to resign. Although gratified, and convinced that she has made a difference in his future, Reed is no longer prepared to marry him, but intends to pursue her career as a congresswoman and possibly marriage to Cole.

The central characters are surrounded by many amusing characters, particularly Reed's pragmatic, witty secretary, played by Shirley Booth, and Reed's college room-mate, Ellen, who thoughtlessly spouts such lines as, "I always say the less women worry about the government, the better" and who thinks the Spanish Civil War was "the one where the Russians were fighting it out with the Nazis or something" (20-22).

The play itself has a conventional three-act, well-made play structure. Kanin felt cramped by that, but accepted it as one of the exigencies of getting a play on-stage in a period when the production of new plays was shrinking. She wrote that she had to limit the size of the cast, and contain the play within one setting, which she found difficult after writing for the screen. "With the costs of production on Broadway at an all-time peak, no writer for the theater today can afford to ignore the practical economies of simplicity [otherwise] the only hearing your play is apt to have is in an experimental theatre or in a living room with your friends as an audience" (Kanin, "Fay Kanin's Trial" 19).

Kanin was wise to make the choices she made since they enabled her to present her ideas successfully on-stage in New York and on the road. It clearly was the play, not just the glamour of Madeleine Carroll as Reed, which carried the play through one of the hottest summers in New York on record to two years on Broadway, because Carroll toured the country and was replaced in New York by Ann Harding. She made a welcome return from acting in films and the social comment in the role called up memories of her first stage hit in Glaspell's socially significant *Inheritors* in 1920.

Kanin was extremely fortunate in the public and critical response to her first play. The demanding *New Yorker* critic Wolcott Gibbs wrote, "The story is an ingenious contrivance permitting Miss Kanin simultaneously to express her political views, to handle an extremely complicated three-way love affair, and to introduce quite a bit of incidental comedy, at which, like the other members of her extensive family, she is often neat and effective" ("Goodbye, My Fancy" 52). (A number of critics commented on the "Kanin theatrical family" and the fact that her husband had produced the play and Garson Kanin and his wife Ruth Gordon came to the opening night.) Richard Watts, Jr. felt the play was superior to most Broadway comedies. His review represented the view of most of the critics: "It is almost certain to be a success and it deserves to be, because it is attractively written, admirably played and has a painless message to present about frightened liberals, college freedom of speech, and spiritual courage in the modern world. It is amusing, it is likeable, and it certainly on the side of the angels, if in a rather superficial way" ("The Brilliant Career" 153). John Chapman called the play "delightfully played and intelligently written. . . . Here is an offering which puts playgoing on an adult basis. In no department is this new hit lacking." He was one of a few critics who put his finger on the theme Kanin was pursuing, that of the education of young women, saying, "This is a forthright theme—a theme, not a message, thank goodness—and it is stated in terms of excellent comedy" ("Goodbye, My Fancy" 154). Robert Garland also noted the mature qualities of the play, calling it "an ardent, adult play with laughter on the surface and, underneath, a fierce, almost frightening call for common sense" ("Palpable New Hit" 152). Even critics who had some quibbles called the play amusing and entertaining. Several implied or stated that the theme was not wholly clarified or integrated, but nonetheless, praised the polished comedy and the excellent acting, particularly by Madeleine Carroll and Sam Wanamaker who also directed. All in all, the critical response was positive, the first-night audience gave a "spontaneous demonstration of approval of the play and players . . . something unusual in the theatre this season" (Watts 154), and lines formed at the box office. Later the play was frequently revived in summer stock, regional theatres, and university theatres. One of these revivals enabled Kanin to develop her acting career, which had taken last place to her other theatrical activities, when she played the role of Congresswoman Reed at the Pasadena Playhouse.

She was not as successful with her first collaboration with her husband as with her solo effort. *His and Hers* opened in 1954. There was positive anticipation of this comedy about playwriting, by two writers who had established themselves as witty and capable in films and onstage. The play has to do with a divorced couple who have each written the same play, sue each other for plagiarism, are awarded joint custody by a comically disinterested judge, and are forced to collaborate on the play. Not surprisingly, they realize they are in love and that their marriage was spoiled by too much emphasis on the need for success. They escape to romance in the country on the opening night of the play, without waiting to see it or the reviews. The performances by Celeste Holm and Robert Preston were excellent, the setting for the wife's apartment delightful, and Holm, in costumes by Oleg Cassini, was dazzling. Unfortunately, the play is not witty enough and there wasn't enough comedy for the stars to play. The funniest scene is in the courtroom which was described as "a novel and refreshing approach to the usual stage trial" (Chapman, " 'His and Hers' Nice, Warm Comedy" 393). The judge thinks the whole case is trivial and wants to go home to dinner. When it is revealed that the two initially discussed the idea of the play in bed, the lawyers fall into inconsequential arguments, and the judge wearily interrupts to say, "Now, where were we? Oh, yes, plaintiff and defendent were in bed [Peering over at Clem.]—talking" (46). As the trial goes on he suggests they both forget this idea and each get a new one, then "we'll all shake hands and go home and start all over again. Now how's *that* for a good idea?" (46). When the couple vow to appeal after his decision, he tells the stenographer, "Off the record. . . . Personally, I don't give a damn. Court is adjourned" (49).

The general feeling was that the Kanins had an amusing idea, but that the play did not rise to the level of *Goodbye, My Fancy*. Wolcott Gibbs said, "It is a routinely plotted piece, interspersed with small, rather limp jokes, mostly of a fairly special nature, and on the whole it is no better and no worse than a dozen like it you have seen before" ("His and Hers" 53). Still he predicted success because of the acting. Walter Kerr also felt the audiences might like the play which he described as "gracefully written," but "almost studiously unhilarious" ("His and Hers" 395). Richard Watts, Jr. had a little fun with the premise that the couple had divorced and were afraid to remarry because they might have another flop: "This, I must say, struck me as a potentially interesting complication. The idea of two loving souls being kept from each other by worry over the characteristic cruelty of drama critics seemed to me a legitimate and provocating one, containing excellent possibilities for menace." He found the play only occasionally amusing ("The Problems of Writing a Play" 396). Robert Coleman offered some consolation to Kanin: "Even the best of playwrights have failures now and then. So, if 'His and Hers' is a pedestrian work, we can remember Mrs. Kanin fondly and gratefully for 'Goodbye, My Fancy,' and wish her better luck the next time out" ("The Kanins" 395). The play was not a failure, but it did not have a long run. The excellent cast attracted audiences for only 76 performances.

Rashomon (1959), the second collaboration between Fay and Michael Kanin, was a major success. It was based on the Japanese stories by Ryunosuke Akutagawa which had been the basis of the beautiful Kurasawa film. It's Pirandellian structure and the use of a revolving stage opened up theatrical possibilities which were not possible in the limiting settings of her first two plays. The play has framing scenes which take place at the Rashomon Gate, previously an architectural wonder, now a decaying ruin where trash and corpses are deposited. A priest and a woodchopper mournfully wait out a rainstorm and discuss a court case in which they were witnesses. Their talk wakes a wig-maker whose cynicism sharply contrasts with the idealistic priest who has been disillusioned by the case. As they describe it to the curious wigmaker (who takes his hair from corpses and has a taste for lurid matter), the scene shifts to the court and then to the forest where the crimes took place. A robber and the woman he raped are the witnesses, and the voice of her murdered husband is heard through a medium. The essence of the play is that each of the witnesses gives a different, and conflicting account of what occurred, and all that can be gathered is that the woman was raped and the husband found dead. The wig-maker sneers at the dismay of the priest and the woodcutter, saying, "people see what they want to see and say what they want to hear" (52).

In the first of the two acts the three versions of the action are given. The thief says he raped the woman while the husband was tied to a tree and that the woman felt so humiliated that she begged the thief to let her samurai husband avenge his honor by fighting. In the fight, he says, he killed the husband and the woman disappeared. The woman's version is that she was totally scorned by her husband after the rape, fainted and woke to find him dead. Believing she killed him she tried to drown herself. The husband says that he saw that the thief had excited a feeling in her that he never had in their marriage, that she wanted the thief to kill the husband, but the thief was disgusted by her and cut the husband's bonds. Freed, he killed himself.

In the second act a surprise occurs because the woodcutter is forced to reveal that he saw the crime and it was entirely different from all three of these stories. In the end the rain stops, the miserable priest prepares to leave, but is held up by the discovery of an abandoned baby. The woodcutter's kindness to it causes him to regain some hope for mankind.

In 1959 critical attention was placed on the difficulty of discovering truth. But today a major interest is the characterization and treatment of the woman. In each of the versions, she is scorned for her lowly background. Because she has been raped (as was, and still is, so often the case), she is disgraced and either feels she should commit suicide or is told she should. She says that she had no existence of her own in her marriage—she tried to be worthy of her exalted husband: "The clothes I wore, he chose. I learned to walk, to talk, to hold the rice bowl as he wished. I lay at his side at night afraid to sleep so that I shouldn't waken and find it all a dream" (29). In the examination of the position of woman in marriage, the Kanins exposed the vulnerable and rigid quality of life a woman often had. Lest it be thought that this related only to the lowly position of Asian women, when the Kanins made a film version, they set it in the American West.

The critics embraced the unusual play with open arms. Praise was lavished upon the play, the stunning settings and costumes by Oliver Messel, the lighting by Jo Mielziner, and the extraordinary cast with Rod Steiger as the thief, Claire Bloom as the wife, Akim Tamiroff as the Woodcutter and Oscar Homolka as the wigmaker—a truly distinguished cast! In this time, the American theatre was dominated by realism and many critics rejoiced in this unrealistic play and setting. Brooks Atkinson wrote, "Renouncing realism, 'Rashomon' is pure art of the theatre. Out of a legend, it conjures a mood. No one need despair of a commercial theatre that can deal in elusive materials with so much delicacy, expertness and charm" ("Rashomon" 398). Robert Coleman gave an effective description of the impressive setting: "On one side of the stage are the ruins of the fabulous Rashomon Gate in Kyoto, with rain falling intermittantly on the venerable and disreputable structure. On the other, a lush jungle of bamboo and ferns mounted on a turntable that gives you the illusion of moving through a forest." He noted that the audience was spellbound by the play and concluded that "'Rashomon' spells exciting theatre. It is delicate and dynamic, sensitive and savage, packed with color, suspense and seamy wit. A triumph of stagecraft" ("Rashomon" 398). Kenneth Tynan (guest critic for the *New Yorker*) said, "I would never have guessed that an audience of Broadway first-nighters could be held by a legend set in tenth-century Japan. But 'Rashomon' held them, hard and fast" ("The Bright Side of Homocide" 81). Despite the general praise for the play, one critic found it dull, and several objected that the introduction of the baby in the concluding scene was tacked on to give a positive ending. In one of the most perceptive reviews, Brooks Atkinson analyzed the play in detail, concluding that "everything about 'Rashomon is superb." He went on to relate the success of the play to the paucity of imagination in Western theatre compared to Eastern theatre. He stated that a major hope for the future Western theatre lay in the non-realistic theatrical methods of the East, and indicated the importance of the Kanins' play in wrenching attention from naturalistic slices of life: "In case our theatre ever recovers from its preoccupation with the psychology of individuals, it will find the quintessence of theatre in the East where for generations declamation, dance and music have created images bigger than life. The disinterested, measured style of 'Rash-omon' is a bold step in the direction of pure art" ("Rashomon" 1). Recent trends in the theatre have born out his hope, and the theatricality and use of Eastern techniques in *Rashomon* was a notable step on the way.

The play enjoyed a run of 143 performances, continued to bring in praise and earnings as a movie called *The Outrage* (filmed in 1964 with another excellent cast), and to be performed in various theatres throughout the country. It is interesting to note that it was a vehicle for Western actors originally, but today provides an opportunity for Japanese actors. The Kanins' exploration of the elusiveness of truth continued to attract audiences long after the Broadway run. By 1985 Fay Kanin had seen it more than fifty times in various parts of America and in many foreign countries (Dudar 6).

The Kanins' musical *The Gay Life* opened in 1961. It was based on the several one-act plays by Arthur Schnitzler called *Anatol*. The Kanins framed these with an element designed to make it attractive to audiences: the rake Anatol, having carried on affairs with many women, determines to find a wife. He announces, "I'm finished with love; I'm going to get married" (qtd. in Nadel, "The Gay Life" 171). There were fifteen scenes, with dozens of characters dancing in and out, in which the various women in Anatol's life appeared. As in the original, the most hilarious scene occurred when he took his mistress, Mimi, to a dinner at the exclusive Sacher's restaurant, intending to break with her. She one-upped him, by ordering a huge expensive dinner and downing glass after glass of champagne, then, wrapping up a piece of squab for later, breaking with him. A poignant scene in sharp contrast to this comedy was the accidental meeting between Anatol and a former lover on Christmas Eve as she prepared to take presents home to her husband and children. The authors created a plot in which it was uncertain whether the amorous Anatol would carry through on his decision to marry Liesl and whether the sweet, innocent girl would be a lively enough companion compared to the dynamic women of various types he had known. In the end, Liesl, herself, wondered if she were too tame for Anatol, but on going to his apartment and finding yet another former lover there trying to get him back, she revealed high spirits and hot temper, knocking the other woman about and throwing china at her and the walls. With the new view of his fiancée, Anatol felt ready to marry her. The book provided opportunities for lush settings by Oliver Smith and costumes by Lucinda Ballard. Especially notable was the plot device which caused all the women in a ball scene to wear red dresses to attract Anatol, with the exception of his fiancée in blue and another woman in yellow.

The first night audience was very enthusiastic. Critics were divided about the musical. On the negative side, some described it as heavy-handed, old-fashioned, and not gay enough. On the positive side it was praised as delightful, beautiful, and constantly entertaining. John McCarten dismissed it in a very short review in which he described it as "a large portion of *Alt Wienerschnitzel* cooked by Fay and Michael Kanin." Like all the critics he praised Barbara Cook as the naive, then volatile Liesl, but concluded that the could not "counterbalance all the dead weight" ("The Gay Life" 118). Robert Coleman didn't particularly care for the musical, but thought it might be popular as, "the initial audience greeted it with explosive applause" ("'Gay Life' Just Isn't Gay Enough" 169). But a number of critics praised the production as a whole, found the book and lyrics pleasant, and predicted success. Of these, Howard Taubman presented the most detailed description of the charm and *gemuchlichheit*, saying that the scene in the famous Paprikas Cafe was the funniest and liveliest in town ("The Gay Life" 38). It seemed that no praise was enough for Oliver Smith's setting with "gracefully revolving water-fountains with real water and a dozen warm Viennese street scenes" (Kerr, "The Gay Life" 170). The play did not fulfill its authors' hopes. It ran for 113 performances which was not a disaster but not a major success. The play could be described in the same way. It is a perfectly satisfactory, cleverly constructed musical which offers great opportunity for spectacle, charm, comedy, and pathos. However, it really does not capture that peculiar subtle fascination which exists in Schnitzler's writing blending comedy and sparkle with irony and ultimate despair. Richard Watts, Jr. came the closest to analyzing this failure: "The trouble, I think, comes from the difficulty of the librettists and the production in finding the right mood for its mingling of the romantic and the cynical. The result is that it moves rather uncertainly between the two spirits" (The Amorous Life" 169).

Fay Kanin's last work for the theatre was typically inventive, challenging, and wonderfully cast. *Grind* was conceived as a film script about a bi-racial burlesque house. This was informed by anecdotes from actors like Phil Silvers who had worked in burlesque. Kanin was also drawing on her own memories of her black housekeeper "whose treasured son had come home with a white wife to encounter rejection at every turn, from his people as well as hers" (Dudar 6). Her play is set in a decaying burlesque house with recreations of burlesque sketches and dances, with the story line focusing on the difficulties of interracial romance and the rigid segregation backstage. Unfortunately, Kanin's book was not entirely successful in conveying her ideas and the lost aura of burlesque. It was also somewhat dated, as critics felt that the treatment of primitive racism in the Depression had been presented often. Harold Prince directed with verve, and the leading performers, including Ben Vereen and Stubby Kaye, delighted audiences. But that was not enough to keep the play going for more than 79 performances. Douglas Watt wrote, "There are just two things wrong with "Grind": the book and the songs" ("A Grinding Halt" 308). Clive Barnes saw many things to admire, but felt there was an "infirmity of purpose and general muddlement plaguing this ambitious, and in some ways innovative, almost despairing innovative, new musical." He remarked in closing, "Some advertisements said: 'Grind as in Bump and Grind. I think it might unfortunately be *Grind* as in teeth, or even ground" ("Too Many Bumps Spoil the 'Grind'" 309). It is unfortunate that Kanin's last ambitious effort in the theatre could not provide Vereen and the others with a truly dynamic and original vehicle. As usual, her initial idea was excellent and there were many wonderful scenes in the 1985 production.

Kanin has described her approach to writing in several interviews and in an article she wrote in 1949. In contrast to some playwrights discussed above, she did not write quickly. Like Franken, Ferber, and several other playwrights, she was highly involved in the production aspects of the plays. She has said that when she wrote her first play she wrote for a year and a half and found it the hardest work she ever had done. "The script she started out with in rehearsal, she soon discovered, was only half the job; the real work came in the four tryout weeks when she had a chance to see it played before audiences." Then she spent night after night alone in her hotel rooms in Toronto, Detroit, etc. (far from her husband and baby) rewriting and making cuts

("Milestone" n.p.). In contrast to most playwrights, Kanin enjoyed seeing the play in production and listening to the audience comments following each act. She turned these comments to good account with each of her plays. Writing when her first play had begun a second-year run, she stated that the major challenge for the playwright was to be able to cut ruthlessly, to "stop loving every word," and to be able "to deliver a new joke that's needed or a new scene or a new act under 'deadline' conditions—knowing that the days are ticking away" (Kanin, "Fay Kanin's Trial" 19). In 1985 she was still enjoying the challenge and told reporter Helen Dudar that the big payoff for her was "working with the people to make the piece come alive" (6). She was working on the musical *Grind* and, as usual, had found the process exhausting, but pleasing. She had initially written a screenplay which was rejected, then she showed the screenplay to Harold Prince with the idea of turning it into a musical. He was enthusiastic, so she spent two years rewriting. (Of course, she was doing a number of other things in that time such as writing *Friendly Fire*.) The rehearsal process was long and demanding, but as Dudar wrote, "Some writers cringe at the never-ending process of shaping musical theater. For her, the way the work evolves during performance is a joy of the job. You won't catch her sitting at home in Santa Monica writing a novel" (6). Kanin enjoyed working in the theatre in part because she had greater control than in the films. She told an interviewer that in film the writer had little to do with the final product and that the work was generally considered finished when the script was completed. In contrast, she had say-so over the casting, line changes, and other aspects of the production in the theatre, sitting in on every rehearsal and rewriting "right up until the opening night" ("Milestone" n.p.).

When she was completing *Grind* Kanin had been working in some form of theatre for fifty years. Although her output was not great compared to Rachel Crothers or Zoë Akins, she produced successful works for stage, film, and television steadily and with enthusiasm. She was able to put forth her own beliefs regarding women in American society and stand as a demonstration of the possibility of success for women in many areas of theatre. She was particularly enthusiastic about encouraging younger women playwrights and so she worked very hard for the American College Theatre Festival. She wanted women to take an equal and active role in life, and she wanted to theatre to be something more than mere escapism. She was awarded the ACLU Bill of

Rights Award in 1987, and what she said about writing for film covers her other writing as well: "Many of us felt (then and now) that there was a place for movies . . . that mirrored the world we live in, that did battle against ignorance and prejudice and poverty, against the abuses of power and privilege—a place for movies that celebrated the human spirit and touched the heart." The Executive Director of ACLU summed up Kanin's life and work when he presented her the award, saying, "Throughout her career she pushed down the barriers—not only for herself, but for her contemporaries and for generations of women who followed" ("Fay Kanin Tribute Packs Them In" n.p.).

Summary

One of the most obvious qualities of the group of playwrights discussed above is the great diversity within their writing. In the first half of the century the theatre offered opportunities for all types of plays in many different venues. Both Josephine Preston Peabody, with her poetic treatment of the Pied Piper legend, and Rida Johnson Young with her popular characterizations of Brown of Harvard and Naughty Marietta were successful in the commercial theatres. Sophie Treadwell's plays, which ranged from Expressionism to realistic social criticism, were produced by Arthur Hopkins and the Theatre Guild. Alice Gerstenberg's experimental dramas, frequently informed by Freudian psychology, were performed by the Washington Square Players, in vaudeville, in major commercial theatres in Chicago and New York, and in the little theatres she founded in Chicago. David Sievers has indicated how much the work of Gerstenberg, Treadwell, Gale, and others discussed in this section "set the stage for new psychological drama" (61). Such writers as Bella Spewack, Clare Boothe Luce, Fay Kanin, Ruth Gordon, Clare Kummer, and Mary Coyle Chase found ready reception in commercial theatres, and were often included in the best plays volumes. Their plays included musicals, satire, light comedy, drama, and fantasy which enriched the commercial theatre. Dozens of play were produced by these women and hundreds by many others— opportunities abounded.

Yet for other women the doors to success and wide production were generally closed. This is most obvious in the case of African-American women playwrights. Describing the work of Georgia Douglas Johnson, Marita Bonner and other African-American playwrights, Doris Abramson wrote,

> They wrote plays about the Black experience and experimented with language and form. Some wrote in dialect; others did not. They wrote serious plays, not for Broadway—which preferred musical revues [by black writers]—but for the "churches and lodges and halls" recommended by W.E.B. Dubois: "If it is a Negro play that will interest us and depict our life, experience, and humor, it cannot be sold to the ordinary theatrical producer, but it can be produced in our churches and lodges, and halls." (Abramson, "Angelina Weld Grimké" 9)

Again, the diversity of these plays, which were rejected by the commercial theatre and even the Federal Theatre Project, is apparent.

They were written in response to the social problems African-Americans faced in the first half of the century, and they were written in an attempt to change the characterization of blacks in the theatre. Writing in 1993, Patricia R. Schroeder pointed out,

> Transforming images of blackness is not a new project for African-Americans, as their artistic endeavors of the early twentieth century reveal. The early decades of this century saw intense upheaval in African-American life and art, as Americans of all races struggled over issues like suffrage, the anti-lynch movement, the demand for birth control information, and mass migration from the rural South to the urban North. Bearing out Amiri Baraka's contention that "for every period of social upheavel there is a corresponding artistic movement," the African-American artistic movement of the 1920s—what we now call the Harlem Renaissance—included much debate about the ways African-American artists could transform prevailing images of blackness and so attempt to alter their situations. (1-2)

These plays contributed to change through the amateur presentations they received and through their publication in journals. Many of them are worthy of production today and should receive more attention from theatre scholars. As Bernard Peterson, Jr. has observed,

> There is perhaps no bigger gap in the history of the American theatre than that represented by the omission or inadequacy of information in most standard reference books on the majority of serious or legitimate black American playwrights prior to 1950, whose works were produced in hundreds of theatres, community auditoriums, churches, schools, and halls throughout the United States and abroad from the antebellum period to World War II. (1)

These plays demand attention now in order to complete the picture of American theatre history and to alter perceptions of African-Americans which still exist on a conscious or unconscious level in the minds of whites. As Jeanne-Marie A. Miller has written, "Since white playwrights had fashioned their own truths about Blacks, it was against such distortions as these that Black playwrights militated, out of necessity, in many of their plays. Black humanity, for the most part, had to be proved to whites" (280).

Not only Blacks found difficulty in getting their works on the professional stage, of course. The perplexing quality of Gertrude Stein's plays insured that no commercial producer would be interested in presenting them, although she was successful with *Four Saints in Three Acts*. She saw few of her plays on the stage, yet this was partially because she was living in Europe and not actively pursuing production on Broadway or in the little theatres of Chicago, New York, and elsewhere. In recent years changes in theatre have increased interest in her plays and today they reach an ever-widening audience. Her plays, more than any other playwright in this section, were experimental and predicted the theatre of the future.

An important element in the plays discussed above is the contribution to the folk play movement. British plays with aristocratic characters were prevalent in the American theatre in the early part of the century, as were American imitations of them. Critics who wanted an American drama grounded in realism, hailed Lula Vollmer and Zona Gale for contributions in this area. Not only were the plays professionally produced, they became favorites with amateur groups throughout the country. Similarly, Eulalie Spence, with *Fool's Errand*, Georgia Douglas Johnson with *Plumes* and *Blue Blood*, and May Miller with *Riding the Goat* enriched the folk play movement. Through their plays, these women assisted in dislodging American theatre from the drawing room.

Directly or indirectly, too, these women contributed characterizations and themes which were informed by feminism. Much has already been said about this aspect of women's plays, but it is important to note how much feminist writing was deplored in general. There was a great fear that emancipation for women would lead to greater discontent on their part and to more divorce. Feminists were perceived as strange creatures whose ideas were perversions of normal outlooks and boded ill for society. When Zona Gale left home to travel to New York, her mother warned her against involving herself with feminists, saying, "I would let that mess of women alone!" (Derleth 100). Nevertheless, Gale wrote *Miss Lulu Bett* and other portraits of disempowered women.

The plays by women in this section made rich contributions to comedy. In an age when people are familiar with comedians such as Lily Tomlin, Roseanne Arnold, as well as many women writers of comedies such as Wendy Wasserstein, it is difficult to comprehend the idea that early in this century it was often stated, and generally accepted, that women had no sense of humor. Perhaps laughter was thought to be too vulgar for the ideal women placed upon a pedestal, above men both in morals and manners. Women playwrights helped to change that idea. Clare Kummer was so fresh, witty, and original that she was often credited with establishing a new type of comedy and audiences flocked to see her plays. The comedy in Stein's plays was not initially perceived or appreciated, but in productions today, it is an important part of the appeal for audiences. Zona Gale quietly blended comedy and the sorrows of quotidienne life in her engaging portraits of Uncle Jimmy, the neighbors in a small town, and the family which "gives" Miss Lulu Bett a roof over her head. Despite the problems addressed by African-American playwrights, even in poignant or tragic plays there are often flashes of humor as in Johnson's play of incest and rape, *Blue Blood*. Ruth Gordon created comic roles for herself and other actresses and was highly praised for the wit in her dialogue. Bella Spewack and her husband created plays in which the comedy was so intense and fast-paced that it could almost be described as surreal. Clare Boothe Luce's plays have not aged well but a reader can still laugh aloud at some of her tart witticisms. Of course, one of the most hilarious plays of the first half of the century was Mary Coyle Chase's *Harvey* in which the dialogue bubbles with laughter. From *Good Gracious, Annabelle* to *Harvey* society changed greatly, but the comedy in many of the plays written by women still holds up. Many of the comedies by these women should be performed now, and it is pleasing to note that professional producers and university theatre departments are taking a second, or perhaps a *first*, look at these comedies.

In fact, that is true of the plays in general. For example, there are new productions of Gerstenberg's *Overtones,* such as the October 1993 production by the Spectrum Stage in New York. However, her name is still unfamiliar to many, and the play was referred to as "Alice Gersten's *Overtones*" in *Theater Week* in a mention of a summer 1993 off-Broadway production of the play with Mary Dixie Carter (Mandelbaum 6). These productions indicate another problem, the tendency to produce the same play by a woman playwright over and over, without exploring the rest of her work. It is true that there was a recent production of Gerstenberg's *Alice in Wonderland*, but the many other plays she wrote which were successfully produced and which are available in collections of her plays are not performed. Similarly, the numerous plays by Sophie Treadwell and Zona Gale are ignored and only *Machinal* and *Miss Lulu Bett* are performed. The former received a sensational performance at the Royal National Theatre in London in 1993 and the latter is being produced throughout the United States in regional theatres. However, there are many more plays from *Rollo's Wild Oat* to *Years Ago* which offer excellent roles, social comment, comedy and drama and a rich diversity of styles and subject matter.

PART THREE

Martha Morton (1865?-1925)

Martha Morton (1865?-1925) achieved success with her first plays in the nineteenth century and by 1909 was referred to as both America's pioneer woman playwright and the dean of American women playwrights. In the years which followed her death little note was taken of her accomplishments as the memory of her plays blended into the mass of commercial vehicles written around the turn of the century. However, in recent years the importance of Morton's efforts to create opportunities for women as playwrights and directors has been acknowledged. Rosemary Gipson's 1982 article "Martha Morton: America's First Professional Woman Playwright" drew attention to her accomplishments and intentions. The latter were often loftier than her playwriting abilities, but she was a major figure in the history of women in the American theatre. Her greatest accomplishment was the formation of the Society of Dramatic Authors in 1907.

It is not surprising that Morton turned to writing as a young girl since she came from a family of writers. One ancestor was John Morton whose play *Box and Cox* delighted audiences for many years both in his original version and in the Gilbert and Sullivan adaptation. There were other authors who encouraged Martha and her brother Michael (who became an actor and a playwright). Morton said that her mother was the chief force in motivating her children to write. She claimed that her mother had memorized most of Shakespeare's plays and encouraged Morton to submit a short story to a journal when she was just a young girl. The magazine accepted it and paid Morton twenty-five dollars, which was quite a lot of money for the time. It was the first hint of the enormous sums she would later earn as a playwright ("Big Earnings" 153).

Morton developed her ability with dialogue in many short stories for popular magazines, fashioning them after French literature. In 1888, she turned some of this material into a play called *Helene*, but could not interest anyone in producing it. So she courageously spent her own money to produce it for one night only at the Fifth Avenue Theatre in 1888. Clara Morris, nicknamed "The Queen of Melodrama" because of her emotional style of acting, was nearing the end of her career. She found Morton's play suited her abilities and performed in it throughout the country for two years. Morton was apparently in her early twenties at this time (her birth date is uncertain) and earned the amazing sum of $50,000 for the play ("Big Earnings" 153). *Helene* is reminiscent of one of Morris' great successes, *Camille*. Set in France, it is the story of a misunderstood woman, love and sin. The plotting is heavy-handed and there are many tearful scenes (at which Morris excelled). However, there were enough obviously theatrical scenes and speeches to engage the popular audience.

Both Morris' style of acting and this type of play were beginning to be criticized as old-fashioned. When Morton sent the play to her uncle Edward Arthur Morton (also a writer and critic), he criticized it as "French trash" and advised her to forget it and write about the life she knew (Patterson 130). She took his advice and wrote *The Merchant* (1891). The play won a contest sponsored by the New York *World* and the young playwright (who had submitted it under a male *nomme de plume*) received $5,000. The play was produced at the Union Square Theatre in 1891. The familiar plot has to do with a banker who speculates on the stock market, a villain who covets the banker's wife, financial disaster and recovery, and a happy reunion of husband and wife at the end. Although not original in story or characterization, the play was a move toward superficial realism and grounding in American subject matter rather than French. The production featured an excellent cast and both Viola Allen and Henry Miller were praised for their performances of the leading roles. Morton was noted as the author of *Helene*, and praised for comedy dealing with some standard character types, including an old-maid. This negative image of a woman surprisingly occurred in several of Morton's plays. The New York *Times* critic said the play was not dull or stupid and had some bright dialogue. He noted that the very enthusiastic audience called the author out for a curtain call ("The Merchant" 5).

Martha Morton was fortunate to catch the eye of the the popular, talented comedian William H. Crane. This actor was working to encourage American playwrights. In 1893 he appeared in the first of several plays Morton wrote for him, *Brother John*. One critic wrote that Crane was to be praised for encouraging new dramatists, but that the result was a disappointment. He described the vehicle as, "this commonplace, overwrought, and often sadly ineffective piece." He concluded that if the play succeeded it would be entirely due to Crane's comic abilities ("Brother John" 13). Morton again used the negative stereotype of a New England spinster for comic effect. The play did run in New York and Crane performed it in a number of theatres.

Considering her position as a career woman who was capable of directing plays as well as writing them, Morton's 1902 play has a surprisingly regressive point of view. *Her Lord and Master* examines the marriage of a vivacious American heiress to an English Lord for his title and position. At first she obeys all his wishes, but when her relatives arrive, according to the *New York Times* reviewer, she disregards "the express commands of her lord and master." The critic said the play was a sort of version of *The Taming of the Shrew* in which "in the end she is humbled." The male reviewer ironically took a more liberal view of marriage than the female playwright and suggested that the American ideal should be that "neither husband nor wife should rule, and that they should both be swayed by comradeship and sweet reasonableness" ("Her Lord and Master" 6).

The period after the turn of the century was one in which many stars were performing on stage and touring throughout the country. The demand for popular material was enormous and Morton and other women playwrights who could tailor their material to accepted formulae and the abilities of the actors could earn great sums. If Morton never achieved the critical success she sought, she certainly achieved monetary success. An article in *Theatre Magazine* in 1913 discussed the large royalties Morton had received for her plays. Three of her plays for Crane had earned her $250,000 and her greatests success, *The Bachelor's Romance*, acted by Sol Smith Russel, earned $250,000 ("Big Earnings of Big Plays" 153). Morton lived with her husband, Hermann Conheim, in a beautiful home near Riverside Drive where she wrote her plays. The library itself housed a collection of 3000 books (Londré, "Martha Morton" 618).

In an interview in 1906 Morton described the opportunities for playwrights and her approach to writing: "There is an almost frenzied demand for plays, especially for the conventional 'star' plays, which can be sold like potatoes. . . . If the author is enough of a juggler to combine all the characters into one grand central light, surrounding it with shadowy, transparent forms, which act the part of echoes or of a Greek chorus, he will never be without work." Morton said that when she got an idea for a play, she wrote a complete scenario then put it away until it was to be altered to fit a star. She worked on several plays at a time "to suit, star, actor and manager." However, she indicated that she wanted to move away from this commercial process: "For those who have served their apprenticeship, as I have done with others in my line, there is a duty to ourselves and to our art. We must create a national drama that shall ring with truth and life" (Frame 265-66).

Although Morton could not be said to have created such plays, she was definitely a pioneer in directing her own plays. Like Crothers, Franken, Kanin, and others who followed her, she felt that much of the work of the playwrght was accomplished after the play was written. She said that writing the play was a small part, but that the important work came in casting, furnishing the stage, and even making-up the actors and costuming them. She felt so strongly about this that she advised women who couldn't do it all to stay out of the business (Patterson 126). Her decision to direct *The Merchant* in 1891 aroused curiosity and doubts on the part of visitors to the rehearsals who were accustomed to seeing a male director. Speaking to the American Dramatist's Club in 1907 she recalled the stir she created and remembered one man who asked her if she intended to make a business of it. Feeling like "Luther before the Council of Worms," she answered, "God help me, I must! Then he put out a friendly hand and crushed my fingers into splinters and gave me the comforting assurance that a woman would have to do twice the work of a man to get one-half the credit." She noted that after that she had been treated "just as well and just as badly as a man" ("A New Society of Dramatic Authors" 85).

Ada Patterson went to observe Morton as she directed when she was writing an article about her in 1914. She gave a picture of a woman who was capable, sensitive, and knowledgeable. She described her as working in the Hudson Theatre, rehearsing not one, but two plays, one in the lobby and one on stage. Patterson noted that she managed this feat with calm and great control (129).

As earlier noted, Morton stated in an interview in 1906 that there were plenty of opportunities for women to get their plays produced. Despite their increasing numbers and their many contributions to the theatre Morton, Rida Johnson Young and other women were not admitted to the prestigious and powerful American Dramatists' Club. The club was founded by Bronson Howard in 1891 and was an important factor in establishing the copyright laws and other legal protection for playwrights. Because such men as Howard, Augustus Thomas, and others viewed the organization largely as a social club, women were not allowed to join. So in 1907 Martha Morton established The Society of Dramatic Authors. Rachel Crothers and 28 other women were part of the group, as well as one male playwright, Charles Klein. Speaking to the men of the American Dramatists' Club, when she announced the formation of the rival group, she said ironically that they should not be blamed for their sex, and that they were welcome to join: "We are not going to ostracise you because *you* are *merely* men—we invite you all!" ("A New Society" ix). In fact, almost all of them did join and Morton achieved success by the amalgamation of the two societies into one with Augustus Thomas as president and herself as vice-president. This really was a major accomplishment.

In the same year, Morton wrote *The Movers* in which she presented a critique of American society. Her characters were obsessed by the desire for pleasure and wealth, so much so that children were viewed as a drain on time and money. Typical of the period, the play was essentially realistic in its settings and costumes and some of the dialogue. In terms of playwriting, it was still a sentimentalized vision of the world with a happy ending. When asked by Patterson if she were a realist she answered that she was in a broad sense, "but realism is commonly looked upon as a synonym for ugliness. In that sense I am not a realist. There is a great deal in life besides its ugliness. I see much sunshine and beauty" (129).

Morton did make one attempt to create a more realistic and challenging view of women in America. She chose to adapt *On the Eve*, a play by the German playwright Leopold Kampf. She felt the play spoke for the changing conditions in our society in which women were beginning to think in terms of education and careers, and were demanding the vote. The play was about a Russian woman who took part in a revolutionary plot at the sacrifice of her love. Kampf's play had been banned in both Russia and Germany, but had been successfully performed in Paris and in America, in German. Morton cast the German actress, Hedwig Reicher from the previous American production as her heroine. The actress triumphed in the role, but Morton's play was attacked as hackneyed and shallow, with some critics saying she had ruined a good play with her adaptation. The critic for *The New York Times* wrote "with the exception of the first act in which to a great extent Dr. Kampf's original is retained, the play is a collection of antiquated theatrical effects." He concluded that Morton had mirrored the slaughter in the play by slaughtering the original work ("On the Eve" 9).

In 1911 Morton's vehicle *The Senator Keeps House* had been a success, and her 1896 play *A Fool of Fortune* was revived for a popular matinee in 1912. In 1915 her play *Three of Hearts* ran only twenty performances despite an excellent cast which included Blanche Yurka. The play was a typical commercial venture produced by the Shuberts on Broadway. In the interview with Patterson in 1909 Morton indicated that the public taste was improving and that it was possible to write more thoughtful, serious plays. She said, "The next play I shall write will be one about suffrage for women. It is the one thing that American women need because it will furnish them a balance. . . . Woman is going out into the world and helping to do the world's work, and adapting herself to the new condition" (128). She never wrote the play and her own technique never moved beyond the type of plays which she saw as she was growing up. Morton wrote plays which were similar to other plays of the period—no better and no worse than those written by Thomas, Belasco, Avery Hopwood and dozens of others others which are forgotten today, even as Morton's thirty-five plays are now forgotten. Her work in the theatre brought her wealth and an enviable position in the ranks of American women writers up until 1915. She will be remembered less for the individual plays as such than for the role she played in opening careers in the theatre to women and gaining acceptance from male playwrights for women writers and directors.

Alice Moore Dunbar-Nelson
(1875-1935)

Alice Moore Dunbar-Nelson (1875-1935) was not a major playwright in any sense of the word, yet her work as a newspaper writer, a playwright, and a poet were very important in the development of African-American playwriting. She was born in New Orleans to Patricia Wright Moore, a seamstress, and Joseph Moore, a Creole seaman. She was an ambitious woman who managed to get an advanced education in a period when this was very difficult for a woman, especially an African-American woman. She attended public schools in New Orleans, and finished a two-year teacher-training program at Straight University in the same city. Later she studied at Cornell and received an M.A. at the Pennsylvania School of Industrial Art. She became a teacher at the age of seventeen and spent most of her life between 1892 to 1931 teaching in high schools and universities. (Williams, "Dunbar-Nelson" 227). A determined woman, she was fired from her position as head of the English Department at Howard High School in Wilmington, Delaware for defying an order to abstain from political activity (Stein "Alice Ruth Moore Dunbar-Nelson" 247).

Dunbar-Nelson was an active writer and speaker whose work served as an inspiration to later writers. In 1895 she published *Violets and Other Tales* and in 1899 *The Goodness of St. Rocque.* Ora Williams noted the importance of her position as an African-American writer, saying, "The high quality of Dunbar Nelson's work insured that it was published in all the black and many white publications of her day; hers was one of the most consistent, secure, and independent voices of the black community" ("Dunbar Nelson" 227). Because of her position she was able to encourage other writers and give them attention in print. She stood as a model to aspiring writers, many of whom acknowledged her importance. According to Williams, "Although she is better known as a transitional figure to the writers of the Harlem Renaissance, her work influenced some of the best writers of that period" ("Dunbar-Nelson 227).

The writer was married to poet Paul Laurence Dunbar, but their marriage was filled with conflict and they separated after four years. One of the conflicts was over the type of writing an African-American should pursue. W.D. Howells, a great supporter of realism in American writing, encouraged Dunbar to write in a "Negro dialect," which she found a prostitution of his art. Her own writing assumes an extra interest since it represents "raceless writing" which many people felt would do more to advance the cause of African-Americans. Dunbar-Nelson objected to writing which involved "dialect and other stereotypical race materials" (Williams, "Dunbar-Nelson" 229). After her divorce from Dunbar, she was secretly married to Henry Arthur Callis. She then divorced him and later married a journalist, Robert J. Nelson.

Another aspect of Dunbar-Nelson's life which was of importance was her newspaper work. For many years she wrote columns for different newspapers, and in them she frequently engaged in drama criticism, actively encouraging African-American playwrights (Hull, "Introduction," *The Works of Alice Dunbar-Nelson* liii). According to Williams, "Many of these contributions were reviews or critiques of novels, poems, movies, plays, and art. The reviews are important because they reflect Dunbar-Nelson's aesthetic concepts, the breadth of her knowledge, and her importance to black literature" (232).

In 1900 Dunbar-Nelson published a one-act satire in *The Smart Set* which is an amusing depiction of the struggle between an author and his wife. It apparently relates to her own marriage to the poet Dunbar. It is interesting in that it reflects the views she wrote to him in 1895 expressing her dislike for writers who "wedge the Negro problem and social equality and long dissertations on the Negro in general into their stories" (qtd. in Williams, "Dunbar-Nelson" 229). The play is a light sketch in which the author tries to work on his book, but the wife and her mother constantly interrupt him and demand attention. Although he keeps on trying to write, he has little success. His mother-in-law talks as he writes, saying, "You, see it's just as I was saying today to Mrs. Blackwell; when John comes home in the evening, Bess and I love to sit in the library while he writes, and watch him and learn repose by keeping still." Just then, his wife tiptoes in with creaking shoes, and announces that some friends have arrived to play cards, and the author exclaims, "Thank Heavens" (238). The most surprising thing about the play for today's reader is the total lack of indication that it was written by or had anything to do with an African-American. Her later plays still have a "raceless" quality in the dialogue, but they are set in African-American homes and relate to the problems of the race.

In 1916 Dunbar-Nelson wrote an operetta for her students to perform. *An Hawaiian Idyll* gave her students an opportunity to play roles outside the usual range for African-Americans. Existing songs which gave the spirit of life in Hawaii were arranged by Etta A. Reach. This was an ambitious project with an attempt at authentic costumes designed by Agatha F. Jones and utilizing an orchestra of native Hawaiian instruments. The operetta was not directed by Dunbar-Nelson, but by Conwell Benton. It was presented as a holiday entertainment at Christmas time at the Howard High School in Wilmington, Delaware. It was not published. Again, Dunbar-Nelson was attempting to write something for her students which was beyond their immediate experience, and unrelated to the problems of African-Americans in the United States.

An early play, *Mine Eyes Have Seen*, was also written for Dunbar-Nelson's students in Wilmington. It was first produced there in 1918. It was subsequently read and acted by many groups after being published in *Crisis* the same year. It has been described as a "patriotic dramatic skit" which reflected Dunbar-Nelson's support for the war effort (Williams, "Dunbar Nelson" 231). She organized the women in nine Southern states to back the effort and speeches in the play reflect her own beliefs.

The play has to do with a young African-American called Chris who is about to be drafted into the army. Chris was raised with his sister, Lucy, and his crippled brother, Dan, in a beautiful home in the South. It was burned down by white men and the family was forced to escape to the North. He cries out his outrage at their lives and the expectation that he should go to fight: "Must I go and fight for the nation that let my father's murder go unpunished? That killed my mother—that took away my chances for making a man out of myself? Look at us—you—Dan, a shell of a man. . . . No, if others want to fight, let them. I'll claim exemption" (242).

But Dunbar-Nelson's beliefs are expressed by the characters who ultimately change his mind by appealing to his pride in his race. Lucy says, "Chris, we do need you, but your country needs you more. And, above that, your race is calling you to carry on its good name, and with that, the voice of humanity is calling to us all—we can manage without you, Chris" (248). The play ends as the several characters express pride in being African-Americans, and a passing band plays "The Battle Hymn of the Republic." Although Dunbar-Nelson had now moved to a depiction of African-Americans and their problems, the characters are not developed through a use of dialect. Because it is essentially realistic, the absence of characterization by means of the dialogue weakens the drama and creates a rather strange effect: there are African-Americans, a Jew, and an Irish woman, but they all sound very much the same with the exception of a slight attempt to depict an Irish accent. Certainly not all African-Americans speak, or spoke, in a dialect, but the fact that everyone speaks the same indicates the playwrights avoidance of one element of realism in the drama. The play is essentially a clear work of propaganda which was effective in its time, but whose message was questioned later. The treatment of African-Americans who returned from both World War I and World War II caused many people to criticize the sentiments expressed by Dunbar-Nelson in this play.

Gone White was written sometime later. It was not published and may not have been produced. It is a more ambitious play in three acts which tells of thwarted love. Allan is a very light-skinned African-American who is capable of passing for white. He wants to be an engineer, but despite his high qualifications, he can't get a job because of race prejudice. He wants marry Anna, but is unaware that his aunt has written to Anna that her dark skin is a handicap to Allan's career. Although very much in love with Allan, she sacrifices her love and gives him the false impression that she is throwing him over for a rich man. Her loveless marriage to a well-to-do man turns into a disaster. Allan passes as white, but spends his life in fear that his white wife or his employers will find out the truth.

He and Anna meet again (coincidence figures largely in the play), and he begs her to run away with him to another country. She is ready to do so, but his interfering aunt talks him into staying in his superior position and trying to get Anna to be his mistress. There are some excellent speeches in the play, one of which occurs when Anna denounces Allan and refuses his offer. It concludes,

> Your white blood and your white training and your imbibing of the Nordic ideals are showing up through your thin veil of decency. You would keep your white wife, and all that that means, for respectability's sake—but you would have a romance, a liaison with the brown woman whom you love, after dark. No Negro could stoop so low as to take on such degraded ideals of so-called racial purity. And this is the moral deterioration to which you have brought your whole race. White Man! Go on back to your white gods! Lowest and vilest of scum. White Man! Go Back. (27).

Once Anna sees what Chris has become, she is freed from his influence, and is able to begin to build a real marriage with her husband.

The play draws attention to several problems for African-Americans including prejudice in the area of employment, the feeling of inferiority imposed upon darker skinned African-Americans by those of lighter skin, and the suffering endured by African-Americans who passed as white. Dunbar-Nelson was one of the first African-Americans to create a play which explored these problems in a dramatic fashion. Hull commented on the characteristics of Dunbar-Nelson's play, saying, "Though mostly poor, the characters are decent, respectable, and above all, well-spoken. There is no dialect here, no comedy, as Dunbar-Nelson tries to live up to her call for a broader, more realistic Afro-American drama" ("Introduction," *The Works of Alice Dunbar-Nelson* l).

Dunbar-Nelson's plays were of importance chiefly in breaking ground for other playwrights who followed. Her relationship with Georgia Douglas Johnson was a significant factor in the latter's career. Perhaps most important was the fact that Dunbar-Nelson promulgated African-American playwriting in her newspaper columns. At a time when drama was developing in the predominantly black colleges, people were engaged in debate about the portrayal of the "stage Negro." By 1928, Dunbar-Nelson had changed the views she expressed earlier. In a newspaper interview it was reported that she "believes that the stage is the best medium for exploiting ourselves; that we must break away from propaganda per se and the conventional musical comedy that starts on a plantation and ends in a cabaret, and present to the American public all phases of Negro life and culture" (qtd. in Hull, "Introduction," *The Works of Alice Dunbar-Nelson* xlix). Although her actual writing for the theatre was small, Dunbar-Nelson was an important figure in the development of African-American theatre. Through reading her diary, plays, poems, and short stories we can gain an understanding of the conflicts which affected African-American writers at the turn of the century and later. Dunbar-Nelson was a courageous figure who encouraged others through her example. She encouraged women, in particular, to take a part in politics and society. In her short story "The Woman," Stein notes, "This piece decries 'this wholesale marrying of girls in their teens, this rushing into an unknown plane of life to avoid work,' and reassures readers that an independent, intelligent woman, a lawyer or a doctor, does not lose her ability to love when she gains a vocation" (249).

Anita Loos (1893?-1981)

Anita Loos (1893?-1981) wrote a number of plays which have been forgotten, but her play Gentlemen Prefer Blondes was one of the biggest hits in the history of the American theatre and is still remembered fondly. It was performed as a straight play, a musical, and two movies, one with Marilyn Monroe. In all, Loos wrote ten plays, five musicals, two hundred film scripts, four novels, and two autobiographies (Harris, "Anita Loos" 557). Although her plays were not viewed as major contributions to dramatic literature, Gigi was selected as one of the best plays of the 1951-1952 season.

Loos was born in California to Richard Beers, a producer and newspaper editor, and Minnie Ellen Smith Loos. Like her close friend of later years, Helen Hayes, Loos was put on the stage at an early age and had a distinctly unusual childhood. In need of money, her father put Loos in a touring company as Little Lord Fauntleroy. Loos really wanted to be a writer, not an actress. Her only education was in a San Francisco high school, but she read widely and had a natural gift for writing. At the age of eight she submitted a rhymed advertisement to a *St. Nicholas* magazine contest for which she won five dollars (*A Girl Like I* 33). At the age of twelve or thirteen, Loos was already writing paragraphs for the New York *Morning Telegraph*. She submitted a screenplay to the American Biograph Company under the name A. Loos and received, as Mr. Loos, a check for twenty-five dollars. Between 1912 and 1915 she submitted one hundred and five scripts, only four of which were rejected (*A Girl Like I* 71). She was often the main support for the family, so it is not surprising that she married to escape. In 1915 she married Frank Pallma, left home, and later had the marriage annulled.

Loos wrote at length about her own romantic involvements and her marriages. She was the antithesis of her most famous character, the gold-digger blonde, Lorelei Lee; from her childhood on she was involved with men who took her money, starting with her father. At the age of nineteen she married the actor turned writer, John Emerson. Throughout the years she gave him screen credits for scripts he had never touched and supported him (and his mistresses) through her enormous earnings. He spent the last eighteen years of his life in a mental institution. She and Emerson wrote several plays together and a large number of screenplays. She worked continually, traveled, and became friends with famous persons throughout the world including H.L. Mencken, Erich von Stroheim, Winston Churchill, George San-tayana, Mussolini, and James Joyce (Bienstock 34). One day Loos took a pair of scissors and bobbed her own hair. With her petite four foot eleven figure and very modern clothes, she was in sharp contrast to such playwrights as Rachel Crothers and Rida Johnson Young. Her biographer Bienstock wrote, "As one of the first women who dared to hike her hemlines and bob her hair, Loos came to epitomize the flap-pers of the 1920s" (34). But her appearance was deceiving: she was an intellectual who read Kant and other philosophers and who turned the works of the French writer Colette into pieces for the theatre. As Lau-rilyn Harris has observed, "She had a combination of brains and talent and a gift for survival that kept her busy and successful while numerous other famous writers fled from Hollywood in dismay or turned to drink out of frustration" ("Anita Loos" 557).

Loos and Emerson wrote *The Whole Town's Talking* together and enjoyed a success in New York in 1923. The play is a combination of Loo's sophisticated view of sexuality and the background material of her Hollywood experiences. As John Corbin described it, it was "an ultra-modern idea treated in the elder manner of slap-dash farce" which took a while to get going but in the second act "hit the true pace of rapid-fire situations, and the last act culminated in a scene of unlimited knockabout and uproarious hilarity" ("The Whole Town's Talking" 8). The simple story offers many opportunities for comedy. Ethel, a would-be sophisticate living in Toledo will only marry a young man, Chester, if he has had at least one affair. To win her, he brags of a romance with a famous screen star and soon the whole town is talking about it. When the star shows up in Toledo with her highly masculine fiancé, complications naturally ensue. In the end, Chester gets the girl and the star returns to Hollywood. Loos and Emerson adapted the play from a European play by Francis Arnold and Ernest Bach. Corbin praised the Americanization, and concluded, "'The Whole Town's Talking' makes its appeal frankly to the whole town. There is small scope for critical appraisal; the only question is just how infectious its humor will prove to be" (8). It was apparently infectious enough, for the play ran for 173 performances. After the Broadway run the couple rewrote the play as a silent film in 1926 and Loos wrote the dialogue for a sound version in 1931 called "Ex-Bad Boy." The play was produced in Harlem in 1929. Laura Bowman was part of the all-black cast in the Lafayette Players production (Tanner 95).

Working with Emerson, Loos next wrote *The Fall of Eve* which was produced in 1925. It was a good vehicle for Ruth Gordon's eccentric comic style. Critics paid more attention to her performance than to the script, noting generally that it was rather loosely constructed but that it provided an opportunity for Gordon to show off her skill. The plot is a complicated story of misunderstandings, a comic drunk scene, and a fight, which all arise from the jealousy of a woman concerning her husband's innocent relationship with an actress. The critic for the *New York Times* summed up the play by saying, "This is no scintillant comedy, perfected to the last detail. But its ambling course through a definite situation provides merriment, and sometimes engages the sympathies" ("The Fall of Eve" 18). The play was not as successful as their first effort, running only 48 performances.

Loos was jealous of H.L. Mencken's attraction for a "golden-haired birdbrain." While taking a train trip she observed the woman, noting that "if she happened to drop the magazine she was reading, several men jumped to retrieve it, whereas I was allowed to lug heavy suitcases from their racks" (*A Girl Like I* 265). Loos decided to satirize that type of woman who used her sexuality as a lure for wealthy men in a novel called *Gentlemen Prefer Blondes* (1925). Lorelei Lee, from Little Rock, knows what she wants, is uninhibited, and expresses herself frankly. A typical statement of hers is, "An American girl has to watch herself or she might have such a good time in Paris that she wouldn't get anywhere. I mean, kissing your hand can make a girl feel very good, but a diamond bracelet lasts forever" (*A Girl Like I* 273). Mencken pointed out that Loos' satire on his girlfriend was a real literary innovation in America, "You've made fun of sex, which has never before been done in this grand and glorious nation of ours" (*A Girl Like I* 267). The whole question of sexuality and comedy was important in Loos' work and, like Mae West, she explored the subject to great advantage. An immediate sensation, the novel was translated into many languages and went through many editions. In 1926 Loos and Emerson turned it into a play.

In the play Lorelei and her brunette girlfriend, Dorothy, travel to Paris on a ship and Lorelei meets rich men and gets something out of each of them. There is little more to be said about the story line. Brooks Atkinson summed it up by saying, "So this international shopping tour at the expense of gentlemen who understand it least, comes off on its own enjoyable terms; it is frantic and rapid, and it manages somehow to land on its feet." June Walker was praised as the upwardly mobile Lorelei, forever improving her mind and affecting incorrect but high-tone sounding phrases, while Edna Hibbard was a funny contrast as the unrefined Dorothy. As Lorelei remarked to her, "We do not have so much that is common" ("Blondes Preferred" 23). Of course the malapropisms which characterized Lorelei's speech in the novel were used verbatim in the play and delighted the audiences. The play ran for 199 performances in New York and was subsequently revived in regional theatre and abroad.

In 1947 Helen Hayes was visiting Loos while on tour in a play. Each night before she went to bed, she found pages of a play, *Blue Lounge*, Loos was writing for her. Unfortunately, she didn't think much of it. Later, with a new title of *Happy Birthday* and the interest of Oscar Hammerstein as producer, Hayes reluctantly agreed to be in it. Joshua Logan directed with little success by the time the play opened in Boston. It was a disaster in Boston. But theatrical miracles do happen, and the play was a hit in New York, ran for a year and eight months, and won Helen Hayes a Tony award (Hayes 162-63). She played a mousie librarian, Addie Bemis, who loves a bank clerk, but can't seem to get him. At a birthday party she gets drunk, dances on the dance floor and the bar, and manages to get her man. Critics and audiences were amazed to see Hayes in such a role after many successes in serious costume plays. Everyone loved the scene in which she drank and danced, and as she "became more intoxicated, the stage became darker, and the bottles lighted up one by one, glowing in brilliant colors" (Laufe, *Anatomy of a Hit* 52). A number of critics did not like the play, but admired Hayes. Robert Garland said Loos' "flights of whimsey seldom leave the ground" ("Happy Birthday" 280). Richard Watts, Jr. expressed the opinion that the writing was weak, but audiences liked seeing Hayes running wild on stage after acting Queen Victoria and Harriet Beecher Stowe ("Miss Hayes Seconds O'Neill on Pleasures of Drink" 281). Howard Barnes praised Hayes, but speaking of the play said, "Actually her material is very shabby" ("Miss Hayes' Party" 282). And, finally, Louis Kronenberger praised Hayes, but said of the play, "It is not in the accomplished Miss Loos' best, or even second-best, manner" ("Cinderella in Newark" 282). Because of Hayes' spectacular performance, Jo Mielziner's spectacular settings, and Joshua Logan's directing, Loos had a big hit which ran for <u>242 performances</u> in the first season and was continued.

In 1949 Loos and Joseph Fields wrote the book for *Gentlemen Prefer Blondes* which had <u>music by Jule Styne</u>. Burns Mantle wrote, "The biggest musical comedy event since the openings of 'South Pacific' and 'Kiss Me Kate' was the premiere of 'Gentlemen Prefer Blondes' at the Ziegfeld. Carol Channing, playing the role of Anita Loos' Lorelei Lee, got the most enthusiastic notices of any musicomedienne of this generation, and the musical was an immense success" (*Best Plays of 1949-1950* 8). Sticking close to the original play and dialogue, the new production was enhanced by such songs as "I'm Just a Little Girl from Little Rock" and "Diamonds Are a Girl's Best Friend," dances by Agnes De Mille, and settings by Oliver Smith. The critical response was expressed succinctly by John Chapman, who said, "Everything about 'Gentlemen Prefer Blondes' is precisely right" ("'Gentlemen Prefer Blondes' Just Perfect" 198). Giving a little history of the play, Ward Morehouse wrote that Loos wrote her novel during the Coolidge administration, "The book was a best-seller of the hemisphere; the play became a hit in New York and on tour, and now 'Gentlemen Prefer Blondes' done with musical trimmings, comes along as a lively and good-looking song and dance show" ("'Blondes' a Jubilant Hit" 199). Brooks Atkinson summed up the whole gala event saying, "Every part of it is alive and abundantly entertaining. And above it all towers the blond thatch of Miss Carol Channing, who is batting her big eyes, murdering the English language and carrying the whole golden world along with her by sheer audacity. 'Gentlemen Prefer Blondes' was always funny. It is even funnier, now that the lustrous Miss Channing has taken such a strangle hold on the part" ("'Gentlemen Prefer Blondes'" 35). The role has since been played by other actresses in revivals. In January 1993, Robert Osborne reported that the musical was tentatively scheduled for a 1994 revival with yet another blonde, Madonna ("Rambling Reporter" 3).

Loos had another major success in 1951 with *Gigi*, her adaptation of the stories of Colette, whom she had met and admired in Paris. Again she had provided a perfect vehicle for a performer, this time <u>Audrey Hepburn</u>. The story is that of a young woman brought up by two famous cocottes to follow in their footsteps. They intend to have a family acquaintance, the notably wealthy and amourous Gaston Lachaille, take Gigi as his mistress. Knowing her too well, and loving her too much, he rejects her as a mistress and takes her as a wife. A notable scene was that in which the young Gigi, still wearing a sailor dress, was given instructions for her métier: she must learn to eat whole small birds, bones and all, to select a cigar for her protector, to hold her head up and walk gracefully—"a woman should float, like a swan" (32-33). Again, Loos was exploring society by examining women whose approach to life is determined wholly by the material things they can acquire through their sexuality. The two cocottes are appalled that after all their training, Gigi will not become a famous cocotte covered with the right jewels (nothing second rate!), but will become a wife.

Many critics felt that in *Gigi* and her 1959 *Cheri* Loos' was unable to convey the qualities which made Colette's provocative works attractive. Brooks Atkinson called the play "a tired stroll through the byways of an old-fashioned Paris and an old fashioned theatre" ("Gigi" 20). But critics found the play an enchanting vehicle for Hepburn and Robert Garland called the evening a "theatrical delight" ("First Non-Musical Hit of the Season" 160). The acting and the production as a whole were praised by all the critics. Despite the cool critical response to the play, itself, Burns Mantle selected it as one of the year's best and audiences loved it. It had a long run, but was unlikely to be revived because of the success of the musical film based on it with Leslie Caron, Maurice Chevalier, and other stars. It won nine academy awards, but Loos did not do the screenplay.

Loos' success with Colette led her to write a play called *Cheri* based on two of her novels. As Robert Coleman's heading indicated, "Loos' Luck Runs Out in 'Cheri'" 267). Loos' story of a young man whose mother was a cocotte and who is interested in women for the money he can get left a sour taste in the mouths of most critics. Coleman spoke of the "Loos' Parisian Zoo. They're not the kind of folk that a normal host would invite to a conventional dinner party" ("Loos' Luck" 267). Frank Aston wrote that Kim Stanley "rose above the mire" of Loos' script ("Cheri" 268). Richard Watts, Jr. called the script, "without emotion, reality, humor or dramatic irony" ("Sad Fate of Two Colette Novels" 269). Although the play was not a success, it was notable in introducing unusual material to the Broadway stage. The sexually heated story of the spoiled young man who falls in love with an older woman, marries a young wealthy one, returns to his old love to find that she is indeed old and then commits suicide was unwelcome in 1959.

In addition to the plays Loos wrote for the stage, she wrote the film scripts for notable works by other women playwrights including Ferber's *Saratoga* (1937), Luce's *The Women* (1939), considered a film classic, and Crothers' *Susan and God* (1940) and *When Ladies Meet* (1941). In her film work and her work for the stage Loos brought sophistication in subject matter, characterization of women, and dialogue. She frequently introduced unorthodox views about sexuality which reflected her own urbanity and wide reading. Her autobiographies *A Girl Like I* (1966), *Kiss Hollywood Good-by* (1974), and *Cast of Thousands* (1977) provide insight into her character and the work she did in films and theatre. She was a very high-profile, dynamic, independent woman who was frequently photographed and written up in the newspapers. Because of that, she created a image which influenced women throughout her long career. Starting with nothing but her own wits and plenty of nerve, Anita Loos created a successful career which spanned the years from 1912 until her 1974 adaptation of *Gentlemen Prefer Blondes,* as yet another musical vehicle for Carol Channing called *Lorelei.* Loos enjoyed working with other women and not the least of her accomplishments was in providing memorable roles for actresses including Helen Hayes (with whom she wrote a book about New York, *Twice Over Lightly*), Audrey Hepburn, Cathleen Nesbitt, and Marilyn Monroe.

Dorothy Heyward (1890-1961)

Dorothy Heyward (1890-1961) began writing under the name Dorothy Hartzell Kuhns, but her most important works were plays written in collaboration with Du Bose Heyward as Dorothy Heyward. These plays were notable for their South Carolina settings and the use of the local dialect. Both *Porgy* and *Mamba's Daughters* were important in the folk theatre movement in America.

Dorothy Kuhns was not born in the South, but in Worcester, Ohio. She attended the National Cathedral School in Washington, D.C. Continuing her education at Radcliffe, she studied playwriting in the famous George Pierce Baker 47 Workshop at Harvard. She also took courses in playwriting at Columbia and the University of Minnesota. She told an interviewer that she had seen only a few plays in her childhood, but "could not remember when she was not trying to write one" (Mantle, *Contemporary American Playwrights* 231).

In 1922 Kuhns was invited to the famous MacDowell Colony for Artists in Peterboro, New Hampshire (Londré "Heyward" 290). Fortunately, in that same summer DuBose Heyward was also a writer in the colony. They felt an immediate interest in each other and shared sympathies and taste which led to a happy marriage. But before that, the hopeful playwright wanted to gain experience in the theatre, so during the next year she toured in a musical as a chorus girl. In 1924, back at Harvard, Kuhns won a prize for her play *Nancy Ann*. This play was produced on Broadway that year but ran only 40 performances. In 1930 she wrote *Cinderelative* in collaboration with Dorothy De Jagers but it only ran for four performances. She wrote several other plays which were produced by amateur groups, but were never published or produced professionally. Following her marriage, Heyward persuaded her husband to give up his work as an insurance salesman and devote himself to writing. They lived in a cabin in the Great Smokies and he wrote the novel *Porgy* in 1925.

The Heywards were drawn to the theatrical possibilities of the Gullah dialect spoken by the African-Americans living in Charleston and even more strongly by those living on the adjacent islands. This patois was an exciting innovation for audiences who saw *Porgy* in 1927. The dramatization of the novel took place in a rather peculiar way. Heyward wanted to work with her husband to turn the novel into a play, but he was busy in 1926 with another novel. So, pretending to be writing a mystery story, Heyward "alone prepared a rough draft of the play, which he then helped to polish for production" (Londré "Heyward" 290). The production of *Porgy* was an important occasion in American theatre history. It could only have been produced on such a lavish scale by the Theatre Guild with its 2,500 subscribers. It was a theatrically historical event when the prestigious Theatre Guild, which had produced the greatest European authors and had scored successes with Sidney Howard's *The Silver Cord* and S.N. Behrman's *The Second Man,* produced a play by two little-known writers with a company of fifty-three African-American actors from Harlem. The Theatre Guild was praised for giving more support to American playwrights with this production as noted by Brooks Atkinson who said, "In producing it the Guild keeps the faith with its subscribers and friends who look to it for leadership, even for pioneering, in modern drama" ("Porgy" 1).

The treatment of the characters, the dialogue, and the settings raised the play above the sordid subject matter. Most people are familiar now with the story of Bess and her lover Crown, her growing love for the crippled Porgy, his murder of Crown, Bess' departure for New York with the "happy dust" peddler, Sporting Life, and the final departure of Porgy in his goat cart, headed for the "nort" to find his Bess. Audiences were excited by the steamy confrontations between Crown and Bess, the colorful aura of Catfish Row and the moonlit scene of Kittiwah Island with its palmettos. There was great theatricality in the scene in which the terrified characters sang hymns during a hurricane and Crown suddenly burst in upon them, mocking their hymns and their fear of death. The conflicting sounds of the storm, the hymns, the hand-clapping, and Crown's raucous songs about women built up to a climax as Crown again ran into the storm, ready for another bout with his "frien" God.

The atmosphere of Catfish Row is established by the colorfully painted small homes, the bright costumes on the various characters, and the sounds of the Honey Man, Peter, who chants, "Here comes de honey man. Yo' gots honey?—Yes, ma'am, I gots honey.—Yo' gots Honey in de comb?—Yes, ma'am, I gots honey in de comb.—Yo' gots honey cheap?—Yes, ma'am, my honey cheap" (10). In other scenes the dialogue contributes to the depiction of the characters. The tragic sexual dependency Bess has suffered is revealed when she encounters Crown on the island. She wants to escape him and tells him,

[Trying flattery]: Yo' know how it always been wid yo', Crown—yo' ain't neber want for a 'oman. Look at dis chest, an' look at dese arm' yo' got! Dere's plenty better-lookin' gal dan me. Yo' know how it always been wid yo'. Dese five year 'now I been yo' 'oman—yo' could kick me in de street, an' den, when yo' ready fo' me back, yo' could whistle fo' me, an' dere I was again a-lickin' yo' han'. What yo' wants wid Bess? She gettin' ole now. [She sees that her flattery has failed and she is terrified.] Dat boat goin' widout me! Lemme go! Crown, I'll come back fo' see you'. I swear to Gawd I'll come on de Friday boat. Jus' lemme go *now*! (98)

But when he puts his "hot hands" on her, she succumbs to the old passion and he hurls her into the thicket, saying triumphantly, "I knows you' ain't change'! Wid yo' an' me, it always goin' be de same. See?" (99) Crown's sexual subjugation of Bess was an innovative and important element in the play. It foreshadowed her later subjugation by Sporting Life through his "happy dust."

The production, not surprisingly, was up to the usual level of the Theatre Guild. The cast was highly praised, especially Jack Carter who was later to perform in the Federal Theatre Project "voodoo" *Macbeth*, and Rose McClendon, later co-director of the Harlem unit of the Federal Theatre Project. Cleon Throckmorton went to Charleston to study the city and based his highly praised design on actual locations. The play was directed by Rouben Mamoulian with terrific pace and a background of continual movement of adults and children. An anonymous critic for the *New York Times* described the funeral scene as one of "splendid theatrical generalship": "In the violence of the religious orgy the lights are deliberately turned down until the stage is illuminated only from the front, and the pale wall behind quickly swarms with a myriad of dancing, swirling, leaping shadows" ("Porgy" 26). The play ran for 367 performances and was chosen as one of the ten best plays of the season.

Freedley and Reeves reported the importance of the production both in terms of subject matter and in terms of opportunities for African-American actors. "*Porgy* gave American audiences their first true portrait of the southern Negro. The people of Catfish Row became real. . . . Several fine actors appeared in the Theatre Guild production including Frank Wilson, Jack Carter, Georgette Harvey, Leigh Whipper and the fine actress, Rose McClendon, who created leading parts in *In Abraham's Bosom*, *Deep River* and *Mulatto*" (596). The general opinion of white critics that the play presented a true portrait of African-Americans has been a bone of contention. However, it is clear, as the authors indicate, that *Porgy* was significant because it provided opportunities for black actors to act in plays by white playwrights, which in turn led to plays by black playwrights with black actors on Broadway: "The success of *Porgy* and *The Green Pastures* opened the stage to a thrilling spectacle, written by a Negro and played by a Negro cast, *Run, Little Chillun* (1933) by Hall Johnson" (596). These developments were immensely important in the long-delayed integration of the American stage—C.W.E. Bigsby comments ironically "It was not for nothing that Broadway was known as the 'Great White Way'" (*Twentieth Century American Drama* 238). Burns Mantle commented that the opportunity for white audiences to see so many fine black performers was a necessary proof that blacks were capable of great success on the stage (*The Best Plays of 1927-28* vii).

Audiences flocked to see the play when it toured. Brooks Atkinson reviewed the third presentation of the play in New York in 1929 "after two years of extraordinary fortunes in New York and other cities of the East and Middle West and after an interlude in London." He said that the play still had the theatrical qualities, turbulent flow of pictures, and racy comedy which he had remembered. He noted some of the moments which had moved so many audiences:

> Again, that singing over the corpse at the close of the first act and the breathless leap of supplicating shadows are breathlessly vivid. The group scenes are rich in vitality. The picnic departure, led by the Jenkins Orphanage Band in scarlet coats; the grotesque comedy of the divorce proceedings; the horror of the buzzard's silent flight; the loud antics in the palmetto jungle—are as original as anything that has come out of our theatre. The huckster, who sings amiably, "Ahm talking 'bout the food ah sell; Ahm talking 'bout steamed crabs," wanders in and out of the performance like a figure in music. On the whole, "Porgy" improves upon acquaintance. It is a folk play, not only as literature, but as theatre—a cyclorama of negro life, directed, you will remember, by a Russo-American. ("Back Comes 'Porgy'" 17)

Of course the great success of *Porgy* lead to an even greater success, *Porgy and Bess* with music by George Gershwin and lyrics by DuBose Heyward and Ira Gershwin. It was first performed in 1935 and has since been performed throughout the world in numerous revivals. As was the case with Lynn Riggs' lovely play *Green Grow the Lilacs*, once the musical *Oklahoma!* appeared, there was little interest in the straight play. So, while *Porgy and Bess* is still popular despite concerns about "racial condescension" from white liberal writers (Gottfried,

"'Porgy and Bess is Back'" 165), *Porgy* has largely disappeared from the stage. Still, it is the touching story of Porgy created by Dorothy and DuBose Heyward which has become "an American legend" (Bzowski 444) and much of their dialogue was used in the folk opera which adhered closely to the original plot. One difference can be noted in the ending. In the original there is a sense of hopelessness and despair in Porgy's exit, but the vibrancy in the final scene of the musical with the song, "I'm On My Way to the Heavenly Land" creates a sense of exultation even though Porgy's journey is hopeless.

Despite the success of the folk play and the folk opera, criticism of both are common. African-Americans have criticized the dialogue and the characters as stereotypical and have objected to the picture of African-Americans as prostitutes, drug addicts, and superstitious, child-like figures. This problem was discussed by most critics in the 1976 reviews of *Porgy and Bess*.

The same criticism was made of *Mamba's Daughters* (1939). This play was also based on a novel written by DuBose Heyward. The play took the form of a prologue and four acts set in several different locations in Charleston and the neighboring islands. It was directed by the prestigious Guthrie McClintic and starred Ethel Waters. The role of Hagar brought a great change in her career. Freedley and Reeves noted, "It was in this role that the musical revue artist, Ethel Waters, was recognized as an artist of the first rank" (596). Another singer who had an opportunity in this play to show that she could act was Alberta Hunter. Jose Ferrer was praised in the role of a sympathetic white man who tries to help Hagar.

The play is essentially the story of family love and sacrifice based on devotion. The playwrights are examining the efforts of three women for female self-actualization. Mamba and her daughter Hagar want to help Hagar's daughter to have a better life than they have had, to give her opportunities to interact with a higher class of people, and to make a career as a singer. Hagar has a beautiful voice, too, but her intelligence is not high and Mamba says repeatedly, "I ain't neber know nuttin' 'bout dat daughter of mine less I got my eye right on her" (8). Hagar is used and abused by men, both black and white, and she knows neither her father nor the father of her child, Lissa. She is a large, strong woman who has been in jail for various fights, and is finally sent to Ediwander Island to work in the fields after beating a man who wouldn't pay her for his laundry. As the years go by she gives

Mamba her wages to bring up Lissa and keep her out of trouble. All their care seems for nought when a fancy talking gambler seduces Lissa and she has an illegitimate child. But in the end the determination of Mamba and her daughters allows Lissa to achieve success and to sing on the radio from New York. Ironically, after hearing the program, Hagar is forced to kill the gambler to keep him from blackmailing Lissa and she then shoots herself.

The critics noted the effectiveness of the characterizations, the poignancy of the story, and the rural charm of the several settings. The characterization of Hagar was praised and audiences and critics loved Ethel Waters in the role. Brooks Atkinson noted the enthusiasm of the first night audience for the play and the acting, but he felt the construction of the play was a shambles. Calling many scenes "boldly and powerfully dramatic" he nevertheless concluded that the play was little more than a "ground-plan of what might have been a finely wrought drama" ("Mamba's Daughters" 6). The play ran 162 performances, toured, and returned for a run in New York. Reviewing the play after its return critics again praised the dramatic scenes, the use of music, and the acting, but criticised the structure. Theodore Strauss called it a "jerry-built play" and felt that the authors had reduced a strong theme to a poor play (10). Writing many years later, Felicia Londré called it "melodramatic and awkwardly constructed" ("Dorothy Hartzell Kuhns Heyward" 291). Despite its surprising flaws in structure, it was a major success for the Heywards. The play was revived in 1953 and although Brooks Atkinson still felt it was a "cumbersome drama with a profusion of scenes" he said, "the simple tale that Dorothy and DuBose Heyward wrote about Hagar, the heroic Negro plantation hand, contains some elementary human truths that are deeply moving." He also noted the success of the performers in the fine roles created by the Heywards. In particular he enjoyed Hagar as performed by Fredye Marshall: "Her selfless, lonely Hagar has both the purity and the power to dominate the drama and express the artless honesty of a valiant woman" ("Mamba's Daughters" 12).

Dorothy Heyward's liberal concerns and hope for tolerance were once again expressed in *South Pacific* (1943) which she wrote with Howard Rigsby. (This has no connection to the Rodgers and Hammerstein musical.) There was great anticipation on the part of critics and audiences—the play starred Canada Lee, was directed by Lee Strasberg, and had settings by Boris Aronson. Once again Heyward had a good theme but did not develop it well. The critic for *Commonweal* expressed his disappointment by saying, "It seems to me that we should have had the most timely and adult production of this year of the war. In dealing with the provocative situation of two American torpedo vic-tims, one Negro, one white, arriving on a Japanese-held island in the South Pacific . . . and in outlining the dilemma of the American Negro in this situation, the authors have presented a theme which is national in implications and must certainly be of burning interest to any citizen" ("South Pacific" 328). Most of the critics praised the intent of the playwright in examining the situation of the American black man who does not feel it is his war. Many critics praised the "sympathetic and truthful sense of what might go on in the mind of a black American," as John Chapman put it ("South Pacific Barely Misses"). Although the play was a failure, it was a serious attempt at meaningful, controversial theatre. Its chief merit was in offering the opportunity for black actors to appear in serious roles.

That was also the case in *Set My People Free* (1948). This was writ-ten by Heyward alone and was based on the true story of a failed slave revolt in Charleston led by Denmark Vesey. The view of most critics was expressed by William Hawkins who called the play "too talky for dramatic effect" ("'Set My People Free' A Historical Drama" 173). Richard Watts, Jr. was one of the few critics to encourage audiences to see the play, noting its flaws, but calling it "a provocative and almost steadily absorbing drama, admirably acted and skillfully staged" ("Carolina Slave Revolt" 174). Brooks Atkinson wrote that Heyward had had to wait seven years for production of her play, which he described as "intelligent and interesting." Like most other critics he praised the acting of Canada Lee, Juano Hernandez, William Warfield, and other black actors. He put his finger on the real importance of the play in 1948, saying,

> Since Negro actors are pretty generally confined to Negro parts on Broadway, they seldom have an opportunity to show how wide their range as actors is. Most of the parts they play are typed and conventional. If Negro players had access to as many parts as white actors have, we would be better acquainted with their versatility and could better appreciate the richness of their artistry. The opportunities in "Set My People Free" are better than most and most of the acting is magnificent. ("Heyward's Negro Drama" n.p.)

Dorothy Heyward wrote many plays, but will be remembered for *Porgy* and *Mamba's Daughters*. At a time when there were few roles at all for African-Americans on the Broadway stage, she and her husband created the memorable roles of Bess, Crown, Sporting Life, Porgy, Hagar, and Mamba which have been performed by outstanding performers including John W. Bubbles, Ethel Waters, Leontyne Price, and William Warfield. In the 1940s she continued to treat provocative subject matter and provide roles for African-Americans. Although Heyward was unable to fulfill her youthful aspirations to be a major playwright, she was important in the history of the American stage.

Zora Neale Hurston (1891-1960)

Zora Neale Hurston (1891-1960) was a flamboyant personality who achieved great fame, suffered disgrace, was forgotten, and in recent years has been rediscovered. Writing in 1978 in the *Washington Post* Jacqueline Trescott said, "Suddenly Hurston, the most prolific black woman writer of her day, a woman who died in near-obscurity and poverty 18 years ago, a woman who was only consistent in the paradox of her moods, postures and ideas, is the center of a cult" ("The Fabulous Zora Neale Hurston" F1). The past few years have seen the publication of many of Hurston's plays, novels, and short stories and the production of *Mule Bone* on Broadway in 1991.

Hurston was born in Eatonville, Florida, the first incorporated all-black town in the United States. Some sources indicate that her father was the mayor. Her education was in bits and pieces after the age of 13 because her mother, Lucy Ann Potts died and she was shunted around from relative to relative when her father, John Hurston, remarried. Then she became a wardrobe girl for a touring actress. When the troupe got to Baltimore, Hurston left and enrolled in the high school division of Morgan College. Perkins writes, "While at Morgan, she was persuaded by May Miller to attend Howard so she could study with Alain Locke and become involved in theatre and writing" (77). Hurston took courses at Howard intermittently from 1918-1924 during which time she naturally met and became friends with Georgia Douglas Johnson. She studied with Brown and Locke and expressed enthusiasm for playwriting. Here she also met Herbert Sheen whom she later married and divorced.

For Hurston a career always came before love. In 1925 she arrived in New York with "$1.50, no job, no friends, and a lot of hope" (qtd. in Howard, "Zora Neale Hurston" 134). She soon had many friends, among them a number of wealthy white women who acted as patronesses for her. She was later criticized for playing the role of a black pet to white dilettantes. Richard Wright said that she was perpetuating a minstrel image of African-Americans (Trescott F1). In her first year in New York, Hurston was recognized as a writer of merit. In the *Opportunity* competition she received second prize for her play *Color Struck* and honorable mention for *Spears*. Miller described Hurston's flamboyant reaction: "Zora loved the tall tales, loved the attention, and she walked into this room, flung a winding, bright scarf around her neck and bellowed, 'Calaaah struuuck!'" (Trescott F1)

With the help of her patronesses, Hurston received a scholarship to Barnard College in 1925. Between 1925 and 1933 she published a number of pieces of fiction and plays, but Hurston's focus was drawn to anthropology by the anthropologist Franz Boas. In 1928 she was the first black to graduate from Barnard (Perkins 77). After her graduation Hurston got a $1,400 fellowship to travel to Florida and collect African-American folklore. She went down again to collect material from Alabama and Florida from 1927 to 1931, supported by Charlotte Osgood Mason. In this same period *Ebony and Topaz* published Hurston's play *The First One* (1927). Hurston then focused intensely on succeeding as a playwright. She wrote more than twelve plays between 1930 and 1935. This notable outpouring began with a collaboration with Langston Hughes.

The idea for a play arose from a suggestion made at a party by Theresa Helburn of the Theatre Guild. She asked Hughes why no black playwrights were writing comedy. Hughes and Hurston lived near each other in boarding houses in New Jersey and had talked of working together to create a "real Negro theatre." They decided to begin by taking a folk tale Hurston had collected, and turning it into a three-act comedy (Hemenway 137). Unfortunately, what should have been a personal and artistic success ended in quarreling and a permanent break between the friends. The resulting play, *Mule Bone*, had to wait sixty years for production.

While working with Hughes, Hurston was also contributing to and writing musical revues such as *Fast and Furious*. In 1932 she wrote *The Great Day*. This, like her other musical revues, was her "attempt to bring pure black folk culture to both northern and southern audiences" (Howard "Zora Neale Hurston" 137).

Hurston worked briefly with the Federal Theatre Project in 1935, but left to accept a Guggenheim Fellowship to collect folklore in the West Indies. She was achieving success with her fiction and wrote few plays. In 1948 Hurston was arrested on a morals charge which was later dropped. Before she was cleared, the newspapers, white and black, made much of the story. Hurston felt people had let her down and even contemplated suicide (Trescott F1). She broke off relationships with her friends of many years and returned to Florida. There she lived in obscurity and poverty, only occasionally surfacing, as when she covered a trial or criticized the desegregation decision of the Supreme Court in 1954. Just before she died, she wrote to her first husband, "We struggled so hard to make our big dreams come true, didn't we? The world has gotten some benefits from us, though we had a swell time, too. We lived!" In 1959 she died in poverty and was buried in an unmarked grave in Florida (Trescott F1).

Color Struck is a play of remarkable vitality which successfully utilizes music, visual elements, and lively characterizations. The play begins on a train as flashily dressed couples from Jacksonville, Florida are on their way to St. Augustine to compete for a giant cake in the yearly cake walk competition. The couples sing and dance and argue, and are generally merry about their chances of winning as long as Emma and John dance: "There couldn't be no cake walk thout y'all. Dem shad-mouf St. Augustine coons would win dat cake and we would have tuh kill 'em all bodaciously" (91). However, Emma's jealousy seems likely to spoil the day. Hurston depicts the jealousy darker skinned African-Americans sometimes feel for lighter ones. At the party before the competition, Emma becomes furiously jealous over a light-colored woman named Effie and refuses to dance. As the scene ends, she miserably watches as John and Effie enter the competition: "Oh, them half whites, they gets everything, they gets everything everybody else wants! The men, the jobs—everything! The whole world is got a sign on it. Wanted: Light colored. Us blacks was made for cobble stones" (97). Twenty years after this scene when John returns to her, she destroys the love he kept in his heart by her jealous rage over his attention to her own dying half-white daughter. He leaves her saying, "So this is the woman I've been wearing over my heart like a rose for twenty years! She so despises her own skin that she can't believe any one else could love it!" (102).

The play was published in the journal *Fire!* in 1926. The mood of the play is mirrored in the changing settings. The charm of the train setting (with a white conductor wishing them well in the contest) and the initial merriment continue into the second scene in a large room divided by a curtain of sheets. Music is played, and the shadows of dancers are seen on the curtain. In the next scene Emma, miserable and alone, flings back the curtains to reveal a dance hall decorated with palmetto leaves and Spanish moss, with the happy couples dancing to the live orchestra around the prize cake. Emma's isolation is emphasized by her distance from the scene of happiness, especially when John and Effie win the cake. Her final despair after bearing an illegitimate child and working as a maid is reflected in the one-room shack which is the setting for the last act. The play reveals Hurston's theatrical sense and ability to write good dialogue.

The First One is summarized by Peterson as a satire on the story of Noah's curse on Ham, the biblical ancestor of the black race. "In this play, which takes place after the Flood, Ham and his family are portrayed as demonstrating many of the traits and characteristics such as ornate attire, laziness, tardiness, ability to sing and dance, and general mirthfulness, which have come to represent the black stereotype" (116). It is possible to turn the view around and say that the play shows Noah and his family engaged in greed, jealousy, and drunkeness—the very vices for which God flooded the world—and Ham represents love of nature, music, and beauty. Mrs. Shem turns Noah away from Ham in order to get his inheritance for her husband, Noah is a drunkard unworthy of God's special attention, and the whole family is haunted by the memory of dead people with their faces up floating around the ark. Although cursed and dramatically changed from white to black, Ham rises above the others, exiting with the lines "Oh, remain with your flocks and fields and vineyards, to covet, to sweat, to die and know no peace. I go to the sun" (88).

Sermon in the Valley is a monologue by a preacher with songs and responses from the congregation. It was performed with great success in Cleveland in 1931, rivived in 1934, and again as part of the Karamu Theatre Festival Week in 1949.

Fast and Furious (1931) was a musical show with sketches by Hurston, Moms Mabley, and others. Hurston wrote three comedy sketches: "The Courtroom," "The Football Game" (in which Hurston played one of the cheerleaders for a game between Howard University and Lincoln University), and "Poker Game." The last seemed to have a very amusing premise—the winner would go to heaven and the losers to hell (Peterson 116). Unfortunately, the uneven show ran only seven performances on Broadway. Hurston had more luck with revues she wrote alone including *From Sun to Sun,* later called *The Great Day* and presented as *Singing Steel* in Chicago. Audiences responded positively to the mixture of "Bahamian dances, conjure ceremonies, club scenes, work songs, and children's games" (Perkins 78). Hurston traveled the country with the revue, but did not make much money.

In 1991 the controversial Hurston was once more the subject of debate. *Mule Bone* was presented in New York. Some denounced it as stereotypical and others praised it as good entertainment. The simple plot tells of two men who fight over a woman, one hitting the other on the head with a mule bone. There is a trial, described as hilarious by many critics, then the two make up because their friendship means more than the woman. The trial scene is comical because it is almost impossible to get to the trial because of the arguments between the Methodists and the Baptists. The sprightly dialogue is enhanced by the vivid language of the provincial Florida people Hurston had studied. A typical exchange reveals the comical irrelevancies, disgressions, and lack of logic characteristic of the play:

SISTER LUCAS:	I got just as much right to testify as you is. I don't keer if I wasn't there. Any man that treats they wife as bad as you can't tell nobody else they eye is black. You clean round yo' own door before you go sweeping round other folks.
SISTER LINDSAY:	(to Nixon) Whut you doing up there testifyin'? When you done let yo' hawg root up all my p'tater patch?
NIXON:	Aw, shut up woman. You ain't had not taters for no pig to root up.
SISTER LINDSAY:	Who ain't had no taters? (to Lige) Look here, Lige, didn't I get a whole crokus sack full of tater slips from you' brother, Sam?
LIGE:	(Reluctantly) Yeah.
SISTER LINDSAY:	Course I had sweet p'taters! And if you stand up there and tell me I ain't had no p'taters, I'll be all over you just like gravy over rice. (116-117)

Howard Kissel wrote, "If the production itself is historic, so is the cast which has actors who have played a role in all the major black ensembles of the last few decades" ("Folk Comedy" 391). Clive Barnes praised those who produced the play, compared it favorably with its use of music (by Taj Mahal) and dance to Alvin Ailey's *Revelations* ("'Mule Bone' Connected to Funny Bone" 392). Linda Winer praised the production, but said, "In the larger cultural contest, "Mule Bone" has missed its real time and now feels more like a vivid work of archeology than a universal work of theatre" ("A Precious Peek" 393). Noting the first publication of the play, John Beaufort wrote, "'Mule Bone' occupies a unique place in the history of the African-American theater. [It] is thus a publishing as well as a theatrical event" ("'Mule Bone' Debuts After 60 Years" 394). He referred to the excellent edition of the play by George Houston Bass and Henry Louis Gates, Jr. It contains the most complete of several existing versions of the play, Hurston's original story, and a detailed history of the "*Mule Bone* Controversy."

Like so many other African-Americans, Hurston never really had the opportunity to develop her theatrical abilities fully. What she left is clear evidence of strong potential, and some success. Today her work is reaching a wide public and an office building in Washington, D.C. has been named for her. George C. Wolfe recently created a successful play based on three of her short stories under the title *Spunk*. The vivacious writer, so avid for life and success, has been awarded the latter long after her death.

Anne Nichols (1891-1966)

Anne Nichols (1891-1966) won a place in American theatre history through the immense, almost unbelievable success of *Abie's Irish Rose*. She spent her life working in the theatre, but most of her plays were never published. But such was the international success of her one remembered play that she deserves a place in any discussion of American women playwrights. Freedley and Reeves wrote of her,

> Regardless of the merit of her work, there is one name that is likely to be long remembered and that is Anne Nichols. She wrote a comic hodge-podge of Irish-Jewish jokes, which had sufficient sentimentality to weave the various racial elements together and made *Abie's Irish Rose* (1922). Audiences everywhere crowded in to see it, and scores of companies played it simultaneously in this country. It was performed almost everywhere in the world but it stubbornly persists in being a bad play shrewdly written to attract audiences. (586)

Anne Nichols has been praised in recent years for her "particularly active and creative" work in the theatre (Harris "Anne Nichols" 690). Born to a strict Baptist family, Nichols had little encouragement to go on the stage, but after six months of business college, at the age of sixteen, she ran away to become an actress. After appearing in some stock plays and vaudeville, she apparently absorbed enough technique to begin writing plays herself. Her first attempt was, to use a title by Kummer, a "successful calamity." She had married Henry Duffy in 1914 and wrote a vaudeville sketch her husband and herself to perform. According to Laurilyn Harris, "Her first effort, a melodramatic tear-jerker, inadvertently turned out to be funny, and audiences laughed hysterically. The delighted theatre manager offered Nichols her first important contract, launching her career as a professional playwright" (689). She wrote several plays in collaboration with other playwrights. One of the most successful was a musical comedy called *Linger Longer Letty* with A. Goodman and B. Grosman with music by Alfred Goodman. Although never published, it was produced as a vehicle for the high-kicking Charlotte Greenwood who revived it on several occasions in succeeding years. *Just Married* was written with Adelaide Matthews and produced successfully in New York, Chicago, and Cleveland. (It was the basis for three films.) None of her early plays established her reputation as a playwright, despite their success, probably because they were simply a part of the popular theatre which was being written by dozens of playwrights, female and male, in the period before movies and television. Apparently Nichols felt somewhat embittered when people said how lucky she was to have a success with her first play, *Abie's Irish Rose* when *Linger Longer Letty* and *Just Married* had been running in New York when the play opened (Harris 154).

Neither her reputation nor her work caused any producer to put on her major play, although many of them were kicking themselves later. Nichols put up her own money and eventually earned a fortune. After the success of *Abie's Irish Rose* she wrote other plays, but never hit the jackpot again. Her last years were spent traveling around keeping tab on productions of her play, making sure people didn't alter the text, ad-lib, or fail to pay royalties.

In addition to her playwriting, Nichols wrote films and acted in films between 1910 and 1912. She produced five plays for the actress Madame Simon in 1924. She also wrote two programs for radio, *Dear John* (1938-1942) and *Abie's Irish Rose* 1941). Her life was darkened by the negative comments of critics about her work over a long period of years, and the fact that nobody remembered any of her plays except *Abie's Irish Rose*. She had divorced her husband and never remarried. Her time was taken up with many lawsuits, and she felt that she was cheated out of money due her when she lost several cases. Late in her life she told Arthur Gelb, "I've always been haunted by *Abie's Irish Rose*" (40).

A typical play by Nichols was *Just Married* written with another woman playwright Adelaide Matthews. She typically collaborated on popular, formulaic comedies, often with Martha Stanley. *Just Married* is typical not only of Nichols work, but of many comedies written which appealed to the popular taste of the time. Alexander Woolcott noted the prevalence of the genre in his review: "Usually a theatrical season is not considered complete unless it can boast from fifteen to twenty of those farces which involve a good deal of getting into the wrong bedroom and considerable screaming about it, together with a liberal supply of honeymoon jokes and quite a lot of marital jealousy. It is considered best to unfold them in hotels or country houses or boats so that there will be plenty of doors to bang " ("Stencil Farce" 21). This is indeed a fair description of *Just Married*. It takes place on shipboard with a newly married couple, a shrew and her would-be roué husband, and another couple who meet in the first act, end up on the same state room (she in fluffy pink pajamas), and agree to marry in the last act after she has got rid of her unsatisfactory fiancé. Woolcott's review is by no means harsh, he simply notes that the story is predictable and talks mostly about the acting (21).

In the same year Nichols wrote a "melody drama," *Love Dreams*. It was a sentimental drama with music which told the story of a girl who becomes an actress in order to pay her crippled sister's doctor bills. It had an unhappy ending which moved the audience to tears. The critical response was generally positive, but as a part of popular culture it was not taken very seriously by anyone.

Abie's Irish Rose opened in 1922. Abramson and Harris give a detailed description of the difficulties Nichols experienced in getting her play on. She experienced rejection by producers, a law suit, and finally had to mortgage her home and produce the play herself ("Anne Nichols: $1,000,000 Playwright" 155-156). In the play a young Jewish man, Abie Levy and an Irish woman, Rose Mary Murphy are secretly married by a Methodist clergyman. In order to deceive, then pacify their fathers (both their mothers died at birth), they assume false identities and try to keep the fathers apart. They are also married twice again, once by a Rabbi and once by a Catholic priest. Many of the critics made reference to the "Jewish Montague" and the "Irish Capulet."

It is rarely noted that there is only one character who is to be laughed at because he is Irish, but there are three characters laughed at because they are Jewish, and they are onstage most of the time. In one exchange Solomon, Abie's father, says, "I want grandchildren—dozens of them." To which Cohen responds, "Right away you talk wholesale" (573).

The initial reviews were nothing out of the ordinary. Some critics dismissed it as popular claptrap or summer fun, others found it quite amusing. Writing in the *New York Times*, William B. Chase remarked on the all-star cast, noted that Nichols had directed the play herself, told the story, and indicated that the audience was very pleased, first "laughing uproariously" and then responding gravely to the sentimental speeches between the priest and the rabbi. He found it amusing and hoped it would run (Chase, "'Abie's Irish Rose' Funny" 22). The critic for *Theatre Magazine* said it was "thoroughly unpretentious and it is visibly preposterous, but it is nevertheless extremely diverting" (qtd. in Hewitt 342). On the whole the critics did not write "money reviews" and the audiences were small. Nevertheless, Nichols kept it open, and

within a couple of months it became clear that she had a major success.

During the five year run many critics wrote attacks on the play. This
was a period in which George Jean Nathan, Robert Benchley, Stark
Young, Kenneth Macgowan and others were attempting to raise the
taste of theatre audiences by encouraging new serious playwrights. So
when writers like Augustus Thomas had successful plays, they tended
to give them very negative reviews. Obviously, Nichols' run-away success was a red flag to these critics. Robert Littell, critic for the *New
Republic,* assuming that his readers would *not* have seen the play, took
a different tack. He went to see it "determined to catch the secret of
Abie's success." He noted that much of the first act was funny and
bore, at times, a resemblance to life, but he was baffled by the audience
which simply roared all the time, except when the priest and rabbi
spoke about all people going to the same place. He found their
speeches embarrassingly sentimental, and wrote, "this hasty bathos and
insincerity, makes one profoundly uncomfortable. All the more
because all one's neighbors seem to like it" ("Abie's Irish Rose" 98).

After seeing the whole play Littell concluded that there was no
secret for the popularity of the play and described the elements of what
would now be called popular culture. The chief impact of the play was
to make everyone in the audience feel happy and warm, there is no
villain, everyone is likable. "The Jews are made fun of, their persons on
the stage are lovable caricatures, they wear skull-caps, eat ham and
don't care for Christmas trees." But he perceptively notes an important
element, "they are never insulted. Patrick Murphy is furious, but he
never calls Levy either Yid, Kike, or Sheeny, which is what he would
do in real life" (99). Finally, Littell notes the fact that, "Nothing succeeds like success. People will go to see Abie's Irish Rose because it has
been running three years, because all their friends have seen it, if for
no other reason" (99).

A recent bibliographer, Kathleen G. Klein, concurs in the description of the appeal to popular taste which Nichols used in this and
other plays: "The varieties of farcical complications which either separate lovers and honeymooners or inadvertently join complete strangers
are reused from one play to the next. Mistaken identities, improbable
coincidences, quarreling lovers, ticket mix-ups, and unimportant but
closely guarded secrets fill each work ("Anne Nichols" 257).

There is no mystery as to why the play should have achieved a fair run in the theatre—everything that Littell and Klein describe would lead to that. What is mysterious is why it ran for five years, was then revived twice in New York and was performed throughout the country and in many foreign countries. Surprisingly, the play was even a big success in Berlin in 1928! A report stated, "Berliners say that they never saw anything so funny and that they now can understand the long American run" ("Berlin Likes 'Irish Rose'" 24) As the author of *Extraordinary Popular Delusions and the Madness of Crowds* makes clear throughout his book, some things inexplicably become the vogue and because they become the vogue, everyone wants to share in the experience (Mackay xx). In the book *S.R.O.* the long-running plays from the American theatre are published, and many of them are very poor plays. No one can really explain why Booth Tarkington's *The Man From Home* (1909) should have run six years, or why *Lightnin'*, by Winchell Smith and Frank Bacon (1918), should have run 1,291 performances in New York and run on the tour until Bacon, its lead, died. Even less understandable is the urge of audiences to go to see Christie's *The Mouse-trap* for over thirty years! A major part of the answer is simply that it became the thing to do, and so people did it.

Ann Nichols' plays are good examples of popular culture which amused audiences in the early part of the century. In time much of the audience for that type of play turned to movies and to television. Contemporary sit-coms rely on the same type of broad humor, stereotypical jokes, and laughter at ethnic types. (In fact, in the 1970s *Abie's Irish Rose* was the basis for a television sit-com, *Bridget Loves Bernie*.) But in Nichols' life-time the audience was still oriented toward the theatre, and in her comedies she successfully appealed to the populace and made a fortune doing so. Klein summed up her work by saying, "In her various theatrical activities, Nichols seldom varied from the trite limits of the well-made farce; nevertheless, her popular success indicates a clear awareness of the public taste and a smooth, competent ability to meet it" (257-58).

Mae West (1892?-1980)

Mae West (1892?-1980) created an unforgettable persona through the roles she wrote for herself. Her plays challenged accepted ideas, particularly about sex, provoked the law, and introduced a new type of comedy. Largely dismissed in her lifetime, only in recent years have her plays been considered seriously by critics and scholars.

She was born in Brooklyn to John "Battling Jack" West, a former prize-fighter and Mathilda Doegler West, an emigrant from Germany who had earned her living as a corset model. West had little education, but her environment and her inheritance gave her the abilities to achieve what she wanted in her personal life and in the theatre. When she was seven she began her career on an amateur night in Brooklyn, and went on to vaudeville and the legitimate stage. Her boxer father taught her physical exercises which she used all her life to keep her figure. She was highly concerned about her health, did not drink or smoke, and followed a careful diet. In 1911, she married Frank Wallace, an actor with whom she had created a vaudeville act; however the marriage swiftly broke up and the act was dissolved. She did not bother to divorce him until 1942.

In the years in which West was performing in vaudeville she often visited Harlem, at first for fun, and then because she had formed friendships with the African-American performers whose dances she had introduced her performances. When she turned to legitimate theatre and film, she was one of the first white performers to write roles for African-Americans and insist that African-Americans play them. Louis Armstrong said that he got his first movie break when West went to the head of Paramount and "told them they'd better hire me or else" (Haddad-Garcia 63).

Not only did West further the opportunities for African-Americans, she opposed repression and constraint in many other ways. She said, "I always fought for the underdog. I thought white men had had it their own way too long, and should stop exploitin' women and blacks and gays.... I knew black people from the beginning, so I realized they weren't stereotypes; they were people like me" (Haddad-Garcia 64). Of course, "America's Sex Goddess," as she was named by the press, pushed hardest at the constraints on sexuality. She both reveled in sex in her plays and made fun of it. Her first play was called *Sex* (1926). As

Daniel Nadon has written, her plays include "infidelity, beauty contests, sexual addiction, prostitution, homosexuality, and interracial
affairs. All of these issues were used to condemn the puritanical views
of sexuality existing in society and echoed in theatrical criticism" (12).
In the late twenties and early thirties, West was very much involved in
the theatre, but in 1932 she moved to films and became the highest
paid performer in Hollywood—some say in the world. In the forties she
wrote another play, *Catherine Was Great,* and then toured Las Vegas
and elsewhere in an act in which she was surrounded by virile young
men, black and white. From 1954 until her death she lived with a
much younger man from her act, Paul Novak. In her eighties she
appeared in *Myra Breckenridge* and *Sextette* which she co-authored. In
all of her plays and movies she played an extension of herself and was
still playing the role late in life. As Gerald Clarke observed: "Mae
West is her own best invention, and no one believes in it or enjoys it
more than she herself" ("At 84 Mae West Is Still Mae West" 65).

A close analysis of all of her plays is not necessary to understand
their appeal and the critical response; it was nearly the same for all.
The critics wrote that some elements of the playwriting were often
effective, though poor on the whole, but her acting was superb. When
asked why she didn't try to write some other types of characters to act,
she responded with incredulity: why would she want to act anyone
other than herself, she asked, when everyone wants to be Mae West.
She frequently noted with accuracy that she had more imitators than
anybody. Certainly audiences loved her; in a review in 1928 Percy
Hammond commented that she was more popular with fans than Lynn
Fontanne or Eva Le Gallienne ("The Rewards of Virtue" n.p.). On
opening nights the clamourous fans always insisted on a curtain speech
from the witty Mae West. In 1931, after appearing in the title role in
The Constant Sinner, West told an appreciative audience (presumably
with a wiggle to her hips and her tongue in cheek), "I'm not like Babe
Gordon, I'm more the home girl type." The critic commented drily,
"She did not confirm, however, reports that she would act next year
for the Children's Theatre in 'Snow White and the Seven Dwarfs'"
(J.B., "Mae West in New Scarlet Role" n.p.). West's plots were weak,
but her dialogue was hilarious. She was famous for her ad-libs which
were often incorporated into scripts. Two of her frequently quoted
lines were, "When I'm good, I'm very good, but when I'm bad, I'm better" and "Is that a gun in your pocket, or are you just glad to see me?"

Her style of repartee alienated many critics and audiences members, but on the whole was an attractive part of her persona which drew audiences to see her year after year.

It was obvious by her choice of title for her first play that West was challenging the established mores. In 1926, *Sex* was not a term used in polite society, and the newspapers would not run ads for the play. Nevertheless, after the opening in New London, Connecticut (with an audience so small that West asked all 85 to come down front where she could see them), the play drew audiences by word of mouth. The audiences for her first plays were largely male—sailors in New London—and very responsive. When *Sex* opened on Broadway the crowds were so large that the prices were tripled. After the forty-first week of performances, West was the victim of a clean-up campaign forwarded by the Society for the Supression of Vice. There was a trial in which West denied that the play was immoral, but she lost. The plot had to do with a prostitute from Canada who falls in love with a young society man, and whose family opposes the match. She, like many a scarlet woman before her, sacrifices her love and follows the fleet.

The critics were not mild in their response. The critic for the *Herald Tribune* said, "Never in a long experience of the theatre have we met with a set of characters so depraved—and so dull" (C.B.D. "Sex Wins High Mark for Depravity, Dullness" n.p.) The *World* called it "a play cheap in conception, gaudy in interpretation and occasionally explicit to the point of nausea" (W.R. "More Spring Drama" n.p.). But an anonymous critic was daring enough to point out that despite the vulgarity, the play was often amusing and that the cabaret scene in Trinidad was filled with effective color and movement. He noted that the writing "ranges from the undeniably adroit to the unbelievably inept" ("Sex" n.p.).

While West was appearing in *Sex*, her next play *The Drag* was being performed in New Jersey. She was warned that it was not safe to bring it into New York. Her plays became the focus of an anti-smut campaign waged by the Society for the Suppression of Vice, there was a trial, and she was fined $500 and sentenced to ten days in jail.

The Drag (1927) was a contrived drama involving a number of homosexuals and their love affairs, plus a scene in which forty men dressed as women, danced and sang. West later wrote, "It was the oddest party every produced on an American stage during a serious drama" (*Goodness Had Nothing to Do With It* 95). The play is a landmark because although homosexuality was still regarded as a perversion, it treated the homosexuals sympathetically (Nadon 6).

Although she complained about the bed and the clothes she was forced to wear in jail, West never lost her sense of humor. Always a reformer and always active, she wrote an article about prison life, calling attention to the hardships of women, and she wrote another play. In a typical generous gesture, she donated the $1000 for the article to the prison library.

Diamond Lil (1928) was West's best play. Percy Hammond, noting that West, now out of jail, was enjoying the "comforts of respectability" called the play one of the hits of the season. He praised her satirical style and noted the crowded auditorium ("The Rewards of Virtue" n.p.). Many of the critics applauded the realism of the piece and the recreation of a former period. Richard Lockridge said the plot had to do with the white slave traffic and a detective disguised as a Salvation Army man and called it hopelessly weak. Noting that some critics had objected to West walking across the stage in a see-through negligee and changing clothes in view of the audience, he pointed out that it really was more amusing than shocking: she was "in an amply protective and very funny corset" which carried him back to the Bowery of thirty years earlier" ("Mae West" n.p.). Several critics said the play was fun and, if one were prepared to overlook the "almost Elizabethan" attitude toward sex, very enjoyable. J.H. wrote, "She was very low-key, tough, and effective in the leading role. The play was improbable and melodramatic, but the whole was done with such a complete gusto, that it lived and breathed with all the garishness of a lurid lithograph seen under a flaring gas jet, and that probably is the reason it was such good fun" ("Diamond Lil" n.p.). West was achieving success with her plays and performances, and enjoying thumbing her nose at the puritans.

She successfully revived the play in 1948. At that time she was cheered by audiences and praised by critics who called her a fabulous performer. Brooks Atkinson called the play a "burlesque of sex" and said it was "about as wicked as a sophomore beer night and smoker" (qtd. in Hassencahl 918). Other critics, too, felt the play laughed at sex, rather than promoting it. John Chapman said the play had been a spoof even when it first opened, but that now it was even funnier. He praised West's performance, but got in a sly dig by calling her, "The

most gifted female impersonator since Julian Eltinge" ("Same Old
Mae" 369).

West capitalized on her success with the first run of *Diamond Lil* by
presenting *Pleasure Man* in the same year. Comparing the play to *The
Drag*, Nadon writes that the two play are very similar:

> The main character of each play is a sexually promiscuous male, ruthless and
> unfeeling, who batters a cast-off lover. . . . The cast [of the former] includes five
> female impersonators, as West was insistent on dealing with the theme of
> homosexuality, if only in a sub-plot. One of the female impersonators is a major
> character, by the name of Paradise. This tough and vulgar drag queen, a sort of
> gay old whore with a heart of gold, provides the humor of the play. (7)

Not surprisingly, the critics attacked the play fiercely. Robert Littell
referred to the fact that the cast had been arrested and then released
to continue the performances, and said the audience should have been
arrested for laughing and applauding the play which was "full of the
revolting innuendo of perversion" and "showed men in women's
clothes dressing and undressing." He noted that there were some
mildly amusing characters and local color of the backstage of a
vaudeville house, but that it was all "smeared with such filth as cannot
be described" ("They Don't Come Any Dirtier" n.p.). Indicating the
outlooks of the time, an anonymous critic for the *Brooklyn Eagle* wrote,
"There is practically no story—just a collection of vaudeville turns.
One or two of the female impersonators were not bad. But if they must
be on the stage, one is enough in any bill. At the Biltmore there were
entirely too many for comfort" ("Mae West Again" n.p.). Even those
who loathed the theme and the vulgarity of the script observed that
the lines were laugh-getters and that hundreds of people were turned
away from the theatre with police required to keep the large crowds in
order.

West toured her plays on the road, reveled in her fame and fortune,
and gave outrageous interviews. She always claimed she didn't know
what all the fuss was about—she never used any four-letter words and
never appeared nude. Her next play divided the critics about its merits
more than her previous ones. *The Constant Sinner* (1931) was high-
class production with settings in Times Square, a Riverside Drive
apartment and Harlem. Howard Barnes said it was a "good piece of
tough and frequently convincing realism which was interrupted continually with stupidly suggestive lines and situations" ("Mae West's

Play" n.p.). Critics praised West as the sexually voracious Babe Gordon who was (amazingly for this period) married to an African-American boxer. The play provided acting opportunities for many African-American actors and George Givot as the boxer was not only praised, but Percy Hammond said he was in the league of actors in the Theatre Guild. He quoted one of the many funny lines in the play spoken by West (playing a woman who moved from gambler lovers to drug peddlers and racketeers), "When I opened my door this morning five of them fell in. I wouldn't have minded but two of them were dead" ("Is There No Flit" n.p.). Despite the usual objections to the "vile speech" there was praise for the interesting characterizations, the fine supporting cast, and the effective settings moved swiftly on Rollo Wayne's revolving stage. West had another hit which introduced unusual subject matter, African-American performers, authentic locations, and a daring reality of subject matter, despite the weakness of the plot. One woman critic, Wilella Waldorf, noted with approval the "generally shocking idea of presenting Harlem scenes with negroes," regretted that there were no songs by Mae West, and praised the supporting cast. One of the most interesting responses to the play came from a critic with very high standards, Joseph Wood Krutch. He had gone anticipating the worst, but was surprised by the play and her performance. In a lengthy analysis he expressed the view that the play was as "dramatically sound and intellectually as respectable as a play like Belasco's 'Lulu Belle' which ran for a year in one of our temples of art." He said the play was superior to many on Broadway because it was not "dull with that discouraging, anemic dullness characteristic of half the respectable plays produced on Broadway." He joked that if anyone would shout, "they ain't done right by our Mae, I, for one will whistle and stamp my feet" ("In Defense of Mae West" 344).

West moved to the movies where she was a dazzling success, and only in 1944 did she write another play. *Catherine Was Great* was another success, though hardly shocking as her earlier plays had been. As Catherine she was surrounded by a mob of handsome, tall, muscle men as her Imperial Guard. West did not disappoint the audience with the curtain speech. She remarked, "Catherine had 300 lovers. I did the best I could in two hours" ("New Play in Manhattan" n.p.). Critics said the play was poor stuff, much worse than *Diamond Lil*. The expensive play was produced by Mike Todd with gorgeous settings by Howard Bay.

As Deborah H. Holdstein has commented "[West's] contributions to American culture are immeasurable, yet—perhaps because her outrageous persona commands so much attention—her written work is virtually unrecognized. . . . She deserves to be acknowledged as a creative and successful comic playwright" (367). That her playwriting technique never was fully developed was a great misfortune. In his review of *The Constant Sinner*, Arthur Pollock wrote, "Other playwrights write of these characters with more polish, but not such effect of reality. If Miss West would take a shrewd collaborator the result might be amazing" ("The Constant Sinner" n.p.). Behind the vulgar façade, West had an excellent mind and great wit. In challenging the limits of the theatre, she was a pioneer in her time.

Dorothy Parker (1893-1967)

Dorothy Parker (1893-1967) co-authored three full-length plays, a one-act, many screen-plays, and contributed to other theatrical works. She is remembered more for her witty poetry than for her plays. However, her strong connection with the theatre and with film, her reputation as a devastating theatre critic with high standards, and her involvement with many theatre projects earned her a place in the history of the American theatre.

Parker was born to a Jewish father, Henry Rothschild, and a Scottish mother, Eliza A. Marston Rothschild. Born in New Jersey, where her parents were vacationing, Parker was raised in New York. She was always keenly aware of her Jewish heritage, and of the anti-Semitism in society. She had an ambivalent attitude toward her heritage, as towards most things. She chose to use her first husband's name rather than the Jewish name Rothschild and felt concerned about being known as a Jew. On the other hand, she was extremely angered by a comment made by George S. Kaufman at an Algonquin Circle Round Table lunch. Some joking remarks were made about Jews and he pretended to take umbrage, remarking, "I shall now walk to the door, and I hope that Mrs. Parker will walk out with me half-way" (Meade 85).

As an adult, Parker recalled her childhood as "unpleasant and stifling." She never felt close to her siblings and when her mother died, her father married a Roman Catholic who sent Parker to the Blessed Sacrament Convent in New York (Holditch 716). Parker's only formal education beyond that was Miss Dana's School in New Jersey, from which she graduated in 1911. Although many young women were attending college at this time, Parker joined the work force. At eighteen she was precocious and adventuresome. In 1912 she began working at *Vogue* writing advertising copy and then moved to *Vanity Fair* where she became the drama critic in 1919. Although she was a discerning critic, like her friends George S. Kaufman, Alexander Woolcott, and Robert Benchley, she often indulged in such vicious satirical commentary on the productions that there were complaints. In one review she wrote that Katharine Hepburn "ran the gamut of emotions from A to B" (Teichman, *Kaufman* 68) and in another dismissed a play by saying, "*House Beautiful* is the play lousy." After one year she was fired as drama critic. She wrote poems, fiction, and reviews for several journals and established a reputation as a writer with intelligence, wit, and an understanding of the social changes taking place. Her stories often featured women of various classes, and ranged from the tragic story of a prostitute ("Big Blonde") to a satirical portrait of an idle rich woman ("From the Diary of a New York Lady"). She was particularly adept at capturing the aura of the Jazz Age in her portraits of foolish young women and men. In the twenties she spent much of her time with her friends in the Algonquin Hotel and her witticisms became known throughout the city. In 1925 Harold Ross founded *The New Yorker* and invited her to contribute. She wrote for it off and on for the rest of her life, reviewing books and plays (when Robert Benchley was on vacation) in her distinctive barbed style.

Although Parker's career flourished and she published a best selling collection of poems, her personal life was troubled. In 1917 she had married Edward Pond Parker II, but she was notoriously unfaithful to her conservative Wall Street broker husband and in 1928 they were divorced. Parker had a weakness for men who took advantage of her, had many casual affairs, and as a result of one quite openly had an abortion. She attempted suicide so many times that Benchley quipped, "Dottie, if you don't stop this sort of thing, you'll make yourself sick" (Keats 104). Benchley and her other friends affected an amused reaction, but in fact were seriously concerned about her depression and her alcoholism. She consulted a psychiatrist briefly, but received little benefit. Despite her intelligence and success, in marked contrast to such friends as Lillian Hellman and Ruth Gordon, she suffered from low self-esteem. She had many affairs with married men and was highly attracted to blonde, young homosexuals. She first lived with Alan Campbell, then married him on their way to Hollywood in 1934. She believed him to be a homosexual, and frequently insulted him in public by calling him a "pansy" or a "fairy" and deriding his acting as effeminate. When they were married, he was twenty-nine and she was forty. He put up with her abuse, cooked and cleaned when they couldn't afford help, and co-authored many scripts with her. Their lives together were nightmarish: they were divorced in 1947 but remarried in 1950. It was supposed by many of their friends that his death in 1963 was a suicide. Their work together, however, was quite productive. Most notable were the many screenplays they co-authored including *A Star is Born* (1937) and scenes and dialogue for Lillian Hellman's adaptation of *The Little Foxes* (1941).

Parker could be charming or absolutely disgusting in her behavior. Both sides were displayed in stage depictions based on her. In 1932 a charming picture of her was created by her friend George Oppenheimer in *Here Today* in which she was portrayed as Mary Hilliard, "lady playwright and one of America's quickest wits" (Keats 163). Ruth Gordon successfully portrayed Parker, and later went on to write her own play, *Over Twenty-One* in which she again acted the role of a delightful character based on Parker. In response to these plays, Parker commented that she "wanted to write her autobriography but was afraid that if she did George Oppenheimer and Ruth Gordon would sue her for plagiarism" (Keats 164). In contrast, she was portrayed as a rather ridiculous character in Kaufman and Hart's *Merrily We Roll Along*. In her later life Parker became embittered and turned against George S. Kaufman and Robert Benchley, and sneered at the Algonquin Circle. She spoke bitterly of the execution of Sacco and Vanzetti, the failure of leftist politics, her own contempt citation by the House Un-American Activities Committee and subsequent blacklisting (Holditch 714). Although such friends as Lillian Hellman supported her and encouraged her to work, she wrote little, saying in 1962, "I read my verse now and I ain't funny. I haven't been funny for twenty years" (qtd. in Israel 24). Her earlier writing, however, still attracted readers and several attempts were made to dramatize her short stories. Three short stories were dramatized for television in the fifties with Margaret Leighton and Patrick O'Neal. They were well received and she received $3,200 for the project. Haila Stoddard, who had been responsible for the successful *The Thurber Carnival* created a production with stories and verses accompanied by Vincent Youman's songs. Parker flatly rejected the script. Her last connection with the theatre was the ill-fated *Candide* for which she wrote one lyric.

The first play on which Parker worked was initially entitled *Soft Music*. She was inspired to write a play in 1924 by her recent separation from her husband and the domestic difficulties of Robert Benchley. Her play has a very simple storyline—so much so that one might have thought it appropriate for a one-act play. When she brought it to Elmer Rice, her prospective co-author, he described it as, "a simple tale of a suburban householder who, bedeviled by a sweetly dominating wife and an insufferable brat, finds solace in the companionship of a neighbor, a former chorus girl; but habit and convention are too strong, and the spark flickers out" (qtd. in Meade 126). The play has been described as "a love letter to Robert Benchley, who had helped her to wrench free of a dying marriage" (Meade 127).

The central characters are Ed Graham, whose wife refuses to let him smoke his pipe or play his mandolin, and Belle Sheridan, a former chorus girl whose playboy husband carries on with other women. Mrs. Sheridan bears a strong resemblance to the nagging, domineering Mrs. Zero in Rice's successful play *The Adding Machine*. In the first act she complains about her husband and ridicules him in the presence of her rich sister, who has come for a visit. In the second act Belle argues with her husband, who spends most of his time in New York, and when he leaves has a scene with Ed, who brings his mandolin. This scene in which they play piano and mandolin and sing, ultimately kiss and decide to run away together was noted as the best in the play. In the last act Belle arrives in the Graham house with her suitcase, but Ed is not courageous enough to leave his family and suburbia and accompany her to New York. However, the play ends on a bright note because she is free of her indifferent husband and Ed seems to be going to take control of his household.

Critics found the play thin, but some noted its quiet charm. Noting that some "fine material" went into the play and that it took a "certain courage" to write the low-key depiction of drab people, Stark Young nevertheless concluded that "this piece seemed only too often to drag. Where there are almost whole acts without anything happening except conversation it is highly necessary that this conversation be not left to lie as it falls." Like other critics, he praised the naive love scene: "The scene where Ed Graham and this new friend of his are at the piano and sing an old song was done to perfection by Mr. Spottswood and Wanda Lyon, and to rounds of discerning applause from the audience" ("Suburban Harmonies" 23). The mild little play ran for only 24 performances.

Parker's own reaction to the play after it closed was to send a telegram to her Algonquin friends saying, "CLOSE HARMONY DID A COOL, NINETY DOLLARS AT THE MATINEE. ASK THE BOYS IN THE BACK ROOM WHAT THEY WILL HAVE" (Keats 103). Later Parker commented about the play, "It was dull. You have my apologies" (qtd. in Keats 102).

In 1924 Parker was involved in a revue called *Round the Town*. She was well-suited for this type of work and wrote excellent lyrics. In 1931 she wrote the lyrics for songs in another revue, *Shoot the Works*. In the same year she adapted her short story *Here We Are*, which was nearly all in dialogue, into a one-act play. In 1934 she adapted her short stories as sketches for a revue *After Such Pleasures* with Edward F. Gardner. Despite her amusing pieces such as *Here We Are* and *You Were Perfectly Fine* and the presence of outstanding performers such as Shirley Booth the revue ran only 23 performances.

Parker's next venture in theatre was a play written with "a young alcoholic radio announcer" Rosser Evans (Israel 24). *The Coast of Illyria* (1949) was based on the life of Mary Lamb. It included scenes with her brother Charles Lamb and other notable nineteenth century writers who were experimenting with drugs. It was produced in Dallas by Margo Jones for a three week run. There were plans to bring the play to New York, but they never materialized and the lugubrious play was never published.

Ladies of the Corridor was written with Arnaud D'Usseau and produced in New York in 1953. Parker had great hopes for the play and was in a merry mood before it opened. It was closely based on her own experiences while living at the Volney Hotel. The play is a grim depiction of the lives of single women, mostly widows, in a good hotel in New York. The central figures are Mildred Tynan, Lulu Ames, and Mrs. Nichols. Mildred is an interesting character, rather unusual for the period. She has left her husband because he is a sadist and carried on with call girls. The horror of her marriage has caused her to become an alcoholic and at the end of the play she jumps out of the window to her death. Lulu resembles Parker in many ways: she has a spoiled little poodle, she is lonely and frightened, she has an affair with a younger man which turns sour, and she spends her days alone in her hotel room. Mrs. Nichols is based on Alan Campbell's mother and her son, Charlie, on Campbell. Parker once purposefully shocked her mother-in-law by asking her, "Where's my homo husband?" (Meade 300). Like Mrs. Nichols, Alan's mother doted on her beautiful child and invested all her interest in him. Parker depicts Charlie's mother as a selfish, ruthless woman who will even reveal her son's homosexuality to a prospective employer to keep him with her. What comedy there is in the play is supplied by a pair of women who keep their eyes on everyone else, gossip, and go to the movies. The intent of the play is to demonstrate the loneliness of the women and therefore the play is a series of scenes of unrelated action.

This is part of the problem in the play. Unlike similar plays such as *Grand Hotel* and the highly successful Ferber and Kaufman play *Dinner at Eight* there is no interaction between the characters which leads to dramatic tension and irony. Additionally, the play was a disappointment to those who expected the famous Parker wit—the play is grim, but not as grim as Parker wanted it to be. In addition to Mildred's suicide and Charlie's permanent bondage to her mother, she wanted to show Lulu miserable and lonely, sinking into the life of the ladies of the corridor. D'Usseau and the producer insisted that the play end on a more hopeful note, with Lulu maintaining her independence and still hoping for happiness. An even more significant problem was the length. In Philadelphia the play closed at 11:40, causing the critics to complain. These critics, however, praised the play on the whole, calling it "basically a meritorious play, brilliantly performed and graced with the Parker touch, however sporadic" (Israel 24). Naturally, they assumed it was still being revised and would be shortened, but the authors cut only five minutes before the New York opening. Five New York critics gave fairly positive reviews and two wrote very negative reviews. Walter Kerr felt the two writers had made their points too frequently, but felt that the direction by Harold Clurman and the performances, particularly by Edna Best and Frances Starr, were excellent. He concluded, "For all the sorrow which the play elaborately details, "The Ladies of the Corridor" has the saving grace of humor. Its quips are frequent, its movement is rapid, and—above all—its characters are stingingly vivid" ("The Ladies of the Corridor" 244). Robert Coleman felt the play never formed an effective whole and that the authors would have been wiser to "eliminate several characters and concentrate their attention on the really important ones" ("Ladies of the Corridor" 245). Brooks Atkinson said the play was less than expected from such playwrights, noted that there were good roles for the actresses and some good scenes, but that the play was loosely contrived and the playwrights "look comparatively destitute of ideas" ("Edna Best and Betty Field are Starred" 33). In a startling evaluation, George Jean Nathan called it the best play of the year (qtd. in Israel 26). His was the minority view and the depressing material was definitely not appealing to audiences, especially the single women who formed much of the Broadway matinee crowd. The play closed after 45 performances.

Parker's theatre career is a major disappointment. With her wit, her imagination, and her sympathy for marginalized people in society, she should have been able to write some memorable plays. If she had ever written with the right collaborator, perhaps she could have. As it was, she made many efforts, but found little success.

Marita Bonner (1899-1971)

Marita Bonner has been described as a forerunner of many of the African-American playwrights in the 1960s both in her technique and in her open expression of anger. Although she wrote only three plays, she was an important influence both in her own time and later. She was born in Boston and received an excellent education at Brookline High School. In 1918 she entered Radcliffe where she continued music studies and pursued an interest in writing. Her ability is indicated by the fact that she was chosen to study with the notable professor Charles Townsend Copeland, "a distinction accorded only 16 students per academic year" (Peterson 34).

After graduation in 1922, she became a high school teacher. Between 1925 and 1930 she taught in Washington, D.C. at Armstrong High School. She was fortunate to become a part of Georgia Brown Johnson's circle and to receive encouragement from her. Bonner was first encouraged to write plays by Brown whose influence is apparent in her first play *The Pot Maker* (1927). Bonner's playwriting career coincided with the time she spent in Washington where she was a member of the Krigwa Players.

In 1930 Bonner married William Almy Occomy and moved to Chicago where she raised three children. However, marriage and motherhood did not stop her writing career. From the 1920s to 1941 she was a steady contributor to *Opportunity* and *Crisis*. She won several awards for her plays, essays, short stories, and her influential reviews. Brown-Guillory notes her importance in this time, saying, "Though her plays were never produced in her lifetime, they were read and savored during the Harlem Renaissance by some of its finest artists, including Georgia Douglas Johnson, May Miller, and Langston Hughes, who would go on to see their own plays produced" (*Wines in the Wilderness* 1).

Not only were her plays influential, but an essay which she wrote was considered very avante-garde in 1925. It's title, "On Being Young—A woman—And Colored" was later echoed in the title of the play about Lorraine Hansberry, *To Be Young, Gifted, and Black*. In her essay Bonner is in revolt against the "Genteel School" and her language and theme are revolutionary. She writes of the disempowerment of a black woman in a society dominated by white and black males.

She is outraged by white friends who advise her not to be bitter, "Who have never had petty putrid insult dragged over them—drawing blood—like pebbled sand on your body where the skin is tenderest" (qtd. in Hatch and Shine 201). She prefigures the rage of the 1960s in statements of her feelings, "You long to explode and hurt everything white; friendly; unfriendly. But you know that you cannot live with a chip on your shoulder. . . . You get hard" (qtd. in Hatch and Shine 201). Joyce Flynn wrote of this essay, "Bonner expresses the dichotomy she sees between an individual's inner reality and the racial and gender roles forced upon one by society. She conveys her own sense of comparative privilege and her feeling of obligation to identify with the black poor, even when such identification heads toward entanglement 'in the seaweed of a Black Ghetto' " ("Marita Bonner Occomy" 223).

Bonner transmuted her anger into three unusual plays which maintain their interest today. *The Pot Maker* (1927) is described by Bonner as a play to be read. She has written an elaborate description of the setting and the characters to help the reader to envision them. The play is set in a small cabin with a low ceiling and smoked walls. As the play begins there are sounds from the garden of the rustling leaves and wind coming up against the house like waves. Despite the obvious poverty of the Jackson family, the house is very neat, with clean white curtains and geraniums in the window. The story is very simple: Elias Jackson feels he has been called by God to preach to his brothers and sisters, and he is about to practice his first sermon before his mother and father, his wife, Lucinda, and her lover, Lew Fox. He takes as a model the parables of Jesus, but finds difficulty in getting going because of the constant interruptions from his family. His mother says, "Jesus ain't never tol' no tales to Pharisees nor run with them either! Onliest thing He ever done was to argue with them when He met them" (6). Nevertheless, Elias begins his parable about a man who made earthenware pots and talked to them. His wife, who alternates between looking at her lover, Lew, and making sneering remarks, says, "What kinder fool was talking to pots?" (6) At the end of the sermon, Lew leaves and she gets dressed up to follow him. She tells her husband in no uncertain terms what a failure he has been as a husband: "Fools can't preach. . . . If you was any kind of man you'd get a decent job and hold it and hold your mouth shut and move me into my own house. Ain't no woman so in love with her man's mother she wants to live five years under the same roof with her like I done" (9). The play concludes with Lew drowning in the well as he sneaks up the house in the dark. Lucinda rages at Elias because he refuses to try to save him, knowing he is her lover. She rushes out to the well, he follows and both are drowned.

Within this simple framework are vivid characterizations, dramatic tension, and fine speeches and characterizations. Although influenced by Johnson, Bonner's folk play has no merriment to lighten the depiction of her suffering characters. As Brown-Guillory comments, "Refusing to romanticize the rural South, Bonner depicts the poverty, illiteracy, and moral decadence that accompany environmentally stifling conditions. On another level, Bonner addresses women who are devalued in a male-dominated society.... Though not condoning Lucinda's affair, Bonner apparently could sympathize with a woman who felt trapped and helpless in a marriage in which the male seemed oblivious to her emotional and fiancial needs" (*Wines in the Wilderness* 2).

The contrast between the woman and the man is apparent. The description of Lucinda is stark: "At once you can see she is a woman who must have sat down in the mud. It has crept into her eyes. They are dirty. It has filtered through her. Her speech is smudged. Every inch of her body, from the twitch of her eyebrow to the twitch of muscles lower down in her body is soiled" (5). In contrast, at the beginning of the play Elias feels he has been called by God and he is aware of the pride his parents feel for him. One could say that Lucinda feels that God has forgotten her existence, but Elias feels specially valued by God.

His parable is a high-point in the dialogue of the play. It tells the story of the pot-maker who makes the pots, then tells them he is going to fill them up and they mustn't spill on the ground. One says it has a crack, and the potter mends it. Warning the pots after they are filled that they mustn't fall over, even when it gets very dark, he leaves. "It kept getting darker. Bye 'n bye noises commenced. Sounded like a drove of bees had travelled up long a elephant's trunk and was setting out to sting their way out thoo the thickest part. "Wah, we's afraid," said some more pots and they spilled right over" (7). The meaning of the parable is that God wants his people to hold their heads up and "Set up and don' spill the things He give you to keep for him" (7). But when Lucinda rushes out of the house in despair, the parable comes home to Elias, and he cries, "God, God, I got a crack in me too!" (10).

The touching little play was published in *Opportunity* in 1927, but apparently not produced in the author's lifetime.

The Purple Flower was written in 1928 but could have been written recently. It's complex imagery, its surrealistic atmosphere, language, and characterization were unique in African-American literature when it was written. The setting is as vague as that of *Waiting for Godot*: "Might be here, there or anywhere—or even nowhere" (191). The time is the "Middle-of-Things-as-They-Are. (Which means the End-of-Things for some of the characters and the Beginning-of-Things for others.)" (191). The play focuses on the plight of "Us" who have worked so hard for so long to get to Somewhere and reach the Flower-of-Life-at-its-Fullest. But Us have been held back by the White Devils who sing "You stay where your are!/ We don't want you up here!/ If you come you'll be on par/ With all we hold dear" (192). The generations of Us are signified by such characters as Cornerstone, Young Us, and Finest Blood. The suffering of Us is expressed in speeches such as, "I'm blind from working—building for the White Devils in the heat of the noon-day sun and I'm weary!" (194). Sweet tells her brother that she is pursued by a White Devil, but when Finest Blood starts to go for him, Cornerstone screams, "Don't go after him son! They will kill you if you hurt him!" Finest Blood halts, but in the end Old Man says there must be a blood sacrifice so the New Man can be born: "Now bring me blood! Blood from the eyes, the ears, the whole body! Drain it off and bring me blood!" (197). Finest Blood exits saying, "White Devil! God speaks to you through me!—Hear Him!—Him! You have taken blood: there can be no other way. You will have to give blood!" The stage directions indicate that the Us listen as the curtain closes: "leaving all the Us, the White Devils, Nowhere, Somewhere, listening, listening. Is it time?" (199).

This powerful, imaginative statement has the qualities to move a reader, and would be very effective on-stage. Perkins notes that there is speculation that the play was never produced because of the "demanding technical requirements, particularly compared to the other plays written at the time" (190). In addition to the many Us who are on stage are "Sundry White Devils" who dance sometimes like men, sometimes like snakes" and there are two levels of staging. Sometimes the characters above crash down through the boards and occasionally yellow, brown, black, or yellow hands are thrust out" (191-192). As Hatch and Shine comment, "For the reader who believes that the concepts of the White Devils and Us, and the Call to Revolution have developed since the burning of Watts, *The Purple Flower*, published in *Crisis* in 1928, will be a revelation" (201).

Exit, An Illusion was published in *Crisis* in 1923. It is a non-realistic, harsh depiction of the plight of an African-American woman who can pass for white, who loves Buddy, but who is dying because of the circumstances in her life. Dot is lying in bed as the play begins, but gets up and starts to put on white make-up, telling Buddy she has a date. She clearly makes up a name, "Exit Mann" and says she has "been knowing him" all her life. As she proceeds to put on the trappings of a white woman, Buddy becomes more enraged, threatening her and Exit Mann. There is suddenly a man standing in the shadow with his back turned. "You wonder how he came there. You wonder if perhaps he has not been there all the while" (204). Buddy shoots and Dot is killed. The lights go out, then suddenly flare up revealing the room as it was at the beginning. Dot asks Buddy to say he loves her before she goes, but she dies before he wakes. His last lines reveal the ambiguity of the black male toward a woman who can pass and go out with white men, "Naw I don't love you! . . . [realizing she is dead] Oh Dot! I love you! I love you! (205). Joyce Flynn writes of the play "it ultimately appears to be about Buddy's destruction of Dot through his permanent suspicion and hatred of the white side of her mixed ancestry" (224). The depiction of the woman trapped through her inheritance and her environment has often been seen, but here it seems fresh because of the theatrical technique Bonner used.

In the *Crisis* contest of 1927 Bonner was given first place on the basis of two short stories and *The Purple Flower* and *Exit, an Illusion*. Bonner's only one other play had the provocative title of *Muddled Dream*. Unfortunately, it has been lost. Had she received productions of her plays and had they been valued more, she probably would have published it and would have written others. She was a playwright with power, imagination, and fine technique. Both her message and her style were "new and different in black women's playwriting" (Brown-Guillory 18).

Maurine Watkins (1900-1968)

Maurine Watkins (1900-1968) had her first theatrical success in 1926. Chicago caught the eye of critics and had a long run. George Jean Nathan subsequently selected the play for the first in a series of plays he would edit called *The Theatre of Today*. In his introduction he praised it as "American to the core; there is not a trace of imitativeness in it" and he predicted future successes for the playwright, saying "it discloses, unless I am badly mistaken, a talent that will go a considerable distance in the drama of the land" (viii). In the event, he was not mistaken about the high quality of the play, but Watkins did not take her talent far in the theatre; *Chicago* was her only success.

Because she contributed so few plays to the theatre, Watkins is rarely discussed by critics. Burns Mantle, writing in 1929 assumed that she would still make contributions to equal or better *Chicago*, and so he devoted several pages to her in *American Playwrights of Today*. It is interesting that he gave her so much attention in contrast to many other playwrights, including Susan Glaspell, Clare Kummer, Ben Hecht, Charles MacArthur, and S.N. Behrman who were given only a short paragraph each at the end of the book in a section called "We Have Also With Us."

Watkins was born Maurine Dallas Watkins in Louisville, Kentucky. Her family moved a fair amount so her education took place in several cities. She went to Hamilton College in Louisville, then to Butler College in Indiana where she edited the college paper (Ogden n.p.). Watkins then went to Radcliffe where she studied the classics and contemplated earning a Ph.D. in Latin and Greek.

While at Radcliffe she began writing plays and submitted one to her favorite actor, Leo Ditrichstein. He paid her a $500 advance and took her away to Chicago in 1924 to work on an adaptation of a novel he had in mind. Nothing major came of her work with the actor, so she resolved to turn to journalism. She was extraordinarily lucky as well as determined. With nothing except her college experience, she got a job as a reporter on the *Chicago Tribune* at the large salary of $50 a week. Much of her work involved murder and crime which provided her with material for *Chicago*. In particular, she covered the sensational Leopold and Loeb murder of Bobby Franks. She interviewed Leopold and Loeb in depth, turned in her interview, and two hours later they confessed so her story was a scoop. Because she showed up in a proper black dress, she was not recognized as a reporter, and was the only one allowed in to witness the funeral of Bobby Franks. According to an interviewer, Clare Ogden, "She became a specialist in murders. That was why she quit reporting." Watkins was quoted by Ogden as saying, "I got to the point where I prayed for murders. Not that you have to pray very long in vain in Chicago. But I prayed for good murders, and then I prayed that I would be sent out on murders. When I realized that I was getting a murder-story complex, I quit" (n.p.).

Deciding she needed more instruction in playwriting, Watkins went to Yale and took a course from George Pierce Baker. During the course she made a draft of *Chicago* which impressed Baker. According to Watkins he gave her 98% on it, which was the highest grade he had ever given ("Broadway's "Miss Chicago" From Kentucky" n.p.). Watkins decided to try to get the play produced in New York. Again, she was incredibly lucky: it was accepted by the first producer to whom she submitted it, and when it was produced she was stunned to find herself famous overnight (Mantle, *American Playwrights* 201-204). Asked later if she had found the opening night thrilling, after a pause, the young woman answered, "Well, no. I don't think it was. We had had a week in Atlantic City and three days in New Haven, you know. It was just sort of a big night, but not so thrilling, I think" (Ogden n.p.) Watkins was widely interviewed and seemed to have a major career ahead of her. She said she intended to write lots more plays and the future seemed very bright. One reporter wrote, "Miss Watkins, lovely and pretty as ever, is under contract to write another play for Horace Liveright about more hardboiled people, and Professor George Baker, it is said, will accept this homework for credit toward the Fine Arts degree at Yale" ("Broadway's 'Miss Chicago' From Kentucky" n.p.).

With this sort of beginning and the personal interest of Baker and Burns Mantle, it seemed likely that Watkins would have a major career in the theatre. But that was not to be, and she ended her life as a lonely recluse, writing greetings for Hallmark Cards with her mother. She she became wholly involved in religion, then in astrology. Each year she sent her agent "checks and thank-you notes for keeping interested producers away" ("'Chicago' Saga" n.p.) Within a few years of the success of *Chicago* Maurine Watkins, the vivacious, charming playwright who dazzled New York became a woman of mystery.

It is not surprising that *Chicago* made such a big impression on critics and audiences. It has a dynamic quality, it is very funny, and it is carefully structured. It tells the story of Roxie Hart, a pretty, vulgar woman (married to a "meal-ticket husband") who shoots and kills her lover when he tries to walk out on her. The short prologue to the play provides a terrific beginning: Roxie stands with a gun pointed at her lover who is going out the door. She shouts, "You damned tightwad! Like *hell* you're through! You Goddamned louse—!" and shoots him. This is great news to the newspapermen and the prosecuting attorney who soon arrive. They anticipate glorious headlines, and the attorney views this as a chance to move into defending murderesses because that's where the real money is. Roxie confesses, saying defiantly, "By God, I shot him!" Jake, the newspaperman, assures her she won't hang: "Ain't this Chicago? And gallant old Cook County never hung a woman yet!" (13)

In this and subsequent scenes, Watkins establishes an aura of corruption and violence which is treated satirically. The jail scenes present rivalry between various murderesses, a funny caricature of a sob sister called Little Mary Sunshine, and an equally amusing satire on defense lawyers with the character Billy Tyler, who doesn't care if she did it or not—he will get her off if he gets $5000 in advance. The court scenes are hilariously burlesqued, with theatrical speeches by the lawyer and pathetic pantomime by Roxie, gowned in innocent white, and supposedly pregnant. When the jury finds her innocent, she tells her husband to get lost, reveals that she isn't pregnant, and that she is booked for ten weeks in vaudeville. But her great moment with the photographers is cut short when another woman shoots and kills her lover and his wife right in the court house. Enraged, she reverts to her former self and shouts, "You God-damn bums walkin' out on me when I want to make a speech!" Jake cheers her up by saying she can get in the picture with "Machine Gun Rosie": "The Jazz-Slayer Meets the Cicero Kid! Shake hands!" When the newest murderess tries to hide her face, Jake speaks the last line, "Come on, sister, yuh gotta play ball: this is Chicago!" (110-111)

The dialogue is snappy and racy and the play has great momentum. It is unified by maintaining the focus on Roxie. She is a character similar to Woody Allen's Zelig, in her chameleon-like ability to latch on to the characteristics and language of the other characters. After seeing a religious maniac who is going to get off on a plea of insanity, she tells the sob sister, "I was mad—crazy—insane! [hastily] Not enough for the asylum, you know—over with right away" (49). When another murderess weeps about her child, Roxie gets the idea of faking pregnancy and snatches up the child's dress the woman was sewing in time for the photographs. She is hard as nails, but amusingly naive about some things. However, she learns quickly. When she blackmails her lawyer out of $100 he notes that she has learned a lot in three months (83). As Judith E. Barlow commented in her introduction to the play in 1981, Watkins

> is not only accurately and wittily spoofing reporters who turn murderers into madonnas; she is also poking fun at all people who insist on seeing women through the gauze of their own fantasies. The cold-blooded Roxie easily convinces the gentlemen of the jury that she is a poor abandoned mother-to-be who wanted nothing more out of life than to stay home and raise a family. (xxiii)

Part of the success of the play related to its accurate portrayal of the atmosphere of the notoriously corrupt city in which murder was a thrilling part of the scene and tickets for hangings were prized as much as tickets for hit plays. The sensationalism extended to vaudeville, as well, with audiences gaping with delight at a range of non-theatrical people and properties, running the range from Bonnie and Clyde's car and Sitting Bull to the sad, little father of the Dionne Quintuplets. The racy language of *Chicago* outdid that of *What Price Glory* two years earlier, but there was an oddity about it's composition. Either because she didn't know what obscenities to use, or because she didn't want to distress the typist, Watkins left blanks which were filled in by the actors and director! (*American Playwrights of Today* 204). Although the play was highly praised by critics, Nathan noted that there was some puzzlement occasioned by the originality of the script—critics with a fondness for pigeon-holing, "have had a hard time laying hold of an appropriate label. It isn't, they feel, quite satire and it isn't merely burlesque, so what is it?" He felt it was truly fresh and unique (vii). Percy Hammond praised the production, calling the play "a flighty panorama in burlesque, depicting Chicago as a merry pleasure ground for murderesses," and noting the excellent role Watkins had provided for Francine Larrimore as Roxie Hart ("'Chicago' a 'Comic Strip' Treating Burlesquely of the Illinois Crime Waves" n.p.). Burns Mantle found it one of the ten best plays of the year and included it in the 1926-27 volume.

The play was taken to London which was apparently not ready for the hard-boiled American dialogue and characters. The critics panned it, with the London *Times* critic saying that "all its persons are uniformly and continuously vile" ("London Dislikes Watkins Play" n.p.). In contrast, not only was the play originally successful in New York, it was made into a silent film in 1927 with Phyllis Haver, and was then turned into a vehicle for Ginger Rogers in the 1942 film *Roxie Hart.* Throughout the thirties people attempted to get Watkins to authorize stage revivals and to allow a musical to be based on the play. However, only a few friends knew where she was, and Sheldon Abend, head of the American Play Company, had to hire a former F.B.I. agent to track her down. He had a few phone conversations with him, but her astrological charts caused her to refuse to meet him or to allow Kander and Ebb to make a musical version for Gwen Verdon, despite letters from Verdon asking her. Then the way seemed clear when Watkins died in 1968, but her mother was just as intransigent, and only after her death was Abend able to acquire the rights. The result was a highly successful musical starring Verdon, Chita Rivera, and Jerry Orbach, although a far cry from the original play.

Returning to 1927 and the opening of *Chicago,* it would be pleasing to say that Watkins followed up her first success with another fresh and original play. However, she chose to dramatize a novel and apparently rushed it into performance. According to Burns Mantle, Watkins immediately moved to capitalize on her success, but her 1927 play *Revelry* (adapted from a novel by Samuel Hopkins Adams) was a disappointment. It had a promising subject in the corrupt Warren Harding administration and his mysterious death (this later proved a success for Lawrence and Lee with *The Gang's All Here),* but the play ran only 48 performances. In fact, it was only the public interest in her career causing a very large advance sale which allowed to it run that long. Mantle described the play as "thoroughly workmanlike" but not in a class with *Chicago.* He anticipated that she might have another success in time to add remarks about her recent success to *American Playwrights of Today* before publication in 1929, but that was not the case (202).

Revelry opened in Philadelphia where it was received as a rather lurid and talky production. Although the *New York Times* critic acknowledged that Watkins had done a reasonably good job of construction, although too much exposition was required to explain the schemes of the crooked politicians. He wrote, "It tells the sordid tale of misplaced trust and unseemly gorging at the public treasury. If the treasury were private, and the personages less conspicuous, the theme would flatten into ordinary melodrama, its luridities less lurid and its dull spots more dull" ("Dramatization of Revelry" n.p.). A failure in Philadelphia, the play was roundly panned in New York. Brooks Atkinson felt the material was very worthwhile but that Watkins' treatment was a severe failure:

> Miss Watkin's play version is a scissors and paste-pot structure of scenes. "Revelry" jumps from poker party to apartment, to Cabinet room with machine-like versatility. Choppy, disjointed, given to generalities in the dialogue, it brings none of the magic of the theatre to the sordid tale it unfolds. Dramatized with ingenuity, power, and critical perspective "Revelry" might not raise the question of its motives for a moment. In its present shabby dramatic form however, it cannot escape the suspicions of those who believe that the exploitation of such material is in bad taste. ("Opening of 'Revelry'" 37)

Watkin's only other play, *Gesture* (1926) was never produced. Watkins' theatrical career is definitely unusual: on the basis of one fine play, for a couple of years she was considered one of the most important American women playwrights. She had training as a playwright, intelligence, and personal charm yet something went wrong and she was unable to fulfill the high expectations her first play created. Walter Kerr was not the only critic to feel that the treatment of the musical was inferior to the stuff of Watkins' play ("'Chicago' Comes on Like Doomsday" 1). Watkins' play *Chicago* revealed a genuine talent and deserves to be produced in the contemporary theatre.

In a bizarre footnote to her bizarre life and career, a young man named John Elliot spent several years "on a bicycle chasing his lady love's ghost around the country." He went throughout the country looking for information about Watkins in order to write her biography. He supported himself by selling T-shirts with a picture of the playwright and arranging amateur readings of *Chicago*. He felt a mystic sort of love between the dead playwright and himself. He did uncover some interesting material about her life: "She never married, and when her father died she left Hollywood and became a recluse. She'd already made a fortune from her plays and film scripts. Then, just before she died, she went all around the country looking for worthy Greek and

Latin scholars. She'd been a classics major in college, and most of her $2 million estate was left to finance translations of Cicero and Sopho-cles and other ancient authors" ("A Roads Scholar Pedals Passionately into the Past" 1). Maurine Watkins, extraordinary life included study with George Pierce Baker, the Leopold and Loeb "Crime of the Century," a great Broadway success, rejection of the world, and Cicero and Sophocles.

Cornelia Otis Skinner (1901-1979)

Cornelia Otis Skinner (1901-1979) was in the theatre for most of her life and to her the theatre was life. She was a playwright, actress, monologist, and biographer. Skinner was the daughter of actress Maud Durbin Skinner and the famous actor Otis Skinner. Her mother left the stage after she was born, but her father toured widely and achieved great fame, particularly in *Kismet*. As a child Skinner was surrounded by members of the theatrical profession and her father wrote her long letters about his work, so it was not surprising that she wanted a theatrical career. As she lived with her mother in the city of Bryn Mawr, it was natural that she should enter Bryn Mawr College in 1918. There she participated in theatre and played Lady Macbeth. She left to study at the Sorbonne and the Jacques Copeau School. While in Paris she also studied acting with Emile Dehelly of the Comedie Francaise. Her fluent French and love of Paris was reflected in her writings about the French. She was made an *Officier* of the Academie Francaise in 1954.

Returning to the United States in 1921 she made her New York debut with her father in *Blood and Sand*. She acted a full range of plays throughout her career including *Candida*, Wycherley's *Love For Love*, Wilde's *Lady Windemere's Fan*, Somerset Maugham's *Theatre*, and S.N. Behrman's *Biography*. Two of her most successful characterizations were Emily in Lillian Hellman's *The Searching Wind* and Kate in *The Pleasure of His Company* which she wrote with Samuel Taylor in 1958. Her last performance was in *The Irregular Verb to Love* in 1964. She was married to Alden Sanford Blodgett in 1928 and had one son, Otis Skinner Blodget. Throughout her long career she also performed many one-person shows which she wrote for herself. Amazingly, she also found time to write many short stories and prose pieces which she contributed regularly to such magazines as *Vogue* and the *New Yorker*. Additionally, she wrote several books of autobiography in which she detailed her career and that of her father, a highly praised biography of Sarah Bernhardt, and other books. Her last book, a biography of playwrights Lindsey and Crouse, was published in 1976 when she was 75. Her plays and monologues reflected her broad theatrical skills, her intellectual curiosity, and her wit.

Skinner's first play *Captain Fury*, written for her father, was produced off-Broadway in 1925. She was encouraged by the production to go on writing for the stage, but she did not publish the play. In the same year she wrote and performed the first of her one-woman shows which won her great fame here and in London. There had been few female performers of this type in the American theatre. Lotte Crabtree was one, and Skinner had been influenced by seeing Ruth Draper. Skinner decided that she should utilize her wit, her enthusiasm for exploring the lives of different types of women, and her ability to switch characters very quickly with only the aid of a prop or a slight change of costume. Audiences were fascinated by her ability to convey complete depictions of many different women through her writing and her acting. She did a great deal of research for her many one-women shows which included the first one which was untitled, then *The Wives of Henry VIII* (1931), *The Empress Eugenie* (1932), *The Loves of Charles II* (1933) in which she played everything from Nell Gwynn to a duchess, *Mansion on the Hudson* (1935), and *Edna His Wife* (1938). In 1952 she wrote another one-person show called *Paris '90* which was quite popular, and also enjoyed success expanded into a book called *Elegant Wits and Grand Horizontals* (1962). In these she created the aura of *fin de siècle* Paris with its famous salons and courtesans. Although successful in New York and London with her monologues, she spent much of the time touring to small towns in America, bringing theatre to areas where people rarely saw any plays. Although many of the shows had foreign settings, throughout the years she created many portraits of American women and their various roles in society. She was a keen observer whose wit was often biting.

The Pleasure of His Company was unusual in several ways. In a period when "angry young men" plays and intense psychological studies dominated playwriting, this was a witty drawing room comedy. Burns Mantle called it "Broadway's first suavely managed drawing-room comedy in several seasons" and included it in the volume of the ten best plays of 1958-1959 (21). Another unusual element was the theme of the play, that a young woman should not rush into marriage and motherhood without experiencing life first. Secondarily, the play presents a criticism of the custom of young women of intelligence and education marrying men indifferent to art, literature, and music just because they are well-to-do and physically attractive.

Jessica Poole is about to have a big society wedding in San Francisco where she lives with her mother and step-father, Kate and Jim Dougherty. Much to their annoyance, her father Pogo Poole, an inter-

national raconteur and playboy suddenly arrives. The role was a fine
vehicle for Cyril Ritchard: "As the debonair, selfish hedonist who discovers the rewards of fatherhood late in life, Ritchard is triumphant"
(Coleman, "'Pleasure' Wise, Witty, Warm" 247). Having missed the
childhood of his daughter, he now decides to break off her engagement
in order to show her the world before she settles down. He disapproves
of the rancher fiancé with great knowledge of bulls and little else, and
Jessica's grandfather concurs. He says early in the play that he disapproves of young Roger and the wedding: "I have a grand-daughter with
wit and intelligence and a sweet love of life. She has an inquiring spirit
and an eagerness to explore, and a capacity for living that delights me.
How will she use them now: cut down in the prime of her life by marriage!" (23). To Kate's extreme irritation, he continues to develop the
theme, expressing ideas which still seemed unconventional in the
1960s. The grandfather objects to the idea of "giving her away" at the
wedding, "Why give her to somebody else to use? She hasn't begun to
use herself! She's hardly begun to know how! Let her hear her own
music, let her step to the beat of her own drummer!" (23).

Not surprisingly, Kate is fascinated by the reality of the wonderful
father she had only read about in the society columns. She tells him
how wonderful her fiancé is, but realizes he is clearly uninteresting
compared to her father. A typical exchange in the play is,

> Jessica He's terribly progressive and has all sorts of wonderful ideas about
>   selective breeding and artificial insemination and all that sort of thing.
>   He sends his semen all over the world!
> Poole You must be very proud. (47)

In addition to the exploration of Jessica's choice of husband, Poole
puzzles about his former wife, Kate (whom he once talked into standing on her head and whistling Dixie in the Place Pigalle!). When he
questions her, she is very defensive, insisting that she has a wonderful
life chiefly spent in charitable works. She admits that she doesn't have
the fun she had with him, but that she has found, "the fun of blessed
tranquillity." When he speaks with regret of the "rage to live" she once
had she says, "Don't you turn it on for me, Pogo Poole! I'm an elderly,
overweight club woman, and I like it, I like it, I like it!" (93). In the
end both Jessica's grandfather and Pogo demand that she be allowed to
see the world with her father. Jessica's view is, "Mother, all my life I've
done the expected. Just for a while, I want to wake up in the morning

wondering: what's going to happen to me today! . . . Mother, you did it all! Give me a chance!" Kate hollers, "Oh, for a gun! If I just had a gun!" (140). But in the end she must give way, and as Jessica and Poole rush out the door, she exclaims, "If ever San Francisco needed another earthquake—it's today" (145).

The response of the critics and audiences was summed up in Walter Kerr's review: "Pleasure is the word" ("The Pleasure" 248). All aspects of the play were praised, particularly the writing. Describing it as "an enormously satisfactory comedy," John McClain went on to say that "the wisecrack is subordinate to the humor emerging from situation and character. . . . The authors have approached a delicate subject with respect and honesty." He concluded, "Charge, don't lope, to the nearest ticket broker" ("Warm and Hilarious" 245). All of the critics praised the urbanity, intelligence, and hilarity of the dialogue. Brooks Atkinson wrote, "The authors write light, ironic dialogue with polish and skill, and manage now and then to quote poets and philosophers without sounding pretentious. It is a long time since the English language has been used with so much dexterity by writers interested in nothing more lethal than having a good time" ("Theatre: 'The Pleasure'" 36). Most of the critics found the subject matter agreeable and concurred with his view. But, in fact, a close analysis reveals that Skinner and Taylor had something "more lethal," perhaps even subversive in mind. When the dream of most mothers and daughters was a big wedding with an attractive, successful man, followed by motherhood, the authors posited the view that a young woman should have the opportunity to be more than a supportive wife and mother. The depiction of the mother shows what happens to a woman who moves into the conventional groove. The depiction of the daughter is unconventional: she rejects her very suitable, but entirely conventional fiancé, and goes out to see the world. In this time simply being an attractive, virile man (the young George Peppard played the role) supposedly made up for lack of sophistication and a stringently limited range of interests. The fiancé talks only of his business and is "exactly the kind who'd scrape French sauce off broiled prime beef" (Aston, "Taylor Comedy [sic] Is a Real Pleasure" 246). The authors are satirizing him and the generally accepted view of women's role in society. Kate defiantly defends her life by saying that she gives the best dinner parties in San Francisco—what else should she want? (92). The playwrights were able to put this satire in the form of a play which was not only accepted but received with open arms. Coleman noted the degree of success the playwrights had achieved: "The first act of 'The Pleasure of His Company' ran for about 56 minutes according to a clocker in the audience. Yet it seemed to us no more than 25 or 30. Now, that's the mark of a good play. Another is the fact that we, along with the rest of the first-nighters, saw the final curtain fall with regret. For here's the literate laugh hit we've been waiting for. A gem and a joy" ("'Pleasure' Wise, Witty, Warm" 247).

As the critics predicted, the play enjoyed a long run. It ran for a year on Broadway and then toured throughout America. It was subsequently made into a successful movie with Fred Astaire and Lilli Palmer.

Skinner's career as a playwright ran from 1924 to 1958 bringing her satisfaction and wealth. As an independent career woman, she informed her play with her own sense of fulfillment. Her autobiographies reflect that, too, and she became the subject of a play when Jean Kerr turned *Our Hearts Were Young and Gay* (1942) into a popular play in 1948. Both through writing and performance Skinner made a real contribution to American theatre and stood as a symbol of female achievement. As Nelda K. Balch concluded in her essay on Skinner, "Always willing to meet with admiring school girls after a performance or to chat with the townspeople brought into the host's home [on tour], she inspired many to explore a career in the theatre" (*Notable Women in the American Theatre* 796).

The stylish writing of Cornelia Otis Skinner set a high standard. The ideas and the ending of *The Pleasure of His Company* challenged the conventions and outlooks of the 1950s. Perhaps most of all, Skinner set a standard for women in the theatre. She was adept in many areas, especially depicting women for the stage. Both as writer and actor, she excelled in depicting a wide range of women from all classes. In *Edna His Wife* she depicted a woman who married for wealth rather than for love, showing her move from an appealing small-town girl to a woman who is "white haired and miserable in the luxury of a New York Penthouse" ("Edna His Wife" *Time* 33). Brooks Atkinson wrote that he had never seen such a play presented with so much talent and intelligence ("Edna His Wife" 30). He also praised her depiction of the women in *Mansion on the Hudson*, particularly Carrie Howland, "the bitter spinster of 1920, who looks with lack-lustre eyes at the ruin of her high-born existence." He concluded his review by saying that it, "discloses the increasing literary stature of the one-woman theatre. It is thoughtfully written, beautifully costumed, and agreeably staged; and in the instance of Carrie Howland it is acted with a fire that communicates the torture of human character. For Carrie is the most vital figure in Miss Skinner's picturesque gallery of interesting women" ("Cornelia Otis Skinner" 20). Skinner's creations of women, both as an actress and as a writer, set an example for one-women shows which have become so important in the American theatre in recent years. When Skinner wrote and performed monologues she was viewed as exceptional, and only in recent years have such performers as Lily Tomlin, Whoopi Goldberg, and Karen Finley made the form familiar in the American theatre.

Elsa Shelley (1905?-1968?)

Elsa Shelley (1905?-1968?) wrote one powerful play which was generally cosidered one of the best plays of the 1943-44 season. This play, Pick-up Girl, was considered a realistic treatment of an alarming social problem. Shelley was an actress with an aspiration to be a playwright. Unfortunately, she did not have much skill in constructing plays, and her good intentions were seldom realized. Shelley's career in the theatre was really unusual: it went unerringly downhill after one major success.

Shelley was born in Russia and brought to America as a child. She did not reveal her birthdate. She went to school in New York and took extension courses at Columbia University before marrying Irving Kaye Davis. She acted in plays from 1928 on, most notably as a seventeen-year-old Juliet to Walter Hampden's Romeo. Her interest turned to playwriting because she was concerned with many social problems and felt they were not being addressed in the theatre. In 1945 she was awarded the Scroll of Merit by the New York University School of Education for service to youth in playwriting.

Pick-up Girl is a very conventional, well-made thesis play, much in the line of Miller's All My Sons, written in 1947. Shelley was very concerned about increasing juvenile delinquency among young girls and did considerable research on the subject, visiting court rooms and reform schools. When she had completed her research, she turned the material over to her writer husband to fashion into a play. Since she had done all the research and was clearly enthusiastic about the need for a play exposing the problem, he encouraged her to write it herself.

The play is slightly reminisicent of Wedekind's Spring Awakening in the characterization of the protagonist and her relationship to her mother. The setting of the play is a court room in which a judge makes decisions regarding the many young criminal offenders who appear before him. Fifteen year-old Elizabeth has been arrested with a forty-seven-year old man, Mr. Elliott, because they were discovered by a policeman in bed together. She and her parents are shattered by the whole affair. Elizabeth clearly doesn't understand why she has done what she has done, why her previous affair with a sailor began, or what her physical and mental condition is. She is essentially a naive, sweet girl who needs love and some pleasure in life. Because her mother is away at work much of the time, she takes care of her siblings, cooks and cleans, and yearns for freedom and fun. A hardened sixteen-year-old Ruby, testifies that she invited Elizabeth to a party to meet some boys, and took her downtown where they met sailors and went to a hotel. Elizabeth reveals that she had an abortion as a result of her affair with the sailor. This material forms the basis of the first act which ends with the appearance of Peter, a young man in love with Elizabeth who wants to testify on her behalf.

In the next two acts the revelations continue, and the tangled web of life of poor people who have suffered because of the Depression is depicted. Most of the youths who appear before the judge have some medical problem, but their parents don't have the money to help them. Because the mothers have to work, the children are not properly supervised and have little motivation regarding school.

The playwright provides a surprising and guardedly optimistic ending. When Elizabeth finds out that she has venereal disease she simply cannot believe it and asks with horror if Peter knows. She then realizes that Peter really loves her because he was willing to escape with her and marry her even though she was diseased. When the judge orders her to go to the hospital, she tells Peter she is going away to try to make herself good enough to deserve him. The play is a little preachy in the last act, but otherwise well-written and engrossing.

The general critical response was expressed briefly by Herrick Brown, who wrote, "it is an honest and frequently moving portrait of a current situation that well merits consideration by the stage" ("Pick-Up Girl" 198). John Chapman described the play as "admirably acted, cleverly directed, and often movingly written" ("Pick-Up Girl" 196). The critics praised her treatment of the sordid subject matter, and Howard Barnes noted that she "never for an instant resorted to sensationalism" ("Adolescent Tragedy" 196). Willella Waldorf was suspicious that the play might have been produced by Mike Todd in order to "attract sensation-seekers to the box-office." Despite her concern, she chose to believe the playwright had "the only decent reason for writing" such a play: to attract attention to "a festering sociological condition" in order to achieve reforms ("'Pick-Up Girl' Opens" 198). Whereas most of the critics praised the play on the whole, but noted weakness in the writing, a few were rhapsodic about the new playwright. Robert Garland said the play is "very, very good. . . . It's the most effective trial play I've ever seen, with the possible exception of

"The Trial of Mary Dugan." . . . In Miss Shelley's honest playwriting hands, abetted by a cast that couldn't be better improved upon, these so-called "little people" add up to something tremendous, important, significant and frightening." He concluded that Shelley should have been considered for the Pulitzer Prize ("Pick-Up Girl" 197-198). In a similar vein, Burton Rascoe urged audiences to see the play even if they had to save their pennies to do so. In a long review he discussed the various scenes and concluded that "the play is perfect in every way" and a "resounding hit" ("See Pick-Up Girl" 197).

Today both Rascoe and Garland seem to have been carried away by the performances and the importance of the subject matter. Although the play is clearly dated, it was important in its time. It only ran 53 performances in New York, fulfilling Garland's prophecy that it was "too outspoken, too-deep-seeing, too relentless for an overnight sensation." However, it did tour the country successfully. Motivated by the urge to present the message of the play to the parents of America and, at the same time, make a profit, Mike Todd decided to present the play in actual court rooms in several states (Rascoe 197). The play attracted so much attention and praise that it was selected by Burns Mantle as one of the ten best plays of the 1943-44 season. It was then successfully produced in Europe, Australia, South Africa, South America, and Israel. Shelley clearly responded to the concerns of the day with her affecting and daring portrait of an female adolescent.

In her next play Shelley focused on another social problem, that of psycho-neurotic ex-soldiers. A young musician, played superbly by Montgomery Clift, returns to his New York home after psychiatric treatment. He is potentially violent, starved for love, and obsessed by the need for permanent world peace. His unsympathetic sister tries to have him committed, but at the end, just as news of the end of the war comes over the radio, he plans to escape with a beautiful model to her parents' farm in Wisconsin.

Many of the critics noted that Shelley's first play had been effective, but this was less so. Howard Barnes expressed the general opinion by saying, "Since the theme and the central performance constantly transcend the writing and the craftsmanship, it is only possible to report that the work is doubly disappointing" ("A Near-Miss" 211). Lewis Nichols called it "languid and repetitious" and concluded that "it emerges as only another promise which a playwright has failed to fulfill" ("Soldier's Voice" 15). Herrick Brown also spoke of the play's weakness and its "blind alleys of talkiness," but concluded that it was "moving and provocative at moments, too. At least, it again stamps Miss Shelley as a playwright worth watching" ("Foxhole in the Parlor" 211). Burton Rascoe continued as a loyal supporter, writing that the play should be on the list of the ten best plays, and calling it "a subtle, exciting and touching drama, beautifully played by a perfect cast" ("'Foxhole'" 212). Wilella's Waldorf's concerns about the author's motivations were reinforced by this play and she wrote a harshly critical review in which she expressed the opinion that Shelley was a "theatrical opportunist" taking advantage of public concern over social problems to write plays which had no depth or skill in the execution ("'Foxhole in the Parlor' Never Gets Below the Surface" 213).

In fact, Waldorf was quite wrong. The chief problem with Shelley's writing was her intense social concern, so that she tended to include too many problems in her plays, leaving a number of undeveloped ideas hanging in the air. As Howard Barnes wrote, "Before the piece is finished it goes off in so many directions at once, that it is difficult to say whether it is a reaffirmation of the tides of Passover or a plea for clandestine love-making" ("A Near-Miss" 211). Shelley's concerns in the play include exploitation of females (an artist pressures his model to pose in the nude, and remarks, "A woman's body is her stock-in-trade" (10)), anti-Semitism, mistreatment of blacks, extreme jealousy as a problem in marriage, intolerance toward artists, and the anguish of war. All of that together resulted in a play with "the highest possible intentions. . . . What to do with them is not made clear" (Garland, "Foxhole" 212). It is unfortunate that Shelley was unable to martial her material more effectively. There are many touching moments and scenes. Particularly effective is the characterization of the black servant, played by Reginald Beane, who used to work in an office but left "because they made unkind remarks about me" (57). The play ran only 29 performances despite the highly praised portrayal by Clift and the timeliness of the central theme.

With A Silk Thread Shelley hit bottom with critics and audiences. Here she tried for a more complex structure, with Claire Boothe Luce playing an older, but still sexy actress who acts in Shaw's *Candida* with a young Marchbanks who is her lover in real life. She developed the theme of obsessive jealousy with her characterization of the actress' husband, prompting one critic to suggest the playwright hated men as much as Strindberg loathed women. The play-off on *Candida* was unfortunate because most critics felt that the play as "hardly theatre at all," especially when compared to Shaw (Barnes "Tiresome" 315).

On the whole, Shelley took a critical beating, with nobody suggesting that she was still a playwright to watch. They noted her tendency toward platitudes and the long boring monologues written for Luce. They complained bitterly that the pleasure of Luce's return to the stage was ruined by the drivel of her dialogue. Even Robert Garland, a close friend of the playwright, confessed that he could not give it a good review because he couldn't even figure out what it dealt with. He ended, "I did so want to recommend Elsa Shelley's *With a Silk Thread*. I can not!" ("Shelley Plus Shaw" 314). Even the attraction of Luce in scanty bathing costumes and the presence of actual sand for the realistic beach setting could only keep the play going for 13 performances.

Despite her pronounced failure with her third Broadway play, Shelley kept on writing. Of her many plays written after 1950, none was produced or published. She turned *Pick-Up Girl* into a novel in 1959, and continued writing until 1965. It is sad to contemplate her theatrical career. Illness prevented her from acting and she was never able to fulfill the promise she displayed as a playwright with her first attempt. Elsa Shelley is only one of many would-be playwrights who had "more zeal than sound dramatic writing" (Brown, "Foxhole" 211).

Carson McCullers (1917-1967)

Carson McCullers (1917-1967) made a major contribution to the American theatre with her play *The Member of the Wedding* (1950) and wrote one other play. Additionally, Edward Albee adapted her novel *Ballad of the Sad Cafe* into a play. In terms of theatre she is largely remembered for her 1950 success which provided fine roles for Ethel Waters, Julie Harris, and Brandon de Wilde and which was made into a superb film with the same actors.

The playwright was born Lula Carson Smith in Columbus, Georgia. Her mother encouraged her toward a musical career which she pursued, then dropped in favor of writing. She was unhappy and unsuccessful in high school, but went on to New York to study creative writing at Columbia. She chose to be called Carson and when she married Reeve McCullers, took his name. Her personal life was filled with sorrow: when she was twenty-eight she had already suffered two strokes and she later suffered from many other illnesses and acute depression. She divorced, remarried, and divorced her husband who ultimately committed suicide. In addition, she also suffered from alcoholism. Despite all of that, she was a determined and disciplined writer and won Guggenheim Grants and other awards. She was encouraged by Tennessee Williams to turn her 1946 novel into a play and many critics considered it better than her novel. Invited each summer in later life to the McDowell Colony in Peterboro, New Hampshire, McCullers wrote short stories and novels. When she died, she was mourned by the many writers who admired her talent and determination.

The Member of the Wedding has been described as Chekhovian in its structure. There is little story line and the interest is maintained by the colorful dialogue and the interesting characters. The play has generally been perceived as a study of an adolescent going through the pangs of emerging sexuality and the angst of feeling an outsider. However, it is also, and perhaps more importantly, a picture of the problems of African-Americans, and the anguish of their lives.

The play has a single setting which reveals the kitchen and back yard of the Addams family. Most of the action involves the daughter, Frankie, her cousin, John Henry, and Berenice who cares for them while Frankie's father works. The story is very simple: Frankie's soldier brother brings home his fiancé, and the twelve-year old girl falls in love with the idea of them and their wedding. She determines to go with them after the wedding, but is hauled out of the car and brought back to the kitchen. In the third act she has acquired some maturity and some friends, John Henry has died, and she is saying goodbye to Berenice and moving to a new home.

On this simple thread of a plot, McCullers built scenes of richness and poignancy. Many of the scenes simply involve the three central figures exchanging stories and pondering life. Frankie is dirty, skinny, and unhappy (the author said she was the character most like herself as a child in all of her writing) and affects a very amusing high-tone way of speaking. When she tells Berenice of her new friendship in the last act, she says, "As the irony of fate would have it, we first got to know each other in front of the lipstick and cosmetics counter at Woolworth's" (115). In contrast to many saccharine or cute portrayals of children in plays, John Henry is delightful and eccentric. Berenice is a rich, beautiful role which Ethel Waters played to perfection.

Her stories have to do with her four husbands and with her half-brother, a musician named Honey Camden Brown. His life has embittered him and when he meets a white man like Frankie's father, he has to fight to control his rage. Mr. Addams says to him, "I'll be so glad when the war is over and you biggety, worthless niggers get back to work. And, furthermore, you *sir* me! Hear Me?" When Berenice says she would like to shake him for acting impudent to Addams, he answers that her friend T.T. "said sir enough for a whole crowd of niggers. But for folks that calls me nigger, I got a real good nigger razor" (68). Ultimately, frustration and rage lead Honey to pull a razor on a white man while under the influence of marijuana. Arrested, he hangs himself in his jail cell. John Henry dies of meningitis, and Berenice is all alone in the final scene. Sadly fingering her one claim to finery, a tired fox fur, she says, "With what has happened in these last two months, I just don't know what I have done to deserve it. Honey gone and John Henry, my little boy gone. . . . Honey dead and John Henry suffering like he did and daisies, golden weather, butterflies—such strange death weather" (115).

The beautiful play presented a problem for critics. It was obviously a wonderful evening in the theatre. The directing by Harold Clurman and the acting were at the highest level, and yet the play itself was, as Robert Garland's review was headed, "Something Special But Not

Quite a Play." Brooks Atkinson praised the play but said it was essentially character sketches and acting. Still, he concluded, "It may not be a play, but it is art. That is the important thing" ("The Member of the Wedding" 26). Robert Coleman called it a "stirring hit" but noted that the playwright had "created a mood rather than a well-made play, but it is a mood that held an audience spellbound" ("'Member of the Wedding' is a Stirring Hit" 397) William Hawkins reported, "I have never before heard what happened last night at the curtain calls for 'The Member of the Wedding' when hundreds cried out as if with one voice for Ethel Waters and Julie Harris" ("Waters, Harris Roles Spark 'Wedding'" 399). All in all, the critics agreed that McCullers had really not mastered playwriting, but had, nonetheless, created a wonderful performance. Richard Watts, Jr. wrote, "Miss McCullers' drama has a strange, haunting and delicate kind of rueful beauty rarely looked for on the contemporary American stage." He said it was not completely successful, "but it's weaknesses as a well-rounded theatrical conception are more than atoned for by its sensitivity of feeling, its delicacy of treatment, and its understanding warmth of human sympathy. There is quality in both its prose style and its compassionate viewpoint" ("A Striking New American Play" 399).

The play ran 501 performances and won the Donaldson Award and the New York Drama Critics Circle Award. It was also selected as one of the ten best plays of the season. McCullers was also awarded a gold medal by the Theatre Club, Inc. which designated her the best playwright of the year.

Given the reservations about the construction of the play and the feeling that the performances and direction contributed greatly to the success of the play, it is of particular interest to look at the history of the play following its original production. Most critics in that time described it as the study of adolescent girl. In recent years the element of racism has emerged as the dominant theme and the play has often been produced as a vehicle for African-American actresses in the role of Berenice. Clive Barnes noted this shift in his review of the 1975 revival, saying, "The black and white elements of the play have become more evident and more poignant in the last 25 years. . . . The present director, Michael Montel, has deliberately emphasized this sociological aspect of the play" ("'Member of the Wedding' Wears Well" 397). Howard Kissel felt that the "strength of the play seems to lie in the lyricism of the situation and the language" ("The Member of the Wedding" 398). Martin Gottfried, too, commented, "The play is filled with the loveliest writing" but felt that the cast was not strong enough and that McCullers, unfortunately, "wasn't one of the better playwrights" ("McCullers Play at Phoenix" 398). Douglas Watt felt the play was a fine choice for the New Phoenix Repertory Company and that it seemed as fresh as it must have been 25 years earlier ("'Member of the Wedding' Affecting" 399).

Since the original production *The Member of the Wedding* has become a standard play in regional theatres. In 1988, Gloria Bailey and Claire Winters starred in it at the Tampa Bay Performing Arts Center's Jaeb Theater and had a success. Another successful regional production was in Sacramento at the Woodland Opera House in 1993 with Erika Rawlins as Berenice. In the same year a musical version of the play was performed by the Theatre in the Square in Atlanta, with Bernardine Mitchell as Berenice and thirteen-year-old Tony Award winner Daisy Egan as Frankie. The music was by Atlanta composers Ellen McQueen and Frank Hamilton.

The play was revived again in 1989 in New York at the Roundabout Theatre directed by Harold Scott. He told a reporter that Harold Clurman had directed the play from a white point of view, but that he was "directing it as a black man who has been through the 1960s" (qtd. in Hodgson 824). Critic Hodgson, who had not seen earlier stage productions or the film, wrote that it was difficult to imagine anyone sitting through the play without "flinching at the sorry picture it presents of race relations. Looking at it now, in the light of all that has gone on since then, Frankie's struggle seems minor compared with the hopelessness of the struggle facing the black characters. . . . By the end of the play, Frankie is ready to become part of the white world. Berenice, the housekeeper, meanwhile, is left with nothing" (Hodgson 824). Reviewing the production for the *Christian Science Monitor,* John Beaufort said, "Carson McCuller's tender genre play is a period piece that speaks for its own time but with a universality that transcends limitations of era and locale. The work's enduring appeal has been conscientiously preverved in the Roundabout Theatre Company revival starring Esther Rolle, most widely known among her many credits for TV's 'Good Times'" ("A Little World, Big in Heart" 11).

With her stunning success, McCullers went on to write a play called *The Square Root of Wonderful* (1957), but this was a failure which ran for only 55 performances. The play, McCullers said, related to her own life. In the introduction to the published version she wrote, "I suppose a writer writes out of some inward compulsion to transform his own experience (much of it unconscious) into the universal and symbolical. . . . Certainly I have always felt alone" (qtd. in Snipes 462). The play centered on a woman who was "twice divorced from an irascible, half-mad writer and who has fallen in love with an architect" (Atkinson, "Mrs. McCullers' Play Opens at National" 40). Although some of the playwright's wistful, poetic qualities permeated the play, on the whole it did not convey anything like the theatrical effectiveness of her first play. Atkinson noted that "Mrs. McCullers is a stylist who evokes strange images from ordinary situations." Like most of the other critics he reluctantly described this play as theatrically ineffective: "Most of 'The Square Root of Wonderful' remains earthbound. . . . Very little of Mrs. McCullers' odd genius has gotten into the fabric of this frail, delicate, though listless play" ("Mrs. McCullers' Play" 40).

McCullers made only one more theatrical attempt, which was a musical version of *The Member of the Wedding* in collaboration with Mary Rodgers. Produced in 1971 as *F. Jasmine Addams*, it ran for only 20 performances. If McCullers' health had been better she might have worked more in the theatre. She will remembered for her fiction and for one wonderful play. As one biographer wrote, "Although not primarily a playwright, McCullers contributed several memorable characters to American theatre in dramatizations which have become legendary" (Freydberg 617).

Summary

When Martha Morton began writing plays she encountered numerous difficulties, although getting her plays produced was not particularly hard. But in the theatre and in the Dramatists' Club she was treated as someone in the wrong place. She told Shirley Burns in 1910, "When I first started in, the idea of a woman directing a rehearsal was unheard of. But now they think nothing of it. In those days, too, women were not admitted to the Dramatists' Club" (Burns 632). By 1910, Morton was considered quite capable of directing her plays and was soon followed by Crothers, Franken, and later many other women playwrights. By that time she was also Vice President of the Society of American Dramatists and Composers. The situation had changed drastically, but was to change more. By the time Carson McCullers was writing her plays she was encouraged by Tennessee Williams, supported by grants and invited to the McDowell Colony to write, and was given the Drama Critics Circle Award.

The rush toward playwriting by women occurred early in the century when it became apparent that it was both acceptable and economically rewarding. Assessing the first decade, a writer for *Theatre Magazine* stated, "Writing for the stage, once such a discredited and even perilous occupation that authors hesitated to sign their names to their manuscripts, has come to be one of the most reputable and profitable of the professions. A successful playwright's income today is considerably larger than that of the President of the United States" ("Big Earnings" 151). Women began writing plays in such numbers that Shirley Burns could only include a small number of the total in her article on women playwrights. She concluded her discussion by saying, "The list of women playwrights is so long, that detailed mention of all of them is impossible." She then added a list of twenty-one women playwrights beginning with Miss Marguerite Merington and ending with Gladys Unger. Some of these women wrote as many as twenty-five plays. They tended to be like those of Martha Morton: tailored for a star and highly conventional. The chief aim of the early women playwrights was economic.

Although such writers as Anne Nichols continued in a purely commercial tradition, along with many male playwrights, other women began writing plays with social causes in mind, with experimental techniques, and with authentic portraits of human beings. Dorothy Heyward devoted herself to creating plays which addressed problems of race and intolerance. Mae West was considered an opportunistic, commercial playwright with limited goals, but, in fact, she shared many of Heyward's concerns, and also was a pioneer in breaking through the puritanical strait-jacket which limited realistic treatment of sexuality and actuality. Of course, Anita Loos pursued greater freedom in the theatre, too, and shared with West a sharp sense of humor and irony. Marita Bonner anticipated contemporary playwriting with her combination of symbolism and violence in *The Purple Flower* and *Exit, An Illusion*. Cornelis Otis Skinner explored new avenues in theatre both in subject matter and form. Her one-person performances, as well as *The Pleasure of His Company*, placed the focus on the many roles of women in society and the appropriateness of their training and goals. Elsa Shelley was driven to write plays packed with social concerns, and achieved success in *Pick-Up Girl* with her depiction of a social problem many critics and audience members preferred to ignore. By 1949, in sharp contrast to the many women following formulae and conventional wisdom early in the century, McCullers wrote *The Member of the Wedding* which was so unconventional that critics were at a loss to describe what made it so successful and appealing.

By 1949 many African-American women had written plays but had made no impact on the professional theatre—that remained for Lorraine Hansberry ten years later. What Barbara Molette wrote in 1976 about the lack of listeners responding to African-American women playwrights is particularly true of the first half of the century. Noting that most media brokers were white males, she said, "The media brokers will not present informative entertainment of the exposition of truths that might be of some use to an oppressed group of people in reducing their oppression. . . . They won't produce Black women's plays because they go against the stereotypes of Black women perpetuated by white America" ("They Speak: Who Listens?" 28-29). Despite the lack of encouragement such playwrights as Alice Moore Dunbar-Nelson, Zora Neale Hurston, and Marita Bonner did write plays which revealed imagination and a determination to change society.

Some of the playwrights had limited success—Elsa Shelley being the clearest example—yet persevered in their playwriting. In some instances, such as the case of Dorothy Parker, the playwright never found the right collaborator whose work and shared enthusiasm could

bring out the writer's potential. Maurine Watkins had training with
George Pierce Baker, experience as a newspaper writer which provided
her with interesting material, and encouragement from many influential theatrical figures. Nevertheless, after her success with *Chicago*, she
achieved little in the theatre. For many of the women discussed in this
section there was as much frustration and disappointment as pleasure
in working as a playwright.

Nevertheless, the women above stand as examples of women playwrights who were able to present their ideas in theatrical form, who
achieved success in one degree or another, and who were identified in
the public mind as visible members of the theatrical profession who
wrote plays and often succeeded in other areas as well. Some of their
plays, such as *The Member of the Wedding* have become classics which
are frequently performed, while others, such as *Chicago* and *The Purple
Flower* deserve productions but have not received much attention.
Still other playwrights created characters and dialogue which were
then developed into musicals and have become classics: *Porgy and Bess*
and *Gentlemen Prefer Blondes* are two obvious examples. Each of the
playwrights considered in this section made a particular contribution
to the American theatre and each will be remembered for at least one
significant play which moved audiences, challenged conventional
ideas, or broke new ground in the theatre.

Conclusion

Brander Matthews wrote *A Book About the Theatre* in 1916 which contained a chapter called "Women Dramatists." In this he examined the dearth of women dramatists throughout the history of theatre. He posed the question, "Why cannot they write a play as well as they can act it?" The initial answer which he put forth came from Fanny Kemble who had both acted and written plays in the nineteenth century. She said it was impossible for a woman ever to be a great dramatist because the female brain was different from a man's and "beside the original female nature, the whole of our training and education, our inevitable ignorance of common life and general human nature, and the various experiences of existence from which we are debarred with the most sedulous care, is insuperably against it" (116). Ignoring the fact that Kemble was writing long before the sweeping changes which had occurred in the education, travel, and work opportunities for women, Matthews analyzed her comments in detail and agreed, first of all, that women "can never know men as men can know women" and that "they lack the inexaustible fund of information about life which is the common property of men" (118). At the conclusion of the chapter he concluded that the reason there were so few women playwrights and the infrequent plays written by women rarely achieved high rank lay in the lack of knowledge women had and the fact that "they are likely also to be more or less deficient in the faculty of construction. The first of these disabilities may tend to disappear if ever the feminist movement shall achieve its ultimate victory; and the second may depart also whenever women submit themselves to the severe discipline which has compelled men to be more or less logical" (125). It is surprising that these remarks were written sixteen years after the turn of the century. Numerous women were earning their living as playwrights and Rachel Crothers, Josephine Preston Peabody, and Susan Glaspell had contributed excellent plays to the American theatre. Yet it is true that articles and chapters in books in the early part of the century questioned women's aptitude in many areas despite the achievements they had demonstrated. One article in a newspaper asked if women could write plays since it was generally believed that they did not have a sense of humor. Even as late as 1941 Joseph Mersand's chapter "When Ladies Write Plays" in *American Drama, 1930-1940* was condescending in tone and ignored many women who had written successful plays.

In contrast to these individuals were the many men who encouraged women to write plays such as George Cram Cook of the Provincetown Players, Lawrence Langner of the Washington Square Players, W.E.B. DuBois of Krigwa, Professor Frederick Koch of the Carolina Playmakers, producers Brock Pemberton and John Golden, critic Burns Mantle (who defied generally accepted attitudes by including Franken's *Outrageous Fortune* in a best plays volume and who selected many other women's plays for inclusion), Dashiell Hammett who encouraged Lillian Hellman, George S. Kaufman who chose to direct plays by many women, Edward Sheldon who first suggested to Ruth Gordon that she write a play, and George Pierce Baker who encouraged Maurine Watkins and other women who studied playwriting with him.

More importantly, women were encouraging women to write plays. Susan Glaspell worked with Edna St. Vincent Millay, Neith Boyce, Djuna Barnes, and other women in the Provincetown Players who directed each others' plays and acted in them. The very popular actress Margaret Anglin announced that she would not act in a play by a man if she could get one written by a woman (Ferguson, *Women Dramatists in the American Theatre* 12). Throughout the first part of the century women were forming organizations to encourage women playwrights. For example women in Evanston, Illinois founded the Drama League shortly after the turn of the century which was a model later copied by other women in the country. Alice Gerstenberg, as founder of the Playwrights Theatre of Chicago, opened the door for production of many plays by women. Similarly, Eva Le Gallienne produced plays by Glaspell and other women. In 1908 at the first banquet given by the American Dramatists Club to which women were invited, Martha Morton's address indicated the fact that women were writing plays and that they were entitled to the same attention as male playwrights. Her statement, "As a business factor, as a creator, woman must needs be reckoned with in our drama" was important. The fact that she, twenty-nine other women playwrights, and one male playwright formed the Society of Dramatic Authors indicated the self-confidence which had developed on the part of women playwrights. The lone male in the group, of course, was soon joined by all the members of the American Dramatists Club. Another important organization was The Playwrights

Fellowship established by playwright Edith Ellis Baker in 1921 to encourage production of plays by women.

Women journalists were also encouraging women to write plays by focusing attention on the many women writing plays after the turn of the century. The economic fact was that women could make more money writing plays than novels and, as Martha Morton said, more plays were needed as the theatre expanded and leading actors and actresses were looking for vehicles. As early as 1906 Virginia Frame drew the attention of audiences and potential producers to women playwrights in her article, "Successful Women Dramatists." Lucy F. Pierce wrote "Women Who Write Plays" in 1908 and four years later, "Women Dramatists." In 1910 S. Burns wrote "Sketches of Several Women Dramatists." In 1917 A. Dale wrote "Women Playwrights: Their Contribution Has Enriched the Stage." Such articles continued throughout the first half of the century, making people aware that dozens of women were writing plays, winning awards for them, and competing successfully with men in the professional theatre. In his book *American Playwrights of Today* written in 1929, Burns Mantle also reflected the current awareness of women playwrights by including a large number of them.

Today it is fairly common to read that a playwright such as Glaspell or Nichols was important because so few women were writing plays. This perception has developed in opposition to the facts. The thirty-five women discussed in this book represent numerous American women playwrights whose names appear in Phyllis Ferguson's dissertation "Women Dramatists in the American Theatre," Brenda Coven's *American Women Dramatists of the Twentieth Century,* on sixteen pages in Chinoy and Jenkins' *Women in American Theatre,* and on page after page of *The New York Times Directory of Theater,* beginning with Laura Adair and ending with Irma Zimmer. Part of the reason that so many women whose plays were quite popular are unknown today is that fewer plays are performed in New York and that revivals of older works, either by men or women, are uncommon. But a more serious reason is the lack of attention given to women playwrights in theatre history books written after 1950. For example Bernard Hewitt's useful book *Theatre U.S.A. (1959)* which "surveys the professional theatre in the United States" includes information about George S. Kaufman in several places, but nothing about Ferber's work, and there are no reviews of plays by Akins, Gale, Crothers, Glaspell, Franken, Peabody,

Kummer, Young, Luce or most of the playwrights discussed in this book. One might conclude from his survey that aside from Anna Cora Mowatt, Anne Nichols, and Lillian Hellman there were no women playwrights. One might also conclude that there were no women drama critics, since all the critics quoted are male. Similarly, Alan Downer's 1951 book, *Fifty Years of American Drama,* focuses chiefly on male playwrights although Hellman, Gale, Vollmer, Ferber, and Spewack are discussed. Just one more example is Doris Abramson's *Negro Playwrights in the American Theatre* (1969). Although the work of the Krigwa Players is discussed, none of the award-winning African-American women playwrights whose plays were performed by them in New York and Washington are mentioned.

In recent years interest in women playwrights has increased and plays ignored for many years are becoming known. Such books as Judith E. Barlow's *Plays by Women,* Wilkerson's *Nine Plays by Black Women,* Rachel France's *A Century of Plays by American Women,* Brown-Guillory's *Their Place on Stage* and *Wines in the Wilderness,* Perkins' *Black Female Playwrights,* and Hatch and Shine's *Black Theatre U.S.A.* have drawn attention to women playwrights from 1900-1950 and made their plays available. Frances Diodato Bzowski recently made a serious contribution to the awareness of plays by American woman with her books, *American Women Playwrights, 1900-1930; a Checklist.* Her interest was raised by a course she took called "Women in Drama" in which half of the plays were by men and half by women. That such a course existed is proof of the increasing awareness of American women playwrights. It is also important to note the increasing number of articles in scholarly journals on these women. In contrast to the period following 1950, there are now panels about these women playwrights at conferences of the Modern Language Association, American Theatre for Higher Education, and the American Society for Theatre Research. As indicated in this book, many of the plays discussed have been successfully revived and theatres are now expected to perform plays written by American women.

We are clearly moving beyond the limited appreciation of women playwrights expressed by Brander Matthews in 1916. In the first fifty years of the century women wrote plays of all types, many of which were the equal of any being written in the American theatre. After the early realism and social criticism which disturbed Augustus Thomas and others, women wrote in various styles, using Expressionism, Surrealism, Freudian symbolism, poetic drama, folk drama, satire, high comedy, and farce. The appendix listing their awards indicates success in all these areas.

The playwrights discussed in this book relate to their time, yet most of these women were unconventional in questioning and challenging the mores of their time through their plays and, in many instances, their own lives. Martha Morton looks the epitome of a woman of fashion at the turn of the century: sitting in her elegant library, her mass of hair piled up on her head, the long, feminine dress not quite covering the high-button shoes resting on a velvet pillow. But Morton challenged the male playwriting establishment. Susan Glaspell's work as a founder of the Provincetown Players presented the most direct challenge to the commercial theatre of the period beginning in 1915. In the 1920s Mae West and Anita Loos both explored sexuality in women's lives through their plays and shocked many people with their efforts to expand the boundaries of sexuality in general. Clare Boothe Luce boldly presented unflattering portraits of the society women of her own time and she played a major part in American political life. The achievements of women playwrights of the first half of the century deserve the attention which is developing. But more plays need to be anthologized, more plays need to be produced, and more plays need to be discussed in classrooms. As we near the end of the century we must pursue knowledge about the women playwrights before 1950 whose rich heritage stands as an example for women playwrights in the second half of the century. New courses discussing women playwrights, new books about them, and panels at conferences indicate the rising interest in their work. Even more importantly, the number of productions rises each year. *Miss Lulu Bett* has been performed throughout the country, and there are many performances of one-act plays by Gerstenberg, Glaspell, and others. Each week such magazines as *Theater Week* list new productions and new adaptations. Furthermore, attantion is now being paid to these plays in foreign countries. For example, Ken Mandelbaum recently wrote, "Sophie Treadwell's 1928 play *Machinal* which had an acclaimed revival by the New York Shakespeare Festival a couple of seasons back, has just joined the Royal National Theater repertory at the Lyttelton [in London]" ("Theater News" 9-10).

Although the long neglect of American women playwrights is presently being addressed, there are many areas for more scholarship.

Mary Papke's excellent book on Susan Glaspell points the way for research and production sourcebooks on the many playwrights listed in this book, and the many more who were not included. New analysis of the plays in terms of changes in society should be written, and new interpretations of the plays presented onstage. As Cynthia Sutherland has suggested, new approaches to analysis of the plays in the area of characterization are also needed:

> As theatre historians and critics, we must now attempt to refine our working lexicon. . . . Only by developing descriptive categories with some historical precision can we hope to account for both formulaic successes and changes in dramatic modes. A more accurate vocabulary for female 'dramatis personae' could help us to understand the interrelationships between the theatre and evolving social milieus. (331)

Paralleling the need for more scholarship on women playwrights is the need for work on women theatre critics, about whom little has been written. American women contributed to the development of American theatre in many ways and their efforts are now being recognized. Only when women playwrights are discussed in classes, included in histories and anthologies, analyzed in articles, and presented more frequently onstage, will the full picture of the history of American theatre appear.

Appendix

Honors and Awards for Women Playwrights Discussed in this Book

American Academy of Arts and Letters

Edna Ferber   Elected to the Institute in 1930*

Rachel Crothers   Elected to the Instutute in 1933

Carson McCullers Recipient of an Academy Award in Literature 1943
                     Elected to the Institute in 1952

Lillian Hellman   Elected to the Institute in 1946
                     Elected to the Academy in 1962
                     Recipient of the Gold Medal for Drama, 1964

Dorothy Parker   Recipient of the Marjorie Peabody Waite Award
                     1958
                     Elected to the Institute in 1959

*Prior to 1993 there were two bodies of this institution. The Academy was the more elite body and was limited to 50 members. One had to be a member of the Institute first in order to be elected into the Academy.

Pulitzer Prizes

1920-21 *Miss Lulu Bett* by Zona Gale

1930-31 *Alison's House* by Susan Glaspell

1934-35 *The Old Maid* by Zoë Akins

1944-45 *Harvey* by Mary Coyle Chase

Drama Critics Circle Award

1941   *Watch on the Rhine* by Lillian Hellman

1950   *Member of the Wedding* by Carson McCullers

1960   *Toys in the Attic* by Lillian Hellman

Antoinette Perry Award (Tony Award)

1949   *Kiss Me Kate* book by Bella and Sam Spewack*

*The was the first time an award was given for the book of a musical.

Crisis Awards

1925   Marita Bonner "On Being Young—A Woman—and Colored"

1926   Eulalie Spence Second Prize *Foreign Mail*

1927   Marita Bonner First Prize for four works including *The Purple Flower* and *Exit, an Illusion*

Opportunity Awards

1925	Zora Neale Hurston	Second Prize *Color Struck*
		Honorary Mention *Spears*
	May Miller	Third Prize *The Bog Guide*
1926	Georgia Douglas Johnson	Honorable Mention *Blue Blood*
	May Miller	Honorable Mention *The Cuss'd Thing*
	Zora Neale Hurston	Honorable Mention *Color Struck* (revised)
1927	Georgia Douglas Johnson	First Prize *Plumes*
	Eulalie Spence	Second Prize *The Hunch*
		Tied for Third Prize *The Starter*

Roi Cooper Megrue Award

1932   *Let Us Be Gay* by Rachel Crothers

1936   *Boy Meets Girl* by Bella and Sam Spewack

1937   *Susan and God* by Rachel Crothers

New York World Playwriting Prize

1891   *The Merchant* by Martha Morton

Howard University Drama Prize

1920   May Miller *Within the Shadow*

Samuel French Prize

1927   Eulalie Spence Best Unpublished Play in Little Theatre Tournament *The Fool's Errand*

Burns Mantle Best Play Series

1909-19   *Good Gracious, Annabelle* by Clare Kummer

1919-20   *Déclassée* by Zoë Akins

1920-21 *Nice People* by Rachel Crothers

1922-23 *Mary the 3rd* by Rachel Crothers

1923-24 *Sun-Up* by Lula Vollmer

1924-25 *Minick* by Edna Ferber and George S. Kaufman

1926-27 *Chicago* by Maurine Watkins

1927-28 *The Royal Family* by Edna Ferber and George S. Kaufman

1928-29 *Let Us Be Gay* by Rachel Crothers

Machinal by Sophie Treadwell

1930-31 *As Husbands Go* by Rachel Crothers

Alison's House by Susan Glaspell

1931-32 *Another Language* by Rose Franken

1932-33 *Dinner at Eight* by Edna Ferber and George S. Kaufman

When Ladies Meet by Rachel Crothers

1933-34 *Her Master's Voice* by Clare Kummer

1934-35 *The Children's Hour* by Lillian Hellman

The Old Maid by Zoë Akins

1935-36 *Boy Meets Girl* by Bella and Sam Spewack

1936-37 *Stage Door* by Edna Ferber and George S. Kaufman

The Women by Clare Boothe Luce

1937-38 *Susan and God* by Rachel Crothers

1938-39 *The Little Foxes* by Lillian Hellman

Kiss the Boys Good-bye by Clare Boothe Luce

1939-40 *Margin for Error* by Clare Boothe Luce

1940-41 *Watch on the Rhine* by Lillian Hellman

1941-42 *Hope for a Harvest* by Sophie Treadwell

1943-44 *The Searching Wind* by Lillian Hellman

Over 21 by Ruth Gordon

Outrageous Fortune by Rose Franken

Pick-Up Girl by Elsa Shelley

1944-45 *Harvey* by Mary Coyle Chase

Soldier's Wife by Rose Franken

1946-47 *Another Part of the Forest* by Lillian Hellman

Years Ago by Ruth Gordon

1948-49 *Goodbye My Fancy* by Fay Kanin

1949-50 *The Member of the Wedding* by Carson McCullers

1950-51 *The Autumn Garden* by Lillian Hellman

1951-52 *Gigi* by Anita Loos

Mrs. McThing by Mary Coyle Chase

1952-53 *My 3 Angels* by Bella and Sam Spewack

Bernardine by Mary Coyle Chase
1955-56 *The Lark* adapted by Lillian Hellman
1956-57 *Candide* book by Lillian Hellman
1958-59 *The Pleasure of His Company* by Cornelia Otis Skinner and
         Samuel Taylor
1959-60 *Toys in the Attic* by Lillian Hellman

Long Runs on Broadway
Abie's Irish Rose 2,327
Harvey 1,775
Gentlemen Prefer Blondes (musical) 740
Claudia 722
The Children's Hour 691
Boy Meets Girl 669
The Women 657
Show Boat 572
Toys in the Attic 556
The Member of the Wedding 501

Works Cited

Books

Abramson, Doris. *Negro Playwrights in the American Theatre, 1925-1959.* N.Y.: Columbia University Press, 1969.

Akins, Zoë. *Déclassée.* New York: Boni and Liveright, 1924.

——. *Déclassée: Daddy's Gone a-Hunting: and Greatness—A Comedy* [Variant title of *The Texas Nightingale*]. New York: Boni & Liveright, 1923.

——. *The Happy Days.* New York: French, 1924.

——. *Magical City.* In: *Forum* May 1916: 507-50.

——. *Mrs. January and Mr. Ex.* New York: French, 1942.

——. *The Old Maid.* New York: Appleton-Century, 1935.

——. *Papa.* Ed. Edwin Björkman. New York: Kennerley, 1913.

Allen, Frederick Lewis. *The Big Change: America Transforms Itself 1900-1950.* New York: Harper, 1952.

Barlow, Judith. *Plays by Women.* New York: Avon Books, 1981.

Bigsby, C.W.E., ed. *Plays by Susan Glaspell.* Cambridge: Cambridge Univ. Press, 1987.

——. *Twentieth-Century American Drama, Volume I, 1900-1940.* London: Cambridge Univ. Press, 1982.

Bloom, Harold, ed. *Gertrude Stein.* New Haven: Chelsea House Publishers, 1986.

Bonner, Marita. *Exit: an Illusion.* In: Perkins.

——. *The Pot Maker.* In: Brown-Guillory, *Wines.*

——. *The Purple Flower.* In: Perkins.

Brown, Sterling. *Negro Poetry and Drama and the Negro in American Fiction.* New York: Atheneum, 1969.

Brown-Guillory, Elizabeth. *Their Place on Stage; Black Women Playwrights in America.* Conn.: Greenwood Press, 1988.

———, ed. *Wines in the Wilderness. Plays by African-American Women from the Harlem Renaissance to the Present.* Conn.: Greenwood Press, 1990.

Bryer, Jackson, ed. *Conversations With Lillian Hellman.* Jackson, Miss.: UP of Mississippi.

Bzowski, Frances Diodato. *American Women Playwrights, 1900-1930: A Checklist.* Westport: Greenwood Press, 1992.

Cerf, Bennett and Van H. Cartmell, eds. *S.R.O. The Most Successful Plays of the American Stage.* New York: Doubleday and Company, Inc., 1944.

———. *Thirty Famous One-Act Plays.* New York: Random House, 1949.

Chinoy, Helen Krich and Linda Walsh Jenkins, eds. *Women in American Theatre.* New York: Crown Publishers, 1981.

Chapman, John and Garrison P. Sherwood, eds. *The Best Plays of 1894-1899.* New York: 1955.

Chase, Mary Coyle. *Bernardine.* New York: Oxford UP, 1953.

———. *Harvey.* New York: Dramatists Play Service, 1943.

———. *Midgie Purvis.* New York: Dramatists Play Service, 1963

———. *Mrs. McThing.* New York: Oxford UP, 1949.

Clark, Barrett H. and George Freedley. *A History of Modern Drama.* New York: Appleton-Century-Crofts, Inc. 1947.

Clements, C.C., ed. *Sea Plays.* Boston: Small, Maynard, 1925.

Coe, Kathryn and William H. Cordell, eds. *The Pulitzer Prize Plays 1918-1934.* New York: Random House, 1935.

Cohen, Stanley. *Rebellion Against Victorianism: The Impetus for Cultural Change in the 1920s in America.* Oxford: Oxford U. Press, 1921.

Cordell, Richard, ed. *Representative Modern Plays.* New York: Nelson, 1929.

Coven, Brenda. *American Women Dramatists of the Twentieth Century: a Bibliography* New Jersey: Metuchen, 1982.

Crothers, Rachel. *Expressing Willie, Nice People, 39 East.* N.Y.: Brentano's, 1924.

——. *He and She.* In: Quinn, Arthur H., ed. *Representative American Plays.* 7th ed.

——. *Let Us Be Gay.* N.Y.: Samuel French, 1929.

——. *A Man's World.* Boston: Badger, 1915.

——. *Mary the Third, Old Lady 31, A Little Journey.* New York: Brentano, 1923.

——. *Nice People.* In: Quinn, *Contemporary American Plays.*

——. *Susan and God.* New York: Random House, 1938.

——. *The Three of Us.* New York: Rosenfield, 1906.

——. *When Ladies Meet.* New York: French, 1932.

Davis, Arthur P. and Michael W. Peplow. *The New Negro Renaissance.* New York: Holt, Rinehart and Winston, 1975.

Derleth, August. *Still Small Voice; The Biography of Zona Gale.* New York: Appleton-Century, 1940.

Dick, Bernard F. *Hellman in Hollywood.* Teaneck: Fairleigh Dickinson UP.

Dickinson, Thomas H. *Chief Contemporary Dramatists.* Boston: Houghton Mifflin, 1921.

——. *Playwrights of the New American Theater.* New York: Books For Libraries Press, rpr. 1967.

——, ed. *Wisconsin Plays*. New York: Huebsch, 1914.

Downer, Alan S. *Fifty Years of American Drama, 1900-1950*. Chicago: Regnery, 1951.

Dunbar-Nelson, Alice. *Give Us Each Day; The Diary of Alice Dunbar-Nelson*. Ed. Gloria T. Hull. New York: W.W. Norton, 1984.

——. *The Works of Alice Dunbar-Nelson*. Vol. 3. Ed. Gloria T. Hull. Oxford: Oxford Univ. Press, 1988.

Eaton, Walter Pritchard, ed. *Washington Square Plays*. New York: Doubleday, Page & Co., 1925.

Estrin, Mark W., ed. *Critical Essays on Lillian Hellman*. Boston: Hall, 1989.

Falk, Doris V. *Lillian Hellman*. New York: Ungar, 1978.

Fabré, Genevieve. *Drumbeats, Masks, and Metaphor*. Trans. Melvin Dixon. Cambridge: Harvard U. Press, 1983.

Faust, Langdon Lynne, ed. *American Women Writers*. New York: Ungar, 1988.

Ferber, Edna. *The Eldest*. In: France A *Century of Plays*.

——. *A Kind of Magic*. New York: Doubleday, 1963.

——. *A Peculiar Treasure*. New York: Doubleday, 1940.

——. *Showboat*. New York: Grosset and Dunlap, 1936.

Ferber, Edna and George S. Kaufman. *Bravo!* In: Schneider, *George S. Kaufman*.

——. *Dinner at Eight*. New York: French, 1935.

——. *The Land is Bright*. New York: Dramatists Play Service, 1946.

——. *Minick*. New York: French, 1925.

——. *The Royal Family*. New York: French, 1927.

——. *Stage Door*. New York: Doubleday, 1936.

Ferber, Edna and Norman Levy. *$1200 a Year*. Garden City: Double-day, 1921.

Flexner, Eleanor. *American Women Playwrights, 1918-1938*. Pref. John Gassner. New York: Simon and Schuster, 1938.

France, Rachel, ed. *A Century of Plays by American Women*. New York: Richards Rosen Press, 1979.

Franken, Rose. *Another Language*. N.Y.: French, 1932.

———. *Claudia*. N.Y.: Farrar & Rinehart, 1941.

———. *The Hallams*. N.Y. French, 1948.

———. *Outrageous Fortune*. N.Y.: French, 1944.

———. *Soldier's Wife*. N.Y.: French, 1945.

———. *When All Is Said and Done*. N.Y.: Doubleday, 1963.

Freedley, George and John A. Reeves. *A History of the Theatre*. New York: Crown, 1941.

Gale, Zona. *Miss Lulu Bett*. In: Coe, *The Pulitzer Prize Plays*.

———. *Mister Pitt*. New York: Appleton, 1925.

———. "Neighbors." In: Dickinson, *Wisconsin Plays*.

———. *Uncle Jimmy*. Boston: Baker, 1922.

———. *Uncle Jimmy*. *Short Plays for Modern Readers*. Ed. Glenn Hughes. New York: Appleton, 1931.

Gassner, John. *Best American Plays: Third Series; 1945-1951*. New York: Crown, 1952.

———. *Twenty-Five Best Plays of the Modern American Theatre: Early Series*. New York: Crown, 1949.

Gerstenberg, Alice. *Alice in Wonderland*. In: *Plays New and Old*. Ed. Stella B. Finney. Boston: Allyn and Bacon, 1928.

———. *Comedies All*. New York: Longmans, 1930.

———. *Fourteen.* In: *Drama*, 10 (1920): 180-4.

———. *Overtones.* In: Dean, *Washington Square Plays.*

———. *The Pot Boiler.* In: Shay, *Fifty Contemporary One-Act Plays.*

———. *Ten One-Act Plays.* New York: Brentano's, 1921.

Glaspell, Susan. *Alison's House.* New York: French, 1930.

———. *Bernice.* London: Benn, 1924.

———. *Inheritors.* Boston: Small, Maynard, 1921.

———. *The Outside.* In: Clements, C.C., ed., *Sea Plays.*

———. *The People and Close the Book.* New York: Frank Shay, 1918.

———. *Plays.* New York: Dodd, Mead, and Co., 1931.

———. *The Road to the Temple.* New York: Stokes, 1927.

———. *Trifles.* In: Gassner, *Twenty-Five Best.*

———. *The Verge.* In: Bigsby, *Plays.*

——— and George Cram Cook. *Suppressed Desires.* In Cerf, *Thirty Best.*

——— and Norman Matson. *The Comic Artist.* London: Benn, 1927.

Gordon, Ruth. *The Leading Lady.* New York: Dramatists Play Service, 1949.

———. *Over Twenty-One.* New York: Random House, 1944.

———. *Years Ago.* New York: Viking, 1947.

Gottlieb, Lois C. *Rachel Crothers.* N.Y.: Twayne, 1979.

Gould, Jean. *Modern American Playwrights.* New York: Dodd, Mead & Co., 1966.

Hamalian, Leo and James V. Hatch, eds. *The Roots of African American Drama.* Detroit: Wayne State Univ. Press, 1991.

Harris, Trudier, ed. *Afro-American Writers from the Harlem Renaissance to 1940. DLB*, 51. Detroit: Gale Research Co., 1987.

Hatch, James V. , ed., Ted Shine, consultant. *Black Theater, U.S.A. New York:* MacMillan, 1974.

Hayes, Helen with Katherine Hatch. *My Life in Three Acts*. N.Y.: Harcourt, Brace, Janovich, 1990.

Hellman, Lillian. *The Collected Plays*. Boston: Little Brown, & Co., 1972.

——. *Scoundrel Time*. Boston: Little, Brown, 1976.

——. *An Unfinished Woman*. Boston: Little, Brown, 1965.

Hemenway, Robert E. *Zora Neale Hurston*. Urbana: Univ. of Illinois Press, 1978.

Hewitt, Barnard. *Theatre U.S.A.* New York: McGraw-Hill, 1959.

Heyward, Dorothy and Du Bose. *Mamba's Daughters*. New York: Farrar & Rinehart, 1939.

——. *Porgy*. New York: Doubleday, Page & Co., 1927.

Hoffman, Michael J., ed. *Critical Essays on Gertrude Stein*. Boston: G.K. Hall, 1986.

——. *Gertrude Stein*. Boston: Twayne, 1976.

Hughes, Langston and Zora Neale Hurston. *Mule Bone*. Eds. George Houston Bass and Henry Louis Gates, Jr. New York: Harper Perennial, 1991.

Hurston, Zora Neale. *Color Struck*. In: Perkins.

——. *The First One*. In: Perkins.

Johnson, Georgia Douglas. *Blue Blood*. In: Brown-Guillory, *Wines*.

——. *Blue-Eyed Black Boy*. In: Brown-Guillory, *Wines*.

——. *Frederick Douglass*. In: Richardson, *Negro History*.

——. *Plumes*. In: France, *A Century*.

——. *Safe*. In: Brown-Guillory, *Wines*.

——. *A Sunday Morning in the South*. In: Hatch and Shine.

——. *William and Ellen Craft*. In: Richardson, *Negro History*.

Kanin, Fay. *Goodbye, My Fancy*. New York: French, 1947.

——— and Michael. *Rashomon*. New York: French, 1959.

——— and Michael. *His and Hers*. New York: Samuel French, 1954.

Keats, John. *You Might as Well Live; the Life and Times of Dorothy Parker*. New York: Simon and Schuster, 1970.

Kinney, Arthur F. *Dorothy Parker*. New York: Twayne, 1978.

Kirkpatrick, John. *She Married Well*. New York: French, 1947.

Krutch, Joseph Wood. *The American Drama Since 1918*. New York: Braziller, 1957.

Kummer, Clare. *Be Calm, Camilla!* New York: French, 1922.

——. *Good Gracious, Annabelle*. New York: French, 1922.

——. *Her Master's Voice*. New York: Samuel French, 1934.

——. *Pomeroy's Past*. New York: French, 1923.

——. *The Rescuing Angel*. New York: French, 1917.

——. *Rollo's Wild Oat*. New York: French, 1922.

——. *Spring Thaw*. New York: French, 1937.

——. *A Successful Calamity*. New York: French, 1922.

Langner, Lawrence. *The Magic Curtain*. New York: Dutton, 1951.

Laufe, Abe. *Anatomy of a Hit*. New York: Hawthorn Books, Inc. 1966.

Locke, Alain. *The New Negro*. New York: Atheneum, 1970.

Loos, Anita. *A Girl Like I.* New York: Viking, 1966.

——. *Gigi.* New York: French, 1953.

——. *Happy Birthday.* New York: French, 1947.

—— and John Emerson. *The Fall of Eve.* New York: Dodd, Mead, 1926.

——. *The Whole Town's Talking.* New York: Longman's, Green, 1925.

Luce, Clare Boothe. *Kiss the Boys Goodbye.* New York: Random House, 1939.

——. *Margin for Error.* New York: Dramatists Play Service, 1940.

——. *Slam the Door Softly.* New York: Dramatists Play Service, 1970.

——. *The Women.* New York: Random House, 1937.

Mackay, Charles. *Extraordinary Popular Delusions and the Madness of Crowds.* London: Bentley, 1841.

Mainiero, Lina, ed. *American Women Writers.* New York: Ungar, 1979.

Makowsky, Veronica. *Susan Glaspell's Century of American Women.* New York: Oxford University Press, 1993.

Maltin, Leonard. *Movie and Video Guide 1993.* New York: Signet, 1992.

Mantle, Burns. *American Playwrights of Today.* New York: Dodd, Mead & Co., 1929.

——. *Best Plays of——.* Annual series.

——. *Contemporary American Playwrights.* New York: Dodd, Mead & Co., 1939.

—— and Garrison P. Sherwood, eds. *The Best Plays of 1899-1909.* New York: Dodd, Mead, 1944.

——. *The Best Plays of 1909-1919.* New York: Dodd, Mead, 1934.

Martine, James J. *American Novelists, 1910-1945*. *DLB*. Detroit: Gale Research Co., 1981.

Matthews, Brander. *A Book About the Theatre*. New York: Scribner's Sons, 1916.

Mazer, Sharon. "Instructor's Manual," *The Anthology of Drama*. New York: Harcourt, Brace Janovich, 1993.

McCullers, Carson. *The Member of the Wedding*. New York: Country Life Press, 1949.

———. *The Square Root of Wonderful*. Boston: Houghton-Mifflin, 1958.

Meade, Marion. *Dorothy Parker*. New York: Villard Books, 1988.

Miller, May. *Christophe's Daughters*. In: Perkins.

———. *Graven Images*. In: Hatch and Shine.

———. *Harriet Tubman*. In: Perkins.

———. *Nails and Thorns*. In: Richardson, *Negro History*.

———. *Riding the Goat*. In: Brown-Guillory, *Wines*.

———. *Sojourner Truth*. In: Richardson, *Negro History*.

———. *Stragglers in the Dust*. In: Perkins.

Moody, Richard. *Lillian Hellman, Playwright*. New York: Pegasus, 1972.

Morehouse, Ward. *Matinee Tomorrow*. New York: McGraw-Hill, 1949.

Nathan, George Jean. *The Theatre, the Drama, the Girls*. New York: Knopf, 1921.

———. *The Theatre Year Book of* ———. Annual Series.

Nichols, Anne. *Abie's Irish Rose*. S.R..O. *The Most Successful Plays of the American Stage*. Eds. Bennett Cerf and Van. H. Cartmell. New York: Doubleday, 1944.

——— and Adelaide Matthews. *Just Married*. New York: Samuel French, 1929.

Papke, Mary E. *Susan Glaspell: A Research and Production Sourcebook.* Westport: Greenwood Press, 1993.

Parker, Dorothy and Arnaud d'Ussau. *The Ladies of the Corridor.* New York: Viking, 1954.

——. and Elmer Rice. *Close Harmony.* New York: French, 1929.

Peabody, Josephine Preston. *The Collected Plays of Josephine Preston Peabody.* Foreword George P. Baker. Cambridge: Riverside Press, 1927.

——. *Diary and Letters.* Ed. Christina Hopkins Baker. Boston: Houghton Mifflin, 1925.

——. *Marlowe.* Boston: Houghton Mifflin, 1905.

——. *The Piper.* In: Dickinson, *Chief Contemporary Dramatists.*

——. *Portrait of Mrs. W.* Boston: Houghton Mifflin, 1922.

——. *Wings.* New York: French, 1917.

——. *The Wolf of Gubbio.* Boston: Houghton Mifflin, 1913.

Peters, Margot. *The House of Barrymore.* New York: Knopf, 1991.

Peterson, Jr., Bernard L. *Early Black American Playwrights and Dramatic Writers.* Conn.: Greenwood Press, 1990.

Quinn, Arthur Hobson, ed. *The Art of Playwriting.* Penna.: U of Penna P, 1928.

——. *Contemporary American Plays.* New York: Scribner, 1923.

——. *Representative American Plays.* New York: Appleton-Century-Crofts, 1953.

Richardson, Willis and May Miller, eds. *Negro History in Thirteen Plays.* Washington: The Associated Publishers, 1935.

Richardson, Willis, ed. *Plays and Pageants From the Life of the Negro.* Washington, D.C.: The Associated Publishers, 1930.

Robinson, Alice M., Vera Mowry Roberts, and Milly S. Barranger, eds. *Notable Women in the American Theatre*. New York: Greenwood Press, 1989.

Schlueter, June, ed. *Modern American Drama: The Female Canon*. New Jersey: Associated Univ. Presses, 1990.

Schneider, Anne Kaufman, ed. *George S. Kaufman and His Collaborators*. New York: Performing Arts Journal Publications, 1984.

Shadegg, Stephen. *Clare Boothe Luce*. New York: Simon and Schuster, 1970.

Shay, Frank, ed. *Fifty Contemporary One-Act Plays*. Cincinnati: Stewart & Kidd, 1921.

Shelley, Elsa. *Foxhole in the Parlor*. New York: Dramatists Play Service, 1945.

——. *Pick-Up Girl*. New York: Dramatists Play Service, 1946.

Short, Kayann, ed. *Ticklish Proceedings*. Boulder: CU Publications, 1991.

Sievers, W. David. *Freud on Broadway; A History of Psychoanalysis and the American Drama*. New York: Hermitage House, 1955.

Simonson, Harold P. *Zona Gale*. New York: Twayne Publishers, 1962.

Skinner, Cornelia Otis. *One Woman Show*. Woodstock, Ill.: Dramatic Publishing Co., 1984.

—— and Samuel Taylor. *The Pleasure of His Company*. New York: Random House, 1959.

Skinner, R. Dana. *Our Changing Theatre*. New York: Dial, 1931.

Sochen, June. *The New Feminism in Twentieth Century America*. Lexington, Ma.: D.C. Heath, 1971.

——. *The New Woman*. New York: Quadrangle Books, 1972.

Spacks, Patricia Meyer. *The Female Imagination*. New York: Knopf, 1975.

Spence, Eulalie. *Episode*. In: Brown-Guillory, *Wines*.

———. *Fool's Errand*. In: Perkins.

———. *Her*. In: Perkins.

———. *Hot Stuff*. In: Brown-Guillory, *Wines*.

———. *Undertow*. In: Perkins.

Spewack, Bella and Sam. *Boy Meets Girl*. New York: Random House, 1936.

———. *Clear All Wires*. New York: French, 1932.

———. *Festival*. New York: Dramatists Play Service, 1955.

———. *Kiss Me Kate*. Lyrics and Music by Cole Porter. New York: Knopf, 1953.

———. *My 3 Angels*. New York: Random House, 1953.

———. *Poppa*. New York: French, 1929.

Stein, Gertrude. *Last Operas and Plays*. Ed. Carl Van Vechten. New York: Rinehart, 1949.

———. Selected Operas and Plays of Gertrude Stein. Ed. John Malcom Brinnin. Pittsburgh: Univ. of Pittsburgh Press, 1970.

Tanner, Jo A. *Dusky Maidens*. Conn.: Greenwood Press, 1992.

Taubman, Howard. *The Making of American Theatre*. New York: Coward-McCann, 1967.

Teichmann, Howard. *George S. Kaufman*. New York: Atheneum, 1972.

Toohey, John L. A *History of the Pulitzer Prize Plays*. New York: The Citadel Press 1967.

Treadwell, Sophie. *Hope for a Harvest*. New York: French, 1942.

———. *Machinal*. In: Gassner, *Twenty-Five Best*.

Vollmer, Lula. *The Hill Between*. New York: Longmans, Green, 1939.

——. *Moonshine and Honeysuckle*. New York: French, 1934.

——. *Sun-Up*. In: Quinn, *Representative American Plays*.

Watkins, Maurine. *Chicago*. Pref. George Jean Nathan. New York: Knopf, 1927.

West, Mae. *Goodness Had Nothing to Do With It*. New Jersey, Prentice-Hall, 1959.

Williams, Mance. *Black Theatre in the 1960s and 1970s*. Westport, Conn.: Greenwood, 1985.

Wilson, Edmund. *The American Earthquake; A Documentary of the Twenties and Thirties*. New York: Doubleday, 1964.

Wright, William. *Lillian Hellman*. New York: Simon and Schuster, 1986.

Young, Rida Johnson. *Brown of Harvard*. New York: French, 1909.

—— and Rudolf Friml. *Some Time*. New York: Schirmer, 1946.

—— and Christy Mathewson. *The Girl and the Pennant*. New York: French, 1917.

—— and Sigmund Romberg. *Naughty Marietta*. New York: Witmark, 1910.

Articles

"About Alice's Stage Mother," *New York Times* 4 April 1915: 5.

Abramson, Doris. "Angelina Weld Grimké, Mary T. Burrill, Georgia Douglas Johnson, and Marita O. Bonner: An Analysis of Their Plays." *Sage* (Spring 1985): 9-13.

——. "Rachel Crothers: Broadway Feminist," *Modern American Drama: The Female Canon*, ed. Schlueter, 55-65.

——. "Rose Franken." Robinson, *Notable Women* 314-316.

Abramson, Doris and Laurilyn Harris. "Anne Nichols: $1,000,000 Playwright," *Women in American Theatre,* eds. Chinoy and Jenkins, 153-157.

"After Nearly Ten Years 'The Piper' in the Playwright's Own City." Unidentified clipping Lincoln Center Library.*

Akins, Zoë. "The Playwriting Passion." *Vanity Fair* 8 June 1920: 61+.

Alexander, J.B. "Revival of the Fittest: 'Boy Meets Girl.'" *New York Post* 12 Ap. 1976: 31.

"American Play Wins Prize." Unidentified clipping Lincoln Center Library.

"Anita Loos." *Contemporary Authors* Vols. 21-22 (1969): 548-549.

Austrian, Delia. "Young Chicago Woman is Novelist and Playwright." *Cincinnati Tribune* 5 Nov. 1916: n.p. Clipping Lincoln Center Library.

Balch, Nelda K. "Cornelia Otis Skinner." Robinson, *Notable Women* 795-797.

Barron, Mark. "Mrs. Chase Makes Million with Plays." *Portland* [Oregon] *Journal* 26 October 1952: n.p. Clipping Lincoln Center Library.

Beckley, Zoe. "Girl Author's Best Seller Based on Story Mother Told of Loveless Spinster." *New York Evening Mail* 21 March 1915: n.p. Clipping Lincoln Center Library.

Beebe, Lucius. "Translating Another Language." *New York Herald Tribune* 8 May 1932: n.p. Clipping Lincoln Center Library.

"Bella Spewack." *Variety* 2 May 1990: 319.

"Bella Spewack Hits Critics of 'Festival.'" Unidentified clipping Lincoln Center Library.

Bennett, Helen Christine. "The Woman Who Wrote 'Mother Machree.'" *American Magazine* Dec. 1920: 34-35+.

Ben-Zwi, Linda. "Susan Glaspell." Robinson, *Notable Women* 341-346.

"Berlin Likes 'Irish Rose.'" *New York Times* 20 Dec.1928: n.p. Clipping Lincoln Center Library.

Berry, Linda S. "Georgia Douglas Camp Johnson." Mainiero, *American Women Writers* 407-408.

"Big Earnings of Big Plays." *Theatre Magazine* (Nov. 1913): 151-155+.

Bienstock, Beverly Gray. "Anita Loos." Mainiero, *American Women Writers* 33-35.

———. "Cornelia Otis Skinner." Mainiero, *American Women Writers* 91-92.

"Bloody Distinguisht." *Vanity Fair* 4 Jan. 1907: n.p. Clipping Lincoln Center Library.

Bowling, R. Peter. "Mae West on Broadway." Unidentified clipping Lincoln Center Library.

Braggiotti, Mary. "The Bone Splintering Career of a Playwright." *New York Post* 19 Nov. 1943: 1.

Breitsprecher, Nancy. "Zona Gale." Mainiero, *American Women Writers* 97-98.

"Brief Sketches of Winners of Pulitzer Prizes." *New York Herald Tribune* 7 May 1934: n.p. Clipping Library Lincoln Center.

"Brilliant Dramatist of the South." *Louisville Times* 15 Nov 1910, n.p. Clipping Lincoln Center Library.

"Bringing 'Lillian' to Life is a Rough Acting Role." *Chicago Tribune* 8 Jan. 1987: 11.

"Broadway's 'Miss Chicago' From Kentucky." Unidentified clipping Lincoln Center Library.

"A Broom For Miss Ferber; City Offers Novelist a Post in Its Clean-up Drive." *New York Times* 26 Ap. 1953: n.p. Clipping Lincoln Center Library.

Burns, Morris U. "Edna Ferber." Robinson, *Notable Women* 269-273.

Burns, Shirley. "Sketches of Several Women Dramatists." *Green Book Album* Sept. 1910: 634.

Bywaters, Barbara L. "Marriage, Madness, and Murder in Sophie Treadwell's *Machinal.*" Schlueter, *Modern American Drama* 97-110.

Carlson, Susan L. "Comic Textures and Female Communities 1937 and 1977: Clare Boothe and Wendy Wasserstein." Schlueter, *Modern American Drama* 207-217.

Carmer, Carl. "George S. Kaufman; Playmaker to Broadway." *Theatre Arts Monthly* Oct. 1932: 807-815.

Cassidy, Joseph. "Edna Ferber, 82, Dies; Author of Showboat." *Daily News* 17 Ap. 1968: n.p. Clipping Lincoln Center Library.

Chapman, John A. "Zoë Akins-Experimenter in the Drama Laboratory." *The Spotlight* 2. Unidentified clipping Lincoln Center Library.

Chase, Mary. "My Life With Harvey." Unidentified clipping Lincoln Center Library.

"'Chicago' Saga." Unidentified clipping Lincoln Center Library.

"Clare Boothe Luce Dies of Cancer." *New York Post* 10 Oct. 1987: n.p. Clipping Lincoln Center Library.

Clark, Barrett H. "Lillian Hellman." *College English* Dec. 1944: 127-133.

Clarke, Gerald. "At 84 Mae West Is Still Mae West." *Time* 22 May 1978: 65-66.

"'Claudia' Royalties Pay for Farm." *New Hampshire Register* 27 July 1941: n.p. Clipping Lincoln Center Library.

Coleman, Robert. "Her Play Gets Premiere Tonight," *Daily Mirror* 1 Mar. 1937: n.p. Clipping Lincoln Center Library.

Conroy, Sarah Booth. "Authors of Change; Locke, Johnson and the Black Renaissance." *Washington Post* (4 Mar. 1990): F1.

"Cornelia Otis Skinner." *Current Biography 1964* 423-426.

"Creator of 'Machinal' Returns to Broadway With Guild Play." Unidentified clipping Lincoln Center Library.

Creelman, Eileen. "Lillian Hellman Discusses Casting and Directing of Her Original 'The North Star.'" Unidentified clipping Lincoln Center Library.

Crothers, Rachel. "The Construction of a Play." Quinn, *The Art of Playwriting* 115-134.

——. "Troubles of a Playwright." *Harper's Bazaar* 14 Jan. 1911: 14.

Dean, Alexander."Preface." Gerstenberg, *Comedies All*.

Dillon, Jane. "Edna Ferber Sees Better Days Ahead." *Christian Science Monitor* 15 June 1943: n.p. Clipping Lincoln Center Library.

"Dinner At Eight-Thirty." *New York Times* 30 Oct. 1932: n.p. Clipping Lincoln Center Library.

Drutman, Irving. "Herman Shumlin's Favorite Dramatist." *New York Herald Tribune* 7 May 1944: n.p. Clipping Lincoln Center Library.

Dudar, Helen. "Woman in the News: Edna Ferber." *New York Post* 1 Oct. 1966: 25.

Duval, Elizabeth R. "Edna Ferber Rings Down One Curtain." *New York Times Magazine* 1 Sept. 1940: 7.

Eaton, Walter Prichard. "Josephine Preston Peabody," *Metropolitan* May 1911: 190-92.

"Edna Ferber Dies at 82." *Newark Evening News* 17 April 1968: n.p. Clipping Lincoln Center Library.

"Edna Ferber, Novelist, 82, Dies." *New York Times* 17 Ap. 1968: 1+.

"Edna Ferber Returns; Novelist Returns From Europe Says She Has Turned Playwright." Unidentified clipping Lincoln Center Library.

"Edna Ferber's % on Giant Film Tops 1 1/2 Million." *Variety* 14 May 1958: n.p. Clipping Lincoln Center Library.

"Edna Ferber's Notion of Fun is Playwriting." *New York Herald Tribune* 13 Nov. 1932: n.p. Clipping Lincoln Center Library.

Eliasberg, Ann Pringle. "Josephine Preston Peabody." Mainiero, *American Women Writers* 358-359.

Engle, William. "Rose Franken Wrote New Play in 6 Days, & So She Says 'out of plain cussedness.'" *New York Times* 4 May 1932: n.p. Clipping Lincoln Center Library.

"Fay Kanin Tribute Packs Them In at ACLU Awards." *Variety* 16 Dec. 1987: n.p. Clipping Lincoln Center Library.

"Fay Kanin's 'Trial by Fire.'" 16 Nov. 1949. Unidentified Clipping Lincoln Center Library.

Ferber, Edna. "My Son, the Show Boat." *New York Times* 17 July 1966: D1+.

Fields, Sidney. "The Playwright Wants to Act." Unidentified clipping Lincoln Center Library.

Fletcher, Winona. "From Genteel Poet to Revolutionary Playwright: Georgia Douglas Johnson" *Theatre Annual* (XXXX 1985), 41-64.

——. "Georgia Douglas Johnson." Harris, *Afro-American Writers* 153-163.

——. "Georgia Douglas Johnson." Robinson, *Notable Women* 473-477.

Forman, Henry James. "The Story of Rachel Crothers, America's Leading Woman Playwright." *Pictorial Review* June 1931: 2+.

Flynn, Joyce. "Marita Bonner Occomy." Harris, *Afro-American Writers* 222-228.

Frame, Virginia. "Successful Women Dramatists" *Theatre Magazine* (October 1906): 265-267+.

France, Rachel. "Susan Glaspell." *Dictionary of Literary Biography*. 7: 215-223.

Franken, Rose. "An Author's Slings and Arrows." *New York Times* 21 Nov. 1943: 1.

Freydberg, Elizabeth Hadley. "Carson McCullers." Robinson, *Notable Women* 614-18.

Friedman, Sharon. "Feminism as a Theme in Twentieth-Century American Women's Drama." *American Studies* (Spring 1910): 68-69.

Fugate, Liz. "Rachel Crothers." Robinson, *Notable Women* 180-85.

Gabbard, Lucina P. "Clare Boothe Luce." Mainiero, *American Women Writers* 48-49.

——. "Mary Coyle Chase." Mainiero, *American Women Writers* 340-42.

Gaines-Carter, Patricia. "New Generation Discovers D.C. Poet May Miller." *The Washington Post* (26 Dec. 1986): B12.

Gerstenberg, Alice. "The Players' Workshop of Chicago." *Theatre Magazine* Sept. 1917: n.p. Clipping Lincoln Center Library.

Gipson, Rosemary. "Martha Morton: America's First Professional Woman Playwright." *Theatre Survey* (Nov. 1982): 213-22.

Goldman, Michael. "The Dangerous Edge of Things" *New York Times Literary Supplement* 5 Dec. 1988: 139.

Gottlieb, Lois. "Looking to Women: Rachel Crothers and the Feminist Heroine." Chinoy, 137-45.

Green Book Sept. 1919: n.p. Unidentified clipping about Rida Johnson Young, Lincoln Center Library.

"Grit and Wit Made Ruth Gordon a Star," *New York Times* 8 Sept. 1985: 10.

Grossman, Ron. "A roads scholar pedals passionately into the past." *Chicago Tribune* 7 Apr. 1982: 1.

Haddad-Garcia, George. "Mae West, Everybody's Friend." *Black Stars* Apr. 1981: 62-64.

Harlitz, Aljean. "To the Top." *People Magazine* 21 Apr. 1980: 18+.

Harris, Laurilyn. "Anita Loos." Robinson, *Notable Women* 555-58.

———. "Anne Nichols." Robinson, *Notable Women* 688-89.

Hart, Lynda. "Bella Spewack." Robinson, *Notable Women* 814-16.

Hassencahl, Fran. "Mae West." Robinson, *Notable Women* 913-18.

Hellman, Lillian. "An Author Jabs Her Critics." *New York Times*: n.p. Unidentified clipping Lincoln Center Library.

Hevesi, Dennis. "Bella Spewack, Author, 91, Dies." *New York Times* 29 Apr. 1990: 36.

Holditch, Kenneth W. "Dorothy Parker." Robinson *Notable Women* 712-16.

"Holds the Record as Woman Playwright." *Chicago Examiner* 3 Apr. 1910: n.p. Clipping Lincoln Center Library.

Holdstein, Deborah H. "Mae West." Mainiero, *American Women Writers* 365-67.

Horwitz, Simi. "A Creative Producer." *Theater Week* 27 Sept. 1993: 16-21.

Howard, Lillie P. "Zora Neale Hurston." Harris, *Afro-American Writers* 241-47.

Hutton, Elizabeth M. "Mary Coyle Chase." Robinson, *Notable Women* 124-26.

Hyams, Joe, "This is Hollywood." *New York Herald Tribune* 17 Aug. 1955: n.p. Clipping Lincoln Center Library.

Inge, Benson. "The Author of Twenty Plays, Zoë Akins, Adds Still Another." Unidentified Clipping Lincoln Center Library.

Isaacs, Edith J.R. "Lillian Hellman: A Playwright on the March." *Theatre Arts* Jan. 1944: 19-24.

Israel, Lee. "The Theater of Dorothy Parker." *Theater Week* 25 May 1992: 24-26.

"It Appears Two Persons Wrote Latest Kaufman-Ferber Play." Unidentified clipping Lincoln Center Library.

Kaufman, George S. "From Mr. Kaufman." *New York Times* 22 Nov. 1936: n.p. Clipping Lincoln Center Library.

"King and Queen See 'Sun-Up.'" *New York Times* 14 Aug. 1925: 13.

Kiper, Florence. "Some American Plays From the Feminist Viewpoint." *Forum* 50 (1914): 921-931.

Klein, Kathleen G. "Anne Nichols." Mainiero, *American Women Writers* 257-58.

Kolb, Deborah S. "The Rise and Fall of the New Woman in American Drama." *Educational Theatre Journal* (May 1975): 149-160.

Koon, Helen. "Ruth Gordon." *Current Biography Yearbook 1972*: 159-61.

Korf, Jean Prinz. "Fay Mitchell Kanin." Robinson, *Notable Women* 483-86.

Kummer, Clare. "The Essence of Drama," *Theatre Magazine* May 1921: n.p. Clipping Lincoln Center Library.

Lester, Elenore. "'The Women': Older But Not Wiser," *Ms.* Aug. 1973: 42-45.

"Lillian Hellman Author of 'The Searching Wind.'" Unidentified clipping Lincoln Center Library.

Londré, Felicia Hardison. "Dorothy Hartzell Kuhns Heyward." Mainiero, *American Women Writers* 290-92.

——. "Josephine Preston Peabody." Robinson, *Notable Women* 721-24.

——. "Martha Morton." Mainiero, *American Women Writers* 229-30.

——. "Martha Morton." Robinson, *Notable Women* 676-78.

——. "Rida Johnson Young." Robinson, *Notable Women* 942-44.

——. "Zoë Akins." Robinson, *Notable Women* 11-13.

——. "Zona Gale." Robinson, *Notable Women* 323-325.

"Lula Vollmer Dies; Writer of Folk Plays." *New York Herald Tribune* 3 May 1958: n.p. Clipping Lincoln Center Library.

MacNicholas, Carol. "Lillian Hellman." *Dictionary of Literary Biography* 1981: 275-95.

Mandelbaum, Ken. "Theater News." *Theater Week* 13 Sept. 1993: 6.

Mantle, Burns. "Watching a Stage Wife Grow Up; Rose Franken's 'Claudia.'" Unidentified clipping Lincoln Center Library.

"The Many Lives of Clare Boothe Luce." *Parade Magazine* 6 Nov. 1983: 4-8.

Mackaye, Milton. "Clare Boothe." *Scribner's Magazine* Mar. 1939: 9-13+.

McGovern, Edythe M. "Rachel Crothers." Mainiero, *American Women Writers* 428-30.

——. "Susan Glaspell." Mainiero, *American Women Writers* 144-46.

Michaelson, Judy. "Edna Ferber: First Person Singular" *New York Post* 13 Oct. 1963: n.p. Clipping Lincoln Center Library.

"Milestone for a First Playwright: Second Year on Broadway." Unidentified clipping Lincoln Center Library.

Miller, Jeanne-Marie A. "Black Women Playwrights from Grimké to Schange: Selected Synopses of Their Works." In: *But Some of Us Are Brave*, ed. Gloria Hull, Patricia Bell Scott, and Barbara Smith. Old Westbury, New York: Feminist Press, 1982: 280-296.

"Miss Ferber's Fox River Valley." Unidentified Clipping Lincoln Center Library.

"Mlle. Manhattan." *New York Telegraph* 1909. Clipping Lincoln Center Library.

Molette, Barbara. "They Speak: Who Listens? Black Women Playwrights." *Black World* (April 1976): 28-34.

Morehouse, Rebecca. "A Theatregoer's Notebook; Clare Boothe Luce." *Playbill* Jan. 1988: n.p. Clipping Lincoln Center Library.

"Mrs. Luce is Contradicted." *New York Times* 29 June 1943: n.p. Clipping Lincoln Center Library.

"Mrs. Rida Johnson Young, Who Has Written ..." Partially obliterated clipping Lincoln Center Library.

Mullett, Mary B. "Clare Kummer's Experience in Play Writing Has Been Unusual." 4 Mar. 1917. Unidentified clipping Lincoln Center Library.

"Mulrain Nettled by Charge of 'Filthy City.'" Unidentified clipping Lincoln Center Library.

"A New Society of American Dramatic Authors" *Theatre Magazine* Mar. 1907: 84-85+.

Nichols, Lewis. "Talk With Edna Ferber," *New York Times* 5 Oct. 1952: n.p. Clipping Lincoln Center Library.

Noe, Marcia. "Susan Glaspell." *Dictionary of Literary Biography* 9: 66-71.

"Novelist Back From Europe." *New York Herald Tribune* 8 Sept. 1932: n.p. Clipping Lincoln Center Library.

Ogden, Clare. "Ex-Reporter, Now Playwright, Tells of High Spots in Career." *New York Telegraph* 9 Jan. 1927: n.p. Clipping Lincoln Center Library.

"One of America's Foremost Writers." *Toledo Times* 24 Aug. 1910: n.p. Clipping Lincoln Center Library.

Osborne, Robert. "Rambling Reporter." *BPI Entertainment News Wire* 28 January 1993: 3.

Ormsbee, Helen. "Miss Hellman All But Dares Her Next Play to Succeed." *New York Herald Tribune* 9 Ap. 1944: 1.

———. "Rose Franken Says Playwriting Like Pie-crust Needs Light Hand." *New York Herald Tribune* 28 Nov. 1943: n.p. Clipping Lincoln Center Library.

Osnes, Beth. "Good Gracious Miss Kummer! A New Kind of Humor for the American Stage." Short, *Ticklish Proceedings* 103-8.

Ozieblo, Barbara. "Rebellion and Rejection: The Plays of Susan Glaspell." Schlueter, *Modern American Drama* 66-75.

"Pancho Villa Source of Material for Play." Unidentified clipping Lincoln Center Library.

Patterson, Ada. "A Chat with the Dean of America's Women Playwrights." *Theatre* Magazine 1909. Clipping Lincoln Center Library.

Pederson, Lucille M. "Clare Boothe Luce." Robinson, *Notable Women* 563-66.

Peterson, Jr., Bernard L. "Marita O. Bonner." *Early Black American Playwrights* 34-35.

———. "Alice Moore Dunbar-Nelson." *Early Black American Playwrights* 71-72.

———. "Georgia Douglas Johnson." *Early Black American Playwrights* 118-20.

——. "Zora Neale Hurston." *Early Black American Playwrights* 114-116.

——. "May Miller." *Early Black American Playwrights* 143-146.

——. "Eulalie Spence." *Early Black American Playwrights* 178-180.

"Plays Given By Blind; Sightless Audience Laughs Over a Comedy by Zona Gale." *New York Times* 18 June 1924: 23.

"Professional Women's Club of Boston Honors Josephine Preston Peabody." *New York Mirror* 23 Ap. 1910: n.p. Clipping Lincoln Center Library.

Puk, Francine Shapiro. "Dorothy Rothschild Parker." Mainiero, *American Women Writers* 343-44.

"Recall Mae West at USC Testimonial; Still Alluring Siren," *Variety* 31 Mar. 1982: 2+.

Reid, B.L. "An Evaluation: 'Think of Shakespeare and Think of Me.' " Bloom, *Gertrude Stein* 81-100.

Robinson, Marc. "Gertrude Stein, Forgotten Playwright." *The South Atlantic Quarterly* 3 (Summer 1992): 621-43.

"Rose Franken Panicking 'Em on the Thames." *New York Times* 8 Jan. 1933: n.p. Clipping Lincoln Center Library.

Ryan, Betsy. "Gertrude Stein." Robinson, *Notable Women* 830-35.

Sartain, Geraldine. "Women Can't Juggle the Rules of Man's World." *World Telegram* 13 Oct. 1932: n.p. Clipping Lincoln Center Library.

Saylor, Oliver. "Some Playwright Biographies." *Theatre Arts Magazine* July 1927: 531-32.

Seeley, Evelyn. "Had to Flee Hollywood, Says Mrs. Spewack, Author." *World Telegram* 1932. Clipping Lincoln Center Library.

Shafer, Yvonne. "Rose Franken." *DLB Yearbook* 1984, 280-85.

——. "Rose Franken's *Outrageous Fortune*." *Exchange* Spring-Summer 1978: 8-15.

——. "Susan Glaspell: German Influence, American Playwright." *Zeitschrift für Änglistik und Amerikanistik* (December 1988): 333-38.

——. "Whose Realism? Rachel Crothers' Power Struggle in the American Theatre." *Realism and the American Dramatic Tradition.* Ed. William Demastes. Forthcoming.

Simonson, Harold P. "Zona Gale." *DLB,* 9: 39-41.

Smith, Susan Harris. "Lulu [sic] Vollmer." Robinson, *Notable Women* 890-93.

Snipes, Katherine. "Carson McCullers." Mainiero, *American Women Writers* 459-62.

"Society Girl Wins Fame In Play That Bares Social Hypocrisy." *Louisville Herald* 26 May 1914: n.p. Clipping Lincoln Center Library.

"Sophie Treadwell." Unidentified clipping Lincoln Center Library.

"Speakers at Book and Author Luncheon." *New York Herald Tribune* 5 Mar. 1947: n.p. Clipping Lincoln Center Library.

Stein, Karen F. "Alice Ruth Moore Dunbar Nelson." Mainiero, *American Women Writers* 247-49.

Stimpson, Catharine R. "The Mind, the Body, and Gertrude Stein." *Critical Inquiry* (Spring 1977): 489-6.

Stinnett, Jack. "New Yorker at Large." Unidentified Clipping Lincoln Center Library.

Stoelting, Winifred L., "May Miller." Harris, *Afro-American Writers* 241-47.

"A Successful Calamity Miss Kummer's Comedy of the Tired Businessman." *Current Literature* 1917. Clipping Lincoln Center Library.

Sutherland, Cynthia. "American Women Playwrights as Mediators of the 'Woman Problem.'" *Modern Drama* (September 1978): 319-36.

Sutton, Charlotte. "Images of Black Washington." *Washington Post* (2 Nov. 1983): B3.

Syse, Glenna. "That rare and durable 'Harvey.'" *Chicago Sun Times* 24 Oct. 1971: 3.

Tai, Amanda and Sharon Lai. "Drama in English Proves Popular." Unidentified clipping Lincoln Center Library.

"Tells of Her Prize Play." *The Sun* 28 Jan. 1911: n.p. Clipping Lincoln Center Library.

Ten Broeck, Helen. "Rida Young 'Dramatist and Garden Expert." *Theatre Magazine* April 1917: 148-49.

". . . that Women Do Have a Sense of Humor." Unidentified clipping Lincoln Center Library.

"The Theatre." *New York Times* 26 April 1925: n.p. Clipping Lincoln Center Library.

"Three Plays Offered by Blind Actresses: Lighthouse Players Show Skill." *New York Times* (4 Mar. 1931): 33.

Toohey, John Peter. "Edna Ferber's Shopping Splurge." *New York Herald Tribune* 8 Jan. 1933: n.p. Clipping Lincoln Center Library.

Townsend, Janis. "Gertrude Stein." Mainiero, *American Women Writers* 153-61.

——. Bloom, "Gertrude Stein." 714-717.

Treadwell, Sophie. "Miss Treadwell Explains Why She Put a $2.00 Top on Her Play." *New York Herald Tribune* 5 Mar. 1933: n.p. Clipping Lincoln Center Library.

Trescott, Jacqueline. "The Fabulous Zora Neale Hurston." *Washington Post* (21 May 1978): F1.

Walker, Cynthia L. "Edna Ferber." Mainiero, *American Women Writers* 24-27.

"Water Warden's Day," *New York Herald Tribune* 14 December 1949: 20.

Weinstein, Marion. "Real Love for the Stage." *Kansas City Times* 10 Sept. 1917: n.p. Clipping Lincoln Center Library.

Weinstein, Norman. "*Four Saints in Three Acts:* Play as Landscape." Bloom, *Gertrude Stein* 113-20.

Wertheim, Albert. "The Comic Muse of Mary Chase." Chinoy 163-70.

West, Mae. "Ten Days and Five Hundred Dollars." *Liberty* (Winter 1975): 6-8.

Westcott, Holly Mims. "Dorothy Heyward, DuBose Heyward." *DLB,* 7: 295-301.

Wilder, Thornton. "*Four in America.*" Bloom, *Gertrude Stein* 25-45.

Wilkerson, Isabel. "A D.C. Poet Reminisces; From Harlem Renaissance to Howard U." *Washington Post* (1 Dec. 1982): DC1.

Williams, Ora. "Alice Moore Dunbar Nelson." *DLB,* 50: 226-233.

"Woman Author of Hit is an Amazing Figure." *New York Mirror* 8 May 1932: 20.

"Young, Rida Johnson." Letter to *New York Telegraph* 16 May 1909: n.p. Clipping Lincoln Center Library.

Yongue, Patricia Lee. "Zoë Akins." Faust, *American Women Writers* 13-15.

"Zona Gale Dies." *New York Herald Tribune* 28 Dec. 1938: n.p. Clipping Lincoln Center Library.

"Zona Gale Memorial Dramatic Collection." Unidentified clipping Lincoln Center Library.

Reviews

"American Folk Play by the Author of 'Neighbors' is Warmly Welcomed." *New York Telegram* 28 Dec. 1920: n.p. Clipping Lincoln Center Library.

Anderson, John. "Lillian Hellman Establishes Self as Major Playwright." *New York Times.* Unidentified clipping Library Lincoln Center.*

———. "Spring Thaw." *New York Journal* 22 Mar. 1938: n.p. Clipping Lincoln Center Library.

Aston, Frank. "Cheri." *New York World-Telegram* 13 Oct. 1959: n.p. *New York Theatre Critics' Reviews 1959*: 268,

———. "Tallulah Plays 'Midgie Purvis.'" *New York World-Telegram* 2 Feb. 1961: n.p. *New York Theatre Critics' Reviews 1961*: 376.

———. "Taylor Comedy Is a Real Pleasure." *New York World-Telegram* 23 Oct. 1958: n.p. *New York Theatre Critics' Reviews 1958*: 246.

Atkinson, Brooks. "Abide With Me." *New York Times* 22 Nov. 1935: 19.

———. "Alderman Schwitzky Goes Free." *New York Times* 24 Dec. 1928: 31.

———. "Back Comes Porgy." *New York Times* 14 Sept. 1929: 17.

———. "Blondes Preferred." *New York Times* 29 Sept. 1926: 23.

———. "Boy Meets Girl." 29 Nov. 1935: 38.

———. "The Children's Hour." *New York Times* 19 Dec. 1952: 35.

———. "Clear All Wires." *New York Times* 15 Sept. 1932: 19 and 25 Sept. 1932: 1.

———. "Cornelia Otis Skinner." *New York Times* 3 Ap. 1935: 20.

———. "Desire in 'Lone Valley.'" *New York Times* 11 Mar. 1933: 18.

———. "Edna Best and Betty Field are Starred." *New York Times* 22 Oct. 1953: 33.

———. "Edna Ferber Begins a Week's Acting Career." *New York Times* 13 Aug. 1940: 15.

———. "Edna His Wife." *New York Times* 8 Dec. 1937: 30.

———. "'Gentlemen Prefer Blondes.'" *New York Times* 9 Dec. 1949: 35.

———. "Gigi." *New York Times* 26 Nov. 1951: 20.

———. "'The Happy Days' Adapted by Zoë Akins from the French." *New York Times* 14 May 1941: 24.

———. "Helen Hayes in Mary Chase's Comic Fantasy." *New York Times* 21 Feb. 1952: n.p. *New York Theatre Critics' Reviews* 1952: 359.

———. "Her Master's Voice." *New York Times* 24 Oct. 1933: 24.

———. "Heyward's Negro Drama." *New York Times* 14 Nov. 1948: n.p. Clipping Lincoln Center Library.

———. "The Hill Between." *New York Times* 12 Mar. 1938: 12.

———. "Holding Both His Sides." *New York Times* 15 Dec. 1935: 3.

———. "In Three Dimensions." *New York Times* 15 May 1932: 1.

———. "Jobyna Howland in a Chronical Drama." *New York Times* 9 Jan. 1936: 24.

———. "Kiss Me, Kate." *New York Times* 31 Dec. 1948: 10.

———. "Kiss the Boys Goodbye." *New York Times* 29 Sept. 1938: 30.

———. "Machinal." *New York Times* 8 Apr. 1960: 27.

———. "Mamba's Daughters." *New York Times* 4 Jan. 1939: 24.

———. "Mamba's Daughters." *New York Times* 21 Mar. 1953: 12.

——. "Mary Chase Studies Problem of Being Young." 17 Oct. 1952: n.p. *New York Theatre Critics' Reviews 1952*: 233.

——. "The Member of the Wedding." *New York Times* 6 Jan. 1950: 26.

——. "Mrs. McCullers' Play Opens at National." *New York Times* 31 Oct. 1957: 40.

——. "Opening of 'Revelry.'" *New York Times* 13 Sept. 1927: 37.

——. "The Play: 'Another Part of the Forest.' " *New York Times* 21 Nov. 1946: n.p. *New York Theatre Critics' Reviews 1946*: 248.

——. "The Play: 'Years Ago.'" *New York Times* 4 Dec. 1946: 44.

——. "Plumes in the Dust." *New York Times* 7 Nov. 1936: 14.

——. "Porgy." *New York Times* 16 Oct. 1927: 1.

——. "Rashomon." *New York Times* 8 Feb. 1959: 1.

——. "Royal Family." *New York Times* 29 Dec. 1927: 26

——. "Ruth Gordon Appears as 'The Leading Lady.' " *New York Times* 19 Oct. 1948: 38.

——. "Sentinels." *New York Times* 26 Dec. 1931: 15.

——. "Show Boat." *New York Times* 8 Jan. 1928: 1.

——. "Susan and God." *New York Times* 8 Oct. 1937 26.

——. "The Theatre: 'Candide.'" *New York Times* 3 Dec. 1956: 40.

——. "The Theatre: 'Pleasure of His Company.'" *New York Times* 23 Oct. 1958: 36.

——. "Three People and Miss Crothers." *New York Times* 16 Oct. 1932: 1.

——. "Troyka." *New York Times* 2 Ap. 1930: 32.

——. "Two Bites at a Cherry." *New York Times* 22 Feb. 1929: 19.

——. "Vine Leaves in a Heap." *New York Times* 26 Sept. 1930: 16.

——. "When All Is Said and Done." *New York Times Book Review* 22 Sept. 1963: 32.

——. "The Women." *New York Times* 22 Nov.1935: 19.

——. "Yes Is For a Very Young Man." *New York Times* 7 June 1949: 27.

B., J. "Mae West in New Scarlet Role." *New York Times* 15 Sept. 1931: n.p. Clipping Lincoln Center Library.

Barnes, Clive. "Liz' Glamour brings glitter to 'Little Foxes.'" *New York Post* 8 May 1981: n.p. *New York Theatre Critics' Reviews 1981:* 232.

——. "'Member of the Wedding' Wears Well." *New York Times* 3 Jan. 1975: n.p. *New York Theater Critics' Reviews 1975:* 397.

——. "'Mule Bone' Connected to Funny Bone." *New York Post* 15 Feb 1991: n.p. *New York Theatre Critics' Reviews 1991:* 392.

——. "Perfect Period Piece." *New York Times* 16 Oct. 1990: n.p. *New York Theatre Critics' Reviews 1990:* 173.

——. "The Royal Family." *New York Times* 18 Dec. 1975: 64.

——. "Too Many Bumps Spoil 'The Grind.'" *New York Post* 17 Ap. 1985: n.p. *New York Theatre Critics' Reviews 1985:* 309.

Barnes, Djuna. "The Tireless Rachel Crothers." *Theater Guild Magazine* May 1931: 18.

Barnes, Howard. "Adolescent Tragedy." *New York Herald Tribune* 4 May 1944: n.p. *New York Theatre Critics' Reviews 1944:* 196.

——. "Fascinating Yankees." *New York Herald Tribune* 4 Dec. 1946: n.p. *New York Theatre Critics' Reviews 1946:* 229.

——. "Fay in Wonderland." *New York Herald Tribune* 2 Nov. 1944: n.p. *New York Theatre Critics 1944-45:* 95.

———. "Miss Gordon's Night." *New York Herald Tribune* 4 Jan. 1944: n.p. *New York Theatre Critics' Reviews* 1944: 298.

———. "Miss Hayes's Party." *New York Herald Tribune* 1 Nov. 1946: n.p. *New York Theatre Critics' Reviews* 1946: 282.

———. "Miss West's Play Opens at the Royale Theater." *New York Herald Tribune* 15 Sept. 1931: n.p. Clipping Lincoln Center Library.

———. "Mystical Confusion." *New York Herald Tribune* 30 Oct. 1945: n.p. *New York Theatre Critics' Reviews* 1945: 132.

———. "A Near Miss." *New York Herald Tribune* 24 May 1945: n.p. *New York Theatre Critics' Reviews* 1945: 211.

———. "'Poppa' Amusing." *New York Herald Tribune* 26 Dec. 1928: n.p. Clipping Lincoln Center Library.

———. "Tiresome." *New York Herald Tribune* 13 Ap. 1950: n.p. *New York Theatre Critics' Reviews* 1950: 315.

"Be Calm, Camilla!" *Vogue* 15 Dec. 1918: n.p. Clipping Lincoln Center Library.

"'Be Calm, Camilla!' Marks New Best for Clare Kummer." *New York Tribune* 1 Nov. 1918: n.p. Clipping Lincoln Center Library.

Beaufort, John. "Be Calm, Camilla!" *Christian Science Monitor* 2 Nov. 1918: n.p. Clipping Lincoln Center Library.

———. "A Little World, Big in Heart." *Christian Science Monitor* 7 Ap. 1989: 11.

———. "'Mule Bone' Debuts After 60 Years." *Christian Science Monitor* 26 Feb. 1991: n.p. *New York Theatre Critics' Reviews* 1991: 394.

Black, John. "Metcalfe's New York Gossip." 11 Feb. 1911. Clipping Lincoln Center Library.

Boehnel, William. "Akins Play at Empire." *New York World Telegraph* 8 Jan. 1935: n.p. Clipping Lincoln Center Library.

———. "'Boy Meets Girl' Wins Applause in London; Critics Find it Full of Laughs." *New York Times* 28 May 1936: 18.

Bradley, Jeff. "'Machinal' Still Jolting." *Denver Post* 1 April 1992: 6.

Broun, Heywood. "Brother John." *New York Times* 26 Mar. 1893: 13.

———. "Ethel Barrymore in 'Royal Fandango'." *New York World* 13 Nov. 1923: n.p. Clipping Lincoln Center Library.

———. "'Expressing Willie.'" *New York World* 17 Ap. 1924: n.p. Clipping Lincoln Center Library.

———. "Good Gracious, Annabelle." *New York Tribune* 5 Nov. 1916: n.p. Clipping Lincoln Center Library.

———. "It Seems To Me." *New York World* 27 Feb. 1924: n.p. Clipping Lincoln Center Library.

———. "'Miss Lulu Bett' is of Fine Fabric Though often Crude." *New York Tribune* 28 Dec. 1920: n.p. Clipping Lincoln Center Library.

———. "Mister Pitt." *New York World* 23 Jan. 1924: n.p. Clipping Lincoln Center Library.

———. "The New Plays: 'The Texas Nightingale.'" Unidentified clipping Lincoln Center Library.

———. "Thirty-nine East." Unidentified clipping Lincoln Center Library.

Brown, Herrick. "Foxhole in the Parlor." *New York Sun* 24 May 1945: n.p. *New York Times Theatre Critics' Reviews 1945*: 211.

———. "Pick-Up Girl." *New York Sun* 4 May 1944: n.p. *New York Theater Critics' Reviews 1944*: 198.

Brown, Joe. "The Enduring 'Miss Lulu Bett.'" *Washington Post* 25 Oct. 1985: 11.

Brown, John Mason. "Diana Barrymore Seen in 'The Happy Days.'" *New York Herald Tribune* 14 May 1941: n.p. Clipping Library Lincoln Center.

———. "The Land is Bright." Unidentified clipping Library Lincoln Center.

———. "Max Gordon Presents Miss Kummer's Pleasant Comedy." *New York Evening Post* 24 Oct. 1933: n.p. Clipping Lincoln Center Library.

———. "Spring Thaw." *New York Post* 22 Mar. 1938: n.p. Clipping Lincoln Center Library.

"Brown of Harvard." *Theatre Magazine* April 1906: 87+.

Cariaga, Daniel. "UCLA Forces Present 'Four Saints' Opera." *Los Angeles Times* 7 Feb. 1989: 4.

Carey, Ralph W. "Among New York Theatres: 'Happy Days.'" Unidentified Clipping Lincoln Center Library.

———. "A Carroll Classic Pleasantly Staged." *New York Times* 24 Mar. 1915: 11.

Chapman, John. "'Candide' an Artistic Triumph." *New York Daily News* 3 Dec. 1956: n.p. *New York Theatre Critics' Reviews* 1956:176.

———. "'Gentlemen Prefer Blondes' Just Perfect." *New York Daily News* 9 Dec. 1949: n.p. *New York Theatre Critics' Reviews* 1949: 198.

———. "Goodbye, My Fancy." *New York Daily News* 18 Nov. 1948: n.p. *New York Theatre Critics' Reviews* 1948: 154.

———. "'Harvey Is Just Wonderful and His Friend Frank Fay is Superb." *New York Daily News* 2 Nov. 1944: n.p. *New York Theatre Critics* 1944-45: 95.

———. "Hellman's 'Autumn Garden' Meaty Comedy Played by Flawless Cast." *New York Daily News* 8 Mar. 1951: n.p. *New York Theatre Critics' Reviews* 1951: 327.

——. "'His and Hers' Nice, Warm Comedy." *New York Daily News* 8 Jan. 1954: n.p. *New York Theatre Critics' Reviews 1954*: 393.

——. "Julie Harris Simply Magnificent in a Beautiful Drama." *New York Daily News* 18 November 1955: n.p. *New York Theatre Critics' Reviews 1955*: 208.

——. "'The Leading Lady.'" *New York Daily News* 19 Oct. 1948: n.p. *New York Theatre Critics' Reviews 1948*: 192.

——. "'My 3 Angels' a Smooth, Engaging Comedy." *New York Daily News* 12 Mar. 1953: n.p. *New York Theatre Critics' Reviews 1953*: 334.

——. "Pick-Up Girl." *New York Daily News* 4 May 1944: n.p. *New York Theatre Critics' Reviews 1944*: 196.

——. "Ruth Gordon Writes Herself a Delicious Comedy." *New York Daily News* 4 Jan. 1944: n.p. *New York Theatre Critics' Reviews 1944*: 298.

——. "Same Old Mae in Same Old Play." *New York Daily News* 7 Feb. 1949: n.p. *New York Theatre Critics' Reviews 1949*: 369.

——. "'South Pacific' Barely Misses Being an Exciting War Drama." *New York Daily News* 30 Dec. 1943: n.p. *New York Theatre Critics' Reviews 1943*: 184.

——. "'Years Ago' Winsome Play." *New York Daily News* 4 Dec. 1946: n.p. *New York Theatre Critics' Reviews 1946*: 232.

Chase, William B. "'Abie's Irish Rose' Funny." *New York Times* 24 May 1922: 22.

Christiansen, Richard. "'Miss Lulu Bett' Suffers at the Hand of Superficial Acting." *Chicago Tribune* 26 Jan. 1988: 5.

——. "'Stage Door' Opens On An Old-Fashioned Treat." *Chicago Tribune* 18 Nov. 1985: 6.

"Clare Kummer Wins Success as a Writer." *Minneapolis Tribune* 3 Feb. 1918: n.p. Clipping Lincoln Center Library.

"Clare Kummer's Comedy 'Rollo's Wild Oat.'" *New York Sun* 24 Nov. 1920: n.p. Clipping Lincoln Center Library.

"Clare Kummer's Smart Dialogue." Unidentified clipping Lincoln Center Library.

Clark, Norman. "Outrageous." Unidentified clipping Lincoln Center Library.

Clurman, Harold. "Alien Corn." *New Republic* 22 November 1948: 28-29.

Coleman, Robert. "'Bernardine' Is Moving Story of Adolescence." *New York Daily Mirror*: n.p. *New York Theatre Critics' Reviews 1952*: 231.

——. "'Gay Life' Just Isn't Gay Enough." *New York Mirror* 20 Nov. 1961: n.p. *New York Theatre Critics' Reviews 1961*: 169.

——. "'Hope for a Harvest' Pedestrian Play." Unidentified clipping Lincoln Center Library.

——. "The Kanins." *New York Daily Mirror* 8 Jan. 1954: n.p. *New York Theatre Critics' Reviews 1954*: 395.

——. "Ladies of the Corridor." *New York Daily Mirror* 22 Oct. 1953: n.p. *New York Theatre Critics' Reviews 1953*: 245.

——. "Lillian Hellman Play Is Depressing Farce." *New York Mirror* 1 Ap. 1963: n.p. *New York Theatre Critics' Reviews 1963*: 303.

——. "Loos' Luck Runs Out in 'Cheri.'" *New York Daily Mirror* 13 Oct. 1959: n.p. *New York Theatre Critics' Reviews 1959*: 267.

——. "'Member of the Wedding' and Its Cast Earn Cheers at the Empire." *New York Daily News* 6 Jan. 1950: n.p. *New York Theatre Critics' Reviews 1950*: 398.

——. "'Montserrat' Well Acted But Script is Bumpy." *New York Daily Mirror* 30 Oct. 1949: n.p. *New York Theatre Critics' Reviews 1949*: 246.

——. "Mrs. McThing is Slapstick Lesson in Kindliness." *New York Daily Mirror* 21 Feb. 1952: n.p. *New York Theatre Critics' Reviews 1952*: 361.

——. "Musical 'Candide" Is Distinguished Work." *New York Daily Mirror* 3 Dec. 1956: n.p. *New York Theatre Critics' Reviews 1956*: 179.

——. "'My 3 Angels' a Wonderful New Hit." *New York Daily Mirror* 12 Mar. 1953: n.p. *New York Theatre Critics' Reviews 1953*: 335.

——. "Rashomon." *New York Daily Mirror* 28 Jan. 1959: n.p. *New York Theatre Critics' Reviews 1959*: 398.

——. "'Toys in the Attic' Sure-Fire Hit." *New York Mirror* 26 Feb. 1960: n.p. *New York Theatre Critics' Reviews 1960*: 346.

Collins, Charles. "Comedy Playlets at the Bandbox." *New York Times* 10 Nov. 1915: 5.

——. "Ideas on Stage Affairs." *Chicago Post* n.d.: n.p. Clipping Lincoln Center Library.

Corbin, John. "Americans in Mexico." *New York Times* 15 Dec. 1922: 26.

——. "Betrayed and Scorned." *New York Times* 17 Oct. 1923: 14.

——. "Mister Pitt." *New York Times* 6 Jan. 1924: 1.

——. "Princess and a Matador." *New York Times* 13 Nov. 1923: 25.

——. "Rachel Crothers Triumphs." *New York Times* 17 Apr. 1924: 22.

——. "Sentimental Comedy." Unidentified clipping Lincoln Center Library.

——. "'Sometime' Comes With Ed Wynn." *New York Times* 5 Oct. 1918: 11.

——. "The Sphinx, Three Marys." *New York Times* 11 Feb. 1923: 1.

——. "The Texas Nightingale." *New York Times* 21 Nov. 1922: 15.

——. "39 East." *New York Times* 1 Ap. 1919: 9.

——. "War Romance in Musical Frame." *New York Times* 5 Nov. 1918: 2.

——. "Wisteria Romance." *New York Times* 1 Ap. 1919: 1

——. "'The Whole Town's Talking.'" *New York Times* 30 Aug. 1923: 8.

Craig, James. "Machinal." Unidentified clipping Lincoln Center Library.

"Crothers Play in London." *New York Times* 27 Ap. 1933: 15.

D., C.B. "'Sex' Wins High Mark for Depravity, Dullness." *New York Herald Tribune* 27 Ap. 1926: n.p. Clipping Lincoln Center Library.

"'Daddy's Gone A-Hunting.'" *Theatre Magazine* November 1921: 315.

Davis, Charles Belmont. "'O, Nightingale' at 49th Street Theater." *New York Tribune* 16 April 1925: 12.

De Casseres, Benjamin. "Let Us Be Gay." *Arts and Decoration* May 1929: 64.

De Foe, Louis V. "'Miss Lulu Bett' as a Play." *New York World* 28 Dec. 1920: n.p. Clipping Library Lincoln Center.

——. "Wild Youth in a Play." *New York World Telegram* 6 Mar. 1921: n.p. Clipping Lincoln Center Library.

Donnelly, Tom. "Best Musical News of Year Is Found in New 'Candide.'" *New York World-Telegram* 3 Dec. 1956: n.p. *New York Theatre Critics' Reviews 1956*: 177.

"Drama Mailbag." *New York Times*. Unidentified clipping Lincoln Center Library.

"Dramatization of 'Revelry.'" Unidentified Clipping Lincoln Center Library.

"Edna His Wife." *Time* 20 Dec. 1937: 33-34.

Ellis, Abby. "Janet Rayor Winning, Effective in 'Years Ago.' " *Denver Post* 24 June 1983: 19.

"Everything But a Play." *Newsweek* 22 Nov. 1948: 80.

F., L.W. "'Poppa' Opens." *American* 25 Dec. 1928: n.p. Clipping Lincoln Center Library.

"'The Fall of Eve.'" *New York Times* 1 Sept. 1925: 18.

"Feral Foxes in Hellman's 'Forest.'" *Chicago Tribune* 29 Sept. 1986: 3.

Field, Rowland. "Broadway: 'Claudia.'" *Newark Eve. News* 13 Feb. 1941: n.p. Clipping Lincoln Center Library.

"Footloose." *Chicago Tribune* 1924. Clipping Lincoln Center Library.

"Footloose." *Theatre Magazine* Jan. 1920: 526.

Freedley, George. "Billy Burke, Frank Craven Provide Entertainment in Zoë Akins Opus." *New York Morning Telegraph* 3 Ap. 1944: n.p. Clipping Lincoln Center Library.

"'Hope for a Harvest' First Truly Adult Play of Present Broadway Season." Unidentified clipping Lincoln Center Library.

"Outrageous Fortune." *New York Morning Telegraph* 28 Dec. 1943: n.p. Clipping Lincoln Center Library.

Gabriel, Gilbert W. "Her Master's Voice." *New York American* 24 Oct. 1933: n.p. Clipping Lincoln Center Library.

Garland, Robert. "At the Fulton." *New York Journal American* 21 Nov. 1946: n.p. *New York Theatre Critics' Reviews* 1946: 248.

——. "A Brilliant Play Written, Acted by Ruth Gordon." *New York Journal American* 19 Oct. 1948: n.p. *New York Theatre Critics' Reviews* 1948: 191.

——. "First Non-Musical Hit of the Season." *New York Journal American* 26 Nov. 1951: n.p. *New York Theatre Critics' Reviews* 1951: 160.

——. "Foxhole in the Parlor." *New York Journal American* 24 May 1945: n.p. *New York Theatre Critics' Reviews 1945*: 212.

——. "Grim." *New York Journal American* 31 Oct. 1949: n.p. *New York Theatre Critics' Reviews 1949*: 246.

——. "Happy Birthday." *New York Journal American* 1 Nov. 1946: n.p. *New York Theatre Critics' Reviews 1946*: 280.

——. "'Mrs. January' Seen." *New York Journal American* 1 April 1944: n.p. *New York Theatre Critics' Reviews 1944*: 236.

——. "Palpable New Hit In Canny Comedy." *New York Journal American* 18 Nov. 1948: n.p. *New York Theatre Critics' Reviews 1948*: 152.

——. "Pick-Up Girl." *New York Journal-American* 4 May 1944: n.p. *New York Theatre Critics' Reviews 1944*: 197-98.

——. "Shelley Plus Shaw Equals Neither." *New York Journal American* 13 Ap. 1950: n.p. *New York Theatre Critics' Reviews 1950*: 314.

——. "Shumlin's Production Completes First Lap of its Notable Run." *New York World-Telegram* 21 Nov. 1935: n.p. Clipping Library Lincoln Center.

——. "Something Special But Not Quite a Play." *New York Journal American* 6 Jan. 1950: n.p. *New York Theatre Critics' Reviews 1950*: 397.

Gassner, John. "Two Folk Plays." *One-Act Play Magazine* April 1938: 1120-1122.

Gibbs, Wolcott. "Goodbye, My Fancy." *New Yorker* 27 Nov. 1948: 52-53.

——. "His and Hers." *New Yorker* 16 Jan 1954: 52-53.

——. "The President's Husband." *New Yorker* 20 Nov. 1948: 60-61.

——. "A Very Nice Piece of Work." *New Yorker* 8 Ap. 1944: 44.

"Gillette Returns in a Brilliant Play." *New York Times* 14 Oct. 1917: 10.

"Glorious Betsy." *Washington Star* 2 Dec. 1908: n.p. Clipping Lincoln Center Library.

"Good Gracious, Annabelle." *Vogue* 15 Dec. 1916: n.p. Clipping Lincoln Center Library.

Gottfried, Martin. "McCullers Play at Phoenix." *New York Post* 3 Jan. 1975: n.p. *New York Theatre Critics' Reviews 1975*: 398.

———. "'Porgy and Bess' Is Back." *New York Post* 27 Sept. 1976: n.p. *New York Theatre Critics' Reviews 1976*: 165.

Greene, Alexis. "Serious Fun!" *Theatre Journal* (May 1993): 256-258.

Grenville, Vernon. "Kiss the Boys Goodbye." *Commonweal* 14 Oct. 1938: 644.

———. "Margin for Error." *Commonweal* 24 Nov. 1939: 118.

Gussow, Mel. "Dinner at Eight." *New York Times* 8 Oct. 1988: 9.

H., J. "Diamond Lil." 10 Ap. 1928. Unidentified Clipping Lincoln Center Library.

Hackett, Francis. "Miss Lulu Bett." Unidentified clipping Lincoln Center Library.

Hammond, Percy." 'Chicago' a 'Comic Strip' treating Burlesquely of the Illinois Crime Waves." Unidentified clipping Lincoln Center Library.

———. "It is Well for 'A Royal Fandango' That Miss Barrymore is Present." *New York Tribune* 13 Nov. 1923: n.p. Clipping Lincoln Center Library.

———. "Is There No Flit." *New York Herald Tribune* 4 Oct. 1931: n.p. Clipping Lincoln Center Library.

——. "'Mister Pitt' by Zona Gale is Good, Though it Needs to be Rewritten." *New York Tribune* 24 Jan. 1924: n.p. Clipping Lincoln Center Library.

——. "O Evening Star." *New York Herald* 9 Jan. 1936: n.p. Clipping Lincoln Center Library.

——. "The Rewards of Virtue." *New York Herald Tribune* 29 Ap. 1928: n.p. Clipping Library Lincoln Center.

Hawkins, William. "'Autumn Garden' Is Rich and Mellow." *New York World-Telegram* 8 Mar. 1951: n.p. *New York Theatre Critics' Reviews 1951*: 325.

——. "'Leading Lady' Called Amiable but Aimless." *New York World-Telegram* 19 Oct. 1948: n.p. *New York Theatre Critics' Reviews 1948*: 192.

——. "'My 3 Angels' Stars Convicts with Halos." *New York World-Telegram* 12 Mar. 1953: n.p. *New York Theatre Critics' Reviews 1953*: 336.

——. "'Set My People Free' A Historical Drama." *New York World-Telegram* 4 Nov. 1948: n.p. *New York Theatre Critics' Reviews 1948*: 173.

——. "Waters, Harris Roles Spark 'Wedding.'" *New York World-Telegram* 6 Jan. 1950: n.p. *New York Theatre Critics' Reviews 1950*: 399.

Hayes, Richard. "Ceremony of Innocence." *Commonweal* 9 May 1958: 153.

Hayes, Suzanne. "After Words." *St. Petersburg Times* 1 Dec. 1991: 11.

"Her Lord and Master." *New York Times* 25 Feb. 1902: 6.

The Highbrow. "'Rollo's Wild Oat' at the Punch and Judy Theatre." *Town Topics* 2 Dec. 1920: n.p. Clipping Lincoln Center Library.

"The Hill Between." *Time* 21 Mar. 1938: 30.

Hodgson, Moira. "'Peer Gynt' [and 'Member of the Wedding']." *Nation* 12 June 1989: 824.

Holden, Stephen. "Gertrude Stein Interprets Faust." *New York Times* 9 July 1992: 15+.

———. "The Opera Ensemble Has Fun With 'Four Saints.' *New York Times* 14 Nov. 1986: 33.

"Hollywood Misery." *Literary Digest* 18 Jan. 1936: 19.

"Homespun and Brocade." *The Nation* 21 Sept. 1921: 325.

Hornblow, Arthur. "Expressing Willie." *Theatre* June 1924: 15-16.

———. "Her Soldier Boy." *Theatre* Jan. 1917: 24.

———. "Little Simplicity." *Theatre* Dec. 1918: 347.

———. "Some Time." *Theatre:* Dec. 1918: 346.

Kalem, T.E. "Witchy Laugh Potion." *Time* 7 May 1973: 88.

Kerr, Walter. "Bernardine." *New York Herald Tribune* 17 Oct. 1952: n.p. *New York Theatre Critics' Reviews 1952*: 233.

———. "Candide." *New York Herald Tribune* 3 Dec. 1956: n.p. *New York Theatre Critics' Reviews:* 179.

———. "'Chicago' Comes on Like Doomsday." *New York Times* 8 Jan. 1975: 1.

———. "The Gay Life." *New York Herald Tribune* 20 Nov. 1961: n.p. *New York Theatre Critics' Reviews 1961*: 170.

———. "His and Hers." *New York Herald Tribune* 8 Jan. 1954: n.p. *New York Theatre Critics' Reviews 1954*: 395.

———. "The Ladies of the Corridor." *New York Herald Tribune* 22 Oct. 1953: n.p. *New York Theatre Critics' Reviews 1953*: 244.

———. "'The Lark.'" *New York Herald Tribune* 18 Nov. 1955: n.p. *New York Theatre Critic' Reviews 1955*: 206.

——. "'Midgie Purvis.'" *New York Herald Tribune* 2 Feb. 1961: n.p. *New York Theatre Critics' Reviews 1961*: 377.

——. "Mrs. McThing." *New York Herald Tribune* 21 Feb. 1952: n.p. *New York Theatre Critics' Reviews 1952*: 362.

——. "The Pleasure of His Company." *New York Herald Tribune* 23 Oct. 1958: n.p. *New York Theatre Critics' Reviews 1958*: 247.

——. "'Toys in the Attic.'" *New York Herald Tribune* 26 Feb. 1960: n.p. *New York Theatre Critics' Reviews 1960*: 348.

——. "A Truly 'Royal' Revival." *New York Times* 11 Jan. 1976: 1.

Kissel, Howard. "Folk Comedy tickles funny 'Bone.'" *New York Daily News* 15 Feb. 1991: n.p. *New York Theatre Critics' Reviews 1991*: 391.

——. "The Little Foxes." *Women's Wear Daily* 8 May 1981: n.p. *New York Theatre Critics' Reviews 1981*: 229.

——. "The Member of the Wedding." *Women's Wear Daily* 3 Jan. 1975: n.p. *New York Theatre Critics' Reviews 1975*: 398.

Klein, Alvin. "Purchase Offers Life According to Stein." *New York Times* 7 Dec. 1986: 24.

Koehler, Robert. "Stage Beat: 'Susan and God.'" *Los Angeles Times* 11 Mar. 1988: 10.

Kroll, Jack. "The Girls in the Band." *Newsweek* 7 May 1973: 109.

Kronenberger, Louis. "The Audience Takes Medicine." *New York Newspaper PM* 29 Dec. 1943: n.p. *New York Theatre Critics' Reviews 1943*:188.

——. "Bad News for 'Harvey' Fans." *PM Reviews* 30 Oct. 1945: n.p. *New York Theatre Critics' Reviews 1945*: 130.

——. "Cinderella in Newark." *New York PM Reviews* 3 Nov. 1946: n.p. *New York Theatre Critics' Reviews 1946*: 282.

——. "A Fine Night With a Rabbit." *New York Newspaper* PM 2 Nov. 1944: n.p. *New York Theatre Critics' Reviews 1944*: 95.

——. "Ruth Gordon is Twice Blessed." *New York Newspaper* PM 4 Jan. 1944: n.p. *New York Theatre Critics' Reviews 1944*: 299.

——. "Ruth Gordon's Likeable Comedy About Her Youth." PM *Reviews* 5 Dec. 1946: n.p. *New York Theatre Critics' Reviews 1946*: 231.

——. "Very Fancy But Very Foolish." *New York Newspaper* PM 4 Nov. 1943: n.p. *New York Theatre Critics' Reviews 1943*: 237.

Krutch, Joseph Wood. "Dinner at Eight." *Nation.* 9 Nov. 1932: 464-5.

——. "In Defense of Mae West." *Nation* 30 Sept. 1931: 344.

——. "Too Good Not To Be Better." *Nation* 7 Nov. 1936: 557-58.

"The Land is Bright." *Life* 1 Dec. 1941: n.p. Clipping Library Lincoln Center.

Lardner, John. "Nostalgia of '23 Skidoo' Days." *New York Star* 20 Oct. 1948: n.p. *New York Theatre Critics' Reviews 1948*: 193.

Lask, Thomas. "Another Language." *New York Times* 8 Dec. 1975: 42.

Lewisohn, Ludwig. "Native Plays." Unidentified clipping Lincoln Center Library.

——. "Scramble." *Nation* 21 Nov. 1923: 587-588.

Littell, Robert. "Abie's Irish Rose." *New Republic* 18 Mar. 1921: 98-99.

Little, Robert. "Let Us Be Gay." *Theatre Arts*: May 1929: 330-33. check.

——. "They Don't Come Any Dirtier." *New York Evening Post* 2 Oct. 1928: n.p. Clipping Library Lincoln Center.

Lockridge, Richard. "The Happy Days." *New York Sun* 14 May 1941. *New York Critics Reviews 1940-41*: 326.

——. "Her Master's Voice." *New York Sun* 24 Oct. 1933: n.p. Clipping Lincoln Center Library.

——. "Mae West." *New York Sun* 10 Ap. 1928: n.p. Clipping Lincoln Center Library.

——. "Miss Hellman Hews to People." Unidentified clipping Lincoln Center Library.

——. "'Spring Thaw' Polite Entertainment." *New York Sun* 22 Mar. 1938: n.p. Clipping Lincoln Center Library.

Macgowan, Kenneth. "Clare Kummer and Roland Young at Their Best in 'Rollo's Wild Oat.'" *New York Globe* 24 Nov. 1920: n.p. Clipping Lincoln Center Library.

——. "Miss Lulu Bett." *New York Globe* 28 Dec. 1920: n.p. Clipping Lincoln Center Library.

"Mae West Again." *Brooklyn Eagle* 2 Oct. 1928: n.p. Clipping Lincoln Center Library.

"'A Man's World.'" *Nation* 10 Feb. 1910: 146.

"'A Man's World.'" *Theatre Magazine* 1 Mar. 1910: 68-69.

Mantle, Burns. "'The Happy Days' Ends Theatre Season." *New York Daily News* 14 May 1941. *New York Theatre Critics 1940-41:* 325.

——. "Her Master's Voice is Great Fun." *New York Daily News* 24 Oct. 1933: n.p.

——. "Lillian Hellman's 'Watch on the Rhine' Enters Season's Best Play Contest." *New York Sunday News* 13 Ap. 1941: n.p. Clipping Library Lincoln Center.

——. "Rollo's Wild Oat." *New York Mail* 24 Nov. 1920: n.p. Clipping Lincoln Center Library.

"Margin for Error." *Time* 13 Nov. 1939: 58.

"'Mary the Third' Interests." *New York Times* 6 Feb.1923: 14.

Maxwell, Perriton. "Trigger." *Theatre* Feb. 1928: 39-40.

"'Maytime' Scores at the Shubert." *New York Times* 17 Aug. 1917: 17.

McCarten, John. "The Gay Life." *New Yorker* 2 Dec 1961: 118.

McClain, John. "A Brilliant Cast and a Sure-Pop Hit." *New York Journal American* 12 Mar. 1953: n.p. *New York Theatre Critics' Reviews 1953*: 334.

——. "Julie Depicts a Vital Joan." *New York Journal American* 18 Nov. 1955: n.p. *New York Theatre Critics' Reviews 1955*: 208.

——. "Mary Chase Gets Snarled in Her Plot." *New York Journal American* 21 Oct. 1952: n.p. *New York Theatre Critics' Reviews 1952*: 360.

——. "Tallulah's Fine—The Play? No!" *New York Journal American* 2 Feb. 1961: n.p. *New York Theatre Critics' Reviews 1961*: 378.

——. "Warm and Hilarious." *New York Journal American* 23 Oct. 1958: n.p. *New York Theatre Critics' Reviews 1958*: 245.

"The Merchant." *New York Times* 5 May 1891: 5.

"Miss Peabody's Play." *Boston Transcript* 16 Jan. 1912: n.p. Clipping Lincoln Center Library.

Morehouse, Ward. "'Blondes' a Jubilant Hit." *New York Sun* 9 Dec. 1949: n.p. *New York Theatre Critics' Reviews 1949*: 199.

——. "Hellman's 'Another Part of the Forest' is a Fascinating and Powerful Drama." *New York Sun* 21 Nov. 1946: n.p. *New York Theatre Critics' Reviews 1946*:250.

——. "Mary Chase's 'The Next Half Hour,' Done at Empire, Gloomy and Exhausting." *New York Sun* 30 Oct. 1945: n.p. *New York Theatre Critics' Reviews 1945*: 130.

——. "'Montserrat' Disappoints." *New York Sun* 31 Oct. 1949: n.p. *New York Theatre Critics' Reviews 1949*: 245.

——. "Mr. Fay's Friend is a Big White Rabbit in 'Harvey,' Enormously Funny Play." *New York Sun* 2 Nov. 1944: n.p. *New York Theatre Critics' Reviews 1944:96.*

——. "'Mrs. January and Mr. Ex,' Presented at Belasco." *New York Sun* 1 April 1944: n.p. *New York Theatre Critics 1943-44:* 235.

——. "'Over-Twenty-One,' by and With Ruth Gordon, an Enormously Funny Show." *New York Sun* 4 Jan. 1944: n.p. *New York Theatre Critics' Reviews 1944:* 297.

——. "Ruth Gordon's Autobiographical 'Years Ago' a Warming and Chuckling Comedy." *New York Sun* 4 Dec. 1946: n.p. *New York Theatre Critics' Reviews 1946:* 230.

——. "Wonderful Atmosphere, Little Play." *New York Sun* 19 Oct. 1948: n.p. *New York Theatre Critics' Reviews 1948:* 190.

Nachman, Gerald. "Strong Staging of Hellman Play at Ashland." *San Francisco Chronicle* 4 July 1992: 3.

Nadel, Norman. "The Gay Life." *New York World-Telegram* 20 Nov. 1961: n.p. *New York Theatre Critics' Reviews 1961:* 171.

Nathan, George Jean. "Arrivals and Departures." *Newsweek* 20 Nov. 1939: 36.

"'Naughty Marietta' Back." *New York Times* 22 Oct. 1929: 26.

"New York's Rehearsal Club Inspires Adroit Comedy." *Newsweek* 31 Oct. 1936: 24.

"The New Play at the Comedy Theatre 'Gringo.'" *New York World* 15 Dec. 1922: n.p. Clipping Lincoln Center Library.

"New Play in Manhattan." Unidentified clipping Lincoln Center Library.

Nichols, Lewis. "Soldier's Voice." *New York Times* 24 May 1945: 15.

Norton, Elliot. "Searching Wind." *Boston Post.* Unidentified clipping Lincoln Center Library.

"O, Nightingale." *Christian Science Monitor* 18 Ap. 1925: n.p. Clipping Lincoln Center Library.

"On the Eve." *New York Times* 5 Oct. 1909: 9.

"The Old Maid." *Variety* 15 an. 1935: n.p. Clipping Lincoln Center Library.

Osborn, E.W. "Mr. Pitt." *New York Evening World* 23 Jan 1924: n.p. Clipping Lincoln Center Library.

"Our Mrs. McChesney." *Nation* 28 Oct. 1915: 527.

"Ourselves." *New York Times* 14 Nov. 1913: 11.

P., H.T. "Toy Theatre: Three Short Plays." Unidentified clipping Lincoln Center Library.

"The Piper." *New York Evening Post* 31 Jan. 1911: n.p. Clipping Lincoln Center Library.

"'The Piper Charms.'" *Billboard* 11 Feb. 1911: n.p. Clipping Lincoln Center Library.

Pollock, Arthur. "Claudia." *Brooklyn Eagle* 13 Feb. 1941: n.p. Clipping Lincoln Center Library.

———. "The Constant Sinner." Unidentified clipping Lincoln Center Library.

———. "' Spring Thaw' a Comedy by Clare Kummer—She Used to Write Delightful Comedies." *Brooklyn Daily Mail* 22 Mar. 1938: n.p. Clipping Lincoln Center Library.

"Porgy." *New York Times* 11 Oct. 1927: 26.

"Presenting Claiborne Foster." *New York Times* 7 Dec. 1927: 32.

"Prize Plays, Critics and Such." *New York Times* 3 Ap. 1941: n.p. Clipping Lincoln Center Library.

"The Propriety of 'Naughty Marietta.'" *Munsey* Feb. 1911: 707.

R., W. "More Spring Drama." 27 Ap. 1926: n.p. Clipping Lincoln Center Library.

Rascoe, Burton." 'Foxhole in the Parlor' Subtle, Exciting, Touching." *New York World-Telegram* 24 May 1945: n.p. *New York Theatre Critics' Reviews 1945*: 212.

——. "'The Next Half Hour' Another Chase Success." *New York World Telegram* 30 Oct. 1945: 12.

——. "Old Concoctions Only in 'Doctors Disagree.'" *New York World-Telegram* 29 Dec. 1943: n.p. *New York Theatre Critics' Reviews 1943*: 189.

——. "'Outrageous Fortune' An Exciting Drama." 4 Nov. 1943: n.p. *New York Theater Critics Reviews 1943*: 237.

——. "See 'Pick-Up Girl.'" *New York World-Telegram* 4 May 1944: n.p. *New York Theatre Critics' Reviews 1944*: 197.

Rathbun, Stephen. "'Ladies Leave' Opens." *New York Sun* 21 Oct. 1929: n.p. Clipping Lincoln Center Library.

Reamer, Lawrence. "Déclassée." *The Sun* 12 Oct. 1919: n.p. Clipping Lincoln Center Library.

——. "Miss Ferguson the Lovely Heroine in Zoë Akin's Play." *New York Herald* 7 Dec. 1921: n.p. Clipping Lincoln Center Library.

Reid, Louis R. "He and She." *New York Dramatic Mirror* 21 Feb. 1920: 16.

Rich, Frank. "The Misses Taylor and Stapleton in 'Foxes.'" *New York Times* 8 May 1981: n.p. *New York Theatre Critics' Reviews 1981*: 228.

——. "A Nightmarish Vision of Urban America." *New York Times* 16 Oct. 1990: n.p. *New York Theatre Critics' Reviews 1990*: 171.

Rogers, W.G. "In Moonlight and Magnolia The Protest Was Lost." *New York Times Book Review* 8 Sept. 1963: n.p. Clipping Lincoln Center Library.

"Rollo's Wild Oat." *Christian Science Monitor* 30 Nov. 1920: n.p. Clipping Lincoln Center Library.

"'Rollo's Wild Oat' Has Suggestion." *New York Herald* 24 Nov. 1920: n.p. Clipping Lincoln Center Library.

Roosevelt, Eleanor. "My Day." *New York World Telegram* 31 Jan. 1941: n.p. Clipping Lincoln Center Library.

Ruhl, Arthur. "The Old Maid." *New York Herald Tribune* 8 Jan 1935: n.p. Clipping Lincoln Center Library.

———. Unidentified clipping reviewing "Machinal" Lincoln Center Library.

Schrader, Fred. F. "His Little Widows." *Toledo Blade* 9 May 1917: n.p. Clipping Lincoln Center Library.

Sherburne, E.C. "Outrageous Fortune." *Christian Science Monitor* 4 Nov. 1943: n.p. Clipping Lincoln Center Library.

"Significance of 'Overtones.'" *Indianapolis News* 3 Feb. 1916: n.p. Clipping Lincoln Center Library.

Skinner, Richard Dana. "The Play: 'Dinner at Eight.'" *Commonweal* 9 Nov. 1932: 49.

Smith, Sol. "Rediscovered 'Machinal.'" *Chicago Tribune* 21 July 1991: 5.

"'Sometime' At Atlantic City." *Christian Science Monitor* 3 Sept. 1918: n.p. Clipping Lincoln Center Library.

"South Pacific." *Commonweal* 14 Jan. 1944: 328.

"The Stage and the Screen: 'Doctors Disagree.'" *Commonweal* 14 an 1944: 328.

"Stage Door." *Commonweal* 6 Nov. 1936: 51.

Sterritt, David. "A Strikingly Modern Look at Feminism." *Christian Science Monitor* 5 June 1980: 19.

Strahler, Steven R. "Theater: 'The Royal Family.'" *Crain's Chicago Business* 7 Mar. 1988: 1.

Strauss, Theodore. "Ethel Waters Returns." *New York Times* 25 Mar. 1940: 10.

"Such Is Life in Carolina." *Current Opinion* December 1923: 701-714.

"Sun-Up." *Theatre* July 1923: 16.

Taubman, Howard. "Drama of Wartime Fails to Come to Life." *New York Times* 6 Mar. 1963: 7.

———. "The Gay Life." *New York Times* 20 Nov. 1961: 38.

———. "Tallulah Bankhead in Mary Chase Play." *New York Times* 2 Feb. 1961: n.p. *New York Theatre Critics' Reviews 1961*: 376.

"The Texas Nightingale." Unidentified clipping Lincoln Center Library.

"Theater Workshop Produces Dramas." *Brooklyn Eagle* 7 May 1917: n.p. Clipping Lincoln Center Library.

"These Be the Players At Home." *Literary Digest* 21 Jan. 1928: 26-27.

Towse, J. Rankin. "The Varying Shore." *New York Post* 6 Dec. 1921: n.p. Clipping Center Library.

———. "Zona Gale's Play Has Good Points." *New York Evening Post* 23 Jan. 1924: n.p. Clipping Lincoln Center Library.

Tynan, Kenneth. "The Bright Side of Homicide." *New Yorker* 7 Feb. 1959: 81-82.

"Valentine of Yesteryear." *New York Sun* 8 Jan. 1935: n.p. Clipping Library Lincoln Center.

Vaughan, Peter. "Theater." *Minneapolis Star Tribune* 9 Ap. 1993: 9E.

Waldorf, Wilella. "Boy Meets Girl." 23 June 1943: n.p. *New York Theatre Critics' Reviews 1943*: 317.

———. "Elsie Ferguson Returns To the Stage in 'Outrageous Fortune.'" *New York Post* 4 Nov. 1943: n.p. *New York Theatre Critics' Reviews 1943*: 239.

———. "'Foxhole in the Parlor' Never Gets Below Surface." *New York Post* 24 May 1945: n.p. *New York Theatre Critics' Reviews 1945*: 213.

———. "Hope for a Harvest." *New York Post* 27 Nov. 1941: n.p. *New York Theatre Critics' Reviews 1941*: 198.

———. "'Lone Valley' Arrives." *New York Evening Post* 11 Mar. 1933: n.p. Clipping Lincoln Center Library.

———. "Mae West Returns." *New York Evening Post* 15 Sept. 1931: n.p. Clipping Lincoln Center Library.

———. "Over Twenty-One." *New York Post* 4 Jan. 1944: n.p. *New York Theatre Critics' Reviews 1944*: 299.

———. "'Pick-Up Girl' Opens." *New York Post* 4 May 1944: n.p. *New York Theatre Critics' Reviews 1944*: 198.

———. "Two On the Aisle: 'Soldier's Wife.'" *New York Post* 10 May 1944: n.p. Clipping Lincoln Center Library.

"Watch on the Rhine." *Cue* 5 Ap. 1941: n.p. Clipping Lincoln Center Library.

Watt, Douglas. "A Grinding Halt." *New York Daily News* 17 April 1985: n.p. *New York Theatre Critics' Reviews 1985*: 308.

———. "'Machinal': Joltingly Executed Drama." *New York Daily News* 19 Oct. 1990: n.p. *New York Theatre Critics' Reviews 1990*: 173.

———. "'Member of Wedding' Affecting." *New York Daily News* 3 Jan.1975: n.p. *New York Theater Critics' Reviews 1975*: 399.

Watts Jr., Richard. "The Amorous Life." *New York Post* 20 Nov. 1961: n.p. *New York Theater Critics' Reviews 1961*: 169.

———. "The Brilliant Career of a Lady Liberal." *New York Post* 18 Nov. 1948: n.p. *New York Theater Critics' Reviews 1948*: 153.

——. "California." Unidentified clipping Lincoln Center Library.

——. "Carolina Slave Revolt in Provocative Play." *New York Post* 4 Nov. 1948: n.p. *New York Theatre Critics' Reviews* 1948: 174.

——. "'The Land is Bright' Reflects America's Past." Unidentified clipping Library Lincoln Center.

——. "Lillian Hellman's Latest Drama." *New York Post* 8 Mar. 1951: n.p. *New York Theatre Critics' Reviews* 1951: 326.

——. "Lillian Hellman's New Play Is Fascinating Drama." *New York Post* 21 Nov. 1946: n.p. *New York Theatre Critics' Reviews* 1946: 250.

——. "Miss Hayes Seconds O'Neill on Pleasures of Drink." *New York Post* 1 Nov. 1946: n.p. *New York Theatre Critics' Reviews* 1946: 281.

——. "Pleasant Memories of Past in Ruth Gordon's New Play." *New York Post* 4 Dec. 1946: n.p. *New York Theatre Critics' Reviews* 1946: 232.

——. "The Problems of Writing a Play." *New York Post* 8 Jan. 1954: n.p. *New York Theatre Critics' Reviews* 1954: 396.

——. "Sad Fate of Two Colette Novels." *New York Post* 13 Oct. 1959: n.p. *New York Theatre Critics' Reviews* 1959: 269.

——. "A Stirring Play About Joan of Arc." *New York Post* 18 Nov. 1955: n.p. *New York Theatre Critics' Reviews* 1955: 207.

——. "A Striking New American Play." *New York Post* 6 Jan. 1950: n.p. *New York Theatre Critics' Reviews* 1950: 399.

——. "The Theatre: 'Claudia.'" *New York Herald Tribune* 23 Feb. 1941: n.p. Clipping Lincoln Center Library.

——. "Trials of the Younger Generation." *New York Post* 17 Oct. 1952: n.p. *New York Theatre Critics' Reviews* 1952: 234.

——. "Unhappy Spring." *New York Herald Tribune* 22 Mar. 1938: n.p. Clipping Lincoln Center Library.

——. "Youth." *New York Herald Tribune* 14 May 1941. *New York Theatre Critics 1940-41*: 324.

Whipple, Sidney B. "Diana Barrymore in Play Adapted by Zoë Akins." *New York World Telegram* 14 May 1941: n.p. *New York Theatre Critics 1940-41*: 324.

Winer, Linda. "A Precious Peek at a Lively Legend." *New York Newsday* 15 Feb. 1991: n.p. *New York Theatre Critics' Reviews 1991*:393.

Winn, Steven. "'Dinner at Eight' is a Stylish Affair." *San Francisco Chronicle* 3 April 1993: 3.

——. "'Harvey' Reappears at San Jose Rep." *San Francisco Chronicle* 15 Dec. 1992: 1.

Winston, Iris. "Foray into Wonderland Worth the Visit." *Ottawa Citizen* 26 Nov. 1992: 7.

Woolcott, Alexander. "'Déclassée' A Brilliant Play." *New York Times* 2 Oct. 1919: 22.

——. "Good Gracious, Annabelle." *New York Times* 5 Nov. 1916: 9.

——. "Miss Treadwell's Play." *New York Herald* 15 Dec. 1922: 14.

——. "Mrs. Marks' Play Revived." *New York Times* 20 Mar. 1920: 14.

——. "Rachel Crothers Herself." *New York Times* 13 Feb. 1920: 16.

——. "A Royal Wild Oat." *New York Herald* 13 Nov. 1923: n.p. Clipping Lincoln Center Library.

——. "Second Thoughts on First Nights." *New York Times*: 23 Jan. 1921: 1.

——. "The Severe Miss Crothers." *New York Times* 3 Mar. 1921: 11.

——. "Stencil Farce." *New York Times* 27 April 1921: 21.

——. "Zona Gale's Play." *New York Times* 28 Dec. 1920: 9.

Wyatt, Euphemia van Rensselaer. "The Drama: 'Outrageous Fortune.'" *Catholic World* Dec. 1943: 298.

Young, Stark. "Cock O'The Roost' Shown." *New York Times* 14 Oct. 1924: 23.

——. "Dinner at Eight." *New Republic* 9 Nov. 1932: 355.

——. "Lulu [sic] Vollmer's New Play." *New York Times* 4 Ap. 1925: 20.

——. "Might It Be Mountains?" *New Republic* 2 Mar. 1934: 246+.

——. "Suburban Harmonies." *New York Times* 2 Dec. 1924: 23.

——. "Two Generations Again." *New York Times* 25 Sept. 1924: 20.

"Zoë Akins of St. Louis." *Vogue* 1 Dec. 1919: n.p. Clipping Lincoln Center Library.

Miscellaneous

Abrahamson, Irving. I. "The Career of Rachel Crothers in the American Theater." Diss. U of Chicago, 1956.

Aldridge, Joyce. "Gertrude Stein: Rose by Any Other Name." Paper at ATHE Conference. Atlanta, 1992.

Austin, Addell Patricia. "Pioneering Black Authored Dramas: 1924-27." Diss. Mich. State U, 1986.

Caldwell, Zoe. Personal Interview. 6 August 1992.

Dale, George. "Jacket Notes." *Kiss Me Kate*. Columbia Records, n.d.

Dorfman, Nat. "Ruth Gordon" and "Ruth Gordon Makes Bow in Own Comedy." Typed press release. Lincoln Center Library.

Franken, Rose. Personal Interview. 7 Oct. 1983.

Ferguson, Phyllis. "Women Dramatists in the American Theatre 1901-1940." Diss. U of Pitt., 1957.

Finizio, Victor. "Clare Kummer: An Analysis of Her Plays and Musicals." Diss. U of Iowa, 1965.

Heck-Rabi, Louise. "Sophie Treadwell: Subjects and Structures in Twentieth Century Drama." Diss. Wayne State U, 1976.

Leach, Wilford. "Gertrude Stein and the Modern Theatre." Diss. U of Ill., 1956.

McCullers, Carson. "Comments by Mrs. McCullers on the Creative Side of Playwriting." Article released by Whitehead-Rea Producers. Lincoln Center Library.

Mielech, R.A. "The Plays of Zoë Akins Rumbold." Diss. Ohio State U, 1974.

Nadon, Daniel Raymond. "Come Up and See Me Sometime! The Sexual Outsider in the Plays of May West." Paper at ATHE Conference, Chicago, 1990.

Pendleton, Austin. Personal Interview. 8 June 1993.

Russell, Helen Johnston. "Social Comment as Depicted in the Plays of American Women Dramatists." Diss. U of Denver, 1958.

Schroeder, Patricia R. "Transforming Images of Blackness: Dramatic Representation, Motherhood, and the Legacy of the Harlem Renaissance." Paper presented at the ASTR Conference, New Orleans 1993.

"Theatre and Social Change Newsletter" Feb. 1991. Published by ATHE.

Zastrow, Sylvia. "The Structure of Selected Plays by American Women Playwrights: 1920-1970." Diss. Northwestern U, 1975.

*Unless otherwise identified, the clippings are in files under the playwright's name in the Library for the Performing Arts at Lincoln Center.

Index

A

Abbey Theatre Company, 236
Abbott, George, 287, 324, 328,
    Broadway, 326
Abend, Sheldon, 437
Abramson, Doris, 24
Ackermann, Jean Marie, 154
ACT (American Conservatory
    Theatre), 94
Adair, Laura, 461
Adams, Maude, 148
Adams, Samuel Hopkins. Revelry
    (novel), 437. (See also Maurine
    Watkins)
Addams, Jane, 217
Ade, George. A College Widow, 207
Adrian, 77
Ailey, Alvin. Revelations, 407
Akins, Zoë, 1, 7, 17, 58-78, 148-54,
    368, 461. Camille (screenplay),
    59, 61. The Crown Prince, 70.
    Daddy's Gone A-Hunting, 64-
    65, 151. Déclassée, 59, 61-65,
    69, 75, 77. The End of the
    Strike, 58. First Love, 70. Foot-
    Loose, 63-64. The Furies, 70,
    152. Greatness (The Texas
    Nightingale), 68-69, 73. The
    Greeks Had a Word for It, 70,
    75. The Happy Days, 74-75.
    Iseult, the Fair, 58. The Magical
    City, 60. The Moon-Flower, 70.
    Morning Glory (screenplay), 59.
    Mrs. January and Mr. Ex, 76-
    77. O Evening Star, 73-74, 149.
    The Old Maid, 58, 61, 71-73,
    75, 77, 124, 131, 151. Papa,
    59-61, 76. A Royal Fandango,
    69-70. Showboat (screenplay),
    59. Thou Desperate Pilot, 153.
    The Varying Shore, 66-67, 152
Akutagawa, Ryunosuke, 362
Albee, Edward. Ballad of the Sad Cafe,
    451. (See also Carson
    McCullers)

Allen, Martha-Bryan, 258-59
Allen, Viola, 378
Allen, Woody, 435
Ameche, Don, 342
American Dramatists Club, 460
Ames, Winthrop, 10, 61, 85, 182,
    242, 256
Anders, Glenn, 116
Anderson, John, 74, 128, 174
Anderson, Judith, 71
Anderson, Maxwell, 128-29. Elizabeth
    the Queen, 56. What Price
    Glory?, 85, 436
Anderson, Robert. Tea and Sympathy,
    112
Anglin, Margaret, 460
Anouilh, Jean. L'Aloutte, 141. (See
    also Lillian Hellman)
Anson, A. E., 183
Apollinaire, Guillaume. The Breasts of
    Tiresias, 192
Archer, William, 50
Ardery, Robert, 118
Arena Stage, 141
Arnold, Francis, 389
Arnold, Roseanne, 372
Aronson, Boris, 400
Astaire, Fred, 444
Aston, Frank, 353, 393
Astor, Mary, 173
Astor Theatre, 212
Atkinson, Brooks, 6, 29, 30, 32, 50,
    70, 74-75, 89, 91, 104, 118,
    126, 136-37, 142, 172, 200,
    262, 264, 266, 289, 293, 305-
    6, 324, 326, 328, 330, 336,
    339, 341, 352-53, 364, 390,
    392-93, 396, 398, 400-1, 417,
    426, 438, 443, 453

B

Bacall, Lauren, 94
Bach, Ernest, 389
Bailey, Gloria, 454
Bainter, Fay, 350

Baker, Edith Ellis, 461
Baker, George Pierce, 178, 226, 395, 434, 439, 458, 460
Balderston, John, 106
Baldwin, James, 160
Ballard, Lucinda, 366
BAM Theatre Company, 23
Bancroft, Anne, 129
Bankhead, Tallulah, 7, 24, 29, 64, 127-29, 353-54
Baraka, Amiri, 160, 371
Barlow, Judith E., 436
Barnes, Clive, 89, 130, 262, 367, 407, 453
Barnes, Djuna, 17, 460
Barnes, Howard, 6, 77, 287, 290, 324, 348, 350, 391-93, 418, 447-49
Barnsdall, Aline, 60
Barrie, J. M., 148, 167, 352. *Peter Pan*, 189, 284
Barrymore, Diana, 75, 98
Barrymore, Ethel, 16, 61, 63-64, 69, 81, 88, 148, 248, 334
Barrymore, John, 87, 93-94, 266, 288, 334
Barter Theatre (Virginia), 307-8
Bass, George Houston, 408
Baum, Vicki. *Grand Hotel*, 93, 426
Bay, Howard, 145, 419
Beane, Reginald, 449
Beaufort, John, 407, 454
Beckett, Samuel, 193, 202. *Waiting For Godot*, 431
Beebe, Lucius, 105
Beecher, Henry Ward, 162
Beechwood Players, 297
Behrman, S. N., 53, 433. *Biography*, 440. *The Second Man*, 396
Belasco, David, 9, 15, 81, 192, 224, 241, 334, 382. *Lulu Belle*, 419
Belcher, Fannin, 160
bel Geddes, Barbara, 76
bel Geddes, Norman, 60
Belmont, Mrs. O.H.P., 335, 339
Benchley, Robert, 311, 412, 421-24
Bennett, Helen Christine, 203-4
Bennett, Joan, 344
Benson, E. F., 181-82
Bentley, Eric. *Are You Now, or Have You Ever Been?*, 121

Benton, Conwell, 385
Bergner, Elizabeth, 99
Bergson, Henri, 328
Berkshire Playhouse/Theatre Festival, 63, 224
Berle, Milton, 344
Berner, Lord. *A Wedding Bouquet* (ballet), 202
Bernhardt, Sarah, 79, 176, 190, 440
Bernstein, Leonard, 142-43
Berry, Wallace, 94
Best, Edna, 105, 426
Biltmore Theatre, 418
Björkman, Edwin, 60
Black, John, 182
Blechman, Burt. *How Much* (novel), 145. (*See also* Lillian Hellman)
Blitzstein, Marc, 154. *Regina*, 129
Blood and Sand (play), 440
Bloom, Claire, 364
Boas, Franz, 404
Bodenheim, Max, 241
Body Politic Theatre, 90
Boehnel, William, 72
Bogart, Humphrey, 332
Bonfils Theatre (Denver), 354
Bonner, Marita, 8, 160, 370, 428-32, 457. *Exit, an Illusion*, 432, 457. *Muddled Dream*, 432. *The Pot Maker*, 428-31. *The Purple Flower*, 431-32, 457-58.
Boone, Pat, 353
Booth, Edwin, 176, 190, 284
Booth, Shirley, 359, 425
Booth Theatre, 10, 242, 281
Boswell, Connee, 342
Bourdet, Edouard. *The Captive*, 109
Bowen Park Theatre Company, 90
Bowman, Laura, 266, 269, 305, 390
Boyce, Neith, 3, 460
Bradley, Jeff, 263
Braithwaite, William Stanley, 229
Braque, Georges, 191
Brawley, Benjamin, 314
Brecher, Egon, 326
Brecht, Bertolt, 99
Bridget Loves Bernie (television), 413.
Broun, Heywood, 6, 21-22, 27, 41, 69, 165, 168, 222, 225
Brown Arvin, 94

Brown, Herrick, 447-48
Brown, Joe, 224
Brown, Joe E., 348
Brown, John Mason, 56, 74, 98, 172
Brown, Sterling, 159-60
Browning, Robert, 179, 182
Bubbles, John W., 300, 401. And Buck, 300
Buckingham, George Villiers, 2nd Duke of. *The Rehearsal,* 250
Bulwer-Lytton, Edward George. *Richelieu,* 176
Burke, Billie, 76-77, 167, 171
Burns, Shirley, 148-49, 456
Burrill, Mary, 309-10
Burton, Richard, 152
Butcher, James, 159
Byron, Lord, 204

C

The Cabinet of Dr. Caligari (film), 38
Cagney, James, 329
Caldwell Theatre Company, 90
Caldwell, Zoe, 121
Calhern, Louis, 94
Campbell, Alan, 193, 422, 425. (*See also* Dorothy Parker)
Carb, David, 50
Carey, Ralph, 75
Cariaga, Daniel, 197
Carmer, Carl, 87-88
Carmines, Al, 201
Carnegie, Andrew, 82
Carolina Playmakers, 460
Caron, Leslie, 393
Carpenter, Edward, 4
Carroll, Lewis, 165, 167, 241-43. *Alice in Wonderland,* 242. *Through the Looking Glass,* 242
Carroll, Madeleine, 360-61
Carter, Jack, 397
Carter, Jimmy, 312
Carter, Mrs. Leslie, 73
Carter, Mary Dixie, 373
Cassini, Oleg, 361
Cather, Willa, 59, 70
Cavett, Dick, 123
Center Theatre (Chicago), 224

Century Play Company (Connecticut), 281
Champion, Gower, 146
Channing, Carol, 392, 394
Chapman, John A., 67, 141-43, 287, 290, 293, 331, 348, 360, 392, 401, 417, 447
Charles, Martie, 160
Chase, Mary Coyle, 346-55, 370. *The Banshee,* 346, 350. *Bernardine,* 352-53. *Harvey (The White Rabbit),* 346-50, 354-55, 373. *Me Third,* 346. *Midgie Purvis,* 353-55. *Mrs. McThing,* 350-53. *The Next Half Hour,* 350-51. *Now You've Done It,* 346. *Sorority Girl* (film), 346. *We Love You, Denver!* 354
Chekhov, Anton, 139, 451. *The Cherry Orchard,* 55. *The Three Sisters,* 284
Cheney, Stewart, 72, 74
Chevalier, Maurice, 393
Chicago Junior League Theatre for Children, 242
Childress, Alice, 161
Christiansen, Richard, 96, 224
Christie, Agatha. *The Mousetrap,* 413
Churchill, Winston, 97, 389
Cicero, 439
City Center Theatre, 33
Civic Repertory Theatre, 50, 56-57
Claire, Ina, 70, 89
Clark, Barrett H., 129, 131, 147
Clark, Gerald, 415
Clark, Norman, 114
Cleveland Playhouse, 154
Clift, Montgomery, 133, 448-49
Clurman, Harold, 99, 426, 452, 454
Cocteau, Jean. *The Ox on the Roof,* 192. *Parade,* 192
Coleman, John, 6
Coleman, Louise, 296
Coleman, Robert, 104, 138, 143, 145, 269, 331, 352, 362, 364, 366, 393, 426, 444, 453
Colette, 389, 392-93
Collier, Constance, 93
Collins, Charles, 164

Comedy Theatre, 302
Communism, 76-77
Community Players (Boston), 183
Connelly, Marc, 233. *The Green Pastures*, 398. (*See also* George S. Kaufman)
Cook, Barbara, 366
Cook, Elisha, 241
Cook, George Cram (Jig), 36-38, 41, 43, 45-47, 53-54, 153, 460
Cook, Michael, 154
Cooke-Reid, Anne, 159
Coolidge, Calvin, 76, 392
Copeland, Charles Townsend, 428
Corbin, John, 21, 26-27, 69-70, 167-68, 213, 224-26, 257, 301, 389
Cornell, Katherine, 24
Cort Theatre, 328
Cowan, Jerome, 328, 331
Coward, Noel, 61. *Private Lives*, 28
Cowl, Jane, 335
Crabtree, Lotte, 441
Craig, James, 261
Crane, William H., 378-79
Craven, Frank, 76-77
Crawford, Cheryl, 89
Crawford, Joan, 33
Crews, Laura Hope, 171
Cromwell, John, 304
Crothers, Rachel, 7-8, 15-35, 102, 148-54, 269, 356, 368, 380-81, 389, 456, 459, 461. As *Husbands Go*, 31. *Every Cloud Has a Silver Lining*, or *The Ruined Merchant*, 15. *Expressing Willie*, 26-28, 31. *He and She*, 3, 20-23, 116, 154. *The Herfords*, 20. *A Lady's Virtue*, 28. *Let Us Be Gay*. 28-29, 151. *A Man's World*, 3-4, 17-19, 21, 104, 149, 151-52. *Mary the Third*, 25-26, 151. *Myself, Bettina*, 16. *Nice People*, 23-25, 28. *Ourselves*, 20. *Susan and God*, 31-33, 394. *Thirty-Nine East*, 16, 21, 64. *The Three of Us*, 16. *Venus*, 28. *When Ladies Meet*, 29-31, 394. (*See also* Anita Loos)

Cukor, George, 33, 89, 92, 94, 338
Cullen, Countee, 229, 311
The Curse of Drink (play), 296

D

Dale, Alan, 69
Dale, George, 329
Daly's Theatre, 303
Darvas, Lili, 99
Davis, Bette, 129, 358
Dawn, Hazel, 284
Dean, Alexander, 252
de Bracco, Robert, 246
de Casseres, Benjamin, 29
De Courcelles, M., 210
Deep River (play), 397
De Foe, Louis V., 25, 222
Dehelly, Emile, 440
De Jagers, Dorothy, 396. (*See also* Dorothy Heyward)
De Mille, Agnes, 392
de Musset, Alfred, 246
Denver Center for the Performing Arts, 354
Denver Center Stage Ensemble, 263
de Wilde, Brandon, 351, 451
Dick, Bernard, 125
Dickenson, Thomas. *Wisconsin Plays*, 217
Dickerson, Glenda, 160
Dickinson, Emily, 54
Ditrichstein, Leo, 433
Dodge, Mabel, 45
Dodson, Owen, 159
Donat, Peter, 94
Donnelly, Tom, 143
Drake, Alfred, 330
Drama League, 460
Draper, Ruth, 441
Dressler, Marie, 73, 94
Du Bois, W.E.B., 229, 232, 272, 275, 309, 460
Dullea, Keir, 138
Dumas, Alexandre. *The Count of Monte Cristo*, 64. *The Lady of the Camellias* (*Camille*), 61, 378
Dunbar Garden Players, 272
Dunbar-Nelson, Alice Moore, 7, 160, 383-87, 457. *Gone White*, 386-

87. *Goodness of St. Rocque*, 383.
An Hawaiian Idyll, 385. *Mine
Eyes Have Seen*, 385. *The Smart
Set*, 384. *Violets and Other
Tales*, 383.
Duncan, Isadora, 216
Duncan, William Cary, 212
Dunnock, Mildred, 136, 292
Dunsany, Lord, 248
Durning, Charles, 94
D'Usseau, Arnaud, 425-26. (*See also*
Dorothy Parker)

E

Eaton, Walter Prichard, 56, 177, 179,
182
Eddy, Nelson, 211
Edmonds, Randolph, 160, 310
Edward, King, 179
Egan, Daisy, 454
Eisenhower, Mamie, 345
Eldridge, Florence, 141, 267, 269,
289-90
Elias, Lois, 323
Elizabeth II, Queen, 345
Elliott, John, 436
Elliott, Maxine, 8, 10, 16
Ellis, Abby, 291
Ellis, Havelock, 4
Eltinge, Julian, 418
Emerson, John, 388. (*See also* Anita
Loos)
Encompass Theatre, 28
Engle, William, 105
Equity Library Theater, 120
Estrin, Mark W., 147
Evans, Rosser, 425. (*See also* Dorothy
Parker)
Expressionism, 36-38, 41-42, 44-46,
51, 70, 152, 242, 259-61, 263,
370, 462

F

Falk, Doris, 145
Fassbinder, Rainer Maria. *Women in
New York* (film), 339
Fay, Frank, 348, 354
Faye, Joey, 328

Fazekas, Imre, 304-5
Fechter, Charles Albert, 176
Federal Theatre Project, 8, 56-57,
231, 234, 237-38, 346, 370,
397, 404
Ferber, Edna, 1, 3, 7, 79-101, 133,
149-51, 153-54, 216, 248, 288,
367, 461-62. *The Eldest*, 83-84,
151. *Giant* (novel), 80. *Old
Man Minick*, 84-87. *Our Mrs.
McChesney*, 81-82. *Saratoga
Trunk* (novel), 98, 394. *Show
Boat*, 90-91, 154. *So Big*,
(novel), 80, 101. *$1200 a Year*,
82-83. And George S. Kauf-
man. *Bravo*, 82, 98-100. *Dinner
at Eight*, 91-94, 96, 99-100,
149, 151, 252, 426. *The Land is
Bright*, 86, 96. *The Royal
Family*, 82, 87-90, 96, 100.
Stage Door, 86, 95-96, 100-
101, 154. (*See also* Anita Loos)
Ferguson, Elsie, 67, 113
Ferrer, Jose, 399
Field, Rowland, 108
Fields, Joseph, 392
Fifer, Elizabeth, 193
Fifth Avenue Theatre, 377
Finley, Karen, 445
Firkins, O. W., 50
Fitch, Clyde, 292. *The Truth*, 310
Flexner, Anne Crawford, 149
Fly's Eye, A (Chicago), 263
Fonda, Jane, 123
Fonteyn, Margot, 202
Foreman, Richard, 202
Forever After (play), 213
49th Street Theatre, 259
Foster, Claiborne, 304
Foxworth, Robert, 137
France, Rachel, 42
Frank Theatre (Minneapolis), 263
Frankel, C. David, 263
Frankel, Gene, 262
Franken, Rose, 1, 7-8, 102-120, 148-
51, 153-54, 367, 380, 456,
461. *Another Language*, 102-8,
118, 120, 149, 151. *Claudia*, 7,
75, 106-9, 116, 119, 148.
Doctors Disagree, 115-16, 119.

Franken, Rose (continued)
  Fortnight, 103. *The Hallam
  Wives,* 103. *The Hallams,* 118-
  19. *Outrageous Fortune,* 109-
  17, 119, 460. *Pattern* (novel),
  102. *Soldier's Wife,* 116-17.
  When All is Said and Done
  (autobiography), 118. *Wings,*
  118. And Jane Lenin. *Mr.
  Dooley, Jr.,* 103
Franks, Bobby, 433-34
Franz, Eduard, 112
Freedley, George, 76, 119, 269
French, Samuel, 230, 275, 305
Freud, Sigmund, 4, 39, 242, 246-47,
  370, 463. *The Interpretation of
  Dreams,* 242.
Friml, Rudolph, 213
Frohman, Charles, 15
Frohman, Daniel, 203

                   G

Gable, Clark, 260, 269
Gale, Zona, 5, 7, 214, 216-28, 230,
  307, 370, 372-73, 461-62.
  Birth, 224-25. *Miss Lulu Bett,*
  217, 219-25, 372-73, 463. *Mr.
  Pitt,* 225-26. *Neighbors,* 217-19,
  223. *Uncle Jimmy,* 226-27
Gallo, Lillian, 357
Gardner, Edward F., 425. (*See also*
  Dorothy Parker)
Garland, Hamlin, 216, 222
Garland, Robert, 77, 125, 136, 138,
  287, 293, 361, 391, 393, 447-
  48, 450, 452
Garrick Theatre, 297
Gassner, John, 130, 307
Gates, Henry Louis, Jr., 408
Gaxton, William, 326
Gelb, Arthur, 410
Germinal Stage (Denver), 291
Gershwin, George, 91, 398. (*See also*
  Dorothy Heyward)
Gershwin, Ira, 398. (*See also* Dorothy
  Heyward)
Gerstenberg, Alice, 2, 8, 241-54, 370.
  Alice in Wonderland, 242-46,
  253, 373, 460, 463. *Attuned,*

  250-51. *Beyond,* 250. *Comedies
  All,* 252. *The Conscience of
  Sarah Platt,* 253. *Facing Fact,*
  252. *Fourteen,* 251-52. *The
  Land of Don't Want To,* 242. *A
  Little World,* 241. *The Menu,*
  252. *Overtones,* 241, 246-48,
  252, 254, 373. *A Patroness,*
  251. *The Potboiler,* 248-50,
  252. *The Puppeteer,* 252.
  Rhythm, 252. *Victory Belles,*
  242. *Water Babies,* 242
Gest, Morris, 322
Gibbs, Wolcott, 77, 99, 115, 360, 362
Gilbert, Gilbert W., 172
Gilbert, W. S., 167. And Arthur
  Sullivan, 377
Gillette, William, 162-63, 165-67,
  190, 284. *Secret Service,* 190,
  199 , 284
Gillmore, Margalo, 112
Givot, George, 419
Glaspell, Susan, 2-3, 5, 7, 36-57, 73,
  149-54, 214, 248, 252, 433,
  459-61, 463-64. *Alison's
  House.* 9, 36, 40, 48, 54-56,
  151. *Bernice,* 40, 47-48. *The Big
  Bozo,* 56. *Close the Book,* 42-43.
  The Comic Artist, 53-54.
  Inheritors, 1, 42, 48-51, 55, 57,
  360. *A Jury of Her Peers*
  (story), 39. *The Outside,* 43-46,
  151. *The People,* 41-42, 46.
  Suppressed Desires, 38-39, 43,
  46. *Tickless Time,* 46-47.
  Trifles, 5, 36, 38-41, 43, 46,
  151, 154. *The Verge,* 3, 43, 51-
  53, 149, 151. *The Visioning,* 37.
  Woman's Honor, 45-46
Glover, John, 224
Godwin, William, 188
Goldberg, Whoopi, 445
Golden, John, 10, 119, 460
Goldman, Michael, 57
Goldwyn, Samuel, 125
Gone With the Wind (film), 340
The Good Little Devil (play), 334
Goodman, Alfred, 409. (*See also*
  Anne Nichols)
Goodman, Kenneth Sawyer, 241

Goodrich, Frances and Albert Hackett. *The Diary of Anne Frank* (play), 142

Gordon, Max, 171-72, 340

Gordon, Ruth, 3, 7, 284-95, 370, 372, 390, 422-23, 460. *The Actress* (film), 289. *Adam's Rib* (film), 294. *A Double Life* (film), 294. *The Leading Lady*, 291-94. *My Side* (memoir), 295. *Over Twenty-One*, 5, 285-88, 290, 295, 423. *Pat and Mike* (film), 294. *A Very Rich Woman*, 294. *Years Ago*, 284, 288-91, 293, 295, 373

Gottfried, Martin, 454

Grautoff, Christine, 99

Greek Theatre (Berkeley), 255

Green, Paul, 310-11. *In Abraham's Bosom*, 273, 397. *Johnny Johnson*, 308

Greene, Robert, 179

Greenwich Village Theatre, 302

Greenwood, Charlotte, 409

Gregory, Montgomery, 158, 311

Greif, Frank, 262

Grenville, Vernon, 341, 343

Griffies, Ethel, 293

Grimke, Angelina, 309-10

Grody, Kathryn, 224

Groody, Louise, 300

Grosman, B., 409. (*See also* Anne Nichols)

Group Theatre, 256

Gussow, Mel, 94

Guthrie, Tyrone, 142

Gwynn, Nell, 441

Gwynne, Fred, 346

H

Hackett, Francis, 228

Hakim, Raphael and Robert, 75

Hall, Dorothy, 70

Hall, Radclyff, 193

Hamilton, Clayton, 72, 245

Hamilton, Frank, 454

Hamilton, Margaret, 112

Hammerstein, Oscar, 391. And Richard Rodgers. *Oklahoma!*, 308, 398. *South Pacific*, 392, 400

Hammett, Dashiell, 121-23, 125-27, 139-40, 460. *The Thin Man* (novel), 122

Hammond, Percy, 69, 72, 74, 225, 415, 419, 436

Hampton, Walter, 446

Hansberry, Lorraine, 2, 161, 311, 457. *To Be Young, Gifted and Black*, 428

Harding, Ann, 50, 57, 360

Harding, Warren, 437

Hardwick, Elizabeth, 129

Harlem Experimental Theatre, 230

Harlow, Jean, 94

Harrigan, Edward, and Tony Hart, 324

Harris, Jed, 88, 285, 291

Harris, Julie, 138, 142, 451, 453

Harris, Mike, 246

Harris, Rosemary, 89

Harris, Sam, 31

Hart, Moss, and Kurt Weill. *Lady in the Dark*, 5, 109, 265. (*See also* George S. Kaufman).

Harvey, Georgette, 397

Hasenclever, Walter, 42

Haver, Phyllis, 437

Hawkins, William, 141, 293, 331, 401, 453

Hayes, Helen, 105, 257, 269, 346, 348, 351, 388, 391. (*See also* Anita Loos)

Hayes, Richard, 344

Hayward, Susan, 357

Hebbel Theatre (Berlin), 198

Hecht, Ben, 241, 326, 433. And Charles MacArthur. *The Front Page*, 326

Hedberg, 186

Heggie, O. P., 85

Helburn, Theresa, 269-70, 404

Hellman, Lillian, 7, 58, 77, 118, 121-51, 153-54, 269, 422-23, 460, 462. *Another Part of the Forest*, 135-37, 144, 153-54. *The Autumn Garden*, 122, 139-41, 146. *Candide*, (operetta), 142-43. *The Children's Hour*, 72,

Hellman, Lillian (continued)
    109, 122, 124-26, 129, 149,
    151. *Days to Come*, 126. *Dead
    End* (film), 147. *The Lark*, 141-
    42. *Montserrat*, 137-39. *North
    Star* (film), 123. *The Little
    Foxes*, 1, 4, 7, 9, 123, 127-30,
    132, 135-36, 146, 153-54, 422.
    My Mother, My Father and Me,
    145-46. *Pentimento* (memoir),
    123, 146. *Scoundrel Time*
    (memoir), 123, 153. *The
    Searching Wind*, 132-34, 440.
    These Three (film), 125. *Toys in
    the Attic*, 144-46. *An Unfinished
    Woman*, (memoir), 123. *Watch
    on the Rhine*, 122-23, 130-32.
    (*See also* Dorothy Parker)
Helpmann, Robert, 202.
Henderson, William Penhallow, 245
Hepburn, Audrey, 125, 392-94
Hepburn, Katherine, 59, 96, 294,
    304, 421
Herbert, Victor, 210-11
Hériat, Phillippe. *Les Joies de Famille*, 294
Hernandez, Juano, 401
Herne, Crystal, 27
Herne, James A., 150
Hewitt, Bernard, 128. *Theatre U.S.A.*,
    461
Heyward, Dorothy (Hartzell Kuhns),
    395-402, 457. *Nancy Ann*, 395.
    Set My People Free, 401. And
    Dorothy De Jagers. *Cinderela-
    tive*, 395. And DuBose
    Heyward. *Mamba's Daughters*,
    395, 399-401. *Porgy*, 395-99,
    401. And Dubose Heyward,
    George and Ira Gershwin.
    Porgy and Bess, 398-99, 458.
    And Howard Rigsby. *South
    Pacific*, 400.
Hibbard, Edna, 257, 391
Hitler, Adolf, 33, 80-81, 96, 98, 132,
    342-43
Hobart, George V., 81
Holden, Stephen, 197-98
Holland, Endesha Ida Mae, 161
Holm, Celeste, 361
Homolka, Oscar, 99, 364

Hopkins, Arthur, 10, 60, 65, 78, 162,
    164, 166, 168, 259, 263, 266,
    270, 370
Hopkins, Charles, 263
Hopper, Hedda, 94
Hopwood, Avery, 9, 81, 382
Horizon Theatre (Washington), 224
Hornblow, Arthur, 28, 43, 211, 213-
    14
House Beautiful (play), 421
Howard, Bronson, 380. *Shenandoah*,
    190
Howard, Sidney. *The Silver Cord*, 103,
    396. *Paths of Glory*, 137. *They
    Knew What They Wanted*, 85,
    267
Howard University Players, 159
Howells, W. D., 384
Howland, Carrie, 445
Howland, Jobyna, 68-69, 73
Hughes, Charlotte, 150
Hughes, Hatcher, 272
Hughes, Langston, 229, 311, 404,
    428. (*See also* Zora Neale
    Hurston)
Hull, Henry, 266
Hull, Josephine, 348
Hunger Artists (Denver), 154
Hunter, Alberta, 399
Hunter, Kim, 126, 340
Hurston, Zora Neale, 8, 160, 229,
    272, 282, 311, 403-8, 457.
    Color Struck, 403, 405. *Fast and
    Furious*, 404, 406. *The First
    One*, 404, 406. *From Sun to
    Sun*, 406. *The Great Day*, 404,
    406. *Sermon in the Valley*, 406.
    Singing Steel, 406. *Spears*, 403.
    And Langston Hughes. *Mule
    Bone*, 403-4, 407-8. (*See also*
    George C. Wolfe)
Husson, Albert, 330-31. *La Cuisine
    des Anges*, 330. (*See also* Bella
    Spewack)
Huston, Walter, 226

                    I

Ibsen, Henrik, 34-35, 64-65, 132,
    134, 150-51, 296. *A Doll*

House, 34, 65, 220, 263-64, 291-92, 336, 344. *The Wild Duck*, 65-66, 139
Immediate Theatre Company, 137
In the Heat of the Night (film), 237
Inchbald, Elizabeth, 188
Inge, Benson, 78
Ionesco, Eugene, 202
Irving, Henry, 79, 216
Isaacs, Edith, 33, 125, 311

J

Jacobson, Lee, 224
Jaeb Theatre (Tampa Bay), 454
Jaffe, Sam, 324
James Adams Floating Palace Theater, 90
James, William, 191
Jansen, Louise, 204. *(See also* Rida Johnson Young)
Johann, Zita, 259, 269, 305
Johnson, Georgia Douglas, 8, 160, 229-40, 272, 309-10, 370, 387, 428, 430. *An Autumn Love Cycle*, 230. *Blue-Eyed Black Boy*, 238. *Blue Blood*, 235, 311, 372-73. *Bronze*, 230. *Frederick Douglass*, 231, 238-39. *The Heart of a Woman and Other Poems*, 230. *Plumes*, 230-31, 236, 372. *Safe*, 237-38, 317. *Share My World*, 210. *A Sunday Morning in the South*, 1, 233-34. *William and Ellen Craft*, 231, 239
Johnson, Hall. *Run, Little Chillun*, 398
Joyce, James, 389
Jones, Agatha F. 385
Jones, Margo, 425
Jones, Robert Edmond, 37, 65, 164, 166, 168, 259, 263, 270
Joslyn, Allyn, 328
Judson Memorial Church, 201
Julia (film), 123

K

Kahn, Michael, 91

Kaiser, Georg, 42. *The Burghers of Calais*, 137. *From Morn to Midnight*, 38, 261
Kalem, T. E., 340
Kalman, Emmerich, 211
Kampf, Leopold. *On the Eve*, 381. *(See also* Martha Morton)
Kander, John, and Fred Ebb. *Chicago* (musical), 437. *(See also* Maurine Watkins)
Kane, Carol, 224
Kanin, Fay, 1, 3, 356-70, 380. *Friendly Fire* (television), 357, 368. *Fun and Games* (television), 357. *Goodbye, My Fancy*, 356, 359-62. *Grind*, 367-68. *Heat of Anger* (television), 357. *Hustling* (television), 357. *Tell Me Where It Hurts* (television), 357. *The Woman's Angle* (television), 356. And Michael Kanin. *The Gay Life*, 365-66. *His and Hers*, 361-62. *The Opposite Sex*, (film), 338, 357. *The Outrage* (film), 365. *Rashomon*, 362-65. *Teacher's Pet* (film), 357
Kanin, Garson, 285, 287-90, 292-94, 360
Kaufman, George S., 72-73, 78, 84-101, 172, 269, 285, 287-88, 337, 350, 421, 423, 460-61. And Marc Connelly, 101. *Begger on Horseback*, 45. And Moss Hart, 101. *The Man Who Came to Dinner*, 89. *Merrily We Roll Along*, 423. *Once in a Lifetime*, 6, 73. *You Can't Take It With You*, 286. *(See also* Edna Ferber)
Kaye, Stubby, 367
Keith, Ian, 293
Kelly, George, 269
Kelly, William J., 293
Kemble, Fanny, 459
Kemble, John Phillips, 188
Kennedy, Adrienne, 161
Kennedy Center, 91
Kennedy, Laurie, 23

Kern, Jerome, 91

Kerr, Jean. *Our Hearts Were Young and Gay*, 444

Kerr, John, 352

Kerr, Walter, 89, 142-43, 145, 352-53, 355, 362, 426, 438, 443

Kingsley, Sidney, 118

Kirk, Lisa, 330

Kirkland, Jack. *Tobacco Road* (play), 266

Kirkland, Patricia, 289

Kirkpatrick, John. *She Married Well*, 157.

Kismet (musical), 440

Kissel, Howard, 130, 407, 453

Klein, Charles, 381

Kober, Arthur, 122

Koch, Frederick, 310-11, 460

Koehler, Robert, 33

Koon, Helene, 292

Kornfeld, Lawrence, 201-2

Kramer vs. Kramer (film), 23

Krigwa Players (New York), 230, 235, 272-76, 311, 314, 428, 460, 462

Kroll, Jack, 340

Kronenberger, Louis, 113, 115, 288, 290, 348, 350, 391

Kruger, Otto, 88

Krutch, Joseph Wood, 93, 96, 148, 419

Kummer, Clare (Rodman Beecher), 162-75, 370, 372, 433, 462. *Amourette*, 171-72. *Be Calm, Camilla!*, 167-69. *Good Gracious, Annabelle*, 4, 162-65, 171, 173, 373. *Her Master's Voice*, 171-73. *Many Happy Returns*, 173-74. *Pomeroy's Past*, 171. *The Rescuing Angel*, 167. *Rollo's Wild Oat*, 163, 169-71, 173, 373. *Spring Thaw*, 172-74. *A Successful Calamity*, 163, 165-66, 169, 173.

Kummer, Marjorie, 163

Kurasawa, Akira, 362

L

Lafayette Theatre/Players, 273, 390

La Guardia, Fiorello, 342

Lakeside Players (Canada), 246

Lamb, Charles and Mary, 425

Lang, Harold, 330

Langner, Lawrence, 37, 252, 269-70, 460. *Matinata*, 47

Langtry, Lily, 79

Lardner, John, 294

Larrimore, Francine, 24, 28, 436

Lask, Thomas, 120

Latouche, John, 142

LaVerne, Lucile, 300

Lawrence, Gertrude, 32-33

Lawrence, Jerome, and Robert E. Lee. *The Gang's All Here*, 437

Lear, Edward, 167

Lee, Canada, 400-1

Le Gallienne, Eva, 9, 50, 56-57, 89, 216, 246, 415, 460

Le Gallienne, Richard, 216

Leighton, Margaret, 423

Lester, Elenore, 340

Leopold, Nathan, and Richard Loeb, 433, 439

Lenya, Lotte, 99

Levant, Oscar, 342

Levene, Sam, 343

Levy, Norman, 82

Lewis, Joan, 160

Lewisohn, Ludwig, 45, 52, 61, 66, 222, 301

Lighthouse 1/Players, 10, 219, 281

Lincoln Center, 129

Lindsay, Howard, and Russel Crouse, 440

Littell, Robert, 412-13, 418

Little, Robert, 29

Little Theatre, 9, 61, 256

Locke, Alain, 158, 229, 236, 272, 309, 403

Lockridge, Richard, 55, 75, 132, 171-72, 336, 417

Loeb, Phillip, 287

Logan, Joshua, 391

Long Wharf Theatre, 94

Loos, Anita, 338, 388-94, 457, 463. *Cast of Thousands* (memoir), 394. *Cheri*, 393. *Ex-Bad Boy* (film), 389. *Gentlemen Prefer Blondes*, 388, 390, 392, 394,

458. *Gigi*, 388, 392-93. *A Girl Like I* (memoir), 394. *Happy Birthday (Blue Lounge)*, 391-92. *Kiss Hollywood Good-by* (memoir), 394. *Lorelei*, 394. *Saratoga* (film), 394. *Susan and God* (film), 394. *When Ladies Meet* (film) 394. *The Women* (film), 394. And John Emerson. *The Fall of Eve*, 390. *The Whole Town's Talking*, 389. And Helen Hayes. *Twice Over Lightly*, 394.

Lorre, Peter, 99

Lovell, John, 159

Luce, Clare Boothe, 3, 7, 80-81, 200, 287, 334-45, 359, 370, 373, 449-50, 462-63. *Abide With Me*, 335-36. *Child of the Morning* 344. *Kiss the Boys Goodbye*, 335, 340-43. *Margin for Error*, 335, 342-44. *Slam the Door Softly*, 336, 344-45. *The Women*, 334-41, 345, 357, 394. (*See also* Anita Loos)

Luce, William. *Lillian*, 121

Lunt, Alfred, and Lynn Fontanne, 98, 415

Lupino, Ida, 282

Lyttleton Theatre (London), 463

M

Mabley, Moms, 406

MacArthur, Charles, 326, 433. (*See also* Ben Hecht)

MacDonald, Jeanette, 211

Macgowan, Kenneth, 52, 148, 170, 220, 412

Mackaye, Milton, 341

MacKaye, Percy, 187

MacLaine, Shirley, 125

MacNicholas, Carol, 137-38

Madame Simon, 410

Madonna (Ciccione), 392

Maeterlinck, Maurice, 183. *The Intruder*, 45. *Pélleas and Mélisande*, 45

Mainbocker, 293

Maltin, Leonard, 105, 125, 304, 329

Mamoulian, Rouben, 397

Mandelbaum, Ken, 463

Mann, Iris, 126

Mann, Thomas, 99

Mannering, Mary, 210

Mantle, Burns, 6, 10, 25-26, 56, 63, 75, 79, 81, 84-85, 89, 92, 102, 113-14, 125, 129, 132, 134, 136, 148, 165, 170, 172, 307, 328, 332, 338-39, 392-93, 398, 433-34, 436-37, 441, 448, 460-61

March, Fredric, 89, 141, 267, 269, 289-90

Markell, Jodie, 262

Marks, Lionel S. 177

Mark Taper Forum, 336

Marlowe, Julia, 58

Marriott, John, 128

Marshall, Alexander, 160

Marshall, Fredye, 400

Martin, Mary, 326, 342

Marvenga, Ilse, 211

Mason, Charlotte Osgood, 404

Mason, Judi, 161

Mason, Marsha, 94

Masters, Edgar Lee, 59

Mathewson, Christie, 205

Matisse, Henri, 191

Matthews, Adelaide, 409-10. (*See also* Anne Nichols)

Matthews, Brander, 462. *A Book About the Theatre*, 459

Matthison, Edith, 183

Matson, Norman, 53, 55, 153

Maugham, Somerset, 61, 148. *Theatre*, 440

Maxwell, Perriton, 304

McCarten, John, 366

McCarthy, Joseph, 141, 153

McCarthy, Mary, 123

McClain, John, 142, 331, 352, 354, 443

McClendon, Rose, 273, 397

McClintic, Guthrie, 72, 78, 256, 399

McCormick, Myron, 116

McCullers, Carson, 451-57. *Ballad of the Sad Cafe*, 451. *A Member of the Wedding*, 5, 451-55, 457-58. *The Square Root of Wonderful*, 454-55. And Mary Rodgers. *F.*

McCullers, Carson (continued)
    Jasmine Addams, 455. (*See also*
    Edward Albee)
McGovern, Edythe M., 57
McGuire, Dorothy, 106
McQueen, Ellen, 454
Meloney, William Brown, 106, 109
Mencken, H. L., 389-90
Menken, Helen, 71
Merington, Marguerite, 456
Merkel, Una, 326
Messel, Oliver, 364
Michaelson, Judy, 99
Mielziner, Jo, 32, 97, 364, 391
Millay, Edna St. Vincent, 460
Miller, Ann, 330
Miller, Arthur, 2. *All My Sons*, 446.
    Incident at Vichy, 137
Miller, Dean Kelly, 230
Miller, Gilbert, 113
Miller, Henry, 210, 378
Miller, May, 8, 160, 229, 272, 282,
    309-21, 428. *The Bog Guide*,
    311. *Christopher's Daughters*,
    311, 316. *The Cuss'd Thing*,
    311. *Freedom's Children on the
    March*, 311. *Graven Images*,
    315. *Harriet Tubman*, 311,
    318-20. *Nails and Thorns*, 316-
    18. *Pandora's Box*, 309. *Riding
    the Goat*, 312-15, 372. *Samory*,
    316. *Scratches*, 311. *Sojourner
    Truth*, 311, 319-20. *Stragglers
    in the Dust*, 1, 314-15. *Within
    the Shadow*, 310. (*See also*
    Willis Richardson)
Mitchell, Abbie, 128
Mitchell, Bernardine, 454
Mitchell, Thomas, 326
Modjeska, Helena, 176, 255
Molette, Carlton, 160
Molière. *The School for Scandal*, 24.
    The Would-be Gentleman, 27
Monroe, Marilyn, 394
Montel, Michael, 453
Moody, William Vaughn, 59, 187
Moore-Forrest, Marie, 159
Morehouse, Ward, 77, 117, 136, 138,
    286, 290, 293, 349-50, 392
Morison, Patricia, 330

Morosco, Oliver, 61
Morosco Theatre, 331
Morris, Clara, 377-78
Morton, Edward Arthur, 378
Morton, John. *Box and Cox*, 377
Morton, Martha, 2, 377-82, 456,
    460-61, 463. *The Batchelor's
    Romance*, 379. *Brother John*,
    378. *A Fool of Fortune*, 382.
    Helene, 377-78. *Her Lord and
    Master*, 379. *The Merchant*,
    378, 380. *The Movers*, 381. *On
    the Eve*, 381. *The Senator Keeps
    House*, 382. *Three of Hearts*,
    382
Moss, Arnold, 97
Mowatt, Anna Cora, 462
Mulatto, (play), 397
Muni, Paul, 270
Murfin, Jane, 304, 338
Music Box Theatre, 287
Mussolini, Benito, 132-133, 389
Myers, Carole, 224

N

Nachman, Gerald, 145
Nadzo, Guido, 172
Nashe, Thomas, 179
Nathan, George Jean, 61, 107-8, 113-
    15, 117-18, 148, 250, 343,
    349, 412, 426, 433, 426. *The
    Theatre of Today*, 433
National Ethiopian Art Players, 273
National Little Theatre Tournament,
    275
Neal, Patricia, 126, 136
Neighborhood Playhouse, 9, 219
Nesbitt, Cathleen, 394
New Phoenix Repertory Company,
    454
New Theatre, 182, 184
New York City Opera, 143
New York Shakespeare Festival, 463
Nichols, Anne, 2, 409-13, 456, 461-
    62. *Abie's Irish Rose*, 409-13.
    Dear John (radio), 410. *Love
    Dreams*, 411. And Alfred
    Goodman and B. Grosman.
    Linger Longer Letty, 409-10.

And Adelaide Matthews. *Just Married*, 409-10
Nichols, Lewis, 448
Nichols, Mike, 129
Norman, Marsha, 2
Norton, Elliott, 134
Norton, Frederic. *Chu Chin Chow*, 213
Nugent, Elliott, 77

O

135th Street Library Theatre, 273-74
O'Brien, Margaret, 344
O'Brien, Pat, 329
Odeon Stock Company, 58
Odets, Clifford, 118, 128-29. *Golden Boy*, 256
Oenslager, Donald, 293
Off-Center Theatre (New York), 354
Offenbach, Jacques. *The Tales of Hoffman*, 211
O'Neil, Patrick, 423
O'Neill, Eugene, 37-38, 40, 45, 52, 54, 57, 64, 78, 128-29, 214, 233, 252, 262, 272, 296, 303. *Bound East for Cardiff*, 38. *Desire Under the Elms*, 85. *The Emperor Jones*, 45, 47, 223, 316. *The Hairy Ape*, 38, 261. *Long Day's Journey Into Night*, 141. *Strange Interlude*, 70, 262
Oppenheimer, George. *Here Today*, 423.
Orbach, Jerry, 437
Ormsbee, Helen, 114
Osborn, E. W., 225
Osborne, Robert, 392
Ouspenskaya, Maria, 112

P

Page, Geraldine, 50, 145
Palmer, Lilli, 444
Papp, Joseph, 271
Parker, Dorothy, 3, 7, 9, 122-23, 142, 285-87, 346, 421-27, 457. *Big Blonde* (story), 422. *Candide*, 423. *Close Harmony*, 424. *From the Diary of a New York Lady* (story), 422. *Here We Are*, 425. *Round the Town*, 424. *Shoot the Works*, 424. *Soft Music*, 423-24. *You Were Perfectly Fine*, 425. And Alan Campbell. *The Little Foxes* (film), 422. *A Star is Born* (film), 422. And Arnaud D'Usseau. *Ladies of the Corridor*, 425-26. And Rosser Evans. *The Coast of Illyria*, 425. And Edward F. Gardner. *After Such Pleasures*, 425.
Parker, Robert A., 52
Pasadena Playhouse, 200, 361
Patterson, Ada, 380
Paul, Alice, 340
Pawley, Thomas, 160
Peabody, Josephine Preston, 2, 59, 176-89, 241, 370, 459, 461. *Marlowe*, 178-79, 184. *The Piper*, 176-84, 187, 189, 370. *Portrait of Mrs. W*, 187-89. *The Wings*, 186-87. *The Wolf of Gubbio*, 184-186
Pegasus Players, 90
Pemberton, Brock, 10, 31, 220, 224-25, 341, 346, 460
Pendleton, Austin, 129
Penn, Arthur, 145
Peppard, George, 443
Perkins, Anthony, 289
Perry, Antoinette, 31, 33, 341, 346
Philadelphia Story (film), 304
Picasso, Pablo, 191-2
Pickford, Mary, 334
Pinero, Arthur Wing, 65, 148. *Mid-Channel*, 29, 61
Pinter, Harold, 45, 202
Pirandello, Luigi, 141, 326, 362
Pitts, Ethell, 160
Players' Workshop of Chicago, 241-42, 248
Playmakers Theatre (North Carolina), 314
Playwrights Fellowship, 460-61
Playwrights Theatre of Chicago, 242, 460
Poe, Edgar Allen, 266
Poitier, Sidney, 237
Pollock, Arthur, 72, 108, 162, 420

Poole, Rosey, 231
Porter, Cole, 326, 329-30. (*See also*
    Bella Spewack)
Porterfield, Robert, 307-8
Preminger, Otto, 342-44
Preston, Robert, 361
Price, Leontyne, 402
Prince, Harold, 154, 367
Princess Theatre, 302
Provincetown Players/Playhouse, 3,
    9-10, 36-38, 40-41, 46, 52, 54,
    57, 81, 83, 152, 236, 297, 300,
    322, 460, 463
Public Theatre, 262
Puget, Claude-Andre, *Les Jours
    Heureux*, 74. (*See also* Zoë
    Akins)

                      Q

Quinn, Arthur Hobson, 23, 33, 35,
    297, 302-4

                      R

Rabb, Ellis, 89-90
Rahman, Aishah, 160
Rathbun, Stephen, 52, 264
Rapport Theatre, 33
Rascoe, Burton, 115, 350, 448-49
Rawlins, Erika, 454
Rayor, Janet, 291
Reach, Etta A., 385
Reamer, Lawrence, 63, 67
Reed, Alan, 269
Reed, John, 37
Reicher, Hedwig, 381
Reid, Louis R., 23
Reinhardt, Max, 99, 335. *The Miracle*,
    184, 335
Revere, Anne, 145
Rice, Elmer, 214, 423. *The Adding
    Machine*, 45, 261, 424. *Dream
    Girl*, 265. *On Trial*, 213
Rich, Frank, 129, 262
Richardson, Howard. *Dark of the
    Moon*, 303
Richardson, Willis, 310. *Mortgaged*,
    310. *Plays and Pageants From
    the Life of the Negro*, 315. And

May Miller, eds. *Negro History
    in Thirteen Plays*, 231, 239, 310
Riggs, Lynn, 118. *Green Grow the
    Lilacs*, 308, 398
Ritchard, Clive, 442
Rivera, Chita, 437
Robards, Jason, 145
Robeson, Paul, 123
Roblès, Emmanual. *Montserrat*, 137.
    (*See also* Lillian Hellman)
Rodgers, Mary, 455. (*See also* Carson
    McCullers)
Rodgers, Richard. (*See* Oscar
    Hammerstein)
Rogers, Ginger, 96, 437
Rogers, W. G., 80
Rolle, Esther, 454
Romberg, Sigmund, 211-12
Roosevelt, Eleanor, 108, 345
Roosevelt, F. D., 80, 97
Rosemary's Baby (film), 284, 294
Ross, Harold, 422
Rostand, Edmund, 183
Roundabout Theatre Company, 454
Royal National Theatre, 373, 463
Ruben, Jose, 257
Rudd, Wayland, 305
Ruhl, Arthur, 72, 262
Rule, Jane, 193
Rumbold, Captain Hugo, 59
Russel, Sol Smith, 379
Russell, Lillian, 73

                      S

Sadler's Wells Opera, 329
Sanchez, Sonia, 160
Sandberg, Carl, 59
San Jose Repertory Theatre, 349
Santayana, George, 389
Saroyan, William, 352
Satie, Erik, 192
Schaeffer, Louis, 52
Schmitz, Neil, 193
Schnitzler, Arthur, 60-61, 242, 246,
    366. *Anatol*, 365
Schroeder, William, 212
Scott, George C., 129
Scott, Harold, 454
Scott, Martha, 116

Scudder, Horace, 176
Selznick, David O., 340
Serena Blandish (play), 291
Shakespeare, William, 64, 170, 176,
    206, 296, 309, 329-30, 377.
    Hamlet, 52, 70, 169, 176. *King
    Lear*, 176. *Taming of the Shrew*,
    329, 379
Sharaff, Irene, 97, 142
Shaw, George Bernard, 34-35, 83,
    167, 334. *Candida*, 292, 344,
    440, 449. *St. Joan*, 141
Shaw, Irwin, 118. *The Harder They
    Fall*, 256
Sheehan, John J. D., 197
Sheldon, Edward, 288, 460
Shelley, Elsa, 1, 446-50, 457. *Foxhole
    in the Parlor*, 448-49. *Pick-Up
    Girl*, 446-48, 450, 457. *With a
    Silk Thread*, 449-50
Sherburne, E. C., 113
Sheridan, Richard Brinsley. *The
    Critic*, 250
Sherwood, Robert. *The Petrified
    Forest*, 71. *There Shall Be No
    Night*, 132
Shine, Ted, 232
Shubert Theatre, 212
Shumlin, Herman, 72, 134, 324, 326
Siddons, Sarah, 188
Sievers, David, 370
Sigaloff, Eugene, 326
Silvers, Phil, 367
Simmons, Jean, 289
Simon, John, 129
Simon, Neil, 2
Simonson, Lee, 246
Skinner, B. F., 191
Skinner, Cornelia Otis, 440-45, 457.
    Captain Fury, 440. *Edna His
    Wife*, 441-44. *Elegant Wits and
    Grand Horizontals* (book), 441.
    The Empress Eugenie, 441. *The
    Irregular Verb to Love*, 440. *The
    Loves of Charles II*, 441. *Man-
    sion on the Hudson*, 441-44.
    Paris' 90, 441. *The Wives of
    Henry VIII*, 441. And Samuel
    Taylor. *The Pleasure of His
    Company*, 440-44, 457

Skinner, Otis, 179, 335, 440
Skinner, Richard Dana, 93
Slezak, Walter, 331
Smith, Alexis, 340
Smith, Loring, 287
Smith, Oliver, 142, 366, 392
Smith, Sid, 263
Smith, Susan Harris, 304, 308
Smith, Winchell, and Frank Bacon.
    Lightnin', 413
Society of Dramatic Authors, 460
Sophocles, 439
Sothern, E. H., 178, 203
Southey, Robert, 188
Spectrum Stage (New York), 373
Spence, Eulalie, 160, 271-83. *Being
    Forty*, 273. *Episode*, 280-81.
    Fool's Errand, 274-75, 282,
    372. *Foreign Mail*, 273. *Her!*,
    273-74, 282. *Hot Stuff*, 278-80,
    282. *The Hunch*, 275-76. *La
    Divina Pastora*, 10, 281. *Ready
    to Love* (film), 282. *The Starter*,
    273. *Undertow*, 5, 276-78, 282.
    The Whipping, 281-82
Spewack, Bella and Samuel, 322-33,
    370, 373, 462. *Boy Meets Girl*,
    322-23, 326-29, 331. *Clear All
    Wires!*, 324-27, 332. *Festival*,
    332. *Golden State*, 323. *Leave it
    to Me!*, 326. *My Three Angels*,
    322, 330-32. *Poppa*, 323-24.
    Swing High Sweeney, 323. And
    Leo McCarey. *My Favorite Wife*
    (film), 332. And Cole Porter.
    Kiss Me, Kate, 322, 329-30,
    392
St. Augustine College Players, 314
Stage Relief Fund, 31
Stanley, Kim, 393
Stanley, Martha, 410
A Star is Born (film), 73
Stapleton, Maureen, 145, 357
Starr, Frances, 426
Steiger, Rod, 364
Stein, Gertrude, 190-202, 344-45,
    371-72. *Counting Her Dresses*,
    195. *Dr. Faustus Lights the
    Lights*, 197-99. *Geography and
    Plays*, 192, 195. *Ladies' Voices*,

Stein, Gertrude (continued)
   193-94. *The Mother of Us All*,
   200-01. *Tender Buttons*, 191.
   *They Must. Be Wedded. To
   Their Wife.*, 202. *What
   Happened*, 192. *The Woman*
   (story), 387. *Yes is For a Very
   Young Man*, 199-200, 344. And
   Virgil Thomson. *Four Saints in
   Three Acts*, 193, 195-97, 201,
   371
Sterritt, David, 23
Stevens, Emily, 64
Stevenson, Robert Louis, 186
Stewart, James, 346, 348
Stickney, Dorothy, 105
Stoddard, Haila, 423
Stowe, Harriet Beecher, 162, 391.
   Uncle Tom's Cabin, 190
Strahler, Stephen R., 90
Strasberg, Lee, 400
Stratford Memorial Theatre Festival,
   181
Strauss, Theodore, 400
Strindberg, August, 37, 40, 242, 276,
   449. *A Dream Play*, 37. *Ghost
   Sonata*, 37. *Miss Julie*, 40
Stritch, Elaine, 121
Styne, Jule, 392
Sullavan, Margaret, 95-96
Sullivan, Barry, 137
Surrealism, 462-63
Swinburne, Algernon, 189
Symbolism, 45

                     T

Taj Mahal, 407
Tamiroff, Akim, 364
Tarkington, Booth. *The Man From
   Home*, 413
Taubman, Howard, 24, 200, 353, 366
Taylor, Elizabeth, 7, 129
Taylor, Laurette, 70
Taylor, Samuel, 440, 443. (*See also*
   Cornelia Otis Skinner)
Teasdale, Sara, 59
Teichman, Howard, 101
Tenniel, John, 245

Terry, Ellen, 216
Theatre Club Incorporated, 73
Theatre Guild, 6, 38, 56, 267, 269,
   297, 370, 396-97, 404, 419
Theatre in the Square (Atlanta), 454
Throckmorton, Cleon, 51, 159, 397
Thomas, Augustus, 152, 193, 225,
   241, 248, 250, 380-82, 412,
   462. *As a Man Thinks*, 3, 19.
   Alabama, 190
Thomas, Brandon. *Charley's Aunt*,
   210
Thompson, Beatrice, 136
Thomson, Virgil, 193, 195, 200-1.
   (*See also* Gertrude Stein)
Thurber, James. *The Thurber Carnival*,
   423
Todd, Mike, 419, 447-48
Toklas, Alice B., 191, 193, 202
Tomlin, Lily, 372, 445
Torn, Rip, 138
Torrence, Ridgely, 216, 233. *Granny
   Maumee*, 157. *The Rider of
   Dreams*, 157. *Simon the Cyre-
   nian*, 157. *Three Plays for a
   Negro Theatre*, 232
Towse, John Rankin, 67, 225
Toy Theatre, 9, 186
Tozere, Frederic, 112
Tracy, Lee, 326
Tracy, Spencer, 289, 294
Treadwell, Sophie, 7, 78, 255-70,
   370, 373. *For Saxophone*, 265-
   66. *Gringo*, 256-57, 259. *Hope
   for a Harvest*, 266-69. *Ladies
   Leave*, 256, 263-66. *Lone Val-
   ley*, 264-65. *Loney Lee*, 257.
   Machinal, 1, 5, 255, 259-65,
   269, 305, 373, 463. *Million
   Dollar Gate*, 256. O, *Nightin-
   gale*, 257-59. *Plumes in the Dust*,
   256, 266. *Promised Land*, 256,
   262. *Rights*, 256
Trentini, Emma, 211
The Trial of Mary Dugan (play), 448
Truex, Ernest, 171
Tucker, Sophie, 326
Tyler, George C., 64, 186, 257
Tynan, Kenneth, 364

U

Unger, Gladys, 456
Union Square Theatre, 378
Untermeyer, Louis, 216

V

Valentino, Rudolph, 69
Van Doren, Mark, 56
Van Druten, John. I Am A Camera, 352
Van Vechten, Carl, 70
Vaughn, Peter, 263
Verdon, Gwen, 437
Vereen, Ben, 367
Vernon, Grenville, 33
Vesey, Denmark, 401
Villa, Pancho, 256
Vollmer, Lula, 225, 296-308, 372, 462. *The American Story* (radio), 307. *Dearly Beloved*, 307. *Dunce Boy*, 302-3 *Grits and Gravy* (radio), 297. *The Hill Between*, 297, 305-6, 308. *In A Nutshell*, 305. *Jule*, 296. *Moonshine and Honeysuckle* (radio and play), 297, 305. *Sentinals*, 305. *The Shame Woman*, 297, 300-2. *Shining Blackness*, 305. *Sun-Up*, 297-301, 303-4, 307-8. *Trigger*, 303-4. *Troyka*, 304-5. *The Widow's Son* (radio), 297
Voltaire. *Candide*, 142. (*See also* Lillian Hellman)
von Stroheim, Erich, 389

W

Waldorf, Wilella, 6, 113, 117, 264, 269, 287, 328, 349, 419, 447, 449
Walker, Celeste, 161
Walker, June, 391
Wallace, Henry, 123
Wanamaker, Sam, 361
Warfield, William, 401-2
Washburne, Annette, 242

Washington, Booker T., 309
Washington Square Players/Playhouse, 9, 60, 81-82, 219, 246, 370, 460
Washington, Walter, 312
Wasserstein, Wendy, 178, 372
Waters, Ethel, 399-400, 402, 451-53
Watkins, Maurine, 433-39, 458, 460. *Chicago*, 433-38, 458. *Gesture*, 438. *Revelry*, 437-38. *Roxie Hart* (film), 437
Watt, Douglas, 262, 367, 454
Watts, Richard, Jr., 6, 74, 89, 98, 107, 128, 136, 141-42, 173, 268, 290, 353, 360, 362, 366, 391, 393, 401, 453
Watson, Minor, 304
Wayne, Rollo, 419
Wedekind, Frank, 242, 334. *Spring Awakening*, 446
Weill, Kurt, 99, 265
Weinstein, Norman, 196
Wertheim, Albert, 347, 353
West, Mae, 7, 213, 341, 390, 414-20, 457, 463. *Catherine Was Great*, 415, 419. *The Constant Sinner*, 415, 418-20. *Diamond Lil*, 417-19. *The Drag*, 416-18. *Myra Breckenridge* (film), 415. *Pleasure Man*, 418. *Sex*, 414, 416. *Sextette* (film), 415.
West, Robert, 160
Westport Playhouse, 53
Wharton, Edith, 70-72, 151. (*See also* Zoë Akins)
Wheeler, Hugh, 143
Where's Poppa? (film), 284
Whipper, Leigh, 397
Whipple, Sidney B., 75
Whitehead, Robert, 351
Whorf, Richard, 193
Wie einst im Mai (play), 212
Wied, Gustav, 60
Wilbur, Richard, 142
Wilde, Oscar, 165, 167, 334. *Lady Windemere's Fan*, 440
Wilder, Thornton, 191, 202, 285, 291. *The Long Christmas Dinner*, 42. *Our Town*, 41, 202. *Pullman Car Hiawatha*, 42

Dinner, 42. Our Town, 41, 202.
  Pullman Car Hiawatha, 42
Williams, Tennessee, 451, 456. The
  Glass Menagerie, 349-50
Wilson, August, 310
Wilson, Edmund, 259
Wilson, Elizabeth, 224
Wilson, Frank, 397
Wilson, Llewellyn, 311
Wilson, Marie, 329
Wilson, Robert, 198, 202
Williams, Allen, 160
Williams, Emlyn, 138
Williamstown Theatre, 90
Winer, Linda, 407
Winn, Steven, 94, 349
Winston, Iris, 246
Winters, Claire, 454
Winwood, Estelle, 166
Wisconsin Dramatic Society/Players,
  217, 219-20
Wolfe, George C. Spunk, 408
Wollstonecroft, Mary, 187-88, 256.
  The Vindication of the Rights of
  Women, 188
Woodland Opera House, 454
Woodruff, Harry, 210
Woodson, Carter G., 309
Woolcott, Alexander, 6, 23, 25, 28,
  63, 67, 69, 88, 148, 162, 164,
  170, 174, 189, 222-23, 257,
  284, 286, 292, 311, 410-11,
  421
Woolf, Virginia, 193
Worth, Irene, 145
Wright, Haidee, 88
Wright, Teresa, 289
Wyatt, Euphemia van Renselaer, 6,
  110
Wycherley, William. The Country
  Wife, 284. Love for Love, 440

Wycherly, Margaret, 52
Wyler, William, 125, 129
Wylie, Elinor, 70
Wynn, Ed, 213

Y

Yeats, William Butler, 236
Youmans, Vincent, 423
Young, James, Jr., 204, 210
Young, Rida Johnson, 9, 203-15, 370,
  380, 389, 462. Brown of
  Harvard, 203-5, 207-10, 214,
  370. Captain Kidd, Jr., 211.
  Cock o' the Roost, 214. The Girl
  and the Pennant, 205. Glorious
  Betsy, 210, 215. Her Soldier
  Boy, 211-12. His Little Widows,
  211-12. "I'm Falling in Love
  With Someone" (song), 211.
  Little Simplicity, 213-14. The
  Lottery Man, 206, 214. May-
  time, 203, 212-13. "Mother
  Machree" (song), 203. Naughty
  Marietta, 203, 210-11, 214,
  370. Sometime, 213.
  "Sweethearts" (song), 212.
  Wanted—a Sister, 210. "When
  Love is Young in Springtime"
  (song), 209
Young, Roland, 163, 166, 169-74
Young, Stark, 85, 93, 148, 201, 214,
  302, 412, 424
Yurka, Blanche, 53, 57, 382

Z

Ziegfeld, Florenz, 171
Ziegfeld Follies, 70
Zimmer Irma, 461
Zweig, Stefan, 99

The author, Yvonne Shafer, in costume as
Rachel Crothers in the performance of
American Women Playwrights